THE AGE OF ROOSEVELT

The Politics
of Upheaval

BOOKS BY
ARTHUR M. SCHLESINGER, JR.

Orestes A. Brownson:
A Pilgrim's Progress

The Age of Jackson

The Vital Center

The General and the President
(with Richard H. Rovere)

The Age of Roosevelt
I. The Crisis of the Old Order, 1919-1933
II. The Coming of the New Deal
III. The Politics of Upheaval

The Politics of Hope

A Thousand Days:
John F. Kennedy in the White House

The Bitter Heritage:
Vietnam and American Democracy, 1941-1966

The Crisis of Confidence:
Ideas, Power and Violence in America

The Imperial Presidency

Robert Kennedy and His Times

The Cycles of American History

The American Heritage Library

THE AGE OF ROOSEVELT

THE POLITICS OF UPHEAVAL

Arthur M. Schlesinger, Jr.

Houghton Mifflin Company · Boston

For information about permission to reproduce selections
from this book, write to Permissions, Houghton Mifflin Company,
2 Park Street, Boston, Massachusetts 02108.

Library of Congress Cataloging-in-Publication Data

Schlesinger, Arthur Meier, date.
    The politics of upheaval.

    (The American Heritage library)   (The Age of Roosevelt)
    Bibliography: p.
    Includes index.
    1. United States—History—1933-1945.   2. Depressions—1929—
United States.   3. New Deal, 1933-1939.   4. Roosevelt, Franklin D.
(Franklin Delano), 1882-1945.
I. Title.   II. Series.   III. Series: Schlesinger, Arthur Meier, date.
Age of Roosevelt.
E806.S347   1988   973.917   88-8207
ISBN 0-395-48904-0 (pbk.)

Printed in the United States of America

S 10 9 8 7 6 5 4 3 2 1

FOR

J. K. GALBRAITH AND

SEYMOUR E. HARRIS

"He that will not apply new remedies must expect new evils; for time is the greatest innovator."

FRANCIS BACON

Foreword to
the American Heritage Library Edition

THE FIRST THREE VOLUMES of *The Age of Roosevelt*, now reissued in the American Heritage Library, were published a generation ago: *The Crisis of the Old Order* in 1957, *The Coming of the New Deal* in 1958, and *The Politics of Upheaval* in 1960. These volumes cover the life and times of Franklin Roosevelt through the election of 1936. Their emphasis, reflecting FDR's own priorities during these years, is on the New Deal and domestic affairs.

The next volume was scheduled to deal with FDR and foreign affairs in the 1930s. But in 1960 many essential foreign policy documents were under official lock and key, protected by government classification from scholarly inquiry. I saw no choice but to suspend *The Age of Roosevelt* until I could gain access to the files. Then, for a number of years thereafter, I was drawn into other matters, political and scholarly.

In these years also the American and British archives were gradually opened to the end of the Second World War (and now well beyond). The fourth volume of *The Age of Roosevelt*, covering FDR and the coming of the war, is at last in the making. More volumes will follow in due course. I regret the delay but take solace in the example of my putative ancestor George Bancroft, who published the first volume of his *History of the United States* in 1834 and, after spirited and interesting digressions into politics and public service, published the tenth (and final) volume in 1874—and then added a two-volume *History of the Formation of the Constitution of the United States* in 1882 (at the age of eighty-two).

When I wrote *The Crisis of the Old Order*, FDR had been dead for hardly more than a decade. His presidency had stirred vivid and intense emotions. Like all great American presidents, he had been a divisive figure in his own time. Most Americans revered him. Some detested and reviled him. Change always provokes resentment and anger, especially on the part of those who benefit from the old order. The passions of the 1930s had not much abated by the 1950s. Many Americans still actively loved Roosevelt. A not inconsiderable number still actively hated him.

Moreover, the 1950s, like the 1920s thirty years before and the 1980s thirty years after, fell in the conservative phase of the political cycle. (In the same way, times of liberalism, reform, and affirmative government come along every thirty years: Theodore Roosevelt and the Progressive era in 1901, FDR and the New Deal in 1933, John Kennedy and the New Frontier in 1961.) The reputation of liberal presidents declines in conservative swings of the cycle, as the reputation of conservative presidents declines in liberal swings.

In any case, presidential reputations tend to be at low ebb in the years shortly after a president's death. When I went to college in the 1930s, Theodore Roosevelt, who died in 1919, and Woodrow Wilson, who died in 1924, were only beginning to emerge from the fashionable judgment that one was an adolescent braggart and the other a Presbyterian fanatic. The combination of the conservative phase of the cycle with the recency of FDR's death accounts for the somewhat defensive tone the reader may find in the foreword to *The Crisis of the Old Order*.

Today, nearly half a century after Roosevelt's death, the bitter passions of the 1930s and 1940s have pretty well subsided. Periodic polls of historians and political scientists routinely rank Roosevelt as one of the three greatest American presidents, with Lincoln and Washington. FDR reshaped scholarly conceptions and popular expectations about the presidency, and his towering personality and astute management of the office have haunted all his successors, as William Leuchtenburg reminded us in his excellent book of 1985, *In the Shadow of FDR*. Even during the conservative 1980s, when the most conservative president since Herbert Hoover mounted a counterrevolution against FDR's New Deal, Ronald Reagan nevertheless spoke with affection and respect of Franklin Roosevelt himself, perhaps because, when younger and possibly wiser, he had cast his first *four* presidential votes for FDR.

But history should never be an exercise in reverence. Franklin

Roosevelt had superb qualities of leadership, superb instincts for the crucial problems of his age, superb ability to select and manage vigorous subordinates, enormous skill as a public educator, and enormous ability to lift the spirits of the republic and to mobilize national energies. He was, however, far from infallible. He made mistakes both in policy and in politics. He had his moments of deviousness, craftiness, vanity, undue casualness, and insouciant cruelty. He combined soaring idealism with tough and sometimes petty realism. He was, in other words, a human being, somewhat larger than life but hardly exempt from human infirmity, frailty, and error.

Those vigorous subordinates in FDR's supporting cast add color and excitement to the age of Roosevelt. When these volumes were first published, their names and personalities—Hopkins, Ickes, Wallace, Hull, Morgenthau, Frankfurter, Tugwell, Berle, Frances Perkins, Tom Corcoran and Ben Cohen, Jimmy Byrnes and Jesse Jones, Robert Jackson and Francis Biddle, Sumner Welles and David Lilienthal—were still well known. What a formidable and dashing group they were! Few of them, alas, are household words today. Still I trust that these pages contain enough about their characters and contributions to explain their impact on those turbulent and agitated times. I had the great luck to know and interview a good many of them, and I hope that their testimony will impart a certain directness to the narrative.

Indeed, the determination to take advantage of living witnesses was an important motive in my decision to attempt *The Age of Roosevelt*. When I was preparing to write *The Age of Jackson*, I benefited greatly, as have all Jackson scholars, from James Parton's wonderful *Life of Andrew Jackson*. In his preface Parton discussed the problems of discovering information "respecting a man whom two thirds of his fellow-citizens deified, and the other third vilified, for a space of twelve years or more." To find out what Jackson was like, Parton, conducting his research a decade after Jackson's death, "conversed with politicians of the last generation, who have now no longer an interest in concealing the truth." He roamed around the country eliciting "the recollections of men and women, bond and free, who knew him well, knew him at all periods of his life, lived near him, and with him, served him and were served by him. . . . Thus it was that contradictions were reconciled, that mysteries were revealed, and that the truth was made apparent."

I cannot pretend to the journalistic skills or literary graces of James Parton. But I was struck by his methods. I was struck too by the frustrations that attend those methods, for the questions Parton asked of his witnesses were not always the questions to which future historians have sought answers. At any rate, I was inspired by his example to talk to FDR's friends, associates, and adversaries (no one was more generous and helpful than the fine man he trounced in 1936, Alfred M. Landon). I do not suppose that I was any more successful than James Parton in asking the questions that will interest scholars of the future, but I hope that at least testimony may have been preserved that might otherwise have perished with the witnesses.

Since these books were published, a very considerable literature has appeared on many facets of the age of Roosevelt. I do not believe that the outpouring of scholarly books, monographs, and articles changes the main outline of the story told in these volumes, but some float ingenious theories and others add valuable details. I will take account of this rich literature in the volumes of *The Age of Roosevelt* yet to come.

The Roosevelt years were above all a battlefield of ideas—ideas about the American past and the American future; ideas about the role of government in guaranteeing the economy and protecting the forgotten man (and woman); ideas about isolationism and internationalism and America's relationship to the world beyond; ideas articulated with uncommon vehemence and ardor and often with authentic brilliance; ideas that intersected with power and helped shape the destiny of the United States and the world.

Today, I believe, a new cyclical change impends in American politics. If the rhythm holds, the nation can be expected to move from the energetically conservative 1980s into an energetically progressive new decade. I would like to think that in this coming period new generations will find power and resonance in the memory of Franklin Roosevelt and the New Deal. Of course the problems of the 1990s will be very different from the problems of the 1930s. But the spirit of experiment, idealism, and concern with which the republic defeated the worst depression and won the greatest war in American history remains, I think, a precious resource as we confront the darkly unpredictable future.

ARTHUR M. SCHLESINGER, JR.

May 21, 1988

Foreword

THIS THIRD VOLUME of *The Age of Roosevelt* carries the domestic history of the administration of Franklin D. Roosevelt through the 1936 election. I have acquired many obligations in the course of writing this volume, and these few words represent a most inadequate acknowledgment. Once again, I want to express my gratitude to my father and mother, Arthur M. Schlesinger and Elizabeth Bancroft Schlesinger, for their patient and helpful reading of the manuscript. Once again, Seymour Harris and John Kenneth Galbraith allowed me to invade busy lives with discussions of bygone economic problems. Their criticisms of the manuscript saved me from much economic error; they are absolved from responsibility for what remains. Herman Kahn and John M. Blum gave the entire manuscript the benefit of their unsurpassed knowledge of this period. I am also deeply indebted to the following for casting expert eyes on parts of the manuscript: Alfred M. Bingham; Benjamin V. Cohen; Thomas G. Corcoran; Morris L. Cooke; Charles P. Curtis; Paul A. Freund; Ruth Harris; Barbara Wendell Kerr; Arthur Maass; Robert G. McCloskey; Joseph L. Rauh, Jr.; Selden Rodman; Morris Schonbach; R. G. Tugwell; Herbert Wechsler; James A. Wechsler; Aubrey Williams. Those who have permitted me to discuss the period with them are too numerous for listing, but I do want to mention here the exceptional gallantry and generosity of Governor Alfred M. Landon in throwing his papers open to me and in allowing me to talk over all aspects of the 1936 campaign with him. All students of this epoch are everlastingly in debt to Herman Kahn and his splendid staff at the Franklin D. Roosevelt Library at Hyde Park. I have a particular additional debt to Paul H. Buck and his excellent staff at the Harvard University Library; I want especially to state my appreciation to T. F. O'Connell for his skill in making unavailable books magically available.

This volume could not have been completed so quickly without the indispensable aid of E. G. Shinner and the Shinner Foundation. I am endlessly grateful for their generous assistance. My secretary Julie Armstrong Jeppson saw the manuscript through every stage with incomparable fortitude and good humor. My wife Marian Cannon Schlesinger bore the making of this book with her usual tolerance and support.

Once again, may I say that I will greatly welcome corrections or amplifications of anything I have written in this text.

ARTHUR M. SCHLESINGER, JR.

February 4, 1960

Contents

THE AGE OF ROOSEVELT

The Politics
of Upheaval

1. Prologue to Stalemate

"HE HAS BEEN ALL BUT CROWNED BY THE PEOPLE," wrote William Allen White, the dean of American editors, after the congressional elections of 1934. "There has been no such popular endorsement since the days of Thomas Jefferson and Andrew Jackson," said William Randolph Hearst, the most powerful of American newspaper publishers. The New Deal, wrote Arthur Krock, the veteran political reporter of the *New York Times,* had won "the most overwhelming victory in the history of American politics." As a matter of course, midterm elections are supposed to go against the party in power. But in 1934, the second year of the New Deal, the party of Franklin Roosevelt made astonishing gains in every category: in senators, in congressmen, in state governors, in popular vote. It all seemed to constitute an unprecedented national endorsement. The Roosevelt administration might well have entered the year 1935 with high hopes.[1]

II

Still, thoughtful New Dealers knew that all was not so well as it looked. The accomplishments so far were no doubt impressive — the laws enacted, the agencies set up, the programs launched. At the end of 1934, national income was up $9 billion — nearly 25 per cent — over 1933. Employment had increased by over 2.5 million; unemployment was down by over 2 million. The national government had moved in a variety of ways to reduce the disorder and cruelty of the economy: floors now existed under wages, ceilings over hours, child labor was abolished, collec-

tive bargaining enjoyed federal sponsorship, the unemployed were
receiving emergency relief, provision was being made for more
permanent security against unemployment and old age, mortgagors
were helped to retain their homes and farms, federal public
works were under way across the country, the government was
assuming control of the national monetary policy, the financial
community was renouncing cherished practices of manipulation
and speculation, the farmers were collaborating cheerfully in
measures to adjust agricultural production and increase farm income, new conservation policies were preserving the nation's basis
in water and land and natural resources.

The downward grind had been stopped; the panic of 1933
had vanished. Businessmen were recovering confidence in themselves and their system. Working people were filled with new
vigor and hope. Mobs of farmers no longer gathered along country roads to stop produce from going to market or to demonstrate
against the foreclosure of mortgages. The American republic
and the democratic system were showing unexpected resources of
vitality and purpose. Two years earlier, no one could have anticipated such a sweeping revision either of the political mood or
of the economic structure. From the perspective of the winter
of 1932–33, it was a record of prodigious achievement.

Prodigious, yes, but was it enough? The 1934 national income
of $48.6 billion, however much better than 1933, was still $10
billion under that of the depression year 1931 and nearly $40
billion below that of 1929, the last year of prosperity. In January
1935 the income of urban consumers was running about 13 per
cent below what it had been in the same month in 1929; cash
income of farmers, in spite of the great improvement since 1933,
was about 28 per cent under the 1929 figure. Most ominous of
all, while the number of unemployed had declined fairly steadily
from 1933, nearly 10 million persons — almost one-fifth of the
labor force — were still out of jobs. "It seems to me," Henry
Morgenthau, Jr., the Secretary of the Treasury, said in 1935, "that
we are not making any headway and the number of unemployed is
staying more or less static." No one knew this better than
Franklin Roosevelt. "The unemployment problem," he wrote an
English friend in February 1935, "is solved no more here than it
is with you."

In the meantime, the policies which had produced the economic and moral revival seemed themselves to be faltering. For two years the New Deal had been living off the momentum of the Hundred Days. Now the grand initiatives of 1933 appeared to be running their course. The central ideas of the early New Deal had been industrial planning, to be carried out through the National Recovery Administration, and agricultural planning, to be carried out through the Agricultural Adjustment Administration. By early 1935 NRA was in a state of turmoil and demoralization; reforms were at last coming from within, but too late to still the criticism from without. As for AAA, while it was in a less precarious condition, it was nevertheless under increasing attack. These agencies had been the chief New Deal weapons in the assault on economic stagnation. Now it looked to some as if they had gone about as far as they could go.

In their day NRA and AAA had done remarkable things. But if they had failed to break the back of the depression when they commanded public enthusiasm, what could be expected of them now that a modicum of recovery was destroying the unity of 1933 and reviving opposition from both left and right? [2]

III

Recovery had proceeded far enough to end despair, but not far enough to restore satisfaction. People still felt that many things were wrong, but no longer felt, as they had in the terrible days of 1933, that their single duty was to trust Franklin Roosevelt and hold their peace. By transforming the national mood from apathy to action, the New Deal was invigorating its enemies as well as its friends. Through 1934 apprehension had spread among businessmen; by fall it had turned to resentment, by winter, to open hostility. And the emergence of dissatisfaction among the conservatives was paralleled by restless and erratic stirrings among the masses, incited by a new set of political prophets, some of whose banners bore exceedingly strange devices. The new political moods infected the new Congress, freshly returned in the fall elections. In March 1933 the 73rd Congress had come to Washington expressing the desperate national desire for unity under presidential leadership. Now, in January 1935, the 74th Congress arrived as the carrier of an inchoate national wish for new departures.

The latent discontent presented a challenge to the President. He, too, sensed the national mood; worse, he evidently shared the national bafflement. Indeed, he had probably anticipated it. In the fall of 1934 he had systematically called in businessmen as well as New Dealers in a search for new ideas in economic and social policy. His interviews had not been productive. As Congress reconvened, it appeared that the President had no bold new proposals to send to the Hill. Certain things were imperative, of course. Roosevelt knew he had to do something about reorganizing the relief and public-works programs. He was already committed to bring in a program on social security. His state-of-the-Union message on January 4, 1935, concentrated on these two issues. For the rest, it expressed a mild and dignified optimism, looking forward to "a genuine period of good feeling, sustained by a sense of purposeful progress." His budget message was equally conciliatory in tone and unenterprising in content. Neither paper displayed any intention of breaking new ground. His hope for recovery seemed to depend on more of the same. Yet more of the same would hardly be enough.[3]

IV

As the 74th Congress gathered for its first session in January 1935, the Roosevelt administration apparently controlled both houses by overwhelming margins. But was this control as reliable as it looked? Too large a majority, by encouraging indiscipline and irresponsibility, might be almost as dangerous as one too small. The new session had barely begun when Roosevelt found himself in trouble. On January 16, 1935, he sent the Senate a special message advocating American adherence to the World Court. This innocuous thought roused the dormant isolationism of the progressive bloc. Hiram Johnson, a Roosevelt Republican from California, took the lead in denouncing the proposal as an attempt to entangle the United States in the affairs of the bad old world. Huey Long of Louisiana, William E. Borah of Idaho, and other members of the Senate's capricious progressive group joined enthusiastically in the attack. The controversy quickly spread from the Senate to the nation. The Hearst papers, Father Charles E. Coughlin, the radio priest of Detroit, and Will Rogers, the popular comedian, all rushed to the support of the Senate isolationists. Letters and telegrams began to pour into Washington in unprecedented number, even for the Roosevelt administration — over fifty thousand in all. The administration's margin, which the majority leader, Senator Joseph T. Robinson of Arkansas, had deemed quite safe, began to crumble. Under the pressure Roosevelt was forced to give ground. By the end of January, the President was ready to accept formulas for conditional adherence which he had rejected two weeks earlier. But it was too late. On January 29 the administration could muster only fifty-two votes — seven less than the two-thirds required — and the World Court was lost. ("Thank God!" said Borah.)

Several members of the administration — Vice-President John N. Garner, James A. Farley, the Postmaster General, Harold L. Ickes, the Secretary of the Interior — thought the fight a grievous political error. And Ickes, watching Roosevelt's reaction, had the impression that the defeat cut deeply. "There seemed a bitter tinge to his laughter and good humor and perhaps a little showing of willingness to hurt those who brought about his defeat."

The Senate, stimulated by its success, proceeded almost immediately to assert its independence of the President on other issues. The works relief bill provided the next opportunity. Rebellious Democrats, Huey Long in the lead, tacked on an amendment, sponsored by Senator Pat McCarran of Nevada and opposed by the White House, providing for prevailing wages on public-works projects. When the Senate adopted it on February 23, the *New York Times* commented that Roosevelt's "legislative program was thrown into a state of confusion bordering on chaos."

Meantime in the House, the social-security bill, the other priority item in the annual message, was encountering unexpected snags. Everything seemed to be going badly. Ickes reported Roosevelt about this time as "distinctly dispirited. I have never seen him in quite such a state of mind. He looked tired and he seemed to lack fighting vigor or the buoyancy that has always characterized him." For the first time since he had come to Washington, Congress was defying him — and getting away with it. "If the

President wants control of that body," Arthur Krock wrote on February 27, 1935, "he must begin to exercise it at once. . . . The legend of invulnerability fades fast." [4]

V

The outlook for 1935 was increasingly troubling. The country already seemed in a condition of economic stalemate. A political stalemate was threatening in the new Congress. On top of all this, the administration was increasingly faced by the possibility of a constitutional stalemate.

For two years the New Deal had managed to avoid judicial tests of its legislative and administrative innovations. Now cases were steadily working their way through lower courts up to the Supreme Court itself. In December 1934 the justices heard arguments on a suit challenging the oil provisions of the National Industrial Recovery Act. On the first Monday after the President's annual message in 1935, the Court decided against the government by an 8–1 vote. The damage to the administration's oil policy could quickly be repaired by the passage of a new law. But the next New Deal case — a suit against the congressional joint resolution of 1933, voiding the clauses in public and private bonds pledging redemption in gold — placed the government's entire monetary policy in jeopardy. And close behind were a swarm of other cases — challenges to additional sections of the National Industrial Recovery Act, including the section assuring workers of the right to organize in unions of their own choosing and the section providing for wage regulation in the coal industry; challenges to the act establishing the Tennessee Valley Authority; challenges to the Agricultural Adjustment Act. By March 2, it was reported, 389 cases involving New Deal laws were pending in the courts.

In the few short weeks from November 1934 to February 1935, euphoria had given way to anxiety. At the end of February, Ernest Gruening, Director of the Division of Territories and Island Possessions in the Department of the Interior, expressed to Harold Ickes his concern over the decline in the popularity of the President. Ickes suggested that Gruening talk the situation over with Colonel Edward M. House, a surviving sage from the Wilson administration. Gruening learned from House that Cordell Hull, the Secretary of State, Homer Cummings, the Attorney General, and Daniel Roper, the Secretary of Commerce — all old friends of House's from Wilson days — had already waited on him with similar worries. The expert consensus was that the administration "was drifting and was losing popular strength." About the same time Oscar Chapman, the politically astute Assistant Secretary of the Interior, declared that the tide was running strongly against the administration and that "unless the President did something to change the current during the next thirty days," he could not be re-elected in 1936. Vice-President Garner said in cabinet that he had not seen so much trouble since he had been in Congress: no sooner did he put out one fire than another broke out somewhere else. Key Pittman of Nevada, the chairman of the Senate Foreign Relations Committee, sent the President a vivid picture of the situation in the upper house. The basic trouble, said Pittman, was that there was "no Democratic Party in the United States Senate." There was an "unscrupulous, regular Republican" group; there were the Progressive Republicans, roaming far to the left; there were Democrats who sympathized more with the progressives than with the administration; there were conservative Democrats who "conscientiously believe they are saving you by destroying you." Why this state of confusion?

> Well, of course, the fault is that there is a lack of confidence in the success of the Administration. There is cowardice. There is discontent with regard to patronage. There is complaint . . . that the Congress is not considered a part of the Administration; that they are supposed to pass bills and not be interested in the result of the administration of act; that strange and peculiar persons have become advisors; that there is no leadership; that thinking is farmed out; that defeat is inevitable; and every man must take care of himself.

The despondency was spreading fast from Washington to the country. Thomas Amlie, the Progressive congressman from Wisconsin, reported in March "a very distinct change" in his letters from home: "the people who write to me express the most profound discouragement about the national administration." Herbert

Bayard Swope told Jim Farley about New York: "things ain't too good. . . . I am referring to a sense of fear that is beginning at the top, growing downward and spreading as it goes, which, lacking realization, takes the form of misgiving about the President." "We have come," said Walter Lippmann in March, "to a period of discouragement after a few months of buoyant hope. Pollyanna is silenced and Cassandra is doing all the talking. . . . Within the Administration itself there is a notable loss of self-confidence which is reflected in leadership that is hesitant and confused." "The air has been filled of late," commented the *Washington Star*, "with the noise of things breaking up." On April 4, as the 74th Congress began its fourth month, no important administration measure had yet gone to the President for his signature.[5]

VI

These were hard days for the President. He knew that things were going badly. On every side he was assailed with demands for action. Yet he felt that he must bide his time. On March 13 he deplored to the National Emergency Council the "jittery feeling" that Congress was not going to accomplish anything. "That, I think, is positively childish. . . . Give them a chance! After all, they love to talk. Let them talk." "I am saying very little, keeping my temper and letting them literally stew in their own juice," he wrote Josephus Daniels. "I think it is the best policy for a while." He told Colonel House that the rest of the session would no doubt be more or less of a madhouse, "every Senator a law unto himself and every one seeking the spotlight." Still, out of it might come "such disgust on the part of the average voter that some well-timed, common sense campaigning on my part this spring or summer will bring people to their senses."

Among those expressing alarm was Molly Dewson of the Democratic National Committee. The President tried to relieve her mind by a special message transmitted through his wife. This message set forth with unusual clarity his instinct on the timing question. "The fact that people are feeling a lack of leadership in him at present and are worried is perfectly natural," Eleanor Roosevelt told Miss Dewson at her husband's behest.

These things go in cycles. We have been through it in Albany and we are going through it here. . . . He says to tell you that Congress is accomplishing a great deal in spite of the fact that there is very little publicity on what they have done. . . . The relief bill and the [social] security bill are bound to go slowly because they are a new type of legislation. If he tried to force them down the committee's throat and did not give them time to argue them out, he would have an even more difficult congress to work with. . . .

Please say to everyone who tells you that the President is not giving leadership that he is seeing the men constantly, and that he is working with them, but this is a democracy after all, and if he once started insisting on having his own way immediately, we should shortly find ourselves with a dictatorship and I hardly think the country would like that any better than they do the delay.

The ups and downs in peoples' feelings, particularly on the liberal side, are an old, old story. The liberals always get discouraged when they do not see the measures they are interested in go through immediately. Considering the time we have had to work in the past for almost every slight improvement, I should think they might get over with it, but they never do.

Franklin says for Heaven's sake, all you Democratic leaders calm down and feel sure of ultimate success. It will do a lot in satisfying other people.

But confidential presidential injunctions to calm down were not enough when Congress seemed out of control, when clamorous new voices, like those of Huey Long and Father Coughlin, were seizing the headlines, and when days went by without a lead of any sort from the White House. Still, Roosevelt stuck obstinately to the waiting game. In March, as Long, Coughlin, and General Hugh S. Johnson engaged in a radio free-for-all, he commented to Colonel House that the fracas was overdue — "better to have this free side-show presented to the public at this time than later on when the main performance starts!" Late in March he explained to Ray Stannard Baker, the friend and biographer of Wilson. "People tire of seeing the same name day after day in the important headlines of the papers, and the same voice night after night over the radio. For example, if since last November I had tried to keep up the pace of 1933 and 1934, the inevitable histrionics of the new actors, Long and Coughlin and Johnson, would have turned the eye of the audience away from the main drama itself! . . . Individual psychology cannot, because of human weakness, be attuned for long periods of time to a constant repetition of the highest note in the scale."

Yet the longer the unprecedented presidential silence lasted, the more disquiet it caused. When would the "main performance" begin? As Professor Arthur M. Schlesinger of Harvard wrote Roosevelt in May, his constant communication with the people during his first months in office "marked an epoch in the history of democratic leadership." It made people a part of government as never before. It brought "that cold abstraction, civic responsibility, down from the clouds" and transformed public affairs into personal affairs. "What troubles me, Mr. President," Schlesinger said, "is that since those early months of your leadership something has happened to drive us apart. . . . I find it more and more difficult to stand by you and your program because I know less and less about what is going on. That is true of a lot of other people I know and it must be true of people all over the country." Roosevelt replied, "I agree with you about the value of regular reporting. My difficulty is a strange and weird sense known as 'public psychology.' "

There is no question that Roosevelt felt a sense of intense frustration over his unaccustomed impotence. Thus in February he planned a speech defying a possible adverse Supreme Court decision in the gold-clause cases; when this defiance turned out to be unnecessary, "his only regret," said Joseph P. Kennedy, the Chairman of the Securities and Exchange Commission, "was his inability to deliver the speech." The Court had deprived him of a chance to regain the initiative. Later in the winter he underwent a minor humiliation when Congress passed a bonus bill over administration protests. Opposition to the bonus was one of the virtuous issues of the day: it was considered to show both an enlightened concern for the public welfare as against selfish special interests and a true dedication to economy in government. Roosevelt had resolved to veto the bill. But he wavered as to

whether he should do this for the record and acquiesce in its
passage over his veto, or whether he should go personally to the
Hill and fight to have the veto sustained. In a late night argu=
ment at the White House, Morgenthau, striding up and down
in front of the President, urged him to make a fight of it. Finally
as Morgenthau described it, Roosevelt's face lit up in a great smile
he raised his two fists in the air and shook them and said, "My
God! if I win I would be on the crest of the wave."

He badly needed to be on the crest of the wave. But it was
not only the "strange and weird sense known as 'public psychol
ogy'" which held him back. The basic reason for his inaction
was that he was simply unprepared to act. It was not that in
February and March he had things in mind which he was saving
up for a more propitious moment to spring upon Congress and
the nation. It was that the inscrutable processes of decision were
moving all too slowly within. He could not lead until he knew
where he wanted to go. The wrangles of the winter, the overhanging threat of the Supreme Court, the play of pressures in
Congress, the three-cornered brawl on the radio, the turbulence
of opinion in the country, all formed the background for his
own effort to feel his way through to "the main performance" —
the performance for which he, as well as the nation, was waiting.[6]

I

The Theology
of Ferment

2. The Rise of the Demagogues

IN THE HALF-DOZEN YEARS before 1935, the American people had been through two profound shocks. The first was the shock of depression, bringing the sudden fear that the national economy could no longer assure its citizens jobs or perhaps even food and shelter. The second was the shock of the New Deal, bringing the sudden hope that the national government offered a magical means of recovery and progress. If the first shock induced a sullen apathy, the second incited a vast discharge of aspiration and energy. The combination of the two shocks — the swift passage from black discouragement to exaggerated optimism — left the people, or at least volatile minorities among them, excited and vulnerable.

The second shock — the impact of the New Deal — terminated the national descent into listlessness and introduced a period of initiative. In the first months this initiative had seemed a presidential monopoly. But soon it began to spread through the country and shoot off in several directions. The people, by uniting their hopes and efforts during the Hundred Days of 1933, regained the energy to fight among themselves in 1934. In the new mood, politics began to recover meaning; the battle of programs and ideas acquired significance once more. Roosevelt, by showing unexpected possibilities in leadership, was exciting others to dream of new leadership (sometimes their own) even more far-reaching and miraculous. The new administration, by restoring a sense of forward motion to American life, was stimulating many Americans to demands which the New Deal itself could not or would not meet.

The reawakening of politics first took place on the right. By the summer of 1934 growing discontent in the business community had led to the formation of the American Liberty League, which seemed for a moment the spearhead of conservative opposition to the New Deal. No doubt militance on the right hastened the rise of a corresponding militance on the left. A diffuse and indignant political activism now appeared, compounded of chaotic but passionate yearnings for recognition, salvation, and revenge. If the opposition to the New Deal from the right was, in the main, traditional in its organization and expression, much of that on the left represented something novel in its methods and its purposes.

The left opposition was slower to emerge. Through 1934 Roosevelt and the New Deal had kept the currents of popular discontent from developing significant outlets of their own. Thus the voices of the new unrest played a generally minor role in the congressional elections of the autumn. But with Roosevelt's attack of uncertainty in the months following, the situation began to alter. The apparent vacuum in Washington gave the new political prophets their opportunity. As the President lingered off-stage in a seeming paralysis of irresolution, their voices began to sound with increasing confidence. As the President maintained this unwonted silence through the winter and into the spring of 1935, the new clamor began to gain the center of the stage. The rise of the social prophets became the primary political fact of the new year. "I do not think it is possible," wrote H. G. Wells, who visited the United States in this period, "to minimize the significance of their voices as an intimation of a widespread discontent and discomfort, and of an impatient preparedness for sweeping changes in the great masses of the American population. . . . The actual New Deal has not gone far enough and fast enough for them, and that is what the shouting is about." [1]

II

In 1926 a Roman Catholic priest presented himself at radio station WJR in Detroit, Michigan. He was just under thirty-five years old, Irish by origin, Canadian by birth, and had recently taken over the parish in the Detroit suburb of Royal Oak. It was

a time and place of intolerance, and a few weeks before the cross
of the Ku Klux Klan had flamed in the young priest's church-
yard. Now Father Charles E. Coughlin proposed to turn to the
new medium of radio in order to explain his faith to his community. His earnestness and conviction impressed the owner of
the station, also an Irish Catholic. Soon Father Coughlin was
able to begin a series of broadcasts beamed directly from the
altar of his Shrine of the Little Flower.

Gradually the Golden Hour of the Little Flower built a following. Coughlin's rolling and resonant brogue, his highly colored
rhetoric, his instinct for the new medium, all increased his weekly
audience. By 1929, stations in Chicago and Cincinnati began
to carry his broadcasts. The Radio League of the Little Flower
was soon formed to pay the bills. Letters and checks flowed in
each week, and he enlarged his staff to deal with his unseen flock.
All this no doubt gave the young priest an unexpected sense of
personal power. Then in 1930 the depression offered him the
opportunity to put the power to use.

Gradually his attention shifted from religion to politics. An
inspired radio journalist — he used to call himself a "religious
Walter Winchell" — he turned his first attention to the Communists, whom he traced to Adam Weishaupt and the Order of
the Illuminati in eighteenth century Bavaria. "Christian parents,"
he would ask, "do you want your daughter to be the breeder of
some lustful person's desires, and, when the rose of her youth
has withered, to be thrown upon the highways of Socialism? . . .
Choose to-day! It is either Christ or the Red Fog of Communism."
Varying the antithesis, he made *Christ or the Red Serpent* the title
of his first book. "I think by 1933, unless something is done,"
he told a congressional committee in 1930, "you will see a revolution in this country."

Still, Coughlin's conception of the Communist threat was considerably more compassionate than that of Hamilton Fish, before
whose committee he delivered his warning. He defended the
workers who marched under Communist leadership and were shot
down by the Dearborn police before the Ford factory. If a revolution came, Coughlin said, it would be due, not to the deviltry of
the Communists, but to the failure of the propertied class to
work for social justice. "The most dangerous Communist," he

said in 1931, "is the wolf in sheep's clothing of conservatism who is bent upon preserving the policies of greed." This wolf now became Coughlin's particular target. With journalistic flair, he began giving the wolf names — Hoover, for example, or "the Morgans, the Kuhn-Loebs, the Rothschilds, the Dillon Reeds," or the Four Horsemen of the Apocalypse — Morgan, Mellon, Mills, and Meyer. Through 1931 and 1932, his weekly discourses became steadily more specific and sensational.

In the meantime, Coughlin began to offer solutions of his own. He had been an apt student of social philosophy (as well as of debating and football) at St. Michael's, a Basilian college at the University of Toronto. The Basilian Order had long emphasized the question of economic justice. From the documents of the medieval church, young Coughlin had learned that interest was usurious and immoral; from Leo XIII's encyclical of 1891, *Rerum Novarum,* that Catholics should renounce economic individualism, help the weak and defenseless, and, while holding fast to the sanctity of private property, not hesitate to use the state as a means of establishing social justice.

In Detroit Coughlin found an atmosphere congenial to the development of his opinions. His bishop, Michael J. Gallagher, had a background in Austrian social Catholicism. He had studied at Innsbruck in the nineties, was an admirer of Monsignor Seipel, the Catholic priest who became Austrian premier after the First World War, and a friend of Engelbert Dollfuss, the Christian-Social premier of 1932. When Dollfuss was murdered in 1934, Gallagher was among those who walked in his funeral procession. The Bishop believed that priests should preach social justice — and construed social justice in terms mistrustful of bankers and sympathetic toward clerical corporatism. And, by a further stroke of fortune, Coughlin found in the Middle West an audience already prepared by Populist memories for an obsession with the money problem.[2]

III

"I oppose modern capitalism," Coughlin said, "because by its very nature it cannot and will not function for the common good. . . . Modern capitalism as we know it is not worth saving. In fact it is a detriment to civilization." "Capitalism," he wrote for Raymond Moley's *Today* in 1934, "has become so identified with abuses which encumber it that its nature is merged with the abuses. Their removal means the burial of capitalism."

He detested capitalism for its callousness, its individualism, its atheism; most of all, for its domination by bankers, and especially by international bankers. "Long enough," Coughlin cried, "have we been the pawns and chattels of the modern pagans who have crucified us upon a cross of gold . . . the filthy gold standard which from time immemorial has been the breeder of hate, the fashioner of swords, and the destroyer of mankind." These "modern Shylocks" had caused depression; now, in their greed for profit, they were preventing recovery. Bankers gained their profits by making money scarce; this artificial shortage of money was the bottleneck which constricted the flow of goods from the factories and farms to the people. Without means of payment, "capitalism could not go on any more than a human being equipped for the operation of breathing air could go on when submerged in the waters of the ocean." Given the money shortage, "the only two ways out are revaluation of our gold ounce, or repudiation of our debts. One way is Christianity. The other way is Bolshevism."

Beginning in 1932, Coughlin began to press his demands for the Christian solution. His orations now bristled with economic statistics and syllogisms. Part of this air of authority came from two New York businessmen, George LeBlanc, a banker, and Robert M. Harriss, a cotton broker, both convinced inflationists. Coughlin also used papers on economic questions written at his order by students at the Brookings Institution. The revaluation of gold was only the first step in a sound — i.e., inflationary — monetary program. Next, he said, must come the remonetization of silver, both to broaden the base of the currency and to enable the Orient to regain its purchasing power. Here again the international bankers, who had driven silver out of circulation many years before, were the villains. Silver, Coughlin warned sententiously, "has a value and always will, long after the slave standard of the Rothschilds will have been forgotten." And if the people were to recapture control over money, Coughlin believed, the government must nationalize the banks, "creating a nationally-owned banking system as sound as our army and as honest as our post office." This demand was the heart of Coughlin's program.

This program was by no means irrelevant. Coughlin was, of course, more correct than the orthodox economists of 1932 in his preference for inflation over deflation. His plea for monetary management was defensible. Certainly these were fairly basic issues. But his economics were nonetheless rudimentary, specious, and incoherent. He gave indiscriminate support to nearly every available monetary nostrum without regard to logic or consistency. A bill drawn up to embody his ideas and introduced by Gerald Nye in the Senate and Martin Sweeney in the House was abysmally vague. For Coughlin economics was a minor branch of rhetoric.[3]

IV

By 1934 Father Coughlin was established as a public figure of definite but uncertain magnitude. He got more mail than anyone in America — at least 80,000 letters in a normal week and, after certain discourses, as many as a million. He received voluntary contributions of probably half a million dollars a year. He required a clerical staff of 150 to handle his affairs. In place of the old frame church of 1926, he had built an imposing new structure, topped by a 150-foot stone tower with a floodlit figure of Christ on the Cross. His office, at the top of the tower, was accessible only by a spiral staircase. There, in the company of his Great Dane, he composed the weekly orations.

Discounting his extravagant publicity all they could, his critics had to concede him a weekly listening audience of at least ten million people — probably the largest steady audience in the world. He was, said Fortune, "just about the biggest thing that ever happened to radio." Polls showed him outranking such favorites as Ed Wynn, Amos 'n' Andy, and Dr. Fu Manchu. In 1931, when the Columbia Broadcasting System, distressed by his attacks on bankers, had demanded the right to screen his talks, Coughlin complained of censorship, and CBS was deluged with angry letters. The next fall CBS terminated the Coughlin contract on the ground that it had stopped selling network time for religious purposes; at three o'clock on Sundays CBS listeners heard the equally sonorous but less controversial tones of the New York Philharmonic. But Coughlin, organizing his own independent network, invaded CBS territory. When WCAU in Philadelphia polled its clientele on Coughlin versus classical music, the result was 187,000 for the priest and 12,000 for the Philharmonic.

Coughlin could even face down the princes of his own church. Once Cardinal O'Connell of Boston, a rigidly conservative prelate, tried to scold him: "You can't begin speaking about the rich or making sensational accusations against banks and bankers, or uttering demagogic stuff to the poor. You can't do it, for the church is for all." O'Connell warned his own flock not to be "whisked off their feet by spectacular talk, mostly froth, but with some poison in it. . . . We do not like to hear almost hysterical addresses from ecclesiastics." But Coughlin, secure in the backing of his own bishop, remained unperturbed. "It would be egotistical for me to disclose the confidence which Bishop Gallagher has oftentimes spoken to me about my broadcasts," he said, immediately disclosing it. And Gallagher was quick to defend Coughlin. "Christ was not setting class against class when he rebuked the abuse of wealth," the Bishop said. To accuse Coughlin of fomenting class bitterness was to "accuse the Popes and to accuse Christ." Gallagher added that, had Coughlin lived in Russia before the Revolution, "and had he possessed the radio facilities," there would probably be no Communism in Russia today.

Father Coughlin seemed to be rising on a mighty tide. He was a big man, sleek and plump, with bland and genial manners. His gray hair, mild blue eyes, steel spectacles, and soft-pink too-smooth face gave him a priestly look; but he added to this a certain brisk worldliness of his own. He chain-smoked cigarettes, liked bridge and the theater, and sprinkled his conversation with "hells" and "damns." Hugh Walpole, the English novelist, thought him "very free in his talk about sex." He was a hard man to dislike: Raymond Swing considered him "likable," and Selden Rodman found him "friendly, tolerant, a good listener." He reminded Frank Kent of Bryan in the timbre of his voice and in his "vibrant personal charm." Walpole saw "a quiet, stocky, gentle and beautiful-eyed man with whom I felt instantly a strong bond. I think he felt it for me. Our eyes constantly met during lunch. . . . His influence on me was quite extraordinary. . . . I shall never forget him." Without irony, Walpole gave the scourge of the international bankers a silver mustard pot that had belonged to the Rothschilds.

Many, like Kent and Walpole, felt some indefinable force of personality. Power evidently excited Coughlin; he knew its temptations and believed that only religion had saved him from a gaudy career of evil, in which he might have become the wickedest international banker of them all. "Why, if I threw away and denounced my faith," he told an adoring female biographer, "I would surround myself with the most adroit hi-jackers, learn every trick of the highest banking and stock manipulations, avail myself of the laws under which to hide my own crimes, create a smoke screen to throw into the eyes of men, and — believe me, I would become the world's champion crook."

If he could not become the world's champion crook, he could at least become the world's champion radio priest. Bishop Gallagher was right in conditioning Coughlin's possible Russian triumphs on the achievements of Marconi. He fitted the new medium superbly, with his musical diction, the low, slow beginning, the trilled r's, the long e's ("unprecedented"), and the prolonged o's, the gradual increase in tempo and vehemence, and finally the sanctimoniously passionate climax. But radio had its drawbacks too. Weekly broadcasts consumed material at a tremendous rate. Coughlin increasingly faced the problem of maintaining momentum from week to week, of avoiding boredom, of coming up regularly with new ideas and new sensations, new heroes and new villains.[4]

v

For a considerable time Coughlin had amiable relations with Franklin Roosevelt. As Governor of New York, Roosevelt had conveyed his sympathy to the priest for his troubles with CBS. Though Coughlin expressed no preferences in 1932, none of his followers could have supposed that he wanted more of Hoover and the Four Horsemen of the Apocalypse. In the first months of 1933, Coughlin hailed the new administration with such proprietary enthusiasm that some thought he was an official representative of the Treasury (and a few wrote irritably to the President about it). He conferred with Roosevelt, reminded the President of the background of the French Revolution ("as I had garnered it from the carefully prepared sermons extant in the archives of the old churches in France"), and dispatched him admiring telegrams and letters of advice. Nor did he neglect the White House staff. Sending Marvin McIntyre a copy of *Quadragesimo Anno,* the good priest added earthily, "Take time off — if necessary go and sit on the toilet while you read the enclosed book."

In a general way Coughlin favored the early program of the New Deal. He believed that government had the duty "to limit the amount of profits acquired by any industry"; moreover, "there can be no lasting prosperity if free competition exists in any industry." He approved of NRA, public works, social security, and the regulation of the stock exchanges. His main objection was to the agricultural program. Writing Roosevelt in September 1933, he denounced Wallace, Ezekiel, and Tugwell, "who have advocated the slaughter of six million pigs and have already defiled the countryside and the Mississippi River with their malodorous rottenness under the pretext that there was a superfluity of pork in this world while millions of Chinese, Indians and South Americans are starving. . . . My dear Mr. President, there is no superfluity of either cotton or wheat until every naked back has been clothed, until every empty stomach has been filled."

Coughlin's solicitude for the unhappy East possibly proceeded as much from his desire to remonetize silver as from his concern for oriental backs and bellies. He led the inflationist crusade in the fall of 1933; and when Roosevelt fell under conservative attack for the gold-purchase policy, Coughlin defended him at the giant rally at the Hippodrome in New York. Testifying before a House committee in January 1934, Coughlin said that if Congress refused to back Roosevelt's gold policy, "I predict revolution in this country and a revolution that will make the French Revolution silly. It is either Roosevelt or ruin." Coming out of the White House the next day, Coughlin told the press, "I discovered that Mr. Roosevelt is about twenty years ahead of the thought that is current in the country today." As late as April 1934 he said, "I will never change my philosophy that the New Deal is Christ's deal." [5]

VI

He did not anticipate, however, the strain to which that philosophy would soon be subjected. Roosevelt's resistance to the silver bloc made him unhappy, and his unhappiness was notably increased when Morgenthau released a list of silver speculators headed by the name of Coughlin's secretary. Coughlin responded with cryptic and angry talk about "gentile silver" and denunciation of the controllers of gold. In this new perspective, Christ's deal was losing its luster. "We now see," Coughlin said bitterly in another fortnight, "the policies of a Hitler, the suggestion of a Mussolini and the dogma of a Stalin more honored in our midst than the ideas of a Washington or a Jefferson."

Coughlin had tricky tactical problems. He could not know whether his popularity would survive a real break with the New Deal. Yet he was driven to excesses by the infernal necessity of keeping his listeners week after week in an appropriate state of tension. So for a year he veered crazily in his attitude toward the administration, one week testing the possibilities of opposition, the next retreating to the safe shelter of support, then again rushing to plant his own standard in exposed ground. His own confusion was compounded by the adroitness of Roosevelt, who saw no point in losing Coughlin's support and regularly despatched emissaries like Joseph P. Kennedy and Frank Murphy to sweeten up the radio priest.

Thus, after his springtime denunciations of Roosevelt and Morgenthau in 1934, Coughlin returned to the air in the fall to proclaim his unwavering faith "in the courage of our President and in the stalwart uprightness and integrity of his Secretary of the Treasury." He would support the New Deal, he said, so long as he retained the power of speech. A week later, however, while retaining the power of speech, he went off on a new tack. "These old parties," he now decided, "are all but dead." They should "relinquish the skeletons of their putrefying carcasses to the halls of a historical museum." The nation needed a political realignment; and he offered his contribution to this end on November 11 by announcing the formation of his own movement, the National Union for Social Justice.

The Union was not to be a party. It was a pressure group

designed to move both parties toward the Coughlin program. Of the sixteen planks in its platform, six dealt with monetary policy. Others called for an annual wage, for the nationalization of such public necessities as power, light, oil, and natural gas, for the protection of organized labor against (mysteriously) "the vested interests of wealth and intellect," and for the triumph of human rights over property rights. One plank called for liberty, specifying conscience and education but oddly saying nothing about speech, press, or political activity. Roosevelt, Coughlin said coldly, "is now willing to hand over the reins to the United States Chamber of Commerce and the international bankers." The President's effort to save capitalism was as hopeless as "removing in a sieve the water from the Atlantic Ocean to the swimming pool of the New York Athletic Club."

But this mood did not last either. In a few days he gave ecstatic praise to the social-security message of January 1935. "Such outworn and unpractical phrases as 'free competition' and 'rugged individualism' and 'laissez-faire,' " Coughlin said, "today are seeking a resting place in the limbo of archaic falsehoods." As for Roosevelt, "Today I believe in him as much as ever." This last statement was doubtless true enough. In a fortnight, Coughlin was leading the fight against the administration proposal that the United States enter the World Court. By March he concluded that the Roosevelt administration had "out-Hoovered Hoover. . . . I will not support a New Deal which protects plutocrats and comforts Communists."

In part, this may all have been the calculated confusionism of a man whose hope lay in chaos. Certainly Coughlin had more than a usual knack for mystification. For all his big talk about abolishing capitalism, he could observe of it in the next breath, "The sane people in this country have always lent their support and will always lend their support to that theory of economics." While denouncing business, he had no compunction about asking businessmen to support him in his crusade against government regimentation. His solution to the challenge of "production for use" was to advocate "production for use at a profit," whatever that meant. "By the nationalization of power, light, oil and natural gas," he once explained, ". . . I do not subscribe to the theory that we should nationalize public utilities." Point 13 of his Union program began, "I believe in the broadening of the base of taxation," and Point 14 ended calling for "the further lifting of crushing taxation from the slender revenues of the laboring class." "If necessary," he said characteristically, "I shall 'dictate' to preserve democracy." There were few issues in these years in which Father Coughlin did not take both sides more resoundingly than anyone else.[6]

VII

For a season, Father Coughlin seemed a point of fusion between Populism and the Encyclicals, between William Jennings Bryan and Cardinal Gibbon. He was aware of the native sources of his appeal. The National Union's platform bore many resemblances to that of the Minnesota Farmer-Labor Party; and Coughlin occasionally invoked such names as Bryan and Charles A. Lindbergh, Sr. Next to the Northeast, his main strength lay in the Middle West (though the fact that New York and Massachusetts had four times as many local units of the National Union as Minnesota and Wisconsin suggests that as early as 1935 his support came more from urban lower-middle class Catholics than from Protestant farmers in the Populist tradition). Yet papal bulls, even supplemented by Populism, were hardly enough to maintain Coughlin against the competition, say, of Governor Floyd Olson of Minnesota, not to mention Franklin D. Roosevelt. Reaching out for new emotional levers to touch, for new sources of support, Coughlin was beginning to manipulate ambiguities which had existed in Populism and in social Catholicism but to which he gave new and crude emphasis. By 1935 the compulsion to produce weekly sensations was bringing doubtful emotions near the surface.

Thus his view of the role of business and especially of labor implied increasingly the pattern of the corporate state. He wanted the Department of Labor to take over the functions of collective bargaining: "let it supplant the AF of L entirely. Why should the workers pay dues to a labor organization to protect a right which is guaranteed by law?" And his hatred of the moneylenders spilled over to an identification of bankers with Rothschilds, Warburgs, and Kuhn-Loebs, and thus to lurking anti-Semitism.

He was, in his mellow way, a racist. Mentioning Alexander Hamilton, he would casually add, "whose original name was Alexander Levine." He freely attacked those "who, without either the blood of patriotism or of Christianity flowing in their veins, have shackled the lives of men and of nations with the ponderous links of their golden chain." Testifying against a. birth-control measure in 1934, he said, "We are being degenerated, and here we are advocating ways and means to uncriminalize the use of contraceptives, and to help America forget its Anglo-Saxon origin. . . . One hundred years from today Washington will be Washingtonski."

For a time, these had been grace notes in his Catholic Populism, clear enough to those who listened for them but imperceptible to most of his audience. In 1935, as he strove frantically to discover a base independent of the New Deal, these themes became more insistent. Yet few detected the fascist implication, and such perceptive figures tended to be discounted for other reasons — Hugh Johnson, because hyperbole was his occupational disease; the Communists, because they considered even Norman Thomas a fascist. Nor did these proto-fascist nuances especially disturb either his Populist or his Catholic followers. Obsession with the money question had long contained an anti-Semitic potential, visible in critics of the banking system from William Cobbett to Henry Adams and including a few Populists. Indeed, Bryan's cherished image of crucifixion on a cross of gold had an obvious, if wholly unintended, racist resonance. By 1935 Milo Reno, the Farmers' Holiday leader, was referring to the "Jew Deal"; James Rorty, scratching Reno's radicalism, reported that he found underneath not only anti-Semitism but fundamentalism. This was Gerald Winrod's brew, too. As for Coughlin's Catholic followers in the cities, economic and cultural collisions had long since predisposed many of them against the Jews.

What threatened to hurt Coughlin far more than this growing ambiguity of his message was his growing hostility toward Roosevelt. His followers wanted to cleave to them both. It was hard to predict how many would remain loyal to the National Union if its leader forced them to a choice. Thus Ruth Mugglebee, who had published a hagiographical life of Coughlin in 1933, recorded his anti-Roosevelt gestures with evident dismay when she brought the work up to date in 1935; and there must have been thousands like her.

By 1935, Coughlin's case against the administration was achieving what was for him almost coherence. So long as the bankers remained untouched, he said, the old economic deal reigned supreme. The administration had sought to nationalize industry while leaving banking in private hands, when it should have nationalized banks and left industry in private hands. "We demand ownership of the banks . . . [but] I protest most vehemently against any government going into business." In such terms, Coughlin was seeking to unite the agrarian radicals and the small businessmen of the cities against the President. If it was not altogether clear in the spring of 1935 that Coughlin was moving away from Leo XIII and Bryan in strange deviations of his own, it was increasingly clear that he was preparing to take the great risk — to gamble his own magnetism against that of Franklin D. Roosevelt.[7]

3. The Old Folks' Crusade

THERE WERE OTHER SYMPTOMS of the vast unrest. No group of Americans, except the Negroes, was harder hit by depression than the aged. There were more old people than ever before: the number of those over sixty had more than doubled since 1900. They were more likely to be sick or disabled than younger people. Where jobs existed, they had far less chance of getting them. In nearly half the states there was no system of old-age pensions; in the rest, pensions averaged around twelve or fifteen dollars a month and were hopelessly inadequate. Nor were these needy old people a rabble of paupers. Depression had brought so-called solid folk into their ranks — men and women who had faithfully worked and saved according to the precepts of the capitalist system and who, in reward for their virtue, had nothing now to keep them in their old age, no savings, no jobs, nothing but relief or charity. Such people were proud and bitter. Their despair was rendered the more poignant by their memories of the America of their youth — a rugged, self-reliant, optimistic land where men always looked ahead to new frontiers.

II

At the same time, this identification with an earlier America gave them a certain incredulity about their present helplessness and thus kept alive the desperate inner conviction that somewhere an answer could be found. So, one morning in the late fall of 1933, Dr. Francis Everett Townsend, an unemployed physician of Long Beach, California, sixty-six years old, looked out his bathroom window while shaving and saw in the alley below, cluttered with rubbish barrels and garbage cans, "three haggard, very old women" — as he later described them — "stooped with great age, bending over the barrels, clawing into the contents." Dr. Townsend had kept his calm through a good deal in the years since the crash. But this indignity to his generation and his country was too much. He broke into a rage of profanity, reminiscent of the days when he had been a doctor in a wide-open town in the Black Hills. He later said, "I let my voice bellow with the wild hatred I had for things as they were." His wife, alarmed, rushed into the room: "Doctor! Oh, you musn't shout like that! All the neighbors will hear you!" To this, Townsend replied, according to his later recollection, "I want all the neighbors to hear me! I want God Almighty to hear me! I'm going to shout till the whole country hears!"

Francis E. Townsend was ordinarily a gentle man; but a lean intensity occasionally gleamed through his thin face, and he carried from his frontier upbringing a deep belief that America was a land of possibility. He had been born in 1867 in a log cabin on an Illinois farm. Growing up in hard times, he roamed the country west to California, trying his hand at farm labor, mining, homesteading, and schoolteaching. "I came to manhood," he later said, "in the severe depression of the Nineties, so you can see I've had my fill of depression, and that I've reason to hate the word. In the Nineties I was thwarted at every step."

In due course, Townsend decided that he wanted a profession. In 1900, having managed to save up $100, he enrolled in the Omaha Medical College at the age of thirty, the oldest man in his class. For a time he paid his way by selling mail orders to farmers on the sod-house frontier. "This experience in salesmanship stood me in good stead later." Eventually one of his professors lent him the money he needed to finish. The friendly professor, an ardent Socialist, also gave young Townsend the vision that "in a poverty-free world we might see an end to vice and disease." He probably first encouraged Townsend to read Bellamy's *Looking Backward*.

In 1903 Townsend went to a small town on the north slope of the Black Hills. He practiced medicine there for seventeen years until failing health led him to move to Long Beach, California. In Long Beach he kept up practice, but in a desultory way; more

of his income came from selling building lots, often for a successful real-estate broker named Robert Earl Clements. Then came
the crash, and for a while Townsend caught on as assistant health
officer. The next three years were a shattering experience. Every day
needy people, many of them old, crowded the health office. Townsend, treating them in the clinic, visiting them in their homes,
saw the depression from the inside — "such distress, pain and
horror," he later wrote: "such sobbing loyalties under the worst
possible circumstances." He was afflicted particularly by the hope-
lessness of the old people, their "spiritual panic." When he lost
his job with a change in city administration in 1933, he was
determined, with all the irrepressible optimism of a man who had
grown up on the frontier and read Edward Bellamy, to find the
road out. "I suppose I have always been more or less socialisti-
cally inclined," he mused in 1959. "I believe we ought to plan
as a nation for all the things we need. . . . I suppose that taking
care of people runs against the American grain — against the
feeling that everyone ought to hustle for himself. But there comes
a time when people can't hustle any more. I believe that we owe
a decent living to the older people. After all, they built our country and made it what it is." [1]

III

In September 1933 Dr. Townsend sent a letter to the *Long
Beach Press-Telegram*. To solve the problem of unemployment,
Townsend said, "it is just as necessary to make some disposal of
our surplus workers, as it is to dispose of our surplus wheat or
corn." But surplus workers obviously could not be disposed of
through slaughter, like surplus hogs. Some means had to be
found to retire them from economic activity. And the natural
class to be retired would be the old people. Townsend's proposal
was simple. Give everyone over sixty federal pensions of $150
a month "or more, on condition that they spend the money as
they get it." This program would both pump new purchasing
power into the economy and open up jobs for younger people.
The pension system, Townsend added, could be financed by a
national sales tax.

Where Townsend got the idea is obscure. In August 1931

Bruce Barton, the advertising man, wrote a satirical article for *Vanity Fair* entitled "How to Fix Everything." His genial proposal was to cure the depression by retiring every one at forty-five (Barton explained that he had just celebrated his forty-fifth birthday) and paying them half what they had been earning. "My plan would fix everything," Barton concluded, "and be so grand in every way that I wonder why I ever thought of it. . . . Wire your congressman! Vote! Organize! Orate!" In 1931 a Seattle dentist named C. Stewart McCord circulated a more serious document along similar lines called "The Mercy Death for Surplus Labor." McCord advocated the retirement of old people from the labor market at pensions of $50 a month, the money to be raised through a sales tax.

Dr. Townsend was hardly a typical reader of *Vanity Fair;* and there is no evidence that he ever saw the McCord memorandum. Still, the idea was plainly in the air. Townsend's particular contribution was to convert the idea into a movement. When his letter set off a mild controversy in the Long Beach press, Townsend advertised for elderly men and women to pass around petitions for the pension plan. The ante was quietly upped from $150 to $200. In two weeks, volunteers had obtained several thousand signatures. Townsend now approached his old real-estate associate Clements to help manage the agitation. At first skeptical, Clements, impressed either by the plan or by the flow of signatures, allowed himself to be persuaded. On January 24, 1934, Townsend and Clements, along with Townsend's brother, who was a porter in a Los Angeles hotel, filed the articles of incorporation for a new organization, Old Age Revolving Pensions, Ltd.

Clements brought to the movement the hustle of a high-pressure real-estate promoter. He was thirty-nine years old, a Texan by birth, hard-eyed and tough, with unusual talents for organization and ballyhoo. Where Townsend could think of little more to do than circulate petitions and answer mail, Clements perceived the need, as he later put it, of keeping the developing enthusiasm "at a high pitch." In August 1934 he began the formation of local clubs. At the same time, he started to take over both techniques and organizers from the Anti-Saloon League (much as the Liberty League was the continuator of the Association Against the Prohibition Amendment). He found unemployed ministers particularly effective as missionaries for the new faith.

IV

The response was rapid and wistful. For old folks who had lived too long in the shadows, the promise of $200 a month offered deliverance and dignity. It told them that the America in which they had grown up, the land of kindliness and faith, was not dead; it meant that their own lives, which they could not but regard as lives of labor and thrift, would at last have their reward in a secure old age. In 1934, throughout the West, pathetic old people — mostly Anglo-Saxon in origin, mostly lower middle class, mostly nonpolitical or Republican — flocked into the Townsend clubs. Some younger people joined them, hoping to be relieved of the burden of elderly relatives or to benefit by the new money thrust into circulation. They all listened with rapt attention to the Townsend orators and obediently sent in their mites to national headquarters.

The atmosphere of the movement was less that of pressure politics than of the old-time religion. The Townsendites sang hymns and interrupted speakers with cries of "Amen." Some among them saw in the plan the fulfillment of the millennial hope. The Townsend ministers were ready to certify authoritatively that the plan was at least "the God-given way." As Dr. Clinton Wunder, former pastor of the Baptist Temple of Rochester, New York, once dean of the Institute of Religious Science and Philosophy of Los Angeles, said at a Townsend convention, "God is with us, and with God all things are possible." (Dr. Wunder's avocation was the writing of letters so unsacerdotal that a congressional investigating committee primly declined to publish the more striking passages.) The Michigan bulletin of the organization described Townsend as "the man whom God raised up to do this job." One letter to Townsend reported, "So many of our citizens have gone so far in their faith now as to declare Dr. Townsend is the embodiment of Jesus Christ." A delegate to a Townsend convention once complained that in 1867 no star had risen over Fairbury, Illinois, to mark his birth. The Founder himself said that his movement would make "as deep and mighty changes in civilization as did

Christianity itself," but "where Christianity numbered its hundreds, in its beginning years, our cause numbered its millions." Once he described the Townsendites as "the instruments through whom the Divine Will proposes to establish on earth the universal brotherhood of man." As the meetings adjourned, the membership sang:

> Onward, Townsend soldiers,
> Marching as to war,
> With the Townsend banner
> Going on before.
> Our devoted leaders
> Bid depression go;
> Join them in the battle,
> Help them fight the foe.

This quasi-religious mood produced an almost hysterical intensity, leading to cruel pressure against nonsigners and to the boycott of merchants who refused to circulate the petitions or put the Doctor's picture in their shop windows. Stanley High, a liberal Methodist minister, wrote Franklin Roosevelt's secretary, Steve Early, about the movement in 1935, "The more I see of it the more I am impressed with its power. It is doing for a certain class of people what — a few years ago — was done by the prohibition movement: giving them a sublimation outlet."

Clements took care that the Townsend organization kept the movement's evangelism under strict control. The new clubs were permitted no autonomy, and even the organizers had to stick carefully to their scripts. Authority remained firmly in the hands of Townsend and Clements; after all, they were not only apostles of a faith, but owners of an organization. In January 1935 Clements launched the *Townsend National Weekly*; by the end of the year its circulation had leaped to more than 200,000. Patent medicine companies filled its pages with advertisements for bladder tablets, gland stimulators, and the like, headed "How To Live 100 Years" or "Married At 120." Clements saw to it that the ownership of this profitable enterprise was vested, not even in the OARP, but personally in Townsend and himself.

It was Clements whose skill transformed Townsendism from one

more crazy California enthusiasm into a crusade. He was quite right
to begin, as he did in 1935, billing himself as the Co-Founder.[2]

v

As the Townsend movement grew, the Townsend Plan itself
began to take on new dimensions. "The plan is only incidentally
a pension plan," Dr. Townsend insisted; "the old people are
simply to be used as a means by which prosperity will be restored
to all of us." The real objective was nothing less than ending the
depression by giving buying power to the masses. "The time has
arrived," Townsend said, "when the citizenry must take charge of
their government and repudiate the philosophy of want and hunger in a land of wealth and abundance."

Originally, Townsend had meant to finance the plan by a retail
sales tax. Then someone pointed out that this would fall most
heavily on those least able to pay. In its place Townsend and
Clements came up with the idea of a 2 per cent transaction tax,
which would hit a commodity, not just at the point of ultimate sale,
but every time it changed hands along the way from raw material to
finished product. For some reason, this tax, which would have been
no more than a multiple sales tax, struck them as more equitable
than a retail sales tax — perhaps because they looked to large returns from stock and bond transactions. At one point Townsend
had thought of starting things off with two billion dollars' worth of
new currency as well; but conservative advisers persuaded him to
drop the idea as inflationary.

The bill was first introduced into the House in January 1935 by
John S. McGroarty, an otherwise conservative Democrat who owed
his election in the fall of 1934 to Townsend support. McGroarty,
who had been chosen poet laureate of California by the state
legislature a few years earlier, was himself seventy-two years old.
His bill guaranteed a $200 monthly pension to all citizens over
sixty on condition that they renounce gainful employment and
agree to spend all the pension within the country in thirty days.
In April 1935 McGroarty introduced a revised bill which abandoned the flat $200 promise in favor of pensions as large as the
reserve fund would permit, but not to exceed $200. (The Town-
send leaders approved this, which did not prevent the *Townsend*

Weekly from declaring calmly a few months later, "There has never been, nor will be, any compromise on the $200 per month provision in the Townsend demands. All statements to the contrary are false.") The revised bill also added some trivial supplementary taxes and called for an income test.

In the meantime, the Plan was meeting a highly skeptical reaction in most informed circles, liberal or conservative. Townsend himself guessed that about 8 million men and women would qualify for the Plan, which meant about $1.6 billion disbursed every month. But experts found it hard to believe that, even with a means test, less than 10 million of about 11.5 million people over sixty would qualify. This would mean an annual outlay of $24 billion, about half the national income and twice as much as combined existing federal, local, and state taxes. The Plan, in short, seemed to the unregenerate a system for channeling half the national income to the one-eleventh of the population over sixty.

The Townsendites rejoined that the stimulus to business activity from the forced circulation of the pension money would raise the national income for all and, at the same time, increase the yield from the transactions tax. But opponents questioned whether forced circulation would materially speed up the rate at which money was spent; most Americans, they claimed, were already spending their money the month they received it. And they denounced the transactions tax as regressive and uncollectible. By raising prices, it would reduce purchasing power; it would wipe out profit margins for small business; it would promote economic concentration (since an integrated business would have fewer transactions to be taxed and therefore would be in a better competitive position). In addition, the Plan's provisions for licensing all sellers and for policing the spending of the pension presented vast administrative problems. Provisions for old age might be a good idea — and, indeed, old-age insurance was about to be enacted in the Social Security bill — but the Townsend Plan was fantasy.

None of this impressed the Founder, who prayed, "God deliver us from further guidance by professional economists!" "Every time a 'brain-truster' says this plan is crazy," Townsend told a congressional committee with satisfaction, "a hundred thousand new converts come to our banner. . . . I myself am not a statistician.

I am not even an economist, for which fact millions of people have expressed thanks. I am simply a country practitioner of medicine." As Congressman McGroarty put it during the debate in the House of Representatives, "I refuse to talk to college professors. Give me the names of some practical people. [Laughter]." As for the old-age provisions of the Social Security bill, the *Townsend Weekly* denounced them as "outrageous." When Harry Hopkins and Frances Perkins expressed skepticism about the Townsend Plan, the *Weekly* lost all hope in Roosevelt and thereafter scathingly attacked all aspects of the New Deal.

The House approached the Townsend bill in the most gingerly way. No one could afford to be against Mother. Hear Congressman John Tolan of California: "She is the sweetest memory of my life, and the hands that used to feed me and cool my fevered brow now touch me only in my dreams. But if she were living today . . . that little, frail mother of mine . . . would say, 'Son, you be good to the old folks, and God will bless you.' " Most members of the House, however, were perhaps less concerned with sentimental memories than with the letters and telegrams flooding their offices, the bundles of petitions, the implacable elderly visitors, and the other manifestations of the crusade. When the division finally came, nearly two hundred congressmen bravely absented themselves, and the rest arranged to defeat the proposal without a roll call. According to the Townsend tabulation, 38 Democrats voted for the Plan, 17 Republicans, 3 Progressives, and 2 Farm-Laborites.

The supporters included a number of congressmen better known up to that point as advocates of sales taxes than of old-age pensions. If the pension feature was radical, the tax feature was, after all, profoundly conservative. The Plan thus seemed an all-purpose political weapon, capable of attracting both men of the left eager to dramatize a national need and men of the right eager to find a new basis of popular support.[3]

VI

Townsend's own personality was well designed to put a reassuring face on what seemed at first a radical idea. And the idea, indeed, was all that remained of his youthful utopianism: the splendid dream of Edward Bellamy was dwindling to a huckster's promise of $200 a month for old folks. "One of the great faults of socialism," Townsend told a reporter, "is that it is too vague, people can't get it through their heads. I used to be a Socialist once." There was nothing vague about him now. Nor did he want to risk misunderstanding at a time when the air was full of talk about production-for-use and other such heresies. "We believe," Townsend headquarters declared, "that the profit system is the very main spring of civilized progress." When Upton Sinclair and his End Poverty in California crusade terrified Californian respectability in 1934, Townsend made his position clear. "We don't endorse any socialistic program. The EPIC plan opposes the profit system. The Townsend Plan represents an attempt to make the profit system function." Privately he commented that Sinclair was "our very greatest menace." The Townsend Plan was too much for Sinclair, who swallowed almost everything else; but Frank Merriam, his conservative Republican opponent, came out for it, and the *Townsend Weekly*, discovering that Merriam savored of "Lincolnism," gratefully endorsed him. Townsend preferred working with Republicans. After all, Roosevelt declined to see him, and the administration had its own social-security program. Stanley High, talking to Townsend in 1935, found him more favorably disposed toward Hoover than toward Roosevelt.

On the surface Townsend remained the same as ever, plain as an old shoe, everybody's next-door neighbor, a player of cribbage who called his wife "Mother" and sprinkled his talk with "bless your souls," a simple country doctor with a kindly bedside manner. "I am ridiculed as a visionary and a dreamer," he once said, "but no one has said that I am a bulldozer. I am always spoken of as a soft-voiced, mild-mannered old chap." But the strain of being a minor prophet was considerable. "Doctor," as his associates called him, was becoming aware of himself as a public figure. He was also becoming aware of the possibilities of his movement. As he wrote Clements in January 1935, "You and I have the world by the tail with a downhill pull on this thing, Earl, if we work it right." As a man with the world by the tail, he could permit himself liberties. His offhand remarks sometimes shocked his disciples. When one brought the rank-and-file of the movement into the conversation, Townsend was reported to have said, "Oh, those old

fossils; they don't know what it is all about anyway." Another witness told of complaining to Doctor that Clements had said,
"We don't give a damn about the old people"; Doctor responded
irritably, "What of it: what of it?"

Clements was infinitely the more cynical of the two. In his
frank promoter's way he called the movement "the racket," and
when he left in 1936, he took $50,000 for his share in the *Townsend
Weekly*. Doctor, on the other hand, let the movement pay no more
than his expenses and a salary; there is no evidence that he used it
to increase his personal bank account. He had higher rewards. A
Townsend state manager once reported the Founder standing before
the Lincoln statue in Washington. "Take this man, for example,"
Doctor said; "just a poor lawyer, no smarter than me and certainly
not better educated than me, but just being at the right moment
before the people with a plea to save the Nation from slavery . . .
and now the world faces a fate worse than slavery and a lowly country doctor comes out of the West to save the world. It might be me
sitting up there." After all, Sheridan Downey of California, once
the lieutenant of Upton Sinclair, now Townsend's counsel, could
say, "Dr. Townsend and Robert E. Clements no longer belong to
themselves, they belong to the American nation. . . . Some day men
will talk of Dr. Townsend and Robert Clements as we now speak
of George Washington and Alexander Hamilton or Abraham Lincoln and General Grant."

VII

Yet already success was bringing trouble. In the course of 1935
there were stirrings among the rank-and-file — doubts about the
rigid centralization of authority, questions about what was happening to the money. For a while Townsend was philosophical.
"There are always hell-rumblings in a Townsend organization at
all times, I guess," he told Clements. Soon he was taking sterner
action against the schismatics, expelling them from the movement,
suing them in court, and authorizing editorials in the *Townsend
Weekly* which compared himself with Christ and his critics with
Judas Iscariot.

Nonetheless, Townsend really believed in his Plan and had the
best interests of his movement at heart. In time he felt obliged

to recognize the demand from below for a more democratic organization. This brought him into conflict with Clements, who had no intention of relinquishing power. The two men had other differences. Townsend felt that the profits of the *Weekly* should go to the movement; Clements thought they belonged personally to the Founder and the Co-Founder. And on issues Townsend was the more liberal of the two. Where Clements was wedded to the transactions tax, Townsend was willing to listen to criticisms of the tax as regressive and entertain Sheridan Downey's proposal that the pensions be paid for through the issuance of tax-free bonds. Perhaps the most important disagreement, however, had to do with the future of the organization. Clements, impressed by the example of the Anti-Saloon League, wanted the movement to remain a pressure group working within both parties. But by late 1935 Townsend was thinking about organizing a new political party.

Few outside the movement were aware of the strains within. To most, the sudden upsurge of Townsendism was the striking political phenomenon of 1935. The passage of the Social Security Act could not arrest it: the old-age provisions left millions of old people uncovered, and in any case payments under old-age insurance would not begin till 1942. In August 1935, Stanley High called the Townsend movement "the most vital and fast-moving extra-orthodox movement now under way"; Senator William E. Borah, "the most extraordinary social and political movement in recent years and perhaps in our entire history." "Townsendism," wrote Raymond Moley in December, "is easily the outstanding political sensation as this year ends." "The battle against the Townsend Plan has been lost, I think," reported the economist E. E. Witte, "in pretty nearly every state west of the Mississippi, and the entire Middle-Western area is likewise badly infected."

Much was repellent about the movement — the slick publicity, the autocratic structure, the cynical exploitation of wretchedness and senility, the anti-intellectualism, the economic illiteracy, the greedy emphasis on "$200 a month," the hysteria of the rank-and-file. And the influence of the movement has often been overrated. The Townsend agitation had nothing to do with the initiation of the New Deal social-security policy. Roosevelt established the Committee on Economic Security in June 1934, when the Doctor was unknown outside Long Beach and before there was a Town-send club in existence. Though the threat of the Townsend Plan no doubt speeded the passage of the Social Security bill and as-sured the inclusion in it of old-age insurance, that bill passed two months before Townsend considered that his own movement "had developed to a size sufficient to justify our calling a national convention."

Yet Townsend and his followers were calling attention in a definitive way to a cruel problem which the American people had too long shoved under the rug. Now the nation could never ignore its old again. And when its chosen issue was not involved, the movement on the whole preserved the old-fashioned kindliness which marked its leader at his best. Though its members were mostly Anglo-Saxon in stock and fundamentalist in faith, Town-send had no truck with racial or religious bigotry. (There were even desegregated Townsend clubs.) He concentrated his own fanaticism and that of his followers on a single goal and for the rest, strove for democracy. Though he himself was wobbled by power, he was not destroyed by it. To the end he kept as best he could the trust reposed in him by millions of elderly people who believed, as he did, that his plan would save them and America. Dr. Townsend had indeed shouted until the whole country heard.[4]

4. The Messiah of the Rednecks

THUS FERMENT held out opportunity to those who could imprint their personalities on despair and offer distressed people an assurance of the millennium. The question remained whether the unrest would shoot off in different directions under a multitude of leaders or whether one man could gather it all unto himself. For all their talents, neither Father Coughlin nor Dr. Townsend was in the tradition of major political achievement. If anyone could organize the discontent on a national basis and use it to propel himself into power, it would more probably be, not a priest nor a doctor, but a politician. The most likely candidate was surely the Senator from Louisiana, Huey Pierce Long, Jr.

II

Louisiana was as natural a breeding place for radicalism as its swamps were for fevers. No state in the Union had been so long misgoverned. The old oligarchy, a dreary alliance of New Orleans businessmen and upstate planters, controlled by the utilities, the railroads, and Standard Oil of Louisiana, had run things without serious challenge almost since Reconstruction. No state had so high a proportion of illiteracy: in 1928, when Huey Long was elected governor, probably one-fifth of the white men on the farms could not read or write. No state treated its children worse: in Louisiana, little boys and girls worked long hours in cane and strawberry fields, in mills and shrimp-packing plants. The system of roads was as run down as the system of schools. And the submerged people of Louisiana had not only been oppressed, they had been bored: no Cole Blease, no Tom Watson, no Heflin nor Bilbo had arisen to make them laugh and hate and to distract them from the drabness of their days. Half a century of pent-up redneck rancor was awaiting release.

Not all the state had acquiesced in the reign of the oligarchy. No part was more recalcitrant than the parish of Winn in the piny uplands of north central Louisiana, where poor white farmers worked the thin red soil for a meager living. During the Civil War, Winn had instructed its delegate to the state convention to vote against secession; it was derisively known as the Free State of Winn. When the Populist insurgency hit Louisiana, Winn was one of its centers. Twenty years later, it was a Socialist stronghold. In 1912, when Debs polled more votes in Louisiana than William Howard Taft, over a third of Winn Parish voted Socialist. The town of Winnfield, where Huey Long was born in 1893, elected an entire Socialist slate.

Young Huey's father, Huey Pierce Long, Sr., was a typical Winn Parish radical. "My father and my mother favored the Union. Why not? They didn't have slaves. They didn't even have decent land. The rich folks had all the good land and all the slaves — why, their women didn't even comb their own hair. They'd sooner speak to a nigger than to a poor white." Life under the oligarchy had left unplumbed depths of resentment. "There wants to be a revolution, I tell you," old Huey said to a journalist in 1935. "I seen this domination of capital, seen it for seventy years. What do these rich folks care for the poor man? They care nothing — not for his pain, his sickness, nor his death. . . . Maybe you're surprised to hear me talk like that. Well, it was just such talk that my boy was raised under."

Young Huey was the seventh of nine children. He was born in a log house, but it was a comfortable four-room unit, and he was not reared in poverty. Still, he could not escape the drudgery of country life. "From my earliest recollection," he later said, "I hated the farm work. . . . Rising before the sun, we toiled until dark, after which we did nothing except eat supper, listen to the whippoorwills, and go to bed." Only politics and religion — both highly revivalist in style — relieved the tedium. A bright, rather bookish lad, Huey was resolved to be anything but a farmer. He read avidly, particularly romantic history and fiction — J. C.

Ridpath's florid *History of the World,* and Scott, Dumas, and Victor Hugo. He attended church, became a champion debater in high school, and spent his free time in the local printing office. He was not a tough boy. His younger brother Earl used to say in later years, "I had to do all of Huey's fighting for him."

In 1910, when Huey was seventeen, his debating talent won him a scholarship to Louisiana State University. But he lacked money for books and living expenses; so he put his volubility to other uses and became a traveling salesman. He sold furniture, soap, groceries, patent medicines for "women's sickness" and a vegetable shortening product called Cottolene. As part of his Cottolene pitch, he organized cooking contests; the winner in Shreveport was a pretty girl named Rose McConnell, with whom he fell in love — or at least so the story went, as certified by all except Huey in his autobiography. In 1912, having strayed as far west as Oklahoma, Long spent a few months at the University of Oklahoma Law School, "the happiest days of my life." When the session ended, he returned to the road. In 1913 he married Rose McConnell, and the next year, with a few hundred dollars of savings and a loan from his brother Julius, he entered Tulane Law School in New Orleans. Now he applied himself with frenzied determination. Studying from sixteen to twenty hours a day, he completed a three-year law course in eight months. Then he talked the Chief Justice of the state into giving him a special bar examination. In May 1915 he was sworn in as a lawyer. He was twenty-one years old.[1]

III

The young man made an office out of the small anteroom over the bank in Winnfield. He put his three law books on a white pine-top table, and a fifty-cent tin sign announced "HUEY P. LONG, LAWYER." The shoe store next door agreed to take his phone calls. Business was slow to come. He was ambitious and sensitive. When he appeared before a legislative committee to plead for a better workmen's-compensation law, he was kidded and laughed at by the senators; this gave him a dislike of legislatures. He failed to receive an expected appointment as Assistant United States Attorney; this, too, wounded him. "Once disappointed over a poli-

tical undertaking, I could never cast it from my mind. I awaited
the opportunity of a political contest."

In the meantime, the United States entered the First World
War. "I did not go," Long later said, "because I was not mad at
anybody over there." A notary public, he claimed draft exemption
as a state official. When State Senator S. J. Harper, an old Winnfield radical, was indicted by a federal grand jury for writing a
book warning that profiteers would take advantage of the war to
establish financial slavery, Long was his lawyer and secured his
acquittal. It was under Harper's influence that Long published a
letter in the *New Orleans Item* on March 1, 1918, under the
headline "THINKS WEALTH SHOULD BE MORE EVENLY DISTRIB-
UTED." In it Long argued that 2 per cent of the people owned 70
per cent of the wealth, that the rich were growing richer and the
poor poorer, and that inequality of educational opportunity was
widening the gap between classes. "With wealth concentrating,
classes becoming defined," he concluded, "there is not the opportunity for Christian uplift and education and cannot be until there
is more economic reform. That is the problem that the good people of this country must consider."

And Huey Long meant to help the good people in their consideration. After a careful examination of the state constitution,
he found that the post of Railroad Commissioner had no prescribed age limit. In 1918, twenty-five years old, he announced
for this office, noisily assailed the big corporations, and won election. During the next nine years on the Railroad Commission
and its successor, the Public Service Commission, Huey seized
every opportunity to dramatize himself as the champion of the
people against the oil companies, the telephone company, the utilities, and the railroads. Nor was this all merely whooping and
hollering. His shrewd and persistent attacks put the companies
on the defensive and brought rates down.

In 1924 he tried to cash in on this record by running for governor. It was too soon; he was barely thirty-one years old. And
he was caught in the cross fire between the Klan and its opponents.
Long straddled this issue; despite his poor white sympathies, he
did not, like Hugo Black in Alabama, join the Klan.

A few months before the 1928 primaries he again showed up as
a candidate, his followers parading under a banner reading (the

phrase was adapted from William Jennings Bryan): "EVERY MAN A KING, BUT NO ONE WEARS A CROWN." Huey campaigned furiously around the state, speaking at dusty crossroads and in shaded courthouse squares, his voice raucous and confiding, his arms pumping up and down, his seersucker suit stained with sweat. The poor white farmers — lean, leather-faced, rawboned men, surly and proud — crowded to see him. When he deluged the prominent figures in the community with unsparing personal abuse, they shouted, "Pour it on 'em, Huey! Pour it on 'em!" The oligarchy bewailed his uncouthness, his vituperation, his lack of dignity. "This State's full of sapsucker, hillbilly, and Cajun relations of mine," Long replied, "and there ain't enough dignity in the bunch to keep a chigger still long enough to go brush his hair." And the sapsuckers, the hillbillys, and the Cajuns, the woolhats and the rednecks, laughed and cheered and voted for one of their own. In 1928 they elected Huey Long Governor of Louisiana. He was now thirty-five.

IV

Thus far it was a familiar southern pattern — the ambitious young politician from the sticks, making his way to the top by rousing the boobs and denouncing the interests. The next step seemed obvious enough; now he would exact his price for peace with the people he had so long assailed. After all, Huey Long was no model of pecuniary virtue. He himself admitted that in the twenties legal fees from large corporations enabled him to build "a modern home in the best residential section of the City of Shreveport at a cost of $40,000." His brother Julius told a Senate committee that Huey's 1924 gubernatorial campaign was largely financed by the Southwestern Gas and Electric Company. Earl Long said that Huey took a $10,000 bribe from a utility executive in 1927. (Huey cried, "That is a God damn lie.") If the interests would pay the price, they could presumably take Long into the same camp they had taken so many others.

And so the merchants and the respectable politicians of New Orleans tendered the Governor-elect an elaborate banquet. But they underestimated their man. Though Huey would occasionally sell for a price, he could never be relied on to deliver. His essential ambition was not money but power, and he did not want to share the power with anybody else. He proposed now to smash the oligarchy and gain undisputed power for himself. Nor, perhaps, was it just for himself. Huey had not forgotten the poor people of Louisiana. As Governor, he was determined to increase school appropriations, to provide free textbooks, to pave highways and bridge rivers, to build charity hospitals and insane asylums. Long knew where the money was coming from — the big corporations, and especially Standard Oil.

He launched his program with characteristic vigor. When the legislature balked, the Governor appeared personally at the Capitol to cajole, threaten, browbeat, and bribe. He ignored the separation of powers, treated senators and representatives with unconcealed contempt, and bulled through enactments with careless confidence. One opponent shoved a volume before the Governor: "Maybe you've heard of this book. It's the Constitution of the State of Louisiana." "I'm the Constitution around here now," Long replied.

In 1929, when Long called a special session of the legislature to place an occupational tax of five cents a barrel on refined crude oil, his enemies decided that the time had come. Standard Oil and other corporations feared the tax as a fatal precedent. Constitutionalists thought that Huey Long's technique of personal government was threatening democracy. The oligarchy saw its power crumbling away before the pile-driver onslaughts of a redneck revolutionist. If they could not buy Long, they would break him. Their response was to demand his impeachment. A scatter-gun indictment accused the Governor of virtually every impeachable act except (oddly) drunkenness; he was even charged with plotting the assassination of an opposition representative. For a moment, Long was on the defensive. But he fought back savagely, haranguing audiences around the state and bringing incessant pressure on members of the Senate. Finally enough senators signed a round robin citing technical objections to the indictment to deny the opposition the necessary two-thirds. Huey was in the clear. The experience only deepened his resentment. He said later, "I used to try to get things done by saying 'please.' That didn't work and now I'm a dynamiter. I dynamite 'em out of my path."

In the next months, as his brother Julius said, "He political-ized everything in the State that could be politicalized." Julius added, "He holds every State office; every State office," and, "There has never been such an administration of ego and pompos-ity since the days of Nero." Huey was now more shameless than ever in crushing out opposition. "They beat a man almost to death, if he does not agree with them," said Julius Long, "and not a thing is done about it. The people that were supposed to enforce the laws in this State have become a howling, lawless mob. . . . A human life is not safe, and neither is his property." "I did not know how they hold elections in Mexico or Russia or any-where else," said Earl Long, "but I do not think they could sur-pass what has been going on in Louisiana."

Dynamiting everything out of his path, Huey moved to complete the humiliation of the oligarchy. In 1930 he announced his candi-dacy for the Senate to succeed J. E. Ransdell, the respectable conservative who had been senator since 1913. At the same time, he made it clear that he would not resign as Governor until he had served out his term lest the anti-Long Lieutenant Governor sabotage his program. And he described the election itself as a referendum on his policies. After a turbulent campaign, climaxed by the kidnaping of two men who threatened to expose corrup-tion in the administration, Long carried the day. The country boy from the red slopes and loblolly pines of Winn Parish was now on the national stage.[2]

v

In his manners, values, and idiom, Huey Long remained a back-country hillbilly. But he was a hillbilly raised to the highest level, preternaturally swift and sharp in intelligence, ruthless in action, and grandiose in vision. He was a man of medium height, well built but inclining toward pudginess. His dress was natty and loud. His face was round, red, and blotched, with more than a hint of pouches and jowls. Its rubbery mobility, along with the curly red-brown hair and the oversize putty nose, gave him the deceptive appearance of a clown. But the darting pop-eyes could easily turn from soft to hard, and the cleft chin was strong and forceful. At times it was a child's face, spoiled and willful; he looked, noted John Dos Passos, "like an overgrown small boy with very bad habits indeed." At times, it was the face of the cunning yokel about to turn the tables on the city slickers around him. At times, it became exceedingly hard and cruel.

In relaxation, Long had the lethargic air of an upcountry farmer. He liked to slump drowsily on a chair or stretch out on a sofa or loll on a bed. In certain moods, he would talk quietly, grammatically, and sensibly, with humor and perception. But he was always likely to explode into violent activity, leaping to his feet, hunching his shoulders, waving his arms, roaring with laughter or rage, emphasizing points by pounding furniture or clapping people on the back. "The phone rang every minute or so while we talked," said James Thurber, "and he would get up and walk through a couple of rooms to answer it and come back and fling himself heavily on the bed again so that his shoulders and feet hit it at the same moment." The jerkiness of his movements reminded one observer of the flickering figures rushing across the the screen in early silent films. This very intensity underlined his coarse and feverish power.

His weakness for conducting business in bed won him his first national notoriety. On a Sunday morning in March 1930, while Huey was recovering from the diversions of the night before in his suite at the Hotel Roosevelt in New Orleans, the commander of the German cruiser *Emden,* in dress uniform, accompanied by the German consul in morning coat, paid a courtesy call on the Governor of Louisiana. Hearing that guests were outside, Huey flung a red and blue dressing gown over green silk pajamas, shuffled on blue bedroom slippers, and ambled affably into the next room. His visitors left somewhat stiffly. Soon after, the German consul complained that Long had insulted the German Reich by his attire and demanded an apology. Long, somewhat amused, explained that he was just a boy from the country. "I know little of diplomacy and much less of the international courtesies and exchanges that are indulged in by nations." The next day, having collected all the elements of formal morning dress except a top hat, the Governor, in tail coat but with a snappy gray fedora, boarded the *Emden* and made his apologies.

The incident delighted the press across the nation, and Huey became for the first time a front-page figure outside Louisiana.

It may also have given him some ideas. For the first time he was receiving friendly notices. All the world loved a character; might it not be that the disguise of comedy could make people overlook or forgive much else? He had always been a jocose figure, given to ribald language and homely anecdotes. From this time forward he began to cultivate a public reputation as a buffoon. And the new public persona happily acquired a name. In the ribbing which took place around the Executive Mansion, Huey took to calling one of his gang "Brother Crawford," after a character in the Amos 'n' Andy radio program; in return he was called "Kingfish," after the head of Amos and Andy's lodge, the Mystic Knights of the Sea. Once someone questioned his right to be present at a meeting of the Highway Commission. "I looked around at the little fishes present," Long explained later, "and said, 'I'm the Kingfish.' " The title stuck. Huey himself used to claim that the name "Long" was hard to get over the telephone, so that it saved time to say, "This is the Kingfish." Also, he added, it substituted "gaiety for some of the tragedy of politics." In the same vein, he started a mock debate over whether cornpone should be crumbled or dunked in potlikker — the liquid left at the bottom of the pot after boiling vegetable greens and pork fat. This became a national issue. Even Franklin D. Roosevelt, Governor of New York but a Georgian by adoption, joined the argument. Roosevelt was a crumbler. Long, a dunker, finally agreed to a compromise.

But all the Kingfish's clowning could not conceal his more formidable qualities, especially his power and speed of mind. His intelligence, Raymond Moley once said, was an instrument such as is given to few men. As Governor, he was an efficient administrator, sure in detail, quick in decision. On his legal mettle, before a courtroom or arguing the case for seating his Louisiana delegation at the Democratic convention of 1932, he displayed a disciplined and razor-keen analytical ability. Still, he did not value his gift. As Moley said, "He misused it, squandered it, battered it, as a child might treat a toy. . . . He used his mind so erratically as to seem, a great deal of the time, not only childish but insane." Alben Barkley once told him, "You are the smartest lunatic I ever saw in my whole life!" (Long rejoined, "Maybe that is the smartest description I've ever had applied to me!")

He was not a nice man. When his brother Julius asked him in

1930 to give their aged father a room in the Executive Mansion, Huey complained bitterly about "base ingratitude and threatened holdups" and refused. "I swear," Julius said later, "that I do not know of a man, any human being, that has less feeling for his family than Huey P. Long has." The yes men and hoodlums who clustered around him were bound to him by fear or by greed, not by affection. He knew he was much smarter than anyone else, and he could not conceal his contempt for others. He told legislators to their faces that he could buy and sell them "like sacks of potatoes." He called officeholders "dime-a-dozen punks." He rejoiced in deeds of personal humiliation. Revenge was always prominent in his mind. His flippant brutality was both evidence of his mastery and a further source of his power.

On the hustings, he played on his listeners with intimate knowledge, deriding them, insulting them, whipping up emotions of resentment and spite, contemptuously providing them with scapegoats. He knew what to say to produce the response he wanted, and, knowing, said it. "If he went in a race up North," Julius Long said, "he would publish up there that there is part nigger in us in order to get the nigger vote."

Vilification was his particular weapon. His blistering frontier invective provided the link between his own superior intelligence and the surging envy of the crowds before him. He expressed what his hearers had long felt but could not say. He was their idol — themselves as they would like to be, free and articulate and apparently without fear. It was only when he had left the platform, when hard-faced bodyguards closed in around him, shoving his admirers back and moving in a flying wedge toward the black limousine, it was only then that it became evident that Huey Long was a coward — the "yellowest physical coward," his brother Earl said, "that God had ever let live."

He carried these qualities to Washington — the comic impudence, the gay egotism, the bravado, the mean hatred, the fear. He was a man propelled by a greed for power and a delight in its careless exercise. "The only sincerity there was in him," said Julius Long, "was for himself." He talked broadly about the need for redistributing the wealth, but these were words. When a reporter tried to discover deeper meanings, Long brushed him off: "I haven't any program or any philosophy. I just take things

as they come." Yet, for all this, there remained the sense in which
his qualities and his ambitions were those of the plain people of
his state writ large — the people from the red clay country and the
piny woods, from the canebrakes and the bayous, the shrimp
fishermen and the moss fishermen, the rednecks and the hillbillies
and the Cajuns. Once, standing before the Evangeline Oak, he
spoke to the Acadians of southern Louisiana and recalled the
legend of Evangeline, weeping for her vanished lover. She was
not, Long said, the only Acadian thus to have waited and wept.

> Where are the schools that you have waited for your children
> to have, that have never come? Where are the roads and the
> highways that you spent your money to build, that are no
> nearer now than ever before? Where are the institutions to
> care for the sick and disabled? Evangeline wept bitter tears in
> her disappointment. But they lasted only one lifetime. Your
> tears . . . have lasted for generations.

His conclusion seemed to come from the heart: "Give me the
chance to dry the tears of those who still weep here."

His strength, observed Sherwood Anderson, lay in "the terrible
South that Stark Young and his sort ignore . . . the beaten, ignorant,
Bible-ridden, white South. Faulkner occasionally really touches it.
It has yet to be paid for." That terrible South was exacting the
price of years of oppression. Huey Long was its man, and he
gave it by proxy the delights it had been so long denied.[3]

                                VI

One day late in January 1932, while Jim Watson of Indiana,
the Republican leader in the Senate, was idling on the floor, a
man dealt him a smashing blow with open hands on his chest and
said explosively, "Jim, I want to get acquainted with you!" Staggered by the blow, Watson said, "Well, who in the hell are you?"
"I," the answer came, "am Huey Long." The Senator from
Louisiana, a year late, was coming to claim his seat.

His debut was all too typical. From the start, he violated every
rule of the club. He picked an immediate fight with his Louisiana
colleague, who thereupon refused to escort him when he took his

oath. Instead of relapsing into the decorous silence expected of a first-termer, he spoke expansively on all subjects. When Joseph T. Robinson, the Democratic leader, refused to back his share-the-wealth resolution, Long called for new party leadership and dramatically resigned all his committee assignments. (Robinson called this a "comic opera performance unworthy of the great actor from Louisiana"; other senators resented it as an escape on Long's part from the hard work of the Senate.) When Carter Glass brought in his banking bill at the end of the year, Long filibustered against it and launched a scornful personal campaign against Glass. And, when his attendance was needed in the Senate, he was always likely to be dashing off to more important business in Louisiana.

It seemed plain that Long could hardly have a lower opinion of the body which regarded itself as the greatest deliberative assembly on earth. He made certain exceptions, especially George W. Norris and Burton K. Wheeler; "they were the boldest, most courageous men I had ever met." But he treated the others like a collection of stuffed shirts. The more revered they were in the club, like Robinson, Glass, and Pat Harrison, the more Long needled and tormented them. Huey in debate, said Alben Barkley, was like a horsefly; "he would light on one part of you, sting you, and then, when you slapped at him, fly away to land elsewhere and sting again." Sitting at a desk where John C. Calhoun had once sat, wearing white flannels, pink necktie, and orange kerchief or some other bizarre combination, Long posed and strutted and stung until most of his colleagues could not endure him. He knew this, and in certain moods regretted it. Then he would bid for popularity by trying for laughs in speeches or by geniality in the cloakroom, or else talk wistfully of resigning because he had "no friends" in the Senate.

But he bided his time in the hope that the new administration would change things. Long had not originally wanted Roosevelt. "He failed with Cox," Long said, "and that should end him. Al Smith would be entirely satisfactory." But Norris brought him around, and Long played an important role in holding southern support for Roosevelt at Chicago. He wanted to play an equally important part in the campaign. When Jim Farley refused to provide him a special train to go from state to state, promising immediate payment of the bonus, Huey, in bad temper, said, "Jim, you're gonna get licked. . . . I tried to save you, but if you don't want to be saved, it's all right with me." Finally he accepted a less ambitious schedule which took him into states where Democratic strategists thought he would do a minimum of harm. Everywhere he went, he was a great success. Farley wrote later, "We never again underrated him."

At first, Long was — or seemed — enthralled by Roosevelt. "When I was talking to the Governor today," he told a newspaperman in October 1932, "I just felt like the depression was over. That's a fact. I never felt so tickled in my life." After the election, he expressed a constant fear that the new administration might be captured by the reactionaries; but his personal susceptibility to Roosevelt remained undiminished. In January he called on the President-elect at the Mayflower in Washington. "I'm going to talk turkey with Roosevelt," he shouted to reporters, "I am going to ask him, 'Did you mean it or didn't you?' Goddam it, there ain't but one thing that I'm afraid of — and that's the people." He then pounded at the door of Roosevelt's suite, an action he obligingly repeated for the photographers. Half an hour later Huey emerged jubilant. "I come out of this room happy and satisfied," he said. "We've got a great President." Some one asked whether Roosevelt intended to crack down on him. "Crack down on me?" said Long. "He don't want to crack down on me. He told me, 'Huey, you're going to do just as I tell you,' and that is just what I'm agoin' to do."

But it was not that easy. Long retained deep suspicions of some of Roosevelt's associates. A day or two before the inauguration, he came to Moley's room at the Mayflower, kicked the door open, chewed on an apple, and said pugnaciously, "I don't like you and your goddamned banker friends!" (Everyone was struck dumb; after Long departed, Moley found a senator hiding in the bathroom.) During the Hundred Days Long's suspicions steadily mounted. He disliked the conservative measures of the first month, such as the Economy Act, strongly supported the inflation drive of April, and in May denounced the administration on the ground that it was dominated by the same old clique of bankers who had controlled Hoover. "Parker Gilbert from Morgan & Company, Leffingwell, Ballantine, Eugene Meyer, every one of them are here

— what is the use of hemming and hawing? We know who is running the thing." The National Recovery Act completed his alienation.

VII

Long's ideological disillusionment was accompanied by — indeed may well have been the result of — an intense if covert political conflict with the administration. In August 1932 Roosevelt had already called Long one of the two most dangerous men in America. In January, reassessing Long's troublemaking potentiality, he suggested to Rex Tugwell, of all people, that an effort should be made to bring him round. There was an apparent period of appeasement. Presumably with Roosevelt's assent, the Senate Committee on Campaign Expenditures, which had been looking into the recent senatorial election in Louisiana, abandoned its inquiry. Nothing was done to reopen a Treasury Department investigation of Huey's income tax, begun under the Hoover administration. But Long grew insistent, particularly on questions of federal patronage. At the same time, the White House was receiving hundreds of complaints about the Long organization from Louisiana.

Sometime during the spring, Roosevelt decided to write Long off — a decision expressed in a determination to deny him patronage. The reasons for this decision are obscure. Long's power in his own state, his national appeal as a rabble rouser, his capacity to make mischief in the Senate — all this argued for a serious effort to keep him in the New Deal camp. Moreover, Roosevelt was quite prepared to get along with tyrannical bosses like Frank Hague of New Jersey or with popular demagogues like Father Coughlin. Yet the President may well have been genuinely persuaded that Long was far more dangerous to the country than the Hagues or Coughlins. If this were so, then he would not let federal patronage or presidential favor strengthen the Louisiana despotism further.

In June 1933 he asked Farley to bring Long over for a talk. Huey breezed into the White House in a light summer suit. On his head was a straw hat with a brightly colored band. He sat down in the presidential office, and the three men began a superficially genial conversation. Then Farley noticed that Long was keeping his hat on. "At first I thought it was an oversight, but soon realized it was deliberate." Farley looked apprehensively at the President. Roosevelt was plainly well aware of what was going on. Huey occasionally took off the hat to underline points, tapping Roosevelt with it on the knee or elbow. But the President declined to be annoyed. His sole interest, Roosevelt kept saying, lay in seeing that good men were named to public office. After a time, Long knew that he could not break through the ring of cool and gracious phrases. As he left the White House, he told the press, "The President and I are never going to fall out. I'll be satisfied whichever way matters go." But he muttered to Farley, "What the hell is the use of coming down to see this fellow? I can't win any decision over him." "I'm never goin' over there again," he told a reporter. His grandfather, Long added, once had a man working for him who picked twice as much cotton as anyone in the entire history of the farm. Naturally grandpappy fired him, saying "You're so smart that if you stayed around here fust thing I know I'd be working for you." "That's the way I feel about Roosevelt," Long said. "He's so doggone smart that fust thing I know I'll be working fer him — and I ain't goin' to."

Soon he defined to his satisfaction the difference between the Hoover and Roosevelt administrations. Hoover, Huey said, was a hoot owl, Roosevelt, a scrootch owl. A hoot owl banged into the roost, knocked the hen clean off, and seized her as she fell. "But a scrootch owl slips into the roost and scrootches up to the hen and talks softly to her. And the hen just falls in love with him, and the first thing you know, *there ain't no hen*." [4]

VIII

In 1930 and 1931 the Bureau of Internal Revenue had begun to receive letters from Louisiana charging illegal activity on the part of the Long machine. In July 1932, Elmer Irey, chief of the Treasury Department's Intelligence Unit, sent in an agent to case the situation. In a few weeks, the agent reported back. "Chief," he said, "Louisiana is crawling. Long and his gang are stealing everything in the state . . . and they're not paying taxes on the loot." Irey despatched a force of thirty-two agents to push the investiga-

tion. Long responded with heavy pressure on the Hoover administration to call the Treasury off. After the 1932 election, Ogden
Mills asked Irey whether he had enough evidence to warrant
indictment. When Irey said that his people had not had enough
time, Mills said, "Very well, then. Suspend your investigation
immediately and write a full report of what you have done and
what you propose doing and submit it to my successor. After all,
the Senator is one of their babies; let them decide what to do with
him."

Irey accordingly stopped the investigation and filed the report.
For the first months of the New Deal, he heard nothing about
Long. Then in August, a few weeks after Long kept his hat on in
the presidential office, the Commissioner of Internal Revenue told
Irey that the White House wanted to know why the Intelligence
Unit had investigated Long; wasn't it a job for the FBI? Irey
pointed out that Long was vulnerable as an income-tax evader,
which made him Treasury business. Then silence again, until
Henry Morgenthau, Jr., became Secretary of the Treasury. "Why
have you stopped investigating Huey Long, Mr. Irey?" the new
Secretary asked Irey brusquely one day. Irey explained that Mills
had told him to stop and no one since had told him to resume.
"What's the matter, Mr. Irey, are you afraid of Huey Long?"
"I'm awaiting instructions," said Irey. "Very well, then," said
Morgenthau. "Get all your agents back on the Louisiana job.
Start the investigation of Huey Long and proceed as though you
were investigating John Doe. And let the chips fall where they
may."

The resumption of the investigation was only one of Long's
headaches. A comic episode in August 1933 further complicated
his life. One night Gene Buck, the song writer, took the Kingfish
to spend an evening at the Sands Point Club on Long Island.
Long was drunk and offensive. It is not clear what precipitated
the denouement — whether his free comments to a woman at a
neighboring table, or an ingenious but misguided effort to urinate
between the legs of the man in front of him while waiting his turn
in the men's room — but someone, goaded beyond endurance, hit
Long in the face and opened a cut over his left eye. There was
considerable merriment over the Kingfish's humiliation; medals
were offered to the assailant, lists printed of men who regretted

they had not committed the assault themselves. Long did not help his own case by asserting that it was a Wall Street plot and that three or four men with knives had ganged up on him, nor by subsequently writing an open letter to Al Capone, then in retirement at the Atlanta penitentiary, suggesting that Wall Street would doubtless arrange to give Capone his freedom if the great racketeer would confess to having planned the Long attack.

At this moment, the Kingfish even seemed in trouble at home. His hand-picked successor, Governor O. K. Allen, impressed no one. As Earl Long put it, "A leaf once blew in the window of Allen's office and fell on his desk. Allen signed it." And everyone regarded him as Huey's responsibility. "There is not a dishwasher here," said Julius Long, "that is more subservient to his master than Oscar Allen is to Huey Long." Mutters against "Long Island Huey" were rising through the state. The Mayor of New Orleans, with whom the Kingfish had patched up an alliance, turned against him. The Senate committee reopened the investigation of the 1932 election. When Long attacked Roosevelt at the South Louisiana State Fair, the crowd broke into a storm of boos. From behind twenty highway policemen, Long screamed back at the hecklers, "Come down here out of that there grandstand and I'll man-to-man it with you. And I won't have five or six men [the number was multiplying] jump on you like they did to me at Sands Point! . . . Come on down here, and I'll make you giggle! I'll give you a dose of castor oil and laudanum!"

The Mayor of New Orleans was re-elected early in 1934 over Long's envenomed opposition, and it looked as if the Kingfish were at last on the ropes. But once again his enemies underestimated Long's resourcefulness. He fought back in two ways. By pushing an ever more radical program through the state legislature — including the abolition of the poll tax, exemptions for the poor from the general property tax, a debt moratorium, and new levies on business — he reawakened support among the poor whites. At the same time, by extending his personal control over the apparatus of government at every level, he transformed the state government into a virtual dictatorship.

The legislature was wholly under Long's domination. Once it shouted through forty-four bills in twenty-two minutes. The Kingfish wandered about the floor, waved aside objections, and briskly declared that whatever he wanted had been passed. "He was like a young father on a romp in the nursery," wrote Raymond Swing after seeing him in action. "Anyone could see how much fun it was being a dictator." Few dared to protest. Even Long's personal life was sacred. As Westbrook Pegler commented after a visit to Baton Rouge, "They do not permit a house of prostitution to operate within a prescribed distance of the state university, but exempt the state Capitol from the meaning of the act."

In a series of seven special sessions in 1934 and 1935, the legislature obediently transferred nearly every vestige of authority from towns and parishes to the state, which meant to Huey. By 1935 local government was virtually at an end. No municipal officer — policeman or fireman or schoolteacher — could hold his job except by Long's favor. If elected officials defied the Long machine, the state could force their resignations by withholding public funds. Another law gave the Governor power to make new appointments once the offices were vacated. If communities continued defiant, the Governor could call out the militia and declare martial law without accountability to anyone. Indeed, Long broke the resistance in New Orleans in 1934 by sending in the National Guard for a long period of military occupation. To insure against an uprising at the polls, the state government had exclusive authority to name all election commissioners; this enabled the machine to count the votes. And the Kingfish's Supreme Court certified the constitutionality of his program. Every man was a king, but only one wore a crown.

IX

In return, the people of Louisiana got a state government which did more for them than any other government in Louisiana's history. The power of the oligarchy, which had for so long sucked the people dry, was now broken. Schools, hospitals, roads and public services in general were better than ever before. Poor whites and even Negroes had unprecedented opportunities. Though Long had standard Southern racial views, he played very little on racist emotions. He regarded the Klan, for example, with contempt; and, when its leader offered to enter the state and campaign against him, Long told reporters, "Quote me as saying that that Imperial bastard will never set foot in Louisiana, and that when I call him a son of a bitch I am not using profanity, but am referring to the circumstances of his birth." He was rather proud of his achievements for the colored people: "Lincoln didn't free the slaves in Louisiana; I did." His greatest pride was what he had done for education, from the free textbooks and school buses in the elementary schools to the new university of Louisiana State. He led the brass band at State, meddled with the football team, and invented the Sugar Bowl. At the same time, he built up a first-class medical school, tried to get men like Wayne Morse of the University of Oregon Law School and Thomas G. Corcoran to become dean of his law school, and subsidized one of the best highbrow quarterlies in the country, the *Southern Review*. (A young man in the English Department at State named Robert Penn Warren was fascinated by the phenomenon of Long; the result was the astute and compassionate novel, *All the King's Men*.) In a way, Louisiana State summed up the Long paradox. Able people pursued their studies without hindrance, and the professional schools flourished; but the president of the University, a Columbia Ph.D. and Long stooge named James Monroe ("Jimmy Moron" or later "Jingle Money") Smith, was meanwhile using half a million dollars in university funds for private speculation in the wheat market.

Long achieved much — certainly more than the oligarchy ever had. But his achievement should not be overestimated. Like an ancient emperor or a modern dictator, he specialized in monuments. He sprinkled the state with roads and buildings. But he did little or nothing to raise wages for the workers, to stop child labor, to reduce the work day, to support trade unions, to provide pensions for the aged, to furnish relief to the unemployed, even to raise teacher's salaries. He left behind no record of social or labor legislation.

Moreover, if within Long's limits government was benevolent and fairly efficient, it was still intricately and hopelessly corrupt. In 1934, to take an example, Long and several close associates set up the Win or Lose Corporation. The state government considerately made it possible for the new corporation to acquire properties in the natural gas fields; the corporation then persuaded natural gas companies to buy the properties by threatening to increase their taxes if they didn't. Using such persuasive sales methods, Win or Lose cleared about $350,000 in 1935. And, where local talent was inadequate, Long invited outside experts into the state to assist his projects of sharing the wealth. Thus he summoned Frank Costello, the New York gangster, to take over the Louisiana slot machine concession.

Government was also increasingly cruel. Those who dared criticize the regime risked not only political and economic reprisals but threats, beatings and kidnappings. The new order, wrote Westbrook Pegler, was "reducing to the political status of the Negro all of the white people of Lousiana who oppose Der Kingfish." Newspaper critics, like Hodding Carter of the *Hammond Courier*, went armed day and night. And as the corruption and the tyranny spread, the opposition, denied legal means of expression, began itself to contemplate desperate measures. "If ever there was need for shotgun government," Carter wrote, "that time is now. . . . Let us read our histories again. They will tell us with what weapons we earned the rights of free men. Then, by God's help, let's use them."

Toward the end of 1934 the legislature enacted an occupational tax on oil refining — the same tax which had led to Long's impeachment five years before. In response, a group of Standard Oil employees, joined by indignant citizens like Hodding Carter, formed the Square Deal Association, put on blue shirts, conducted military drill, and talked of overthrowing the dictatorship. In January 1935 Long's militia dispersed the Square Dealers in an abortive engagement at the Baton Rouge airport. Later in the year, when the anti-Long leaders met secretly in a New Orleans hotel, they could only say to each other despairingly, "I wish somebody would kill the son of a bitch."

Nothing helped Long more than the bankruptcy of his opposition. It included many brave and gallant individuals; but, as an organized political force, it seemed only the old oligarchy again — hardly more honest than Long himself, and far more boring, stupid, and reactionary. "Part of our failure," Hodding Carter wrote years later, "arose from an unwillingness to approve any Long-sponsored proposal for change, regardless of its merits. We offered none of our own except a plea for democratic rule, and that sounded hollow in contrast." But Carter could rightly add, "Yet, at the end, it became the one thing of importance in Louisiana." [5]

X

Long thus built his kingdom — the nearest approach to a total-itarian state the American republic had ever seen. And Louisiana was only the beginning. Now that Frank-lin De-La-No Roo-Se-Velt (as he called him, giving unctuous emphasis to each syllable of the hated name) had turned out to be a stooge of the bankers, the Kingfish was out to save all America.

The ideological basis for his national movement lay deep in Long's experience — back to the letter to the *New Orleans Item* in 1918, farther back to the poor white Populism of Winn Parish ("Didn't Abe Lincoln free the niggers and not give the planters a dime?" his father said. "Why shouldn't the white slaves be freed?"), back to the twenty-fifth chapter of Leviticus, the year of jubilee, when liberty would be proclaimed throughout all the land unto all inhabitants thereof, and all property would be redistributed, and every man would be returned unto his posses-sion, and no man would oppress another.

As Long looked at America, he conceived the maldistribution of wealth to be the cause of all social and economic distress. "When one man decides he must have more goods to wear for himself and his family than any other ninety-nine people, then the condition results that instead of one hundred people sharing the things that are on earth for one hundred people, that one man, through his gluttonous greed, takes over ninety-nine parts for himself and leaves one part for the ninety-nine." But one man could not eat the food intended for ninety-nine people, nor wear the clothes, nor live in the houses. And, as the rich grew richer and the poor poorer, the middle class was threatened with extinction. "Where is the middle class today?" Long asked in 1933. "Where is the corner groceryman, about whom President Roosevelt speaks? He is gone or going. Where is the corner druggist? He is gone or going. Where is the banker of moderate means? He is vanishing. . . . The middle class today cannot pay the debts they owe and come out alive. In other words, the middle class is no more." Its only hope of resurrection, Long suggested, was to follow him.

His actual program underwent a succession of versions. The share-the-wealth resolution of 1932 proposed that the government take by taxation all income over $1 million and all inheritances over $5 million. In 1933 he added a capital levy which would reduce all fortunes to somewhere around $3 million. By 1934 he was emphasizing the result more than the method: government would furnish every American family with a "homestead allowance" of at least $5,000 and an annual income of at least $2,000. There were, in addition, fringe benefits. Hours of labor would be limited. Agricultural production and consumption would be balanced through government storage and the control of planting. Everyone over sixty would receive an "adequate" pension (this was first to be $30 a month, but the competition of Dr. Townsend changed that; as Gerald L. K. Smith, the director of Long's movement, explained, "We decided to put in the word 'adequate' and let every man name his own figure. This attracted a lot of Townsendites to us"). Boys and girls of ability would receive a college education at government expense. And no one need worry about money; "taxes off the big fortunes at the top will supply plenty of money without hurting anybody."

Share-the-wealth was, in short, a hillbilly's paradise — $5,000 capital endowment without work, a radio, washing machine, and automobile in every home. It was the Snopeses' dream come true. It had almost no other quality. While Coughlin and Townsend at least went through the motions of economic analysis, Long rested his case on rhetoric and the Scriptures. "I never read a line of Marx or Henry George or any of them economists," he once said. "It's all in the law of God." In 1935 he was still using the same statistics he had used in 1918. He wildly overestimated what the government would gain from confiscation; he under estimated the number of families who would need to have their income jacked up to the $5,000 limit; he ignored the problems involved in redistributing nonmonetary wealth; and he showed little interest in such a mundane issue as economic recovery.

XI

And yet, as economic fantasy, it produced a response. Wealth *was* unfairly distributed. Many of the poor were consumed with envy and rancor. The New Deal seemed awfully complicated and, to some, very far away. Encouraged, the Kingfish decided in January 1934 to convert his aspiration into a crusade. He launched the Share Our Wealth Society and called on Americans everywhere to organize local chapters. "Be prepared for the slurs and snickers of some high ups," he warned. ". . . Be on your guard for some smart aleck tool of the interests to come in and ask questions. . . . To hell with the ridicule of the wise street-corner politician! . . . Who cares what consequences may come following the mandates of the Lord, of the Pilgrims, of Jefferson, Webster and Lincoln? He who falls in this fight falls in the radiance of the future."

Gerald L. K. Smith, his chief assistant in the movement, was a fundamentalist preacher and political sensationalist who, a year before, had been writing William Dudley Pelley offering to set up "the first Silver Shirt storm troop in America." But he shifted quickly enough to Long, whom he worshiped (or did when Huey was alive; Smith, writing his spiritual autobiography in 1952, noted that he had experienced a "call" in 1933, but did not mention the name of the caller). "Huey Long," said Smith, "is a superman. I actually believe that he can do as much in one day as any ten men." To Raymond Swing, Smith explained Louisiana democracy as "the dictatorship of the surgical theater. The surgeon is recognized as being in charge because he knows. Everyone defers to him for that reason only. . . . They are not servile, they believe in the surgeon. They realize he is working for the welfare of the patient." "No great movement has ever succeeded," Smith once said, "unless it has deified some one man. The Share-the-Wealth movement consciously deified Huey P. Long."

Smith was, if possible, a greater spellbinder than Huey himself. On the platform, his mighty voice sounded for blocks. Sweat stained his blue shirt and streamed down his face, his arms flailed in the air while he denounced the Kingfish's foes as "dirty, thieving drunkards" or, in a swift change of pace, invoked Christ on the Cross. A favorite Smith device was to ask his audience: "All of you that ain't got *four* suits of clothes raise your two hands." As arms shot up, he would ask again, "Three suits? — two suits?" Then, a sob in his voice: "Not even two suits of clothes! Oh, my brethren, J. P. Morgan has two suits of clothes. He has a hundred times two suits of clothes." He could continue in this vein for two hours. "Share, brothers, share," he would conclude, "and don't let those white-livered skunks laugh at you." From the crowd would come a chorus of "Amens" as they surged forward to sign up for Share Our Wealth. H. L. Mencken, a connoisseur of oratory, pronounced Smith more impressive than Bryan. Throw together, Mencken said, "a flashing eye, a hairy chest, a rubescent complexion, large fists, a voice both loud and mellow, terrifying and reassuring, *sforzando* and *pizzicato,* and finally, an unearthly capacity for distending the superficial blood vessels of his temples and neck, as if they were biceps — and you have the makings of a boob-bumper worth going miles to see."

By July 1935 Smith claimed seven million adherents for Share Our Wealth. This was wild exaggeration, but there could be no question that Long was having an impact. Early in 1935 Dan Tobin of the Teamsters expressed his concern to Louis Howe about the increase in Long's popularity. "I have several letters from our members," he said, "most of them decent and honest fellows inquiring about and asking me if they should proceed to organize clubs." And Louis Howe, passing on Tobin's letter along with a letter from a Montana banker describing Long as "the man we thought you were when we voted for you," said to Roosevelt, "It is symptoms like this I think we should watch very carefully."

As for Huey, he saw his movement more and more as the alternative to the major parties. The Democrats and Republicans, he said, reminded him of the patent-medicine vendor with two bottles, one marked High Popalorum, the other Low Popahirum. When asked the difference, the vendor explained that High Popalorum was made by taking the bark off the tree from the ground up and Low Popahirum, by taking the bark off the tree from the top down. "And these days the only difference between the two party leaders in Congress that I can see is that the Republican leaders are skinning the people from the ankle up, and the Democratic leaders are taking off the hide from the ear down. Skin 'em up or skin 'em down, but skin 'em!"

More and more people sang Huey's song:

> Ev'ry man a king, ev'ry man a king,
> For you can be a millionaire

But there's something belonging to others.
There's enough for all people to share.
When it's sunny June and December too,
Or in the winter time or spring
There'll be peace without end
Ev'ry neighbor a friend
With ev'ry man a king.[6]

XII

At the beginning of 1935, in his forty-second year, Long gave
off a sense of destiny. Would there be a third party in 1936?
"Sure to be. And I think we will sweep the country." Foreign
visitors found him impressive, though unattractive. Rebecca
West detected the steely intelligence behind the Mardi Gras mask
of his conversation: "He is the most formidable kind of brer fox,
the self-abnegating kind that will profess ignorance, who will
check his dignity with his hat if he can serve his plans by buffoon-
ery." She said later, "In his vitality and his repulsiveness he was
very like Laval." He reminded H. G. Wells of "a Winston Churchill who has never been at Harrow."

Yet the nature of this destiny remained obscure, even to him.
All he had was a sense of crisis and of opportunity. Once during
the Hundred Days he had said to a group in the Senate cloakroom, "Men, it will not be long until there will be a mob assem-
bling here to hang Senators from the rafters of the Senate. I
have to determine whether I will stay and be hung with you,
or go out and lead the mob." ("That statement," Senator Richard
B. Russell reported later, "evoked very little laughter.") Was he
a demagogue? "There are all kinds of demagogues," he said.
"Some deceive the people in the interests of the lords and masters
of creation, the Rockefellers and the Morgans. Some of them
deceive the people in their own interest." He often said, with
his impish grin, "What this country needs is a dictator." But he
also said, "I don't believe in dictatorships, all these Hitlers and
Mussolinis. They don't belong in our American life. And Roosevelt is a bigger dictator than any." Then again: "There is no
dictatorship in Louisiana. There is a perfect democracy there,
and when you have a perfect democracy it is pretty hard to tell

it from a dictatorship." He told a gullible interviewer from the *New Republic,* "It's all in Plato. You know — the Greek philosopher. I hadn't read Plato before I wrote my material on the 'Share the Wealth' movement, and when I did read Plato afterwards, I found I had said almost exactly the same things. I felt as if I had written Plato's 'Republic' myself."

In 1935 some people wondered whether Long was the first serious American fascist. Long himself, when George Sokolsky asked him about it, laughed it off: "Fine. I'm Mussolini and Hitler rolled in one. Mussolini gave them castor oil; I'll give them tabasco, and then they'll like Louisiana." But he was no Hitler or Mussolini. He had no ideological preoccupations; he never said, "When the United States gets fascism it will call it anti-fascism," nor was he likely to think in such terms.[7] Read *Mein Kampf,* and one sees a man possessed by a demonic dream which he must follow until he can purge all evil from the world. Read *Every Man A King,* and one finds a folksy and rather conventional chronicle of political success. Read Long's *My First Days in the White House,* ghostwritten by a Hearst reporter in 1935, and one has a complacent picture of a painless triumph, with Rockefeller, Mellon and the du Ponts backing President Long in his project of sharing the wealth (the book did have one engaging impudence: in choosing his cabinet, Long appointed as his Secretary of the Navy Franklin D. Roosevelt). Long's political fantasies had no tensions, no conflicts, except of the most banal kind, no heroism or sacrifice, no compelling myths of class or race or nation.

He had no overriding social vision. According to Raymond Daniell, who covered him for the *New York Times,* he did believe in Share Our Wealth "with all his heart"; but it was as a technique of political self-aggrandizement, not as a gospel of social reconstruction. Part traveling salesman, part confidence man, part gang leader, he had at most a crude will toward personal power. He had no doubt about becoming President: the only question was whether it was to be in 1936 or 1940. He told Forrest Davis that he planned to destroy both major parties, organize a single party of his own, and serve four terms. To Daniell he disclosed "the whole scheme by which he hoped to establish himself as the dictator of this country." His hero was Frederick the Great, and he no doubt saw himself as a kind of

Frederick the Great from the piney woods. ("He was the greatest son of a bitch who ever lived. 'You can't take Vienna, Your Majesty. The world won't stand for it,' his nitwit ambassadors said. 'The hell I can't,' said old Fred, 'my soldiers will take Vienna and my professors at Heidelberg will explain the reasons why!' Hell, I've got a university down in Louisiana that cost me $15,000,000, that can tell you why I do like I do.")

At bottom, Huey Long resembled, not a Hitler or a Mussolini, but a Latin American dictator, a Vargas or a Perón. Louisiana was in many respects a colonial region, an underdeveloped area; its Creole traditions gave it an almost Latin American character. Like Vargas and Perón, Long was in revolt against economic colonialism, against the oligarchy, against the smug and antiquated past; like them, he stood in a muddled way for economic modernization and social justice; like them, he was most threatened by his own arrogance and cupidity, his weakness for soft living and his rage for personal power.

And, like them, he could never stop. "I was born into politics," he once said, "a wedded man, with a storm for my bride." A man of violence, he generated an atmosphere of violence. Early in 1935 Mason Spencer, one of Long's last foes still on his feet in the Louisiana legislature, sent the Kingfish a solemn warning.

"I am not gifted with second sight," Spencer said. "Nor did I see a spot of blood on the moon last night.

"But I can see blood on the polished floor of this Capitol.

"For if you ride this thing through, you will travel with the white horse of death." [8]

5. The Dream of Fascism

For a moment in 1935, intelligent observers could almost believe that the traditional structure of American politics was on the verge of dissolution. The old parties no longer appeared adequate to contain the new energies. Millions across the land were turning to the new prophets of unrest. And, though Coughlin, Townsend, and Long were preaching competing gospels, their adherents seemed to represent a common group and to express a common impulse.

The followers of the demagogues mostly came from the old lower-middle classes, now in an unprecedented stage of frustration and fear, menaced by humiliation, dispossession, and poverty. They came from provincial and traditionally nonpolitical groups in the population, jolted from apathy into near-hysteria by the shock of economic collapse. They came, in the main, from the ranks of the self-employed, who, as farmers or shopkeepers or artisans, felt threatened by organized economic power, whether from above, as in banks and large corporations, or from below, as in trade unions. To a considerable degree, they came from the evangelical denominations; years of Bible reading and fundamentalist revivalism had accustomed them to millennial solutions. They were mostly men and women of native-born old-immigrant (Anglo-Saxon and German) stock; if Coughlin's Irish Catholic supporters seemed an exception, the exception was more apparent than real, for the Irish were beginning to see themselves as part of the old immigration rather than the new. In sum, they seemed to represent Old America in resentful revolt against both contemporary politics and contemporary economics.

As yet, their leadership presently divided rather than united them. But some Americans, themselves weary of the disorder of free society and angry at the rise of new elements in American life, saw in this situation of lower-middle-class discontent a deep analogy — and hence an exciting possibility. Could not these manifestations of demagogic protest be rallied to form the basis for a movement of patriotic regeneration of the kind which had already revitalized Italy and Germany? A few intellectuals, especially attuned to the woes of the nonpolitical old-American, xenophobic middle class, were sure that the way to national revival lay in promulgating an American brand of fascism. As the old political system appeared to disintegrate in 1934 and 1935, they now tried to offer the all-inclusive fascist mystique which the demagogues, with their commitment to particular nostrums, had thus far failed to supply.[1]

II

In April 1933, a few weeks after Franklin Roosevelt took office, a new magazine called the *American Review* made its appearance. Discreet in its cover, conservative in its typography, it was obviously addressed to the thoughtful minority. Its editor was Seward Collins, a man of thirty-four who had gone to Hill School and Princeton and in the twenties had published the *Bookman*. The point of the *American Review,* he announced, was to provide a forum for what he called the "Revolutionary Conservatives" or the "Radicals of the Right." He meant those attacking society from a traditionalist basis; and he included the New Humanists in the school of Irving Babbitt and Paul Elmer More, the English Distributists after Hilaire Belloc and G. K. Chesterton, the Southern Agrarians, whose manifesto *I'll Take My Stand* had been published in 1930, and the Neo-Thomists.

Collins's panel of Radicals of the Right obviously represented a set of disparate emphases. The New Humanists had no political program at all, beyond Babbitt's vague hope that, if necessary, an American Mussolini would appear to save the country from an American Lenin. The Distributists idealized the Middle Ages, denounced the "servile state," and were susceptible to eccentric monetary ideas, particularly the Social Credit schemes of Major C. H. Douglas; like many monetary cranks, some of them inclined toward anti-Semitism, and Collins seems to have been particularly influenced by Belloc in this and other respects. The Neo-Thomists, like the New Humanists, lacked a political program; like the Distributists, they admired the Middle Ages. The Agrarians were, in the main, a collection of Jeffersonian fundamentalists who wanted to preserve the traditional South (or their magnolia-scented dream of it) against the temptations of industrialism.

From the start, Collins began to outdistance his fellow Radicals. In 1933 he called Mussolini "the most constructive statesman of our age." As for Hitler, "even if the absurd atrocity stories were all true," Collins wrote, "the fact would be almost negligible beside an event that shouts aloud in spite of the journalistic silence: the victory of Hitler signifies the end of the Communist threat, *forever.*" By 1934 Collins, describing himself frankly as a fascist, told Jews to decide between "relinquishing some of the forms of participation in national affairs temporarily won for them by liberalism and turning more for their happiness to themselves . . . or having this outcome forced on them in strife, agony and bloodshed." "We are offered," Collins said, "our choice of Communist collectivism or personal liberty under Fascism." All this was too much for Agrarians like Herbert Agar and Allen Tate, who were democrats, individualists and anti-fascists. Tate, speaking for most of the Agrarians, responded that, if he had to take Collins's choice, he would choose Communism.

As it sloughed off its original associates, the *American Review* became the spokesman for a reactionary (in the precise sense of the word) form of fascism, based not on anticipations of a new order but on a desire to restore the old — as Collins put it, on "the revival of monarchy, property, the guilds, the security of the family and the peasantry, and the ancient ways of European life." Collins himself disliked the cruder manifestations of fascist militancy. While rejecting Jews in his own courteous Park Avenue way, he professed himself repelled by uncouth anti-Semitic propaganda like the Protocols of Zion. "I suppose I will be called anti-Semitic," John Roy Carlson reports him saying, "but I don't particularly care so long as I am not mixed in with the crackpots and the bums. I want to be interpreted honestly and not washed in the same water with the rabble." But Collins evidently could not find enough fascists who had gone to Princeton. His standards steadily declined; by the end of the decade he was ·putting up bail for pro-fascist agitators like Allen Zoll and for the wife of the Nazi agent Ignatz T. Griebl.[2]

III

Collin's descent to the rabble he so much disdained was doubtless a confession of his failure to appeal to his own class; perhaps, also, evidence of the attraction primitive virility has often had for upper-class exquisites. Similarly, in December 1934, two young Harvard men, Philip Johnson, a brilliant architect, and Alan Blackburn, announced that they were forsaking the Museum of Modern Art, where they were employed, to go to Louisiana and study Huey Long. Johnson and Blackburn planned to form a National Party inspired by the writings of Lawrence Dennis and dedicated to the thesis that there should be "more emotionalism in politics." "We shall try to develop ourselves," Blackburn said. ". . . We may learn to shoot, fly airplanes and take contemplative walks in the woods." Unhappily, the Louisiana pilgrimage did not work out; the Kingfish's entourage had snobbish suspicions of Harvard men. Blackburn and Johnson turned up later as associates of Father Coughlin.

There was an air of wistful ineffectuality about the intellectuals in search of fascism in the United States. Indeed, the most serious talent to partake of this mood wasted no time at all on American fascism, but went straight to the source in Italy. This was Ezra Pound. Like so many others, Pound took off from an obsession with the magic of money. His grandfather, a congressman from Wisconsin in the seventies, was a monetary reformer who issued his own scrip ("Chippewa Lumbering Co. will pay bearer in lumber or merchandise"). His father seems to have had monetary delusions. Pound himself, springing from this line of monetary cranks, could remark as late as 1958 that it would be a good thing if "some of the sanity of the Greenback Party could have been restored." From his early days in England before the First World War, Pound showed a weakness for Guild Socialism and then Distributism, which led him to Social Credit and eventually to Mussolini.

The source of evil, in Pound's view, was usury, and the enemy

to be extirpated was the group which thrived as a result of usury
— *i.e.* the Jews.

> with usura, sin against nature,
> is thy bread ever more of stale rags
> is thy bread dry as paper

In the days of the Adamses, Jefferson, and Van Buren, America
had been strong and pure. But "usury spoiled the Republic."
The money power had taken over; the "gombeen men" were
in control. Usury, "the power of hell . . . which is the power
of hogging the harvest," was enthroned.

> Usura slayeth the child in the womb
> It stayeth the young man's courting
> It hath brought palsy to bed, lyeth
> between the young bride and her bridegroom
> CONTRA NATURAM

Usury brought more than oppression and poverty: it also brought
cultural degeneracy. "A tolerance of gombeen men and stealers
of harvest by money, by distortion and dirtiness, runs concurrent
with a fattening of all art forms." Liberalism could do nothing
to save the nation — it was, said Pound "a running sore, and its
surviving proponents are vile beyond printable description"
(and Pound's idea of what was printable was broad). Usury
was "the cancer of the world, which only the surgeon's knife of
Fascism can cut out of the life of the nation."

Mussolini offered the twentieth-century way of vindicating the
dreams of the founders of the American Republic. "The heritage
of Jefferson, Quincy Adams, old John Adams, Jackson, Van
Buren," wrote Pound in 1935 in *Jefferson and/or Mussolini*, "is
HERE, NOW in the Italian *peninsula* at the beginning of fascist
second decennio, not in Massachusetts or Delaware." With this
announcement, Pound turned his back on his native land (though
in 1934 he struck up a correspondence with William Dudley
Pelley's Silver Shirts), denounced Franklin D. Roosevelt and "the
Nude eel," and settled down in Rapallo to enjoy the Second
Coming of the gentile Christ.[3]

IV

Collins, Pound, and the other literary fascists were figures in a sideshow, without significance in American politics. One intellectual, however, brought to the advocacy of fascism powers of intelligence and style which always threatened to bring him (but never quite succeeded) into the main tent.

This was Lawrence Dennis, a dark and saturnine figure from Georgia, who, after an early career as a boy evangelist, abruptly changed his way of life, went to Exeter and Harvard, became a first lieutenant in the First World War and for some years in the twenties served as a foreign-service officer in Rumania, Honduras, and Nicaragua. His front seat on American intervention in Central America gave Dennis a cynical picture of the motives of capitalist foreign policy; and when he abandoned diplomacy to enter the banking firm of J. and W. Seligman and Company, he acquired an equally low view of business. He was an impressive witness against Wall Street in the Pecora investigation. In the third year of the depression he discharged his accumulated pessimism in a book entitled *Is Capitalism Doomed?*

In 1932 this was still an open question for Dennis. He had little doubt of the stupidity of business or of "the futility of liberalism"; and he greatly feared the consequences of the cult of international cooperation. "The international bankers and American liberals of internationalist leanings," he wrote, "have been leading this country straight towards communism." But he wrote as one who believed that stern measures of discipline might yet save the system. The hope lay in a new spiritual leadership expounding a philosophy "that is essentially true to the people . . . a notion of their objectives which they can believe without internal conflict." Such a philosophy, Dennis implied, would be realistic and nationalistic, and such a leadership would call for sacrifice and order.

To state the argument of *Is Capitalism Doomed?* in these terms perhaps does it some injustice. On its face, the book was a closely argued attack on the policy of allowing the investment bankers to determine the use and allocation of capital, a process which, Dennis held, was inevitably destructive of the public welfare. But notes of romantic desperation throbbed underneath. "I am a fatalist," Dennis wrote in a private letter of this period. "I am prepared to take my medicine in the bread line, the foreign legion or with a pistol shot in the mouth, and I ask no sympathy and would resent any indication of pity just as I would have neither sympathy or mercy on thousands of people now in the seats of the mighty if I came into power. I should like nothing better than to be a leader or a follower of a Hitler who would crush and destroy many now in power. It is my turn of fate now to suffer. It may some day be theirs."

The implicit themes of *Is Capitalism Doomed?* took shape in the next years and culminated in the publication of *The Coming American Fascism* in 1936. His question of 1932 was now settled in Dennis's mind: capitalism *was* doomed "by the irresistible trend of prevailing social forces." It could not return to the nineteenth-century pattern of imperialist expansion. It could not keep itself going by deficit spending (here Dennis departed from the position he had taken before the Senate Finance Committee in 1933, when he saw "no reason" why government spending could not be continued indefinitely). And its internal rigidities and vested interests would prevent it from undergoing any basic reorganization.

If capitalism could not survive, the choices, as Dennis saw them, were Communism, fascism, or chaos. While conceding the charms of Communism, Dennis had several reasons for preferring fascism. "I am in favor of a middle-class revolution," as he put it, "and against a proletarian revolution." Seeing himself as "an American and a nationalist," he felt that "any ethic which does not put a man's country above all else is a stench in my nostrils." There were, in addition, technical objections. A Communist revolution would involve a high degree of violence and disorder; it would mean the liquidation of many competent managers and experts; while fascism, because it was prepared to utilize the skills of the present bosses, could economize the human resources of society.

Dennis had no patience with the argument that the American nation had some inherent immunity to fascism. Quite the contrary: big business had made fascism logical for the United States. Americans were "the most organized, standardized, regimented and docile people in the world." "We have perfected techniques in propaganda and press and radio control which should make the United States the easiest country in the world to indoctrinate with any set of ideas, and to control for any physically possible ends. . . . No country has been better prepared for political and social standardization." Nor would their passion for freedom lead Americans to resist regimentation: 90 per cent had no grasp "whatever" of the supposed ideological content of their system. Their responses to words like "liberty" or "representative government" were only conditioned reflexes; all they wanted was the symbol, not the reality. "A fascist dictatorship," Dennis said, "can be set up by a demagogue in the name of all the catchwords of. the present system."

v

Though Dennis professed himself more concerned with philosophy than with program, his writings yielded vivid glimpses of his fascist America. States rights and the tripartite division of federal powers were to be abolished in favor of "a highly centralized government which would exercise the powers of a truly nation State." Since a multiparty system was "utterly incompatible with the successful pursuit of any possible scheme of national interest," there would have to be a single national party. This party would probably have a "militarized type of organization"; "no country boasts more militarized organizations, which wear distinctive uniforms and have discipline, than the United States." Unemployment would be eliminated by government spending, banks and basic monopolies would be nationalized, the rest of business would be placed under strict public regulation. Farmers should be content with subsistence and "aim at security and self-sufficiency rather than profits." Women would be barred from employment except under special license.

Above all, a regime of discipline was essential. "There must be no nonsense about tolerance in an absolute or unlimited sense." No one could be permitted to assert private ideas or values against the national plan. "Truth, right, justice, and reason," Dennis emphasized, "are whatever serves the fulfillment of this purpose." If minorities persisted in opposing the oncoming fascism, they would render fanaticism inevitable; "undoubtedly the easiest

way to unite and animate large numbers in political association
for action is to exploit the dynamic forces of hatred and fear."
A fascist revolution, Dennis courteously warned, might be tainted
with "some of the unfortunate race and religious prejudices now
cherished by large numbers of our people."

Who would bring about the revolution? At this point Dennis
talked in vague and contradictory terms about the elite. Whether
by design or confusion, he was never precise about who the elite
were. At one moment he defined it as everyone with an income
of more than $3,000 a year; at another, as that one-fourth to
one-third of the population which was "actually or potentially
more powerful and influential" than the rest, a definition including all businessmen, professional men, and farmers. When he
spoke of the "frustrated elite of the lower middle classes," however, he meant something more specific. It was from these "sinking
members of the middle class who are by way of being declassed"
that he basically expected his revolutionary impulse to come.

In 1935 Dennis found evidences of lower-middle-class insurgency on every side. Long and Coughlin, he wrote, were "in
far closer harmony with the logic of mass needs" than any liberal
or conservative politicians of the day. "I hail these movements
and pressure groups, not because their members are as yet fascists
or friends of fascism, but because they are making fascism the
alternative to chaos and national disintegration." What was now
required was a leader to "exploit the weaknesses and opportunities
for action presented by the situation." And in Huey Long Dennis
saw "the nearest approach to a national fascist leader" the country had yet known.

Obviously influenced by Long, Dennis wrote in 1935 that "the
road to national control" lay "through acquiring the control of
state governments, one by one." And perhaps the leader could
accelerate the process. Let Long get up before five hundred
of our industrialists in a secret meeting, and he would give them
a proposition they would prefer to the Roosevelt disorder! "I
have no ambitions," Dennis added for himself. "It takes a man
like Long to lead the masses. I think Long's smarter than Hitler,
but he needs a good brain-trust. . . . He needs a Goebbels."

An unaccustomed access of modesty stopped Dennis, but one
can assume that he had his own idea who the American Goebbels

might be. Dennis, indeed, had Goebbels-like qualities. His style was clever, glib, and trenchant. His analysis cut through sentimental idealism with healthy effect. He tried to shift attention from words and symbols to the realities of power. His "realistic" writing, for all its flashy and vulgar quality, had an analytic sharpness which made it more arresting than any of the conservative and most of the liberal political thought of the day.

Still, underneath his pose of toughness he was (again, like Goebbels) an incurable romantic. Though his myth-making was less Wagnerian, he lived even more fully in the world of myth; Goebbels, after all, had a government to transform dream into reality, and Dennis, only the Harvard Club. Dennis's fascism had practically no points of contact with American actuality, a fact which an increasing arrogance about his own infallibility as a prophet obscured for him but for few others. Like Seward Collins, Dennis soon began to follow a rake's progress in an increasingly desperate pursuit of authentic American fascists. Collins had a fastidious passion for the Middle Ages; Dennis saw himself as the sophisticated spokesman of a revolutionary elite in a technological epoch; but whether looking forward or back, each had progressively to lower his sights in order to find anyone in America in the thirties to agree with him. For both, the elite which was to save civilization eventually turned out to be a collection of stumblebums and psychopaths, united primarily by an obsessive fear of an imaginary Jewish conspiracy. What began as an intimation of the apocalypse ended as squalid farce.[4]

VI

The *farceurs* — the activists of American fascism — were mostly local adventurers or fanatics hoping somehow to capitalize on anxiety and unrest. Their ambitions gave these years a background of furtive and trivial melodrama. Many turned for a model to the dictators of Europe — to Mussolini, who had led his triumphant Fascists into Rome eleven years earlier, and even more frequently to Hitler, who had come to power only a few weeks before Franklin Roosevelt. As such students applied the lessons of European fascism to the American scene, the veterans of the First World War obviously stood out as a group crucial to the fascist revolution. The debacle of the Bonus Expeditionary Force at Anacostia Flats signified only a wasted opportunity, not a wrong conception. After all, the ex-doughboys were the one body of men in America expressly dedicated to patriotism and expressly trained for violence. If unemployed veterans, now agitating again for the advance payment of the bonus, could only be rallied under bolder leadership, might they not overthrow the government and reorganize the system?

This thought had occurred to more than one ambitious man at Anacostia. W. W. Waters, the leader of the B.E.F., had had the vision himself. But he disappeared from the nation's consciousness in the summer of 1932 as quickly and mysteriously as he had appeared in the spring. A quasi-veterans' organization remained, however, as a sort of illegitimate offspring of the B.E.F. Its name — the Khaki Shirts — suggested its fascist inspiration. Under the leadership of "General" Art J. Smith, a professional soldier who had fought in Africa and China, it dedicated itself to what it called "manocracy: a new philosophy of economics"; and its program included the abolition of Congress, the payment of the bonus, the revaluation of silver at 16:1, and the largest Army and Navy in the world. Its headquarters were in Philadelphia, where Smith, wearing a khaki shirt, riding breeches, a brown suede riding coat decorated by four stars, and a plumed headdress, spouted political nonsense and sold shirts and boots to his followers.

Mussolini having marched on Rome, Smith proposed to march on Washington: a million and a half veterans, under his leadership, were scheduled to invade the capital on Columbus Day 1933. But the movement was in trouble long before October. In July radicals tried to break up a Khaki Shirt rally in a New York suburb. When a heckler persisted in challenging Smith from the floor, a Khaki Shirt aide fired a shot. Knives flashed, lights went out, panic ensued, and by the time the police arrived, Smith's critic was dead and twenty-four people were injured. With presence of mind, Smith immediately identified a member of the radical group as the killer. The Socialists (over bitter Communist opposition) took up the cause of the accused man; Norman Thomas became chairman of his defense committee.

Then, on the eve of Columbus Day, a police raid on Smith's

Philadelphia headquarters uncovered an impressive collection of revolvers, knives, clubs and swordsticks. Smith himself promptly disappeared with a part of the organization's funds. Disgruntled followers said that their commander-in-chief had given them orders to take over the city of Philadelphia and ransack three armories before moving on to Washington. The police, scoffing at Smith as a revolutionist, called him a confidence man and his organization a shirt-selling racket. In December, at the New York murder trial, a witness who had originally supported Smith's testimony now recanted; he had backed Smith, he said, because Smith threatened that he would "kill all the Jews in America," and the witness did not want to be the first. Ultimately a Khaki Shirt confessed to having fired the fatal shot, and Smith, who received six years in prison for perjury, vanished from history.[5]

VII

The Khaki Shirt story was characteristic enough of the seediness of the movements in which two-bit demagogues, part racketeers, part prophets, preyed upon simpletons and deadbeats. Nor were the leaders by any means confined to the big cities. One of the most influential, William Dudley Pelley, operated out of Asheville, North Carolina.

By his own account, Pelley, a screen writer and real estate promoter in California, had died in the twenties. However, he returned to life a few moments later and promptly wrote an article about his heavenly interlude entitled "Seven Minutes in Eternity." In the next years Pelley preserved his transcendental contacts. In 1929 he was "inspirationally instructed" that, when a young house painter became the head of the German people, Pelley should regard that as a signal to follow his example in the United States. Accordingly, the day after Hitler became Chancellor of Germany, Pelley launched the Silver Shirts. The initials expressed his admiration for the Nazi SS, Hitler's elite guard.

The Silver Shirts, Pelley said, represented "the cream, the head and the flower of our Protestant Christian manhood." Pelley himself, a little man in his forties with gleaming malignant eyes and a dirty-gray goatee, strutting in silver shirt and riding breeches, did not look like the cream of anything. Yet he cast a kind of spell on ignorant and disturbed people. He was obsessed with the international Jewish conspiracy — with the "Dutch Jew" Rosenfelt, with the "half-Jew" Alfred E. Schmidt, and with Bernard Baruch, the "uncrowned prince of the Jewish nation in the western hemisphere." His magazine *Liberation* was a mad mixture of astrology, spiritualism, radiotherapy, anti-Semitism and Nazism. There was "but one issue in these United States," it declared in March 1934, "and that is the forcible removal of the Jew from office." "This great Christian Militia," said the Silver Legion's official Despatch No. 1, "nation-wide in its ramifications, means to suddenly become an active, dynamic, vigilante organization that shall . . . put in political office men from its own ranks."

Pelley's followers, to meet their leader's astrological standards, had to register the hour and minute of their birth on their application blanks. They devotedly bought and read the anti-Jewish and pro-Nazi material distributed by his publishing house, the Galahad Press. In San Diego, California, the Silver Shirts were armed and used a convenient target range for practice and maneuvers. In Minneapolis, a retired businessman who was a Silver Shirt showed a young reporter his stores of canned goods, laid up against the day of Communist revolution, and said, "If it be God's will that I fall as a martyr to the cause at the hands of these beasts, I shall die here, in my Christian home, defending my dear wife to the end."

A Kansas fundamentalist minister named Gerald B. Winrod harped on similar themes in a millennial context. Winrod's magazine, *The Defender*, with a circulation of 40,000 in 1934, strove to alert the Protestant community against the anti-Christ — first identified with the Catholics and then increasingly, in the thirties, with the Jews. In Winrod's view the New Deal was a Jewish Communist racket, and a trip to Germany in 1934 persuaded him of Hitler's righteousness. He told his wife that he would become "dictator of the country after the revolution," assuring her that in the meantime he would take her to a hide-out in Wyoming in case of trouble. At the same time he lived in constant fear of powerful enemies and used to prowl around his house behind drawn curtains, gun in hand. Like Pelley, he flooded the mailboxes of devoted followers with weird writings.

Pelley and Winrod were not alone. George W. Christians had

his white-shirted Crusaders for Economic Liberty, Harry A. Jung, his American Vigilantes; Elizabeth Dilling, George E. Deatherage, Robert E. Edmondson, and other patriots were beginning their activities. To pathetic people in back parlors who hated themselves or their lives, these men and women presented hatred itself as a gospel. Depression aggravated anxieties; Nazism provided a model, and its success, an inspiration; the Jew became increasingly the favorite target. In 1934 and 1935 the American fascists were in the main a collection of crackpots working the back alleys. Still, observers noted ominously, this is what people had once said about Hitler.[6]

VIII

Nor was fascism merely a disease of the lower middle class. More exalted circles from time to time shared or were suspected of sharing the infection. The Sentinels of the Republic, an organization which opposed the Child Labor Amendment and the Social Security Act and advocated the repeal of the general-welfare clause of the Constitution, was subsidized by some of the country's most glamorous financial figures. Its president, Alexander Lincoln of Boston, instructed a correspondent that "the Jewish threat is a real one." Again, an Army captain testified before a House committee that a Wall Street financial counsel named Jackson Martindell had discussed forming a group to be called the American Vigilantes, half a million strong, who, when the inevitable revolution came, would be ready "to take over the reins of the government" with Martindell as "head of the organization." Fantasies or actualities, such stories registered a marginal mood of the times.

Most spectacular of all was the story told by Smedley D. Butler, a retired major general of the Marines, a holder of two Congressional Medals of Honor, a Republican and a Quaker, whose devil-may-care personality might well have attracted people in search of a man on horseback. In 1933, Butler told a House committee, a New York bond salesman named Gerald C. Mac-Guire offered him $18,000 in one-thousand-dollar bills to defend the gold standard at the American Legion convention. Butler refused. MacGuire then took a trip to Europe on behalf of a group called the Committee on Sound Currency and a Sound Dollar. One purpose of the trip, judging by the reports MacGuire

sent back to New York, was to study fascist veterans' movements.
The Croix de Feu particularly impressed MacGuire; "these men,"
he said, "will be the bulwark upon which France will be saved."
Returning to the United States, MacGuire asked Butler to head
a similar group in America. A reporter testified that MacGuire
had told him, "We need a Fascist government in this country. . . .
The only men who have the patriotism to do it are the soldiers
and Smedley Butler is the ideal leader." What about Roosevelt?
"We might go along with Roosevelt and then do with him what
Mussolini did with the King of Italy." But Butler rejected the
proposal with his accustomed pungency. "If you get the 500,000
soldiers advocating anything smelling of Fascism," he said, "I am
going to get 500,000 more and lick the hell out of you, and we
will have a real war right at home."

No one quite knew what to make of the Butler story. It seemed
as ridiculous as Dr. Wirt's fantasies. MacGuire himself denied
most of the statements attributed to him. Most people agreed
with Mayor La Guardia of New York in dismissing it as a "cocktail
putsch." But James E. Van Zandt, national commander of the
Veterans of Foreign Wars and subsequently a Republican congressman, corroborated Butler's story and said that he, too, had
been approached by "agents of Wall Street." As for the House
committee, headed by John McCormack of Massachusetts, it declared itself "able to verify all the pertinent statements made by
General Butler" except for MacGuire's direct proposal to him,
and it considered this more or less confirmed by MacGuire's European reports. No doubt MacGuire did have some wild scheme
in mind, though the gap between contemplation and execution
was considerable and it can hardly be supposed that the republic
was in much danger.[7]

IX

As yet, the dream of fascism remained misty and confused. But
what was clear in 1935 was the impression that new forces had
somehow been released in American politics; and that these
forces drew their strength from stirrings in the nonpolitical,
xenophobic lower middle classes. The new activists had little
experience of party politics and little understanding of democracy. Moved by envy and suspicion, they would follow any

leader who promised to advance their status and foster their self-respect. Their passions threatened to overstrain the existing organization of politics; and the threat acquired an ominous urgency in the light of the success in Europe of Mussolini and Hitler.

In 1935 Raymond Swing, a thoughtful newspaper correspondent who had spent many years in Europe, assessed the prospects for fascism in the United States. On the basis of the experience of Italy and Germany, Swing suggested that four conditions made fascism probable: the impoverishment of the middle class; economic stagnation; the paralysis of democratic government; and the threat of a strong Communist movement. The first two prerequisites, he said, already existed in the United States; as for the third, if democratic government was not in a state of paralysis, it was at least in a state of acute crisis. There remained only the threat of Communism. Obviously nothing existed in the United States equivalent to Italian Communism before Mussolini or German Communism before Hitler. Yet, Swing contended, there now seemed to be a concerted effort to fulfill the fourth precondition of fascism by persuading the American people that they were in imminent danger of Communist revolution.

In 1934 William Randolph Hearst, who had followed a long trajectory from left to right in his forty years as a newspaper publisher, visited Nazi Germany. "Hitler is certainly an extraordinary man," he wrote back after an audience with the German Chancellor. "We estimate him too lightly in America." The Führer's claim to have saved Germany from Communism particularly impressed Hearst. "This is the great policy, the great achievement," he said on his return to the United States, "which makes the Hitler regime popular with the German people, and which enables it to survive very obvious and very serious mistakes." Two months later, in November 1934, Hearst declared that there was no fascist movement in America "AS YET." "Fascism will only come into existence in the United States," he added, "when such a movement becomes really necessary for the prevention of communism."

A strategy, conscious or unconscious, seemed to be emerging. Whether, as he claimed, to avert fascism, or, as his enemies charged, to create the demand for it, Hearst began in November 1934 a crusade to rouse America to the dangers of Communism.

The red peril was, of course, no recent discovery of Hearst's. Though he had strongly advocated the recognition of the Soviet Union fifteen years earlier, he had come in the twenties to see the Bolshevik in a more baleful light and to respect the Communist skill at infiltration and subversion. "Clever chaps those disciples of Lenin and Stalin in the Government at Washington!" he admiringly remarked in the midst of the Hoover administration. His early support of the New Deal thrust his Communist preoccupations into the background. But in 1934 the revelations of Dr. Wirt, followed by the San Francisco strike, refreshed his recollection. It was then that he described the administration as "more communistic than the communists." His visit to Hitler gave anti-Bolshevism new urgency.

There were other factors promoting an anti-Communist mood. One was the growing recognition in 1934-35 that the Soviet regime was one of something less than perfect benevolence. The Hearst press broke in America the story of the ghastly Russian famine of 1932–33 (though Hearst, with his instinct for getting things wrong, placed the famine a year later and tried to prove it by photographs taken a dozen years earlier). Another factor was the dawning realization that a Communist conspiracy was, in fact, at work in the United States.

In March 1934, the House of Representatives authorized an investigation into "un-American" activities by a special committee headed by John W. McCormack of Massachusetts and Samuel Dickstein of New York. In the following months the McCormack-Dickstein Committee inquired into Nazi operations in America, exposed William Dudley Pelley and the Silver Shirts, looked into Smedley Butler's allegations, and called the Communist leaders up for testimony. Its manner of investigation commanded special respect. McCormack used competent investigators and employed as committee counsel a former Georgia senator with a good record on civil liberties. Most of the examination of witnesses was carried on in executive sessions. In public sessions, witnesses were free to consult counsel. Throughout, McCormack was eager to avoid hit-and-run accusation and unsubstantiated testimony. The result was an almost uniquely scrupulous investigation in a highly sensitive area.

The work of the McCormack-Dickstein Committee might have

given Hearst a context of responsibility in which to conduct an anti-Communist campaign. But Hearst had other methods and, very likely, other objectives. "Does anybody want the bloody despotism of Communism in our free America," Hearst asked in January 1935, "except for a few incurable malcontents, a few sap-headed college boys and a few unbalanced college professors?" His primary object was evidently less to uncover genuine Communists than to frighten liberals out of expressing opinions on public affairs. The brain trust was reaping its whirlwind.

The warfare against the colleges began in November 1934, when Hearst operatives, disguised as students, sought to entrap professors at Syracuse University into radical remarks. In a few weeks, his *New York Journal-American* tried the same thing at Columbia; but, alerted by the Syracuse experience, Professor George Counts of Teachers College penetrated the masquerade and interviewed the interviewers. This did not prevent the Hearst press from portraying Teachers College as a hotbed of disloyalty, nor from moving on to expose Professors Sidney Hook and James Burnham of New York University as subversive figures. When President Harry Woodburn Chase refused to fire Hook and Burnham, Hearst asked whether N.Y.U. was to be classified hereafter "as an active center for treasonable plotting for the overthrow of the American Government."

x

This was only the beginning. Richard Washburn Child, Mussolini's American patron, wrote impassioned articles for the Hearst papers: "Keep the boys and girls out of those institutions where investigation shows red degeneracy is found." When someone mentioned academic freedom, Hearst responded irritably, "Academic freedom is a phrase taken over by the radical groups as a new camouflage for the teaching of alien doctrines." The enthusiasm spread. Some students themselves pleaded for rescue. Thus a Johns Hopkins undergraduate, writing on "Sinister Forces on Campus" for the *National Republic,* asked "the sane and the understanding" to tear "these undergrowths out by the roots and remove by one carefully conceived and deliberately executed campaign an evil which may otherwise effect damage beyond repair."

And there were pathetic moments of family conflict. When Henry Bedford-Jones, the pulp-magazine writer, wrote under a pseudonym an article for *Liberty* entitled "Will the Communists Get Our Girls in College?" his daughter Nancy, saying that her father's allegations were drawn from her own experience, replied bitterly in the *New Masses* under the title, "My Father Is a Liar!"

In the spiritual turmoil of the year, the Hearst crusade found an immediate response, especially among troubled members of the lower middle class, already apprehensive over their status, resentful of the foreigner, and suspicious of sex and radicalism. For them "Communist" did not mean a man under the discipline of the Communist party or an agent of the Soviet Union; it meant a dissenter or a foreigner, if not simply an outlander who drank and smoked. Hearst promoted this confusion. With almost faultless precision, his campaign avoided any identification of authentic Communists, and whipped up the mob against liberalism, sometimes of the most innocuous variety. Thus he attacked Nicholas Murray Butler and the Carnegie Endowment for International Peace — "the most SEDITIOUS proposition ever laid before the American public." He even denounced Representative John J. McSwain, the conservative chairman of the House Military Affairs Committee and a sponsor of anti-Communist legislation, as "a communist in spirit and a traitor in effect."

The publication in 1934 of a singular volume by Elizabeth Dilling, entitled *The Red Network: A 'Who's Who' and Handbook of Radicalism for Patriots,* compounded the confusion. *The Red Network* was a list of about 500 organizations and 1,300 individuals presumably implicated in a Communist conspiracy to take over America. Mrs. Dilling cast a wide net. She listed such names as William E. Borah, Newton D. Baker, Chiang Kai-shek, Monsignor John A. Ryan, Donald Richberg, Felix Frankfurter, Eugene Lyons, William C. Bullitt, Eleanor Roosevelt, H. L. Mencken, and Mahatma Gandhi; and such organizations as the Foreign Policy Association, the Federal Council of Churches, the American Federation of Labor, and International Ladies' Garment Workers Union, the National Education Association, the Consumers' League, and the Union Theological Seminary. Though she did bring the red scare into an authentically Marxian world, it was, alas, more Groucho than Karl.

The twelve months from June 1934 to June 1935, according to the American Civil Liberties Union, "recorded a greater variety and number of serious violations of civil liberties than any year since the war." Forty-four states considered sedition and teachers' oath legislation. Charles R. Walgreen, the head of the drugstore chain, withdrew his niece from the University of Chicago where, he said, she was exposed to Communistic propaganda and free love; and the Illinois legislature, egged on by the Hearst press, sought evidence of Communism in Illinois schools. The Wisconsin legislature did likewise, hinting darkly of sex orgies among faculty members at the University of Wisconsin, denouncing President Glenn Frank, who was being mentioned as a possible Republican presidential candidate, and concluding that the University of Wisconsin was an "ultra liberal institution in which communistic teachings were encouraged and where avowed communists were welcome."

There were shrill counterattacks, particularly in the colleges. Students organized boycotts of Hearst newspapers, magazines, and newsreels. The publisher was burned in effigy, and for a moment the agitation seemed to transform him into a serious political figure. "There is not a cesspool of vice and crime," said Charles A. Beard, "which Hearst has not raked and exploited for money-making purposes." Hearst himself remained majestically calm before the uproar. "Whenever you hear a prominent American called a 'Fascist,'" he said in October 1935, "you can usually make up your mind that the man is simply a LOYAL CITIZEN WHO STANDS FOR AMERICANISM." And he clung to his faith that he knew best how to deal with dissent. "Perhaps the only way to restrain any one in an hysterical frenzy," he said, "is in a straitjacket until he recovers his sanity." [8]

XI

"No one can move about America," John T. Flynn wrote in the fall of 1935, "without being aware of the deep breathing and pompous chest expansion of the one-hundred percenters. Any public proposal that seems to hit some entrenched interest is promptly branded as 'un-American' or 'communistic.' As soon as that label is tacked on a proposal or movement, further argument becomes unnecessary." The fascist movement, Raymond Swing

predicted, would be in its first stage radical and strongly nationalist; then it would combine with big business in a coalition; "from
that moment democracy is doomed." So thought William Allen
White, too: "Fascism always comes through a vast pretense of
socialism backed by Wall Street money. . . . Huey Long is the type
we must fear. Huey Long backed by the Wall Street money on
the quiet, rabble-rousing the morons into a belief that he was going
to give them pancakes three times a day, is a menace."

But could fascism really come to America? Swing thought it
could. "The usual complacent assumption that we cannot become
fascist, simply because America is 'different,' or too large, does not
bear analysis. We are not different enough to produce all the
attendant phenomena of fascism except its salutes and shirts."
After all, the nation had accepted something much like a fascist
tyranny during the war and would accept it again if it found it
again wanted unity more than freedom. "War is not the only
crisis that can unite a sprawling nation. Economic despair also
can do it."

Swing's pessimism found vivid support toward the end of 1935
in *It Can't Happen Here,* a new novel by Sinclair Lewis. While
the Lewis novel was more properly classified as the literature of
warning than of prophecy, it nonetheless put the case for a possible American fascism in arresting and uncomfortably plausible
terms. Part of the plausibility lay in the ease with which Lewis
produced American counterparts of the leading Nazis. Thus Senator Buzz Windrip, Lewis's Hitler, was obviously based on Huey
Long, with a touch of Gerald B. Winrod; Lee Sarason, the
Goebbels, could have reminded readers of Robert E. Clements;
Dewey Haik, the collaborating general, might have been suggested by Douglas MacArthur. And Lewis was able to add a set
of distinctive American types to his fascist gallery: Bishop Prang
and the League of the Forgotten Men recalled Father Coughlin and
the Union for Social Justice; Mrs. Gimmitch was an evident transportation of Mrs. Dilling; and even William Dudley Pelley was
cited by Buzz Windrip as one of his inspirations.

Like Swing, Lewis wondered whether a nation of Babbitts really
had the passion for freedom which would lead them to resist
fascism. "Why, there's no country in the world," said Doremus
Jessup, Lewis's country editor, "that can get more hysterical —
yes, or more obsequious — than America." Look at Huey Long

and Tammany Hall, Aimee Semple McPherson and Mary Baker Eddy, Tom Heflin and Tom Dixon, the Kentucky night riders and the Klan, the red scares and the Catholic scares. "Where in all history has there ever been a people so ripe for a dictatorship as ours!" America had a tradition of cruelty, too: it was hardly necessary for an embittered radical to remind Doremus Jessup, suffering in a Vermont concentration camp, of the Scottsboro boys and Tom Mooney. "In the humorous, friendly, happy-go-lucky land of Mark Twain, Doremus saw the homicidal maniacs having just as good a time as they had had in central Europe."

It Can't Happen Here had defects as a novel — its slap-dash journalism, its occasional weakness for burlesque, the abysmal failure of all its women. Nonetheless it swept the reader along in a torrent of rude feeling. And it had a sharp understanding of the emotions which might generate an American fascism — emotions usually associated, not with public policy, "but with baptism by immersion in the creek, young love under the elms, straight whiskey, angelic orchestras heard soaring down from the full moon, fear of death when an automobile teeters above a canyon, thirst in a desert and quenching it with spring water." All these were concentrated in Berzelius Windrip, the Professional Common Man, whose qualities were so magnified by his oratory that "while the other Commoners could understand his every purpose, which was exactly the same as their own, they saw him towering among them, and they raised hands to him in worship."

It Can't Happen Here had a disturbing resonance. "There is a history of terror in the bowels of every nation," observed R. P. Blackmur of the Lewis novel, "only awaiting the moment's impetus to be articulated and made general." In Britain, a lonely foe of Nazism saluted Sinclair Lewis. "Such books render a public service to the English-speaking world," said Winston Churchill. "When we see what has happened in Germany, Italy and Russia we cannot neglect their warning." [9]

XII

But the pessimists underestimated the American people — possibly their faith in freedom, possibly their ultimate boredom with bogeymen. In time, the stuck whistle of the red scare began to make the audience shut its ears. After all, despite the buildup he received in 1935 as the scourge of the campus, William Randolph Hearst was always a flop as a crusader. He had hardly won a campaign since he helped get the United States into the Spanish-American War nearly forty years earlier. He had failed to achieve his own ambitions to become mayor, governor or senator in New York. He had failed in his fight for municipal ownership. He had failed to keep America out of the First World War. He had failed to bring about the recognition of Russia. He had failed to deny the Democratic presidential nomination to Al Smith. He had failed to put over universal military service, to abolish capital punishment, or to end vivisection. He had not even been able to make Marion Davies a popular movie star. It was predictable that he would fail again.

Moreover, he raised up opposition in Washington more serious than that of the parading college students. This opposition did not come directly from the President. Roosevelt himself, while he had no use for the red scare, disappointed some of his supporters by refusing to speak out against it. Evidently he feared that a public stand would provoke congressional opposition to the administration's social and economic program. In the spring of 1935, for example, when Harold Ickes wanted to appoint as Undersecretary of the Interior a Chicago lawyer who had represented John Strachey, the British Marxist, under deportation charges as a supposed Communist, Roosevelt seemed "disturbed." As Ickes noted in his diary, the President was "anxious just now not to do anything to stir up William Randolph Hearst."

Feeling this way, Roosevelt did not provide the executive branch clear guidance when the War and Navy departments supported legislation in the 1935 Congress which civil libertarians thought dangerous. Asked about some of the bills in press conferences, Roosevelt took refuge in evasion ("I was asked about that last week and I said I would look it up and I haven't. So I can't comment on it"). He finally denied, however, that the proposed legislation had administration support.

On the other hand, Roosevelt did nothing to discourage members of his administration from speaking out for civil liberties, and he tended to choose people who were ready to speak out. "President Roosevelt's official family," said Lucille Milner of the

American Civil Liberties Union, "read like a roster of the Civil Liberties Union. . . . We found an open door to all of the Federal Departments." Ickes himself was foremost in the counteroffensive. In April 1935 he condemned the agitation in a speech before the Associated Press. "Why should we be so fearful of half-baked ideas?" he asked. "Why are we so bent on forbidding the advocacy of theories the absurdity of which should be apparent to all if they were allowed freedom of expression? . . . Surely our institutions are not so poorly grounded that they may not be exposed to the buffetings of criticism." In June he delivered at the University of Alabama a ringing defense of academic freedom — "freedom to trail the truth into its most secret hiding place; freedom to proclaim the truth when found and verified; freedom to live one's life with the window of the soul open to new thoughts, new ideas and new aspirations." While he described Communism and fascism as "equally abhorrent," he considered the real issue in the United States between fascism and the America of the Founding Fathers. "Communism," he said in Detroit in December, "is merely a convenient bugaboo with which to frighten those who are in their political childhood."

In a similar vein, Governor George H. Earle of Pennsylvania told the American Legion in August that the influence of Communism in America was negligible. The greater danger, Earle said, was in permitting "our men of wealth to send us on a wild-goose chase after so-called radicals while they continue to plunder the people." Earle optimistically called on the Legion to hold fast to liberalism and "block the attempt of organized wealth to deliver us into fascism and dictatorship." Others asserted that Communism owed more to the irresponsibility of the rich than to the agitation of the poor. As Franklin Roosevelt's old neighbor Herbert Pell wrote in July 1935 to Ralph M. Easley, head of the National Civic Federation and a leading scourge of radicalism, "Mitchell [of the National City Bank] has made more Radicals than Marx. There are more opponents of our system who owe their conversion to [Harry] Sinclair and Insull than there are who were convinced by Lenin and Trotsky."

The issues were ventilated in congressional hearings over anti-Communist bills recommended by the McCormack-Dickstein Committee. One bill, for which there seemed a reasonable prima facie case, proposed to make it a crime to incite members of the armed forces to disobey the official laws and regulations. Communists for some time had been trying to undermine the loyalty of the services, through leaflets and pamphlets. "You must refuse to fight in the interests of the bosses," proclaimed a typical throwaway. ". . . Use your military training against your real enemy, the capitalist class that exploits us and plunges us into wars! You must refuse to fight against the Soviet Union."

On the other hand, the proposed remedy seemed to contain its own dangers to freedom. The bill would appear to make it a crime to criticize the recent cut in Army and Navy pay. A newspaper editor denouncing the use of militia to break strikes might well bring himself within the purview of such a law. Some critics of the bill sentimentally pointed out that even a mother writing a letter urging her soldier son not to shoot down strikers might be sent to prison for two years. As Professor Karl Llewellyn of the Columbia Law School put it, "We are dealing here with a penal law so loose, so broad, so indefinite, and so impossible of clean-cut application that it is a menace to anybody." The bill, said the conservative *New York Herald Tribune,* was "not only superfluous but dangerous."

Nor did such a departure seem justified by a threat to the republic which would not be met through existing statutes (such as those dealing with efforts to cause disaffection in the services). Brigadier General H. E. Knight testified that Communists had made "very little" headway in the Army; asked whether there was any tendency for the CCC boys to fall for Communist propaganda, he said, "none whatever." General D. C. McDougal said for the Marine Corps, "It has made no headway"; and Assistant Secretary H. L. Roosevelt added, "The Navy Department has every confidence in the loyalty of its personnel." Wherein, congressmen asked, lay the danger? It was, said Representative Maury Maverick of Texas, like using a twelve-inch gun to kill a gnat. The Communists, Maverick added, "do not amount to anything. They are a lousy crew, and they have no influence." Earl Browder? "That man has no more influence in this country than a jackrabbit."

It was an insult to American soldiers and sailors, said Maverick, who had been badly wounded in the First World War, to prevent them from reading whatever they pleased. "Get this: Freedom of speech and of the press is a safety valve for the protection of our social order. It acts as an escape for steam for such ideas as are hair brained. . . . If we stop them with force, if we give them more attention than they deserve, then the boiler may burst. Let's don't get excited." Or, as William Allen White said, he disliked "the whole business of denying fools their folly instead of letting them prove their folly."

XIII

In time, the Maverick-White attitude prevailed. Secretary of War George Dern, who privately thought the red scare exaggerated, withdrew his endorsement of the armed forces bill; and, along with a proposed sedition bill, it died in the House. Bills offered by Representative Martin Dies of Texas to stop the radical threat by suspending immigration and deporting suspicious aliens got nowhere. In another year the counteroffensive reached the point where Bob La Follette could obtain Senate passage of a resolution authorizing a special investigation of violations of workers' civil liberties. Only nine state legislatures, despite the clamor, enacted teachers' oath bills, and two of these were vetoed. (The best known among those to stay on the books was the act sponsored in the New York legislature by a Republican assemblyman named Irving Ives.) In Chicago, Charles R. Walgreen succumbed to the urbane blandishments of President Robert M. Hutchins and made a large gift to the university from which he had so recently rescued his niece.

By 1936 the pressure against civil liberties was visibly receding. While this was all to the good, the red scare left an unfortunate and ironic residue in the form of undue complacency about Communism. Where nearly everybody to the left of Herbert Hoover seemed a "Red" in the eyes of the Hearst press — "because I laugh at the threat of communism," wrote William Allen White plaintively, "I am supposed to be a sympathizer of it" — then few could take such charges seriously, even when they happen to be true. "Let anyone step out in defense of a popular right," said Professor George Counts of Columbia, "and he will be labelled a Communist." Because the red-hunters saw "Communists" everywhere, they made it harder for responsible persons to get a hearing when they saw the real thing anywhere. Perhaps the worst result of the red scare of 1935 was to set back intelligent anti-Communism in America by a decade.

As the red scare passed away, the fascist dream also waned. Democracy in its constitutional forms still had a vitality and leadership which the American fascists could not match. Lawrence Dennis soon became an intellectual curiosity, to be summoned as the only literate fascist when a journal of opinion or the Town Meeting of the Air wanted to display the spectrum of political philosophies. To the intelligent pro-fascist, the lesson soon became clear. If fascism were to come to America, it would not do so under its own steam. It could happen here only as a by-product of fascist triumph in the world. Insofar as the American fascists had a serious existence after 1935, it was only as agents, conscious or inadvertent, of Adolf Hitler.[10]

6. Revolt in the Old Northwest

THE TIME of stagnation was over. By 1934 and 1935 America was suddenly composed of activists, moving furiously in all directions. Part of the clamor was more or less incoherent demagoguery. But activism took other forms: another part was a more or less thoughtful and ordered radicalism. While both were expressions of upheaval, they appealed to somewhat different groups and expressed their unrest in very different language.

II

The radicals differed from the demagogues in two main ways. One was the intellectual quality of their argument. The demagogues were hawking economic patent medicines, compounded of ignorance, faith, and swamp water. The radicals were making a serious effort to think through the problems of economic society, and their results, though often perverse and wrong, were generally in the realm of rational discourse.

The other difference was subtler. The demagogues found their following among old Americans dismayed by the prospect of social and economic decline. The radicals (with the partial exception of Upton Sinclair of California) found theirs among new Americans excited by the hope of social, economic, and political advance. The depression produced, among other things, a profound shaking-up of American society: it led to a general discrediting of the older ruling classes, locally as well as nationally, and a sudden opening of opportunity for men and ethnic groups on the way up in the competition for position and power. If the politics of upheaval was to a degree the politics of economic privation, it was also to a degree the politics of social status — of upward or of downward movement within the social order. It was natural enough that people on the way down should turn to the demagogues and that people on the way up should turn to the radicals; for those on the skids yearned for the consolations of pap and fantasy, while those on the make demanded a program that sounded as if it might work. Those who followed the demagogues feared the future; those who followed the radicals rushed to possess it.

So behind Governor Floyd Olson of Minnesota there seethed the ambitions of Scandinavians, Catholics, and Jews pushed around too long by the dominant Yankeedom of Minneapolis and St. Paul. Behind Mayor Fiorello La Guardia in New York City there surged the Italians and Jews of Manhattan, weary of the monopoly of municipal power wielded by the Irish of Tammany Hall. The pattern had local variations. Thus silk-stocking Yankees, also long shut out of power in New York City, had become in local terms an underprivileged class and formed an indispensable part of the La Guardia coalition. Nor should one exaggerate the tidiness of the distinction between the radicals and the demagogues. The situation in California, where the bankrupt lower middle class was challenging the ruling dynasties of San Francisco and Los Angeles, was made to order for demagoguery; by accident, Sinclair, a utopian radical, was able to capture the natural clientele of Dr. Townsend and Huey Long. Long himself represented a mixed phenomenon. In Louisiana, where in important respects he was a radical, he led a revolution of vigorous poor whites against a decadent oligarchy. As a national leader he was plainly a demagogue, appealing to the threatened lower middle class: it was no coincidence that his program for the nation made much less sense than his program for Louisiana.

In the main, as the declining, frightened, nonpolitical old-American lower middle class tended to put its stamp on the demagogues, so the alert, rising, new-immigrant lower class tended to put its stamp on the radicals. And this complex of social and ethnic aspiration also distinguished grass-roots radicalism from the liberalism of the Roosevelt administration. The social and ethnic radicalism was more inchoate, more rancorous, more ambiguous, more sweeping, and more transient than the sometimes abstract and academic progressivism of the New Dealers, with which it nonetheless felt a broad kinship. Where the demagogues were basically oriented against the New Deal and represented people who in many cases had been Republican and could easily become so again, the radicals mostly felt, sometimes against their better judgment, a largeness and sympathy in Franklin Roosevelt and his program to which they could not help responding. A good deal of the time, program and purpose brought the New Dealers and the grass-roots radicals into a working alliance. On July 4, 1934, an orator at Macon, Missouri, expressed the common aspiration. "We want everyone to have the power to make a living adequate to his ability," said Judge Harry S. Truman. ". . . We are in the midst of the greatest evolution mankind has known. We are trying to reach the stage of pure freedom; a plane upon which the greeds and lusts of men shall not be allowed to interfere with the rights of others to life, liberty and the pursuit of happiness." [1]

III

In 1934 the most formidable of state radical leaders was Floyd Bjerstjerne Olson, who had been governor of Minnesota since 1932.[2] Olson, who was forty-three years old in 1934, had been born of Norwegian and Swedish parents in a Jewish neighborhood on the north side of Minneapolis. He graduated from high school and spent a year at the University of Minnesota, where he tried to stir a revolt against compulsory military training. Then he left Minnesota for the Far West, going to Alberta, serving as a scowman on the Frazier River, joining an Alaskan gold rush, and ending as a longshoreman on the Seattle docks and member of the Industrial Workers of the World. In 1913, at the age of twenty-one, he returned to Minneapolis and began a career of law and politics.

At the start, Olson's politics were tentative and cautious. He was a nominal Democrat who avoided the Nonpartisan League agitation of 1919 and somehow kept on good terms with the Republicans. In 1920, under Republican sponsorship, he became county attorney for Hennepin County, a job he held for a decade and discharged with efficiency. By 1924 he decided that his future lay with reform. In that year, although only thirty-three and

largely unknown outside the Twin Cities, Olson captured the Farmer-Labor nomination for governor. During the campaign,
Charles A. Lindbergh, Sr., who had been the Nonpartisan League
candidate in the bitter gubernatorial contest of 1918, gave Olson
his apostolic blessing. Olson ran well, but was defeated; he did not
run for state-wide office again until his successful candidacy for the
governorship six years later.

His followers liked to think of him as a Viking in politics.
Certainly Olson looked the part. He was tall and lean, with broad
shoulders, great hands, and strong Scandinavian features. He exuded jovial vitality; Sherwood Anderson described him as "a big
laughing man who gives you the impression of being alive and
aware." This overflowing energy gave vigor to his political leadership, power to his oratory, and magnetic charm to his personality.
Underneath his easy openness of manner, there was a notable
capacity for coldness and toughness. He was highly intelligent,
terribly ambitious and a little cynical. Though a Farmer-Laborite
and a tobacco chewer, he was essentially an urban type, who slicked
back his reddish-blond hair, dressed nattily, and liked to relax in
night clubs. For diversion, he chose, not thoughtful conversation
with earnest Farmer-Labor colleagues, but gambling, carousing
and practical joking with political enemies, the hard-drinking
businessmen and lawyers of the Minneapolis Athletic Club and the
Lake Minnetonka set.

For all his jauntiness, Olson conveyed a deep and biting dislike
for the existing economic system. "You bet your life I'm a radical,"
he told one interviewer. "You might say I'm radical as hell!"
And he rode upon a tradition of social conflict which had torn
his state from the days of Ignatius Donnelly and the Populists.
The Nonpartisan League and radical leaders like the older Lindbergh had carried the tradition of agrarian resentment well into
the twentieth century; and the long war between the labor movement of the Twin Cities and the Citizens' Alliance only added
new elements of civil strife. The violent truck strike of the spring
and summer of 1934 showed the degree of genuine class bitterness.
In addition, even middle-class Scandinavians had long chafed
under their exclusion from places of social and business prestige
by the old New England families of Lowry Hill. Feelings were
explosive, and Floyd Olson was prepared to give these feelings
full expression.

IV

Shortly after Roosevelt's inauguration, Olson told him that this was no ordinary depression but a collapse of the economic order. "If the so-called 'depression' deepens," Olson said, "I strongly recommend to you, Mr. President, that the Government ought to take and operate the key industries of the country." Unless and until this were done, he repeated in August 1933, there could be no "economic security for the common man." He wanted the government to begin by using unemployed workers in production-for-use factories which, by underselling private firms, would gradually put them out of business, until the major part of industry would be government-owned, producing for use, not for profit. At other times he talked of abolishing the profit system through the extension of co-operative ownership and control, presumably on the Scandinavian model. Within Minnesota, he promised to call out the state militia if that were necessary, to see that the hungry were fed and the homeless sheltered. "I shall declare martial law. A lot of people who are now fighting the [relief] measures because they happen to possess considerable wealth will be brought in by the provost guard." "You go back to Washington," he told an emissary of Harry Hopkins's in the anxious days of 1933, "and tell 'em that Olson is taking recruits for the Minnesota National Guard, and he isn't taking anybody who doesn't carry a Red Card." "Minnesota," he boasted, "is definitely a left-wing state."

Such pronouncements were enormously exciting to American intellectuals seeking indigenous radical leadership. Here at last was a practical and successful politician, authentically American, governor of the very state which had inspired Gopher Prairie and Zenith, who yet saw coolly through the pretenses of capitalism and proposed in his rough Midwestern way to build the good society. By 1934 he was an object of attention in the national liberal press. Olson was amused and flattered. He received the pilgrims from the East, signed articles for their magazines, and played affably with the general idea of a new party and a new society.

But he always hung back when it came time for commitment. An episode in 1934 showed the limitations of his radicalism. He opened the convention of the Minnesota Farmer-Labor party with an impassioned keynote address. He declared that he was tired of tinkering and patching and wanted to change the system; and that he could not see why government ownership could not provide a gradual transition to "the ultimate cooperative commonwealth." "I am frank to say that I am not a liberal. I enjoy working on a common basis with liberals for their platforms, etc., but I am not a liberal. I am what I want to be — a radical." He added, "When the final clash comes between Americanism and fascism, we will find a so-called 'red' as the defender of democracy."

Having said all this, Olson, who seemed bored with Farmer-Labor conventions, departed for Washington. But Howard Williams of the League for Independent Political Action, as chairman of the platform committee, interpreted these phrases as a mandate for an open declaration of war against capitalism. In an evening of emotion, the convention solemnly resolved "that capitalism had failed and that immediate steps must be taken by the people to abolish capitalism in a peaceful and lawful manner, and that a new, sane, and just society must be established; a system in which all the natural resources, machinery of production, transportation, and communication, shall be owned by the government." A public ownership plank spelled out the varieties of business — including factories, banks, and mines — to be acquired by the state.

Olson, taken aback by the ardor with which his followers construed his rhetoric, now proceeded to "interpret" the public ownership plan. First he limited it to public utilities and key industries. Public ownership of factories, he said, applied only to idle plants making goods for the unemployed; there was no thought of "any general ownership and operation of business." Soon he defined the Farmer-Labor goal as "essentially a championing of private business," though, he added, "of business carried on for mutual aid and not avaricious profit." In time he authorized a revision of the platform which diluted the public ownership plank still further and placed it under "ultimate aims." Yet Olson always retained enough fiery language about "production for use" as his eventual goal to keep the enthusiasts — a good many of them, at least — happy.

The episode was instructive. And its lesson was confirmed by Olson's role in the Minneapolis truck strike, where he used his power less to help the strikers than to vindicate the public authority. When it came to making decisions under the burden of responsibility, Olson was careful, practical, and even a little cautious. "Changes so far reaching come slowly," he once said, "and the change must be especially slow in a social and economic system as complex as this we live in." When asked whether he believed in revolution, he answered, "I believe in evolution. When we are ten steps ahead of the Bourbons, they will be forced to take one."

v

Olson's radical rhetoric was not insincere. It was genuinely responsive to a mood. But it was not intended as a guide to action. It was a radicalism of emotion rather than of policy; it served to release the resentments of the submerged people of Minnesota. After all, he had grown up among these people and knew their feelings. He spoke Norwegian, Swedish, Danish, and Yiddish. His wife was a Czech. "These people of the Old World," he said in 1936, "are breaking through these barriers seeking a new deal." This awareness of pent-up ethnic aspiration, combined with a tough pragmatism on economic matters, set Olson's political style. For all his flirtation with the doctrinaire left, he was fundamentally uneasy in the presence of doctrinaires: "the trouble with the leftists and ritualists — they want to ride on a white horse with a pennant flying hell bent for the barricades."

Marxists irritated him particularly. "I have never read a line of Karl Marx or Lenin," he said in 1934, "and it seems to me that the Russians have been too drastic and dictatorial in their methods." When John Strachey came to expound Communism in America, Olson said in a public debate, "I am an opportunist, and I hasten to call myself one before Mr. Strachey does." An opportunist, said Olson, was one who tries to do what can be done; "the Communists wait for 'the day' and won't tell what they are going to do when it comes." ("The British mind was incapable of appreciating Mr. Strachey," Olson later commented, "but in the United States he discourses brilliantly at swanky dinners causing delightful shudders to run down the spine of capitalists of both sexes.") For the Communist party, he had only contempt: "bogged down with Marxist dogma, and clumsy Stalinite strategy, [it] offers no hope." He felt keenly the differences between Communism and American radicalism.

The Communists believe in the abolition of private property. We believe in its creation. The Communists would confiscate whatever little private wealth the ordinary man has. We would give him an opportunity to earn more. The Communists believe the individual is created for the service and benefit of the state. We believe that the state is created for the service and benefit of the individual. The Communists would abolish Christian morality. We would give Christian morality the first real test in commercial relations it ever had. The Communists would reduce all people to a dead level. We would uplift all people to a happier life.

It was characteristic that, where his intellectual admirers disdained Roosevelt, Olson admired him above all other politicians.

They had first met at the Governors' Conference at French Lick, Indiana, in 1931, where Olson was much impressed by Roosevelt's plea for planning. Olson backed Roosevelt in 1932, worked with the liberal wing of the Democratic party in Minnesota, and in 1934 received Roosevelt's tacit support against a conservative Democrat ("in Minnesota," Roosevelt wrote Farley, *"hands off"*) in his hard-fought contest for a third term. For a time, Olson thought the NRA "the only plan" that could end the depression, though he condemned Washington's failure to use the licensing power; and he came to accept AAA and "that amiable philosopher Henry Wallace," though he had a more extreme farm program of his own, based on price-fixing and licensing of processors.

As governor, Olson urged a state income tax, unemployment insurance, public power, and mortgage readjustment. Such proposals kept him constantly embroiled with the legislature, and only a small part of his program was enacted. In the meantime, he faced other problems. He had chronic stomach ulcers and was harassed by appendicitis and hernia; physicians began to suspect cancer. While his tremendous vitality still concealed the ravages of disease, ill health was reducing his effectiveness. He could no longer exercise tight control either over his state administration or over his political party.

The Farmer-Labor party, now in office at last, was accommodating itself to success with disconcerting enthusiasm. Power turned some of its leaders into hardboiled machine politicians, prepared, not just for routine political deals, but possibly even for inde-

fensible understandings with Communists or Minneapolis gang-
sters. Walter W. Liggett, a free-lance radical journalist who ran
a political scandal sheet in Minneapolis, charged Olson with personal connections with the underworld; "instead of being a radical,
he is a racketeer." "I think I can finish him off," Liggett wrote
V. F. Calverton, the Trotskyite critic, late in 1935, " — that is if
he doesn't have me shot in the meantime as he did poor Howard
Guilford [another anti-Olson pamphleteer]." Three days later
Liggett was murdered. No evidence ever implicated Olson, and
Minneapolis seems to have been full of people waiting to settle
scores with Liggett. But it can be said against Olson that in 1934
and 1935 he did all too little to arrest the degeneration of his
party.

Outside Minneapolis he continued to impress radicals as their
most likely national leader. *"A third party must arise,"* he wrote
bravely in *Common Sense* in 1935, *"and preach the gospel of government and collective ownership of the means of production and
distribution. . . .* American capitalism cannot be reformed so as to
give happiness to the masses." Privately he confided to Harry
Hopkins that he planned to support Roosevelt in 1936, that he
doubted whether there would be a third party, that he hoped to
reach an understanding with the Democratic National Committee,
and that Roosevelt should use Leo Crowley of Wisconsin in
dealing with the Midwestern states. Publicly he kept options open,
if only as a means of maintaining pressure on Washington. "You
can't have abundance with a capitalistic system," he told a New
York audience in November. "You can't have profits and have
abundance. There must be a third party." "Whether there will
be a third party in 1936, seeking more radical legislation," he
told one interviewer, "depends mainly on Mr. Roosevelt." If there
were a third party, he told another, probably Bob La Follette or
Burt Wheeler would head it; "I think I'm a little too radical."
The interviewer persisted: "How about 1940?" "Maybe by then
I won't be radical enough," said Floyd Olson.[3]

VI

In neighboring Wisconsin, insurgency was for Bob and Phil La
Follette a family tradition. Their father, a patriarch of the old

school, had indoctrinated his sons with a sense of radical mission; and the tightly knit family, in which the women were as dedicated as the men, could hardly wait to vindicate the lost crusade of 1924. Moreover, they took pride in maintaining the state reputation for reform. "It is no accident," Phil used to say, "that nearly every forward-looking, concrete achievement in American public affairs during the past thirty years has had its origin in action in Wisconsin." Old Bob's legacy had gone two ways. Young Bob had inherited his intellectual gifts — his reflectiveness, his critical intelligence, his studious mind, his cool mastery of facts. To Phil had gone his tempestuous passion — those inner fires which sometimes burned so fiercely that they seemed beyond control. Bob, two years the elder, had been struck down in college by a debilitating illness; and the family had looked to the more vigorous Phil to become the new leader. When their father died, however, Phil was too young to qualify for the Senate; so it was Bob who took over the family seat. He went to Washington as a Republican, the Progressive party not having survived the debacle of 1924.

This was in 1925, when Bob himself was only thirty. Nine years later he had fully established himself in his own right. He was a small man, meticulously groomed, his manner unfailingly pleasant and courteous, his personality sensitive and conscientious. He was broader and more impersonal than most of his progressive colleagues. Where they sometimes uncritically accepted the premises of rural individualism, Bob La Follette had a more philosophical cast of mind; his reading of Frederick Jackson Turner had convinced him that the frontier was closed and that American life had to seek new terms of existence. And where the other progressives were mostly a group of prima donnas, Bob La Follette was untemperamental and selfless, working always to unite the members of the insurgent bloc, when their inclinations were to go their brilliant ways alone.

Phil La Follette was also short, slight, and boyish. But he was emotionally flashier. Like his father, he wore his hair in a bush and had a glittering eye. Where Young Bob was self-contained on the platform, Phil was passionate and evangelical. Where Bob was lucid and factual, Phil was often swept away in the torrent of his own rhetoric, uttering words which sometimes meant more to him than to his audience. He was a furious campaigner. Throwing himself into Republican politics in 1930, he won both the gubernatorial nomination and the governorship itself.

His ambitious social program quickly alienated the conservative Republicans. The year 1932 proved disastrous for the La Follettes. The Progressive Republican faction, caught between the conservative Republican organization and a resurgent Democratic party, was nearly ground to pieces. Phil La Follette himself was defeated for renomination in the primary; and, after the election, the La Follette group retained only one state office. Its situation did not improve in the next two years. A group of wealthy Germans was consolidating its control of the state Republican party; the Irish had a stranglehold on the state Democratic party. Middle-class Scandinavians and Germans felt themselves shut out by both ruling cliques. There seemed little hope of carrying the primaries in either major party in 1934. The more radical Progressives — especially Congressman Thomas Amlie and William T. Evjue of the *Madison Capitol Times* — boldly concluded that the only way to save the Progressive position was to re-establish a separate Progressive party.

VI

The La Follettes balked at first. But in the end they had no choice as leaders save to get in front of their followers. In May 1934 the party was launched. The preamble to its platform described it as "a new national party"; hardly a quarter of its forty-three planks dealt with Wisconsin issues. But it was organized only in Wisconsin. In the fall it offered a full slate, headed by the two La Follettes — Phil standing again as candidate for governor, and Bob running for re-election as senator. Roosevelt, asked in a press conference about Bob, replied off the record, "I would love to see Bob La Follette back here because he is a very old friend of mine and has been very helpful." He added that he could not command the Democrats of Wisconsin to nominate him but reiterated his "personal hope . . . that they will find some way of sending Bob La Follette back."

The election justified the militants. Not only did both La Follettes win, but the party elected seven out of ten Wisconsin congressmen. Going to Washington to keep a luncheon date with the President, Bob La Follette mused, "I am convinced that this economic crisis is fundamental in character and will produce a political realignment; just when, or how, it is coming, I don't know." Phil, swept up in campaign euphoria, had, as usual, fewer doubts. After all, Fiorello La Guardia, stumping Wisconsin for the La Follettes, had cried, "The Progressive party of the State of Wisconsin is not a third party. It is destined to be a new national party." Phil himself announced the new vision. The "insanity and cruelty" of the economic system, he told reporters, should "require no proof." The need was for a realignment which would put "the exploiting reactionary on one side and the producer and consumer on the other." First, there would be a spread of radical state parties, on the model of Wisconsin's and Minnesota's; "finally by a consolidation of sectional armies we shall have a national third party — a real leftist party. There is no reason why this can't be accomplished before 1940."

With a new alignment, it would at last be possible to change the system. "We are not liberals!" Phil said, "Liberalism is nothing but a sort of milk-and-water tolerance. . . . I believe in a fundamental and basic change." What sort of change? "I think a cooperative society based on American traditions is inevitable." But it appeared that he was sharply against socialism. European precedents — particularly the Marxist theory of class conflict — seemed to Phil irrelevant and odious. "We Americans, I insist, are different from the Europeans. . . . We in the North here skipped feudalism entirely, while Europe still has a terrible psychological hangover from it. For hundreds of years we were the freest people the sun ever shone upon. The frontier has influenced our minds, our manner in personal intercourse, our political methods." This meant that "the idea of classes has no vital tradition in our American past." Any attempt to install it would only "produce endless dissension among many who now have nothing against each other." (Phil said these things with such emphasis to John Strachey that the British Marxist, returning to New York, called him a potential leader of American fascism. "Phil and Bob La Follette cannot — I mean *cannot* — understand Russia," complained Lincoln Steffens.)

"We Progressives," Phil La Follette emphasized, "believe in the right of men and women to own their homes, their farms, and their places of employment. . . . Nationalization of all property breaks down with the unmanageable task of administration." The curse of the present system, he thought, was the greed of corporate owners. "Our aim," he would remark vaguely, "is to restore to those who work on the farm and in the city the ownership that has been wrung from them by the exploitation of private monopoly." His mood was more radical than his program. But it was the mood which was important; and along with Olson, Phil La Follette, with his shrewd half-smile, his flashing eye, his thick, graying pompadour, seemed evidence that America was at a new political turning.[4]

7. Utopia in the Far West

IF MINNESOTA AND WISCONSIN provided the ablest of the radical leaders of 1934, California provided the most picturesque of the radical uprisings. No state outside the South had a stronger tradition of social violence. Depression was now offering that tradition new and bitter scope. In the spring and summer of 1934 the San Francisco general strike and a series of fierce strikes by agricultural workers in the Imperial and San Joaquin valleys heightened the civic tension. The steady drift into California of fugitives from the dust bowl, dispossessed farmers from Oklahoma and Arkansas, Kansas and Texas, made antagonisms even more acute. The large ranchers, who at first had encouraged the migration out of a desire for cheap labor, now turned savagely against what they regarded as an invasion of wandering mendicants. And the cities were filled with the racially oppressed — Mexicans, Filipinos, Japanese, Chinese, Indians, Negroes — long denied any fair chance in California life.

II

Depression added men and women capable of giving this fluid unrest voice and leadership. Indeed, the crash changed life less for those in California who were already impoverished than it did for those who were living on savings or who were counting on a speedy rise in the world. The golden state had more than its share of the retired old and the ambitious young. Both groups regarded the depression as the betrayal of the promise of American life; and this betrayal seemed worst of all in the state where, if anywhere, fulfillment of that promise was presumed to be guaranteed. People felt personally aggrieved and angry. They yearned for a solution.

Nor did the existing political setup provide adequate outlets for their resentment. The Republicans had dominated the state since the progressive governorship of Hiram Johnson; but Johnson himself had retired in lonely pugnacity to the United States Senate, and his successors in Sacramento had shown themselves steadily more complacent and inert. At the same time Johnson's political reforms, especially the cross-filing system, prevented the emergence of the Democrats as an effective opposition. In 1930 there were more than three times as many registered Republicans as Democrats. William G. McAdoo, a Democrat, won the senatorial contest of 1932, as a result partly of the Roosevelt sweep, partly of a middle-class defection from a wet Republican candidate. But neither McAdoo nor his Wilsonian colleague George Creel, the favored Democratic candidate for governor in 1934, had enough social evangelism to appeal to the gathering grass-roots revolt.

The disaffected lower middle class knew little about politics. Most of its members had been Harding Republicans until the depression hit them. "These were people," Walter Davenport wrote in *Collier's,* "who threw Gene Debs in jail; who spat upon the war objectors as they marched through the streets to prison." Now they could no longer escape economics, and they turned to social prophets with the same credulous faith so many of them had but recently expended on Aimee Semple McPherson. Technocracy was an active cult in southern California long after the rest of the nation had forgotten it; Howard Scott was even imported for a time as resident high priest. In July 1933 three unemployed businessmen under the sway of Technocracy concocted the Utopian Society, which added the mysteries of a secret fraternal order to the promise of economic salvation. The movement spread rapidly through the environs of Los Angeles; one of its special appeals was the fact that it did not draw the color line. Soon Utopians were storming the Hollywood Bowl to watch a series of tableaux which presented the evils of capitalism and, in an ecstatic climax, exhibited Utopia itself, where everybody "produces what he uses and uses what he produces." A few months

later at Long Beach, Dr. Townsend looked out his window and saw
the sad old women clawing at the garbage can.

III

There were veteran social agitators in California, too; and, two
months after Roosevelt's inauguration, one of them contributed a
tract called *The Way Out* to the spreading discontent. Upton
Sinclair, who lived in Beverly Hills, was now fifty-four years old.
He had written forty-seven books and uncounted articles in
thirty years as the amiable scourge of the capitalist system. In
1906 *The Jungle* had exposed the horrors of the meatpacking
industry and helped bring about the Pure Food and Drugs Act.
In the years since, he had exposed religion, the press, education,
the liquor industry, the oil industry, the film industry, the coal
industry, the Sacco-Vanzetti case, and most other aspects of
American life. The last of the prewar muckrakers, Sinclair somehow kept a gentle but durable innocence while all around him —
Steffens to his left, Mark Sullivan and Hearst to his right —
capitulated to images of power and success. His books were brisk
and sentimental, saturated with fact and suffused with moral
indignation. They possessed a transparent sincerity and a sweetness of temper which distinguished them from the smart-aleck de-
bunking of the twenties and the overwrought proletarianism of
the early thirties. Sinclair believed more things, H. L. Mencken
said with affection, than any other man in the world. "As always, you are right," Mencken once wrote Sinclair, " — save on
matters of politics, sociology, religion, finance, economics, literature, and the exact sciences." He was, said Ezra Pound, not a
monomaniac (a breed Pound could recognize) but a "polymaniac."
Sinclair remained voluble without being aimless, self-centered
without being egotistical, and persistent without being finally
unbearable.

His ostensible creed was socialism. But it was a romantic,
old-fashioned socialism in the tradition which had sprinkled America with utopian communities in the nineteenth century. A
quarter of a century before, he had founded the Helicon Home
Colony in New Jersey (where young Sinclair Lewis worked briefly
as a handyman); he had lived at various times in single-tax

colonies; and he would have been thoroughly at home at Fruit-lands or Brook Farm. *The Way Out* showed little change in Sinclair's thought since his book of 1907, *The Industrial Republic,* "The only remedy which has any meaning," he wrote, "is one whereby the community as a whole comes into possession of the natural resources of the country and the means of producing useful goods."

He had twice run for governor and once for senator on the Socialist ticket. But three years of depression gave his program far more relevance than when Sinclair's last gubernatorial can-didacy had picked up a bare sixty thousand votes. In August 1933 an obscure Santa Monica Democrat, once a Populist and now a monetary crank (and, Sinclair later discovered to his dismay, a believer in the Protocols of the Elders of Zion), proposed that Sinclair announce himself as a candidate for the Democratic nomination for governor. Other admirers of *The Way Out* sec-onded the idea. After some hesitation, Sinclair, on September 1, 1933, slipped into the city hall at Beverley Hills and formally registered as a Democrat. A few weeks later he published his central campaign document — a pamphlet entitled *I, Governor of California and How I Ended Poverty: A True Story of the Future.*[1]

IV

Sinclair had been a Socialist for thirty years, and the decision to leave the party was not an easy one. But he had been a Democrat before that, and he sprang from an old Democratic family. And he also had come to feel that both doctrine and vocabulary cut Socialism off from American life. "What we want and must have," he wrote, "is a movement based upon American conditions, and speaking the American language. Ours is not a working-class country. Our workers act and speak and dress middle-class. . . . This depression has been just as hard on the middle-class as on the workers, and they are looking for help and ready to join anybody who shows them the way out."

If they wanted a way out, Sinclair was their man. "I say, posi-tively and without qualification, we can end poverty in California. I know exactly how to do it, and if you elect me Governor, with a Legislature to support me, I will put the job through — and

I won't take more than one or two of my four years." His
campaign slogan was brief and direct: END POVERTY IN
CALIFORNIA! And his plan — the EPIC plan, as it was soon
known from the first letters of the slogan — was equally brief and
direct.

He set it forth with engaging simplicity in *I, Governor of California*. Casting his argument in the form of a utopian narrative,
Sinclair wrote about his nomination, his campaign (features of
which he predicted with astonishing accuracy), his victory, and his
triumphant execution of the EPIC program. The basic problem,
as he saw it, was the existence of idle land, idle factories, and
idle people. Why should not the state acquire unoccupied land
(much of it already due for tax delinquency) and let the unemployed grow food for their own consumption? Why should not
the state rent or purchase deserted factories and let the unemployed make their own shoes and clothes and shelter? And why
should not the unemployed exchange these goods among themselves through an issue of scrip, good only within the system?
"Let the people go to work again, and take themselves off the
backs of the taxpayers."

Sinclair looked to the ultimate establishment of a network of
land colonies, model factories, and workers' villages, all envisaged
in terms which would have delighted Owen and Fourier. When
these units had paid off their debts, they would become "self-
governing communities, production units managed by the workers
under charters from the state." Thus a production-for-use
system would grow up next to the production-for-profit system
of capitalism. Sinclair had no doubt which would win in a free
competition. "Public industry will put private industry out of
business everywhere it is given a chance. . . . The Cooperative
Commonwealth will come as fast as we can prepare ourselves to
administer it." By 1938, according to his narrative, the old order
had "crumbled like a dry-rotted log," and the "political situation
had changed forever." Governor Sinclair, after careful investigation, could find only one poor person in the state — a religious
hermit who lived in a cave. "Therefore he considered his job
done, and he purposed to go home and write a novel." As the
example of the EPIC units converted California, so the example
of California would in time convert the nation. And EPIC was

indefinitely extensible: by 1935 it meant End Poverty in Civilization.

In July 1934 over two hundred thousand copies of *I, Governor* were in print; the End Poverty League, Incorporated, was in operation with a weekly paper and a corps of organizers; and hundreds of local EPIC clubs were sponsoring barbecues, picnics, and sewing circles. The movement even acquired an emblem — a golden honey bee with wings spread wide and the legend "I produce, I defend" (it was later suggested that a wasp with the legend "I sting, I buzz" might have been more appropriate). Sinclair himself was soon going from meeting to meeting, white-haired, thin-faced, confident, expounding his doctrine with soft-voiced, good-humored, and scholarly fanaticism to rapt audiences (Yea, Brother, and Amen).

The first test was the Democratic primary. George Creel, Sinclair's main opponent, came from San Francisco, had the support of McAdoo and other regular Democrats of Los Angeles, and represented the old-fashioned Democracy of the state. But Creel did not understand the fevers raging in the south. "When I crossed the Tehachapi into Southern California," he later wrote, "it was like plunging into darkest Africa without gun bearers." In the primary in August 1934 Sinclair not only beat Creel handily, but piled up more votes than all his eight opponents put together. A few weeks later, at the Democratic state convention, Sinclair and Creel collaborated on a platform which in Creel's view surrendered and in Sinclair's affirmed the essence of EPIC. In late September, Sinclair, as the leader of a united Democratic party, seemed to have an excellent chance of election in November on a platform pledge to put "the unemployed at productive work, enabling them to produce what they themselves are to consume." [2]

v

The rest of the nation watched the rise of Upton Sinclair with mixed emotions. Conservatives portrayed him as a beamish crackpot whose EPIC really stood for Empty Promises in California. His old Socialist comrades thought he was reviving the "colonizing" heresy they had extirpated thirty years before — the notion that the co-operative commonwealth was to be achieved by the Socialist capture of state governments. Norman Thomas, dismissing EPIC as "economically and politically absurd," said that Sinclair's election would prove "a tragedy to himself and to the cause of radicalism." Marxist scholars recalled Lenin's description of Sinclair as "an emotional socialist without theoretical grounding." The Communists were even harsher. EPIC, they said, was "another addled egg from the blue buzzard's nest"; "no greater threat to the American workers' standard of living has appeared." By August, the *New Masses* declared that the class line was being drawn in California more sharply than ever before, and Sinclair was taking his position "on the Fascist side of that line."

His nomination confronted the Democratic party with delicate problems. From Washington's viewpoint, politics on the West Coast had always seemed incomprehensible. "California is certainly one H —— of a State," Louis Howe wrote Harry Hopkins in March 1934, "and whenever they come to me on matters political, I crawl out and tell them that James A. Farley is handling all political matters today." But James A. Farley would have rather liked to crawl out, too. When Sinclair won the primary, Farley finally said, "If Sinclair is the choice of the Party, there's nothing else we can do but congratulate him. The Party has never failed to support its nominee." As for the President, he had announced early in the year, in connection with a factional feud in New York, a "hands-off" policy toward local contests. After his primary victory, Sinclair now proposed to come east to talk over EPIC and his campaign with Roosevelt. Marvin McIntyre replied that the President would be glad to see him, but that he had declared his intention not to take part in state elections and could not discuss politics.

It was early September when Sinclair drove from New York City along the Albany Post Road to Hyde Park. The sumac was turning red along the Hudson, and Sinclair found logs burning in the fireplace of the library where Roosevelt sat in a large leather chair, a stack of documents a foot or two high on the table beside him. "I do not think I have ever been more curious about any man in my life," Sinclair later wrote. In the past, he had condescended toward Roosevelt. New Deal policies,

Sinclair had said in June 1933, "will not postpone the crisis for a few days; they are plasters put upon a cancer." He had relented somewhat in *I, Governor*, allowing that Roosevelt was "headed in the right direction, towards government control of business and industry — and I am shoving!" Now Roosevelt greeted him in high good humor, offered him iced tea and told the story (which, however unlikely, is endorsed by Eleanor Roosevelt) that his mother used to spoil his breakfast many years before by reading aloud to him from *The Jungle*. He next launched into a series of tales about politics and finance in California. "I have met two Presidents in my life," Sinclair said to him after a time. "The other was Theodore, and I don't know which of you is the more indiscreet." F.D.R. threw back his head and laughed heartily. Then they discussed EPIC. Roosevelt displayed interest in the idea of production-for-use among the unemployed, gave Sinclair an enthusiastic picture of what the state of Ohio had been doing in this field with federal support, and suggested that the problem required further study. As the genial talk neared its end, Sinclair assured the President that he need not worry about newspaper talk of Sinclair as a presidential candidate. Roosevelt interrupted Sinclair's disclaimers, saying cheerfully that he wouldn't mind putting the burden off on somebody else and coming back to Hyde Park to write books.

From Hyde Park, Sinclair went to New York for a meeting with Farley, who startled the renowned author by holding out his hand and saying, "Call me Jim"; then to Washington, for cordial but noncommittal conversations with Hopkins, Morgenthau, Ickes, and Jesse Jones. On his way back to California, he stopped off at Royal Oak, Michigan, and secured the endorsement of EPIC by Father Coughlin. And in the meantime a group of intellectuals — among them, Stuart Chase, Clarence Darrow, Archibald Mac-Leish, Theodore Dreiser, Morris Ernst, and Dorothy Canfield Fisher — signed a national appeal on his behalf. "To me," said Dreiser, "he is the most impressive political phenomenon that America has yet produced. . . . Personally I think the man has done a much more brilliant job than either Mussolini or Hitler."

Sinclair returned from the eastern trip immensely taken by the Roosevelt personality and also persuaded that Roosevelt was going to make speeches for his program late in October. No doubt, like so many others in the excitement of the presidential audience, Sinclair construed affability as assent. Or he may have transferred a Rooseveltian speculation from the future conditional to the future; a dozen years later, Sinclair, defending his rendition of a talk between the President and Lanny Budd, said that Roosevelt's more "socialist" assertions came in response to questions about the nature of his program "in the event of another economic breakdown."

But Sinclair was not mistaken about Roosevelt's friendliness. Roosevelt told J. F. T. O'Connor, the Comptroller of the Treasury and a veteran California politician, that Sinclair had made a "favorable impression" on him. To the President, EPIC represented the impulse to experiment, which he considered so much the essence of America. Sinclair was a crank, no doubt, but cranks had contributed a good deal to social progress; the extravagance of his claims seemed to Roosevelt only part of the natural ferment of democracy. As the President remarked to his press conference two days later, EPIC as a state-wide program was "impossible, absolutely impossible, on a scale anything like that"; yet, he added, citing Ohio again, "on the other hand, there is real merit and real possibility in the community plan based on the same principle." "If Sinclair has any sense in him," Roosevelt concluded, "he will modify at least in practice this perfectly wild-eyed scheme of his and carry it on as a community experiment. It will do a lot of good work that way." When Frances Perkins complained that EPIC was dangerous and fanatical, Roosevelt replied calmly, "Perhaps they'll get EPIC in California. What difference, I ask you, would that make in Dutchess County, New York, or Lincoln County, Maine? The beauty of our state-federal system is that people can experiment. . . . If a new, apparently fanatical, program works well, it will be copied. If it doesn't, you won't hear of it again." [3]

VI

California took Sinclair with far less equanimity. The propertied classes saw in EPIC the threat of social revolution by a rabble of crazed bankrupts and paupers — a horrid upheaval from below, led by a Peter the Hermit, which could only end in driving all wealth and respectability from the state. They responded by directing against it the first all-out public relations *Blitzkrieg* in American politics. Under the direction of the firm of Lord and Thomas, aided by the Republican state chairman, Louis B. Mayer of Metro-Goldwyn-Mayer, the smartest advertising people of the state (including so promising a pair as Clem Whitaker and Leone Baxter) were mobilized in a campaign to discredit and destroy Upton Sinclair as expediently and as permanently as possible.

Few candidates could have been more peculiarly vulnerable. For more than a generation Sinclair had carried on most of his thinking, daydreaming, and soul-searching in public. Now his writings were ransacked, his oldest books and most fugitive pamphlets resurrected, his most careless phrases torn from context. "Out of his own mouth shall he be judged," said the opposition, scattering across the state leaflets designed to unveil Sinclair in his own words as an atheist, a Communist, an anarchist, a vegetarian, a believer in telepathy and free love, and enemy of Catholics, Christian Scientists, Mormons, Seventh Day Adventists, and Boy Scouts. "We had one objective," Leone Baxter said many years later: "to keep him from becoming Governor. But because he was a good man, we were sorry we had to do it that way."

Where his own words did not suffice to damn him, his opponents had no scruple about fabrication and forgery. Thus he was freely confused with Sinclair Lewis and denounced for having written *Elmer Gantry*. Fliers were circulated endorsing Sinclair signed by the "Young People's Communist League. Vladimir Kosloff, Secy.," though no such organization or person existed. Affidavits asserted that Sinclair had trampled on the American flag at San Pedro, that he had cursed the Constitution, and that, when forty-eight sailors had been killed in an explosion on the battleship *Mississippi*, he had expressed the wish that it had been forty-eight hundred. Aimee Semple McPherson denounced him as "a red devil."

Hollywood lost no time in getting into the act. A group of producers, rallied by Mayer, raised half a million dollars, partly by assessing directors and stars one day's salary. Hollywood studios turned out fake newsreels in which substantial community leaders and gentle old widows (played by bit actors) declared for Frank Merriam, the Republican candidate, while bearded figures with heavy Russian accents explained why they were voting for Sinclair: "vell, his system worked vell in Russia, vy can't it work here?" Other newsreels and photographs pretended to depict an invasion by hordes of tramps and bums, attracted to California by Sinclair's promises. The *Los Angeles Herald and Express* printed a picture of a typical group of such indigent hoodlums, only to have spoilsports identify it as a still from a Warner Brothers film *Wild Boys of the Road.* (Mayer's methods boomeranged. A group of film stars, led by Jean Harlow and James Cagney, rebelled against his "Merriam tax"; and Morrie Ryskind and Gene Fowler organized a writers' committee for Sinclair.)

In September, Sinclair was felt to be running ahead. But the publicity barrage had stunning effect. "The campaign against Upton Sinclair," exulted the *Hollywood Reporter,* "has been and is DYNAMITE. It is the most effective piece of political humdingery that has ever been effected." Sinclair's denials of false charges (thus he sardonically said of vegetarianism, "I abandoned this evil practice twenty-five years ago") were ignored by press and radio. Except for vilification, press coverage of the Sinclair campaign practically disappeared. The three big Los Angeles papers, said *Time,* "simply quit reporting news of EPIC and its sponsor." When he issued *Immediate EPIC,* a pamphlet of his own with a final statement of his plan, George Creel pronounced it a violation of the platform compromise and used it as a pretext to stay out of the campaign. By the third week in October, Creel publicly repudiated Sinclair. ("It's a choice between catalepsy and epilepsy," said Creel. "Sinclair has a fantastic, impossible plan and Merriam is as modern as the dinosaur age.")

VII

"At this distance," Roosevelt told Key Pittman early in October, "it looks as though Sinclair will win if he stages an orderly, common sense campaign but will be beaten if he makes a fool of himself." When Moley urged Roosevelt to disengage the administration from Sinclair, Roosevelt commented that Merriam had come out for the Townsend Plan, which was surely no less crazy than EPIC. California Democrats received a letter from the National Chairman, signed in Farley's green ink, calling on them to support the whole state ticket, including Sinclair. But more and more the pressure from California was on the President to back away. Hiram Johnson wrote Ickes of Sinclair, "Unfortunately, he is erratic and, I think, irresponsible, and his so-called EPIC program is simply damned foolishness." Early in October Moley denounced EPIC in a *Today* editorial which Sinclair's opponents were happy to interpret as an administration brush-off.

An excited Sinclair wrote Roosevelt that only the President or possibly Hiram Johnson could undo the damage of the Moley piece. "I am cherishing your promise to come out in favor of production for use about the 25th of this month," Sinclair concluded. "If you make it strong enough, it will serve the purpose!" Telegrams followed: RESPECTFULLY REMIND YOU OF THAT PROMISE TO BROADCAST IN FAVOR OF PRODUCTION FOR USE. (F.D.R. might have recalled the message Cousin Teddy had sent to Sinclair twenty-eight years before, "Your second telegram has just come: really, Mr. Sinclair, you *must* keep your head.") As it became plain that Sinclair was falling behind, Roosevelt decided to abandon him. When Eleanor Roosevelt inquired what attitude she should take, Steve Early replied, "The President's instructions on Sinclair's candidacy in California are (1) Say nothing and (2) Do nothing." Sinclair still waited with eager anticipation for October 25. But the President said nothing and did nothing. Then on October 26 Jim Farley disowned his letter of endorsement; it was a form letter, he belatedly explained, with a rubber-stamp signature. The same day a newspaperman asked Roosevelt to comment on Sinclair's claim that every statement he had made concerning the President was in rigid conformity with an understanding between the two men. Roosevelt replied, "I cannot take part in any state campaign."

In the meantime, Sinclair's opponent, an exceedingly conservative Republican, had been transformed by the public-relations experts into a stanch progressive. Merriam not only swallowed the Townsend Plan, but, to please the publisher of the *Los Angeles News*, came out for Major Douglas's currency nostrum of Social Credit (which Merriam called "Social Credits") and even declared himself "heartily in accord with President Roosevelt's policies."

In the last few days, the Sinclair campaign fell to pieces. A. P. Giannini of the Bank of America and others tried to get him to withdraw in favor of Raymond Haight, the Progressive candidate; Sinclair thought about it, then refused. Whatever chance Sinclair may have had left was finally destroyed when J. F. T. O'Connor came to the coast and cemented a tacit alliance between the conservative Democrats and Merriam. In a secret meeting, Merriam assured O'Connor that, if elected, he would say that his victory could not be interpreted as a defeat for the New Deal and could not have come about without Democratic support. "In fact," Merriam told O'Connor privately, "our Republican organization was shot and the Democratic organization gave us our most effective leaders." O'Connor was acting for himself, and not for Roosevelt or Farley. Yet he came to California with the prestige of a high administration figure; and it could be assumed that he was not defying administration policy. Indeed, Roosevelt retrospectively endorsed the O'Connor strategy by suggesting after the election that O'Connor become Federal Reserve agent in San Francisco and take the party leadership in California.

By election day, the Sinclair movement was in disorderly rout. Merriam won by 250,000 votes, and the state of California was saved from vegetarianism and Bolshevism. When she heard the news, Mary Craig Sinclair, who had feared for her husband's health, sank to the floor in tears, crying, "Oh thank God! Thank God!" Merriam said to Jefty O'Connor, "I appreciate what you did." As for Upton Sinclair, he quickly announced the serialization of his new book, *I, Candidate for Governor: And How I Got Licked.*[4]

VIII

Sinclair got licked all right. But the manner of his licking reshaped California politics for a generation. The Republican success marked a new advance in the art of public relations, in which advertising men now believed they could sell or destroy political candidates as they sold one brand of soap and defamed its competitor. Humdingery and dynamite dominated California politics from then on. In another twenty years, the techniques of manipulation, employed so crudely in 1934, would spread east, achieve a new refinement, and begin to dominate the politics of the nation.

As for Sinclair's followers, the shock of the campaign pushed them sharply to the left. In local EPIC headquarters people broke down and wept; at least one person committed suicide. Sinclair was beaten, it seemed, because rich businessmen had corrupted the democratic process. The success of this effort led some to wonder whether democracy and the business system were compatible. California's susceptibility to Communism in the next years dated in part from the trauma of the Sinclair defeat.

The prophet himself took defeat more serenely. "In my heart were things such as this: I can drive my own car again! I can go and take my walks! I can sleep with my windows open!" The experience merely confirmed the conclusions of a lifetime's muckraking; and writing a new book offered its usual solace. He saw no point in a third party so long as Roosevelt resisted reaction; it would only elect a Republican reactionary in 1936 and lead very likely to civil war followed by fascism. As for Communism, "No EPIC worker can have anything to do with Communists, or with any of the camouflage organizations into which the Communists seek to lure the workers." "American conditions," he added, "require American thinking and American methods of action. First and foremost of these is insistence upon democratic methods in bringing about necessary social change." "We are now the Democratic party," he said, "and we intend to remain the Democratic party."

Sinclair himself made no serious attempt to stay in politics. But his candidacy had given the California Democratic party a new set of leaders. What was once a lethargic minority party under safe conservative control suddenly found itself bursting at the seams with a collection of irrepressible personalities, propelled by a vague and often eccentric but generous-hearted desire to make a better world. One such was a Sacramento lawyer named Sheridan Downey, who had argued in a book called *Onward, America* that the private control of credit was the root of economic evil. He was originally skeptical about EPIC, but eventually he and Sinclair narrowed their differences; and Downey agreed to go on the ticket as candidate for lieutenant governor. After EPIC

collapsed, Downey moved on to the Townsend movement. Another such personality was the EPIC candidate for state senator
from Los Angeles County, an earnest and idealistic lawyer named
Culbert L. Olson. Another was the EPIC candidate for state assemblyman from the forty-ninth district, an intelligent ex-Socialist
schoolteacher named Jerry Voorhis. Men like Downey, Olson,
and Voorhis spoke for quite a different version of California Democracy from that of McAdoo and Creel.

The EPIC campaign thus left behind a ferment of local radicalism not unlike that stirred by Floyd Olson and the La Follettes —
a new popular militancy, fairly loyal to Roosevelt and the Democratic party but constituting a leftward pressure on the New Deal.
It was committed to a thesis of American exceptionalism and
sharply opposed to the Communists.[5]

IX

California was not the only West Coast state in a radical mood.
In the state of Washington, the Continental Committee on Technocracy led to the formation of the Commonwealth Builders, an amalgamation of Technocrats, production-for-use people, and the Unemployed Citizens' League. In 1932 these groups had helped
send Homer Bone to the Senate and Monrad C. Wallgren, Knute
Hill, and the unfortunate Marion Zioncheck to the House. In
1934 the Commonwealth Builders developed an End Poverty in
Washington program. They also played an active role in electing Lewis B. Schwellenbach to the Senate, nearly half the members
of the state legislature, and a young man named Warren Magnuson as prosecutor in King County.

By 1936 the Commonwealth Builders had become the Washington Commonwealth Federation. Under the resourceful direction of Howard Costigan, the WCF brought together labor, the
organized unemployed, the Old Age Pension Union and Democratic politicians in a coalition which captured the Democratic party in the state and committed it to "public ownership
of natural resources, munition plants and public utilities" and
"federal ownership and operation of national banks," and declared that a national plan of production for use was "urgent,
pressing, and vital." One of the silent partners in the WCF was

the Communist party, and this was later to distract and finally to destroy the Federation. But the Communists were clambering aboard a movement which had gathered momentum for other reasons. The existence of the WCF was one more indication of the spread in 1934 and 1935 of radical movements dedicated to the idea of social reconstruction to attain an economy of abundance.[6]

8. The Melting Pot Boils Over

ACROSS THE CONTINENT in New York City there was ferment, too. Here a number of currents converged. In the foreground were the ostensible issues — the simmering outrage of all good citizens over years of misrule by Tammany Hall, and now, with the depression, the intensifying problems of unemployment and relief. In the background were less articulate but no less powerful emotions, in particular the pent-up frustration of those whom the Irish Catholic monopoly shut out of local politics, whether civic-minded, old-family Yankee Protestants from the East Seventies, or ambitious Italians and Jews, representatives of the new immigration, seeing in politics, as in the theater and the fight ring and crime, a means of speeding the climb to status and power.

By the early thirties, Tammany was already on the defensive. Since the death of Boss Murphy in 1924, its leadership had been mediocre. Its opposition to Roosevelt had reduced its prestige and influence. When Roosevelt induced its popular and flashy mayor, James H. Walker, to resign in 1932, it lost control of the top office in the city. Walker was replaced by Joseph V. McKee, President of the Board of Aldermen, and a protégé of Ed Flynn, the pro-Roosevelt boss of the Bronx. An honest, efficient, rather conservative figure, McKee did an excellent job as acting mayor. But in the special election Tammany, repelled equally by his integrity and by his closeness to Flynn, succeeded in putting over Surrogate John P. O'Brien as Walker's successor, despite an astonishing write-in vote for McKee.

It took O'Brien only a short time to show himself a hopeless bumbler. As the regular election of 1933 approached, more and more people talked of McKee. Then in May 1933 McKee, resigning from the Board of Aldermen to become a bank president, declared himself out of politics. The good government forces, hoping for a "fusion" between independent Democrats and Republicans behind an anti-Tammany candidate, had to look elsewhere. Increasingly attention turned to the colorful figure who had enlivened New York and national politics for over fifteen years — Fiorello H. La Guardia.

II

La Guardia was born in a New York tenement in 1882. His father was Italian, but, in the Garibaldi tradition, anticlerical and agnostic; his mother was Italian of Jewish extraction and faith. The elder La Guardia, a musician who had once accompanied Patti, had come to America three years before. Soon after his son's birth he joined the United States Army as a bandmaster. For the next years the family lived in a series of army posts, ending up in Arizona. "All my boyhood memories," La Guardia later said, "are of those Arizona days." This western interlude gave the slum kid from Varick Street an identification with a frontier America most immigrants never knew. Later in life he took pride in always wearing a broad-brimmed black Arizona hat.

On the outbreak of the Spanish-American War, Fiorello's father went with his regiment to Florida, where he fell ill from eating the "embalmed beef" sold the Army by crooked contractors. Discharged from the Army, he took his wife and children back to live with his wife's family in Trieste. When he died there in 1901, Fiorello, then eighteen years old, managed to get a job in the American consulate in Budapest. In 1903, still under twenty-one, he became consular agent at Fiume, presiding over the flow of South Slav emigrants to America. Denied promotion in the consular service, he decided in 1906 to return to the United States. He was by now a cocky and exuberant youth whose experience stretched from the Arizona frontier to the crowded steerages of immigrant ships and to the multinational complexities of the Austro-Hungarian Empire.

Back in New York, he worked as an interpreter on Ellis Island.

Here, at the other end of the immigrant stream, he encountered the problems facing the bewildered men, women, and children from Southern and Eastern Europe, many without English, some unable to read or write, crowding into the new world in flight from oppression and poverty of the old. Young La Guardia soon spoke Italian, German, Yiddish, Croatian, French, and Spanish. In the evenings he attended law school at New York University.

Law was primarily a pretext for politics. Hating Tammany from the start, adoring Theodore Roosevelt, La Guardia became a Republican. In 1914 he got a presumably meaningless congressional nomination in a district which the Republican leaders had for years conceded to the Democrats. Against all the rules, the unabashed young Italo-American proceeded to make a contest of it. With his backing among the new immigrants, he nearly beat his opponent, an Irish saloon-keeper. Two years later, he did win.

In Washington La Guardia's Arizona background asserted itself, and he discovered his natural allies among the western progressives. The men he found most inspiring, he once said, were Robert M. La Follette and George W. Norris. In their spirit he fought valiantly against war profiteering and against the repressive provisions of the Espionage Act. On the war itself, however, he differed from La Follette and Norris; here his European experience was decisive. He spoke ardently for the draft. When an opponent asked how many of those so eager to send American boys to war were prepared to go themselves, La Guardia was one of five who promptly stood up; a short man, he waved his hand above his head, so none could miss him. In the summer of 1917, he enlisted in the Air Service.

He served most of the war in Italy, where he combined flying on combat missions with propaganda work among the Italians, and emerged a much-decorated major. Re-elected to Congress in 1918, he ran a year later in the special election to pick a successor to Al Smith as President of the Board of Aldermen in New York City. La Guardia won, resigned from Congress, and expected to be the Republican candidate for mayor in 1921. But the Republican organization passed him over; and when he challenged the decision in the primaries, he was badly beaten. The death of his wife and baby daughter that year completed his dejection. For a time he sank into a depression and brooded sullenly about the future.

But William Randolph Hearst, for reasons of his own, saw value in keeping La Guardia alive in politics. His newspapers offered La Guardia a forum, and La Guardia used it so effectively that the Republican organization decided to buy him off by giving him the congressional nomination in the twentieth district. This district, covering East Harlem, from Central Park to the East River, had a large Italian and Jewish population, with a smattering of Negroes. It elected La Guardia in 1922; this was the contest in which La Guardia, accused of anti-Semitism, blandly challenged his non-Yiddish-speaking Jewish opponent to a debate in Yiddish. The Twentieth re-elected him in 1924 as a La Follette Progressive, and re-elected him every two years thereafter as a Republican until the Roosevelt sweep of 1932. But throughout this period the city beckoned him. In 1929, he even seized the Republican nomination and ran for mayor, only to be badly defeated by Jimmy Walker.

III

La Guardia's Republicanism was nominal, and his relation with the state organization tenuous. He had his own personal machine — a collection of young Italians known as the Gibboni, a combination of political club and street gang. Their leader was La Guardia's special protégé, a young Italo-American with political gifts almost as remarkable as La Guardia's own. His name was Vito Marcantonio.

In Washington, La Guardia soon made himself the most influential progressive in the House. As he modestly described his role, "One of the weaknesses of the Progressive group was that each was a prima donna. Team work was lacking. It was not until the 71st and 72nd Congresses that I succeeded in providing a certain degree of leadership." With his idol George Norris, he put through the Norris–La Guardia Act outlawing the yellow-dog contract. He fought for public power and the forty-hour week. He denounced prohibition. He attacked immigration restriction for its "vicious, cruel discrimination against Italians and Jews." With the depression, he called for public works, unemployment insurance, and regulation of the stock exchanges. When farmers revolted against foreclosures, La Guardia spurred them on: "Fight, farmers, fight. Fight for your homes and your children. Your names will live with Paul Revere's." When the bankers pleaded for government aid, La Guardia was unmoved. "The bastards broke the People's back with their usury," he said, "and now they want to unload on the Government. No, no. Let them die; the People will survive." His politics fused Western progressivism with the needs and emotions of the city working class and the foreign-born. Tom Amlie, the Progressive congressman from Wisconsin, said, "I don't think that any one in Congress typified the Farmer-Labor sentiment there better than Major La Guardia."

By now La Guardia had begun to strike the national fancy. Short, stocky, swarthy, with rumpled black hair and glistening dark eyes, he was possessed of demonic energy. For him life was a perpetual combat, in which he was forever fighting the people's fight against the wicked schemes "they" were trying to put over against the people. "They" were the bankers, the politicians ("I loathe the professional politician"), the judges, the big businessmen, the racketeers; and he abused them all, with enormous zest and enthusiasm. His love was as exuberant as his hate. He identified himself passionately with the oppressed and the defenseless — with the poor, with the foreign-born, with children. "Although the politicians try to kick us around," he once told Maury Maverick of Texas, "the people will stand by us if we play it straight and fight with both fists."

He carried on his combat with operatic gusto. Wherever he went there was noise and movement, explosive laughter, pounding on the desk, farce, and melodrama. He was an unscrupulous and sometimes vicious campaigner: "I can outdemagogue the best of demagogues." Everything about him was extravagant: the sinister broad black western hat; the high-pitched voice, rasping shrill epithets; the petty dictator's arrogance and ingratitude; the actor's repertoire of moods, from ferocious rage to impish satire to demure pleas for forgiveness; the headlong physical courage; the boundless compassion. His mind was sharp, quick, and merciless; his disposition was endlessly mercurial. His loyalty went to principles rather than people. "Anyone who extends to him the right hand of fellowship," said Alva Johnston, "is in

danger of losing a couple of fingers." Something always goaded
him to violent self-assertion. In part, it was surely his determination
to make his fellow-Americans eat their patronizing words about
"wops" and "dagoes." In part, perhaps, it was just his size. Once
when an adviser thoughtlessly dismissed someone as too small,
La Guardia turned white, leaped from behind his desk, drew
himself to his full five feet two inches, stamped the floor and
shouted, "WHAT'S THE MATTER WITH A LITTLE GUY?
WHAT'S THE MATTER WITH A LITTLE GUY? WHAT'S
THE MATTER WITH A LITTLE GUY?" A furious compound of egotism and idealism, he galvanized everything he
touched.[1]

IV

In the spring of 1933 La Guardia was only one of several as-
pirants for the reform nomination. But it would have been
hard to find a man better qualified to lead a combined civic and
ethnic revolt against political misrule and racial monopoly. La
Guardia stood with passion for honesty and progressivism in
government. More than that, he charged these sometimes dreary
positions with a free-swinging Latin exuberance which made reform as exciting as corruption. And he carried his insistence
on new faces and races in politics to the point of demagogic manipulation of racial grievances and memories. After a series of wearying negotiations, he received the Republican-Fusion designation.

In the meantime, the Democratic party seemed stuck with the
unfortunate John P. O'Brien. On the day after the primaries in
September, President Roosevelt suggested that Ed Flynn put McKee
in the race as an independent candidate. This appealed to Flynn
as a means of at once showing up Tammany and of strengthening
the prestige of his own Bronx organization. Accordingly he set
up a new party — the Recovery party — as the vehicle and persuaded McKee to change his mind about retiring from politics.
A number of Roosevelt associates — Jim Farley, Raymond Moley,
Averell Harriman, and others — came out for McKee. Flynn
thought that he had in addition the promise of a presidential
endorsement, though Farley's recollection was that Roosevelt,
while agreeing to invite McKee to the White House, had said
he would take no part in the campaign.

But Roosevelt was not even to come through on the White House invitation. Early in October, Adolf Berle, a close La Guardia associate, declared at a La Guardia rally, "No one without the direct authority of President Roosevelt has the right to attempt to steal his name and prestige." When Flynn rushed to Washington to inveigle Roosevelt into support for McKee, the President was affable but evasive; in the end he did nothing. Meanwhile O'Brien had dropped to a bad third; the race was plainly between La Guardia and McKee. A fortnight before the election, La Guardia dug up an article written twenty years earlier by McKee for the *Catholic World*. Though the intent of the article was innocent, and though McKee's subsequent career had been free of bigotry, a passage taken from context gave La Guardia an excuse to denounce McKee for anti-Semitism. It was a piece of unscrupulous demagoguery. McKee replied by calling La Guardia "a communist at heart." The campaign ended with the two champions of civic virtue engaged in sordid name-calling. On election day La Guardia won by a quarter of a million votes.[2]

v

For La Guardia the mayoralty was much more than just another job. He construed "good government," not in traditional American terms of economy and efficiency, but in the Central European sense of a loving supervision of the community in all its aspects. "You know," he told a reporter, "I am in the position of an artist or a sculptor. . . . I can see New York as it should be and as it can be if we all work together. But now I am like the man who has a conception that he wishes to carve or to paint, who has the model before him, but hasn't a chisel or brush." As one observer put it, La Guardia became not so much New York's mayor as its burgomaster. "Too often," La Guardia once said, "life in New York is merely a squalid succession of days; whereas in fact it can be a great, living, thrilling adventure."

As head of the city, he put its finances on a sound basis, reorganized the municipal administration, tried to root out graft and corruption and began to rebuild and beautify Manhattan Island. He did it all with the usual mixture of irascibility and charm. Robert Moses recalls La Guardia in his first day at City

Hall, tossing letters at a secretary and shouting, "Say yes, say no, throw it away, tell him to go to hell." "There is only room for one demagogue in this administration," he told subordinates, "and I'm the one." "When I make a mistake, it's a beaut." When he changed his mind, he said, it was in Macy's window. Like Haroun Al Rashid, he roamed his domain in person, appearing suddenly as a magistrate in night court, at the head of police raiding parties, at baseball games or concerts, or riding on the hook-and-ladder, a fire helmet on his head. Watching the organist play one day at the Radio City Music Hall, La Guardia told Newbold Morris, "That's how our city must be run. Like the organist, you must keep both hands on the keyboard and both feet on the pedals — *and never let go!*" It was personal government, yet government continuously dedicated to civic ideals. Unlike other reform mayors, La Guardia was never a bore. Unlike other reform mayors, he could be re-elected.

In his wake there came a political revolution. He ended the Irish monopoly on city government and offered both the older and the newer nationalities a chance. Silk-stocking Republicans like Newbold Morris and Clendenin Ryan were able to break into local politics. Intellectuals like Adolf Berle and, later, Rexford G. Tugwell were brought into the city administration. For the first time in history, a Negro was appointed city magistrate. Above all, the Italians and the Jews at last saw the pathway to political power clearing before them. Bad elements sought to exploit the racial breakthrough as well as good. "There is no reason for the Italians to support anybody but La Guardia," as Joe Adonis, the racketeer, said in 1933; "the Jews have played ball with the Democrats and haven't gotten much out of it. They know it now. They will vote for La Guardia. So will the Italians." But the crooks did not last when La Guardia discovered who they were. And responsible people among the new immigrants at last had their chance at public service. The result was a release of ambition and energy which reconstructed New York political life.

Italians and Jews were developing other instruments of political influence, especially Sidney Hillman's Amalgamated Clothing Workers and David Dubinsky's International Ladies' Garment Workers. Hillman and Dubinsky were Socialists or ex-Socialists

(Ben Stolberg once described their variety of Socialism as "purely nostalgic, like a Wall Street broker's memories of his Iowa childhood"). They stood with La Guardia — all somewhat to the left of the New Deal, all hostile to the Communists, all personally devoted to Roosevelt. They had no passion for a third party, though they wanted to keep the idea in reserve in case reaction blocked the New Deal. Thus La Guardia, as noted, spoke of a new national party in Wisconsin in 1934. In 1935 Dubinsky discussed "independent political action by labor," and Hillman added that, if the conservatives stopped the New Deal, "it is my judgment that labor, farmers and others who make up 90 percent of the population of this country will turn to a new political party."

The New York brand of ethnic and ideological insurgency was a factor of growing importance in the New Deal coalition. And as La Guardia played the broker among nationality groups in New York, so he played the broker between New York radicalism and the progressivism of inner America. Knowing Arizona as well as Ellis Island, he seemed destined to serve as the bridge between men in the European Social Democratic tradition, like Hillman and Dubinsky, and men in the Progressive or Populist tradition, like Norris, Floyd Olson, and the La Follettes. It was a mutually beneficial contact, saving one side from dogmatism and the other from provincialism. The result was further to define the lineaments of an authentic American radicalism.[3]

9. Insurgency on Capitol Hill

LA GUARDIA'S TRANSLATION to New York did not leave radicalism without experienced spokesmen in Washington. Despite the prevailing conservatism of the twenties, during that decade Congress had served to an astonishing degree as a forum for heretical political opinion; on many issues it had been far to the left of visible public sentiment. Many veterans of the congressional wars against Coolidge and Hoover were still around. Some had preserved their progressive faith from the pre-war times of Theodore Roosevelt and Wilson. Others expressed the agrarian resentments of the prosperity years, when farmers had been left out of the general well-being. Many of them had been shaped, even perhaps deformed, by the experience of having been part of what seemed for so long a permanent minority. As men who valued their sense of inner righteousness more than anything else, many were happier in opposition than in power. Still, they were nearly all men of ability, imagination, and courage. For thirty years they had represented the future: they had provided the channels through which new ideas made their slow way into the minds of conventional party leaders. If the New Dealers found it hard at times to live with them, they must have known that the New Deal could never have come into being without them.

II

The radicals in the Senate were mostly old Progressives — Republicans or ex-Republicans like Norris, La Follette, Bronson M. Cutting of New Mexico and Gerald P. Nye of North Dakota;

along with a few affiliated Democrats like Burton K. Wheeler of Montana, who had been the elder La Follette's running mate in 1924, and Edward P. Costigan of Colorado and Homer Bone of Washington, who had started out as Progressive Republicans. In general, these men followed the progressivism of the elder La Follette rather than that of Theodore Roosevelt: they were agrarian rather than industrial in their domestic orientation, isolationist rather than internationalist in their foreign policy. They did, of course, traverse the spectrum of responsibility in their attitude toward public matters, from George Norris, who had the insight of wisdom, and the younger La Follette, who had the strength of intelligence, to some one on the other extreme like Gerald Nye, the fluent and angry embodiment of small-town prejudice. Essentially the Senate Progressives were a collection of brilliant individualists, united by mood rather than by program. Each had preoccupations of his own, and each was sufficiently persuaded of his own superior intellect or virtue to resent discipline or leadership. Indeed, the progressive conviction of rectitude gave some outsiders an impression of offensive self-righteousness. Harry S. Truman, a first-term Democratic Senator from Missouri in 1935, felt that Norris and Cutting, for example, looked down on him "as a sort of hick politician who did not know what he was supposed to do."

Norris was unquestionably their sage and mentor. With Hiram Johnson increasingly dour and conservative and William E. Borah increasingly oratorical, Norris remained the one Progressive of the prewar generation who had kept contact with a changing world. He was seventy-four years old in 1935, and a recent succession of victories — the Tennessee Valley Authority, the Twentieth Amendment, the Norris–La Guardia Act — had given him a new tolerance and serenity. There were still moments of melancholy in which he sighed heavily, assumed a posture of profound discouragement, and said that, exhausted by years of struggle, he now wished only to go back to his little house in Nebraska: already he was threatening retirement at the expiration of his term in 1936. But his deep confidence in Roosevelt was far more important than his occasional disappointments about the Roosevelt administration. At last the old warrior on the Hill had found someone at the other end of Pennsylvania Avenue whom he felt he could trust. The trust was fully reciprocated; no one in the Senate had such moral authority at the White House as Norris. This sense of security mellowed Norris's later years.[1]

III

Of the younger men, La Follette was generally regarded as the most responsible and Wheeler as the strongest and boldest. If Roosevelt thought of any of the Progressives as his successor, it was certainly the quiet, tough-minded Senator from Wisconsin; but outside observers tended to put their money on the Senator from Montana. Wheeler, who was born just four weeks after Franklin Roosevelt, was fifty-three years old in 1935. He was the tenth son of a Quaker shoemaker in Hudson, Massachusetts. As a young man, fleeing family poverty, he migrated to Michigan, where he worked his way through law school. Continuing his westward movement, he went to Colorado and then to Montana. Apparently he meant to go all the way to the coast. But card sharps fleeced him one day playing stud poker, and, put on his mettle, Wheeler decided to settle down in Butte. In a short time he was well established as a lawyer. In 1910, the same year that Roosevelt went to the New York State Senate, Wheeler was elected to the Montana House of Representatives.

Roosevelt may have faced a tricky situation in bucking Tammany over Blue-eyed Billy Sheehan. But this was tea-party stuff compared to the ferocious politics of Montana. In 1910 the Anaconda Copper Company sought to run the state like a huge company town. The politician who defied the Company risked not only his political future but his livelihood, even his physical safety. Wheeler, moved by an instinct for the underdog, decided to enlist behind Thomas J. Walsh in the savage guerrilla war against the Company. The Battle of Anaconda turned Burt Wheeler into a rough-and-ready alley fighter who had to learn to bite and kick and gouge in order to save his political life.

The First World War further toughened Wheeler's hide and deepened his rancor. Appointed United States Attorney through Walsh's solicitation, he found himself confronted in Montana by a war hysteria of surprising virulence. Honest citizens convinced themselves that all German-Americans or pacifists or Wobblies were German agents. Some even discerned gun emplacements on inaccessible peaks or reported German planes flying over the Bitterroot Mountains. Faced by a clamor to indict all suspicious figures, Wheeler, who did not approve of the war anyway, declined to act. This seemed ample proof that he himself was a hireling of the Kaiser, if not of the Bolsheviki. In 1918, rather than embarrass Tom Walsh's campaign for re-election, Wheeler resigned.

But he tried to come back in 1920 as the Nonpartisan League's candidate for governor. This was an exceptionally bitter contest. Wheeler was accused of pro-Germanism; he was nicknamed "Bolshevik Burt"; in Dillon, a mob of angry patriots ran him out of town. He was beaten at the polls, but two years later, with the state prostrate because of the postwar depression, Wheeler won election to the United States Senate. There he immediately joined Tom Walsh in conducting the investigations into the scandals of the Harding administration. Harry Daugherty, Harding's Attorney General, called Wheeler "the Communist leader in the Senate," and sent FBI agents into Montana to build a case against him. (The Assistant and then Acting Director of the Bureau in this period was an ambitious young man named J. Edgar Hoover.) "Agents of the Department," Wheeler later said, "raided my offices. . . . They stationed men at my house, surrounded my house, watched persons who went in and came out, constantly shadowed me, shadowed my house, and shadowed my wife." An investigator named Blair Coan portrayed Wheeler as a key figure in a huge subversive conspiracy in a book called *The Red Web*.

Eventually the Department of Justice tried to hook Wheeler on the charge of improperly using his influence to get oil leases for a Montana client. But the case had all the earmarks of a frame-up. Both a Senate investigating committee and a Montana jury cleared Wheeler in short order. In the meantime, Wheeler forced Daugherty's resignation — a remarkable achievement for a junior senator. In a few months, Wheeler was a national figure. In 1924 he ran for Vice-President with La Follette on the Progressive ticket.

No Senator perhaps had more personal reasons to feel that the rich and powerful would ruthlessly manipulate the system to punish those fighting for the underdog. "What is a radical?" he asked in 1926. "A radical is a progressive who knows what he wants,

and believes in the things that he advocates. . . . Has the movement
become a class struggle? It has always been a class struggle. Every
economic struggle is a class struggle." Once the journalist
Clinton Gilbert commented to him that McAdoo had no progressive convictions, that all he had was a promoter's feud with Wall
Street. Wheeler said grimly, "That is enough." For him progressivism was not a theory but a fight. He had come, so to speak,
out of a mining camp, and he had the temperament and passion
of a vigilante.

Only the pleasure of being a member of the senatorial club
and, in the end, a certain indolence tempered his bitterness. The
indolence was intellectual. No one could be more active when it
came to an investigation or a debate; but Wheeler often could
not bring himself to do the necessary preparatory work. His
central ideas — bimetallism, trust-busting, nationalization of the
railroads — were straight out of William Jennings Bryan, with little
allowance for the world's having grown more complicated in the
interval. The columnist Jay Franklin suggested that his early
success in 1924, at the age of forty, had lulled him into unwarranted self-confidence. "If he would study current problems as
Bob Wagner and young Bob La Follette study them, he would
be a much more effective man."

He had been the first member of the Senate to call for the
nomination of Franklin D. Roosevelt, and he had worked hard
for Roosevelt at the Chicago convention. But their relations
thereafter began to cool. Perhaps it started at the convention itself, when Wheeler may have been disappointed in the hope of the
vice-presidential nomination. He was subsequently pleased by
Tom Walsh's appointment as Attorney General; this would give
the men from Montana a chance to clean up the mess in the
Department of Justice and the Federal Bureau of Investigation.
But Walsh's death just before the inauguration created new troubles. Whether or not Wheeler wanted the job himself, he resented
the designation of Homer Cummings to the vacancy. Though
Cummings was a good friend of Walsh's, he was also a good friend
of J. Bruce Kremer, the Democratic national committeeman from
Montana and an old enemy of Wheeler's. Through Cummings,
Kremer seemed soon to be exerting more influence in the adminis-
tration, especially on patronage matters, than Wheeler. And in

the Department of Justice, J. Edgar Hoover, Wheeler's old antago-
nist, appeared to grow stronger than ever.

IV

By 1934 Wheeler began to feel himself frozen out of the New
Deal. If any Senator was entitled to a voice in inner administration councils, it was Wheeler. But Roosevelt rarely consulted
him. Wheeler, who had conducted for years a lonely fight for
progressivism in the Democratic party, now saw southern conservatives like Joe Robinson, Pat Harrison, and Jimmy Byrnes
installed as White House favorites. Wheeler, who had been an
ancient champion of free silver, now saw the credit for the silver
policy go to Key Pittman. The ingratitude seemed deliberate:
when Wheeler was up for re-election in 1934, Roosevelt traversed
the state without mentioning his name, and then went on to
Wisconsin to pay tribute to La Follette as well as the conservative
Democrat Ryan Duffy. All this played upon the instinct for
grievance which lay just under the surface of Wheeler's breezy
Montana geniality. He now both rationalized and aggravated his
resentment by pouncing on every evidence of conservatism in the
administration.

Roosevelt's treatment of Bronson Cutting in 1934 gave Wheeler
and the Progressives a specific reason for anger. Cutting was
unique among the Progressives and adored by them. Where the
others were mostly sons of dirt farmers or poor shopkeepers,
Cutting had been born to wealth on Long Island. He attended
Groton half a dozen years after Franklin Roosevelt; at Harvard, he
was a member of the class of 1910, along with Walter Lippmann,
Hamilton Fish, John Reed, T. S. Eliot, and Heywood Broun,
and was a favorite student of George Santayana's. But he suffered from tuberculosis, and after graduation migrated to New
Mexico for his health. As he regained his strength, he bought
a newspaper, signed up in the Bull Moose movement, and went
off to the First World War. When he came back, he went seriously
into politics and led a successful fight in the New Mexico Republican organization against Albert B. Fall. Through skillful use of
his newspaper, his money, and his linguistic ability, Cutting built
a tight political organization of his own. His genuine liking for

the Spanish-American people and culture made him something
of a hero in the eyes of the "natives." He went to the Senate in
1927 and quickly won a place as a hard-working and courageous
radical. A bachelor and aesthete, reserved and sensitive, speaking
slowly in an unmistakable Harvard accent, he conveyed in Washington a genuine sense of aristocratic high principle, which mingled somewhat strangely with the tough political machine he
maintained in New Mexico.

Every aspect of family and upbringing should have made Roosevelt feel closer to Cutting than to the other Progressives; it was
no doubt this fatal similarity which estranged them. After his
election, Roosevelt offered Cutting the Interior Department, but
Cutting preferred to stay in the Senate, partly perhaps because he
mistrusted Roosevelt's progressivism. In the special session, Cutting
fought hard against Roosevelt's attempt to reduce veterans' pensions. This produced, according to Moley, Roosevelt's single outburst of anger during the whole Hundred Days. Roosevelt was
willing to forgive in other Progressives the bad taste of supporting
the bonus, but he evidently considered it inexcusable on the part
of a man who had been to Groton and Harvard. Or perhaps both
Roosevelt and Cutting, as Grotonians in an unfamiliar territory,
looked on each other with automatic suspicion and rivalry, like
explorers suddenly meeting in the jungle. In any case, Roosevelt said that Cutting had made disagreeable personal remarks
about him, and he later tried to validate his dislike by saying
that he did not approve of the Cutting organization. "I am
personally mighty fond of him and have known him since he
was a boy," Roosevelt told Norris in January 1934, when Norris
complained that federal patronage was going to Cutting's enemies.
"I do not want to do anything to hurt him, but a lot of Bronson's
retainers in New Mexico are not considered especially fine
citizens."

When Cutting came up for re-election in 1934, he was the only
Progressive the administration opposed. It was an uncommonly
dirty campaign, even for New Mexico; money was spent freely
and improperly; and Cutting finally emerged the apparent victor
by slightly over a thousand votes. His Democratic opponent,
Dennis Chavez, instituted — with administration approval — a
contest for Cutting's seat. Progressives in the Senate considered

this a wretched performance on Roosevelt's part, and Progressives in the administration, like Ickes, agreed with them.

In the spring of 1935 Cutting had to go to New Mexico to get affidavits in connection with the contested election. On his way back to Washington the plane crashed in a dense fog over Missouri. Cutting, who was forty-six years old, was killed. What would probably have been a career of genuine distinction was brought to an end. When the news was announced in the Senate, Norris put his head in his hands, Borah wept, La Follette broke into tears and would not go on the floor. Soon after, a Democratic governor appointed Chavez to take Cutting's seat. When the new Senator appeared to be sworn in, Norris, La Follette, Nye, Hiram Johnson, and the Farmer-Laborite Henrik Shipstead walked out of the chamber. (Chavez ignored the demonstration and, after taking his oath, shook hands with his deskmates, Theodore Bilbo and Harry S. Truman.) Some of the Progressives blamed Roosevelt for Cutting's death.

v

On February 1, 1935, Wheeler dined at Rex Tugwell's house in the company of William E. Dodd, the historian and Ambassador to Germany, Jerome Frank and Paul Appleby of the Department of Agriculture, John Franklin Carter, who wrote political comment under the name of Jay Franklin or The Unofficial Observer, and others. Throughout the dinner Wheeler railed against Roosevelt and the administration. He said that the President, for all his fine talk, really preferred conservatives to progressives; the treatment of Cutting, Wheeler said, was typical. He defended Huey Long as the one man who could get rid of Robinson and Harrison and thus smash the conservative leadership of the Senate. (When Dodd expostulated about Long, Wheeler said cryptically, as Dodd remembered it, "We shall soon be shooting up people here, like Hitler does.") He looked forward to a third party in 1936, backed by Long, Coughlin, Floyd Olson, Sinclair, and La Follette. He then roamed into the foreign field and said that it was not the job of the United States to prevent Hitler from unifying Europe (including England) or the Japanese from unifying the Far East. He said this so emphatically as to give Dodd the impression that he was advocating German and Japanese expansion. (When Dodd described the conversation to Roosevelt without mentioning the Senator's name, Roosevelt promptly said, "It sounds like Senator Wheeler.") [2]

It was a stormy evening, and undoubtedly expressed Wheeler in a passing rage. Yet, if a third party were to emerge, Wheeler in many respects seemed its obvious candidate. He was not a great mass leader, like Long or Coughlin, but this very fact might make it easier for the charismatic personalities to support him rather than each other. And, as Jay Franklin pointed out, he had better connections with more groups than any of the other radicals. He was a close personal friend of Long's. His record on inflation and silver commended him to Coughlin. He had excellent relations with John L. Lewis and with railroad labor. As the heir of the Progressive party of 1924, he might expect support from the La Follettes. His Nonpartisan League past made him acceptable to Olson and the Farmer-Laborites. He had a solid base in his own state of Montana. He was sufficiently serious to appeal to the radicals and sufficiently reckless to appeal to the demagogues. This tall, vigorous man, with his jovial manner, his incessant flow of conversation, his eternal cigar clamped in his big mouth, his shrewd, sharp prosecutor's mind and his vigilante's audacity and ruthlessness was plainly the most formidable of the Senate radicals.[3]

VI

The election of 1934 brought a lively generation of radicals into the House of Representatives. Shortly after the opening of the 74th Congress, a number of them joined together in an informal bloc. Their leader was a vivid Texan named Maury Maverick.

Maverick was the grandson of the man whose failure to brand his cattle had added a word to the American language — a word soon applied, by extension, to unbranded and roaming figures in politics. Maury lived up to the patronymic tradition. He was reared on the *Appeal to Reason,* the old Socialist magazine; he had met Gene Debs; and he remembered as a boy seeing Francisco Madero, with his spiked beard, talking intensely in the San

Antonio sun before returning to Mexico to overthrow Porfirio Díaz. During the First World War he served with distinction in France, was terribly wounded at the Argonne, and received the Silver Star. In the twenties he was a lawyer and businessman in San Antonio.

In the new Congress, Maverick looked as if he might become another La Guardia. Like La Guardia, he was short, stocky, and explosive, with a small man's cockiness and pugnacity. Like La Guardia, he was colorful in his language and extravagant in his personality, an engaging mixture of wit, humanity, and irascibility. He looked on San Antonio with the same proprietary devotion that La Guardia lavished on Manhattan, and his solicitude for the Mexicans of Texas was akin to that of La Guardia for the immigrants of New York. And like La Guardia, Maverick was a radical but not a socialist; in essence, he was a pragmatic American politician who wanted the oppressed to get a better break. Still, he was more ideological than the New Yorker; and he took particular pride in his capacity to state a radical philosophy in the American idiom. He loathed what he later called (in his own contribution to the language) "gobbledygook." The catch-phrases of the New York radicals — "proletarian ideology," "economic determinism," "class struggle" — seemed to him book-words without substance or sense; they were "a stumbling block in the path of anything progressive or sensible." His determination was to save American radicalism from "the Manhattan mind." His heroes were, not Marx and Engels, but Norris ("the greatest living American") and La Follette.

"Democracy, to me," Maverick once said, "is liberty *plus* economic security. To put it in plain language, we Americans want to talk, pray, think as we please — and eat regular." The objective of "freedom plus groceries" implied a good deal in the way of immediate action; and in March 1935 Maverick collaborated with a young Wisconsin Progressive, Gerald J. Boileau, in drafting a manifesto for a group of radical congressmen. In time, there were about thirty-five in the Maverick group — Democrats like Maverick and Mon Wallgren, Wisconsin Progressives like Boileau and Tom Amlie, Minnesota Farmer-Laborites like Ernest Lundeen, and eccentric Republicans like Usher Burdick and William Lemke of North Dakota and Vito Marcantonio of New York. Marcantonio, who had succeeded to the old seat of La Guardia, his patron, and Lundeen were somewhat apart from the rest because of their close (though unavowed) ties with the Communists. But the others regarded the Communists with indifference, or, like Maverick, with derision. The logic of their native American radicalism was best expressed by Tom Amlie, the most intensely ideological of them all.[4]

VII

Amlie, who was thirty-eight years old in 1935, was a tall, slow-moving man, with an earnest Norwegian face, a manner of calm dignity, and an impressive personal presence. In the twenties he had been a Nonpartisan League organizer and then a lawyer in Beloit and Elkhorn. In his spare time he worried about the economic system, reading Marx, Sombart, and Veblen. The depression crystallized his ideas. In a striking speech at a conference of radicals in September 1933, Amlie set forth his reaction to the apparent collapse of capitalism.

The capitalist system, Amlie argued, required incessant expansion in order to survive. When the frontier disappeared, it began to get into trouble. Various expedients — overseas imperialism, the First World War, the automotive boom, foreign lending — only staved off the debacle. The crash of 1929 registered the inevitable conclusion. The large investors had decided that there was no further profit to be made by reinvesting capital in productive machinery. As private investment declined, the system could be kept going only by an increase in public spending; and Roosevelt, Amlie said, had not called for the only thing which might have saved capitalism — a twenty-billion-dollar works program. In any case, *"whether capitalism could be kept going for another period of years or not, it is not worth saving."*

What was the solution? Amlie had no faith in piecemeal change; this would only destroy capitalist incentives without putting anything in their place. The hope was total transition from production-for-profit to production-for-use. As a first step, Amlie, a loyal Veblenian, proposed a constitutional amendment confiscating all absentee-owned property and abolishing absentee ownership. But, he added gloomily, "Very frankly I do not believe that the change will be brought about by orderly constitutional means." As dis-integration set in, there would come an increasing demand for the restoration of "order." "Unless we have an organization ready to step into the breach," Amlie said, "it is clear that a movement of this kind will come from the right, and this is what we have come to know as 'fascism.' "

No speech better expressed the mood of American radicalism in the first year of the New Deal. The Chicago conference had been initiated by the League for Independent Political Action, which Paul H. Douglas of the University of Chicago and John Dewey had organized in 1929. La Guardia, Lundeen, A. F. Whitney of the Railroad Trainmen, along with radical farm leaders signed its call. *"We are living on top of a volcano,"* the call declared. "If we are not prepared we will go to smash as Rome and former civilizations went to smash." The meeting resolved, "We the masses of the people must rise up and win economic and political control. We must organize to establish a new social order, a scientifically planned system. We must own and control the means of production and distribution." It concluded by establishing a new organization, the Farmer-Labor Political Federation, with Dewey as honorary chairman and Amlie as chairman.

The magazine *Common Sense,* the organ of native radicalism in these years, observed in 1936, "Amlie's life from the Conference of September 1933 on has been the life of the Third Party movement in this country." In Congress and around the country, Amlie expounded the radical gospel. "I believe that a change is inevitable," he said, "from the profit motivated economy . . . to the planned production that will take its place, and as I see it, planned production cannot take place unless the Government owns and controls the operation of that which is to be planned." He continued pessimistic about the prospects of reaching the new economic order peaceably. "But I think, if it comes, in America, it will be Meade at Gettysburg, not John Brown at Harpers Ferry."

Through this period, Amlie remained adamant in opposition to the Communists. The 1933 conference proposed to exclude Communists from the new federation. "I have tried working with the Communists for fifteen years," said Amlie grimly, "and I feel their course is inevitably what it is." He called the United States "psychologically classless" and expressed the hope that the great majority of the middle class could be swung behind the radical program. "If this gets into the arena of the class struggle," he said, "we are going to lose what perhaps it is going to take generations to regain." Marxism, he added, was "dialectics adrift." A girl from the *New Masses* reported sadly that Amlie employed "some of the slanders and virtually every crude distortion in the Red-baiting handbook." A *New Masses* editorial pronounced the Communist judgment on the Amlie effort: "Such movements bulwarked behind radical phrases, are the stuff out of which fascism comes." But Tom Amlie, speaking in his slow, unhurried way, insisted day in and day out that Americans must find an American road to the co-operative commonwealth.[5]

10. Radicalism: American Plan

WHILE the rough-hewn Amlie was the most drastic voice of native radicalism in national politics, the leading theoretician of the movement was a young easterner from a sharply contrasting background. Alfred Bingham was the son of a highly conservative Republican senator from Connecticut and himself a graduate of Groton and Yale. Born into the secure old-family Yankee world of which Hiram Bingham, the archaeologist of the Incas and the friend of the Connecticut Manufacturers' Association, was so notable a figure, Alfred Bingham found himself coming into maturity at the very time his father's world was beginning to disintegrate. A young man of curiosity and energy, he decided in 1931 to inspect other worlds. He visited the Soviet Union and was impressed by the immense emotional force of the Communist experiment, even while he recoiled from its cost in lives and terror. He was impressed, too, in Italy, where Mussolini told the young man of his admiration for Communism — "Fascism is the same thing" — and emphasized the power of the new social religions "to move mountains" by faith. Back in the United States, Bingham concluded that the world of Binghams and Tiffanys was gone beyond recall. "I found at the end of my world tour, almost to my horror, that I was arguing the inevitability of revolution with everyone I met."

With Russia and Italy striving to master economic forces, why should America stand helpless and impotent? "Why are we hungry, jobless, panic stricken, in the richest country on earth? Why are banks closed, factories shut down, office buildings empty, farms mortgaged and cities bankrupt, in a land of plenty? . . . All that is clear is that those in power are unable to understand, much less

control, events." With these words, Bingham, after his return to
the United States in 1932, launched a new magazine called *Common Sense*. As co-editor, he brought in another Yale man, Selden
Rodman, whose radicalism in culture and art matched Bingham's
in politics. Together they proposed to prepare the way for a non-
Marxist anticapitalist peaceable "made-in-America" revolution.

Bingham's belief in a distinctively American approach soon
brought him into an alliance with the League for Independent
Political Action. *Common Sense* became the LIPA organ and got
in exchange a circulation list and a string of contacts around the
country. Bingham became executive secretary of the new Farmer-
Labor Political Federation. In the next four years *Common
Sense* became the most lively and interesting forum of radical
discussion in the country.

II

Bingham's own major contribution was *Insurgent America:
Revolt of the Middle-Classes,* a book published in 1935. Marxism,
he wrote, contained much wisdom, but one basic error invalidated
it as a guide to action. That error was its gross underestimate of
the middle class. Marx had supposed that capitalist evolution
would wipe out the middle class and consolidate the power and
will of the working class. Instead, modern capitalism was obviously enfeebling the working class and enthroning the middle
class. The new technology was reducing the number of manual
workers and increasing the number of white-collar workers. The
new abundance was eliminating the old social distinctions. And
the working class was not only in numerical decline; it had already
— in America, at least, where even most workers thought of themselves as members of the middle class — lost the psychological
battle. To believe that the American working class would be
the prime mover in bringing about revolutionary change was
fantasy; to glorify the proletarian was a waste of time, if, indeed,
it might not be the means of frightening the middle classes into
fascism. The new group rising to dominance, said Bingham, was
"the technical and managerial middle-classes." The problem for
an American radicalism was to win this group for social reconstruction.

Bingham's particular proposal was, in effect, an extension of the EPIC idea. Its essence was the taking over of what Bingham called a "vertical cross-section" of the national economy and operating it on a production-for-use basis. By this means, the unemployed could be put to work producing and exchanging the goods and services they themselves required. "As production-for-use proved its superiority for those engaged in it to production-for-profit, the great bulk of the population engaged in private enterprise would clamor for admission to the new system. The life-blood of the old system would be gradually drained away, and it would be left an empty shell. A transition to an economy of abundance would have been effected."

III

Insurgent America was an arresting book. Bingham pushed aside the reigning radical clichés and took a fresh look at the social phenomena of his day. The result was a number of striking insights into underlying trends — the obsolescence of the proletariat; the evolution of organized labor into a conservative force; the emergence of the managers; the rise of suburbia; the implications of automation; the understanding that fascism was a political and not an economic system and a bourgeois rather than a capitalist movement.

Its ultimate thrust was toward a technocratic utopia of a peculiarly American sort. While Bingham shied away from the excesses of the "mysterious and hyperbolic" Howard Scott, he was much impressed by the more sober residue of the original Technocrat movement, now associated with Harold Loeb and his National Survey of Potential Product Capacity. "Whatever legitimate doubt may have been cast upon individual statements," wrote Bingham in 1934, "there is no longer any question but that the basic conclusions of Technocracy are true."

What cheered Bingham and Rodman now was the apparently spontaneous rise through the nation of groups dedicated to production-for-use and to the economy of abundance. Most important, they thought, was the Minnesota Farmer-Labor party. Floyd Olson became *Common Sense*'s special hero; at last there was a consummate practical politician who seemed nonetheless authentically radical in attitudes and convictions. For his part, Olson looked with tolerance on Bingham and Rodman, signed the articles they wrote for him and enjoyed the resulting national attention. In Wisconsin there were the La Follettes; in California, Sinclair; in Washington, the Commonwealth Federation; in North Dakota, the Nonpartisan League. In addition, the millions flocking behind Long and Coughlin and Townsend might still be won to a rational program. Bingham, convinced that this radical ferment was ready for crystallization, dedicated himself to organizing a third party.

The Farmer-Labor Political Federation advocated a new party in 1934; and early in July 1935, a meeting convened in Chicago in response to a call demanding "a fundamental program striking at the roots of the profit system," and signed by Amlie, Lundeen, Marcantonio, and two other radical congressmen. Two issues complicated the meeting. One was the evident resistance on the part of many delegates to any action which might split the progressive vote and thus endanger the New Deal; the other was the old issue of collaboration with the Communists. On the first, Tom Amlie agreed to call, not for a third party, but for a "political federation" to be held ready, if necessary, for 1936. On the second, Amlie said, "Our aim is to unite all groups who want a change to come through the ballot box, which excludes communists." However, he was able to sustain this position only with difficulty, and Marcantonio and Lundeen finally withdrew, saying they were opposed to excluding anyone.

The 1935 meeting resulted in a new organization — or rather, perhaps, in a new name designed to give the impression of a more inclusive coalition. The success of the Canadian Commonwealth Federation across the border suggested the name American Commonwealth Political Federation. Amlie, Bingham, and Paul Douglas were the top officers; the platform reaffirmed the old aims and spoke hopefully of a mass radical party. But though Olson sent the conference a message, the Farmer-Laborites held aloof as a party, and the La Follettes would not even permit the use of their names. Organized labor showed no interest; only the most radical farm groups paid any attention. The movement lacked political reality. Looking back years later, Bingham commented, "It was all only make-believe." Still, in the confusion of the time, anything seemed possible; and many things in America must have seemed far less possible than the American Commonwealth Federation.[1]

IV

What *Common Sense* expressed most clearly was the tradition of the intellectual progressivism of the twenties — the progressivism of national economic planning, developed by such men as John Dewey, Thorstein Veblen, Herbert Croly, and Charles A. Beard, and finding inspiration as far back as Edward Bellamy. For a moment, indeed, it almost looked as if there were a Bellamy revival. "Bellamy's epic dream," said Beard, "served as a torch from which were lighted the aspirations of multitudes in the United States." "It is encouraging to know," John Dewey wrote in *Common Sense* in the spring of 1934, "that Bellamy Societies are starting almost spontaneously, but with the aid of a central organization, all over the country. It is a good omen." *Looking Backward* and *Equality*, said Alfred Bingham, contained "the best full-length descriptions" of the ideal economic system. "Back to Bellamy" was the title of a Heywood Broun column. Early in 1935, when Beard, Dewey, and Edward Weeks of the *Atlantic Monthly* made independent selections of the most influential books of the last half-century, *Das Kapital, The Golden Bough,* and *Looking Backward* headed each list.

Of the liberal ideologues of the twenties, Veblen and Croly were dead by 1930; but Beard, who was sixty-one in 1935, and Dewey, who was seventy-six, were undiminished in energy and power. They were now the patriarchs of *Common Sense.* Beard, Alfred Bingham once said, probably represented "the American genius better than any man alive"; Dewey's *Liberalism and Social Action* was "a pinnacle of the human mind." Together Beard and Dewey laid down the main lines of a native American radicalism, critical both of the Marxism of Europe and the pragmatism of the New Deal.[2]

V

Beard in particular was possessed by a profound conviction of the uniqueness of America. Though an offshoot from Europe,

America was no mere copy, Beard used to say, of European ideas and institutions. The transition to the new world had left behind aggregations of barbaric laws and historic cruelties. In particular, America was "not feudal`and clerical in the roots of its economy and its thought . . . a fact of immense significance to which little attention has been given by those who write glibly on American life." Divorced from "the feudal and theological heritage," American civilization had a specific identity of its own, "fundamentally different from civilization in Europe." Beard's great work of 1927 had traced what he called *The Rise of American Civilization*. The idea of the American civilization dominated him even more through the thirties, as he worked on the two last volumes of *The Rise: America in Midpassage* and *The American Spirit*.

Venturing a "distillation of American history" in 1932, Beard summarized the goals which he believed the American nation had set for itself: the first was "national planning in industry, business, agriculture and government." How were these goals to be attained? Beard believed that the logic of what he called "engineering rationality" was carrying the American mind to the conclusion that full mass production could not be achieved under traditional capitalistic practices, and that these practices must therefore give way to whatever extent necessary to meet the laws of mass-production economy. "The actually integrating economy of the present day," he wrote in 1934, "is the forerunner of a consciously integrated society in which individual economic actions and individual property rights will be altered and abridged." The next America would be a "collectivist democracy." By this he meant, as he explained in *Scribner's* in 1934, a "workers' republic," without the degradation of poverty, on the one hand, or of luxury and waste on the other. He had a moving vision of what this America might be — "one vast park of fields, forests, mountains, lakes, rivers, roads, decentralized communities, farms, ranches, and irrigated deserts. . . . A beautiful country — homes beautiful; communities and farms beautiful; stores and workshops beautiful." "Sheer Utopianism, my masters will say," wrote Beard defiantly, but "let it be clearly understood then that there are elements of Utopianism in all of us."

Though he showed little interest in the economic strategy of his new society — in questions of fiscal, monetary, wage, or invest-

ment policy — Beard wrote a good deal about its problems of economic organization and structure. The United States "in the
nature of things" was meant to be "a great continental, technological society." Big business was here to stay, more integrated,
efficient, productive than ever. Trust-busting, said Beard, was a
"farce," antimonopoly, a "racket." The attempt to restore littleness only prolonged dangerous tensions in American society. "If
all we can do is to snap at the heels of big business, while our
economic machine runs at about 50 percent of efficiency and ten
or twelve million people sink into the degradation of permanent
unemployment, then we might as well give it up and go to whis-
tling, not in the wind, but in the graveyard." The thing to do,
Beard said, was "to make the Federal government powerful enough
to cope with private bigness."

VI

In these terms Beard welcomed the early New Deal. Indeed,
the NRA and AAA were from the same ideological cupboard as
his own Five-Year Plan for America of 1931. "Although a member
of the same Jeffersonian party," wrote Beard cheerfully in 1934,
comparing Roosevelt and Wilson, "President Franklin D. Roosevelt repudiates the New Freedom in economy, accepts the inexorable collectivism of American economy in fact, and seeks to
work out a policy based on recognition of the main course of our
economic history." The New Deal, concluded Beard in his first
evaluation (called *The Future Comes,* and published in 1933),
signalized "a break with the historic past and the coming of a
future collectivist in character."

Next year in *The Open Door At Home* Beard introduced a
caveat about Roosevelt: he had "not yet brought the foreign policy of the United States entirely into line with his domestic theory."
The logic of national planning, Beard suggested, called for a policy
of "least possible dependence on foreign imports," both to minimize the "frightful prospects" of world war and to accelerate
the changes in internal organization necessary to bring the economy abreast of the new technology. In 1934 Beard saw distant
intimations of Wilsonian internationalism in the New Deal. By
early 1935 he thought these intimations were assuming a dangerous

reality. The idea of central planning, he now wrote, had gone on the defensive: the New Deal was evidently losing its *élan*. "Banks have not been nationalized, nor the railways taken over by the Government. Not a single instrumentality of economic power has been wrested" from the party of business. "Confronted by the difficulties of a deepening domestic crisis and by the comparative ease of foreign war, what will President Roosevelt do?" Beard was ready to hazard a gloomy answer. "Judging by the past and by his actions, war will be his choice." Beard hated war for its blood and agony and waste. He hated it, too, because it besmirched the ideal of American civilization, unique and sacred. But, as an historian, he discerned a fatal rhythm in American liberalism. "The Jeffersonian party gave the nation the War of 1812, the Mexican War, and its participation in the World War. The Pacific War awaits." [3]

VII

Beard, as an historian, had concrete habits of mind which compelled him to take account of what was happening around him. This led him for a season to detect promise in the New Deal. But John Dewey, as a philosopher, was more inclined — for all his invocations of experience in the abstract — to mistake preconceptions for facts. Before Roosevelt's election he predicted that a Raskob would dominate a Walsh or a Wheeler in the Roosevelt administration; and, between election and inauguration, he concluded that the Democratic party was "thoroughly incapable" of doing what had to be done. Committed to these premises and relatively indifferent to programs, Dewey did not have to follow the details of the Washington performance. The New Deal, by prior logic, simply could not work. As Dewey's colleagues in the League for Independent Political Action put it in 1933, "Any amount of changes and reforms in the capitalist system will not rid it of its fundamental defects any more than changing the rigging will give motion to the windjammer when it runs into a dead calm. . . . That is why capitalism must be destroyed; that is why it must inevitably be superseded by some form of cooperative society based on production for use and not for profits." Dewey himself concluded in 1934 that, while the Roosevelt effort showed a commendable bias toward a "controlled and humanized capitalism" as against the brutality of laissez-faire, "the necessary conclusion seems to be that no such compromise with a decaying system is possible."

What was for a moment puzzling was to reconcile Dewey's longtime advocacy of the experimental method in public affairs with his flat rejection of the New Deal. But it became apparent in the thirties that Dewey advocated experimentalism in a restricted and special sense. "Experimental method," Dewey wrote in 1935, "is not just messing around nor doing a little of this and a little of that in the hope that things will improve. Just as in the physical sciences, it implies a coherent body of ideas, a theory, that gives direction to effort." Experimentalism for Dewey did not mean trial-and-error pragmatism; it meant action according to systematic hypothesis. For all his nominal dislike of absolutism, he held social policy to the requirements of ideology. Paradoxically, the New Deal, preferring experiment to abstraction, became repugnant to this theoretical experimentalist.

VIII

But no one in America, as his chief critic Reinhold Niebuhr wrote in 1935, "has a more generally conceded right to speak in the name of liberalism than John Dewey." Dewey's book of that year, *Liberalism and Social Action,* summed up the case for American radicalism. In great part, the book was a thoughtful recapitulation of his familiar views about the role of scientific method in the construction of a new social order. But the pressure of depression had given Dewey's philosophy a new sternness. He affirmed his contempt for piecemeal action. " 'Reforms' that deal now with this abuse and now with that without having a social goal based upon an inclusive plan, differ *entirely* from effort at re-forming, in its literal sense, the institutional scheme of things." Organized social planning, put into effect for an order in which business was "cooperatively controlled" and "socially directed," was, he said with unaccustomed dogmatism, "the *sole* method of social action by which liberalism can realize its professed aims." The old liberalism was obsolete; its ends, he declared, could be achieved *"only* by reversal of the means to which early liberalism was committed."

The sense of urgency which led Dewey to use such words as *entirely, only,* and *sole* led him even to belittle his old faith in individual freedom and political debate. "The idea that the conflict of parties will, by means of public discussion, bring out necessary public truths is a kind of political watered-down version of the Hegelian dialectic, with its synthesis arrived at by a union of antithetical conceptions. The method has *nothing* in common with the procedure of organized cooperative inquiry which has won the triumphs of science in the field of physical nature." Discussion and argument were "weak reeds to depend upon for systematic origination of comprehensive plans, the plans that are required if the problem of social organization is to be met."

If such views had grave implications for political freedom, Dewey elided this by talking disparagingly of "the formal concept of liberty" which would be replaced by genuine liberty once the new order had been won. Nor did he appear to doubt that some group (alas, not specified in his text) could provide objective solutions to social and economic problems if only the nonsense of politics were abolished. Liberalism, Dewey concluded, must "socialize the forces of production, now at hand, so that the liberty of individuals will be supported by the very structure of economic organization." With strong and pensive logic, Dewey rejected the whole philosophy of the New Deal.[4]

IX

The Social Gospel, which had endorsed the liberal view of planning in the twenties, now also tended to more drastic conclusions in the thirties. Early in 1934 about 21,000 clergymen responded to a questionnaire sent out by the *World Tomorrow.* One question asked whether they thought capitalism or the "cooperative commonwealth" more consistent with the ideals of Jesus. Capitalism was chosen by only 5 per cent. Of the 95 per cent who favored the co-operative commonwealth, 10,700 came out for "drastically reformed capitalism," and nearly 6,000 declared outright for socialism (which led the veteran Kirby Page to exult, "Among all the trades, occupations, and professions in the country, few can produce as high a percentage of Socialists as can the ministry").

This movement of clerical sentiment was confirmed by resolutions in church conferences. The Protestant Episcopal House of Bishops resolved that Christ demanded a new order "which shall substitute the motive of service for the motive of gain." The Methodist General Conference pronounced the existing social system "unchristian, unethical and antisocial because it is largely based on the profit motive which is a direct appeal to selfishness." The General Council of the Congregational Christian Churches called for the abolition of the profit-seeking order "by eliminating the systems, incentives and habits, the legal forms which sustain it and the moral ideals which justify it." The Conference of American Rabbis said, "It is not safe for society to leave the basic social enterprise in the control of private groups that operate those enterprises for private profit instead of for the service of the community."

The followers of the Social Gospel shared with Dewey a general faith in the goodness of man, the plasticity of human nature, the inevitability of progress, and the attainability of the millennium. And some churchmen who clung to older Christian views on these matters still approached Dewey's mood in contemporary politics. "The real authors of violent and bloody revolution in our times," said the Bishops of the National Catholic Welfare Conference, "are not the radicals and communists but the callous and autocratic possessors of wealth and power who use their position and their riches to oppress their fellows." [5]

X

So intense were the premonitions felt by liberal intellectuals that Reinhold Niebuhr, the most searching critic of the rationalism and utopianism of the official liberal tradition, had himself a political position indistinguishable from the utopians and the rationalists. Niebuhr saw man fully as capable of evil as of good, human nature as inherently limited, progress as doubtful and precarious, and the Kingdom of God as not of this world. His book of 1932, *Moral Man and Immoral Society*, was a somber and powerful rejection of the politics of love and reason. To the followers of Dewey he denied that scientific knowledge could ever achieve impartial wisdom. To the champions of the Social Gospel he

denied that moral piety could bring about social perfection. Individual egoism and love of power, said Niebuhr, were not to be
tamed by either "the development of rationality or the growth of
a religiously inspired goodwill."

Where both Dewey and the Social Gospel minimized the significance of power, to Niebuhr "all life is an expression of power,"
and therefore all politics had to begin and end with power. He
vigorously emphasized "the necessity of reducing power to a minimum, of bringing the remainder under the strongest measure of
social control; and of destroying such types of it as are least
amenable to social control. For there is no ethical force strong
enough to place inner checks upon the use of power if its quantity
is inordinate." If this analysis were right, he concluded, "an uneasy balance of power would seem to become the highest goal to
which society could aspire." In his book of 1934, *Reflections on
the End of an Era,* Niebuhr called for a political theory which
would be radical "not only in the realistic nature of its analysis
but in its willingness to challenge the injustices of a given social
system by setting power against power until a more balanced equilibrium of power is achieved."

Such an analysis of power and human frailty would seem to
lead to gradualism and a mixed economy rather than to revolution
and a socialist state. But the pressure of the time was so great
that even Niebuhr found himself forced beyond the implications
of his own general theory to utopian positions. Like Dewey,
Niebuhr had decided in the interval between Roosevelt's election
and his inauguration that liberalism was a "spent force" and that
"next to the futility of liberalism we may set down the inevitability
of fascism as a practical certainty in every Western nation." In
Reflections on the End of an Era (the very title expressed apoca-
lyptical urgencies) he argued that the sickness of capitalism was
"organic and constitutional," rooted in "the very nature of capitalism," in "the private ownership of the productive processes."
There was no middle way; economists like Keynes and Stuart
Chase might offer their advice, but they could not hope to arrest
the drift toward fascism: "the drift is inevitable." Middle-class
politics seemed to him hopeless in 1935, "rushing us at incredible
speed from the futilities of Rooseveltian 'liberalism' to the worse
confusion of a political program concocted by a radio priest and a

Louisiana 'kingfish,'" The New Deal figured in his writing as "whirligig reform," an image of aimless and incoherent triviality; Roosevelt himself, not as a leader pledged to a specific program, but as a messiah "more renowned for his artistic juggling than for robust resolution."

In the case of Dewey, his disdain for the New Deal and his commitment to socialization proceeded logically enough from his disregard of power in society and from his faith in human rationality and scientific planning. But for Niebuhr, who was realistic about man and who wanted to equilibrate power in society, the commitment to socialization was both a sign of indifference to the achievements of piecemeal reform and a symptom of despair. Where Dewey spurned the New Deal because of his optimism about man and his belief in science, Niebuhr spurned it because of his pessimism about man and his belief in catastrophe. Together they secured both radical flanks; and their joint testimony presented a formidable intellectual case against the possibilities of a middle way between reaction and revolution.[6]

XI

The influence of Dewey and Niebuhr, fortified somewhat by that of Beard, gave powerful impetus to either-or tendencies of thought in American radicalism. When the New Deal asserted that a middle way was possible, many radicals preferred to follow eminent intellectual authority in dismissing this faith as an illusion. Bingham himself pronounced the New Deal "a fraud and a sham in spite of its humanitarianism." "When an egg is rotten," *Common Sense* said, "painting it pretty colors won't improve it." What, after all, was the New Deal's purpose? "It is the clear intention of the Roosevelt Administration," *Common Sense* disapprovingly observed, "to make capitalism work. And since it is impossible today to make capitalism work for long, the New Deal is doomed to failure. With this in mind no intelligent or courageous radical can support Roosevelt."

In the fall of 1934 William Harlan Hale wrote a repentant article for *Common Sense* entitled "The Opium Wears Off: A Liberal Awakens From the New Deal." "Many liberals are saying good-bye to hoping and praying," Hale concluded. "They are learning that in this time there is no middle ground." So, too, Robert S. Lynd, whose intellectual idols were Dewey and Veblen, worked through the decade on his *Knowledge For What?*, a militant expression of faith in central planning in the older liberal tradition. As late as 1944, Lynd condemned America to the choice between fascism and socialism; "there is no possibility beyond perhaps the next decade of straddling the two systems."

John T. Flynn was a radical rather than a socialist, but he gave the prevailing rationalism and utopianism sharp expression. Appraising the New Deal in the fall of 1934, he concluded that it had been a failure in recovery and a failure in reform. NRA, AAA, the Stock Exchange and Securities acts, monetary policy, labor policy — all were terrible; only TVA and the spending policy received his endorsement. "Mr. Roosevelt up to now," Flynn wrote, "has been using the rich resources of his political talents to preserve the capitalist system intact and he has resisted in every possible way any attempt to make any breaches in the shaky walls of that system." Flynn warned radicals to be especially wary when Roosevelt pretended to talk the language of radicalism: "it is under cover of such talk that he always moves another step or two to the right." As things grew worse, Flynn predicted, Roosevelt would turn even farther to the right. "That way lies [sic] his tastes, his dreams, his friendships, his convictions. He could do no other. And that turn would be in the direction of fascism." And meanwhile the ordinary citizen, Flynn wrote, "thinks our economic society ought to be planned. And he is right. . . . Let us have an intelligent, deliberate, calm attempt at national planning." Let us have a national economic council with power to put its measures into effect. "And if there is regimentation, as there will be, it will be in the interest not of profits, but of social well-being." Roosevelt's failure, he thought, gave the radicals their opportunity. "The historic moment will have arrived for the launching of a powerful third party upon modern radical economic issues." [7]

XII

And so in 1935 the intellectual radicals contemplated the New Deal with dislike. They had a splendid idea of what America might be: they saw the means of abundance rusting on every side; they had no patience for a government too mean-spirited or incompetent not to use every resource of the machine age in an all-out assault on poverty. Roosevelt, for all his decent intentions, seemed the prisoner of the past; indeed, his vague humanitarianism threatened to relieve things just enough to drain off the demand for basic reform.

What kept them buoyant was their conviction that palliatives could have only a passing effect. William Saroyan, who heard over the radio a huckster's pitch about aspirin becoming a member of the NRA, expressed their general conviction that aspirin was not enough. "All I know is this," he wrote: "that if you keep on taking aspirin long enough it will cease to deaden pain. And that is when the fun begins. That is when you begin to notice that snow isn't beautiful at all. That is when your hair begins to freeze and you begin to get up in the middle of the night, laughing quietly, waiting for the worst, remembering all the pain and not wanting to evade it any longer, not wanting any longer to be half-dead, wanting full death or full life. That is when you begin to be mad about the way things are going in this country. . . . That is when, weak as you are, something old and savage, and defiant in you comes up bitterly out of your illness and starts to smash things . . . pushing you into the sun, getting you away from evasions, dragging you by your neck to life." [8]

Radicalism: European Plan

ONE OTHER SENTIMENT united the native American radicals: a dislike of Communism. The radical politicians, from Floyd Olson and the La Follettes to Sinclair and La Guardia, abhorred the Communists as troublemakers and doctrinaires. The radical ideologists had an equal abhorrence for Communist ideas. All shared a profound conviction that, though Karl Marx might have been a formidable social thinker, Marxism in general and Communism in particular were irrelevant to the United States.

II

The intellectual rejection of Marxism began with the liberal elders. Charles A. Beard thought that Marxism "from start to finish" denied all notion of individual freedom, personal rights, and democracy. Communism, he said, confronted the idea of American civilization with "the most thoroughgoing opposition which it had ever met in the long course of its development." Dewey declined for years even to read Marx. When Max Eastman asked him to preside over a debate between himself and Sidney Hook on whether Marx was a pragmatist, Dewey replied contentedly, "I don't know enough Marx to go into the scheme and I don't see the least probability of my getting the time to acquire the needed knowledge."

Because he was more tempted by Marxism than the others, Reinhold Niebuhr was more articulate in explaining both its immediate attraction and its ultimate unacceptability. Rebounding from the liberal belief in the inevitability of progress, Niebuhr was for a moment all too susceptible to an equally extreme belief in the inevitability of catastrophe. The recurrence of the "end of an era" formula in his writings of the thirties suggested his appalled fascination with the idea of some basic turn in history. He pronounced the Marxist appreciation of the "fact of judgment and catastrophe . . . closer to the genius of Hebrew prophecy than liberalism, either secular or religious."

As Marxist catastrophism corrected liberal optimism for Niebuhr, so Marxist cynicism about the power of self-interest corrected liberal idealism; so Marxist collectivism, with its emphasis on the need for community, corrected liberal individualism; so Marxist determinism, with its sense of the implacability of history, corrected liberal faith in the perfect plasticity of man and society; so the Marxist commitment to the working class corrected the self-righteous complacency of the middle class. At one point Niebuhr called Marxism "an essentially correct theory and analysis of the economic realities of modern society"; even Communism seemed an indispensable myth, "a very valuable illusion for the moment; for justice cannot be approximated if the hope of its perfect realization does not generate a sublime madness in the soul."

Yet Niebuhr's leaning toward Marxism was strictly provisional. On reflection the madness generated by Communism appeared less sublime than sinister. "Only a sentimentalist," he wrote in 1931, "could be oblivious of the possibilities of Napoleonic ventures in the forces which are seething in Russia." In 1932 he condemned the abuse of power by Communist bureaucrats, predicting that it would grow worse as the revolutionary idealists were supplanted by men who cared only to stay in power. "If the Russian oligarchy strips itself of its own power, it will be the first oligarchy in history to do so." As for his momentary tolerance of Communism as a myth, he wrote ruefully in 1935, "I once thought such a faith to be a harmless illusion. But now I see that its net result is to endow a group of oligarchs with the religious sanctity which primitive priest-kings once held."

By 1935 Niebuhr was ruling out the Communists as "a hopelessly sectarian movement." And though he remained a nominal member of the Socialist party, he dismissed American Socialism as impotent and futile. He was now highly critical of the whole Europeanization of American radicalism; left-wing politics in the

United States had been dominated too long by the irrelevant controversy "between a discredited German social democratic system and a Russian religion which has far more relevance to Asia than to the western world." He resented particularly the Marxist attempt to reduce all American liberalism to a simple expression of middle-class self-interest. He assailed the notion that "American constitutional rights are nothing but a façade for capitalism." These rights, he said, were the means by which a strong liberal movement could achieve substantial reforms. "Democracy," Niebuhr declared, "has certain universal values which transcend bourgeois and capitalist interests." The Marxists were ignoring "the elements of the American tradition which might become resources for an American radicalism." [1]

III

An episode in February 1934 sharpened the native radical detestation of the Communists. The Socialist party and a number of trade unions called a meeting at Madison Square Garden to protest the slaughter of the Social Democratic workers in Vienna by the Dollfuss regime. The Communists, professing to regard the sponsors of the meeting as a gang of social-fascists and labor fakers, marched to the Garden several thousand strong, shouting such edifying sentiments as "Down with the Fascist La Guardia" and "We'll hang Matt Woll to a sour apple tree." Ushers could not stop them from storming onto the floor of the auditorium. When the meeting began, Communist boos and yells drowned out the chairman and the speakers. Fights broke out all over the Garden as Communists tried to force their way to the platform; furriers' knives flashed in the dark, people threw chairs down from the balcony. After David Dubinsky, the Socialist head of the International Ladies' Garment Workers Union, gave up trying to speak in the uproar, Clarence Hathaway, the Communist leader, leaped onto the stage and seized the microphone. Several men jumped him. rushed him across the floor and pushed him over a railing into the pit. Soon he was ejected into Forty-ninth Street where, with cut face and bleeding nose, he harangued a small crowd. Finally the police cleared the hall. A German trade unionist who was present, a fugitive from Nazism, observed, "It was precisely such spectacles as that staged here today that led to the triumph of Hitlerism."

There could be no question about the studied Communist intent to break up the meeting. This pointless exhibition of brutality and stupidity consolidated a growing anti-Communism among radical intellectuals. As recently as 1932, the Communist presidential ticket had attracted the public support of such novelists as Theodore Dreiser, Sherwood Anderson, John Dos Passos, Erskine Caldwell, and Waldo Frank; such critics as Edmund Wilson, Newton Arvin, Malcolm Cowley; such professors as Sidney Hook and Henry W. L. Dana. After Madison Square Garden, Wilson, Dos Passos, John Chamberlain, Lionel Trilling, Clifton Fadiman, and others addressed a sober letter of protest against the Communist tactics. The Communist response, self-righteous and strident, increased the estrangement. Never again would the party as such command much support among serious American intellectuals.[2]

IV

But the demi-intellectuals remained. If, after 1933, the American Communist party had astonishingly little backing from major poets, novelists, critics, or scholars, it nonetheless had a steadily widening influence till the very end of the decade in the lower ranks of the intelligentsia. For the discontented magazine writer, the guilty Hollywood scenarist, the aggrieved university instructor, the underpaid high-school teacher, the politically inexperienced scientist, the intelligent clerk, the culturally aspiring dentist — as well as for a diminishing number of genuinely creative people — Marxism as a system of explanation and consolation carried great appeal.

Its primary attraction lay in its apparent capacity to deal in a realistic way with the brute historical facts of the age — the depression, the moral and intellectual exhaustion of laissez-faire capitalism, the rise of fascism. In a time of confusion and despair, Marxism provided certitudes, while liberalism and conservatism alike mumbled in the corridor. Moreover, these certitudes met not only intellectual but psychological needs. The resentful intelligentsia generally combined a sense of guilt over possessing more than the workingman with a sense of grievance over possessing less than the banker; Marxism at once exorcised the guilt and rationalized the grievance. Above all, Marxism offered light at the end of the dark cave. It held out the hope of the classless society, the collectivist utopia; to the best disciplined Marxist sect (though by no means to all Marxists) this hope had already found its embodiment in the Soviet Union. The Marxist world view thus seemed historical, rational, and tough; at the same time, it provided subtle justification for the multiplicity of hopes and guilts which were estranging men and women from the existing order.[3]

v

Literature mirrored the spreading mood. Malcolm Cowley was a representative writer of the twenties; he had left Harvard to drive an ambulance in France during the First World War, was a friend of Dadaists in Paris and of Hart Crane in New York. Nothing had mattered less than politics. Now, in 1934, brooding over the experience of the "lost generation," he published a book called *Exile's Return*. A thoughtful and generous-minded critic, Cowley was finding in the social struggle a new fulfillment; for a moment the social conflict seemed far more significant than all the literary exuberance of the twenties. Artists, he said, must not be deceived by the surface mellowness and liberalism of the ruling class. These were "merely the ornaments of its prosperous years; in times of danger they gave way to brutality, direct and unconcealed." Capitalism condemned the artist to an isolation which dried up the springs of creativity. The hope for artistic renewal lay in cultivating the world of struggle — "the outer world that is strong and colorful and demands to be imaginatively portrayed." Artists "can't stay out of the battle without deliberately blinding and benumbing themselves." Accepting the workers' cause as their own was the road to salvation. It could offer "an end to the desperate feeling of solitude and uniqueness that has been oppressing artists for the last two centuries. . . . It can offer instead a sense of comradeship and participation in a historical process vastly bigger than the individual. . . . It can offer the strength of a new class."

It was a powerful dream, given urgency by a sense that history itself was at a breaking point. Jack Conroy, a proletarian writer, expressed it crudely: "To me a strike bulletin or an impassioned leaflet are of more moment than three hundred pretty and fault-lessly written pages about the private woes of a gigolo or the biological ferment of a society dame as useful to society as the buck brush that infests Missouri cow pastures and takes all the sustenance of the soil." So much for Proust and Henry James! Even an author like Dos Passos could not understand Scott Fitz-gerald's writing on so trivial a subject as his own nervous break-down: "Christ, man, how do you find time in the middle of the general conflagration to worry about all that stuff? . . . We're living in one of the damnedest tragic moments in history." Men whose every instinct pulled them in the opposite direction were impressed by the Marxist vision. An exceptionally sensitive younger critic, confronting the work of E. M. Forster, acknowl-edged its appeal while announcing its obsolescence. "Although the future does not belong to his kind of novel, ethically based on individual 'understanding' and 'tolerance,'" Lionel Trilling wrote a little wistfully, "in personal life these virtues are still real. In political life, however, history has proved them to be catchwords that becloud reality in the service of the worst 'passion and interests.'"

The Communist party, of course, sought to organize the new mood. Through its elaborate cultural apparatus — the *New Masses, Partisan Review, The New Theater,* the John Reed Clubs, the Theater Union, the Film and Foto League — it concentrated partic-ularly on promoting the cult of "proletarian literature." The first burst of proletarian fiction had come in 1932, the year before the New Deal, when, by W. B. Rideout's computation, eleven proletarian novels were published. In 1933 and 1934, twenty-eight more came out, presenting the set themes of bourgeois decay and working-class virility, the blinding flash of conversion and the solidarity of comrades on the barricade.

But the mood was much larger than the Communist party. Though Communists organized the American Writers' Congress in 1935, many non-Communist writers attested to their acceptance of the prevailing state of mind by signing the call. "The capitalist system crumbles so rapidly before our eyes," the call began, "that . . . today hundreds of poets, novelists, dramatists, critics and short story writers recognize the necessity of personally helping to accelerate the destruction of capitalism and the establishment of a workers' government." Among the names inscribed on this document were John Dos Passos, Theodore Dreiser, James T. Farrell, Waldo Frank, Lewis Mumford, Richard Wright, Malcolm Cowley, Nathanael West, Erskine Caldwell, Nelson Algren. "My premise and the premise of the majority of writers here assembled," said Waldo Frank, who served as chairman, "is that Communism must come and must be fought for. . . . To agonize within the present system, to refuse to get clear by the social revolution of the working classes, means the plunge of Western man into a darkness." (Yet Frank, Farrell, and Dos Passos all insisted at the Congress on the autonomy of art as against politics; all were soon to condemn the Moscow trials; none would be present when the Writers' Congress next met.) [4]

VI

For most of the writers involved, this revolutionary mood was only a rush of emotion, a vague but excited salute to a new historical epoch. And emotions were transient. If Marxism were to survive in America, it needed a structure: it had to come across not as mood alone but as doctrine.

The two ablest American students of Marx at this time were Sidney Hook, a professor of philosophy at New York University, and Max Eastman, a veteran of *The Masses* in the First World War, a friend of Leon Trotsky's, a Bohemian Communist of the pre-Stalin, pre-depression, Greenwich Village era, and a skilled and versatile journalist. Eastman and Hook were less interested in the economics and politics of Marxism than in its philosophical and cultural aspects. Both came quickly to see through the pretenses of the Stalinist dictatorship — a perception which guaranteed their books scurrilous reviews in the Communist press, involved them in a wearying series of sectarian disputes and, in effect, cut them off from the main stream of organized Marxism.

The Communist party, of course, had its corps of house ideologists. But for them thinking consisted of memorizing the latest bulletins from the Comintern; and their application of Marxist ideas to the American situation was uniformly mechanical and sterile. Only one American Marxist of the orthodox sort made any impress at all. This was the curious figure who wrote in the thirties under the name of Lewis Corey, but whose name fifteen years before, when he had played a leading role in founding the American Communist party, was Louis C. Fraina.

Fraina's early eminence in the American Communist movement had won him enemies within the party itself. In 1920 someone denounced him as an agent of the Department of Justice; and, though a party investigation cleared him of what was evidently an unfounded charge, his position was badly shaken. Subsequently the Comintern removed him from the American scene by sending him on a mission to Mexico. Fraina, bitter and disillusioned, decided to resign from the party. He took with him about $4,000 of Comintern funds. In spite of a later offer of repayment, this action became the basis for stories of embezzlement which dogged him the rest of his life.

In 1923 Fraina returned quietly to New York and became a proofreader for Street and Smith. But he was still a Marxist with a consuming interest in American economic problems. In 1926 he began to write articles for the *New Republic* under the name of Lewis Corey. In 1929 the Brookings Institution gave him a fellowship. In 1930 he published *The House of Morgan*, and in 1931 he became an associate editor of the *Encyclopedia of the Social Sciences*. In the meantime he had cautiously returned to political activity, not rejoining the Communist party but working actively for the Communist ticket in 1932.

During these years he labored on a massive work which was published in 1934, entitled *The Decline of American Capitalism* (which he rewrote somewhat and published again in 1935 under the title *The Crisis of the Middle Class*). The *Decline* was a long-winded and pretentious book, turgid in style, abstract and pedantic in its approach, filled with irrelevant learning and dedicated to the thesis that "precisely because it is the most highly developed, American industry offers the fullest confirmation of the analysis Karl Marx made of the laws of capitalist production." Corey detested the notion that the American experience might compel the slightest modification in Marxist theory. The depression signified "a fundamental, permanent crisis in the economic and social relations of American capitalism." Capitalism now faced the choice between fascism and communism. But communism would not come of itself; "only the revolutionary consciousness and action of the proletariat and the understanding, strategy and tactics of its communist party make socialism inevitable." Decaying capitalism was threatening the "death of civilization"; but Corey perceived the usual hope: "life is already triumphant over death in the developing socialism of the Soviet Union."

The Communists greeted *The Decline of American Capitalism* with enthusiasm (subsequently moderated, however, when headquarters began to perceive in Corey a possible threat to the party pundits). Nearly everybody else was unmoved. Corey, Alfred Bingham commented in *Common Sense*, took Marxism "as an absolute finality, to which every present-day fact can and must be fitted." He ignored American life. His was a work, not of sociology, but of theology. "This book," said Bingham, "is a symbol of the poverty of radical political and economic theory in America." [5]

VII

It is no wonder that, given the hurdy-gurdy monotony of American Marxist writing, literate Americans interested in Marx turned quickly away from Lewis Corey and even more quickly away from Earl Browder, V. J. Jerome, M. J. Olgin and the sages of Twelfth Street in order to read Marxists who could at least write the English language. As a result, Englishmen shaped the Marxist ethos in America far more than any of the native faithful. John Strachey's *Coming Struggle for Power* had defined the problem in compelling terms in 1933; in 1935 he followed it with *The Nature of Capitalist Crisis* and an American lecture tour. But the Englishman who, through his writings, his personal relations, and his American visits, had the greatest effect on American left-wing thought in the thirties was a professor at the London School of Economics, Harold J. Laski.

Laski knew America well. In 1916, as a twenty-three-year-old prodigy a few years out of Oxford, he received an appointment in the Government Department at Harvard. In a short while, he made enduring friendships with Felix Frankfurter, Oliver Wendell Holmes, and Louis D. Brandeis; he met Herbert Croly and

Walter Lippmann and became a contributor to the *New Republic;* and his support of the Boston police strike of 1919 won him a permanent place in the history of academic freedom in the United States. Harvard alumni demanded his dismissal. He was damned in Boston clubs. The *Harvard Lampoon,* a supposedly humorous undergraduate publication, devoted an issue to a vicious personal attack on him as a Jew and a radical. While President Lowell strongly defended Laski's right to free utterance, Laski gained the impression that his future in Cambridge was limited. It was an unsettling experience for a sensitive and very aspiring young man of twenty-six. In 1920 he returned to England.

As a political theorist, Laski in his book of 1919, *Authority in the Modern State,* had sought to vindicate the rights of groups against the state. His pluralism was, for the moment, deeply felt. But it was fundamentally a means of strengthening the position of the people against an aggressive capitalist government; it carried the plain implication that the need for pluralism would disappear as soon as the people took the government away from the capitalists. "No one would object to a strong state," he wrote, "if guarantees could be had that its strength would be used for the fulfillment of its theoretic purposes." This theory would allow him to move quietly from pluralism to Marxism; and events were already providing the impetus. The Harvard episode badly shook his early liberalism. Then the British general strike of 1926 strengthened a growing belief that in moments of stress, capitalism would always turn against democracy.

By 1930, Laski began to question whether peaceful transition from capitalism to socialism would ever be possible. So long as capitalism was in its expansionist phase, then the capitalist class could afford concessions to the workers. But when capitalism entered the phase of contraction, continued movement toward equality would be impossible without the steady abandonment by the ruling class of its privileges. How long would a beleaguered capitalism consent to a policy of "piecemeal surrender"? "Will a class," Laski asked, "which has hitherto enjoyed a virtual monopoly of effective authority in the state, acquiesce peacefully in its own extinction?"

In the spring of 1931 Laski dealt with this question in a series of lectures at the University of North Carolina. Later in the year the downfall of the British Labour government under what seemed intense pressure from the bankers confirmed Laski's growing pessimism. As he prepared the North Carolina lectures for publication, the book, he said, was burning inside him. "I would go to the stake for it, and I think it is the most creative book I have ever written." He called it *Democracy in Crisis;* and its purpose was to show "how near our feet lie to the abyss." The epoch which had begun with the French Revolution — the age characterized by a search for individual liberty — was drawing to a close. The system of private ownership was at the end of its tether. Every moral and material force demanded a new social order. Theoretically the capitalists might co-operate in their own liquidation. But of this hope, "it is only necessary to say that it envisages something entirely new in historic experience." With the best will, Laski could not easily see an alternative to catastrophe. "No new social order," he concluded, "has so far come into being without a violent birth."

VIII

If this were so, nothing could be more futile than efforts at reform. Laski condemned as sharply as Herbert Hoover the notion that America could spend its way into recovery. Pump priming, Laski said with horror, would lead to inflation or heavy taxation or wasteful expenditure; it would be a "dangerous interference" with the automatic processes of adjustment; it would mean "an unbalanced budget with the disturbance of confidence (an essential condition of recovery) which this implies"; it would bequeath "a bill of staggering dimensions" to future generations. "Government spending as anything more than a temporary and limited expedient," he concluded, "will necessarily do harm in a capitalist society." The only way out was a planned economy "based on the public ownership of the means of production." The next year in *The State in Theory and Practice* Laski further derided the conviction that one could build "a *via media* between capitalism and socialism directed by the state in the interests of the whole community but without any change in the essential structure of class-relations." He explicitly rejected the Fabian belief in gradualness: "in the period of capitalism's decline, its result would, I think, be to give to the owning class a supreme opportunity to organize itself for counter-attack. The real lesson of post-war Germany is the futility of trying to reorganize the economic foundations of capitalism by half-measures."

Nor would Laski exclude America from these somber calculations; "as soon as crisis came, it was obvious that the central American problem was no different from that of the European. . . . What evidence is there, among the class which controls the destiny of America, of a will to make the necessary concessions? Is not the execution of Sacco and Vanzetti, the long and indefensible imprisonment of Mooney, the grim history of American strikes, the root of the answer to that question?" He wrote this in *Democracy in Crisis*, which made a deep impression on the American left. Thus Henry Hazlitt wrote: "Mr. Laski's analysis of the world's present political dilemma is in many respects the most persuasive and penetrating that has yet appeared. . . . It is hard to see how one could avoid accepting the broad lines of his analysis." (In due course, Hazlitt himself discovered how this could be done.) And Laski reiterated his pessimism in a series of articles in American magazines in 1934 and 1935. The belief that the New Dealers might "somehow make all things new," he wrote, "seems to me an act of faith denied by the very postulates of the system they propose to regenerate." "I miss my guess," he observed improbably of Earl Browder in 1935, "if the failure of the Roosevelt experiment does not leave him, or some successor, one of the outstanding figures in the American scene."

And yet Laski's position was not so clear-cut in emotion as it was in theory. For he had a great affection for America and Americans; and the personality and example of Roosevelt, the "exhilarating spectacle" of the New Deal, challenged his essentially spirited nature. As he wrote to Holmes, their friend Frankfurter had a deeper faith in the New Deal than Laski could permit himself. "But he can't outdo me in admiration for Roosevelt as a person even though I don't believe he can succeed. America excites us all as never in my lifetime. Even at this distance one has a sense of something big being tried." As a man, Laski could not restrain an enthusiasm which, as an ideologist, he could not bring himself to endorse. Even in Britain he expended his life in a gallant struggle to realize the constitutional revolution which his theory had pronounced impossible.

This was characteristic: few influential political theorists of the time combined a greater generosity of feeling with a greater sterility of thought. Ironically, the warmth of his manner won a tolerance for his analysis that his thin logic could never have commanded on its own. The facile elegance of his writing, his graceful notes of regret for the doomed past, his brave acceptance of the inevitabilities of the future, his poses of romantic despair and hope — all this gave him an influence in the United States far beyond that of any native Marxist. And his personality — the kindliness to the poor and defenseless, the wide-ranging sympathy, the fascinating if often far too fanciful accounts of his influence on great events — further increased his American appeal. If Dewey, Beard, and Niebuhr were the mentors of a native American radicalism, it was appropriate that a European should be the missionary of Marxism to the American infidels.[6]

IX

The native radicals and the Marxists had large and crucial areas of disagreement. But radicals and Marxists alike agreed in rejecting piecemeal methods and half-measures. Neither would settle for anything less than drastic change on the basis of fixed and comprehensive ideology. When R. G. Tugwell revisited Columbia in 1933, he rashly bragged of the New Deal's freedom from "blind doctrine." The *Columbia Spectator,* edited by a brilliant undergraduate in the Marxist orbit named James Wechsler, seized on this boast as the fatal weakness of Tugwell's argument. "This is the crux of the problem," the *Spectator* said; "the blind stumbling in the most chaotic fashion — experimenting from day to day — without any anchor except a few idealistic phrases — is worthless. It is merely political pragmatism."

Political pragmatism: to the radicals, whether finding their inspiration in Bellamy or in Marx, this was evidence, not of wisdom, but of bankruptcy. In 1935 two American journalists, Benjamin Stolberg and Warren Jay Vinton, presented the sophisticated Marxist case against Roosevelt in a witty pamphlet called *The Economic Consequences of the New Deal.* The essential fact of American life, they said, was that the interests of big ownership and of the American people were completely opposed; "they can neither be theoretically reconciled nor realistically compromised." The logic of history presumably compelled Roosevelt to choose between them. "Conceivably he could choose either, but he could not choose both. But, like Buchanan, he did." From this all else in the New Deal followed. Its admirers had sought to rationalize opportunism into a philosophy; but pragmatism, wrote Stolberg and Vinton, was "the philosophy of having no philosophy"; it was "an apologetics for side-stepping the class struggle."

The result reminded them of the Russian peasant who cut some cloth from the front of his pants to patch the hole in the seat, and then from the leg of his pants to patch the front. "After repeating this operation a dozen times he wound up, very much like the New Deal, with his pants all in patches and the migratory hole still there." No one should be taken in by Rooseveltian rhetoric: the New Deal consists largely "in moving one speech forward and two steps backward." The conclusion summed up the case: "There is nothing the New Deal has so far done that could not have been done better by an earthquake."

Stolberg and Vinton were having too much fun for most Marxists, but what they said gaily others said portentously. In this perspective the New Deal became a form of self-deception which could issue in only one result. Capitalism in any form meant fascism; "if we maintain the Capitalist system," said John Strachey, "there is no other possibility." And he added:"There is no way at all in which capitalism can be 'reformed' into giving decent or efficient results." "Roosevelt's policies can be welded into a consistent whole," wrote I. F. Stone, "only on the basis of one hypothesis . . . that Mr. Roosevelt intends to move toward fascism." A young American political scientist, whose fluency, knowledge, and generosity reminded many of Laski, stated it in 1935 with brutal directness. "The essential logic of the New Deal," wrote Max Lerner, "is increasingly the naked fist of a capitalist state."

Convinced of the hopeless fragility of the system, the radicals conceived themselves as the forerunners of apocalypse. Adam Smith had said that nations had a lot of ruin in them; but they had no use for Adam Smith. "American commercial agriculture is doomed," wrote Louis Hacker, the Marxist historian. Capitalism was doomed too, and the party system, and the traditional American way of life. "Never was soil more favorable for revolution," cried Elliot Cohen in 1934. ". . . The Marxist revolutionaries are few and the obstacles facing them stupendous. But what odds would those sound Britishers, Lloyds, have quoted on Lenin and his tinier band in 1914?" In 1934 Sidney Hook, James Burnham, Louis Budenz, V. F. Calverton, James Rorty and others addressed "An Open Letter to American Intellectuals." "We cannot by some clever Rooseveltian trick," the letter warned, "evade the unfolding of basic economic and political developments under capitalism. . . . Let us not deceive ourselves that we shall not have to face here also the choice between reaction, on the one hand, and a truly scientific economy under a genuine workers' democracy on the other."

In June 1935 the *New Republic* stated with magistral simplicity the argument of the radicals against the New Dealers, of New York against Washington, of the Marxists against the pragmatists: "Either the nation must put up with the confusions and miseries of an essentially unregulated capitalism, or it must prepare to supersede capitalism with socialism. *There is no longer a feasible middle course.*"

Radicalism, like conservatism, thus ended in the domain of either-or. The contradictions of actuality, which so stimulated the pragmatists of Washington, only violated the proprieties and offended the illusions of the ideologists. Dewey and Laski wholly agreed with Herbert Hoover and Ogden Mills that one must have either capitalism or socialism; any combination of the two was impossible. The protagonists on both sides saw themselves as hardheaded realists. But in fact they were all unconscious Platonists, considering abstractions the ultimate reality.[7]

x

For those who demanded drastic change and denied the feasibility of the middle course, the New Deal was almost as hopeless as the old order itself. Some more thoroughgoing political instrumentality was required than so flimsy and compromised a vehicle as the Democratic party. To meet this need, the native radicals, as we have seen, dreamed of organizing a third party of their own. As for the radicals in the Marxist orbit, they had two parties already in existence, based on European models and dedicated to fundamental social reconstruction in America. One was a party of soft revolution, the Socialist party; the other, a party of hard revolution, the Communist party.

The Socialist party was in the tradition of the European Social Democratic parties of the Second International. It had been active in American politics for more than a generation, though in the years after the First World War it never approached its high point of 1912. Yet in 1932 it was on the ballot in forty-three states and polled 882,000 votes in the presidential election — more votes than it had polled since 1920, and nearly nine times as many as the Communists in 1932. Moreover, its perennial candidate, Norman Thomas, had a significant personal following throughout the country. His humane and appealing version of Socialism was winning many disciples in the churches and on the campuses: where Debs had Americanized Socialism for the working class, Thomas Americanized it for the middle class.

Nonetheless, there were grave weaknesses in the Socialist position. In 1932, after three years of depression, total membership was only about 15,000; and this tiny group was badly divided within itself. The Old Guard, led by the veteran Morris Hillquit, had already looked with misgivings on Thomas's free-wheeling and undoctrinaire radicalism. Now it regarded with distinct alarm a rush of impetuous younger men into the party. In the 1932 convention, Hillquit barely retained his post as national chairman against an uprising of the Militants, as the insurgent faction called itself. With Hillquit's death in October 1933, the Old Guard lost its single leader with enough authority to prevent an open breach.

The issues were partly of temperament, partly of doctrine. The Old Guard consisted in the main of older men, largely immigrants, who had made good in America as lawyers or businessmen. They had grown up with the party and regarded it more or less as their private property. Their interest in socialism was sentimental and rhetorical rather than activist. They looked forward genuinely enough to the revolution, but supposed that it would come under its own steam. The Militants were mostly of a younger generation, middle class rather than working class in origin, native-born rather than foreign-born, new to socialism, responsive to the left-wing fantasies of the day, and uncomfortably ardent in their enthusiasm. The extreme Militant wore a blue shirt and a red tie and delighted in giving the clenched-fist salute and singing the Internationale ("he solves problems of the class war here and abroad," said an Old Guard leader sourly, "with the ease that he flicks his ashes from his cigarette"). The most leftish of the Militants were hard to tell from Communists in their catastrophism as well as in their admiration for the Soviet Union and their willingness to work with American Communists. The Old Guard considered the Militants a collection of dilettantes and irresponsibles; the Militants considered the Old Guard a collection of stuffed shirts. Probably both judgments had their points.

While not a member of the Militant caucus, Thomas regarded the Militants with sympathy. "The Socialist Party is coming close to suicide," he said, "when it is so much quicker to see the sins of Communism than the sins of capitalism or of the embryonic Fascism in America." The conflict came into the open at the Detroit convention in June 1934. Here the Militants, with Thomas's support, demanded a resolution pledging, in case of war, "massed war resistance . . . to convert the capitalist war crisis into a victory for Socialists." In another resolution, the Militants said that, if capitalism should collapse, the Socialist party, whether or not it commanded a majority, should "not shrink from the responsibility of organizing and maintaining a government under the workers' rule."

It could not have mattered less what the American Socialist party decided to do in case of war or economic collapse. But the resolutions, with their tacit advocacy of force and violence, symbolized the differences between respectability and radicalism within the party. Louis Waldman of the Old Guard denounced the resolutions as "anarchist, illegal, and communistic." John Haynes Holmes called them "communism pure and simple." The Militants responded with vehement revolutionary declamations. In the end, the convention adopted the resolutions, and this action was ratified, though by a thinner margin, in a national referendum.

For the next few months, as leaders on both sides concentrated on mobilizing their forces for a final showdown in 1936, the party lost whatever forward drive it had. A writer in *Common*

Sense portrayed it without much exaggeration: "The Left Wing leans to the side of revolution, the pacifists withdraw from the idea of violence, the Westerners get distrustful of the New York Jewish legal crowd, the trade unions resent the highbrows." An infusion of ex-Communists in 1935 — Lovestonites, Trotskyites, Gitlowites, Fieldites, Zamites — only multiplied the intrigues. The orgy of factionalism disgusted many party members. In the year after September 1934, over seven thousand — nearly a third of the membership — left the party.

XI

If the internal difficulties were not enough, the Socialist party confronted in the New Deal an unexpected problem of external competition. Norman Thomas himself had first watched Roosevelt with sympathy. Getting the American people to accept a measure of collective control, Thomas wrote in the fall of 1933, "constituted nothing less than a genuine revolution." It was, he quickly added, "a revolution to state capitalism," not to socialism. Still, he thought that Roosevelt had probably gone as far as he could *"until Americans organize to give power to fundamental demands."* By 1934 he was less sympathetic, speaking of the "essential impotence" of the New Deal and affecting to discern a "growing disillusionment of the masses." Other Socialists, especially of the Militant school, were blunter. "The greatest fraud among all the utopias," said an author in the *American Socialist Quarterly* in 1935, "is the 'New Deal.' Based on no philosophy, it is the apotheosis of opportunism."

In part, the attack on the New Deal was essential if the Socialists were to maintain an identity of their own. But in Thomas's case it also stemmed from a growing moral concern over aspects of New Deal policy. He feared the militarism of the Roosevelt administration. He sharply criticized its indifference to the plight of tenant farmers and sharecroppers. He raised his voice courageously and insistently on questions of civil liberties and of civil rights. His essential contribution, indeed, was to keep moral issues alive at a moment when the central emphasis was on meeting economic emergencies. At his best, Thomas gave moving expression to an ethical urgency badly needed in politics, to a sense of the relation between means and ends and of the inestimable value of the individual human being — to the hope for "the end of the long night of exploitation, poverty and war, and the dawn of a day of beauty and peace, freedom and fellowship."

But on economic issues, Thomas moved fairly soon into the either-or camp. His economic thought was jejune; like Herbert Hoover and Harold Laski, he worried over the "crushing burden" of the national debt. By 1935, he could find only the TVA to approve in the New Deal, "a beautiful flower in a garden of weeds." "One cannot successfully marry planning for the common good and the supremacy of the profit system," he concluded. ". . . Sooner or later we shall swerve sharply to a fascist right or to a Socialist left."

Thomas could not take all his followers with him in his rejection of the middle course. After all, in 1932 he had himself campaigned for an essentially reformist program. A year later, most of those who voted for Thomas were shouting for Roosevelt. In New York, Paul Blanshard, once a Militant leader, joined the La Guardia administration. In California, Upton Sinclair became the Democratic candidate for governor. Labor leaders with Socialist affiliations, like David Dubinsky and Sidney Hillman, were now the cheerful beneficiaries of the NRA, while the Socialist party officially denounced it as a step toward fascism. Al Smith was claiming that the New Deal had enacted, not the Democratic, but the Socialist platform of the previous election.

Even if the Socialist party had not achieved impotence on its own, even if it were internally vigorous and united, it still would have found itself hopelessly squeezed on the political stage, with little room for maneuver between the reformism of the New Deal and the revolutionism of the Communists. In 1928 the wife of the Socialist candidate for governor of New York, on meeting the Democratic candidate, told her husband: "Roosevelt is the most formidable opponent that the Socialist Party will ever have in the United States. He will charm your working class away from you." Many years later Norman Thomas confirmed the prediction: "What cut the ground out pretty completely from under us . . . was Roosevelt in a word. You don't need anything more." [8]

12. Growth of a Conspiracy

FOR MANY of those adrift in Marxism, Socialism was not enough. Norman Thomas gave off an atmosphere too reminiscent of the settlement house, the pulpit, and the college bull session. It was all too polite, tolerant, middle class; in a word, too *liberal*. Why stop at Socialism? To some, every factor which created the broad susceptibility to Marxism — the deepening depression, the exhaustion of laissez-faire, the rise of fascism — led to Communism as the irresistible conclusion. "I tell you," said Lincoln Steffens, the old muckraker, "nobody in the world proposes anything basic and real, except the Communists"; only the Communists offered "a scientific cure for all our troubles."

The Socialist party had too much conscience and too little discipline to be serious in a revolutionary age. Something more was surely needed — something drastic, something devouring, above all, something *hard*. A poem uncovered in 1934 by a FERA investigator in Ohio expressed the new passion. Written by an unemployed youth, it cried for a "radiant leader" to crush the enemies of the poor:

> We care not if Thy flag be white or red,
> Come, ruthless Savior, messenger of God,
> Lenin or Christ, we follow Thy bright sword.

The image of the sword was central to the Communist appeal at a time when the olive branch seemed to open the way to oppression, fascism, and war. The world had deferred too long to bourgeois ideas of freedom and truth and right. "Get the notion of liberty out of your head," said Steffens. ". . . The Truth from now on is always dated; never absolute, never eternal. . . . We want liberty for us, but not for Hitler and Mussolini." "We would deny democratic rights to Fascists, to lynchers," said the Communist *New Masses*, "to all those who wish to use them as a means of winning mass support for reaction." Was not the goal worth the swift moment of violence? Aspirin, after all, was not a member of the Communist party. Bolshevism was surgery.

A Communist leader sketched out the future in 1933. "The economic crisis could be easily solved if we, the workers, took over the industries and government. We would open the warehouses and feed and clothe the hungry and naked. We then would once more start the wheels of industry moving. Everybody would be given a job including those who don't want to work. He who would not work would not eat. . . . Workers' families would be moved into the spacious apartments of the rich. . . . Hunger and cold would be unknown." And the Communists offered evidence to confound scoffers. "This is not a fantastic dream. Such a society is at this very moment being built in the Soviet Union." [1]

II

After 1933, the rise of Hitler gave the need for ruthless salvation international urgency. Marx had not anticipated fascism; but, when fascism came, it was quickly absorbed into the Marxist system as capitalism *in extremis*. If this analysis were correct, then only a faith which challenged capitalism could hope to master fascism. The impression spread — in spite of the facts of Communist collaboration with the Nazis in the assault on German democracy — that the Communists were alone in resisting the new barbarism inside Germany. And in the gathering European conflict, the Soviet Union stood out as the one apparently unconditional enemy of Hitler, the one reliable friend of peace.

It was the Soviet Union which at home and abroad validated the Communist mystique. The Russians, as Steffens said, had made the great turning. The workers and peasants had taken over. They had abolished the exploitation of man by man, had destroyed the causes of economic crisis, had eradicated the motives which drove nations to war. had established the classless society. Jane

Addams called it the greatest laboratory experiment in social science of all time. "Russia just now is a sort of heaven," Steffens wrote to Edward A. Filene in 1935, "where humans have got rid of the great primitive problems of food, clothing and a roof. And therefore of all the other mean problems that go with business for private profit. That leaves the Russians with minds for philosophy, art and science. Now civilization may begin." (When Filene demurred, Steffens told him, "There is no third way, but you always hoped for one, the impossible.")

In point of fact, the Soviet Union in the early thirties was much nearer a sort of hell. Millions of Russians had perished in the famine of 1932–33. Other millions were deported to forced labor in Siberia. The power of the NKVD was growing every day. Stalin was tightening the screws of a tyranny which eventually even his closest collaborators would repudiate. But the facts, when they filtered through to the West, were simply not accepted. Communist doctrine supplied the true believer a built-in means of discrediting all criticism. If capitalism was by definition corrupt, obviously the capitalist press would be full of lies. "The first thing to remember," said Granville Hicks, "is that it is not safe to believe all you read." And there were always the assurances of the returned travelers. "The Soviet Union is the only country I've ever been in, where I've felt completely at ease," said Paul Robeson, the actor and singer, in 1936. ". . . I don't see how one can come to any other conclusion than that the Soviet way is the only way." Foreign correspondents contributed to the illusion, minimizing the nightmare and portraying instead a country governed by stern but benevolent and far-seeing statesmen working selflessly to improve the lot of the people. The existence of limitations on freedom in Soviet Russia was conceded; but, as Granville Hicks suggested with an air of reasonableness, the majority had in certain ways more freedom than had ever been enjoyed by the masses of any land; "it is a pity, no doubt, that they cannot have the right to advocate the restoration of capitalism, even though they do not want it back. But they have other rights, rights that directly concern their daily lives, and these may be more important."

This idyllic version of the U.S.S.R. met the requirements of the bad conscience of the West. Obviously capitalism had failed; its end-products were depression, war, and fascism. Civilization could endure only by a transfusion of moral energy from some new faith, austere in its severity, uncompromising in its dedication. The decadent west had everything to learn from the U.S.S.R. — the arts of planning, the arts of racial equality, the arts of peace, the arts of culture. (Even the arts of film-making; in 1935 Cecil B. De Mille could write, "In the fifteen years since the Soviet cinema was instituted as a national medium of expression, it has grown to a point where it can now teach its teacher.")

The pro-Communist liberals, as Eugene Lyons suggested, were inventing a utopia. The old honorable hope of the co-operative commonwealth had somehow got mixed up with the Soviet dictatorship; and dream, as so often happens, proved stronger than reality. "One reads of expert city planners traveling over Siberia in a special train," an American city planner wrote with envy, "leaving the ground plans of new communities behind them as they go." This fantasy of benign social reconstruction overpowered everything else. To doubt was to speak for privilege against the world which promised to end exploitation. With perfect sincerity, magazines like the *New Republic* and the *Nation* week after week refuted "slanders" about the Soviet Union. They did this, not in the service of Communism, but of their old ideal of social betterment. "The facts of life do not penetrate to the sphere in which our beliefs are cherished," Proust once wrote; "as it was not they that engendered those beliefs, so they are powerless to destroy them; they can aim at them continual blows of contradiction and disproof without weakening them; and an avalanche of miseries and maladies coming, one after another, without interruption into the bosom of a family, will not make it lose faith in either the clemency of its God or the capacity of its physician." [2]

III

"Put one more S in the U.S.A." sang Langston Hughes, the Negro poet,

> To make it Soviet
> One more S in the U.S.A.
> Oh, we'll live to see it yet.

When the land belongs to the farmers
And the factories to the working men —
The U.S.A. when we take control
Will be U.S.S.A. then.

The Bolshevik was the man of the future; and the worker-hero of the Soviet Union became the model for his American counterpart. The American Communist organizers, impersonal and tough in their Russian-style leather jackets, who knew all, comprehended all, and always had the hard tenderness to sacrifice the lesser good to the greater, were already making their appearances in the proletarian novel and the proletarian play; even, perhaps, on a picket line or two. Steffens, perpetually romantic, described them as "thoughtful, rather silent men and women, terribly overworked but poised in their manifold activities, loyal, uncompromising, daring and very understanding."

Measured against the Bolshevik, with his infinite courage and his terrible calm, the American bourgeois could only feel a sense of his own unworthiness. When the Communists invited Steffens to join the party in 1934, he replied in terms of liberal self-abasement, "I think I am not to be trusted in the party or in the front ranks of the struggle. . . . We liberals must not have power, not ever; we must not be leaders, we must not be allowed to be parties in the leadership. . . . We, who have fitted successfully into the old culture, are to the very degree of our education and adjustment, — we are corrupted and unfit for, — the kingdom of heaven."

Liberals were soft; they were betrayed by foolish scruples. But Communists were hard; they preferred the deed to the word. "There comes a time [Steffens again] to close our open minds, shut up our talking, and go to it. Lest Hitler do things his way. That time is when we don't need good fellows and liberal compromisers who want to get together. The goal is in sight and we must be Bolsheviks and — do it." *Do it:* this was the irresistible Communist commandment. And it carried with it the unspoken implication of access to power to get things done. As Dwight Macdonald once observed, Communism allowed people to identify themselves with power without feeling guilt.

Nothing expressed this ambiguous imperative better in 1935 than

an explosive little play called *Waiting for Lefty*. It was written
by a Communist playwright, Clifford Odets, and presented by the
Group Theatre, a producing organization well within the Marxist
intellectual orbit, though backed (according to the fashion of the
day) by bourgeois angels like John Hay Whitney.

Waiting for Lefty opened on a bare stage. A fat man, well
fed and confident, the archetype of a labor boss, seeks to dissuade
a group of workers from a strike. "We workers got a good man
behind us now," he urges. "He's top man of the country — looking
out for our interests — the man in the White House is the one
I'm referrin' to." A derisive voice interrupts him from the
audience. The fat man shouts back: "Stand up and show yourself, you damn red!" He adds confidingly, "Give those birds
a chance and they'll have your sisters and wives in whorehouses,
like they done in Russia."

The crowd, unsatisfied, begins to call for Lefty, the chairman
of the workers' committee. But Lefty is not there; and, as the
workers wait for Lefty, other members of the committee tell their
stories. In a series of flashbacks, each re-enacts the moment of
economic desperation which brought him to this platform. Then
back to the strike meeting: the fat man again denounces those
who want to strike as reds. "If we're reds because we wanna
strike," one replies, "then we take over their salute too!", and out
shoots the clenched fist. As excitement mounts, speakers plead for
the strike. "Don't wait for Lefty!" one says. "He might never
come. Every minute ———." Then a man running down the center
aisle from the back of the auditorium on to the stage, interrupts
him. "Boys, they just found Lefty!" he cries. ". . . Behind the
car barns with a bullet in his head!" And the audience, swept
away night after night by the brilliance of the staging and the
drama of the denouement, would join the cast in the final thundering affirmation of proletarian power:

> AGATE *crying:* When we die they'll know what we did to
> make a new world! Christ, cut us up to little
> pieces. We'll die for what is right! put fruit
> trees where our ashes are!
>   To audience: Well, what's the answer?
> ALL: STRIKE!

AGATE: LOUDER!
ALL: STRIKE!
AGATE and OTHERS on stage: AGAIN!
ALL: STRIKE, STRIKE, STRIKE!!! [3]

IV

In the confusion and anxiety, many were tempted by certitude
and sacrifice — none more so perhaps than some of the young,
flung helplessly into the world they never made, a world described
by Whittaker Chambers as "wracked by global wars and social
struggles." The *American Magazine*, carried in 1935 an article
by a young man entitled "Almost a Red." It was written in the
spirit of breathless enthusiasm in which the *American* a few years
earlier would have recorded other ambitions ("Almost a Bank
President"). "Since I came to New York," the author said, "I
have seen continuous, militant, idealistic activity by only one
political organization — the Communist Party." With "something
like envy," he watched young men and women on soapboxes in
Columbus Circle and Union Square, their eyes aflame, exciting
crowds with the vision of a new world. He saw the police break
up the meetings and send the young Communists flying, with
bloody noses and bruised bodies; "and back they came the
next day, crying bravely for a new world. That's what got under
my hide. It was thrilling. Here was an opportunity for action,
service, sacrifice. . . . These youngsters had fortitude, courage,
idealism — all the virtues that are young America's. Frankly, I
was stirred."

No doubt, the writer continued, Communism was "a philosophy
for the defeated, the thwarted, and the baffled. But do not these
words describe thousands of young Americans today? They describe me politically." Like the others, he wanted an organization
that would define the freedom for which the nation stood; he
wanted to build an America that would be beautiful, tolerant,
and just. The Communist party "appealed to me because it offered
me an immediate opportunity to participate actively and adven-
turously in the cause of idealistic government." In the end he
could not bring himself to join a party sponsored by a foreign
nation to overthrow his own government. "But even though I

rejected it, I still believe that it is the only daring, militant, dramatic, and appealing political movement in America today. I say that with shame for my country."

The author of the *American* article was unusually intelligent in balking at — or even in perceiving — the fact of foreign control. Others did not look beyond the façade of Communist promises. "The future looked black for my generation just emerging from school," said Lee Pressman. "At the same time, the growing specter of Nazism presented to my mind an equally grave threat. In my desire to see the destruction of Hitlerism and an improvement in economic conditions here at home, I joined a Communist group." "The free enterprise system in 1932–33 seemed on its last legs," said Nathaniel Weyl. "Faith in it, particularly among students, was practically zero. . . . The conclusion I came to, very slowly and very reluctantly, was that fascism could be beaten and destroyed only by a disciplined organization which would not shrink before violence." "Only the Communists," wrote John Gates, "were able to infuse youth with idealism, missionary zeal and a crusading spirit." Often interior anxieties moved in counterpoint with the mixed-up world outside. Chambers noted that Alger Hiss, like himself, had come from a proud but impoverished middle-class family, shadowed by insanity and suicide; "like me, I believe he saw in the decline of his family the image of a society in decline." For them all, the party, the embodiment of history, offered intellectual understanding and emotional surcease. Above all, it meant a chance to change the world.

It is dangerous to exaggerate. Murray Kempton's estimate, adding the young Communists and Socialists and Trotskyites together, is that at no time did all the young Marxists total more than 15,000 — about three-tenths of one per cent of the student community. And, in joining the Communist party, most of them did not feel they were choosing between America and Russia; one could look with hope on the Soviet experiment, they believed, without being the less loyal to their native land. Nor did most feel they were choosing between freedom and totalitarianism; for they supposed they were clasping hands with the only power in the world unconditionally opposed to the totalitarianism of fascism. Nor did most even feel they were choosing between democracy and dictatorship, for they considered they were challenging a class dictatorship in the name of a classless paradise, "a sort of heaven."

They saw themselves primarily as friends of mankind. Granville Hicks, fired from the faculty of Rensselaer Polytechnic Institute during the red hunt of 1935, asked his eight-year-old daughter: "Do you know why?" She answered, "Because you're a Communist." Hicks pressed on: "What is a Communist?" Tearfully she answered, "He wants all the poor people to be helped." Hicks said, "Are you glad I'm a Communist?" And still crying over the uncertainties ahead, the little girl said, "Yes." "By insisting on acting as Communists must," wrote Whittaker Chambers in retrospect, "we found ourselves unwittingly acting as Christians should. I submit that that cuts to the heart of one aspect of the Communist appeal." 4

v

It was a touching ideal. Nothing was more dismal than the gap between the individual hope and the organizational reality. For all the illusions of its supporters, the American Communist party was a pliant instrument of Soviet policy. As its general secretary, Earl Browder, told the McCormack-Dickstein Committee in 1934, the CPUSA was "a section of the Communist International," which he described as "a world party." The policy of the American party followed that of the Comintern because of the happy fact, as Browder blandly observed, "that the leadership of the party in the United States was in agreement with the action that was taken" in Moscow.

International Communist policy was currently in its third period. The Sixth World Congress of the Comintern in 1928 had laid down a policy of revolutionary militancy — no compromise with a decaying social order. Capitalism led inevitably to fascism, and all who collaborated with bourgeois democracy — especially Social Democrats and trade unionists — were "social-fascists." There was only one way to abolish the capitalist state, and that was to smash it by force. The job of Communists was everywhere to intensify the revolutionary struggle.

The American leadership conscientiously applied this drastic line to the American situation. In *Toward Soviet America* in 1932, William Z. Foster explained with grim satisfaction how the Communist revolution would overthrow the capitalist order, abolish the party system, and set up the United Soviet States of

America. Foster was the party's major link with traditional American radicalism and had been its presidential candidate in 1932. But a heart attack in the midst of the 1932 campaign disabled him; he did not make a public speech again until 1935. In any event, Earl Browder had been the effective party leader since the Comintern intervened to reorganize the American leadership in 1929. A native-born American whose ancestors had come over well before what the Communists liked to call the First American Revolution, Browder had the drab and harassed appearance of a small-town bookkeeper from Kansas. This, indeed, was exactly what, by profession, he was. But his father had been a Populist and Socialist; and young Browder grew up in the Socialist movement, serving a term in Leavenworth because of his opposition to the First World War. Afterward, he joined up full-time with the Communists. A series of overseas assignments brought him to favorable attention in Moscow and eventually gained him the party leadership.

Faithful to the directives of the Sixth Congress, the American Communist party waged bitter warfare against the New Deal. "Roosevelt's program," said Browder in 1934, "is the same as that of finance capital the world over. It is a program of hunger, fascization and imperialist war. . . . In political essence and direction it is the same as Hitler's program." "Roosevelt and his New Deal," he went on, "represent the Wall Street bankers and big corporations — finance capital — just the same as Hoover before him, but [are] carrying out even fiercer attacks against the living standards of the masses." The *Daily Worker* was even more violent. "Roosevelt, himself a rich cotton planter . . . personally is interested in making money out of the destruction of cotton. . . . This is the 'New Deal' in all its stark nakedness. Every move, every action of the Roosevelt regime strengthens the powerful lever of the exploiters crushing the masses to the ground." This in 1933; and in 1934: "Is not this trickery the hallmark of this Wall Street tool, this President who always stabs in the back while he embraces? How unctuous is his empty solicitude for the ragged, hungry children . . . with the ruthlessness of a devoted Wall Street lackey spending billions for war and profits, and trampling on the faces of the poor." And in 1935: "The New Deal is striving toward fascism and war in order to hold the workers in industrial slavery."

No New Deal measure found favor with the Communists. NRA? "The claws of the Blue Eagle are the grasping hands of the parasite rich." Section 7a? "New chains for labor." The Wagner labor-relations bill? It would take away "the last remaining rights of labor." Agricultural policy? "The Roosevelt program has attempted to plough under the farmer along with the crop. . . . The Federal Government has established what is in effect a state of serfdom." The work-relief program of 1935? "Positively vicious . . . it will mean a country-wide pauperism hitherto known only in the most backward Southern states. No words are strong enough to condemn this piece of pre-Victorian poor-law legislation." The Works Progress Administration? "The WPA is doing more to destroy the American standard of living than any group of reactionary industrialists in the country." The social security program? "Designed . . . to provide security for the rich who dominate the country." On every side, the party called for "the increasing fight against the unmasked dictatorship of capital represented by Roosevelt." [5]

VI

If the Communists hated the New Deal in this period, the New Dealers could hardly have cared less. Absorbed in the end-less day-to-day task of keeping the battered economy afloat, they had not time nor taste for apocalyptic visions. Concerned with events in the United States, they had only the most academic interest in developments in Utopia. In July 1933 Raymond Robins, the veteran Bull Mooser who had striven so valiantly for Soviet recognition in 1918, called his old friend Harold Ickes. "He has just returned from Russia and wants an opportunity to tell me all about it," Ickes noted in his diary. "God knows when I am going to get time to listen to a long recital on Russia." Returning from a European trip in August 1934, Harry Hopkins similarly dismissed the European experiments: "It is clear that we have to do this in an American way. . . . Instead of copying foreign schemes we will have to devise our own."

The New Dealers, after all, believed in capitalism. They wanted to reform the system, not to destroy it. Their social faith was in private ownership tempered by government control. As Ickes put it in 1934, America could achieve a decent living for all its citizens;

"what is more, we can attain it completely, I believe, under the Constitution and under the capitalistic system." "Although the profit system, as it has worked recently, seems to have worked poorly." said Jerome Frank in December 1933, "most Americans believe that, properly controlled, it can work well." (Frank put it more satirically one day when Stuart Chase came to lunch at the Department of Agriculture. "We socialists are trying to save capitalism," he said, "and the damned capitalists won't let us.") Hopkins said simply, "I am committed to the capitalistic system." Raymond Moley could write in the fall of 1934, "This Administration is as far from socialism or communism as any group ever assembled in a national government."

As the Communists rejected the middle way which was the New Deal's faith, so they rejected the experimentalism which was the New Deal's method. Browder condemned pragmatism as the philosophy of "the bourgeoisie in ascendancy." Now that capitalism was in crisis, pragmatism was in crisis too; it "has failed its class creators in the crucial moment. It is unable to give capitalism any answer to the question, What way out?" And its effect in confusing the working class, Browder complained, was "very poisonous." In place of pragmatism, the Communists insisted on the dogmatism of dialectical materialism. All this the New Dealers found philosophically absurd. "Let no man," wrote Archibald MacLeish, "miss the point of Mr. Roosevelt's hold upon the minds of the citizens of this republic." Roosevelt fired the world's imagination because mankind wanted to break out of the cage of dogma; people were sick of both the great bankers and the great revolutionaries, each resting their case on the idea of immutable ideology. "It is only to the free, inventive gestures of the human soul that men wholly and believingly respond." "It is just possible," said Adolf Berle in an acid review of Lewis Corey's *Decline of American Capitalism*, "that all of the social inventiveness of the world was not exploded between the two poles of Adam Smith and Karl Marx." [6]

VII

And Communist dogmatism was more than absurd. It was evil in the repression and persecution to which it led. "Its leaders," said MacLeish, "the writers and journalists who shape its thought, are for the most part intellectual terrorists." MacLeish derided the dream of "that far, far distant, classless society which Karl Marx permitted his congregations to glimpse over the million heads of many sacrificed and immolated generations — that classless society which retreats as rapidly as communism with *its* privileged class advances." "One hears from time to time," wrote Felix Frankfurter, "much shallow talk about the elimination of politics, as though politics — the free exchange of opinion regarding the best policy for the life of a society — were not the essence of a free and vigorous people. . . . We have been nauseated by 'purges' both in Berlin and in Moscow." "Like all civil liberties people," said Upton Sinclair, "I encounter difficulties in defending the rights of Communists who themselves repudiate freedom of speech, press and assemblage, and do everything they can to deprive others of those rights."

The essence of Communism was revolution; the essence of the New Deal was evolution; and the two faiths could hardly have been more distinct. The first, MacLeish noted in a remarkable article in 1934, was based on hatred, the second, on hope, and the gulf was impassable. The revolutionary movement was "a movement conceived, delivered, and nurtured in negatives. . . . Its one convincing aim is the destruction of the existing order. Its one vital dream is the establishment of a repressive control." Its portrait of the future was cruel and sterile. To replace Samuel Insull by that which would make Insull's return impossible would be to grant Insull the greatest privilege one generation could grant another — the kingly privilege of fixing the succession to the throne. "If only an iron tombstone will keep Mr. Insull from rising then it is Mr. Insull who has designed the iron tombstone." The whole question, as MacLeish saw it, came down to this: "shall we in America be driven by our hatred of the existing system or drawn by our hopes for the new?"

The New Deal commitment was to gradualness. Mary van Kleeck, a sympathizer with the far left, had advanced a condescending Marxist critique of the gradualist ideal in an address on "Illusions Regarding Government" before the National Conference of Social Work. Piecemeal change, she said, could do nothing; the only hope was to change the system. Her audience consisted of social workers immersed in the everyday miseries of depression, and New Dealers present found their response disturbing. "Never in a long experience of conferences," said one spectator, "has this observer witnessed such a prolonged ovation." David Cushman Coyle was quickly summoned to reply; and he came up with a powerful piece for the *Survey* entitled "Illusions Regarding Revolution." The debate well defined the differences between the Marxist and New Deal approaches. "Violent revolution," Coyle wrote, "like all forms of violence, with its prospect of emotional release and its illusion of easy victory, is a tempting prospect for those who are weary of the long struggle against inertia and stupidity. But after the first elation of bloodshed, the long struggle settles down again with new wrongs, new intolerance of reason, new horrors." Violence, he suggested, aggravated every problem of social change. For that reason Americans should muster all their intelligence without forcing a trial by blood.

There was value, too, Coyle added, in recognizing the limitations of human wisdom. Some disagreeable functions, like death and dislocation, were best left, so far as possible, unplanned by human agency. Power did not insure infallibility. "Being the Lord God Jehovah is no bed of roses. The bankers had their try at it and wrecked the country." He warned against the utopianism which really masked an escape from responsibility.

> If you can believe that nothing is happening now and that the real struggle is still in the future, then you can draw aside and retreat into the dream world where Communism makes faces at the wicked capitalist. There you may have the satisfaction of shrewd blows given and received in argument, and of having all manner of evil said against you falsely.
>
> But all these are shadows. In the real battle the danger is not that people will call us bad names and tell lies about us but that we may go into battle and, through our own weakness or through lack of your support, or through the mistakes of our own friends, we may fail our country in time of storm and may be responsible for suffering and evil to come. . . .
>
> The Communist state is not concerned with anything that is happening in the United States. . . .
>
> We had better win this fight now while we have a chance.

For such reasons, the leading New Dealers abominated Communism. "I abhor the bitterness and violence," said Henry Wallace, "which characterize the Communist approach." "The true American," said Ickes, "will not tolerate a dictatorship either of the right or of the left. Facism and Communism are equally abhorrent to us. Both are tyrannies. Both should be resisted with all our strength." Show me a Communist, Ickes added, "and I will show you a man who, equally with the Fascist, has no respect for the rights of the individual; who would destroy for the sake of destroying." "The principles and methods of the Communist party," said Frances Perkins, "appear to me to be destructive and disintegrating, and their economic and political views to be unsound or untrue. Communism, in my opinion, has no place in American life." 7

VIII

While disliking Communism, the New Dealers could not bring themselves to take it very seriously. It would become dangerous, they thought, only if economic conditions grew much worse. In 1934 Raymond Moley laid out a five-point program to combat Communism:

1. Avoid not only injustice, but the appearance of injustice. The Mooney case has been a powerful aid to Communism.
2. Avoid violence. . . . Communists grow on street violence.
3. Improve living conditions, notably housing; wipe out slums, open up play spaces.
4. Maintain the process of democracy in a healthy condition, no matter how much power the government assumes. . . .
5. Let every government official and every government agency learn to make clear to the public what he is doing and why he is doing it. The germ of Communism flourishes in dark corners of misunderstanding.

"Communism is no menace," Moley concluded. ". . . Communism has failed to grow in this country because the organism it is seeking to attack is strong and vigorous. So long as this healthy condition continues we should save our fears for something else."

Most New Dealers agreed with Moley. The Communists, they

supposed, were a collection of bores and screwballs. They were to be regarded with contempt ("nowhere in our time," wrote MacLeish, "is it possible to discover a more devious self-contradiction and defeat than among the intellectuals of the Left") but not with alarm — a nuisance, not a threat. This group of squabbling malcontents just did not seem a serious problem for a great nation. And nothing that the Federal Bureau of Investigation or other intelligence agencies dug up was concrete or convincing enough to alter this view.

Moreover, the Americans who shouted that Communism was a menace had so long been proved so fanciful in their definition both of "menace" and of "Communism" that it was difficult to take them seriously. The New Dealers who had seen every piece of reform legislation in their time denounced as "socialistic" or "communistic" remained unmoved when they heard the same old cries from the same old criers. William Randolph Hearst, Hamilton Fish, and the National Civic Federation had called wolf too often. As Henry Wallace once put it, "If Jefferson were living today, he would be called a Bolshevik by some of our red baiters." Red-baiting was discounted as the conditioned reflex of those opposed to social change.

There was, too, the impression that red-baiting was becoming a highly profitable racket. "The Red menace sparkles on every side," wrote John T. Flynn in an article thoughtfully (from the viewpoint of his subsequent career) entitled "To Get Rich Scare the Rich." ". . . This is the natural atmosphere for the rich man's terrors. Therefore the first thing to do is to play upon those terrors. Scare him some more. Then invent some racket for protecting him from those perils." And some saw a deeper purpose in the assault on Communism — an attempt to distract people's attentions from the real problems. "You know as well as I know that the contest today in this country is not between communism and democracy," said Sidney Hillman, who had long warred with the Communists in his own union. ". . . The danger we face is in the kind of industrial control, that is in all but the form Fascism."

In addition, some certainly felt a bond of sympathy, vague but real, with Communism. The Communists, after all, were underdogs; they were supposedly working for the common man; in the greedy business leader, Communists and New Dealers shared an

enemy. Nor was the Russian hope yet blighted for this generation. Many American liberals agreed with Keynes's wish that the
Soviet Union would overcome its brutality and dogmatism.

How much rather, even after allowing for everything, if I were
a Russian, would I contribute my quota of activity to Soviet
Russia than to Tsarist Russia! I could not subscribe to the
new official faith any more than to the old. I should detest
the actions of the new tyrants not less than those of the old.
But I should feel that my eyes were turned towards, and no
longer away from, the possibilities of things; that out of the
cruelty and stupidity of Old Russia nothing could ever emerge,
but that beneath the cruelty and stupidity of New Russia some
speck of the ideal may lie hid.

Persuaded of the impotence of the Communist movement, believing in free speech and free assembly as social safety valves,
weary of routine invocations of the Red menace, confronted with
a thousand immediate crises at home, the New Dealers felt they
had far more important things to do than to worry about the
American Communist party. They were quite right. Yet at the
same time they underestimated their adversary. They failed to
recognize how deadly serious the Communists were.[8]

IX

At the beginning of 1931, according to Communist figures, the
membership of the party was a little over 8,000. By 1933 it had
doubled, and was well on its way to doubling again. While party
leaders professed to regard the growth as gratifying, the fact that
after five years of depression, with millions of people unemployed,
the Communist party could show a membership of but slightly
more than 30,000 was not impressive. Moreover, as Browder told
the Communist convention in 1934, the "most serious problem of
the party" was "fluctuation in membership." Most members had
been in for less than two years, and two out of every three tended
to fade away after a short time.

An important reason for the Communists' relative failure was
the bleakness of the party line. The attacks on the New Deal,
organized labor, the Socialists, and the rest appealed only to a

minute fraction of sectarians. By preaching revolution at a time of vast enthusiasm for reform, the Communists succeeded only in isolating themselves. They were uneasily aware of their plight. Fortunately the Sixth World Congress had left them one way to break out of their isolation — the tactic of the "united front from below."

Where the "united front from above," in the Communist vocabulary, meant negotiations with leaders of other movements in order to secure common action on a given policy, the "united front from below" supposed that leaders of other movements were hopelessly corrupt. It meant therefore an appeal by the Communists to the rank-and-file of a movement over the heads of their leaders. Browder denounced Norman Thomas and those like him as "left social-fascists," "the most dangerous enemies of the workers' struggles today." "Unity behind these gentlemen," he said, "means a united surrender to the capitalist attacks." The workers needed a different kind of unity. "We need a united fighting front of the workers against the capitalists and all their agents. But that means that unity must be built up, not *with* these leaders, but *against* them."

The "united front from below" provided the Communists the means of making contact with the masses from which their revolutionary militancy had so effectively separated them. Their method was to invent or penetrate organizations dedicated to a plausible cause and to use agreement on this cause as a means of implicating people in a Communist-dominated movement. Between 1933 and 1935 the Communists concentrated particularly on pushing such organizations in the field of peace, youth, and culture. By February 1935 Browder could boast before a congressional committee (with figures subject to the usual Communist discount), "If you want a gage on the mass following of the Communist Party, a better gage [than party membership] would be the membership of organizations which endorse the various proposals of the party, which number about 600,000."

Probably the most successful of the Communist fronts was the American League against War and Fascism. This was the American offshoot of the World Congress Against War, a movement organized by the Comintern's European specialist in fronts, Willi Muenzenberg, as part of the Comintern's effort to defend the

Soviet Union against the threat of war. A Soviet agent named Urevich, posing as a German banker, started the American group in 1932. By 1933 it had become an aggressive outfit, seeking to mobilize all Americans devoted to the cause of peace — then, as subsequently, an appealing objective. Its first chairman was Dr. J. B. Matthews, a garrulous and unstable figure, who in time proved unreliable and was replaced by a professor of Christian ethics at the Union Theological Seminary, Dr. Harry F. Ward. But no one could doubt who ran the show. As Browder himself said in 1934, "In the center, as the conscious moving and directive force of the united front in all its phases, stands the Communist Party. Our position in this respect is clear and unchallenged." And the fine print of the League's platform, with the stock denunciations of the NRA, the CCC, and so on as proofs of America's warlike purposes, and the stock endorsements of the Soviet Union, was plainly Stalinist in its inspiration.

Next to peace, youth was the main object of Communist solicitude. The American Youth Congress of 1934 was non-Communist in its origin; but a coalition of youthful Communists and Socialists took the group over at its first convention and drove out the original sponsors. Sponsored by Theodore Draper of the National Student League, a Communist group, Gilbert Green of the Young Communist League, and Gus Tyler of the Young People's Socialist League, the Congress attacked the CCC ("identical to the steps taken by Fascist Germany, Poland and Italy to militarize the young generation"), the NRA, the subsistence homestead program, and other aspects of the New Deal, and declared that the Soviet Union offered "the only constructive proposals toward peace." The Communist youth next tried to inveigle the Socialists into a common organization. Through 1934 the Socialists, led by Joseph P. Lash of the Student League for Industrial Democracy, resisted the Communist embrace. But they co-operated on specific issues. In April 1935, on the eighteenth anniversary of American entrance into the First World War, student groups under Communist leadership organized a nation-wide "strike" against war. It was reported that 175,000 students had left their classrooms; many of them repeated the Oxford pledge not to support the government in any war it might conduct.

In the cultural field, the Communists had set up the John Reed

Clubs as a meeting place for writers and artists. In the fall of 1934 Alexander Trachtenberg, a party functionary, proposed that the club call a Writers' Congress to "strike a blow at the growing fascist enemy, the rapidly developing White Guard and fascist criticism, and the Roosevelt-fostered national chauvinist art" and to "organize American revolutionary culture against the imperialist war plans." While it would be hard to imagine a serious writer who would be impressed by such explosions of jargon, the American Writers' Congress of April 1935 nonetheless produced its roster of innocents.

By such means, the Communist party acquired an influence among many who could not bring themselves to accept the Communist program. These people recoiled from Communist extremism. Yet they were persuaded that this extremism represented an excess, not of corruption, but of zeal. Some secretly envied the superior purity of the Communist commitment. Many had too much inner uncertainty — even guilt — of their own to be certain that the extremists were not right. They consequently saw no reason why they could not work with Communists for specific objectives. And they showed an "enlightened" interest in Communist ideas and Communist literature. Between 1929 and 1934, according to the *New Masses*, the annual distribution of publications by the party house, International Publishers, increased from 50,000 to 600,000. In two months 80,000 copies of Stalin's *Foundations of Leninism* were distributed.

The success, such as it was, of the front organizations gave the Communist leaders a cheap sense of influence and no doubt advanced their reputations with the home office in Moscow. Moreover, the fronts provided a recruiting ground for party membership, and they helped build a broad sympathy for Communist activities. Yet, on the whole, the Communist leaders exaggerated the importance of the fronts. For most of the non-Communists involved, participation in them was a meaningless experience; for some it was in retrospect only comic. Browder's figure of 600,000 meant, if it meant anything, that several hundred thousand Americans cared so much about joining organizations for peace or youth or culture that they did not scrutinize the credentials of the organizers. It did not mean that 600,000 Americans were under Communist discipline. Americans had always been a nation of joiners. Good-hearted liberals tolerated the Communists, as high-minded Romans might have tolerated the early Christians. And they themselves were tolerated by the Communists, as the early Christians were tolerated by the lions.[9]

X

The fronts — the exercises of boring-from-within and uniting-from-below — constituted only the first line of covert Communist activity. There remained, buried deep, unknown even to many members, the party's underground section. And this had layers of its own — a layer dedicated to infiltration into key capitalist institutions; an even deeper layer dedicated to espionage.

Every government in the world, of course, liberal or conservative, democratic or fascist, constituted a target for Communist penetration. The United States government probably rated low in the order of priorities. There are suggestions of Communist activity in Washington as early as the Coolidge administration; and Harold Ware, the most successful underground operator in the federal government, held his only public job under Hoover. All this seems, however, to have been the result of accident, not of plan. When new people swarmed to Washington to work in the emergency agencies in 1933, some among them were Communists or Communist sympathizers. Again, so far as existing evidence shows, this was by accident. A planned infiltration would have placed Communists in far more strategic positions.

Still, the presence of Communists in Washington gave the party an opportunity to develop covert activities in the federal government. An underground apparatus already existed, evidently concentrating on industrial and military rather than governmental penetration. Its chief seems to have been a mysterious figure named J. Peters, who worked out of New York. He now decided to extend his organization to Washington. He had, of course, to take his Communists where he found them, which is why Communist cells sprang up in such unlikely (and, from the Communist viewpoint, not very useful) places as the Agricultural Adjustment Administration. In setting up party units, Peters followed the standard underground practice of establishing parallel groups, kept in careful ignorance of the activities and even of the existence of the others. Special agents (one was Whittaker Chambers) maintained liaison with party headquarters in New York. By 1935 there were perhaps half a dozen groups through the government, with a total of seventy-five or eighty members and associates.

For most of the participants, these were essentially study groups, where earnest people gathered together to receive Marxist-Leninist instruction. They thought that capitalism was dying and that a socialist revolution was inevitable. They believed, as one of them, Nathaniel Weyl, later put it, that "when the Communists took control in America, there would be need for men who knew government, politics, something about the management of public affairs. They would be part of this group of men with know-how." But, for most of them it was all rather abstract and romantic. Perhaps on a few issues, here and there, they could shove a government decision in the Communist direction; but they did not often confront decisions on which the Communist line made much difference. They kept their participation secret because knowledge of their activities would ruin their careers. They were passive rather than active revolutionaries, laying side-bets on a Communist revolution while working hard at immediate tasks in a reform government. As with the Communist party elsewhere, the rate of turnover was considerable.

The Ware group in AAA remained probably the most important — or, at least, it is the one we know most about. Its activities illustrated compactly the double purpose of the cells. If, for most of their members, these furtive meetings were seminars in Marxism, they were, for a few, something more sinister: they were the means by which Soviet intelligence picked, tested, and recruited its espionage agents. Not many even of the underground Communists knew about the Soviet espionage effort. Nathaniel Weyl, a member of the Ware group, later said, "I wasn't aware of it until I read about the Canadian spy ring in 1945. . . . I think most Communists at the time I am speaking of didn't know about espionage." Yet, according to Whittaker Chambers, eight other members of the Ware group sooner or later worked with a Soviet espionage apparatus.

XI

Involvement in espionage meant a break with regular party activities, even for secret party members. People passed, in Chamber's distinction, from the American Communist underground to the Soviet underground. Attempting to influence government policies in a Communist direction was one thing; spying on that government was another; and the two missions had to be kept sharply distinct. The stereotype so popular in the early 1950's of government officials who argued for Communist policies by day while they microfilmed documents by night ran counter to the Soviet theory of espionage. As Alexander Foote, who ran the Soviet spy ring in Switzerland during the Second World War, has written, "It is an elementary rule that Soviet agents should not appear to be Soviet sympathizers." If he heard government officials showing sympathy for Communism, he concluded right away "that they were *not* part of a Soviet spy network." A person recruited for espionage was told that "he ought not to join the party or express sympathy with it or in any other way make himself conspicuous."

Thus Whittaker Chambers had been known as a Communist and as an editor of the *New Masses* when he was chosen for underground work. His first boss in the underground told him, "In our work, you will never go near the *New Masses*. You will never have anything to do with party people again." Henry Julian Wadleigh, who had worked for Hoover's Federal Farm Board and then for the Department of Agriculture, offered his services to the Communists in 1935, seeking an opportunity "to do something practical in checking the great menace of fascism in the world." His offer was accepted, and he served as a Soviet spy for four years. But Chambers, who was his underground contact, warned him not to express pro-Communist views. "I think you would do well," Chambers once said to him, "to let it be thought around the State Department that your views are shifting gradually to the right." Wadleigh was never even a member of the party.

The espionage operations were complicated by quarrels between the Soviet intelligence agencies. Thus Chambers worked (though for a long time he did not know it) for the Fourth Section of the Soviet Military Intelligence (GRU). But the Foreign Department of the NKVD — the Soviet state police — also ran its networks in the United States. Each Russian agency had its representatives in this country — men like Valentin Markin and Vasili Zubilin of the NKVD and Colonel Boris Bykov of the GRU.

The rivalry between the NKVD and the GRU even extended to the recruitment of American agents.

In 1935 Hede Massing, an NKVD operative, had been cultivating a young man in the State Department named Noel Field. Field, who came from a Quaker background, was an intense and idealistic figure, restless in his personal life, fascinated by Marxism, in passionate quest of some form of authority or certitude. Hede Massing recalls him standing one night at the top of the steps of the Lincoln Memorial, singing the Internationale in Russian. But, as Mrs. Massing sought to sign him up for the NKVD, she learned that one of his State Department colleagues was tapping him for another apparatus. Mrs. Massing insisted on meeting her competitor. So, if Mrs. Massing is to be believed, she was introduced to Alger Hiss one night at dinner at the Fields'. "I understand that you are trying to get Noel Field away from my organization into yours," she said. According to her report, Hiss smiled and said, "So you are this famous girl who is trying to get Noel Field away from me?" Field finally decided to work with the NKVD but declined to spy against his own country. Instead, he accepted a post with the League of Nations and moved to Geneva. Here he became an important Soviet agent, did a remarkable intelligence job for the Soviet Union against Germany in the Second World War, and was repaid by years of imprisonment in Communist jails.

Such men thought they were serving in a noble cause. They were not consciously seeking personal aggrandizement or material reward. "The desire for personal power was there psychologically," reflected Nathaniel Weyl, "but I wouldn't overstress it — if you are dealing with people like Alger Hiss, for instance, they could have had more power by staying away from Communism." No money changed hands; the Bokhara carpets which Chambers gave Hiss and Wadleigh as Christmas presents in 1936 "from the Soviet people" were accepted as symbols of solidarity (if given as guarantees of complicity). "When the Communist International apparently represented the only world force effectively resisting Nazi Germany and the other aggressor powers," Wadleigh wrote later, "I had offered my services to the Soviet underground in Washington as one small contribution to help stem the fascist tide." If caught, "I would have derived some moral support from the conviction that I was acting right." Espionage, said Chambers, appeared to the convinced Communist as a moral act, committed in the name of the future against a system which was historically bankrupt.

The spies thus began as idealists, dedicated to peace and justice. But, along the way, they became dedicated also to Communism. Their tragedy was that their dedication to party corrupted their dedication to principle. In the end, the party line threatened every decent instinct. The attitude toward Roosevelt of the mild and considerate Hiss, a practicing Quaker and a devoted bird-watcher, startled even Chambers — not because of Hiss's contempt for the President as a political leader, which Chambers, of course, shared, but because of the pleasure Hiss took (if Chambers is to be believed) in brutal references to Roosevelt's physical condition as a symbol of middle-class breakdown.

It was this contained fanaticism that made the years of espionage possible — the years of tedious reporting of meaningless facts, an endless monotony relieved only by an infinite risk. Nothing reported seemed very important in itself, and it is doubtful that the sum of the espionage of the thirties added up to very much. Chambers found the papers he received so boring that he stopped reading them. "I concluded that political espionage was a magnificent waste of time and effort . . . because the secrets of foreign offices are notoriously overrated." Yet, if the damage to the state was limited, the damage to the individuals involved would never end. Chambers's memories of underground Washington sum up the human sacrifices — Hiss, with his tired but "invariably gracious" smile, coming back from the State Department to find Chambers waiting for documents in his Georgetown house; Wadleigh, hatless, his hair bristling, standing alone in a nighttime street, peering nearsightedly to determine the source of approaching footsteps; George Silverman of the Treasury talking incessantly while racing his Ford car through swarming Washington traffic; Colonel Bykov, meeting Chambers furtively in the back of Brooklyn movie houses.[10]

XII

No legal bar kept Communists from working for the American government. The Department of Agriculture directive of this period — "A man in the employ of the Government has just as much right to be a member of the Communist Party as he has to be a member of the Democratic or Republican Party" — accurately registered the law; and Congress did not choose to change the law until 1940. But Communists themselves knew that knowledge of their affiliations would end their usefulness; so Communists working in Washington concealed their party membership. As Nathaniel Weyl later wrote, "There was nothing illegal about Government officials being Communists. Yet if it had been known, it would have wrecked their careers."

"It might be worthwhile," Henry Wallace wrote to Attorney General Cummings in 1934, "to keep tab on the source of the money of both the communists and the fascist brethren." In 1935 Roosevelt asked Frances Perkins about a Communist leader in California, "How does Sam Darcy get in and out of this country? I think he is not a citizen but a native of Russia? Also, how about Harry Bridges? Is he not another alien?" And again: "Will you talk with the Acting Attorney General in regard to these two cases and also in regard to the case of others against whom we can prove propaganda directed at the destruction of the Government?" In May 1934 Roosevelt had ordered the Federal Bureau of Investigation and the Secret Service to undertake a general intelligence investigation of fascist and Nazi groups. In August 1936 the President directed J. Edgar Hoover, the FBI chief, to broaden the investigation to include Communist groups.

Yet the Communist spies seem to have had little trouble eluding the counter-intelligence agencies. While the secret meetings were taking place, while documents were changing hands, while Russian intelligence agents gave orders in drugstores and cafeterias to their American operatives, neither the FBI nor G-2, the intelligence branch of the Army, nor the Office of Naval Intelligence developed enough evidence to cause the prosecution of a single case of espionage in the civilian side of government in Washington.

Something was known — mainly through Soviet bungling — of industrial and military espionage. One Soviet agent was caught in New York trying to pass phony $100 Federal Reserve notes and sentenced to fifteen years in prison. Another was picked up in Los Angeles because he left compromising documents in a suit sent out for dry cleaning. Others were arrested on passport charges. Where evidence existed, prosecution followed.

But there were no prosecutions in Washington, where Communist spies evidently emptied their pockets before sending suits to the cleaners. Nor was it that the "higher-ups," so prominent in the folklore of espionage prevalent in the early fifties, "protected" the spies. It was rather the astonishing fact that the FBI and G-2 and ONI just never had the evidence to warrant indictment. They kept zealous watch on avowed Communists or fellow-travelers or plain liberals, while the spies, secure in protective coloration, filled briefcases unmolested. The enforcement of the laws against espionage was the job of the counter-intelligence agencies, and they did it poorly. The American government knew no more spectacular failure than this in the decade of the thirties.

In the meantime, the Communist conspiracy hung on, an underground creature, pallid but vicious, negligible and even comic in many of its aspects, yet still a great potential challenge to American democracy.[11]

II

The Coming of the
Second New Deal

13. Ordeal by Indecision

1935 OPENED as a year of acute political turbulence. Squalls were making up in every quarter, while the skipper stalled and vacillated, now beating to windward, now turning and running before the blow. On the one side, Roosevelt faced the organized business community, its morale reviving, its purpose gaining clarity, its determination to halt the New Deal gathering strength each day. On the other side, he faced the tumult of mass opinion, so ardently stirred by the radicals and demagogues. Overhanging all was the threat of judicial action against New Deal laws and programs.

Under the combined pressures his position in Congress continued to deteriorate. His World Court message on January 16, 1935, was followed the next day by a message calling for a social-security program. By February the social-security bill seemed hopelessly bogged down in the House of Representatives. The work-relief bill was in trouble in the Senate. A bill for banking reform, emanating from the administration though without direct presidential endorsement, headed into immediate difficulties in committee. In March the President sent Congress a recommendation for the regulation of public-utility holding companies; this only deepened the resentments of the business community. Roosevelt, suddenly silent and irresolute, seemed to have lost his touch. The administration appeared to lack coherence both in policy and in strategy. The New Dealers were troubled and distraught. After all, who could prepare himself for the battle when the presidential trumpet gave so uncertain a sound? "The disintegration of President Roosevelt's prestige," as Charles A. Beard wrote in

April, "proceeded with staggering rapidity during February and early March." [1]

II

The President's uncertainty reflected the confusion of counsel among his advisors. The New Deal of 1933 had rested on a faith in centralized co-ordination — on the notion that modern technology had produced an integrated economy and that modern man must therefore produce an integrated polity. In the crisis of 1933, men from Tugwell on the left to Baruch on the right subordinated their differences to work together in that common faith. But partial recovery was breaking up the Hundred Days' coalition. By 1934, among those accepting the concept of a business-government partnership, the question was growing acute whether business or government was to be the senior partner.

The split between Moley and Tugwell was symptomatic. In the spring of 1934 Moley announced, "The New Deal is practically complete." A few weeks earlier, Tugwell had said, "This battle for a New Deal is not yet over; indeed, I suspect it has just begun." With Moley were ranged the advocates of business-government 'co-operation,' like Richberg and Johnson, the conservative Democrats on the Hill, and all who felt that the pressing need was to restore business 'confidence' and who wished, in the distinction of the day, to subordinate 'reform' to 'recovery.' With Tugwell stood most of the young lawyers and economists in the administration and the progressives in Congress, all sharing a mistrust of business and a conviction that the economic house must be swiftly set in order before the popular demand for change evaporated.

As for Roosevelt himself, he veered from one group to the other, according to mood and circumstance. He had staked his program in 1933 largely on the thesis that, as he had put it, business leaders could be relied on to operate for the general welfare and that "industry would not violate a great public trust." In this faith, he had appointed business leaders to posts of high responsibility. In February 1934, when he dismantled the Civil Works Administration, and again in the fall, when he had gone through the motions of a *rapprochement* with the bankers, he had tried to renew business support by moderating his reform policy.

Yet it seems probable that real hopes of business-government co-operation had faded pretty steadily in his mind throughout the year. In December 1934, when Secretary of Commerce Roper spoke of business's intention to co-operate, Roosevelt said only half mischievously, "Well, Dan, all I can say is that business will have only until January 3 to make up its mind whether it is going to cooperate or not."

Nevertheless, perhaps because he had no better ideas of his own, Roosevelt still seemed early in 1935 to be drifting back into a pro-business policy. By mid-February *Time* could cheerfully list the evidence of this new turn: the purge of liberals in AAA; Richberg's antilabor policy in NRA; the conservative social-security program; the opposition to prevailing wages on public-works projects. The liberal publisher of the *New York Post* declared, "I am very much worried about the President's trend towards the right. . . . Of late it seems to me that he has been shifting more and more towards big business." Later that month Tugwell and Ickes held what must have been a fairly typical conversation in New Deal circles. Tugwell said that the President was slipping, that big business had him stopped, and that the administration had done all that it was likely to do in the way of social advance. Ickes, according to Tugwell, seemed "discouraged and bitter." "F.D.R. will have to recoup somehow," Tugwell noted afterward in his diary," — but the way is far from clear." By April even the ebullient Thomas G. Corcoran was depressed. If things didn't improve, he told Ickes, he would have to reconcile himself to waiting for ten or twelve years for Bob La Follette to come along.

Bruce Bliven, visiting Washington for the *New Republic,* found the liberals "a sad lot, shivering in the wintry wind. . . . They do believe that the President has let them down badly. I do not think that anything he might do now could restore their confidence in him." Charles A. Beard interpreted the collapse of leadership in February and March as meaning that the President was "at the end of his resources" so far as domestic policy was concerned. Francis Brown summed up the predominant impression for the *New York Times.* The New Dealers, he reported, "have little faith left in either the President or his chief assistants. Sometimes they try to recall that faraway age when people worked day and night to inaugurate the New Deal, when the lights burned to all hours in the Commerce Building, when, if human endurance held out, it seemed certain that a new America could be created. Was it, they ask, only a bitter joke?" [2]

III

If external pressures assailed the New Deal from both right and left in early 1935, the President's lot was further complicated by this internal disagreement between those who wanted friendship with business at the expense of reform and those who wanted reform at the expense of friendship with business. Nor was this all: even those who agreed on the need for reform were divided by the old and acute differences between the heirs of the New Nationalism and the heirs of the New Freedom — between those who wanted to use government in the style of Theodore Roosevelt to dominate an organic economy and those who wanted to use government in the style of Woodrow Wilson to restore competitive enterprise. All these layers of disagreement made the formation of policy more difficult.

The heirs of the New Nationalism had dominated the First New Deal. As AAA had been their characteristic instrumentality in agriculture, so NRA had been their instrumentality in industry. AAA had worked well enough. But NRA was in increasing trouble. And NRA's troubles, in a sense, were blotting the planners' copybook. "NRA could have been administered," Tugwell later said, "so that a great collectivism might gradually have come out of it, so that all the enormous American energies might have been disciplined and channelled into one national effort to establish a secure basis for well-being." But it had not been so administered; and its failure threatened to discredit the whole organic approach.

In September 1934 Roosevelt had asked Tugwell to come to Hyde Park for the Labor Day weekend to go over the NRA problem. They chatted in Roosevelt's bedroom before church on Sunday morning, the President in an old sweater amidst a clutter of Sunday papers, fitting one cigarette after another into his long holder as he talked. His doubts were plain enough. Did not the NRA experience show that the nation was not yet ready to function as an integrated economy on the basis of national planning?

The trouble, Tugwell replied, was, not in the idea, but in the execution. Roosevelt reminded him that he himself had approved of Johnson as administrator. Yes, yes, this turned out to be wrong; but the fact that the experiment had gone badly this time did not prove that it would never succeed. Tugwell begged for an extension of NRA, suggesting that Johnson be replaced by a board. Roosevelt seemed to agree.

By now it was time for church. They set out down the road, driving in the big open car through September sunshine, Tugwell reflecting on their talk. As the car came up to the church door, Tugwell had a sudden perception that he had failed. Roosevelt might keep on with NRA for a while. But it would only be improvisation and expediency. "I was asking too much. It was not only NRA, it was the whole organic conception of the living nation, equipped with institutions for foresight, conjecture and balance. It was not yet time for it. . . . I knew that NRA was done for; and I hardly expected to see another attempt of the sort in my lifetime." [3]

IV

Roosevelt actually retained more of the vision than Tugwell suspected. And, in any case, all was not lost right away: there was still the NRA board, of course, and the attempt early in 1935 to reform and extend the experiment. And, if NRA should finally collapse, there remained the bare possibility that Roosevelt might move on to a more serious form of industrial planning. With this in mind, Tugwell and other Department of Agriculture economists began in 1934 to design a scheme of industrial control aimed at producing, not the co-ordinated scarcity of NRA, but co-ordinated economic expansion.

The key figure in this effort was the agricultural economist Mordecai Ezekiel. Though his name evoked scurrilous speculations about alien influences in the New Deal, Ezekiel, like his father, grandfather, and great-grandfather before him, had been born in Richmond, Virginia, and he had joined the government in the Harding administration. In economics, he was of the institutionalist school and much influenced by Veblen. As he analyzed the economic problem, the great need seemed to be for the balanced expansion of production and income. But under the present system, "we don't increase production and income up to our potentialities because our business concerns are not organized in such a way as to make it the direct job of businessmen, and to their interest, to increase production." It wasn't that businessmen would not like to produce more; it was, Ezekiel said, in an echo of Veblen, that the system condemned them "to think primarily in terms of making more money, not of making more goods."

Nor could the competition beloved by classical economics be relied on to stimulate production. The business structure of the 1930's differed from that contemplated by Adam Smith in 1776 as an airplane differed from a stagecoach. In the course of economic evolution, Ezekiel argued, practically all the conditions necessary to make competition serve as a means of maximizing production had disappeared. He restated the familiar institutionalist analysis: the rise of bigness, the dominance of administered prices, the unimportance of freely competing small units. If the price system had failed as an automatic governor of the economy, then something else was required.

The "something else" was a program for "industrial adjustment" or, as Ezekiel later called it, "industrial expansion." The first plan was submitted by Henry Wallace to the Executive Council in October 1934. It was subsequently revised and enlarged in various Department of Agriculture memoranda and in two books by Ezekiel — *$2500 a Year: From Scarcity to Abundance* in 1936 and *Jobs For All Through Industrial Expansion* in 1939. The essential idea behind the program was, as Ezekiel put it, "AAA in reverse." In order to expand production in industry, the government was to use the same techniques — especially the voluntary contract with the individual producer and the benefit payment — which had worked so well in curtailing production in agriculture. The strategic industries of the country, operating through bodies like NRA code authorities, would prepare tentative programs for expanding output and payroll in the year ahead. After an Industrial Expansion Administration had reconciled the various industry programs in a master plan, or "a national blueprint for abundance," each co-operating concern would be given advance orders for the planned production through contracts providing for public purchase of unsold surpluses. The surplus goods would be stockpiled in an "ever-normal warehouse," and appropriate modifications would be made in next year's programming. The plan as a whole would be financed by an industrial processing tax to provide a fund for benefit payments to co-operators. If it worked, it would force all industry to expand simultaneously and in balance, so that the market for one product would be provided by the increased output of the others.

The Ezekiel proposal struck the planning-minded wing of the liberals as the ideal rationalization of the whole NRA effort. As Tom Amlie put it, "The Industrial Expansion Act merely takes the instruments of public control which the New Deal has already sold to the American people to promote scarcity, and uses them to achieve abundance." Even Hugh Johnson conceded, "It is the Blue Eagle reincarnated with as many teeth as an alligator. I don't know whether it lies in the mouth of this writer to condemn it." The plan soon picked up a measure of support — not only Henry Wallace in the cabinet, but the Maverick-Amlie group in the House of Representatives and the *Common Sense* group in the liberal community.

Yet most liberals, discouraged by the NRA experience, regarded the idea with extreme wariness. It seemed as if Ezekiel had carried the agricultural analogy too far; the forecasting of demand for industrial products, for example, was surely quite a different thing from forecasting demand in agriculture. How could any government board hope to anticipate the shifts in requirement and fashion in a volatile and dynamic economy? More than this, while the distribution of benefit payments to farmers under AAA was relatively simple, the division of benefits among industrial claimants would only aggravate existing tensions between the employer, the union, and the consumer. "There are a lot of people in the country," Senator Wagner told Ezekiel, "who will want, not only a larger slice because the pie is larger, but also a larger proportion of the pie, no matter how large it is. That to my mind is the real problem." The industrial expansion plan never faced this problem head-on. Moreover, the proposed technique for expansion — the Industrial Expansion Authority and the national master plan — appeared to some a bureaucratic monstrosity committed to an impossible system of minute physical controls. Such a system, many feared, would discourage innovation, introduce new rigidities, impose a straitjacket on the economy and, in the long run, slow up economic growth. Such fears themselves seemed a trifle rigid and dogmatic; the war experience later showed that physical planning was compatible with a highly dynamic and creative economy. But the existence of these fears in New Deal circles doomed the Industrial Expansion idea.[4]

v

After NRA, the Ezekiel program seemed simply too detailed, too complicated, and too gimmicky. Nonetheless the *idea* of production planning retained adherents among those who felt that, at the moment, information was inadequate for a specific plan. Its main base, apart from the Ezekiel group in the Department of Agriculture, was the Gardiner Means group in the Industrial Section of the National Resources Committee.

Late in 1934 Means, shortly before shifting from Agriculture to the NRC, prepared a powerful statement of the need for general planning in a pamphlet entitled *Industrial Prices and Their Relative Inflexibility*. He cogently argued that administered prices had superseded market prices in vital parts of the economy, and that this was a necessary phase in economic growth. "Administrative coordination — the very thing that has made modern technology and a high standard of living possible — has destroyed the effectiveness of the market as an overall coordinator." This confronted the nation, Means said, with a basic choice. It could either atomize the units of business to the point where inflexible administered prices disappeared and the market mechanism could again become effective; or it could supplement the market mechanism with institutional arrangements sufficient to allow the economy to achieve balanced growth in the presence of and in spite of inflexible prices.

The first course, Means contended, would mean the breaking up of large industry, a decline in productive efficiency, and the lowering of the standard of living; the cost was too great. As for the alternative, it would not, he said, necessarily involve the abandonment of the market; rather it called for the establishment of an institutional framework within which corporate enterprise could continue to function and through which key industrial decisions could be made — the decisions which had to be made in the public interest if the economy was to survive. When he came to describing the new institutional framework, however, Means became vague, doing no more than citing NRA code authorities and AAA crop-control committees as examples.

His real feeling was that no one knew enough to draw up a general plan; exercises like Ezekiel's seemed to him premature. "If general economic planning is undertaken as essential to the integrity of the American economy," he wrote, "it means a long, hard process of research and analysis." It was no doubt important to consider techniques for obtaining compliance, he told the National Resources Committee in October 1935, but "the immediate problem would seem to be not so much — how can conformity be obtained, but — is it possible to draft a pattern of action toward which it is worth seeking conformity." With this in mind, he proposed a series of studies of the structure of the American economy. There would be three phases, he explained: the collection of data; the integration of data to produce a series of production-consumption patterns; the development of a general production-consumption pattern to be considered for possible adoption. He added, "It is doubtful if tangible results can be expected short of two or three years."

The result was to absorb Means in a series of vast descriptive studies of the economy. If Ezekiel was thus too specific in his recommendations, Means was not specific enough. Between them, the policy momentum of the managed-economy idea began to peter out. All that was left were the instruments of economic management, now battered and wobbling after two years of experience — AAA and, above all, NRA.[5]

VI

The very problems which depressed the heirs of the New Nationalism gave hope to the heirs of the New Freedom. If the experiment in direct planning was in trouble, was this not an argument for the government's getting out of the planning business and concentrating its efforts rather on redesigning the structure of competition? So at least felt the old Justice who had supplied the rationale for Wilson's domestic program twenty years before.

He was approaching his seventy-ninth birthday in 1935, but his questions from the bench were as searching as ever and his interest in public affairs, as keen. In all his years in Washington, Louis D. Brandeis perhaps never enjoyed such influence on public policy as in this third year of the New Deal.

The old man had watched the New Deal thus far with mixed feelings. His deepest faith of all was in the right to intelligent experiment: "if we would be guided by the light of reason, we must let our minds be bold." He exulted in Roosevelt (Jefferson, Cleveland, and Wilson had their qualities, he said, "but none of them could match this fellow"), in the brave new spirit Roosevelt brought to government, in the fine young men (some — like Dean Acheson, James M. Landis, Calvert Magruder, Paul Freund — his own former law clerks) he summoned to public service. When someone asked him in 1933 whether he thought the worst was over, he said serenely, "Yes, the worst happened before 1929."

But the basic philosophy of the First New Deal — the philosophy of co-ordination and control — repelled him. Insofar as NRA was a means of rationalizing and humanizing competition, he welcomed it, as in its fair-trade provisions; but insofar as it accepted bigness as inevitable and desirable, he was against it. As he had told Harold Laski a dozen years earlier, the challenge was to develop "vision, wisdom and ingenuity enough to adjust our institutions to the wee size of man and thus render possible his growth and development." The corporate system, he said to Henry L. Stimson, had outgrown the capacity of the brain to manage it; and the remedy lay, not in superimposing public giantism on private giantism, but in whittling down power to fit the capacity of men. He wrote in January 1935, "We must come back to the little unit."

Brandeis was not by any means a foe of public authority as such, or even, for all his devotion to local experiment, of federal authority. He believed that the Constitution had conferred on Congress wide national powers to regulate commerce, to tax, and to spend. Localism was for him a moral preference, not a constitutional injunction. Moreover, he knew that only the national government could exorcise the curse of bigness. Since bigness, as he saw it, arose, not from technological efficiency, but from financial manipulation, government could act to halt the march of bigness by reforming the financial arrangements of modern capitalism. It could do this in several ways. Through progressive taxation it could reduce the advantages and profits of bigness. Through legislation regulating securities issues, the stock exchanges, and holding companies, it could limit the power of finance to build bigness for speculative purposes. Through antitrust legislation, it could stop combination and merger. Through resale price maintenance and other fair-trade measures, it could protect the small merchant against his large competitors. And, in the meantime, the growth of the labor and co-operative movements could provide new means of offsetting the power of the people who lived by their manipulation of other people's money. He looked toward a diversified economy and a decentralized society. When people grew excited about the experiments of Soviet Russia, Brandeis would say, "Why should anyone want to go to Russia when one can go to Denmark?"

Brandeis invested this program with the penetrating moral force of an austere and formidable rationalism. His was a life of intense self-discipline. "When you learn that this is a hard world," he told his daughter, "things will be so much easier for you." The unadorned Victorian apartment on California Street in Washington and the plain, rambling house at Chatham on Cape Cod expressed a passionate dedication to reason and conscience. When the new Supreme Court building was completed, Brandeis refused to use the suite assigned to him; it was, he felt, too grand for the work of justice. The conservation of time and energy was a moral imperative. He had no time for indulgence — for gossip or novels or movies, for dining out or chatting over drinks till late in the evening. Seated underneath the framed photographs of classical antiquities, he talked intently on serious matters to the men and women who came to the weekly teas — talked and listened as well; he was a man of natural and deep humility.

He was also a man of intense feeling. In a moment of irritation Laski once complained to Brandeis's intimate friend Oliver Wendell Holmes, "He is intransigent and dominating, and unnecessarily prone to read evil motives into obvious actions." It was the caustic intensity of a man who enlisted ruthlessness in the service of the moral and rational life. Alvin Johnson called Lincoln and Brandeis "the two most serenely implacable democrats in all history." "The essential postulate of Mr. Justice Brandeis," said Felix Frankfurter, "is effective and generous opportunity for the unflagging operation of reason." As a person, he shone with an intellectual and moral luminosity. He had the mien of a figure from the Old Testament, with his strong and beautiful face, his great, dark, kindly eyes, his pensive and brooding expressions. After meeting him, Harold Ickes wrote, "I felt as if I were sitting at the feet of one of the fine old prophets." Franklin Roosevelt used to refer to him as Isaiah.[6]

VII

There gathered round him a group of the able young men of the country. Each year Felix Frankfurter would send along to Brandeis (as he also did to Holmes) a top Harvard Law School graduate to serve, sight unseen, as clerk. "We are the fortunate ones," Dean Acheson later said, "but what he has meant to us is not very different from what he has meant to hundreds of young men and women who have grown up under his influence."

Brandeis inspired them with a sense of social responsibility. When his law clerks suggested a joint visit on his eightieth birthday, he told them that, even more, he would welcome a message from each telling what public service he had lately performed. He inspired his young men with the idea of making their life in their own community; when they asked him what they should do, he always told them to go back to their "hinterland." A young Oregon newspaperman asked whether he should accept a job in New York. "Dear Richard Neuberger," the Justice replied: "Stay in Oregon. Cordially, Louis D. Brandeis." (Another, subjected to the same counsel, replied gloomily, "But Mr. Justice — Fargo, North Dakota!" And another: "But I have no hinterland. I'm from New York City." The Justice replied bleakly, "That is your misfortune." In time Oregon sent Neuberger east anyway.) Above all, Brandeis inspired everyone he could with his faith that the wellspring of moral vitality was individual identity, and that identity could be made safe only through the decentralization of power.

A wide variety of people came to him. The weekly teas were attended by government lawyers and economists, by writers and reformers, by congressmen and senators (for example: Harry S. Truman of Missouri), each waiting for a few moments' chat with the Justice, as Mrs. Brandeis sternly kept the guests in circulation. But the main channel of Brandeis's influence on the New Deal was through his intimate friend from the Harvard Law School, Felix Frankfurter, and Frankfurter's Washington representatives, Thomas G. Corcoran and Benjamin V. Cohen.

Frankfurter, like Brandeis, was in the tradition of Jefferson and Wilson. Competitive enterprise had to be at the basis of the American system, "not because of the opportunity it affords a few to make fabulous or unearned fortunes, but because of the encouragement and freedom of action it gives to men to shape their own lives and to plan their own destinies." In view of the "limitation of men," said Frankfurter, the general interest would be best served, "not by the minute orders of an all-directing state, governed by non-existent supermen but through the multitudinous activities, experiments and strivings of all those whom Lincoln called the common people." The greatest threat to the competitive system was the trend toward concentration. "If that trend is not reversed there is a danger of a private socialism in this country as alien to traditional Americanism as state socialism. . . . In a truly democratic community the average citizen must have a stake worth preserving in the economic system."

In one vital area Frankfurter extended with brilliance the implications of Brandeis's views. Where the idea of the disinterested expert had been implicit in the "Brandeis brief" and in Brandeis's whole approach to social policy, Frankfurter now used the idea as the basis for a philosophy of government service. He was deeply impressed by the intricate problems thrown up by industrial civilization; "merely to analyze these issues requires a vast body of technical knowledge." Obviously such complex matters could not be left to Jacksonian theories of versatile improvisation. Frankfurter used to quote with contempt William Jennings Bryan's apothegm, "Any man with real goodness of heart can write a good currency law." Democracy, he said, depended on knowledge and wisdom beyond all other forms of government. It was "the reign of reason on the most extensive scale"; the grandeur of its aims was only matched by the difficulties of their achievement.

If democracy were to meet the challenge of modern society, it had to have traditions of public service powerful enough to enlist the best brains of the country. Frankfurter was a confirmed Anglophile; and for him the British Civil Service supplied the answer. "Without a permanent professional public service, highly trained, imaginative and courageously disinterested, the democratic aims of our society cannot be solved." For years he had carried on the fight for such a public service, with little success. "The whole tide of opinion," he wrote sadly in 1930, "is against public administration as a career for talent." "The whole mental and moral climate of our times — the impalpable but terrific pressure of current standards of achievement . . . [are] overwhelmingly on the side of private gain."

The New Deal brought a stunning change. Partly because government now provided the greater challenge, partly because jobs were not available elsewhere, the young men flocked to Washington. Frankfurter rejoiced: "The political law of gravitation has operated as it usually operates when new problems call for new endeavor." It was not accident, he asserted, that the founders of the republic had mostly been youngish men. Disinterested enthusiasm, freedom from imprisoning dogmatism, capacity for fresh insight, unflagging industry, ardor for difficulties, resilience, co-operativeness, release "from complicated ramifications of private life" — these were qualities which the times demanded and which, in the main, youthful years could best supply. The one-man employment office was now working overtime. And Frankfurter, with his flair and sparkle and sense of excitement, attracted the brightest of the young men.

Brandeis, with his classical severity of temperament, won respect by purity of character, whereas Frankfurter, with his Viennese exuberance, won affection by charm and high spirits. He loved food, drink, gossip, and parties; his technique of influence was, not systematic cross-examination, but mischievous provocation and challenge; he was sparkling, contentious and diffuse. His intellectual gaiety had captivated Roosevelt, whom Frankfurter had known when he was a junior at Carter, Ledyard, and Milburn and had worked with on labor matters during the First World War, as it captivated Henry Stimson, Holmes, and Brandeis, and as it captivated the generations of students he was now guiding

into public service. In 1933 Roosevelt had proposed that Frankfurter enter the government as Solicitor General, but Frankfurter
replied that he could be of more use to the administration as a
professorial free-lance than as a full-time public servant. In the
winter of 1933–34 he was out of the country as Eastman Professor
at Oxford. By the fall of 1934 he was back at Harvard, commuting
regularly on the Federal to Washington.[7]

VIII

With his concern for public administration and his admiration
for the more systematic practices of Downing Street, Frankfurter
was particularly troubled over the helter-skelter responsibility imposed on an American President. The problem of subduing any
Roosevelt to any system seemed, as ever, insuperable. But Frankfurter argued to the President that he could diminish his burdens
somewhat if he would take on an able young man as a trouble-
shooter and general aide. Moreover, Frankfurter continued, he
thought he knew the man.

Frankfurter's candidate was Thomas G. Corcoran, a member of
the legal staff of the Reconstruction Finance Corporation. Corcoran's legal brilliance, adorned by Irish ebullience and wit, had
first attracted Frankfurter's attention ten years before at the Harvard Law School. In 1926 Frankfurter sent him on to Washington
as clerk to Justice Holmes. Holmes is supposed to have described
him as "quite noisy, quite satisfactory, and quite noisy." From
Frankfurter, Corcoran gained a sense of the responsibilities of
government and the high dignity of public service ("Make me civil
service commissioner ten years from now," he used to say in the
early thirties, "and I'll be content"). From Holmes, Corcoran took
away an appreciation of style in public life and a conviction of
the indispensability of variety and experiment in a free state, as
well, perhaps, as more than a trace of Holmes's corrosive skepticism. Five years of Wall Street practice perfected Corcoran's
education. Cotton and Franklin was a first-class firm, aware of all
the devices of high finance without being under the compulsion
to regard them as high statesmanship. But the yearning for public
service still touched Corcoran more deeply than anything else.
When Eugene Meyer, staffing RFC in 1932, applied for suggestions

to George Franklin, who had been his general counsel in the War Finance Corporation, Franklin nominated Corcoran, and Corcoran leaped at the opportunity.

After Roosevelt came in, Frankfurter commended Corcoran to Moley, and Moley soon found him indispensable in dealing with the securities and stock exchange legislation. It was then that Corcoran fell in with Benjamin V. Cohen, the gentle and sagacious lawyer whom Frankfurter had summoned in 1933, along with James M. Landis, to rescue the securities bill. Cohen subsequently went to work for Harold Ickes, first in the Public Works Administration and later in the National Power Policy Committee. Corcoran and Cohen made an ideal combination. Corcoran's brashness supplemented Cohen's shyness, as his perpetual high spirits offset Cohen's occasional moodiness. In the same way Cohen's wisdom balanced Corcoran's impetuosity, and Cohen's rectitude, Corcoran's opportunism. Cohen was the man of ideas and reflection; Corcoran, though he had plenty of ideas, was preeminently the salesman and promoter. The idea of the Corcoran-Cohen team — this alliterative partnership of an Irishman and a Jew — caught the popular fancy. They reminded *Fortune* of "those minor state counselors in Shakespearian comedies who serve the Duke, make astute comments, and are always perturbed at developments."

On questions of policy, Cohen and Corcoran were both in the Brandeis tradition. Experiments in central planning of the NRA-AAA type left them cold. What they cared about was the revitalization of competitive enterprise through an attack on the chicanery of finance; and they took pride at outwitting the Wall Street lawyers in their own field. The New Deal, said Cohen in 1934, "recognizes that far-reaching reforms are necessary to preserve that individualism which was achieved in a simpler and less complicated society through laissez faire." He added that "reform of the existing order to effect a revival of true individualism" was intellectually more difficult than the attempt to govern by central plan. "It involves a penetrating understanding of the complicated character and functioning of modern economic life, a delicate sense of balance, and alert sensitivity to constant change." The New Deal was "deliberately flexible and unlogical in its approach to conditions rather than theories" because it recognized "that necessity of dealing with multitudinous concrete instances which is the essence of government."

Cohen, from the beginning a disciple of Keynes as well as of Brandeis, argued that government spending was the only way of making up for the timidity of private capital. Corcoran agreed. In 1934, trying to persuade Amos Pinchot to become a director of RFC, Corcoran suggested that the right way to restore buying power and bring about recovery was to pour money into circulation in the greatest possible quantities and at the highest possible speed. The ideal thing, he said with characteristic high spirits, would be for fleets of airplanes to fly over the country, discharging money as they went, so that anyone needing cash could pick it up from the ground.

IX

Cohen and Corcoran gathered around them a brilliant group of younger lawyers, whom Corcoran placed in key agencies. "What is a government?" Corcoran once asked. "It's not just the top man or the top ten men. A government is the top one hundred or two hundred men. What really makes the difference is what happens down the line before — and after — the big decisions are taken." The old Frankfurter employment agency was now enlarged to epic proportions under Corcoran's tireless direction. "The spectacle of a good man jobless or a good job manless," as Joseph Alsop and Robert Kintner put it, "drives him to a frenzy." Whenever an agency needed a lawyer, Corcoran was ready with a candidate, someone he had known at Harvard or in Wall Street, or someone Frankfurter or Brandeis told him about, or anyone who had a reputation for legal ability and aggressive liberalism.

While nominally domiciled in the RFC, Corcoran by 1934 was operating all over Washington. Soon introduced into the White House circles, he made an instant impression. He knew the law and the Constitution, was a master of legal technicality and artifice, had a unique ability to direct the operations of a team, was single-minded in his determination to get things done, and never slept. More than this, he had an extravagant personal charm which served as a cloak for his boundless talents as a manipulator and an *intrigant*.

With older men he seemed almost to overdo deference. One senator objected that the ingratiating Corcoran had said "sir" to him twice in the same sentence. But toward his contemporaries he mixed a light-hearted cynicism with an idealist's respect for hard work in a compound that most of them found beguiling; and he won the devotion of his juniors with his combination of solicitude, discipline, and inspiration. His personal warmth was as irresistible as his intellectual resourcefulness was unlimited. This compact chunk of a man, an accordion strap swung over his stocky shoulders, his rich voice singing songs at once gay and melancholy ("Tim Toolan" in a Pawtucket brogue or "Vive la Garibaldi" in San Francisco Italian, or "The Yellow Rose of Texas"), soon became a fixture at New Deal parties. The party over, Corcoran (who never smoked and rarely drank) might well go on to read to Justice Holmes, now in his nineties, or spend the rest of the night, sustained by dextrose and hot coffee, working on a brief or preparing for a hearing in the morning.

With the tacit consent of Jesse Jones and the active co-operation of RFC's general counsel, Stanley Reed, Corcoran turned RFC into a base for operations which extended through the government. A fluid and emergency-minded organization, RFC was a reservoir of expert talent for any contingency. It provided not only lawyers but comptrollers, treasurers, bank examiners, personnel experts, public-relations experts, secretaries — not to speak of telephone operators who could get anyone anywhere in the world in five minutes. It furnished Corcoran the facilities he needed — the office space, the all-night secretaries, the long-distance wires, the mimeograph machines. It supplied a means of bringing down new men, looking them over, and putting them on a payroll until something opened up for them. It became in effect the springboard from which the old departments (especially Justice, Interior, and the Federal Reserve) could be reorganized and the new agencies required by the new legislation launched and staffed. "In a practical sense," Corcoran later put it, with slight but pardonable exaggeration, "the new organizations were all 'spin-offs' from an RFC prototype."

Stanley Reed became the particular protector of the Harvard Law School crowd. RFC and, after Reed became Solicitor General in 1935, Justice served as the intelligence switchboard and the operational base for the web of Frankfurter-Corcoran relationships through the new agencies. Whenever a crucial law had to be drafted or crucial brief written, Corcoran conjured up a task force from his young men around the government, who then completed the job in a spurt of intense concentration and furious energy. Little could have been harder than to raise the standards of legal performance in a government hectically expanding in size and purpose. Corcoran's invention of the *ad hoc* task force provided in its time an effective solution.

For its success, this solution required a flexible conception of the way government should operate. This Roosevelt, of course, had; and men like Ickes, Hopkins, Jones, and Reed, instead of insisting on the sacredness of channels and flow charts, were prepared to tolerate, even encourage, the Corcoran-style operation so long as it produced results. For its success it also required a flexible conception of the way lawyers should operate. "We lawyers," one of the most resourceful of the New Deal lawyers, Oscar Cox, once said, "are frequently — and many times justly — accused of having negative minds. Too often we are disposed to search out the reasons why something necessary can *not* be done rather than to seek out the means whereby it *can* be done." This was precisely what Corcoran sought to change. He saw the government lawyer as the man whose job it was to find constitutional ways to do what had to be done. As Roosevelt himself used to challenge his successive chiefs of the Department of Justice: "If you are a good Attorney General, tell me how I can do it."

The New Deal lawyer was thus a freewheeler and an activist. He was also, most probably, a young man. The New Deal's readiness to bet on youth created problems; it also nurtured ability and assured loyalty. Charles E. Wyzanski, Jr., a twenty-six-year old graduate of the Harvard Law School, was told, on his first day in Washington as a prospective solicitor for the Department of Labor, that his immediate job was to draw up a public-works bill. Frances Perkins brought him up to meet the President after they had all taken part in a White House conference on public works, and Wyzanski thought he should explain that he had voted for Hoover. "I don't care," Roosevelt replied. "What I want you to do is to have on my desk tomorrow morning a draft of a bill carrying out this idea that you've heard discussed." Wyzanski, appalled, called Tom Corcoran, who gave him a quick briefing on the things to watch out for. By the next morning a bill was on the President's desk. "This was such an initiation," Wyzanski later said, "as no man would ever forget. I never could be so scared again. . . . This in one moment was plunging into the furnace. If you lived and got out of it, there could be no other fire which you would have to particularly fear in Washington."

Those who lived and got out of it were bound together by a sense of common experience on the firing line. The result was a group of lawyers dispersed through Washington agencies and departments, but united by a strong loyalty to Corcoran and Cohen, to each other, and to the New Deal. Some even lived with Tom and Ben in a convivial house in Georgetown — "the little red house on R Street" which, to the devotees of Dr. Wirt, was the headquarters of revolution. Tom's pretty secretary Peggy Dowd, whom, when he had time, he eventually married, was the Missy LeHand of the second echelon, stroking the brows and sustaining the spirits of a volatile collection of talents. The existence of the Harvard Law School network gave Corcoran a unique instrument both for finding out what was going on and for getting things done. He used the instrument to the hilt.[8]

X

Corcoran and Cohen, like Brandeis and Frankfurter, were working mainly behind the scenes. Moreover, all four men, as lawyers, were more inclined to respond to specific cases than to develop a general rationale. Accordingly, the most rounded presentation of the Brandeis position in 1935 came from a nonlawyer outside government, David Cushman Coyle.

A civil engineer by profession, Coyle had turned some years before to the semipopular writing of economics. His engineering background gave him special qualifications with which to discuss national planning. Thus no one understood better the fallacies packed in the expression "social engineering," a phrase Coyle exposed with relish as based on false analogies. Engineering operations required conditions which free society could not fulfill: definite physical objectives, accepted technical procedures, and the capacity to impose absolute discipline within the area of activity.

Ultimately, total planning meant total tyranny. Coyle liked the capitalist system because, "with all its faults and wastes," it was "the breeding ground of free men and the guarantee of free speech."

From this vantage point, Coyle had sharply attacked Mary Van Kleeck's conception of a planned paradise. From the same vantage point he now criticized milder theories of direct planning on the model, for example, of NRA. When government undertook detailed decision, he suggested, it was bound to get into trouble — or into tyranny. "The American people, rightly or wrongly, do not like strict discipline." Moreover, the world was always changing and the modern world of high technology was changing faster than anything previously seen on earth. "The truth once for all delivered to Andrew Mellon or Karl Marx is only for a day." Reality would forever astonish and frustrate the planners. In the end, either free men must destroy the master plan, or the master plan destroys free men.

His own rejection of master planning by no means implied a return to laissez faire. Coyle called instead for a policy of economic decentralization — not planning for control, but planning for freedom. Such a policy meant drastic income and inheritance taxes to prevent oversaving in the hands of a wealthy few (taxation, Coyle said, was "the main road to freedom"); social-security and old-age insurance to put money in the hands of the many; strict regulation of securities and of holding companies; federal control of bank credit. Those who profited by economic centralization would, of course, resist such a program. This, in Coyle's view, defined the "irrepressible conflict" in American life — the conflict which he described, following Brandeis, as between business and finance. It was finance which created big business by merging small firms in order to float watered stock; it was finance which was methodically strangling the free market. "There will be no peace," Coyle wrote in 1935, "till high finance is destroyed. If the financial cancer can be extirpated before the system dies and turns to disorder, business will be able to decentralize itself into a healthy group of small and widely distributed industries." In addition to the reform program, he advocated public spending in the magnitude of ten to fifteen billion dollars as the means of economic recovery.

All this amounted, no doubt, to planning of a sort, but it was indirect rather than direct planning. It did not impose precise rules as to how people should make specific economic decisions; rather, it used the powers of government to bring about desired general results. Such plans, Coyle said, "call for a minimum of daily discipline. Most of them the ordinary citizen would never feel or know about; the effect upon him would be merely that he would have had a job at good wages."

The conclusion, Coyle argued, would not be a uniform and logical economy, and that would be all to the good. He envisaged an America which included at least six economic systems ("and we may invent more if we feel like it"); an old-fashioned classical capitalist system, ruled by supply and demand; finance capitalism, made up of producers who fixed production according to price rather than price according to production; public enterprise; private nonprofit business — universities, churches, foundations, voluntary societies; the co-operative system; and the underworld. There was positive value, he suggested, in diversity. "There is a curse on trying to be too big, too perfect, too logical, and too efficient. . . . The preservation of a mixed economic order is of the greatest importance to democracy and to freedom." In the end, the justification for the free market lay, not in itself, but in the opportunities it created for human fulfillment. "Free men we must have in order to keep our Government awake. Free initiative in business we must have as a nursery for free men. A free price system we must have, because the price of free initiative is free prices." And again:

> Though reactionaries shout for liberty and try to suppress free speech, and though radicals curse the reactionaries and plan to follow their example, the fact remains that no way is known of getting good sense into human affairs, except to have somewhere a reservoir of free men.

Coyle was not an original economic thinker. He combined Brandeis's faith in small-scale enterprise with an underconsumptionist analysis he traced to Hobson and Malthus; and he presented the result in a plain-spoken, vigorous, rough-and-ready way that commanded a sizable audience as published in the National Home

Library Foundation's 25-cent pocket-size hard-back editions. (Tom
Corcoran helped raise the money to underwrite the Coyle publications.) In 1936 Roosevelt read excerpts from Coyle's book of
that year (*Waste*) to his press conference, adding, "It is a grand
book. You ought to read it."

What Coyle did was to articulate the reaction against the First
New Deal with special force and clarity. Rexford G. Tugwell,
after the appearance of Coyle's July 1935 *Virginia Quarterly Review* article, "Decentralize Industry," told its author that he had
never read anything with which he disagreed so much. Jerome
Frank said, "For gosh sake, Dave, you haven't gone Brandeis, have
you?" Coyle replied, "Hell, I've always been Brandeis." Norman
Hapgood, reporting the exchange to Brandeis, added, "The big
battle is coming on." [9]

XI

Hapgood was right: the big battle was coming on; indeed, it
had been in the making for some time. From the start, the ideologists of the First New Deal had known their enemy. Adolf
Berle had stated the issue when he considered, in the preface to
The Modern Corporation and Private Property, whether the
"corporate revolution" was permanent. "Mr. Brandeis struggled
to turn the clock backward in 1915," he wrote; "Professor Felix
Frankfurter is inclined to believe even now that it cannot last.
To us [himself and Gardiner Means] there is much to indicate that
the process will go on a great deal further than it has now gone."
Donald Richberg, seeing bigness as "the product of an irresistible
force which if now misdirected should be harnessed and wisely
directed in the service of mankind," said of Brandeis, "Our
civilization must protect itself against the destructive experiments now being carried on by its well-meaning but ruthless
friend." Moley explicitly rejected the Wilson-Brandeis philosophy,
which he defined as the faith that "America could once more
become a nation of small proprietors, of corner grocers and smithies
under spreading chestnut trees."

The two groups of New Dealers thus disagreed on the diagnosis
— whether bigness was inevitable or reversible; and they disagreed
on the cure — whether there should be affirmative economic

planning or merely an attempt to revitalize the market; whether government should try and do things itself or whether it should simply try and reform the rules of the game. They agreed on nearly everything else, of course, and from the outside seemed indistinguishable from each other. But, within the family, each regarded the other with wariness. Thus in April 1933 Tugwell and Wallace paid a call on Brandeis. It was not a success. Tugwell tried to maintain that bigness needed only direction, submission to discipline; but Brandeis replied sternly that bigness was always badness. (One of the Justice's images stuck in Tugwell's mind. After seventy years, he said, life was like living in Poe's room, the walls of which continually converged.) A year later, Tugwell noted in his diary that Brandeis had sent a message through Gardner Jackson to Jerome Frank and himself, "in effect, that he was declaring war." "Jerry and I have seemed to fail in working with him," Tugwell reflected. "Frankfurter shares his prejudices but doesn't feel so strongly about it. . . . Tom Corcoran, who is sincere, adroit and a little of a schemer, represents his point of view." Tugwell added, however, "There are no differences here we cannot compromise." When Norman Hapgood, the old Wilsonian, once said he feared he had not been able to learn anything since 1912, Tugwell, understanding the implication, responded, "I do not see why your crowd and ours cannot work together"; then, in a parenthesis: "not Brandeis."

In April 1934, Moley, anxious to hold things together, put to Tugwell and Corcoran the idea of setting up a group like the old brain trust to unite both viewpoints. Nothing came of this. By 1935 the difference among the New Dealers who believed in co-ordination and those who believed in competition was growing acute. "Nothing but a common loyalty to the President," wrote Moley, "prevents this difference from flaring into public attention." The First New Dealers objected now, not to the philosophy of the Brandeis group; they also (except for Tugwell and Jerome Frank) objected to the antibusiness relish with which the neo-Brandeisians voiced their views. But by 1935 they were on the defensive. In February someone asked Roosevelt at a press conference, "Is there some feeling that bigness of business is of itself undesirable?" "I should say yes," the President replied. "I think there is. . . . If you center in the hands of a very small number of people a great many interlocking companies, you get a control of industry of the nation in too few hands. We are a great deal better off if we can disseminate both the control and the actual industrial set-up as a whole." His message to Congress of March 12, 1935, calling for the regulation of public-utility holding companies, was a portent of the mounting neo-Brandeisian influence.

The plight of the First New Dealers was only partly the result of the failure of their devices for integration; after all, the NRA seemed salvageable and AAA was a relative success. It was mainly their own failure. By 1935 they had ceased to offer any common counsel. They united in diagnosis, but they could never unite in prescription. And in the meantime, a recklessly articulate lot, they asserted, argued, speculated, and denounced, dissipating energy in debate rather than decision. Tugwell put it wistfully when he wrote later, "It was after Jerome came that we began to talk too much. . . . Our fundamental philosophy was well-enough developed. But the way of carrying out that philosophy was not at all clear." If Tugwell and Richberg agreed that bigness was inevitable and co-ordination necessary, they agreed, in 1935, on little else; and Tugwell, at the same time, agreed with Brandeis that private bigness could not be trusted. The co-ordination boys — Moley, Berle, Tugwell, Johnson, Richberg, Frank, Charles Beard — were, as Jay Franklin suggested, brilliant but anarchic; they fielded a team which had plenty of star backs but no line. "This was in marked contrast to the unity and discipline of the Little Hot Dogs, who knew only one play but had plenty of substitutes and a will to win." In short, the champions of central planning had no teamwork and hardly remained on speaking terms with each other, while the foes of central planning had the best-integrated machine in the New Deal.[10]

XII

Yet the First New Dealers retained one nominal advantage. Theirs was a program for both reform and recovery, while the Brandeis program, in its antibigness essentials, was a program only for reform. To accentuate this contrast, some of the First New Dealers began to lay particular stress on recovery as their distinctive contribution, causing some, both then and later, to minimize the extraordinary amount of reform that had in fact accompanied the attempt to reorganize economic institutions in 1933 and 1934.

For their part, the more thoughtful Brandeisians knew that the assault on the concentration of wealth and economic power, however necessary, would not by itself produce prosperity. Happily for them, a third body of economic doctrine, differing both from the faith in national planning and the faith in littleness and freedom, was beginning to crystallize. This was the belief — still rudimentary, inchoate, and somewhat opportunistic, but nonetheless growing steadily more systematized and analytical — that the way to achieve recovery was through public spending. The spending policy was essentially neutral on the issues which divided the First New Dealers from the Brandeisians. It could in theory fit equally well with a program of bigness or a program of smallness, a program of national planning or one of competition. Yet certain external features predisposed it to an alliance with the Brandeisians.

The First New Deal, in the main, distrusted spending. Its conservatives, like Johnson and Moley, were orthodox in their fiscal views and wanted a balanced budget; and its liberals, like Tugwell and La Follette, disliked spending as a drug which gave the patient a false sense of well-being before surgery could be completed. Tugwell, recalling Simon Patten's argument for pay-as-you-go financing during the First World War, regarded deficit spending as an upper-class device for transferring the burden to future small taxpayers; better, he thought, to clean up as they went through taxes.

The neo-Brandeisians, on the other hand, had no such inhibitions. Brandeis himself urged on Moley in February 1933 a comprehensive public-works program on the ground that business could no longer find enough attractive opportunities for investment and that the government must fill the gap. Though Frankfurter had been a budget-balancer as late as 1931 ("I cannot characterize the attempts of the Administration to deal with its deficits without increasing taxation as otherwise than cowardly fear"), his year in England in 1933–34 gave him a full exposure to the view, associated with John Maynard Keynes, that public spending should be used to offset declines in private spending. He sent Keynes a letter of introduction to Roosevelt and himself returned wholly sympathetic to the idea of compensatory fiscal policy. Coyle had long advocated spending, and Cohen and Corcoran were Keynesians.

But the organized argument for public spending had already arisen independently in the government, and its source was not Keynes, but rather a group of American economic heretics. William Trufant Foster in his books of the twenties, written in collaboration with Waddill Catchings, had long since summed up antidepression policy in a single maxim: "When business begins to look rotten, more public spending." When Roosevelt came to office, Foster reiterated his old views in a more congenial climate. "Recovery from a major depression through government leadership," he wrote in December 1933, "involves an increase of public debt. . . . Public debts should be increased in hard times and paid off in good times." After a few years of depression, such ideas were gradually beginning to penetrate the economic profession. In January 1933 a group of eleven University of Chicago economists and political scientists — among them Paul Douglas, Jacob Viner, H. C. Simons and H. A. Millis — recommended a deliberate policy of deficit spending. "The federal debt should be permitted to increase in times of depression," the Chicago statement said, "and be rapidly retired in prosperous times." [11]

XIII

The first effective champion of these ideas in the Roosevelt administration was a Utah banker named Marriner S. Eccles. Insofar as Eccles was influenced at all by economic theorists, it was by Foster. He quoted Foster on his first appearance before a congressional committee; and when a senator observed that he evidently had Foster in the back of his head, Eccles responded, "I only wish there were more who had." But the main influence on Eccles was undoubtedly his own sharp and probing intelligence working on a varied business experience.

Eccles was forty-four years old when Roosevelt made him a governor of the Federal Reserve System in November 1934. His father had been a poor Glasgow Scot who was converted to

Mormonism and emigrated to Utah. There he entered business, made a fortune and, before polygamy was abolished, married two wives. Young Marriner, one of twenty-one children, went as a youth on a tour of duty as Mormon missionary in Scotland and returned to become a bank president at the age of twenty-three. By the age of forty, he was a provincial tycoon — the head of a holding company controlling twenty-six banks in the intermountain region, the president of milk, sugar, lumber, and construction companies, and the director of hotels, railroads, and insurance companies. A highly successful businessman, he believed implicitly that hard work and thrift were the keys to national prosperity.

The crash of 1929 came as a shock. "During 1930," he later wrote, "I awoke to find myself at the bottom of a pit without any known means of scaling its sheer sides." The pit was intellectual rather than economic. He was a sufficiently shrewd businessman to bring his interests through the depression in fairly good shape. But he discovered that he *knew* very little about the system in which he operated so successfully; and his ignorance tormented him. More and more he began to reflect on the policies which, as a responsible banker, he felt compelled to pursue. When in the depression bankers forced the liquidation of loans and securities to meet the demands of depositors, when they tightened credit instead of easing it, were they not saving their banks at the expense of the community? "Seeking individual salvation, we were contributing to collective ruin." He drew the logical conclusion. As individuals, they were helpless. "There is only one agency in my opinion that can turn the cycle upward," he told the Utah State Bankers' Convention in 1932, "and that is the government."

What could the government do? Following Foster, Eccles decided that the key lay in placing purchasing power in the hands of the people who needed it. Everything else — the balanced budget, monetary policy, tax policy — should be subordinated to this. Having reached this conclusion, Eccles explored its implications with the energy of a successful businessman and the zeal of a missionary. "As the pursuit of money had been the organizing principle of my life for almost twenty years, the pursuit of an idea of economic balance now replaced it." In February 1933 he went over to Salt Lake City to hear Stuart Chase speak to a business-

men's luncheon. When a snowstorm delayed Chase's train, Eccles
was asked to speak. Chase arrived while Eccles was expounding
his new ideas. Afterward, the two men talked. "Why not get
yourself a larger audience?" Chase said. Someone remarked that
Eccles was to testify before a Senate committee in Washington later
that month. "In that event," Chase said, "why don't you go up to
New York and see Rex Tugwell?"

Eccles made his national debut before the Senate Finance Committee in February 1933. A small, slender man with dark eyes
glowing out of a pale, sharp face, he spoke softly but with fluency
and precision. After the barrage of orthodoxy to which the committee had been subjected, this Mormon banker with his radical
proposals made a strong impression. Instead of the usual budget-
balancing generalities, he offered a definite program designed "to
bring about, by Government action, an increase of purchasing
power on the part of all the people." Not till this was done,
he warned, could the government hope to balance the budget. Nor
could this be done by monetary stimulus of the Bryan–Elmer
Thomas variety, for printing-press inflation provided no method
"for getting the increased supply of money to the ultimate consumer." The only answer was government deficit spending
through unemployment relief, public works, and the domestic
allotment plan in agriculture. Ultimately the banking system
would have to be unified under the Federal Reserve in order to
make effective control of monetary policy possible. There would
also have to be a refinancing of farm mortgages; high income and
inheritance taxes to control capital accumulation; federal certifi-
cation of capital issues; federal minimum wage, old-age pension
and unemployment laws; and a national planning board.

Having delivered himself of this mouthful, Eccles took the
next train to New York to meet Tugwell. They lunched together
agreeably in a drugstore near Columbia; but Eccles felt that Tugwell was so preoccupied with questions of economic structure
as to be unaware of the possibilities of fiscal policy. Having completed his eastern mission, Eccles returned, as he thought, to
decent obscurity in Utah. He watched Roosevelt's economy drive
of the Hundred Days with gloom, despatching Cassandra-like
letters to Tugwell, to his old friend George Dern, and to Bob
La Follette. NRA pleased him little more. The New Deal ap-

peared hardly better than the Hoover administration. "New York, as usual, seems to be in the saddle, dominating fiscal and monetary policy." In October 1933 he was surprised by a letter from Tugwell, suggesting another Washington visit. When Eccles arrived, Tugwell introduced him to a number of leading New Dealers. Eccles made his usual argument for deficit spending in a series of vehement evening discussions; but again Washington seemed to lead nowhere and again he returned to Utah.

Then, early in 1934, Henry Morgenthau, Jr., invited him to come to Washington as assistant to the Secretary of the Treasury. And in June Morgenthau proposed Eccles for a vacancy in the Federal Reserve Board. Roosevelt asked what Eccles thought should be done with the Federal Reserve System. Eccles answered by preparing (with the aid of a young Treasury economist named Lauchlin Currie) a confident memorandum describing precisely how the Federal Reserve Board could establish more effective control over the nation's monetary mechanism. Roosevelt discussed the memorandum at length with him, and in November announced Eccles's appointment.

In the next months Eccles worked hardest on proposals for a new banking law. But he still had time to develop arguments for spending in cogent memoranda for the National Emergency Council in March and April 1935. Currie, whom Eccles brought along to Federal Reserve, doubtless gave a Keynesian sophistication to the ideas; but the central theme was the one which Eccles had been pressing independently for at least four years. He favored an unbalanced budget as "a deliberate measure of economic policy" and dismissed existing deficits as "comparatively small" in relation to the strength of the deflationary forces it was necessary to reverse. As for the alarm over the growing national debt, Eccles pointed out that the current carrying charge was only $800 million, less than in any year between 1919 and 1925. The nation, he said, could easily support a much larger debt.

Circumstances helped Eccles. The government was having to spend for human reasons, and it comforted people to think that the policy made economic sense, too. Thus men like Hopkins and Ickes were attracted to the Eccles policy. Even George Dern — doubtless responsive to his fellow Utahan — could write Roosevelt in December 1934, "My own feeling is that public spending has

not been large enough and it will probably have to be larger."
On every possible occasion Eccles repeated his formula. "I believe that there is only one way by which we will get out of
the depression," he kept reiterating, "and that is through the
process of government spending until such time as private spending and private credit expand." The Brandeisians, badly needing
a recovery program to match the recovery-reform combination of
the First New Deal, now began to shape a fateful alliance with
the spenders.[12]

14. Roosevelt in Retreat

AND so in the early months of 1935 the New Dealers argued among themselves, while their leader remained unwontedly irresolute and unwontedly reticent. The appearance of presidential weakness naturally stimulated the opposition. Huey Long and Father Coughlin had only been flexing their muscles when they led the fight in January against adherence to the World Court. Victory, in the setting of presidential indecision, now spurred them on in their determination to cash in on the apparent stagnation of the New Deal.

II

Long, ever audacious and now irrevocably estranged, assumed the lead. He was mad at Farley, who had given federal patronage in Louisiana to his enemies. He was mad at Ickes, who had suspended Public Works Administration projects in Louisiana because of defects in the supporting state legislation. He was mad at Morgenthau, whose Treasury agents were investigating his activities and preparing to indict his associates. He was mad, above all, at Roosevelt. With Louisiana now bound and gagged, he came to Washington in a fighting mood, ready to take on the New Deal and all its works.

From the World Court, he moved on to a swashbuckling attack on Farley. Claiming that the Postmaster General had profited personally out of post-office construction contracts in New York, Long demanded a Senate investigation. Farley, Long said, had "shiny, roamy tentacles" as well as a "gloomy, smoky, opaque look that only a searching eye can fathom." The administration leaders dared not oppose Long's move for a preliminary investigation. It produced, however, no evidence of wrongdoing on Farley's part. But this was a rare setback. In the main, no member of the Senate wished to tangle with the Kingfish. Confident and patronizing, the Louisiana senator jeered at his colleagues with the swaggering assurance of the neighborhood bully. One day he ridiculed the Democrats. "You aren't even trying to legislate. You've thrown up the sponge. You've turned your powers and duties over to the Wallaces, the Tugwells, and the Richbergs." Then he walked over to the Republican side of the chamber and said, "When the New Deal blows up, you old mossback Republicans need not think you'll get the country back. It won't go to you, and it won't go to those Democrats over there." It was obvious enough where the Kingfish thought it would go.

The Senate, which had seen demagogues rise and fall, preferred to let him career along. But the White House, perceiving Long's impact on the country, was less complacent. Louis Howe in particular kept needling the President by sending him letters demonstrating the spread of Long's influence. And Roosevelt did not seem to require much needling. "In normal times," he wrote Henry Stimson early in February, "the radio and other appeals by them would not be effective. However, these are not normal times; the people are jumpy and very ready to run after strange gods. This is so in every country as well as our own." The analogy with European fascism was evidently on his mind. "We, too," he wrote Breckinridge Long, his ambassador to Italy, "are going through a bad case of Huey Long and Father Coughlin influenza — the whole country is aching in every bone. It is an internal disease, not external as it seems to be in Europe."

Behind the scenes, Roosevelt stepped up the administration's cold war against Long. On February 5, when the Louisiana situation came up before the National Emergency Council, the President said sharply, "Don't put anybody in and don't keep anybody that is working for Huey Long or his crowd! That is a hundred percent!" The ensuing dialogue expressed the administration impatience.

Garner: That goes for everybody!

Roosevelt: Everybody and every agency. Anybody working for Huey Long is not working for it.

Hull: It can't be corrected too soon.

Roosevelt: You will get a definite ruling any time you want it.

Publicly, however, Roosevelt maintained his silence.

More impetuous spirits yearned for a counteroffensive. On March 4, 1935, the editors of *Redbook* gave General Hugh Johnson, the former head of the National Recovery Administration, a banquet at the Waldorf Astoria in New York. There is no evidence that the White House inspired what Johnson had to say; Johnson himself denied that he had consulted anybody in the administration. Yet it seems likely that Johnson was not unaware of the President's feelings. Under the title "The Pied Pipers," he launched into a brilliantly demagogic attack on the demagogues. "You can laugh at Father Coughlin — you can snort at Huey Long — but this country was never under a greater menace." Long, Johnson said, was "a dictator by force of arms and Adolf Hitler has nothing on him any way you care to look at both." In fact, "Hitler couldn't hold a candle to Huey in the art of the old Barnum ballyhoo." Johnson even mimicked the Kingfish: " 'Ahm not against de Constitution. Ahm fo' de Constitution. Ahm not against p'ivate p'op'ety. Ahm fo' p'ivate p'op'ety.' " Added to this, Johnson continued, "there comes burring over the air the dripping brogue of the Irish-Canadian priest . . . musical, blatant bunk from the very rostrum of religion." One might respect Coughlin as an agitator or revere him as a preacher. "But we can neither respect nor revere what appears to be a priest in Holy Orders entering our homes with the open sesame of his high calling and there, in the name of Jesus Christ, demanding that we ditch the President for Huey Long."

Johnson's thesis was that an open alliance had been formed "between the great Louisiana demagogue and this political padre."

These two patriots may have been reading last Summer's lurid story about an American Hitler riding into Washington at the head of troops. That would be definite enough to Huey because he knows what part of the horse he can be, but we

have a right to object most vigorously to the sanctification
of such a centaur by having the head wear the collar of Rome
and come intoning the stately measures of the church in pious
benediction on such a monstrosity.

Between the team of Huey and the priest, Johnson said, there
was "the whole bag of crazy or crafty tricks possessed by any
Mad Mullah or dancing dervish who incited a tribe or people
through illusion to its doom."

Stripped to the facts — and whether consciously or not — these
two men are raging up and down this land preaching not
construction but destruction — not reform but revolution
— not peace but — a sword. I think we are dealing with a
couple of Catilines, and that it is high time for somebody
to say so.

Johnson called on the people to show that they were not in the
market for this "magic financial hair tonic put up by partnership
of a priest and Punchinello guaranteed to grow economic whiskers
on a billiard ball overnight." No one, he concluded, agreed with
everything Roosevelt had done. "But I think our sole hope lies
in him; I believe that we are still in deadly danger."[1]

III

"Last night, while I was about to undertake to throw myself
into the arms of Morpheus," observed Huey Long in the Senate the
next day, "I thought I heard my name being mentioned over the
radio in the next room. I listened for a little while, and, lo and
behold, I become convinced that perhaps I was being mentioned
in some unimportant connection." With this mild beginning,
the Kingfish whirled into a violent assault on Johnson, Bernard
Baruch, Roosevelt, Farley, and, in the end, Joe Robinson. "Beware! Beware!" Long said to the majority leader. "If things
go on as they have been going, you will not be here next year."
    While the galleries roared with appreciative laughter and Long,
his unbuttoned coat and vest revealing his bright pink shirt, swaggered to his seat, Robinson, who had been pushed around too
much, rose in fury. "Egotism, arrogance, and ignorance," he said,

"are seldom displayed in the Senate of the United States. They require a measure of talent possessed only by the Senator from Louisiana." With blunt phrases, he pounded away at Long. "I realize," he said at one point, "that there are those who are listening to me who will say, 'Why pay attention to the ravings of one who anywhere else than in the Senate would be called a madman?'" But the Senate was at last beginning to feel that its honor might be at stake. Month after month, said Robinson, the Senate had permitted Long to bulldoze his fellow senators as well as to assail from the privileged floor those outside who had no means of replying to him. "Now it is about time," Robinson said, "that the manhood in the Senate should assert itself." Before the angry debate was over, Bailey of North Carolina, McKellar of Tennessee, and other senators joined the attack. (Long, unperturbed, patted Robinson impudently on the shoulder as he sauntered off the floor.)

The belated revival of manhood in the Senate was the first consequence of Johnson's challenge to Long and Coughlin. His speech, said the *New York Times,* with unaccustomed enthusiasm, was "like the break-up of a long and hard Winter"; it would release others from the "moral terrorism" set up by the demagogues. This was certainly true. But the Johnson speech also offered the demagogues themselves an unprecedented chance for a national audience. Both Long and Coughlin moved quickly to take advantage of the opening.

Three days after Johnson, Long made a full-dress reply over nation-wide radio. With everyone expecting a blast of invective, Huey, with his flair for the unexpected, appeared instead as the embodiment of reasonableness and humility. "It will serve no useful purpose to our distressed people," he began, "for me to call my opponents more bitter names than they called me. Even were I able, I have not the time to present my side of the argument and match them in profanity." The administration was obviously out to destroy him, Long said good-naturedly; it all reminded him of Davy Crockett, who kept firing at what he thought was a possum in the top of a tree and finally discovered it to be a louse in his own eyebrow. He described the confusion in Washington. "What do you call it?" he asked. "Is it government? Maybe so. It looks more like the St. Vitus dance to me." And how inexcusable when the way out was so simple! "The billingsgate and the profanity of all of the Farleys and Johnsons in America cannot prevent the light of truth from hurling itself in understandable letters against the dark canopy of the sky." He then set forth the Share Our Wealth program before the largest audience of his life. At the end of the week Turner Catledge reported to the *New York Times* from Washington that Johnson and Roosevelt had "probably transformed Huey Long from a clown into a real political menace."

Coughlin followed Long to the microphone on March 11. Less astute than the Kingfish, the priest tried to match Johnson in abuse. "The money-changers whom the priest of priests drove from the temple of Jerusalem," he said, ". . . have marshaled their forces behind the leadership of a chocolate soldier for the purpose of driving the priest out of public affairs." With elaborate contrivance, he heaped epithets on Johnson — "a political corpse whose ghost has returned to haunt us," "the New Deal's greatest casualty . . . who never faced an enemy nor successfully faced an issue," "a cracked gramophone record squawking the message of his master's voice," and so on. But Coughlin's vituperation seemed a little studied and fancy beside the General's spontaneous abundance.

Coughlin's essential point was that Johnson was the servant of the international banking conspiracy. "I will dare confront the Herods by name and by fact," Coughlin announced with relish, "even though my head will be served on a golden platter, even though my body be sawed in twain." He recalled to his audience that this second possibility had been the unfortunate lot of the prophet Isaias for having scorned a prince by the name of Manasses. "Today there is another Manasses, your lord and master, General Johnson. I refer to Bernard Manasses Baruch . . . Him with the Rothschilds in Europe, the Lazzeres [sic] in France, the Warburgs, the Kuhn-Loebs, the Morgans and the rest of that wrecking crew whose God is gold and whose emblem is the red shield of exploitation — these men I shall oppose until my dying days." . . . "If you put quotations from Hitler and Father Coughlin in parallel columns," commented Johnson, "you can't tell them apart, including anti-Semitism. I think the Union for Social Justice is a Fascist movement." [2]

In his speech, Johnson had actually exaggerated the possibility of a Long-Coughlin alliance — chiefly, perhaps, in order to prevent its coming about. From the outside, such a coalition might have seemed reasonable enough. But at the start of 1935 Long and Coughlin had different tactical positions. Long had burnt his bridges to the White House; and he had the inestimable advantage of operating from an impregnable base of his own. But Coughlin had not yet finally broken with Roosevelt, in part because the National Union for Social Justice hardly gave him the same security that the state of Louisiana gave the Kingfish. In addition, Coughlin looked on Long with some personal distaste. When Walter Davenport asked him, about this time, whether he would entrust the principles of social justice to Long, Coughlin said sharply, "No, no. Let's not talk idly."

Aside from the public pleasure it afforded (which was considerable), the main result of the Johnson speech was to prevent the consolidation of any such coalition. Where Long had freely attacked Frank-lin De-La-No Roo-Se-Velt, Coughlin in a slight panic scurried back to the President. Only the evil influence of Baruch, he said, had prevented "a magnificent leader from rescuing a nation still bound to the rock of depression by the chains of economic slavery. . . . I still proclaim to you that it is either Roosevelt or ruin. I support him today and will support him tomorrow."

If the experience thus briefly chastened Coughlin, it only provided a new stimulus for Long. Nothing deterred him in the Senate; soon newspaper statisticians computed that he had filled over 10 per cent of the 748 pages printed in the *Congressional Record* thus far that session. And his eye was roaming farther afield. He was laying plans to topple Joe Robinson in Arkansas and Pat Harrison in Mississippi. He was in touch with Governor Eugene Talmadge in Georgia, and he held conversations with Robert E. Clements of the Townsend movement. He said he would back the Republicans if they nominated Borah in 1936. Late in April he appeared under the auspices of Milo Reno at the convention of the Farmers' Holiday Association in Des Moines. "The Lord has called America to barbecue," Huey said, "and fifty million people are starving." His monologue was, as usual, pungent and arresting. (The Chicago English professor Robert Morss Lovett found him on this occasion "an engagingly boyish figure, jovial and impudent, Tom Sawyer in a toga.") Henry Wallace and his associates, Long said, "should be hung. . . . Moses would have hung every damned man in the department." Father Coughlin? "I like Coughlin. I think his ideas are sound." Cries of "Amen" arose at intervals from the audience.

Coughlin had refused an invitation to speak, and his two observers at the convention warily declined to sit on the platform. Yet Coughlin, too, was maneuvering toward a break with the administration. A few days after the Des Moines meeting, he opened a new drive in Detroit for the National Union for Social Justice, with a selection of politicians — including Gerald Nye, Elmer Thomas, and William Lemke — sitting on the dais beside him. ("Father Coughlin has a damn good platform," said Huey Long quickly, "and I'm 100 percent for him. . . . What he thinks is right down my alley.") The priest went on to New York, attacked the New Deal, and told an audience at Madison Square Garden that, if relief wages were not adequate, "then this plutocratic capitalistic system must be constitutionally voted out of existence." But still he vacillated. A few days later, he informed his audience, "I am more optimistic as to the final outcome of the New Deal at this moment than ever before." [3]

v

In February and March the administration refrained from joining the melee. But the old battler Harold Ickes, watching the fun, found it increasingly hard to stay on the sidelines. Early in April he spoke out at a press conference. If Long insisted on using his "Longislature" to put all federal spending in Louisiana under his control, Ickes said amiably, "The Emperor of Louisiana is creating a situation down there where all allotments might have to be canceled." Huey quickly retorted that Ickes could go "slap damn to hell" and that one sovereign state was left in the country run by people "who don't give a damn about the combination between Stalin and the Nourmahal." "The trouble with Senator Long," Ickes said a few days later, "is that he is suffering from halitosis of the intellect. That's presuming Emperor Long has an intellect." (Roosevelt told Ickes at cabinet that this was the best thing that had been said about Long.) Long's response was an omnibus attack on all his New Deal hates — Farley, "the Nabob of New York"; Ickes, "the Chinchbug of Chicago"; Wallace, "the Ignoramus of Iowa"; Johnson, "the Oo-la-la of Oklahoma"; and Roosevelt, "Prince Franklin, Knight of the Nourmahal." Ickes fired back before the Associated Press in New York. Without mentioning names, he indicted "the man of crooked intellect" who peddles share-the-wealth schemes as "base and loathsome . . . beyond my powers of description." For good measure, he denounced "the other voice of the cloistered individual whose rich but undisciplined imagination has reduced politics, sociology and banking to charming poetry," and added some contemptuous words for the impractical visionary who dreams "an effervescent dream" of a utopia where all over sixty would have $200 a month.

Ickes, like Johnson, was going ahead on his own. But Roosevelt, as he soon told Jim Farley, had "no objections" to what Ickes was saying about Long and Townsend, though he did regard the reference to Coughlin as "very unwise." While Roosevelt permitted himself moments of irritation at Coughlin — he even mused about complaining to the Apostolic Delegate — he well knew the importance of the Catholic vote, and he had confidence in the ability of Frank Murphy and Joseph P. Kennedy to keep Coughlin sweet. But he was quite ready to take on the Kingfish. When former Governor Dan Moody of Texas turned down Morgenthau's request that he serve as government's attorney in presenting the case against the Long ring to a grand jury, Roosevelt's personal intervention persuaded him to change his mind. The President even wondered for a time whether the constitutional guarantee to states of a republican form of government might not serve as a basis for action against Long. A memorandum from Alexander Holtzoff of the Justice Department pointed to the ambiguities of the constitutional provision and killed the idea. Later Felix Frankfurter inquired for the White House into the possibility of a congressional investigation. "The wisdom of doing it," he reported to Roosevelt, "is opposed to the unanimous judgment of the leaders of the party in both House and Senate whom I have consulted. . . . In light of this expert political advice, I assume the matter is to be dropped." For a moment Roosevelt even played with the idea of a boycott of Louisiana by Federal agencies; but Monte Lemann, the eminent New Orleans lawyer and a leading opponent of Long's, persuaded him that this would be a mistake. Thwarted on every side in the hope of direct action, Roosevelt finally wrote Lemann, "We can only hope that even if the situation grows darker for a while, it will be but the prelude to the restoration of free government for the people of your city and state." And meanwhile he supported any weapon which might counter Long — even the demagogic Theodore Bilbo of the neighboring state of Mississippi. Thus, when Bilbo reported a success against "that madman Huey Long" in a Mississippi primary, Roosevelt replied hopefully, "I am watching your smoke."

Democrats in the Senate were also showing a new spirit. Though Robinson left Long alone after their scrimmage in March, a group of freshman Democrats, organized by Lewis Schwellenbach of Washington and Sherman Minton of Indiana, felt that, if their seniors would do nothing about Long, they would act themselves. "We are not going to let him continue to use the Senate," Schwellenbach said, "as a medium for making himself the Fascist dictator of America." When Huey heard their declaration of war, he told a newspaperman ironically, "Just say that I view with alarm the uprising of the young Turks." But they subjected him to relentless hazing. When Long rose to speak, they left the Senate. When he tried to filibuster, they refused him the usual courtesies by which the Senator could depart for relief without losing the floor. On one occasion, an inconspicuous member of the freshman group was in the chair while Long addressed a nearly empty chamber. Afterward, Long asked him, "What did you think of my speech?" "I had to listen to you," Harry S. Truman replied crisply, "because I was in the chair and couldn't walk out." Long never spoke to him again.

Senatorial snubs did not affect Long's popularity in the country. At Jim Farley's request, Emil Hurja of the Democratic National Committee conducted a rudimentary poll of third party possibilities in the summer of 1935. The result showed surprising support for Long in the farm belt, along the Great Lakes, and even on the eastern seaboard. Nearly 17 per cent of those on relief said they liked Long. Hurja counted him far stronger than Coughlin and estimated that, if he became a candidate, he might get as much as 2.75 million votes in 1936.[4]

VI

If the assault of the demagogues was seizing the headlines in the early months of 1935, the New Deal was experiencing at the same time another attack which, though less noisy and spectacular, was far more serious and effective. The source of this attack was the federal judiciary.

In 1933 the New Deal had been faced with a choice of tactics in presenting its legislative experiments to the courts. It could have sought immediate tests of constitutionality in the hope that the feeling of national emergency would influence judges to uphold the new legislation. Or it could have delayed such tests as long as possible in the hope that the laws, by demonstrating their practical value, would create a vested interest in their preservation. For various reasons — partly, no doubt, because people were busy doing too many other things in 1933 — the New Deal decided on the waiting strategy.

One reason, certainly, was fear of what the Supreme Court might decide. As Judge Learned Hand of the Second Circuit Court complained in 1934 of constitutional questions, "Who in hell cares what anybody says about them but the Final Five of the August Nine?" And of the August Nine, the Final Five, it had seemed in 1933, were inclined to strike down social legislation which, in their view, threatened the sanctity of private contracts. This, at any rate, had appeared the moral of the Oklahoma Ice case of 1932, when the Court set aside an attempt by the state of Oklahoma to require certificates of public convenience and necessity for entry into the ice industry.

Yet in his dissent in the Oklahoma case Justice Louis D. Brandeis had given powerful expression to larger views of governmental power. The emergency of depression, he said, was "more serious than war"; democracy's answer to economic crisis must be "the right to experiment." And in the next two years the Brandeis view seemed to be gaining new adherents among his brethren. In two crucial decisions on state economic legislation in 1934, Chief Justice Charles Evans Hughes and Associate

Justice Owen Roberts apparently swung over to the liberal side, transforming a minority of three into a majority of five.

First came the Minnesota Mortgage case, in which the Court, by a 5-4 vote, upheld the right of the Minnesota legislature to declare a moratorium on mortgage foreclosures. "The economic interests of the State," Hughes wrote in the majority opinion, "may justify the excuse of its continuing and dominant protective power notwithstanding interference with contracts." He sharply dismissed the suggestion that the words of the Constitution had to mean to "the vision of our time" exactly what they meant to the founders; and he laid special stress on the role of the emergency in justifying state intervention. "While emergency does not create power," he said, "emergency may furnish the occasion for the exercise of power." In a strong dissent, Justice George Sutherland denounced the decision as carrying "the potentiality of future gradual but ever-advancing encroachments upon the sanctity of private and public contracts."

This was bad enough, but a few weeks later, in the Nebbia case, came something worse. Here the Court — again by 5-4 — vindicated the right of the state of New York to set minimum milk prices. In a cogent opinion, which abandoned even Hughes's limiting emphasis on the concept of emergency, Roberts declared, "Neither property rights nor contract rights are absolute. . . . Equally fundamental with the private right is that of the public to regulate it in the common interest." The power to promote the general welfare, he continued, was "inherent in government." He then reaffirmed traditional canons of adjudication:

> With the wisdom of the policy adopted, with the adequacy or practicality of the law enacted to forward it, the courts are both incompetent and unauthorized to deal. . . . Times without number we have said that the legislature is primarily the judge of the necessity of such an enactment, that every possible presumption is in favor of its validity, and that though the court may hold views inconsistent with the wisdom of the law, it may not be annulled unless palpably in excess of legislative power.

In a bitter dissent, Mr. Justice McReynolds said that the logic of the majority threatened "an end to liberty under the Constitution." As for Roberts's plea for judicial agnosticism on the substance of policies — a plea that Hughes had made in the Minnesota case and even Sutherland had endorsed in his dissent — McReynolds said grimly, "Plainly, I think, this Court must have regard to the wisdom of the enactment. . . . Unless we can affirm that the end proposed is proper and the means adopted have reasonable relation to it, this action is unjustifiable."

Though the two decisions applied only to state laws, the Court's apparent readiness to defer to the legislative judgment, so robustly expressed by Roberts in the Nebbia decision, cheered the New Dealers. Conservatives were correspondingly depressed. James M. Beck, who had been Harding's Solicitor General, called the Nebbia case "as unfortunate as the Dred Scott decision." The two decisions, McReynolds observed darkly to Beck, meant "the end of the Constitution as you and I regarded it. An Alien influence has prevailed." [5]

VII

But state power was one thing, federal, another. The Court had yet to pronounce on cases involving New Deal legislation. And the strategy of delay was at last running out. In December 1934 the justices heard argument on a suit challenging the provisions of the National Industrial Recovery Act. On the first Monday after the President's annual message in 1935, the Court by an 8-1 vote decided the case against the government, holding unconstitutional the section of the act authorizing the President to forbid the interstate shipment of "hot" oil — that is, oil produced in violation of state production quotas. Hughes, speaking for the majority, declared the delegation of power to the President too vague. Justice Benjamin N. Cardozo replied in his solitary dissent that the preamble of the act supplied adequate standards for delegation and that laws designed for emergencies and "framed in the shadow of a national disaster" could not be expected to provide rigidly in advance for a host of unforeseen contingencies.

There had been serious technical defects in the government's case, including drafting errors in the executive order amending the code; one result was the establishment of the *Federal Register*, to provide for the official publication of such orders. But the mistakes involved seemed easily remediable, and the administration took the adverse decision philosophically. As the President told his press conference, he was reminded of the village constable serving under defective orders as a traffic cop at a dangerous intersection; he may have been employed illegally but still, in the meantime, he had saved lives. "You and I know that in the long run there may be half a dozen more court decisions before they get the correct language, before they get things straightened out according to correct constitutional methods." [6]

VIII

In a few weeks, the passage of a new law restored the administration's oil policy. But the next New Deal case involved far more critical issues. In 1933 Congress had by joint resolution voided the clauses in public and private bonds pledging redemption in gold; instead, all obligations were declared dischargeable in legal tender currency. This resolution provided the basis for devaluation and, indeed, for the nation's entire monetary policy. Now bondholders were challenging its constitutionality and demanding that their obligations be paid in their full gold value — i.e. $1.69 for every $1.00 on the face. If the Court were to affirm the absolute sanctity of contract and find for the bondholders, then the public debt would instantly increase by $10 billion, and the total debt of the country, by nearly $70 billion. Even more important, Congress would lose control of the power to regulate the currency, supposedly bestowed on it by the Constitution. As Roosevelt later described the situation, "The entire currency program and the entire gold and silver policy of the Government, which were among the chief foundations of the whole recovery program, would have been invalidated."

With so much at stake, Homer Cummings decided to present the gold case himself, in association with Stanley Reed of the RFC. "I have spent so much time, day and night, on these briefs and in the preparation of my oral arguments," he wrote Miss LeHand before going over to the courtroom, "that I begin to feel a bit like King Midas." The country had realized only slowly the significance of the issue. But, as Cummings opened his argument in the hushed courtroom on January 8, 1935, a sense of what hung on the outcome was beginning to agitate both Washington and Wall Street. Against the "supposed sanctity and inviolability of contractual obligations," the Attorney-General insisted on the government's "power of self-preservation." "That a written understanding must yield to the public welfare," he said, "has been so often reiterated that it is not necessary to dwell upon it any further." In dealing with the currency, government was merely "exercising a prerogative of sovereignty." And denial of this power to government in the midst of depression would have awful consequences. "The stupendous catastrophe . . . is such as to stagger the imagination. It would not be a case of 'back to the Constitution.' It would be a case of 'back to chaos.'" He concluded on a note of fervent appeal: "I feel the walls of this courtroom expand; I see, waiting upon this decision, the hopes, the fears, and the welfare of millions of our fellow citizens."

Cummings's concern was not simulated. Though Congress could mitigate some consequences of an adverse decision — for example, by limiting the right to sue the government for damages — it still could not hope to avert a chain reaction of confusion and bankruptcy. The situation called attention to the extraordinary power of the nine justices over national policy. In cabinet Vice-President Garner cited a pamphlet written about a hundred years earlier (perhaps John Taylor's *Construction Construed, and Constitutions Vindicated*) which predicted that the Court, through self-aggrandizement, would precipitate a major political crisis. Cummings observed that, if the Court ruled against the government, the number of justices should be at once increased to create a favorable majority.

As for the President, he felt strongly about the gold case. The power to regulate the currency seemed to him an attribute of sovereignty which the executive and legislative could not conceivably surrender to the judiciary. In addition, the bondholders clamoring for payment in gold were in his book no better than racketeers. No man holding a government bond could prove loss, the President thought, because the depreciated dollar of 1935 bought more than the gold dollar of 1926. As George Creel wrote after a talk with Roosevelt, "What these swarming litigants want, in the President's opinion, is $1.69 for their dollar, and he views it as an essentially dishonest demand."

With the magnitude of the issues at stake, both Cummings and Roosevelt contemplated desperate resorts. On January 14, Roosevelt actually told Morgenthau that he wanted the Treasury to keep things as unsettled as possible while the Court was making up its mind. Bonds and foreign exchange should move up and down, he said; if things were in a turmoil, then, in the event of a bad decision, the man in the street would say, "For God's sake, Mr. President, do something." Roosevelt added, "If I do, everybody in the country will heave a sigh of relief and thank God."

Cummings, who was present, egged Roosevelt on. But Morgenthau was deeply shocked. "I argued harder and more intensely than I have ever before in my life," he wrote in his diary. "Mr. President," he said earnestly, "you know how difficult it is to get this country out of a depression and if we let the financial markets of this country become frightened for the next month it may take us eight months to recover the lost ground." The stabilization fund had been given him by Congress as a trust; he could not use it to encourage uncertainty. As Roosevelt kept pressing him, Morgenthau finally pointed his finger at him and said, "Mr. President, don't ask me to do this." Roosevelt said, "Henry, you have simply given this thing snap-judgment. Think it over."

Morgenthau, thinking it over, was more certain than ever he was right. And Roosevelt, who thought it over himself, was evidently impressed, as he was on other occasions, by the upright Morgenthau's appeal to conscience. The next day the President and his Secretary of the Treasury met at the Vice-President's dinner. Mrs. Garner sat between them. Roosevelt leaned back in his chair and said, "Well, Henry, I am glad to see that you are smiling again." Then, turning to Mrs. Garner: "You know, Henry was very serious for an hour yesterday. . . . I was arguing with him about the gold case and in arguing I often take the side of the opposition in order to bring out the various points, but of course I didn't believe in these arguments." As the relieved Morgenthau said later, "He was notifying me that I had won." [7]

IX

This episode revealed the rising nervousness in Washington. And, for its part, Wall Street was equally nervous; the financial markets jittered up and down without governmental stimulus. By early February the national anxiety was so marked that Hughes permitted the unprecedented announcement after conference on Saturday, February 2, that the decision would not be handed down on the next Monday. He did the same thing a week later. In the meantime, the Court trooped to the White House for the annual dinner at which the President entertained the justices. "I suspect we will be as popular there," said Associate Justice Harlan Stone, "as a skunk in a hen house."

On February 16 the Court failed to repeat the announcement of the previous two Saturdays. Obviously the nine justices had completed their deliberations. The President had completed his deliberations, too. He now had in reserve a dissent of his own in the shape of a set of proclamations and orders nullifying an adverse Supreme Court decision. "To stand idly by and to permit the decision of the Supreme Court to be carried through to its logical, inescapable conclusion," Roosevelt was prepared to say in a radio address, "would so imperil the economic and political security of this nation that the legislative and executive officers of the Government look beyond the narrow letter of contractual obligations, so that they may sustain the substance." He meant to quote Lincoln's warning from his first inaugural against the people resigning the government into the hands of the Supreme Court; he meant to carry the fight to the country. (After reading the speech to Morgenthau, Roosevelt observed of the chairman of the Securities and Exchange Commission, "Joe Kennedy thinks the statement is so strong they will burn the Supreme Court in effigy.")

On Monday morning there was excitement everywhere — in the Treasury Department, where Morgenthau's people had been drafting proclamations and messages; in the Securities and Exchange Commission, where Kennedy was laying plans to close the exchanges; at the Supreme Court, where lines began to form three hours before the judges were due to assemble; and in Wall Street. Only the presidential office seemed calm: at 11:55 A.M., five minutes before the Court assembled, Miss LeHand called up Kennedy and said blandly that, since it was such a nice day, the President had decided to go for an automobile ride and would not be back till the late afternoon or evening.

Morgenthau, surrounded by aides, was already in the Cabinet Room at the White House. As word came over the ticker that

Hughes was beginning to read the decision, the President wheeled
in to join them. Then Kennedy called to relay the findings.
Meanwhile, at the Court, Hughes was summarizing a complex
opinion. So far as private contracts were concerned, the Court upheld the abrogation of the promise to pay in gold, but it went on
to deny the power of Congress to do the same for government
bonds. However, it quickly cancelled out the practical effect of
this conclusion (which would have raised the national debt 60
per cent) by adding that no actual damage had been shown and
that the aggrieved bondholders had no claims on the government;
indeed, payment of their claims would be "an unjustified enrich-
ment." (Not all were satisfied; a few weeks later a Cincinnati
lawyer, seeing possibilities despite the opinion, filed suit in the
Court of Claims to recover at least $1.07 for each dollar invested
in gold bonds. His name was Robert A. Taft.)

Hughes's opinion was a masterpiece of judicial legerdemain
hardly matched in the annals of the Court since Marshall's opinion
in *Marbury v. Madison*. Through dexterous legal reasoning, he
sought to sustain at once the rights of property and the powers of
the state, voting simultaneously for the immovable obstacle and
the irresistible force. The desire to temper without destroying
the government's power to repudiate contractual debts was intel-
ligible; but Hughes as a logician lacked the magistral power
of Marshall in Marbury. Harlan Stone's cogent concurrence only
slightly muffled his contempt for the Hughes talent (as he wrote
privately) at facing both ways. Though Stone felt that the government had behaved so immorally that for a time he thought he
could never buy another government bond, he had no doubt about
its right so to behave. "To countenance the repudiation of solemn
obligations is abhorrent to me," he told a friend, "but to say that
the Government's power to regulate currency and fix the value
of money can be set at naught by public or private contracts is
equally distasteful." He felt, moreover, that if Hughes believed
that no damage could be shown to the bondholders, he should, by
all rules of the judicial art, have stopped there instead of going on
to decide constitutional questions not necessary to the decision.
Learned Hand, dismissing the Hughes opinion as "pettifoggery,"
was even harsher in his verdict. "What you said was refreshing,
honest and direct," he told Stone. "Everybody dealing with a

sovereign knows he is dealing with a creature who can welch if he wants to welch. To trick up a lot of international stuff as though it were law frankly makes me puke, as dear old Holmes used to say."

The other side of the Court felt even more strongly about the decision. After Hughes finished for the majority, McReynolds, his face set and red, his high-pitched southern voice quivering with cold anger, held forth extemporaneously for about twenty minutes on behalf of the four dissenters. "To us," he said, "the record reveals a clear purpose to bring about confiscation of private rights and the repudiation of national obligations. . . . It is almost impossible to overestimate the result of what has been done here this day. The Constitution as many of us have understood it, the Constitution that has meant so much to us, has gone." Roosevelt, he said, was "Nero in his worst form."

As for Nero, listening to the result at the White House, he was enormously relieved, sorry only that he could not give his speech. The next day Roosevelt wistfully read passages to Tugwell and Moley. Moley observed drily that the President better save the language for the time when NRA would be declared unconstitutional.[8]

x

Roosevelt himself was under no illusion about the constitutional status of the rest of his program. "In spite of our rejoicing," he wrote a few days later to one of the lawyers who had argued the gold cases, "I shudder at the closeness of five to four decisions in these important matters!" And he had reason to shudder. On February 22 a district court judge in Alabama found that TVA could not constitutionally sell power in competition with private utilities. On February 27 a district court judge in Delaware found Section 7a of the National Industrial Recovery Act unconstitutional when applied to companies not engaged in interstate commerce — and held that the Weirton Steel Company was not so engaged. On the same day a district court judge in Kentucky found wage regulation in the coal industry under NRA unconstitutional. The judicial counteroffensive against the New Deal was gathering momentum on every side.

Was the Department of Justice in shape to handle this on-
slaught? Attorney-General Homer Cummings was himself a man
of genuine ability, wily in the law, experienced in politics, courageous and tough. His conduct in the case of Harold Israel, when
as state's attorney in Fairfield County, Connecticut, he braved public opinion to demand the dismissal of an indictment against a man
he believed innocent, was a classic of court history. With his tall,
stooping figure, his long nose, his blue eyes peering mildly through
a gold-rimmed pince-nez, his slowness in speech and movement, he
had the appearance of a wise old country lawyer in an old-fashioned play. But for all his capacity, he was also easy-going and
somewhat indolent; and, in the rush when he unexpectedly took
over the Department of Justice following the death of Thomas J.
Walsh, he affably allowed it to be stuffed with second-rate political
appointees. He spent most of his own time, in addition, working
on the reform of federal crime legislation and on the unification
of practice and procedure in the federal courts.

None of this need have mattered if Cummings had had an able
Solicitor General. But in the early confusion the job went to an
estimable but ineffectual old gentleman from North Carolina
named J. Crawford Biggs. From the first Biggs showed his unfit-
ness for the responsibility, losing ten of seventeen cases in his first
five months. On one occasion Chief Justice Hughes publicly rebuked him: "Mr. Solicitor General, you have talked forty-five
minutes already. You had better take the next fifteen minutes telling us what you want this court to do." As for Assistant Attorney-
General Harold Stephens, who argued the "hot" oil case, Ickes
said of him, "It makes me sick when I think of the way [Stephens]
handled our oil case before the Supreme Court last week, and yet
men on my legal staff think he was the best man in the whole Department to handle it."

Cummings now began to reorganize the Justice Department
for the impending crisis. In the middle of March, Biggs resigned
as Solicitor General, to be replaced by Stanley Reed. Through
Reed, an able, hard-working, and generous-minded chief, the alert
group of young Harvard Law School graduates, recruited by Frankfurter, led by Corcoran and Cohen, began to make their influence
felt in the Department. One result was an immediate improvement
in the technical quality of draftsmanship and argumentation. In

the next months Roosevelt and Cummings further strengthened the Department by bringing in top lawyers from the operating agencies — men who had acquired a first-hand substantive knowledge of the laws in controversy, John Dickinson from Commerce, Robert H. Jackson from the Treasury, Charles E. Wyzanski, Jr., from Labor, Alger Hiss from AAA, and Paul Freund from RFC.

Watching the rising conservative storm, conservatives began to feel happy for the first time since the 1934 election. For a year they had increasingly seen the Constitution as the issue which would save the country — if only someone could be found to save the Constitution. Now, at last, the judiciary appeared to be coming to the rescue. They looked on the future with new hope.[9]

15. The Death of NRA

In the spring of 1935 Roosevelt, seeking a new burst of policy to dynamite the economic and political stalemate, had several possibilities of varying promise. The legacy of the First New Deal was now fragmenting in a bewildering way: the President could, with Johnson, Moley, and Richberg, return to quietist government and economic orthodoxy; or he could, with Tugwell and Ezekiel, move on to more tightly controlled planning; or he could, with Means and the National Resources Planning Board, vanish into long-term research. None of these courses offered what he wanted most — a program for positive and dramatic action. Unconsciously, he was drawn to the new directions urged on him by Frankfurter, Corcoran, Cohen, and Eccles. But, as usual, he avoided ideological commitment. As usual, he even avoided intellectual clarity.

Thus his decision to send the holding-companies message to Congress in March did not necessarily mean full acceptance of the neo-Brandeisian analysis, any more than his support of the Eccles banking bill through the late winter and spring meant that he advocated (or even understood) the bold use of fiscal policy. The spenders, indeed, were colliding with one of the few economic doctrines which Roosevelt held in a clear way — that an unbalanced budget was bad. When Roosevelt cabled the American delegation in London in 1933 to "lay further stress on absolute necessity of every nation large and small living within income and starting to reduce national debts," he was unquestionably speaking his deep private conviction. In 1934 he had announced the achievement of "a completely balanced budget" by June 30,

1936, as "a definite objective." Yet even this he qualified. A reporter asked in January 1935 whether he saw any limit beyond which the debt could not be permitted to rise. Roosevelt replied by asking what he would do if five million people were starving: "would you let them starve in order to keep the public debt from going beyond a specific amount?" "Of course not, Mr. President," the reporter said. "There you are," said Roosevelt: "I don't know." [1]

II

Events were imposing policy on him. With well over nine million people unemployed, federal relief remained a critical need. But the existing character and pattern of relief were clearly unsatisfactory. The unemployed, with some justice, thought the amount of relief wretchedly inadequate; in May 1934 the average monthly grant per family was only $24.53. The business community, on the other hand, thought that too much was being spent on relief and that cutbacks were imperative if the nation was to move toward the cherished goal of the balanced budget. For the same reason, most businessmen believed that, if relief were necessary at all, it should be in the less expensive form of direct relief — the dole — rather than in the form of the provision of jobs by the government. But Harry Hopkins, the director of the Federal Emergency Relief Administration, detested direct relief; work relief, he said, "preserves a man's morale. It saves his skill. It gives him a chance to do something socially useful." In the costly but effective experiment of the Civil Works Administration in the winter of 1933–34, Hopkins had shown some of the possibilities of work relief, Harold Ickes, the director of the Public Works Administration, agreed on the superiority of work relief but naturally favored concentration on heavy public works. Henry Morgenthau, Jr., the Secretary of the Treasury, was torn between compassion for the hungry and concern for the budget; his main present objective was to bring coherence into federal spending programs by establishing a single point of review for all relief and public-works spending.

All these considerations made a reappraisal of relief policy inescapable. In October 1934 Roosevelt opened a series of meetings with Hopkins, Ickes, and Morgenthau by expressing his own general view: that federal direct relief should come to an end by a specified date; that all direct relief thereafter should be the pauper relief supplied by local government; and that Washington should try to give every employable worker a job through a massive public-works effort, costing perhaps $5 billion the first year and less in succeeding years. Hopkins and Ickes both favored this policy in its broad outline. By November Roosevelt's thinking was sufficiently settled for him to explain the new policy to his press conference.

Setting the general design was easy. What remained were a series of tough decisions over the actual composition of the works program. The decisions involved both issues and personalities. Roosevelt confronted the question whether the new program should favor light or heavy public works and the related question whether Hopkins or Ickes, both able and aggressive men, should run it.

In their own rough-and-ready way, Ickes and Hopkins had got along pleasantly enough in the first two years of the New Deal. In an unguarded moment a few months before, Ickes had even told Marvin McIntyre, "I have never worked more happily and understandingly with anyone than I have with Harry." Ickes, however, was under the fatal illusion that he could outmaneuver Hopkins. In mid-November 1934 he blandly suggested to Roosevelt that Hopkins be assigned to PWA as his deputy or perhaps as associate administrator in charge of rural housing and subsistence homesteads. "I don't think he is equipped to do a housing job as is contemplated," Ickes confided thoughtfully to himself, "and so far as Subsistence Homesteads is concerned, he won't have any easier task there than I have had." Ickes wrote in his diary, he was willing "to run the risk of getting along with Hopkins."

It was a greater risk than he suspected. One fine November day Hopkins, driving with members of his staff for an afternoon at the races at Laurel, Maryland, suddenly announced, "Boys — this is our hour. We've got to get everything we want — a works program, social security, wages and hours, everything — now or never. Get your minds to work on developing a complete ticket to provide security for all the folks of this country up and down and across the board." They retired to the St. Regis in New York for days of furious labor. By Thanksgiving a program was ready, and Hopkins was on his way to Warm Springs to present it to the President.

Roosevelt now summoned Ickes, Hopkins, and Morgenthau for new conferences. The differences of emphasis were sharpening. Ickes proposed a program of long-term public works designed to stimulate capital investment and ornament the nation, Hopkins, a program of short-term public works designed to stimulate consumption and mop up unemployment. Implied, too, was a further difference: the Hopkins program (at least as Raymond Moley interpreted it) assumed that rather rapid private re-employment would come about without a permanent spending policy. The Ickes program (as Tugwell saw it) assumed that a long-range spending policy was necessary and that PWA was the best vehicle to assure spending where spending mattered. The Hopkins program, moreover, avoided competition with private employers, while the Ickes program, especially in areas like housing and public power, not only seemed to businessmen to compete for skilled labor (largely a false issue: plenty of skilled workers needed jobs), but also was alleged to deter capital investment in these fields.

The growing personal resentments complicated the discussions. "Ickes and Hopkins," commented Tugwell, "are so worried about who is to do the job that they can hardly think of the job itself." Morgenthau, depressed by the "definite feeling of antagonism," told the President they could get nowhere until he chose between the rivals. Roosevelt replied curtly, "I will get a program within forty-eight hours. I am going to get my program first and I will not settle as to who is going to run it until I get my program."

Conditions were again shaping the President's decision. His main interest was in doing something as quickly as possible about the unemployed; and he tended therefore toward the program which promised to provide the most people the most jobs and money at the least expense to the government. Here the Hopkins approach had obvious superiorities. In the Hopkins program, about 75 per cent of the expenditures went for wages and 25 per cent for materials and other nonlabor costs. In the Ickes program, about 70 per cent went for materials and 30 per cent for wages. Moreover, PWA gave many fewer people direct employment; each man directly employed under PWA cost the government far more than under a civil-works program; and since PWA hired in the general labor market instead of concentrating on the relief rolls, it had only a secondary impact on the plight of the jobless. In addition, on the strictly economic side, Hopkins could argue plausibly for support of demand: "Recovery through governmental expenditures requires that Government money automatically goes to the lowest economic strata. It is there that occurs automatically the greatest number of respendings." [2]

III

What finally emerged from Warm Springs was the broad idea of a $5 billion program, made up, in a proportion yet undecided, of both short-term and long-term public works, though with the President obviously inclined toward the Hopkins approach. The next hurdle was the budget. Morgenthau and Daniel Bell, the Acting Director of the Bureau of the Budget, were determined, as zealous guardians of national solvency, to hold federal spending down. In the end-of-the-year conferences with Roosevelt on the budget message, they insisted stoutly on the dangers of inflation and the need for controlling the spending agencies. ("I am going to accomplish just what [Lewis] Douglas wanted a year ago," Morgenthau noted in his diary, recalling Douglas's attempt, before he left the administration, to require emergency agencies to obtain Budget Bureau approval before further funds could be obligated, "only I am going about it in a roundabout way and am sugar-coating it so that I hope they will not recognize it.") The President seemed surprisingly tractable during the budget talks; he never got irritated, never raised his voice, agreed to the insertion of a sentence (written by Charles Merz of the *New York Times*) pledging that all expenses beyond relief and works would be covered by Treasury receipts, and contented himself by saying philosophically at the end, "Well, my Budget Message is so tory that I will have to put in all of my radical suggestions in my message to Congress."

The message to Congress of January 4, 1935, contained vigorous language on the relief problem. "Continued dependence upon relief," Roosevelt said, "induces a spiritual and moral disintegration fundamentally destructive to the national fibre. To dole out relief in this way is to administer a narcotic, a subtle destroyer of the human spirit. . . . The Federal Government must and shall quit this business of relief." The only answer, Roosevelt suggested, was to provide *work* for all those able to work. "We must preserve not only the bodies of the unemployed from destitution but also their self-respect, their self-reliance and courage and determination."

To this end he advocated (adopting Hopkins's proposal) a national program aimed at putting 3.5 million men to work on an appropriation of $4 billion (plus $880 million unspent from previous appropriations), the sum to be allocated at the discretion of the Executive and to be administered by a unified works agency. The President laid down a set of criteria: the work undertaken should represent a permanent contribution to the nation; the wage paid should be a "security wage" — higher than relief dole but not so high as to deter people from private employment; as far as possible the projects should employ a large number of people, should be self-liquidating, should be located in distressed areas, and should not compete with private enterprise. As for those now on federal relief who would not fit into a works program — the unemployables — these, Roosevelt said, except for certain categories scheduled for aid under the pending social-security program, should be cared for by their communities as they had been before the New Deal.[3]

IV

The new proposal, submitted in the form of a joint resolution, now began a slow passage through an unenthusiastic Congress. The resolution asked, in effect, for a lump sum to be allocated pretty much at presidential discretion. Its congressional managers had no detailed information about how the funds would be used. And because Roosevelt still had not decided who would be in charge, no administration official was able to take responsibility for future policy in the hearings. Both Ickes and Hopkins testified as if in an administrative limbo, their language displaying wariness as well as hope.

The House passed the resolution with dispatch late in the month. Then it bogged down into two months of debate in the

Senate. Warren Austin of Vermont, expressing the conservative reaction, declared he was never "so stirred to the depths" as when he read the proposal. "The audacity, the boldness of the declarations contained in that joint resolution should have caused us unanimously to rise up against it." Jouett Shouse, rallying opposition from without, described the possible passage of the resolution as "a certain indication of the disintegration of the form of government under which we have lived." Many liberals, on the other hand, regarded the measure as inadequate: $4.8 billion seemed far too small to do the job. Some, like Bob La Follette, wanted to raise the appropriation to $9 billion. Others, like the social worker Edith Abbott, criticized the bill because turning back the unemployables to local poor relief seemed regressive and cruel.

The question of the "security wage" produced particular controversy. The American Federation of Labor, fearing that the relief wage would tend to break down general wage rates, argued that it should be increased to the level of the local prevailing wage. A senatorial bloc, led by Senator Pat McCarran of Nevada, introduced an amendment to that effect. Some members of the bloc, like McCarran himself, accompanied their defense of the higher wage with a desire to reduce the total appropriation. Others, like La Follette, Bronson Cutting, and Robert F. Wagner, mistrusted McCarran's motives but felt they had no choice save to go along. For a time, the McCarran amendment threatened to derail the whole program. But Roosevelt strongly opposed it, and in the end the threat of presidential veto saved the security wage.

The price, however, was delay, legislative confusion, an exposure of administration vulnerability, and retreat on other important issues. Thus Democrats in Congress had long been bitterly complaining to the White House that appointments to New Deal agencies in the states, especially in the relief field, were going to Republicans and independents. Now Roosevelt was compelled to accept a provision requiring senatorial confirmation for all appointees under the new program to jobs paying more than $5,000 a year. This single amendment guaranteed that politics would play a much larger part in the new works administration than it had in FERA or CWA. Other disabling amendments forced on the administration a bad system of statutory allocation of the funds; a requirement that, other things being equal, the new

agency should give preference to private contractors; and a provision, demanded by Senator Borah, denying the use of relief
funds to build warships or munitions. With these restrictions,
the Emergency Relief Appropriation Act of 1935 went to the
President, who affixed his signature early in April.[4]

v

The condition of the unemployed imposed policy in one direction. The state of mind of the business community imposed policy
in another. The authorization of a $4.8 billion relief program, at
a time when the budgetary deficit was approaching what to businessmen of 1935 was the appalling point of $3.5 billion, sharpened
discontent on the right. The New Deal of 1933 had relied in
great part on government-business co-operation. But, beginning
in the winter of 1933–34, Roosevelt confronted new business
moods. In January 1935 Tugwell, speaking to a presumably
friendly business group at a dinner arranged by Raymond Moley
in New York, encountered little of the old-time geniality. Present,
among others, were Wendell L. Willkie of Commonwealth and
Southern, Bruce Barton of Batten, Barton, Durstine and Osborne,
Lewis Brown of Johns-Manville, and Colby Chester of General
Foods. "Throughout the evening," Tugwell noted in his diary,
"there was not a single constructive suggestion." (Willkie, Tugwell added, "did a good deal more than his share of complaining.")
At the end, according to Tugwell, the discussion degenerated into
angry remarks about "the attitude of the mob, as they called it,
and the administration's responsiveness to it." Tugwell commented unhelpfully that this sounded like fascist talk to him, and
on this discordant note the meeting ended.

And the Moley dinners involved chiefly the more or less well-
disposed businessmen. Others, who had been morosely silent in
1933 and only muttering in 1934, were now regaining full power
of speech. At the end of April 1935 the United States Chamber
of Commerce held its annual meeting in Washington. Here businessmen from all over the country had a long-awaited opportunity
to express their pent-up indignations in the very shadow of the
White House. The result was to provide what many New Dealers
regarded as a conclusive test of the validity of the partnership
thesis of 1933.

Not all businessmen were in all-out opposition. The Chamber of Commerce meeting showed the existence of a deep rift between those who wanted at least to maintain diplomatic relations with the New Deal and those who insisted on war against it. The first class was made up to a degree of big businessmen, living in big cities, college-educated, many associated with the very Wall Street the New Dealers were working so hard to subject to public control. These men were less affected personally by New Deal measures than were small businessmen. A large corporation could absorb the impact of wages and hours regulation, of unemployment insurance, of trade unions; its president could even win a gratifying reputation for industrial statesmanship by a display of tolerance for such new ideas. Appreciating the importance of public relations, appreciating in some cases the problems of government, men of this sort inclined to view Roosevelt's efforts, if not with positive sympathy, at least with the conviction that they could exert more influence from the inside than from the outside.

The second class consisted mostly of medium-sized and small businessmen, largely from small towns, in the main less educated, less wealthy, and less sophisticated than the others. These men were directly hit by New Deal measures as the big men never were, in terms of status as well as of profits. They felt injured by political hostility and threatened by social change. They could not understand what in the world was going on in Washington. They were determined to dig in their heels and fight for the America they knew. The intransigents among the big businessmen played on their fears and provided them with leadership.

In 1931 the United States Chamber of Commerce had endorsed what its president called "the philosophy of a planned economy." In 1933, when the NRA emerged as a partial response to the Chamber's program, the delegates gave Roosevelt a rising ovation. In 1934, they were somewhat critical of the New Deal; but, if the President did not address them in person, still he sent along a not unfriendly message. Now in 1935 it was known even before the meeting convened that there would be no presidential appearance, not even a presidential greeting. And the old leadership of the Chamber, still disinclined to break openly with the New Deal, discovered that it could not hold the rank-and-file in line.

"We have floundered along for two years without knowing whether we were going to be locked up or not," cried Silas H.

Strawn of Chicago. "I think we have the right to know where we are going. Businessmen are tired of hearing promises to do constructive things, which turn out to be only attempts to Sovietize America." In this spirit, the Chamber, only so recently the citadel of planning, enthusiastically voted its opposition to the proposed two-year extension of NRA, to the social-security bill, to legislation on public utility holding companies, to the government's banking bill, to pending amendments to AAA and to all labor legislation.

A few big business leaders took care to dissociate themselves from this outburst. "As a member of the United States Chamber of Commerce," Thomas J. Watson of International Business Machines wrote the President the next day, "I deeply regret the sweeping criticisms of the Administration, but I am sure their action does not reflect the sentiment of businessmen in general." The Business Advisory Council — including among others, Watson, Henry I. Harriman, the outgoing president of the Chamber, Winthrop Aldrich of the Chase National Bank, Walter S. Gifford of American Telephone and Telegraph, W. Averell Harriman of Union Pacific, Myron Taylor of United States Steel, Gerard Swope of General Electric, and Robert E. Wood of Sears Roebuck — called at the White House and came out for the two-year extension of NRA and other administration measures. But this did not modify the public impression of an across-the-board repudiation of the New Deal by organized business.[5]

VI

The Chamber of Commerce meeting crystallized Roosevelt's growing exasperation with the business community. To Watson he replied that the speaking program was obviously packed from the start; "that was due to childlike innocence or to malice of forethought on the part of somebody!" At his press conference, he added, "I don't believe there was a single speech which took the human side, the old-age side, the unemployment side." And to both Watson and the newspapermen he spoke earnestly about the role of business associations played in misrepresenting the American businessman. Decent businessmen, Roosevelt said, disliked bad working conditions as much as anyone else. Yet business organizations always fought reform. He recalled the Triangle Fire, the workmen's compensation act, the act to limit working hours for women and children to fifty-four hours a week. "It makes me very sad," he told Watson,

> to think that because of the action of a few Associations the country as a whole has it pretty well in mind that business-men are "agin" every improvement and have been consistently for more than a generation. An actual inspection of the rec-ord will show, for example, that our own Chamber of Com-merce in New York has a one hundred per cent record of opposition to things like factory inspection, excessive hours, elimination of child labor, old age pensions, unemployment insurance — year after year the same old story. They may have been right in opposing some of the measures but certainly not the great majority of them. Furthermore, in all this time, dur-ing my own experience of twenty-five years in public life, the same Chamber has never yet initiated and pressed one single item of social betterment.

As Roosevelt looked back over his administration, he thought he had displayed great forbearance. The New Deal, he believed, had saved the position and the profits of the businessmen. He had forgiven their errors of the past and their lack of ideas for the future. And now organized business was assuming what he re-garded as a posture of indiscriminate, stupid, and vindictive oppo-sition. Nothing seemed more unreasonable than the business com-munity. As Elmer Davis once put it, business constantly proclaimed its lack of confidence and expected it to be taken as final con-demnation. "But if anybody ventures to imply some lack of con-fidence in Business, Business is terribly hurt, and calls him a crackpot and a Communist." The rich may have thought that Roosevelt was betraying his class; but Roosevelt certainly supposed (as Richard Hofstadter has suggested) that his class was betraying him.

All those who had been telling Roosevelt that government could not rely on business now saw business prove their point. Bob La Follette called the Chamber's attack most fortunate. The Chamber's meeting, said Tugwell, "is perhaps one of the best things which has happened politically. The President must begin to consolidate the support which is natural to him among the workers and the farmers." And, a few days after the businessmen stormed out of Washington, the President summoned a group of progressives to the White House. From the cabinet were Ickes and Wallace; from the Senate, La Follette, Wheeler, Norris, Costigan, and Hiram Johnson; and from the outside, Felix Frankfurter and David K. Niles, head of the liberal Ford Hall Forum in Boston and a La Follette Progressive of 1924. The group told the President that the time had come for him to assert leadership. Frankfurter said that Brandeis had sent word it was "the eleventh hour." All agreed that business would in no circumstances support the President; Ickes observed that the administration could capitalize on this opposition. La Follette reminded the President that Theodore Roosevelt had not hesitated to take issue with members of his own party; perhaps the time had come for Franklin Roosevelt to do the same.

The talk was candid and unrestrained. Ickes left with the impression that Roosevelt meant to take a progressive stand and force the fighting on that line.[6]

VII

In the meantime, the administration was under mounting pressure on the judicial front. It had won a narrow if ambiguous victory in the gold cases; but in March and April 1935 it suffered a new series of setbacks in lower courts. And on May 6 the New Deal lost its next constitutional test when the Supreme Court, by a 5–4 decision, found the Railroad Retirement Act unconstitutional.

The majority opinion, written by Mr. Justice Roberts, was drastic in its implications. It rejected, not just this particular act, but the whole basic proposal involved; not only the law before it, but all conceivable laws addressed to the same end. "The gravest aspect of the decision," said Chief Justice Hughes in dissent, "is that it does not rest simply upon a condemnation of particular features of the Railroad Retirement Act, but denies to Congress the power to pass any compulsory pension act for railroad employees." The majority, as Hughes pointed out, had declared the whole subject of railroad pensions beyond the reach of the congressional authority to regulate interstate commerce. "I think that the conclusion thus reached," said the Chief Justice, "is a departure from sound principles and places an unwarranted limitation upon the commerce clause of the Constitution." Moreover, in laying down his total constitutional prohibition, Roberts went far beyond what was necessary to dispose of the case before him. Mr. Justice Stone, who joined Hughes, Brandeis, and Cardozo in dissent, told a friend that he would have voted against the act as a member of Congress, "but to say that it is beyond the range of constitutional power puts us back at least thirty years. . . . How arrogant it must well seem to those unaccustomed to judicial omniscience." He later described the decision as "the worst performance of the Court in my time."

With the National Industrial Recovery Act now making its way up through the lower courts, the sweep of the railway pension decision alarmed the administration. Still, there were grounds for hope. After all, the National Industrial Recovery Act did have plausible constitutional foundations. There seemed good reason when the act was passed in June 1933 for supposing that the Court, following the tendency of recent decisions, might concede Congress the power to regulate wages, hours, and trade practices in interstate commerce. The theory of "a current of commerce," which Justice Holmes had broached as early as 1905, had significantly broadened the application of the commerce clause; a series of railroad regulation cases — the Shreveport case, *Wilson v. New* and the Dayton–Goose Creek Railway case — had further affirmed federal power to control local commerce even when effect on interstate commerce seemed tenuous. As for the delegation of legislative power, one law-review article in 1934 concluded that the act should have no great difficulty on that score; "previous acts of Congress going as far or further have been upheld." Moreover, Hughes himself, in the Minnesota Mortgage case, had suggested that a national emergency could furnish the occasion for special exercise of governmental power. And beyond the rigorous constitutional argument lay an appeal, much favored by Donald Richberg, to inherent rights of government. "It is a pitiful concept of sovereignty," Richberg liked to say, "that would emasculate the Constitution and paralyze the protection of all our liberties by denying to our Government the elementary powers of self-preservation."

Nor did constitutional experts widely question the act. Thomas Reed Powell, Harvard's eminent authority on constitutional law, said in November 1933 that, if the Court threw out NRA, "it would assume a dictatorship without parallel even in this day of dictators. . . . No judicial statesman could for a moment think the judiciary a fit instrument to assume command in a situation like this." Even James M. Beck, who was forever on the verge of declaring the federal government itself unconstitutional, wound up a tirade against NRA with the statement, "I am not saying that the National Industrial Recovery Act may not in some way pass the gauntlet of the Supreme Court." Indeed, up to April 1935, NRA had a fair record of success in the courts. In March, on the eve of NRA's day of trial, Hugh Johnson could write, "I think the rock of our deliverance is the Supreme Court."

Johnson's optimism was soon to receive its test. For a considerable period, the administration had been divided about the merits of carrying an NRA case to the Supreme Court. Some thought the law should be allowed to expire in June 1935 without final adjudication; then Congress could pass a new act with more definite standards. But Richberg felt that the administration must fight for the existing law if local NRA enforcement was not to break down. Accordingly, when a federal judge in Alabama held the National Industrial Recovery Act unconstitutional, Richberg favored an immediate appeal to the Supreme Court.

This case involved the proprietor of a lumber mill, W. E. Belcher, who had admittedly worked his employees longer and paid them less than provided for in the Lumber Code. The Belcher case had certain advantages. There was no argument about the facts; nor could there be much argument that his lumber fell within the domain of interstate commerce. But the case presented difficulties too, as Stanley Reed discovered when he took over as Solicitor General in March. The Lumber Code, one of the very early codes, contained production quotas — a device which the NRA itself was unwilling to defend by 1935. Moreover, the record of the Belcher case, because there was no dispute over the facts, was singularly bare of the social and economic data which the NRA felt essential to its cause. Richberg, admitting these drawbacks, still felt it would be better to take the chance with the Court than to encourage further violation of the codes by dropping the case. Hugh Johnson, on the outside, regarded it as a case "truly presenting the real Constitutional issues" in "a great natural resource industry of national extent." Reed and the Department of Justice disagreed, however, and Felix Frankfurter endorsed their judgment. On March 25 the government asked for the dismissal of its appeal in the Belcher case, two weeks before it was due for argument.

As Richberg had anticipated, the reaction was bad. The Lumber Code Authority threw up its hands and announced that it saw no point in trying to enforce the code further. The NRA staff felt itself abandoned by the government. People in general wondered why they should obey a law which the government was unwilling to test in the courts. Just at this point, a new case was projected into the picture. On April 1 the Second Circuit Court, in the case of *United States v. A.L.A. Schechter Poultry Corporation,* upheld on vital issues the constitutionality of NRA.[7]

VIII

The function of the live poultry industry could hardly have been more elevated: it existed to provide kosher chickens for orthodox Jews. Live chickens, shipped in from the countryside, were sold to slaughterhouses, where they were killed according to the proper ritual by a minor religious official and then delivered to retail butchers for sale to the faithful. But few trades in the nation were more squalid. It was a fiercely competitive industry, dwelling on the margin of the underworld and abounding in vicious practices. A witness for the Schechters had testified that live poultry traders were "looked upon as the worst type of businessmen in the world." The Live Poultry Code tried, among other things, to use its fair-trade provisions as a way of cleaning up the industry. Thus the Schechter brothers had been convicted in a lower court of violating the code not only by filing false sales and price reports but by selling diseased poultry, unfit for human consumption.

It was this last aspect which prompted Hugh Johnson to call it the "sick chicken" case. To Johnson it seemed "an absurd case on which to hazard a great and sweeping policy." Yet, while live poultry was precisely the sort of petty trade which NRA officials now generally wished they had never got into, nonetheless the case presented certain advantages from the government's viewpoint. Thre was no more respected court in the country than the New York Circuit Court. Its opinion, fortified by a concurrence from Learned Hand, clearly approved the delegation of legislative power, the process of code-making, and the fair-trade provisions in the code, though it invalidated the wages and hour provisions on the ground that slaughterhouse employees were not directly engaged in interstate commerce. Moreover, a year before, a unanimous Supreme Court, speaking through Justice Butler in an antitrust case, had declared the live poultry industry subject to federal regulation. If the industry was interstate for purposes of the Sherman Act, there seemed good reason to suppose that it was equally interstate for purposes of NRA.

Richberg, desperately anxious to save NRA enforcement from total demoralization, wanted to carry the case immediately to the Supreme Court; and he converted Cummings and Reed to this view. On April 3 Richberg cabled Roosevelt, who was away from Washington for a week's fishing on the *Nourmahal*, that, as a result of the Belcher dismissal, ENFORCEMENT CODES GENERALLY IMPOSSIBLE AND HOSTILITY OF CONGRESS TO NEW LEGISLATION GREATLY INCREASED. Prompt action on the Schechter case, he said, WILL REVERSE GENERAL RETREAT AND STRENGTHEN ENTIRE SITUATION. . . . OTHERWISE PRESENT DISCOURAGEMENT WILL GRADUALLY DESTROY INDUSTRIAL RECOVERY PROGRAM. The next day Felix Frankfurter learned to his dismay that Cummings planned a press conference that afternoon to announce an appeal on the two counts the government lost in the circuit court. As Tom Corcoran cabled Roosevelt, FRANKFURTER SUGGESTS MOST IMPOLITIC AND DANGEROUS TO YIELD TO ANTAGONISTIC PRESS CLAMOR NOW BECAUSE FUNDAMENTAL SITUATION ON COURT NOT CHANGED. FURTHER SUGGESTS YOU WIRE CUMMINGS NOT TO TAKE HASTY ACTION. Roosevelt wired Cummings to hold the situation in abeyance until his return. But the message arrived too late. (Corcoran believed that it was deliberately held up.)

The Frankfurter group thus failed to halt the appeal. In point of fact, the government could not have dodged the case anyway.

Even if the Department of Justice had declined to appeal the counts it had lost, the Schechter brothers were resolved to appeal the counts the government had won. Frederick H. Wood of the Cravath firm, an eminent corporation lawyer, had taken over for the defense. So prosecution and defense applied jointly early in April for *certiorari*. This was immediately granted by the Court, with argument scheduled for early May.

Cummings, who had his doubts about NRA and evidently wished to share the responsibility for advocacy, now asked Richberg to participate in the argument. Richberg, fearing that Reed did not know enough about NRA operations to make the most effective presentation, accepted with alacrity. On May 2 and 3 the case went before the Court. This was one of the Court's last sessions in the old Senate chamber in the Capitol, a small semicircular room with domed ceiling, classic columns, mahogany furniture, and two great fireplaces. Richberg, arrayed in wing collar and cutaway, joined with Reed in arguing for the government in terms of constitutional precedent and of social need. Wood replied that if the government could regulate the live poultry industry, "it could regulate all businesses and, carried to its logical conclusion, the concept would ultimately find Congress in charge of all human activity."

Three and a half weeks later, at noon on Monday, May 27, the justices filed into their places. They were evidently in a cheerful mood. As the crowded room waited with intense interest, Justice Sutherland read an opinion rebuking the President for having summarily removed a Federal Trade Commissioner who had sought to thwart administration policies. In discharging Commissioner William E. Humphrey, Roosevelt had followed what was thought to be a rule clearly set forth by the Supreme Court in the Myers case of 1926. Brandeis had dissented in the Myers case, and a unanimous court now endorsed his result. What gave the Court's opinion a sting of personal animus was its failure to acknowledge that the President, in removing Humphrey, was acting as far as he knew in conformity with the Constitution as interpreted by Chief Justice William Howard Taft and a previous Court majority. Indeed, before making the removal, Roosevelt had consulted with James M. Landis, who had been Brandeis's law clerk at the time of the Myers decision; and Landis pointed to language inserted deliberately and after discussion in Taft's opinion to cover the very case of the independent commissions (the original case had involved a postmaster). But the new decision conveyed the clear impression, not that the Court had changed its mind, but that Roosevelt's action had been high-handed and lawless.

Hardly had this blow fallen when Justice Brandeis, again for a unanimous court, pronounced the Frazier-Lemke Act for the relief of farm mortgagors unconstitutional. (Two unanimous circuit courts and five district judges — a total of eleven judges — had sustained this act. Two district judges and now the nine Supreme Court justices voted against it. Noting the eleven to eleven score, Cummings said sarcastically to Roosevelt, "Manifestly the law is 'an exact science.'") Then came the moment of climax. Chief Justice Hughes announced that he himself would read the opinion in the Schechter case. Moving forward in his chair, his arms rigid on the bench, occasionally stroking his beard, speaking with unaccustomed vehemence in the quiet courtroom, Hughes, for a unanimous court, knocked down with a series of blunt strokes the entire edifice of NRA.

In the room below, Donald Richberg looked suddenly pale and tired. Later he said that the decision ranked with the repeal of the Missouri Compromise "as a tragic event in the history of self-government." As the crowd dispersed, a page tapped Tom Corcoran on the shoulder and asked him to come to the robing room. Corcoran entered to find the justices disrobing. Brandeis, holding his arms aloft for a page to take off his robe, looked to Corcoran for a moment like a black-winged angel of destruction. The old Justice had rejoiced in Hughes's opinion; he had noted on the draft, "This is clear and strong — and marches to the inevitable doom." Now he said triumphantly to Corcoran, "This is the end of this business of centralization, and I want you to go back and tell the President that we're not going to let this government centralize everything. It's come to an end. As for your young men, you call them together and tell them to get out of Washington — tell them to go home, back to the states. That is where they must do their work." To his former law clerk Paul Freund he said, "Now we can move ahead." . . . This was the Black Monday of the New Deal.[8]

IX

The Court made two great points against NRA.

The first dealt with the question of delegation. The doctrine that a legislature could not delegate its powers had been, since the time of Locke, a commonplace among lawyers. However, before 1935, it had never been taken very seriously in the testing of federal law. The Founding Fathers, for example, though wholly familiar with the phenomenon of delegation, had seen no reason to ban or limit it in the Constitution. Until the "hot" oil case of January 1935, the Supreme Court had never once invoked the delegation doctrine to invalidate a federal law. The extent of delegation in NRA had given no trouble to so conscientious a judge as Learned Hand. Yet Hughes raised this as the first decisive count in his indictment. He declared he could find no standards or rules of conduct to govern the delegation. The discretion of the President in prescribing codes seemed "virtually unfettered." He thus condemned the code-making authority conferred by the act as unconstitutional. And Justice Cardozo, distinguishing his opinion in the Schechter case from his dissent in the "hot" oil case, condemned the law as "delegation running riot." (In 1937 he told a law clerk that he was a lot surer he had been right in dissenting in the "hot" oil case than in concurring in Schechter.)

The Court did not state with precision what it meant on the delegation point. Professor E. S. Corwin was probably right when he suggested that it was "the huge *number* of codes, rather than the delegated power represented by any particular code," which appalled the justices. Certainly Cardozo's objection was not to delegation per se, but to delegation running riot. No previous act of Congress had involved so much delegation; in this respect, NRA was novel and extreme; and this perhaps justified Hughes in blowing up the delegation concept into a major constitutional doctrine. The doctrine did not, however, long survive this decision; delegation without a standard (though never delegation in the quantity of NRA) subsequently became not uncommon in federal law.

Having invalidated the act on the issue of delegation, the Court, according to the discreet practice of the judicial art, might have stopped there. Instead, Hughes — like Roberts in the railway pension case — went on to place not only the technique but the subject matter of the legislation beyond the reach of federal power. The Chief Justice's second decisive count dealt with the substance of regulation under the commerce clause.

Seeking to narrow the application of the clause, Hughes revived an older distinction between the "direct" and "indirect" effects on interstate commerce — a distinction he alleged to be "a fundamental one, essential to the maintenance of our constitutional system." Though the bulk of the Schechter poultry came from without the state, Hughes argued that it came "to a permanent rest within the State" (*i.e.* was eaten there), and thus sale within the state was not part of the flow of commerce. Moreover, he rejected the argument that the indirect effects of the live poultry business on economic standards and stability, however great, could ever warrant federal intervention. He even cited with approval a dictum from an earlier decision applying to more formidable industries: "building is as essentially local as mining, manufacturing, or growing crops."

Cardozo and Stone agreed with Hughes's result in the particular case — that is, that the Schechter brothers were engaged in local business. But they backed away from what Stone privately called Hughes's "mechanical" distinction between "direct" and "indirect" effects. As Cardozo suggested in his concurrence (in which Stone joined), the difference was one not of principle but of size. "The law," Cardozo wrote, "is not indifferent to considerations of degree." Thus, where Hughes would presumably deny that indirect effects on interstate commerce even of great magnitude would qualify an industry for national regulation, Cardozo and Stone were evidently willing to consider the concrete situation in each case — a difference of vast potential importance. "I hope," Stone wrote Reed Powell of Harvard, ". . . you noted that two members of the Court did not join in proclaiming the distinction between direct and indirect effects upon Commerce to be the universal touchstone of Constitutionality."

The Schechter decision raised even larger questions than the problems, important as they were, of delegation and of the commerce clause. Together with the railway pension case, it showed an apparent determination on the part of the Court to go

beyond the needs of the immediate litigation and announce broad
constitutional conclusions. Instead of deciding constitutional
cases in the usual manner, as narrowly as possible, the present
Court was evidently resolved to decide them as broadly and pro-
spectively as possible. In these cases it was deciding more than
was required, and, in addition, deciding things that did not have
to be decided at all.

Why should it be doing this? The answer seemed plain enough:
The Court was warning the President and the Congress. This
technique of adjudication, wrote Reed Powell, was obviously intended "to ward off future congressional action." Felix Frankfurter and Henry Hart (a former Brandeis law clerk), added,
"Against such advisory pronouncements the constitutional theory
and practice of a century and a half unite in protest." Frankfurter and Hart concluded their review of the 1934–35 session, by
reminding the Court of its own traditions: as social problems
became more intense and complicated, "the deep wisdom of the
Court's self-restraint against undue or premature intervention,
in what are ultimately political controversies, becomes the deepest
wisdom for our times." [9]

X

The public reaction to Black Monday was an indecipherable
mixture of dismay, delight, and confusion. There was no clear
crystallization of popular sentiment: an American Institute of
Public Opinion poll on the revival of NRA, taken a year later,
showed 49 per cent of those with opinions in favor and 50 per cent
opposed. The one group unaffectedly angered by the decision
was labor. As Sidney Hillman said bitterly, recalling Brandeis's
fight against bad working conditions in the garment industry,
"Having then closed the sweatships, he has now cleared the way
for their reopening." "The great masses of the American people,"
said the *American Federationist*, "do not agree with the Supreme
Court that the promotion of social ends is not a proper purpose
for the use of government regulation." "The average man and
woman," said the *United Mine Workers' Journal*, "cannot understand how such a beneficent law could be destroyed on such a
pretext." And the radical press was equally indignant. "We are

thrown, tied and branded by the Grand Lamas of legalism on the Supreme bench at Washington," said Joseph Medill Patterson's *New York Daily News.* "They are our real rulers. We have got to curb these men." "When men like Stone, Cardozo, Brandeis and Hughes believe that the Constitution compels them to decide as they did in this case," said the *New Republic,* "there is no point any longer in saying that the Constitution is infinitely flexible. . . . To have a socialist society we must have a new Constitution."

Congressmen, on the whole, took the verdict in their stride; NRA had few all-out defenders on Capitol Hill. "I raise my hand in reverence," said Huey Long, "to the Supreme Court that saved this nation from fascism." The conservative press could not have been happier — "a tyranny overthrown," said the *New York Herald Tribune.* "We are back to fundamentals," exulted Frank Kent. ". . . The bottom has been knocked out of the New Deal." Businessmen were at first jubilant; then, with second thoughts, somewhat apprehensive. "The NRA was no sooner pronounced dead," reported Arthur Krock of the *New York Times,* "than many who had attacked it began to appeal to the White House for a substitute to preserve some of its great achievements."

In the White House itself there was much coming and going. Richberg, Tugwell, and other advisers descended on the President. Hugh Johnson and Felix Frankfurter appeared from afar with their opposing views on the merits of NRA. Meanwhile, Roosevelt himself bided his time. At his Wednesday press conference, two days after the decision, he equably dodged comment. When someone asked whether he had heard anything about limiting the power of the Court, he replied with a laugh that he had had about fifty different suggestions, going all the way "from abolishing the Supreme Court to abolishing the Congress, and I think abolishing the President."

Two days later the President held his next press conference. As he was dressing, Steve Early came in for the usual preconference rehearsal. Early told Roosevelt that he had driven to the office with his brother-in-law George Holmes, head of the International News Service bureau in Washington. "George says," Early continued, "that those boys up there think that this is still the horse-and-buggy age." The President made no response. In a

few moments he casually suggested to the Felix Frankfurters, who
were staying at the White House, that they might enjoy attending
the conference. Frankfurter, who disliked the limelight, decided
not to come; the law professor and the President had no other
conversation that morning about the Court.

The conference was twenty minutes late in starting. Mrs. Roosevelt was there, knitting steadily away at a blue sock. Mrs. Frankfurter sat beside her. The President finally arrived, radiating his
usual good humor. The sheaf of yellow telegrams on the desk
beside him suggested that he might have something special to
say. He began by reading some of the wires — pathetic appeals
from people across the country pleading for the restoration of
NRA or something like it in order to protect standards of life
and labor. Then he turned to the implications of the decision.
It was, he began "more important than any decision probably
since the Dred Scott case." He did not resent the decision —
"nobody resents a Supreme Court decision" — but he felt justified
in calling the country's attention to its probable consequences.

He considered briefly the question of delegation. Much wartime
legislation, he observed, was "far more violative" of the supposed
ban against delegation then the recovery act. In any case, the
objections to delegation would have been curable in a new act.
What was really serious, he said, was what the Court had done
to the commerce clause. In recent years the Court had tended
to interpret the commerce clause broadly with a view to the
needs of a highly organized and interdependent economy. But
the Schechter decision, by rejecting the notion of "indirect"
effects on interstate commerce, was reverting to the old view that
the clause applied only to goods in actual transit across state
lines. The decision, Roosevelt said, denied the economic interdependence of the nation; it turned back the Constitution, he
suddenly said, to "the horse-and-buggy days" when the economy
was, in its essence, local and most people were self-supporting
within their own communities. (Had George Holmes's phrase, which
Roosevelt permitted the reporters to quote, recalled to his mind
the dictum of Woodrow Wilson's: "The Constitution was not
meant to hold the government back to the time of horses and
wagons"?)

He next examined the "implications" of this decision, "if carried to their logical conclusion." Listing the five major economic activities of the nation — transportation, construction, mining, manufacturing, and agriculture — he pointed out the Court evidently excluded the last four from federal jurisdiction. "Does this decision mean," he asked, "that the United States Government has no control over any national economic problem?" The nation, Roosevelt concluded, now faced the issue "whether we are going to relegate to the States all control over social and working conditions throughout the country regardless of whether those conditions have a very definite significance and effect in other States. . . . That actually is the biggest question that has come before this country outside of time of war, and it has to be decided." So far as the Court was concerned, "we have been relegated to the horse-and-buggy definition of interstate commerce."

Talking calmly and lucidly without a note, never hesitating over words, pausing only to fix a cigarette in his long ivory holder, Roosevelt spoke for an hour and twenty-five minutes. It was an impressive intellectual performance. And, contrary to subsequent myth, his discourse was neither intemperate nor angry. The *New York Times* described the tone as "courteous and serious . . . outward good humor but only slightly masked irony." Most of the time he had a smile on his face; only once did he seem bitter, when he cited a comment from the Hearst press that, with the end of NRA, the rule of Christ was restored. For those present, it was a persuasive job. "By the time the President had finished his public examination," Arthur Krock reported, ". . . he had changed the viewpoint of many who first thought the decision wholly constructive." By defining the implications of the constitutional choice, "the President once more had turned what seemed a retreat into a firm advance against a more important salient."

His discourse did assume, perhaps unjustly, that the Court planned to carry its concept of interstate commerce to the logical conclusion. The action of the Court in pushing forward gratuitous reinterpretations of the commerce clause in both the railway pension and Schechter cases explained, but hardly justified, this presidential assumption; doubtless he, like they, was seeking to ward off future action. And though those who heard the President's disquisition found his tone and argument impressive, those who read secondhand accounts in the press (except for the horse-and-buggy phrase, nothing was directly quoted) were less favorable. Henry Stimson sternly pointed out to Roosevelt that the Court had steadily expanded the commerce clause through its history, "For you to speak as if a single decision could overthrow this long honorable growth, adjusting itself intelligently to the growing needs of our country and . . . throw us back to a 'horse and buggy' age, was a wrong statement, an unfair statement and, if it had not been so extreme as to be recognizable as hyperbole, a rather dangerous and inflammatory statement." "Dear Harry," Roosevelt wrote in a good-humored response. "That is a good letter of yours and I rather imagine that somewhere between your thought and my Friday statement the truth lies!" He had been speaking, he explained, not of what the Court had thus far done, but where the logic of its decision pointed. "Meanwhile I can assure you that I am trying to look at several angles and that I hope something practical can be worked out. I am mighty glad you wrote me." This mild rejoinder expressed his generally philosophical mood over the setback. As he wrote to William C. Bullitt in Moscow in the midst of the clamor, "We have had much excitement here due to the decision of the Supreme Court. However, the fact remains that the principles of NRA must be carried on in some way." [10]

XI

The problem remained how the principles of NRA were to be carried on. From every side, advice dinned in on the President. The air now sounded not only with economic but with constitutional jargon. As Reed Powell commented on the shift of power from Hugh Johnson to Charles Evans Hughes, "Government by hullabaloo may have been succeeded in part by government by abracadabra."

The series of excited White House conferences after Black Monday produced, as usual, several distinct viewpoints. Some — Johnson, Richberg, Moley — wanted to attempt a constitutionally permissible form of NRA — perhaps, as Moley proposed, through a system of voluntary trade association codes, covering both trade practices and wages and hours, to be enforced by contract and by public opinion. This could be combined with a federal authority empowered to reconcile the codes with the antitrust laws. "The principles of NRA will prevail and return in the end as sure as sunrise," said Johnson. "That is true because they are both necessary and right." He and Richberg agreed on this, if on nothing else (except on blaming the other for NRA's downfall). Others had different answers. Moley, Garner, James F. Byrnes, and Robert M. La Follette, Jr., all advocated a constitutional amendment to enlarge the powers of Congress over industry. Tugwell wanted Roosevelt to come out for Ezekiel's Industrial Expansion plan and for an amendment redefining the commerce power to include everything which affected the stream of commerce. Garner suggested that any power remaining to NRA be given to the Federal Trade Commission and that the Wagner labor bill be brought along to take the place of NRA's labor provisions.

The sharpest debate was between Frances Perkins and Homer Cummings. Charles E. Wyzanski, Jr., the Labor Department solicitor, read the decision on the high seas on his way to Geneva for an International Labor Organization meeting. He cabled Miss Perkins that in his opinion Schechter was not fatal, and that the Court might well uphold a more carefully drafted piece of legislation expressly directed to interstate commerce. "It is at least arguable," Wyzanski contended in a subsequent memorandum, "that the Supreme Court did not lay down precise rules on Federal power over prices, production, hours and wages, but indicated that such power could only be exercised in a way that the court felt did not upset the equilibrium of national and local power." Miss Perkins in addition advocated a "public contracts" bill designed to salvage part of NRA. This proposal, based on a suggestion of Frankfurter's, would have the government write into its public contracts specifications concerning not only the character of the goods purchased but the conditions under which they were to be produced; in this way, it could enforce NRA standards on all firms with which there was public business.

Cummings thought that all this was useless. "I tell you, Mr. President, they mean to destroy us," he said, pounding his fist into his hand and striding the room in anger. He went on (as Frances Perkins later recalled it): "This decision of the Supreme Court is absolutely unnecessary. They could just as well have decided in the other way. This is in line with their old-fashioned,

their archaic, their reactionary decisions in the old *Hammer v.
Dagenhart* case. . . . Mr. President, this is all over. You can't do
anything of that kind any more. They have set their face against
us. We will have to find a way to get rid of the present membership of the Supreme Court." When Miss Perkins mentioned
Wyzanski's theory that something could be salvaged, Cummings
responded, "It is not worthwhile to try to salvage something.
We will do better to let it ride and let the people know who is
responsible for the destruction of the New Deal."

The President, as usual, listened to the avalanche of advice,
and in his own mysterious way proceeded to decision. He was
doubtless influenced by a sort of relief, in part unconscious, over
his deliverance from the NRA mess. "It has been an awful head-
ache," Miss Perkins remembers his saying to her. ". . . We have
got the best out of it anyway. . . . I think perhaps NRA has
done all it can do. I don't want to impose a system on this country
that will set aside the anti-trust laws on any permanent basis."
The Johnson-Richberg idea, he believed, would only confuse the
public; he refused to raise the hope that the problem could be
solved within the Court's charter because, he said, no voluntary
or state system would work. "If ninety percent of industry
honestly works for social betterment and ten percent pulls the
other way, we get nowhere without some form of government enforcement. Secondly, if forty states go along with adequate
legislation and eight do not — again we get nowhere!" As he told
the cabinet, he would not permit the people to believe that he
was a magician who could pull rabbit after rabbit out of the
hat.

Fundamentally he agreed with Cummings and Tugwell that
the constitutional issue was basic. "I suppose you and I are rather
dumb," he told Tugwell, "because all the smart people think
that what we should do is compromise and temporize with the
situation, but I am inclined to fight!" The rather cool reception
to his May 31 press conference, however, persuaded him against
any immediate campaign on the constitutional issue. Instead, on
June 4, he announced his post-NRA policy. So far as NRA itself
was concerned, he perfunctorily recommended its extension to
April 1, 1936, as a "skeleton organization," devoted primarily to
liquidation and to the analysis of records. Of the sixteen other

agencies affected by the NRA decision, six were to be salvaged and ten (mostly NRA labor boards) to be forgotten.

In place of NRA, the President now recommended a program looking, not to central control of the economy, but to the patrolling of separate sectors by separate laws. Speaking with a decisiveness new that session, he called for the passage. of the Wagner bill to replace Section 7a; for a law enforcing wages, hours, and anti-child-labor provisions on public contractors; and for the Guffey bill to replace NRA in the coal industry.

The gradual movement toward decision was evident through the week before Black Monday. On May 22, the President had gone in person to the House of Representatives to deliver his veto of the veterans' bonus bill. The next day the Senate upheld him; he was at last approaching the crest of the wave. *Time* summarized the change in typical style. "Newshawks at the White House could not miss it: Franklin Roosevelt's mood had changed. His whole legislative program was in the pot and boiling. At last everything was coming to a head. . . . Suddenly the irritability which had marked his recent actions dropped from him. His 'winter peeve' was over. Once more he was the President of two years past, taking the political initiative, breaking precedent with verve and satisfaction." The Schechter decision finally severed the ties which bound him to the Hundred Days. The ordeal was over. With energy and zest, Franklin Roosevelt returned to the game of leadership.[11]

16. Breakthrough

FOR MONTHS Roosevelt had been in a stew of indecision, trying in the midst of stalemate to see where his administration could develop new sources of energy. Whatever else the Court had done in the Schechter case, it had seemed to close the door on the sort of structural change which was the heart of the First New Deal. Roosevelt could go no further along these lines; and, however far he had gone before Black Monday, it was not far enough. What remained was a relinquishment of the organic conception of the economy; a retreat from central planning; a revitalization of the competitive sector; a substitution of indirect controls — taxation and fiscal policy — for direct controls; and a new lunge ahead. With such strategy, he could act again. With the Schechter decision, the last constraint upon such action disappeared.

The decay of national planning had already lent momentum to various measures in separate areas; Hopkins's relief bill; Frances Perkins's social-security bill; Robert F. Wagner's labor bill; Marriner Eccles's banking bill; the Cohen-Corcoran public utilities holding company bill; Joseph F. Guffey's coal bill. In a conference with House and Senate leaders on June 13, 1935, the reinvigorated Roosevelt, reportedly pounding the table for emphasis, placed the bills which had not been passed on a "must" list and demanded swift action.

As yet, these measures did not add up to an explicit pattern of policy. Still, they shared certain common assumptions and a common spirit. The First New Deal was plainly dead; the Second New Deal was plainly under way. And as the President himself began to glimpse a new design, his hesitation left him. "Things are not as well economically and socially as they appear on the surface," he wrote to a friend on June 10; " — on the other hand, they are better politically than they appear to be on the surface. These are reasons why a campaign of inaction would be bad for the country as well as for the party!" [1]

II

Of the critical bills, relief had already passed in April 1935. The Wagner labor bill had been regarded with suspicion by the White House ever since its introduction in the spring of 1934; but Wagner nonetheless got it through the Senate in mid-May 1935; and toward the end of the month Roosevelt finally indicated that he wanted it passed in some form in the House. Then the invalidation of NRA, with its guarantee of collective bargaining in Section 7a, made it imperative to do something about labor. The Wagner bill rushed through the House in June, and the President signed it in early July. Meanwhile social security was moving ahead to become law in mid-August. All three laws had their roots in earlier years, and none bore the distinctive mark of the Second New Deal.*

Of the measures introduced for the first time in 1935, the one which had been longest on Capitol Hill was the banking bill. This bill had a double origin. It was partly a relatively noncontroversial effort to regularize the federal deposit insurance system and clarify certain features of the emergency banking legislation of 1933. But the heart of the bill was Marriner Eccles's proposal for reconstructing the Federal Reserve System along the lines he had discussed with Roosevelt before accepting appointment to the Federal Reserve Board.

The Federal Reserve System, as Eccles saw it, had been designed as a combination of private and public interests. But in the twenty years since its establishment, the individual Federal Reserve banks had gained such dominance as to reduce the public Board in Washington to impotence. During the twenties, for example, it was the New York Reserve Bank rather than the Board which

---

* For the Social Security and Wagner acts, see *The Coming of the New Deal*, pp. 297–315 and 400–406.

had come nearest to exercising central banking powers. As a result, Eccles felt, the System tended to serve the interests of the bankers (and especially of New York bankers) rather than the general interests of the country. The great need was to increase public control over monetary policy. Once this was done, the Board and the System could make an effective contribution to recovery. "If the monetary mechanism is to be used as an instrument for the promotion of business stability," Eccles said, "conscious control and management are essential."

Now the Board, in Eccles's view, already had in its hands two of the three necessary levers of monetary management. It had long enjoyed authority to change the rate at which banks borrowed from the Federal Reserve; and since the famous Thomas amendment of 1933 it had possessed authority to change the ratio between dollar reserves and deposits in member banks. But it still lacked what Eccles regarded as "the most important single instrument of control over the volume and the cost of credit" — control over open-market operations.

Under open-market operations, the System bought or sold government securities in order to influence the reserves of member banks and thus to enlarge or contract the base of the money supply. Because the public debt was negligible when the Federal Reserve Act was drawn up, no one had then appreciated the potential importance of operations in government securities. But after the First World War, when the debt increased twenty-sevenfold, it became evident that the purchase or sale of government securities would have great impact on the money market. Accordingly, in 1922 the Federal Reserve banks appointed an informal committee of representatives to manage open-market operations. This committee won statutory recognition in the Banking Act of 1933. Eccles found it objectionable because it vested the power over the money market in a group of private bankers. Henry Morgenthau, Jr., of the Treasury agreed: the open-market committee, in his view, had made little effort to support the Treasury's low-interest-rate policy as, for example, by purchasing government securities in the open market. Both Eccles and Morgenthau wanted to concentrate authority and responsibility for open-market operations "in a body representing a national point of view"; this body, they thought, should be the Federal

Reserve Board itself. Reserve banks should be required to carry out the Board's instructions and denied power to undertake open-market operations on their own. If open-market authority were thus joined in the Board with the control of the discount rate and the control of reserve requirements, then, Eccles and Morgenthau believed, monetary policy could at last become an effective instrument of economic stability.

The bill contained, in addition, a number of more technical proposals. Eccles wanted to reorganize both the Board and the System in order to streamline the whole Federal Reserve structure and to increase the authority of the Board. He also wanted to broaden the eligibility of paper receivable by Federal Reserve banks, making "soundness" rather than "liquidity" the criterion. This, he contended, would encourage banks to extend credit over longer periods and thus promote recovery.

Eccles's attempts to justify the banking bill as a recovery measure were not always convincing. In the matter of broadening eligibility, for example, banks already had large reserves of unused credit; readiness to accept more paper was not likely to transform the situation. And fundamentally, as Eccles well knew, monetary policy was not a potent weapon against deflation; it was, if anything, a string around the balloon of credit, and, in a phrase of the day, you could pull — but not push — with a string. In his more careful moments, Eccles fully acknowledged its limitations. "Without a properly managed plan of Government expenditure and without a system of taxation conducive to a more equitable distribution of income," he said, "monetary control is not capable of preventing booms or depressions." There remained an obvious way in which his bill might contribute to recovery — that is, by making it easier for the government to finance its spending programs; but this argument presupposed policies which Eccles was reluctant at that time to bring into the open.

In any case recovery was not the central issue. That issue was the control of the money market. In this respect, Eccles's proposal was from some viewpoints excessively cautious. Advocates of all-out central banking, like the Committee for the Nation, Frank A. Vanderlip, former Senator Robert L. Owen of Oklahoma, and others, dismissed the Eccles bill as inadequate. Advocates of nationalization like Father Coughlin condemned it for confirming the ownership of the System in the hands of the private bankers. Still, for all its relative conservatism, the Eccles bill was clearly pointed in the direction of transferring control over the money market from the bankers to the government, from New York to Washington.

This was the essence of the measure: whether the power to increase or decrease the supply of money was an attribute of sovereignty, to be exercised, not by a private group with financial interests of its own at stake, but by a public agency. "Bankers and businessmen," Eccles said, "are less likely to select men who will think in terms of the broad interest of all society than a President of the United States acting under the immense and sobering trust of his great office." Such sentiments naturally infuriated men who regarded their personal control of the money market as almost a natural right. Roosevelt, who perceived the explosive implications of the Eccles proposal, at first did little more himself than acquiesce in it, sending it along to the Senate and House Banking Committees in February 1935, with a note describing it guardedly as "a tentative draft." To Eccles he said, "Marriner, that's quite an action program you want. It will be a knock-down and drag-out fight to get it through." [2]

III

Nor would the bankers be the only knock-down and drag-out fighters. Eccles had to encounter something even more formidable — that is, the frail and fierce figure of the senior Senator from Virginia. Carter Glass had long been regarded as the oracle of the Democratic party on public finance. Though the heresies of the New Deal had diminished his general authority, one area in which he remained unchallenged was Federal Reserve policy. After all, twenty years before, Glass had been chairman of the House subcommittee which planned the Federal Reserve System. His original scheme, envisaging substantial banker control of the system, actually underwent some revision when the progressives of the Wilson administration, notably Bryan and McAdoo, got to work on it. Nonetheless, in the mist of memory, Glass felt total emotional identification with the Federal Reserve Act as finally passed.

Glass, seventy-seven years old in 1935, still overflowed with intellectual and temperamental vigor. He was short, slight, and prickly, with large scornful eyes, an aggressive brush of white hair shooting back from his forehead, and the defiant, contemptuous bearing of a man who feared nobody. His habit of talking out of the left corner of his mouth gave his face a peculiar twisted expression well adapted to his snarls and snorts. He was the only man in Washington, someone said, who could whisper in his own ear. He was intensely vain and intensely honest. He abominated the New Deal but adored Franklin Roosevelt, and hated his own weakness before the presidential cajolery.

Above all, he regarded the Federal Reserve System as his personal property. "Next to my own family," he told J. F. T. O'Connor, the Comptroller of the Currency, in January 1935, "the Federal Reserve System is nearest to my heart." As another old Wilsonian, Josephus Daniels, wrote Roosevelt, Glass was "obsessed with the idea that the Federal Reserve Act, of which Carter thinks he is the sole author, makes no other legislation whatever necessary. . . . Carter's mind is both closed and sealed to new ideas." When Roosevelt named Eccles to the Federal Reserve Board without consulting Glass, the Virginian was hurt and indignant. It is not clear why Roosevelt by-passed Glass — whether he just forgot about him, or whether, feeling certain that Glass would object, he decided to present him with a *fait accompli.* In any case, everything the Senator's banking friends told him about Eccles increased Glass's suspicions.

Eccles, though himself a proud and brusque man, decided to try conciliation. In January 1935 he promised that Glass would be the first person outside the administration to see the projected bill. Unhappily, as a result of last minute drafting snags and misunderstandings, the bill went to Congress before Glass received a copy. When Eccles tried to explain, Glass suggested furiously that he was lying. Breathing fire, Glass now resolved to wrest control of the bill from Senator Duncan U. Fletcher, the chairman of the Senate Banking and Currency Committee. He did succeed in winning the bill for his own subcommittee on banking matters, though Fletcher managed to enlarge the subcommittee and thus somewhat to dilute Glass's influence.

The House Banking Committee, under the chairmanship of Henry B. Steagall of Alabama, was more sympathetic. While

Glass wrathfully held up both the confirmation of Eccles's appointment and the bill itself, the House opened hearings on the bill in late February. Eccles personally testified for eleven days, answering a wide variety of questions with invariable confidence and precision; Arthur Krock called it "a personal triumph." A special committee of the American Banking Association endorsed the substance of the bill, though asking for banking representation on the new Open-Market Committee and seeking to limit somewhat the power to change reserve requirements. There was support from bankers outside New York, especially in areas of potential economic growth where public control appeared to promise easier money than the *rentier* mentality of New York: thus A. P. Giannini of California's Bank of America said flatly, "I favor the banking bill." Despite rumblings of opposition (Father Coughlin assailed the bill wildly from the left as "nothing more than a marriage license between a prostitute who has wrecked our home and the government who has deserted his wife, the American people"), the House committee recommended it in mid-April in essentially the form Eccles desired, and the House passed it on May 9 by a vote of 271–110.

IV

In the meantime, feeling was rising against the bill, especially in the domain of the New York Federal Reserve Bank. New York bankers had two main objections: that the bill provided for the "political control" of the Federal Reserve System; and that public management of open-market operations would make it easy for the government to undertake deficit spending or inflation by forcing government securities on the banks. In March Professor H. Parker Willis of Columbia, who had been Glass's collaborator in drafting the original Federal Reserve Act, denounced the Eccles bill as "the most dangerous, the most unwarranted, the most insidious measure" of the entire New Deal. A committee of academic economists, including Joseph Schumpeter, James W. Angell, and O. Glenn Saxon, declared, "The passage of such a measure will invite ultimate disaster." Ogden Mills said curiously, "The proposed law would throw us back five hundred years."

Bankers at first had been reluctant to testify against the bill

— James P. Warburg, spoke of "the amazing reticence" of his profession — but by the time Glass, unable to stall any longer, opened the Senate hearings in mid-April, the mood was changing. Departing from the usual procedure, Glass strove to insure an impression of hostility to the bill by leading off with opposition witnesses before Eccles was given a chance to present the case for the measure. Warburg himself opened the attack, saying that "no amount of changes" would improve the bill and citing "all history" to show what happens "when the long arm of the Treasury reaches out into the control of the credit machinery." "I am not one who sees a Communist under every bed," Warburg said, "but I sometimes wonder if the authors of these bills realize whose game they are playing." Winthrop Aldrich, who had signed the report of the ABA's special committee, suddenly reversed his ground and discovered the bill to be packed with iniquity. "This is not liberalizing the Federal Reserve System," he told the Senate subcommittee. "It is making it over into an instrument of despotic authority. . . . This is a concentration of authority such as has not been known heretofore in the United States."

Glass's strategy was to try and kill off Title II of the bill, which contained the Eccles program, and enact the rest — that is, the provisions concerning the Federal Deposit Insurance Corporation and those providing for unified bank examination. In this effort he had the hearty support of two professional Democratic politicians, both now involved in currency matters in the executive branch, J. F. T. O'Connor, the Comptroller of the Currency, and Leo Crowley, head of the FDIC. O'Connor feared that the revitalized Federal Reserve Board would diminish his own power; Crowley feared that association with the controversial Eccles proposals might jeopardize his own FDIC amendments; and, though Crowley and O'Connor detested each other, they now used their considerable influence on the Hill to back Glass's move to break the bill up into its constituent parts. Since the only chance for Federal Reserve reform that session lay in making it part of an omnibus bill, the Glass strategy of three separate bills obviously would doom the Eccles program.

Glass pursued his campaign with vigor. In March, a few weeks after the introduction of the bill, he told Morgenthau (and doubtless many others) that the President had said he wanted only the FDIC provisions and unified bank examinations. As for the Federal Reserve proposals, Glass said firmly, "The President is not interested. This is Eccles's bill." A few days later Morgenthau repeated this to Roosevelt. "All the color left the President's face," Morgenthau noted in his diary, "and he said nothing for a few moments." Then he insisted that he had told this to Glass in January, but that in March he told Glass he was keeping his mind open about the Federal Reserve System until the picture developed further. Morgenthau asked what he should meanwhile say before congressional committees. Roosevelt told him to endorse the items mentioned by Glass and, in addition, the proposal to place the Open-Market Committee under the Federal Reserve Board and a proposal that the government buy stock in Federal Reserve banks.

The administration policy was now complicated by a growing divergence between Morgenthau and Eccles. However much they agreed on broad objectives, they disagreed somewhat on methods and, through the spring, began to look on each other with increasing suspicion. Thus Morgenthau opposed Eccles's formula for the composition of the new open-market committee. He feared in addition that such a committee, however constituted, might be susceptible to pressure; and consequently he thought more and more favorably of Roosevelt's casual suggestion that the government purchase the stock of the Federal Reserve System and thereby decide once and for all the question of Federal Reserve control. In May, testifying before Glass's subcommittee, Morgenthau, after endorsing "the principles of Title II," added that government ownership of the stock of the System would be the best way of securing the Board against both political and banking pressure.

That afternoon newspapermen asked Roosevelt what he thought of the Morgenthau proposal. "I think it would solve a great many questions," the President replied. Jackson's Secretary of the Treasury, he continued, had proposed during the Bank War that the government buy a majority interest in the Second United States Bank. "That's a hundred years ago," Roosevelt said, "but it would have solved the banking situation at that time in a much more satisfactory way." Having said this, he put his remarks off the record and made no effort to press his views on members of the Glass committee. Publicly he remained enigmatic on the issue of banking reform.

v

This was May 17, 1935. In the next fortnight the log-jam began to break. In his post-Schechter mood, the President spoke out with sudden new clarity. At last seeing the direction in which he had to move, he left no doubt that he wanted Federal Reserve reform that session. He had no intention of giving in on Title II. Morgenthau and Eccles were to settle their differences. Action was essential.

In the meantime, Carter Glass, zestfully rewriting the House measure, brought a new version of the banking bill on to the floor of the Senate and urged its passage. The Senate bill differed from the Eccles-House draft in giving the bankers representation on the open-market committee, in somewhat limiting the Board's power to alter reserve requirements, and in other more or less minor concessions to the banking community. The differences were not of primary importance; but they gave Glass a joyous sense of triumph over Eccles; and he strengthened a public impression that the Senate was repudiating Eccles by vengefully attacking him in debate as a man hungry for power and as the greatest inflationist in the country. Eccles responded with a speech intended to move the Virginian by recalling to him the Wilsonian fight against the bankers over the Federal Reserve Act: "You are hearing the same cry — political control and inflation." Glass remained unmoved. (Years later in his autobiography, Eccles suggested that his story of the banking bill of 1935 was but a transposition of the story Glass himself had written about the Federal Reserve fight. In retrospect, he wondered whether the antagonisms of 1935 might not have been due to the fact that he and Glass had so much in common. Both were proud men, incapable of suppressing their feelings; each was devoted to his own Democratic President and to his own design for public finance. They even looked a little alike: commenting on a photograph showing Glass and himself in profile, Eccles wrote, "We seem to be father and son, which perhaps accounts for our troubles.")

At the time, Eccles was less philosophical. He complained of the Senate bill to Morgenthau and did his best to persuade the House-Senate conference committee to produce a bill more along the lines of his original recommendation. Roosevelt helped, sternly warning Glass against the advice of his old friend H. Parker Willis: "he belongs to that little group of Americans who are appendages or appendices — whichever part of the anatomy you prefer — on the large body of international bankers of London, Paris, Shanghai, etc." The conference committee finally produced an acceptable compromise, which Roosevelt signed on August 24, 1935.

Practically everyone, from Eccles to the president of the American Banking Association, issued statements praising the bill. After signing, Roosevelt handed one of the pens to Glass. Someone whispered, "He should have given him an eraser instead." But Glass, secure in his conviction of victory, was contented. What he did not note was that the Banking Act of 1935 was, in every essential respect, Eccles's original idea, if as Walter Lippmann put it, "dressed up as a defeat." Whatever was lost in detail, Eccles's basic philosophy of monetary control, his determination to transfer control of the money market from New York to Washington, survived intact. With the new law, the national government acquired indispensable powers for the management of the economy.[3]

17. The Utilities on the Barricades

THE BILL to deal with public utility holding companies had also begun a weary legislative struggle in February. But Roosevelt had more clear-cut views on this issue than he at first had on the banking legislation. He had long felt a righteous personal indignation (perhaps self-righteous, in view of his own financial dreams of the twenties) against those who exploited gaps and quirks in corporation law to use other people's money to gain money and power for themselves. "One year ago," he had written in March 1934 to a banker friend who begged him to trust the assurances of the business community, "we were assured that pools and manipulations would be ended. Last summer pools and manipulations were still in full swing. Pools and other manipulations are not only possible but probable under present conditions." The securities and stock exchange legislation were fine so far as they went; but they did not wipe out all the devices of financial chicane.[1]

II

Of the devices remaining, the holding company seemed to Roosevelt especially objectionable. At a meeting of the National Executive Council in December 1934 he denied that his power policy was injuring the financial position of the utility operating companies; the holding company, he suggested, was the real enemy. "The only utility securities which are all wrong," he said, "are the securities of holding companies, which securities represent no cash invested in electrical development itself. They represent merely financial transactions." If it were not for the money pumped out of operating companies by holding companies, Roosevelt continued, power rates to the consumer could be reduced everywhere in the country, and the private utilities would have nothing to fear from TVA. He was equally concerned about the political consequences of the holding-company system. He was tired, he told his cabinet a few days later, of eighty men (he had in mind James W. Gerard's list of the eighty most important Americans) controlling the destinies of 120 million people. The only way to curb this control, he added, was to do away with the holding companies.

The holding-company problem, more acute in the utility industry than anywhere else, thus seemed to Roosevelt a major piece of unfinished business in the fight against financial concentration. This fight, of course, was the one which the neo-Brandeisians had been urging on him from the start. And even the First New Dealers acknowledged the need for action. Tugwell thought a holding-company program was necessary, if a risky diversion. Moley, in early January 1935, wrote that the growth of the utility holding companies "bore little relation to business or economic need," but sprang rather from the desire for "inordinate profits." Holding-company legislation, he added, would merely be "a recognition of the break-down that has already come from within, a break-down that signifies what may be termed the downfall of private socialism in America."

There was ample raw material for the legislative mill. The Federal Trade Commission had been investigating the utility holding companies since 1928, the House Interstate Commerce Committee, since 1930. Both investigations were reaching completion, and the leading figure in each — Judge Robert E. Healy, whom Calvin Coolidge had appointed counsel to the FTC, and W. M. W. Splawn, special counsel for the House inquiry, whom Roosevelt had just named to the Interstate Commerce Commission — had legislative proposals. In addition, the National Power Policy Committee was preparing a report of its own on the problem. The NPPC report, finished in early March 1935, summarized effectively the volumes of intricate and tedious fact patiently dredged up by Healy and Splawn.

By 1932, the NPPC said, thirteen holding groups controlled

three-quarters of the privately owned electric utility industry. The three largest groups — United Corporation, Electric Bond and Share, and Insull — controlled some 40 per cent themselves. These holding companies had grown up, not because managers wanted efficiency, but because bankers and speculators wanted profits. Far from rationalizing or integrating the industry, the holding company made it more confused. Operating companies were thrown together in a single "system" without regard to type or location; holding companies were piled on top of them, sometimes to the sixth or seventh degree, each level providing the occasion for new security write-ups or issues; and the whole dizzy process of pyramiding enabled an astute promoter to build a gaudy empire on a trivial investment of his own cash. The holding companies preyed voraciously on the operating companies, selling them management, engineering, and construction services at excessive fees, profiting hugely on the purchase and resale of materials, even receiving loans "upstream" from their subsidiaries. The extra cost imposed by the holding company passed into the rate base and was paid for by the consumer. "The holding company system," said Judge Healy, "is to a degree more or less of a parasite and excrescence on the actual operating companies." And it was not only a source of waste; it was a source of corruption. "It is not easy to choose words which will adequately characterize various ethical aspects of the situation without the appearance of undue severity," said the Federal Trade Commission. "Nevertheless, the use of words such as fraud, deceit, misrepresentation, dishonesty, breach of trust and oppression are the only suitable terms to apply."

Nor could this increase in the concentration of private economic power be justified in terms of increased productive efficiency. "These holding companies manufacture nothing, so far as I can find out," said Splawn, "except securities." And they were relatively impervious to state regulation — designedly so, through every tactic which could occur to the fertile minds of Sullivan & Cromwell. As Felix Frankfurter had pointed out in 1930, holding companies were "practically immune" to existing law.

Not all holding companies did wicked things at all times. Some of them, the NPPC dimly conceded, might have performed a useful function in the remote past. But enough of them did bad things enough of the time, in the eyes of the NPPC, to warrant a rejection of the system. "Such intensification of economic power beyond the point of proved economies not only is susceptible of grave abuse but is a form of private socialism inimical to the functioning of democratic institutions." The only remedy, the NPPC concluded, was "the practical elimination within a reasonable time of the holding company where it serves no demonstrably useful and necessary purpose." [2]

III

When Roosevelt made his State-of-the-Union address to Congress on January 4, 1935, he misdelivered one sentence in his text. His manuscript spoke of restoring sound conditions in the public utilities field through "abolition of the evil features of holding companies." Before Congress, however, Roosevelt read it as "abolition of the evil of holding companies." He explained in a subsequent press conference that he meant to say "the evils of holding companies," not intending to suggest that everything about holding companies was evil. Nonetheless Freud was right, and there was great truth in the slip.

Two alternatives were before Roosevelt — to regulate holding companies or to destroy them. Corcoran, Cohen, and the National Power Policy Committee proposed rigid limitation as a road to eventual elimination. Robert H. Jackson and Herman Oliphant of the Treasury proposed abolition as soon as possible by immediate imposition of a stiff intercorporate dividend tax — a tax, that is, on the money taken by one company from another. A few days after his annual message, Roosevelt called both groups to a White House meeting to consider a draft bill prepared by Cohen.

It quickly became evident that Roosevelt himself preferred abolition. If holding companies survived at all, he seemed to feel, they might gain a new lease on life under a more complaisant administration; better clear them out of the picture while the going was good. Cohen tried in vain to argue that his bill went as far in that direction as seemed feasible — that it did go beyond regulation and required holding companies to simplify their capital structure and to limit their operations to a single integrated system. The meeting, while adopting the NPPC rather than the Treasury approach — that is, a direct attack on structure rather than an indirect attack through taxation — strongly supported Roosevelt's desire for a red-hot bill. The conception which Cohen and Corcoran had brought to the meeting was of a bill designed to sound as moderate as possible; the conception which emerged was of a bill designed to sound radical and drastic.

Actually there was not vast substantive difference between the two drafts. And Corcoran at least, remembering the chipping away at the stock exchange bill, was glad to build up the draft in order to leave room for "sweat-down" in the legislative process. What the meeting produced was a new emphasis on a clause providing for the gradual extinction of the holding company. This provision, which soon became famous as the "death sentence," became the heart of Title I. The title as a whole empowered the Securities and Exchange Commission to undertake the simplification of the holding-company system and its reintegration on a basis which would make geographical and economic sense. As far as possible, this process was to be voluntary; but after January 1, 1940, as provided in the death-sentence clause, the SEC would have power to *compel* the dissolution of every holding company which could not establish an economic reason for its existence — whose continuation, in other words, was not necessary to the operation of a geographically and economically integrated system. Other provisions of Title I regulated securities issues and intercompany transactions, laid down the principle that a holding company should not benefit from dealings with its own subsidiaries, and demanded uniform systems of reporting and accounting.

If Title I, which dealt with holding companies, was the more controversial, Title II, which dealt with operating companies, was probably more far-reaching in its consequences. Where Title I authorized the SEC to dismantle the holding-company system and free the operating companies, Title II authorized the Federal Power Commission to integrate the operating companies into regional systems on the basis of technical efficiency, not of speculative manipulation. The bill carefully called for federal action only as a means of supplementing state action, but it obviously aimed at the national co-ordination of electric power resources. Title II had emerged from the experience of the Federal Power Commission and had been submitted in earlier

Congresses in somewhat different form by Senator James Couzens. Title I, however, excited the main opposition. And it raised larger issues than the future of public utility holding companies. While it could have been supported on a number of grounds, its particular backers identified it with the philosophy of economic littleness. "Its spirit," said Burton K. Wheeler, introducing the bill in the Senate, "is the spirit of the bill I propose for a Federal tax on bigness. . . . Both these bills are essentials in what I consider the only program that can eventually restore to us the reality of that theory of economic and political democracy by which we fondly like to think this Nation lives." "The idea of the capitalistic system," Tom Corcoran told the Senate Commerce Committee, "is that we have competitive free enterprise. What we are afraid of when we talk about socialism, is that one directing, benevolent hand will have the disposition of all business. . . . There is more socialism in that set-up right there . . . more concentrated disposition of business in one hand and more killing of competition than you could get in any system of State socialism that we could possibly set up in this country." Confronted with such a concentration of private power, Corcoran said, the state could take the system over, or it could permit the system to take over the state, or it could break up the system so that "free enterprise can function again."

Where the men of 1933 might have thought of converting the holding-company system into a mechanism of government planning, the men of 1935, possessed by the Brandeisian vision, wanted to stop the system from choking individual enterprise and creativity. Once it had achieved its simplification and co-ordination, the bill proposed little further interference with the decisions of private management. It was an exercise, not in regimentation, but in revivification: not in handing down, but in setting free. "The spirit of Section 10," Walter Lippman truly commented of the death-sentence provision, "is the spirit of American individualism in its original form." The holding-company bill was, in fact, a profoundly conservative conception.[3]

IV

It was not so received, however, by American conservatives.

No sooner had the bill been introduced by Wheeler in the Senate and by Sam Rayburn of Texas in the House early in February than the business community rushed to defend the holding-company system as if it were the ark of the American covenant.

The holding company had clearly played a considerable role in building the American electric power system. But the issue in 1935 was whether there was a case for its indefinite continuation. According to its defenders, the holding company was necessary to bring operating companies capital and credit; it was necessary to bring operating companies skilled management; and it was necessary because compulsory dissolution under the "death sentence" would destroy the funds innocently invested in holding companies by millions of Americans, largely (apparently) widows and orphans. Friends of the bill, of course, were ready with answers. They denied that the holding company was necessary to help finance the operating company, arguing that operating companies enjoyed higher credit ratings than holding companies, and that holding companies had failed all over the place since 1929 while no operating company had yet closed down. They declared that problems of management could be solved otherwise than by perpetuating a wasteful and corrupt financial system. And they contended that the SEC could manage dissolution in a way that would protect all legitimate interests of investors, pointing out that such compulsory dissolution was nothing new, having been successfully carried out in a number of cases under the Sherman Act.

The most effective spokesman for the power companies was Wendell L. Willkie of Commonwealth and Southern. Taking at first a reasonable and constructive line, Willkie persuasively reformulated the standard holding-company case. He freely admitted the delinquencies of individual holding-company executives. "No radical public ownership advocate," Willkie said, "hates half as much as I do the men who profited from engineering services rendered to their companies, and who acquired property only to put it on the books at excessive values." But such excesses suggested, were in the past; "there was a crazy period when men went crazy and did a lot of foolish things and I am not attempting to speak for that situation." He pointed out that his own company, for example, had not under his presidency pursued these evil practices, which was substantially true; it seemed hardly wise or right to destroy the whole system because of the irresponsibility of an unrepresentative minority. "The indictment that is being made is not the indictment of the utility holding company," he said. "It is the indictment of a period and the indictment of a system of doing business. . . . [The holding company] is an indispensable element in the utility business . . . more so than any other business in the country." The answer, Willkie said, lay in regulation. Similarly, Owen D. Young opposed the bill, while admitting privately that holding-company structures had become "so complicated that I feel sure that most of the men responsible for operating them were misled by their own mechanisms."

In the course of the spring, Willkie produced a regulatory scheme of his own. But the defenders of the bill regarded the Willkie plan, which relied basically on state regulation, as hopelessly inadequate. In any case, Roosevelt's position obliged them to deny that permanent regulation was a possible solution. "You just cannot handle them that way," said Corcoran. "It is just a sheer problem of arithmetic. How much money have you against how much money? How many good lawyers have you against how many good lawyers? Those are the actualities of the regulatory process — the drip, drip, drip of pleasure and influence; the out-maneuvering, the out-braining, which will simply make it impossible to handle these aggregations of power." David Lilienthal said that the holding companies themselves had destroyed any hope of solution through regulation when they decided to enter politics. Flourishing an editorial from *Electrical World* which exhorted utility men to "make politics their major concern," Lilienthal said that the utilities, by thus attempting "to seize the political control of the country," were making regulation impossible. "The only regulation for 100-ton trucks going up a village street," Corcoran concluded, "is that you cannot have them going up a village street at all."

v

Howard C. Hopson, head of Associated Gas & Electric, later distinguished two phases in the utility campaign — the appeal to reason and the appeal to emotion. In the later phase, as in the earlier, Willkie, with his husky charm, his formidable articulateness, and his prodigious energy, was the dominant figure. When Lilienthal in a New York debate described the holding company as a tapeworm sucking the nourishment out of the operating companies, Willkie in his evangelical mood replied by praising Samuel Insull as a "forceful, dynamic and attractive figure," and declaring, "I am the president of a holding company and I make that statement with pride." Warming to his theme, Willkie dismissed his past life as war veteran, as battler for the League of Nations, as champion of civil liberties, and gravely said: "No duty has ever come to me in my life, even that in the service of my country, which has so appealed to my sense of social obligation, patriotism and love of mankind as this, my obligation to say and do what I can for the preservation of public utilities privately owned. All that I have observed, all that I know and all that I read teaches me that I could do nothing nobler for the future financial stability and political good of my country."

Fired with so splendid a sense of mission, Willkie missed no opportunity to press his case. If the Wheeler-Rayburn bill passed, he told the famous Chamber of Commerce meeting in May, the utility industry would be thrown "into a chaos of liquidation and receiverships," holders of utility stocks would suffer "practically complete" losses, and a "great bureaucracy in Washington will be regulating the internal affairs of practically all utility operating companies in the United States." The backers of the death sentence, Willkie charged, were trying "to 'nationalize' the power business of this country."

More and more businessmen began to accept increasingly apocalyptic interpretations of the bill. Preston Arkwright of the Georgia Power Company, asked what would happen if Congress passed the bill, said, "Well, you would paralyze the Nation." "I believe the eventual outcome of the passage of this bill," said Samuel Ferguson of Hartford Electric Light, "would be the nationalization of the industry." S. R. Inch, president of Electric Bond & Share said that the bill "will nationalize these industries just as sure as I am standing here." Philip Gadsden, chairman of the Committee of Public Utility Executives, identified "nationalization and municipalization of the entire electric industry" as "apparently the ultimate object of this legislation." In May, to a conference of bankers, Thomas N. McCarter, president of the Edison Electric Institute, gave currency to ugly rumors already in circulation in the industry: "The President has an obsession on this subject," McCarter said. "It is a condition of mind that even many of his closest associates in Washington do not understand." A few weeks later, before twelve hundred utility officials at the Institute's annual meeting, McCarter repeated his crack about the President's "obsession." "It is up to the industry to fight for its life," he added. "The kid-glove stage has passed." At the same meeting, when Merle Thorpe, editor of the Chamber of Commerce magazine, *Nation's Business,* called for the return of the "old order," the power executives rose to their feet in a thunder of applause.

The concern spread outside the industry. John W. Davis told the American Bar Association that the holding-company bill was "the gravest threat to the liberties of the American citizen that has emanated from the halls of Congress in my time"; it was "the most unexcused and unexcusable grasp of power" he had ever seen. And through the spring the evidence suggested that thousands of Americans shared this concern. From early February, letters and telegrams began to come to Capitol Hill, ostensibly from ordinary people who held utility stock and feared to see a lifetime's savings blasted away. A few such communications could have been ignored. But they arrived in ever-increasing quantities with ever-more forceful language.

"Representatives of the public utilities lobby came to see me," reported a quiet freshman senator from Missouri, "and asked me to vote against the bill. I told them that I was personally opposed to the monopolistic practices which were squeezing the consumer to death and that I would vote in favor of the bill. Next the lobby sent people out to Missouri to get the Democratic organization there to exert pressure on me. That failed also. And finally a propaganda campaign financed by the utility magnates was launched in the state of Missouri among my constituents, many of whom held securities. I was swamped with letters and telegrams." But this failed, too. Harry S. Truman burned the thirty thousand messages which piled up his desk and stayed with the bill. Other members of Congress, less persuaded on the merits, saw no choice but to go along with the people in what seemed an extraordinary revolt against the administration.[4]

VI

The Wheeler-Rayburn bill had only informal presidential blessing when introduced in February. The rising storm of protest
meant that something more was required. On March 12 Roosevelt
transmitting to Congress the holding-company report of the National Power Policy Committee, accompanied it by a message expressly advocating holding-company legislation. He had been
watching with interest, he said "the use of investors' money to make
the investor believe that the efforts of Government to protect him
are designed to defraud him." This had resulted in so much misrepresentation that it was important to state the actual facts. The
proposed law would not destroy legitimate business or productive
investment. It would surround the necessary reorganization of the
holding company with safeguards to protect the investor. As for
the holding company itself, "except where it is absolutely necessary
to the continued functioning of a geographically integrated operating utility system," it must go. "Regulation has small chance
of ultimate success against the kind of concentrated wealth and
economic power which holding companies have shown the ability
to acquire." It was time, Roosevelt concluded, "to make an effort
to reverse that process of the concentration of power" which had
changed Americans from independent proprietors to men and
women dependent on the favor of a few. "I am against private
socialism of concentrated economic power as thoroughly as I am
against governmental socialism. The one is equally as dangerous
as the other; and destruction of private socialism is utterly essential to avoid governmental socialism."

When the message was read in the House, there was an ovation.
"Say, did you read about what Mr. Roosevelt said about those
'holding companies'?" wrote Will Rogers. "A Holding Company
is a thing where you hand an accomplice the goods while the
policeman searches you." But pressures against the bill mounted
even faster. Rogers soon was forced into defiant explanations of
his careless wisecrack. Messages came to Wheeler that, if he persisted in his fight for the bill, his political career would be finished. (He replied, "Tell them that to me a holding company is
Jesse James without a horse, and you can't scare me out of this
fight.") As the vote neared in early June, Wheeler encountered

a persistent rumor that Roosevelt himself was ready to compromise on the death sentence.

Wheeler rushed to the White House to learn the worst. It was early in the morning; the President was still in bed, propped up by pillows. Calling for paper and pencil, he scribbled a statement for Wheeler to show to anyone who raised the question. Any amendment going to the heart of the death sentence, Roosevelt wrote, "would strike at the bill itself and is wholly contrary to the recommendations of my message." (Wheeler later framed the message and hung it on the wall of his office.)

The administration was standing firm. A conservative Democrat pleaded with Garner for a milder policy toward the holding companies. "They have brought it upon themselves," the Vice-President replied. "They cannot be permitted to go on as they were." Someone argued for regulation; "I have no more sympathy in the attempt to regulate them," said Hugo Black, "than to regulate a rattlesnake." On June 11 the death sentence came up for vote. The administration Democrats, backed by the progressive Republicans, barely won by a vote of 45–44. Then the bill itself, complete with death sentence, passed the Senate by 56–32.

VII

The battle now shifted to the House, where the bill was still deadlocked in the Commerce Committee. The House was ordinarily the more acquiescent of the two bodies; but its members — out of simmering resentment over White House pressure, or out of a principled objection to the death sentence, or perhaps because their two-year terms made them peculiarly vulnerable to threats from the utilities — were showing signs of restiveness. At the White House conference on June 13, John J. O'Connor of New York, the conservative Democratic chairman of the House Rules Committee, advised compromise on the death sentence. The President told him confidently not to worry: the House would accept the whole bill once it was presented in a clear-cut fashion and on the basis of party loyalty.

But it was not that easy. A week later, the House Commerce Committee reported the bill, striking out the mandatory death sentence, though still giving the SEC power to order dissolution if in the public interest. The essential difference between the Senate and House bills was now whether the burden of proof lay on the company to prevent dissolution or on the commission to compel it. In talks with his leaders in the House and in his press conferences, Roosevelt insisted more strongly than ever on the disputed provision in its original form. It was not a death sentence, he said, but an emancipation proclamation. It would restore to local communities the control over their own utilities. It would break up the concentrated financial power of New York. Above all, it would wreck the political power so long exerted by the power companies in state capitals and now on display in Washington. "You talk about a labor lobby. Well, it is a child compared to this utility lobby. You talk about a Legion lobby. Well, it is an infant in arms compared to this utility lobby." This was, Roosevelt said, "the most powerful, dangerous lobby . . . that has ever been created by any organization in this country."

That lobby had evidently never been more active. According to the computation of the Scripps-Howard press, it had more representatives in Washington (660) than there were members of Congress (527). The hammering on legislators never ceased. And the campaign was getting tough: the kid-glove stage was definitely over. McCarter's remarks about Roosevelt's "obsession" and "condition of mind" were having their effect. One enterprising advertising man suggested to the chairman of Electric Bond & Share "a whispering campaign designed to create popular suspicion that the 'new dealers' and especially the 'New Dealer-in-Chief' are either incompetent or insane." The letter illustrated a mood rather than an influence; it received no reply for some weeks, when the assistant to the chairman responded perfunctorily that the suggestions were "very pertinent." But the whispering campaign, however stimulated, was clearly under way by the end of June. By mid-July *Time* reported that Washington correspondents were being plagued by queries from their home papers asking whether the President was not on the verge of mental collapse. "He had, according to the tales roaring through the country in whispers, grown mentally irresponsible. Hadn't you heard that during a press conference he had a fit of laughter, had to be hurriedly wheeled out of the room? Why, his intimates were taking the greatest care not to have him make a spectacle of himself on public occasions. And when he heard the Supreme Court's NRA verdict, he was supposed to have succumbed to a violent fit of hysterics." [5]

VIII

The utilities relied even more, however, on pressure on Congress from the folks at home. Sometimes this was exercised behind closed doors, as when local power executives made clear to congressmen their intention to defeat anyone who voted for the death sentence. Sometimes it was exercised in the open, as when letters and wires heaped up in congressional offices. And the flood of messages to Congress — about 800,000 in the last two weeks of June — was undeniably impressive.

Or was it? On June 27 and 28, Denis J. Driscoll of the Twentieth Pennsylvania District received 816 telegrams from the Borough of Warren. Looking them over in the evening, he noticed two things. The names appeared mostly to begin with the first four letters of the alphabet; and, though he knew Warren fairly well, he had never heard of most of his correspondents. Where he did recognize names, he sent letters explaining why he was supporting the Wheeler-Rayburn bill. On July 1, friends began to reply that they had sent him no such telegrams. Meanwhile he was receiving new bundles of telegrams against the bill from the town of Meadville. Driscoll now sent wires himself to a few of the Meadville names. Western Union reported that the addressees were unknown in Meadville.

While Congressman Driscoll was pursuing his researches, the House was already debating the bill. The White House, fighting hard for the death sentence, had loosed its own lobby on the Hill. Led by Tom Corcoran on his first major political assignment, administration emissaries argued with congressmen, hectored them, talked significantly about past and future favors, and pushed all the levers of executive persuasion. Caught between equally harassing pressures, congressmen in the hot Washington summer grew irritable and angry. The debate over the bill became bitter, and the willingness to frustrate the President increased. The congressional leadership successfully thwarted Sam Rayburn's efforts to get a roll-call vote on the death sentence. Rayburn, suddenly

smitten with gloom, refused to push the fight, letting the reins fall
to John Rankin of Mississippi. "The reason he gave," Rankin observed of Rayburn, ". . . seemed about as thin as the proverbial un-
seasoned soup made from the shadow of a chicken that died of
starvation." But Rankin could do no better. In the greatest tension of the session, the House finally turned the death sentence down
on July 1 by an unrecorded vote of 216–146. The next day, after rejecting the death sentence again, it passed the diluted bill by a vote
of 323–81.

Roosevelt, who had thrown his whole prestige into the fight,
was now decisively rebuffed. It was a bitter blow to the White
House. More than that, the methods used by the presidential lobbyists caused deep resentment. The Washington correspondent of
the *New Republic* even doubted whether the President could regain his mastery over Congress. "His reputation as a political
wizard, with mysterious powers, has vanished. Half a dozen representatives spoke against him in the House, and no thunderbolts
struck them down." This was, said the *New York Times,* "the
most decided legislative defeat dealt to President Roosevelt since
he assumed office." [6]

IX

In the midst of the final House vote, there was suddenly a
new excitement. Representative Ralph Owen Brewster of Maine
(he had not yet dropped his first name) rose in the House to say
that Tom Corcoran, approaching him in Statuary Hall just before
the vote on July 1, had threatened to stop construction on the
Passamaquoddy Dam in his district unless Brewster voted for the
death sentence. The House promptly authorized an investigation
by the Rules Committee.

There were inherent implausibilities about the charge. PWA
had long since made the allotment for Passamaquoddy; indeed,
Vice-President Garner was scheduled to set off the opening blast
on July 4. Calling off the project three days before might have
been beyond the powers even of Tom Corcoran. On the other
hand, the project needed certain state legislation to protect the
government's interest; and the decision to go ahead was based in
part on Brewster's assurances to Corcoran that the required legisla-

tion would be forthcoming from the Republican legislature. Corcoran told the Rules Committee that he had said to Brewster in Statuary Hall, "If, as you say, your political situation is such that you are not a free man and you have to take the power companies into account . . . you know perfectly well I cannot trust you on the 'Quoddy project in the future, and you know perfectly well I can no longer trust your assurance that you will protect the 'Quoddy legislation." Conceivably Brewster may have interpreted this as a threat to hold up the project until the legislation was on the statute books. He could not have interpreted it as much more than this.

And even this would have been only Brewster's interpretation. The investigation showed clearly that Corcoran had not uttered the precise threat charged by Brewster. The incident had taken place before a witness — Ernest Gruening, an old personal friend of Brewster's, who had originally introduced Brewster and Corcoran to each other. Gruening backed up Corcoran's account, including Corcoran's statement that Brewster had offered to absent himself from the vote. (When Corcoran made that statement in the hearing, Brewster shouted, "You are a liar.") Corcoran's own testimony was evidently impressive; as *Time* described it, "With cold, lucid, driving fury, he tore Ralph Brewster's tale to shameful shreds." Moreover, the inquiry showed that Brewster had taken part in at least one strategy conference of the pro-death-sentence diehards; that, as Brewster himself admitted, his colleagues at the conference were "warranted" in the assumption that he was for the death sentence; that he had given these colleagues the impression that he would speak for the provision; and that he had actually called Senator White of Maine and asked him to abstain from the death-sentence vote in the Senate. Eight congressmen, including Brewster's two Maine colleagues, took the stand to testify that they regarded him as definitely favorable to the death sentence. It was evident that Corcoran had every reason for surprise and indignation when he learned on the morning of the vote that Brewster not only was not prepared to speak for the measure but was intending to vote against it. He might well have concluded that Brewster was not to be trusted on further power issues. And Brewster might well have made his subsequent charges to cover an otherwise inexplicable retreat.

On July 6 Roosevelt had sent Corcoran a note asking for "a complete statement of all your dealings" with Brewster. This was to give Corcoran an opportunity to put the facts of the case on the record, which he did with relish and despatch and to the President's satisfaction. "I can't tell you how much I appreciated your 'stout fellah,'" Corcoran wrote three days later. ". . . I do feel that I may have convinced the Committee this morning that, however few effective guns I carry I'm a man o' war flying one flag — and that Mr. Brewster is just a shady privateer with forged letters of marque from both sides!"

There were elements of pathos in Brewster's capitulation. As Governor of Maine, he had led the fight against the Insull interests. The opposition of the utilities had been largely responsible for his defeat when he had previously sought election to the Senate and to the House. "I went through hell," Brewster said, "because I would not succumb to pressure of that character." When it became clear in the angry exchange in Statuary Hall that he was at last succumbing, as the tense little group broke up and Brewster walked into the chamber to vote, his old friend Gruening said to him, "You will be a man without a country. You have always fought the reactionaries. They have always hated you. If you run out on the progressives, they will have no use for you. They will feel you have betrayed them and you will simply be nowhere." [7]

X

The Brewster-Corcoran tangle had one further effect. Both House and Senate announced their intention to investigate the lobbyists. The House investigation was confided to the Rules Committee and John J. O'Connor. However, O'Connor's brother Basil, Roosevelt's former law partner, had been retained by Associated Gas & Electric, and though no misconduct was alleged against Basil, liberals for this and other reasons were suspicious of the O'Connor investigation. The Senate, meanwhile, appointed a special committee under the chairmanship of that experienced investigator Hugo Black. It was to this committee that the administration turned for what it hoped would be a searching exposure of the power lobby.

Black, as usual, wasted no time. His investigators promptly surprised Philip Gadsden, the chief utility lobbyist, in the offices of the Committee of Public Utility Education at the Mayflower Hotel, and hustled him off to appear without preparation at the first hearing. Fortified by subpoenas, the investigators then searched Gadsden's files, both business and personal, and extracted whatever seemed of likely use. Under Black's unfriendly and brilliant questioning, Gadsden began the reluctant process of revealing the dimensions of the utility campaign.

But Black had still juicier prospects in mind — especially Howard C. Hopson, the man who had largely built up Associated Gas & Electric, one of the most dazzling examples of the holding company art. A. G. & E. now consisted of over 160 lesser companies — holding companies, management companies, engineering companies, electrical-appliance companies, operating companies. It offered for sale three classes of common stock, six of preferred, four of preference, seven issues of secured bonds and notes, twenty-four classes of debentures, and four series of investment certificates. But while the structure beneath expanded mysteriously and dizzily, Hopson kept tight personal control over the two companies at the summit of the pyramid. He exemplified nearly every iniquitous practice in the Wheeler-Rayburn book. Reputable holding-company figures, like Wendell Willkie, had little use for him.

In the last week of July Black issued a subpoena for Hopson. Then Hopson simply disappeared for a fortnight. When he surrendered, it was not to Black, but to the House Committee, whose chairman's brother was under his retainer. For two days, Black and O'Connor scuffled for possession of the witness. Finally the House committee defied its chairman and turned the witness over to Black. Hopson made a repellent impression on the stand. His testimony perfected Black's case. As *Time* put it, Hopson "dug a pit into which the utility tycoons of the United States fell and writhed in despair."

Congressman Driscoll of Pennsylvania told the Black Committee about the peculiarities of the telegrams which had flooded his office, and Black summoned the head of the Western Union office at Warren. According to the Western Union manager, his New York office had notified him that the utility companies would be filing messages on the Wheeler-Rayburn bill and that he should be co-operative. Shortly after, the Warren manager of Associated Gas & Electric appeared to say he was under orders to send

Driscoll at least one thousand telegrams from Warren. For a few days the utility manager came regularly into the telegraph office for an hour or two and dictated telegrams to be sent at the right time to Driscoll. For signatures, he took names from the early pages of the city directory, or paid a messenger boy named Elmer (who became a day's delight in the headlines) three cents a head for any he could procure. When debate began in the House, he told Western Union to send Driscoll a specified number of wires each day. Later, when Driscoll began to ask embarrassing questions, the original messages were burned in violation of both company and Federal Communications Commission regulations.

In its canvass of the field from utility magnates like Gadsden and Hopson all the way down to Elmer, the Western Union boy, the Black Committee built up a formidable picture. Wendell Willkie had disarmingly portrayed the utilities as "essentially a technical development, devoting their normal energies to engineering and construction work and possessing no natural means of articulation." The Black investigation failed to substantiate this notion of an affable, inarticulate giant. Instead, it seemed to bear out George Norris's old thesis that the utilities were the source of all corruption and David Lilienthal's contention that the power trust was out to take over the government. Early in August Black reported that, on the basis of highly incomplete returns, the utilities had spent at least a million and a half dollars to generate the storm of apparently spontaneous protest. They had evidently paid for more than 250,000 telegrams and stimulated perhaps 5,000,000 letters. "The books of your local company," Black added, "will show these expenses as a part of the cost of delivering electricity to you. . . . In other words, you will pay the bill." William Allen White's *Emporia Gazette* summed up the popular reaction: "In this town and in this State there is no great excitement among the widows and orphans [over] the death sentence to holding companies. But a lot of telegrams and letters left the State and this town, indicating a general uprising. It was pure fake." [8]

XI

The methods employed by Black to procure these results underwent much criticism then and later. Certainly his was no model of fair and impartial investigation. He was criticized most for his use of subpoenas *duces tecum* — dragnet subpoenas, requiring the production of all messages between specified persons and specified dates. "If telegrams that a Senator does not like can be seized and published without restraint, even if they advocate or involve nothing illegal," said the *New York Times,* "then there is no reason why private letters cannot be seized out of the mails." "Once a precedent like this gets established," said the American Civil Liberties Union, "there is no limit to any means taken by a governmental agency to get information. . . . It justifies wiretapping. It justifies any kind of unreasonable search and seizure."

In response, Black contended persuasively that he was "proceeding in exactly the same line of policy and under the same type of proceedings" that had characterized every investigating committee since 1792. In 1936 attempts were made to enjoin the Black committee from further blanket seizure and use of telegrams. "If any judge ever issued an injunction to prevent the delivery of papers that were sought by this body through subpoena," Black said angrily in the Senate, "the Congress should immediately enact legislation taking away that jurisdiction from the courts." The Senate backed Black, voting unanimously a $10,000 appropriation to pay the costs of fighting the injunction. Eventually a Court of Appeals decided that, while the seizure of the messages was illegal, the court had no power to prevent their use by the congressional committee — that the legislative discretion in discharge of its constitutional functions, whether rightfully or wrongfully exercised, was not a subject for judicial interference. The government has readily used such blanket subpoenas, especially in antitrust cases, ever since.

Once he obtained his documents, Black employed them without mercy to trip and trap his witnesses. "You have me on the hip, of course, as I don't know what you are reading from," protested Hopson; and again, "You have me on the hip, because you have copies of these things and I have not." Nor did Black often permit his witnesses to amplify their answers when they deemed "yes" or "no" inadequate or misleading. "I want the truth," he told Hopson, "but I do not care to have any discussions or arguments or philosophies. We are asking for facts. If we want philosophies, we will ask for them." To witnesses who declined to answer questions, Black observed menacingly, "In each instance with which I am familiar, the House and Senate have steadfastly adhered to their right to compel reply, and the witness has either answered or been imprisoned." (In the untutored thirties, people rarely pleaded the Fifth Amendment.) His posture throughout was that of the relentless prosecuting attorney.

At this time Black regarded congressional investigations as "among the most useful and fruitful functions of the national legislature." As he suggested to David Lawrence, so long as Congress was investigating for the purpose of framing legislation, it could not be restrained in any way by the courts, even when protection was sought under the Constitution. By later standards, including his own, Black undoubtedly pushed the investigative power rather far. "Today it is Senator Black out after the unpopular utility lobbyists," wrote Walter Lippmann in a powerful column in March 1936.

> Yesterday it was an Aldermanic committee out after the social workers of New York City. A few weeks ago it was the Nye committee out to prove that Mr. Morgan put us into the war. A few months ago it was a committee out to ruin Chicago University. A few years ago it was a committee out after Jane Addams and John Dewey. Against whom and what will this engine be turned next? I do not know. But I do know that when lawlessness is approved for supposedly good ends, it will be used even more viciously for bad ones.
>
> So I say it is high time the legislative investigations were investigated, and that some one had the courage to raise the issue and bring home to the American people that until reasonable safeguards are established in these proceedings, they are tolerating a very dangerous breach in their institutions and in their tradition of how justice is to be administered.

It was a prescient argument. Still, the standards of the day were different. Black was unquestionably right in insisting that he was following in the footsteps of eminent predecessors — Walsh, Wheeler, Pecora. Nor did the conduct of his investigation really offer much comfort to the committees of the forties and fifties which brought congressional investigation into such spectacular disrepute. Black's subpoenas were general, but they were issued only when the committee had reasonable grounds to suppose activities were taking place within the scope of its inquiry. His questions were harsh, but they were designed to elicit information essential to legislation (provisions requiring registration of lobbyists were inserted in the holding-company bill itself, and further legislation regarding lobbying was introduced in 1936). His manner was tough, even brutal, but it was impersonal. He questioned the motives of few and the patriotism of none. He did not slander reputations, drag in innocent persons, or indulge in promiscuous character assassination, even when confronted with so tempting a possibility as Howard C. Hopson (whose reputation emerged from the Black committee in such good shape that he could proceed to defraud stockholders of some millions of dollars, for which he was sent to prison in 1940). Above all, the Black Committee inquired into people's actions, not their opinions; into what they did, not what they thought. Nothing in the behavior of the Black Committee refutes Chief Justice Warren's dictum in the Watkins case, "In the decade following World War II, there appeared a new kind of congressional inquiry unknown in prior periods of American history." [9]

XII

The administration counted heavily on the Black investigation to induce second thoughts on the death sentence. The Wheeler-Rayburn bill was now in conference; but on August 1, 1935, Sam Rayburn, reopening the matter on the floor of the House, moved to instruct the House conferees to accept the death sentence. To general astonishment, the House held firm, voting the death sentence down by 210–155. For the next two weeks, the conference settled down to a tedious wrangle, enlivened by the successful efforts of the House conferees to prevent Burt Wheeler from bringing Ben Cohen inside the conference room. On August 17 the *New York Times* reported "every indication" that the bill would die before adjournment. In the White House, Felix Frankfurter worked hard for a formula which might save the bill. Then, in mid-August, he counseled letting it go over to the next session to give congressmen a chance to discover that their constituents wanted a bill with teeth.

Alben Barkley, however, continued to press the Frankfurter compromise in conference. This compromise directed the SEC to permit a holding company to control more than one integrated public-utility system if the additional systems could not economically stand alone and were not so large or so scattered as to impair the advantages of localized management, efficient operation, or effective regulation. The Senate version would not have permitted any holding company to survive which controlled more than a single integrated system. Roosevelt finally acceded, grumbling, "Felix sounds just like John W. Davis." The House happily accepted the formula, and on August 26 the President signed the bill.

From the viewpoint of the power companies, the final bill was no better than the earlier versions. Hardly had it passed when its opponents, taking hope from the mood of the courts, resolved to contest its legality every step along the way. Until the Supreme Court itself had approved each comma in the statute, the holding companies were determined to ignore it. An unrepentant Wendell Willkie spoke for the industry in December. "I have only one possible regret," Willkie said bitterly, "namely, if by spending more money legitimately the Commonwealth & Southern could have prevented this destructive act from being passed, I regret I did not authorize such additional expenditures." [10]

18. Triumph and Tranquility

THROUGH June and July 1935 Roosevelt pressed the Congress steadily for legislative results — for the social-security bill, the holding-company bill, the banking bill, the Wagner bill, the Guffey coal bill. And, as his new mood of confident leadership expanded, he even entered an area where earlier in the session he had intended no action. This was the field of taxation.

The motives behind Roosevelt's new departure were oblique but hardly obscure. In his budget message in January, he declared that he saw no need "at this time" for new tax legislation. Nothing happened in the interval to alter the revenue situation: indeed, in March tax collections were reported to be better than the Treasury had anticipated. But a good deal happened to alter the political situation — above all, the mounting strength of Huey Long. It was this development which seems to have precipitated his decision to reconsider his January tax disclaimer.[1]

II

The early turbulences of the year, working on Roosevelt's unaccustomed sense of political impotence, gave him a mild sense of alarm. "I am fighting Communism, Huey Longism, Coughlinism, Townsendism," he told an emissary of William Randolph Hearst in May. "I want to save our system, the capitalistic system; to save it is to give some heed to world thought of today. I want to equalize the distribution of wealth." He cited Huey Long's statistics and his solution. "To combat this and similar crackpot ideas," Roosevelt said, "it may be necessary to throw to the wolves the forty-six men who are reported to have incomes in excess of one million dollars a year. This can be accomplished through taxation." He would raise the income taxes in the top brackets, and he would add a federal inheritance tax. "The thinking men, the young men, who are disciples of this new world idea of fairer distribution of wealth, they are demanding that something be done to equalize this distribution. . . . We do not want Communism in this country and the only way to fight Communism is by ——" The Hearst official interjected "neo-Communism." The President threw back his head and laughed. To Moley, Roosevelt used the phrase "steal Long's thunder."

The first public talk about inheritance and gift taxes had come a week earlier when Henry Morgenthau, Jr., told Congress such taxes would be necessary if it insisted on the bonus that session. But the Treasury had privately presented a sweeping tax program to the President as early as December 1934, proposing not only inheritance and gift taxes, but the intercorporate dividend tax, designed to break up holding companies, a graduated tax on corporate income, which would have the effect of penalizing corporate size, and a tax on undistributed corporate profits. Morgenthau also had the utopian dream of reducing depletion allowance for oil, gas, and mining, and he wanted to end tax-exempt securities. This program plainly derived only in part from a desire to increase revenue. It also expressed a policy of combatting economic bigness — a policy which proceeded from Morgenthau's own mistrust of large concentrations of economic power as well as from the views of his exceedingly able general counsel, Herman Oliphant, a quiet but radical member of the neo-Brandeisian group.

Roosevelt, after a few weeks' consideration, had laid aside the Treasury proposals in February 1935. Then the share-our-wealth clamor, rising through the spring, brought them to the fore again. In his new zest for action following the post-Schechter breakthrough, the President was increasingly attracted by the idea of a message to Congress on tax policy. Such a message would enable him simultaneously to confound those on the left who were complaining that he had not gone far enough and to place on the defensive those on the right who were leading the assault on his other legislative proposals. It would consolidate his recovery of the political initiative.

Accordingly, in June Roosevelt revived the Treasury program. Frankfurter now appeared to work with Morgenthau on a message to Congress; his participation made the neo-Brandeisianism of the tax program even more explicit. As for Morgenthau, he was delighted by the adoption of the Treasury program. But he wanted to seize the occasion to press his own orthodox views on fiscal policy and urged Roosevelt to insert a sentence in the draft beginning, "Looking forward to balancing the budget. . . ." Roosevelt said irritably, "We have Lew Douglas with us again," and needled Morgenthau on the point till the aggrieved Secretary reminded the President of his one message to the London Economic Conference calling on the nations of the world to balance their budgets. (When Morgenthau finally got up to go, the President seized his arm and said, "I have been having a grand time teasing Henry all evening." Morgenthau noted in his diary, "That was his way of showing me that he had been unnecessarily unkind and felt sorry.")

Raymond Moley, who was also summoned to aid in the drafting, objected to the whole program as a soak-the-rich scheme, rendered distasteful to him by its political opportunism as well as by its neo-Brandeisian philosophy. He succeeded in persuading the President to drop the Treasury proposal for a tax on undistributed corporate profits and to limit the range of the corporate income tax. For the rest, Roosevelt remained light-heartedly determined. Of the conservative chairman of the Senate Finance Committee, Roosevelt remarked cheerily, "Pat Harrison's going to be so surprised he'll have kittens on the spot." Reading the message aloud to Ickes, he said he thought it the best thing he had done as President. At one particularly succulent passage, he exclaimed, "That is for Hearst." "The sense of regaining the whip hand," said Moley, "gave him the first buoyant, cheerful moment he had known for weeks." [2]

III

On June 19, 1935, the message went to the Hill. In the House it won a rising ovation from the Democrats. But the Senate listened in silence. There was a notable exception. As the clerk read the text, Huey Long was sauntering cockily around the chamber. When he heard the existing tax structure condemned for having done little "to prevent an unjust concentration of wealth and economic power," he stopped abruptly in front of the rostrum, grinned broadly, rolled his eyes, and almost danced with pleasure. As the reading continued, he swaggered about, chuckling, pointing to his chest and confiding to other Senators that Roosevelt was stealing his program. At the conclusion, he arose and announced with a straight face, "I just want to say 'Amen.' "

The Kingfish, as usual, claimed too much. The message expressed the gospel according to Long much less than it did the gospel according to Brandeis. One argument after another assailed the philosophy of bigness. Large accumulations of wealth, Roosevelt said, meant "the perpetuation of great and undesirable concentration of control in a relatively few individuals over the employment and welfare of many, many others"; therefore, inheritance and gift taxes were required to check "inherited economic power." Higher personal income taxes in the top bracket would further reduce "the disturbing effects upon our national life that come from great inheritance of wealth and power." As for the modestly capitalized small firm, "without such small enterprises our competitive economic society would cease"; therefore, the tax law should discriminate in their favor, and the corporation income tax, instead of requiring small business to pay the same rate on net profits as big business, should be graduated according to the size of the profits. An intercorporate dividend tax would prevent large companies from trying to evade the graduated corporation income tax by pretending to split up into smaller subsidiaries. The pervading thesis of the message was the neo-Brandeisian conviction that cutting down towering fortunes and breaking up massive corporate empires would help the small man and stimulate "creative enterprise."

The message was frank in conceiving taxation as a weapon of social policy. It did not even make a nominal claim that its recommendations would greatly increase revenue; indeed, very little was said about revenue except for a meaningless suggestion about earmarking the proceeds from the inheritance tax for debt reduction. And it was ambiguous as to when its proposals should be carried out — whether they were ideas tossed out for study, like the social-security message of June 1934, to be acted on by some future Congress, or whether the President wanted a tax bill in the next few weeks. Nor did the President resolve the ambiguity by disappearing to New London for the Harvard-Yale boat race, leaving his astonished congressional leaders to speculate as to what was in his mind.

There was no delay, however, about public reaction. William Randolph Hearst, alert to his cue, immediately wired his editors, "President's taxation program is essentially Communism," adding that this "bastard" proposal should be ascribed to "a composite personality which might be labeled Stalin Delano Roosevelt." Conservative and business opinion took this general line, though not always achieving the same vigor of expression. And, on the left, Huey Long, belatedly detecting the lineaments of the scrootch owl in Share-Our-Wealth's newest convert, had sobering second thoughts. His first solution was to send an open letter to Roosevelt, invoking "Jefferson, Madison, Webster, Emmerson [sic] and . . . such lesser lights as myself" as originators of the plan and expressing the hope that Roosevelt would prove himself fit for so august a company. By early July, Long was dismissing Roosevelt as "a liar and a faker," adding, "He's copying my share-the-wealth speeches now that I was writing when I was fourteen years old. So he's just now getting as smart as I was when I was in knee breeches."

IV

In the Senate, the progressive bloc was enthusiastic about the prospect of action on taxes. Of the progressive senators, none knew more about taxation than Robert M. La Follette, Jr. From the start of the depression, La Follette had been a spender; but he was never — except involuntarily — a deficit spender. He had faithfully contended both for large programs of relief and public works and for "taxation to make possible the extraordinary expenditures necessary" to carry such programs out. He realized that strict pay-as-you-go would be impossible until business improved; but he feared for the government credit and a little anxiously defined the alternative in 1935 as "higher taxes or uncontrolled inflation." Through the spring La Follette had called for "drastic increases in the taxes levied upon wealth and income." He also wished to reduce exemptions and broaden the tax base in the belief that the payment of a direct income tax, no matter how small, would increase every citizen's sense of participation in government and therefore his sense of civic responsibility.

La Follette now applauded Roosevelt's message as providing an opportunity for reforming the tax structure. But La Follette's viewpoint remained distinct from Roosevelt's. He disagreed, for example, with the neo-Brandeisian philosophy of the tax message. Though his father had believed passionately in the competition of small units, La Follette was much closer to the philosophy of the First New Deal. "Of all the progressives of that time," said Tugwell, La Follette "had made the most complete transition to modernism." Still, La Follette welcomed the Roosevelt message because it at least conceived of taxation as an instrument of social control. And, most urgently of all, he welcomed it as a means of gaining enough new revenue to keep the national debt from billowing out of sight.

Already pending before the Senate was a joint resolution to extend a miscellany of excise taxes due to die on June 30. La Follette's first thought was to attach a new tax program to the nuisance-tax resolution. When the Democratic leadership rejected this and seemed indifferent to the whole idea of new taxes that session, La Follette, backed by Norris, Borah, and Hiram Johnson, organized a round robin, soon signed by twenty-two progressive senators of both parties, saying that Congress should stay in session until taxes were passed. The idea behind this, as Gerald Nye explained, was to test Roosevelt's sincerity. Joseph T. Robinson, the Senate leader, eventually supported the progressive initiative, though Pat Harrison, chairman of the Finance Committee, wanted to delay action till 1936. Whatever Roosevelt's intention when he sent the message down, he now found himself — between Huey Long's sarcastic letter and La Follette's solemn petition — in a dilemma. If he now did nothing about taxes in 1935, he would dissipate the political gains of the tax message. In his post-Schechter mood of decision, he did not hesitate. Calling the congressional leaders together on June 24, he demanded full speed ahead on tax legislation.

Roosevelt's precipitate action plunged the legislative situation into an unseemly mess. His Senate leaders emerged with the impression that he wanted the tax bill to be attached, as La

Follette had proposed, to the nuisance-tax resolution, the whole
thing to be hurried through Congress before July 1. Pat Harrison
obediently came up with tax rates designed to mediate between
Roosevelt's social policy and the congressional demand for increased revenues. But both in Congress and the country there
arose a protest against rushing through such important legislation
in four days. Even the pro–New Deal *New York Daily News* reminded Roosevelt, "It took six days to make the world!"

Feeling the recoil, Roosevelt forty-eight hours later blandly
denied to newspapermen that he had ever wanted the tax bill
passed by June 30; he had no such power over Congress; he was
only "the little fellow who recommends things." It was a stormy
conference. The newspapermen, led by Raymond P. Brandt of
the *St. Louis Post-Dispatch,* harried him without mercy. On the
Hill, Harrison and Robinson, true professionals, swallowed once
or twice and accepted the responsibility for this misbegotten
strategy. To keep La Follette from offering his amendments anyway, Harrison had to promise that the Finance Committee would
report out a tax bill that session. As the nonsense subsided, Congress now got down to the serious business of considering tax
legislation.[3]

v

On July 8 the House Ways and Means Committee began hearings. For three weeks it stewed over the problem, finally reporting
out a bill which, in the main, followed the President's recommendations, except for a severe dilution of the graduated corporate income tax. To make up for this, the committee added a tax on excess corporate profits. On August 5, the bill passed the House by
a vote of 282–96.

In the meantime, difficulties had been multiplying in the Senate. Pat Harrison had not only a conservative Democrat's dislike
for the social policy of the bill, especially the inheritance tax;
he was also mad at both Roosevelt and Morgenthau because one
of his candidates had failed of appointment to the Board of Tax
Appeals. All this was only barely offset by his instinct for party
loyalty. Moreover, La Follette was more zealous than ever in his
fight for a wider tax base. For a day or so, he persuaded the com-

mittee to cut exemptions to such a point that even single persons on relief would have to pay income tax. The President himself seemed to Morgenthau to waver for a moment on the question of the inheritance tax. Nor did Morgenthau help matters by retiring into an imperturbable agnosticism when Harrison tried to elicit Treasury views ("The Treasury has not, and as long as I am Secretary, is not going to have any views on how to write an income-tax bill").

As the hearings proceeded, revenue seemed to become more and more the predominating purpose of the bill. Robert H. Jackson, the general counsel of the Bureau of Internal Revenue, made a powerful effort to wrench the program back to the President's original conception. In several days of impressive testimony before the Senate Finance Committee, Jackson outlined the problem which, in his view, the tax bill was designed to remedy. The Roosevelt administration, he said, had inherited an inequitable tax structure. In 1933, 58.3 per cent of federal revenues came from taxes based on consumption — taxes which especially hit the poorer classes; only 41.7 per cent came from income, gift, estate, capital-stock, and excess-profits taxes — taxes based on ability to pay. Since 1933, Jackson reported, there had been a "steady drift toward a heavier burden upon the consumer and a lighter burden upon those classes which we rate as being able to pay." This was not only unjust; it also drained away mass purchasing power essential for economic recovery. On top of this, Jackson continued, there was the problem of growing economic concentration. Hence the need for inheritance and gift taxes, for higher surtaxes, for graduated corporate income taxes.

The drive to replace the graduated corporate income tax by the excess-profit tax, Jackson felt, drew the social issue. The first tax, which the House had already weakened, would, of course, fall more lightly on small business than on large. The second, which the House had added to the bill, would, as Jackson pointed out, "fall upon small and large concerns alike" and thus favor big business, since "the risks facing small concerns are generally far greater than those facing large business organizations."

But his arguments were unavailing. From every side, resentment was boiling up. Even New Deal sympathizers, like Governor Herbert H. Lehman of New York, questioned aspects of the bill. (Roosevelt replied to Lehman, "Past records seem to show that the larger the estate the greater the success in avoiding inheritance taxes. . . . If everybody were as honest as you are and as I try to be the problems of Government would be easier, especially in connection with the richer members of the community!") As for the business community, already angered by the holding-company fight, its resentment against Roosevelt reached new heights of absurdity. Moley had no sympathy for the bill, but he found he had even less for businessmen who wailed "that the President must be pursuing a private vendetta against his old friends of Groton and Harvard, that dangerous communists were scuttling in and out of his presence like messenger boys in a broker's office." The most ridiculous accusation was that Roosevelt was committing some kind of sin against the Constitution by viewing taxation as an instrument of social policy (even Herbert Hoover had once said, "To those who believe taxes should not be designed to promote economic or social objectives, I would remark that this Republic has been doing it ever since the first tax bill was signed by George Washington"). Irritated by the uproar, Roosevelt struck back by accusing the very rich of tax avoidance; the fifty-eight individuals with incomes of over one million dollars a year, he said in press conference, had paid no tax whatever to the Federal government on 37 per cent of their net incomes. "Tax avoidance," the President said sardonically, "means that you hire a $250,000-fee lawyer, and he changes the word 'evasion' into the word 'avoidance.'" Such remarks were not calculated to tranquilize the atmosphere.

Under the pressure, the Senate Finance Committee cut out the inheritance tax and retained the graduated corporate income tax in only a token form. On August 15 the Senate passed the bill 57–22. Efforts in conference to restore the inheritance tax failed; instead, the estate tax was increased (that is, the tax on the gross estate rather than the individual inheritance). The intercorporate dividend tax, which the House had rejected, was put back. Late in August the bill went to the White House. The President signed it on August 31.

It cannot be said that the tax bill of 1935 was much in itself. What began as an essay in neo-Brandeisianism lost its sting as Congress tried to rewrite it as a measure to raise money. This divergence in purpose emptied the bill of most of its social content without making it potent as a producer of revenue. The result was a feeble measure, expected to ·deliver only about $250 million of additional revenue, which meant that it would do little either to balance the budget or to redistribute the wealth. What was significant was not the bill but the philosophy behind it. The message of June 19 represented the dramatic repudiation of 1933 — of the belief that integrated bigness was the essence of modern society. This new and explicit commitment to small competitive enterprise made the tax message the first crucial document of the Second New Deal.

The tax message represented only one part, however, of the Second New Deal coalition — the Brandeis group. The advocates of fiscal policy regarded the La Follette program of raising taxes in depression as madness. The fear of inflation, said Eccles in March, was "largely imaginary"; tax increases in the lower brackets would do nothing but mop up necessary purchasing power. Taxation had in Eccles's mind quite another function. "The banking system," as he put it, "can influence the volume of money . . . and the tax system, it seems to me, must influence the velocity of money." In other words, taxation should transfer money from those who would save it to those who would spend it. Such a thought was far from the minds of most of those who drafted the Revenue Act of 1935. Yet the President's willingness to use tax policy as an instrument of social policy gave the spenders hope that in the future he would be willing to use it as an instrument of economic policy. Less important than either the purpose or the achievement of the 1935 law was Franklin Roosevelt's evident readiness to add a powerful new weapon to his economic armory.[4]

VI

The congressional session which had begun as a rout was now beginning to take on the appearance of a triumph. Another bill which had gained new urgency from the demise of NRA was the Guffey coal bill, descendant of a long line of bills designed to stabilize the soft coal industry. Under NRA, the Bituminous Coal Code had provided a testing for the stabilization effort. The Code's success in halting the disintegration of the industry persuaded many northern operators to join John L. Lewis and the United Mine Workers in demanding permanent legislation.

Joseph F. Guffey himself, as he liked to say, was born in the shadow of a bituminous coal tipple. Elected to the Senate in 1934 after a picturesque career in Pennsylvania finance and politics, Guffey perceived with clarity that the future of the New Deal — or at least his own political future — lay with labor and the minority groups. One of his first acts early in the 1935 session was to introduce the coal stabilization bill drafted by the United Mine Workers. After the NRA decision, the measure was revised in an effort to ward off constitutional objections. It proposed, in effect, an NRA for the coal industry — a national coal commission with codes governing minimum prices, trade practices, wages, hours, and collective bargaining. Compliance with the codes was to be secured through the use of the taxing power — a 15 per cent excise tax was to be levied on the entire industry, with co-operating producers allowed a 90 per cent rebate.

James W. Carter, president of the Carter Coal Company, was quick to denounce the bill as "the first step in the socialization of all industry." The owners of the captive coal mines also disliked the bill, since overproduction in the industry meant cheaper coal for their steel mills. The American Liberty League and the organs of official conservatism united in condemning it. But many — perhaps most — of the independent operators, considering the choice to be between regulation and chaos, stayed with Lewis and Guffey.

Still, the post-NRA redrafting did not dissipate the constitutional questions; and doubtless many who disliked the bill on other grounds were happy to rest their opposition on constitutional scruple. To clear away this obstacle, Roosevelt, on July 6, 1935, sent a letter to Congressman Samuel B. Hill, chairman of the sub-committee considering the measure. "The situation is so urgent," Roosevelt said, "and the benefits of the legislation so evident that all doubts should be resolved in favor of the bill, leaving to the courts, in an orderly fashion, the ultimate question of constitutionality." The quicker the Supreme Court could decide on the bill, he continued, the sooner the government and the coal industry would know the constitutional limits within which they must operate. "I hope your committee will not permit doubts as to constitu-

tionality, however reasonable, to block the suggested legislation."
Roosevelt's point was orthodox enough, but the expression
was unquestionably maladroit. He might better have written
"doubts as to unconstitutionality," which was what he meant;
and the phrase "however reasonable" threw the opposition into
new fits of professed apprehension over the imminence of dictatorship. "President Roosevelt has come perilously close to what some
people call impeachable grounds," said Congressman Bertrand
Snell. The House Ways and Means Committee, unmoved by the
presidential plea, kept the bill bottled up for another five weeks.
Finally on August 13 it received a favorable report by a 12–11
vote. In the meantime, John L. Lewis, employing for the first
time a tactic with which the nation would soon become dismally
familiar, was threatening a nation-wide coal strike. By mid-August
Roosevelt twice succeeded in getting the strike postponed on the
assurance that Congress would at least vote on the measure. On
the floor of the House, it provoked a sharp Democratic split.
"Communism, pure and simple, is what's behind this bill," said
Congressman Claude Fuller of Arkansas. "Socialism in its wildest
dreams never went so far." But on August 20 it finally passed
by a vote of 194–168. Three days later, in the end-of-session rush,
the Senate passed the Guffey bill 45–37, constitutional doubts and
all.[5]

VII

The session ended much as it began: Huey Long was once
again on the rampage. On August 9 he had read to an inattentive
and skeptical Senate what he asserted was a transcript, recorded
by dictaphone, of a meeting held by his political opponents on
July 21 in Room 506 of the De Soto Hotel in New Orleans.
According to Long, one voice, regrettably unidentified, had said,
"I would draw in a lottery to go out and kill Long. It would
only take one man, one gun, and one bullet." Another had said,
"I haven't the slightest doubt but that Roosevelt would par-
don anyone who killed Long." When Long reported that a third
voice had suggested that the killing take place in the Senate chamber in Washington, his colleagues broke out in derisive laughter.
(It eventually emerged that four Louisiana congressmen and the

Baton Rouge district attorney were among those present at the De Soto; if there was idle talk about murder, it was because the subject generally came up when Louisianians discussed Long. When Long was present, he often brought it up himself.)

Two and a half weeks later, with every other member of Congress straining for release from their long ordeal, Long again went into his act, this time filibustering against a deficiency appropriation bill because the administration refused to increase AAA loans on wheat. He told the wheat senators that, in return, he expected their support "the next time we have anything to do in the Senate"; then, moved by his obsession with death, that pale horse, the storm as a bride, Huey added, "provided I am back here — I may not be back here. This may be my swan song, for all I know." Swan song or not, it was a success. The Senate leadership finally gave up on the deficiency bill and, amid closing scenes of tumult and indignation, the session came to an end.

Few Congresses in American history had achieved so much: the institution of a revolutionary new system of social insurance; the establishment of government guarantees for labor organization and collective bargaining; the reconstruction of the banking system; the reorganization of the power system; the reform of public utility holding companies; massive provisions for relief and public works; the enactment of a program to stabilize the coal industry; the beginnings of important changes in the tax structure; new railroad-retirement and farm-mortgage laws to replace those invalidated by the Supreme Court — on top of all this, far-reaching changes (to be discussed in the next volume) in neutrality legislation. "Seldom, if ever, in the long history of Congress," wrote Charles A. Beard, who only a few months earlier had pronounced Roosevelt at the end of his rope, "had so many striking and vital measures been spread upon the law books in a single session."

It was a prodigious comeback, set off, it would seem, by a new vision of policy. But it was purchased at the cost of bitter emotions. The holding-company fight, the labor fight, the banking fight, above all, the tax fight, had intensified the alienation of the business community.

On the day Congress adjourned, Roy W. Howard, head of the friendly Scripps-Howard chain of newspapers, wrote the President commenting on the rise of opposition among businessmen "at a time when there is no commensurate dissatisfaction being evidenced by others of the electorate." So long as this was only the opposition of financial racketeers, Howard said, it could be disregarded. "But any experienced reporter will tell you that throughout the country many business men who once gave you sincere support are now, not merely hostile, they are frightened." They feel that, as in the tax bill, your administration is motivated by revenge — "revenge on business." They feel that there can be no real recovery "until the fears of business have been allayed through the granting of a breathing spell to industry, and a recess from further experimentation."

On September 1 Ray Moley, whom Roosevelt had asked to draft a reply, motored up to Hyde Park, where the President had retired for a rest. Moley found the President more relaxed than he had seemed for months. He took Moley's conciliatory notes without cavil, even inserting further gracious words of his own. The letter began as a courteous defense, conceding nothing, of the legislation of 1935. "Duty and necessity required us to move on a broad front for more than two years." But the basic program, Roosevelt disarmingly concluded, "has now reached substantial completion and the 'breathing spell' of which you speak is here — very decidedly so." The announcement produced a highly favorable public reaction. The acrimony of the spring and summer seemed to be fading away in a season of autumnal tranquility.[6]

VIII

The atmosphere, now clearing on the right, cleared suddenly and violently on the left. For Huey Long, there seemed no rest. No sooner did responsibility end in Washington than it began in Baton Rouge. The Kingfish had to spend the day of September 8 supervising his legislature as it rushed to enact a miscellany of bills designed to perfect control of his kingdom. Eventually, in the early evening, Allan J. Ellender, the Speaker of the Louisiana House, declared the session adjourned.

Followed by the usual retinue of bodyguards and hangers-on, Huey swaggered back across the rotunda of the Capitol to the

xTRIUMPH AND TRANQUILITY

339

-Governor's office. It was nine-twenty in the evening. Quietly, out of the shadows, stepped a young man in a white linen suit. Quietly, before Long and the others knew what he was doing, he drew a .32 caliber automatic pistol from his pocket, pressed it against Long's abdomen and fired. Then, with seconds long as hours, while the victim, moaning with surprise, held his hand over his torn side, while the murderer paused and prepared to fire again, the others came out of their trance. Someone knocked up the murderer's gun; then revolvers and submachine guns went into action, shot after shot pouring into the sagging body of the assassin. The medical examiners later found 30 bullet holes in his front, 29 more in his back, 2 in his head.

"I wonder why he shot me?" said Huey Long as the car sped him to the hospital. The putative assassin was a young Baton Rouge doctor named Carl Austin Weiss. (Some in Louisiana would always wonder whether Long was not killed by his own bodyguards, either accidentally, when they misinterpreted Weiss's desire to hold Long in a moment's conversation, or purposely, in revenge for a long history of humiliation, and whether the body-guards did not then riddle Weiss's body with bullets to cover their error, or crime. Why, people asked, was there never an autopsy?) Weiss plainly had not been in Room 506 of the Hotel De Soto on July 21. But he had his reasons for disliking Long. A sensitive, quiet man, he had been a student in Vienna when Dollfuss's soldiers had shot down the Socialist workers; he had strong views about dictators. Moreover, his father-in-law, a district judge who refused to bow to Long, was the target of one of the bills Long had hustled through the legislature that very after-noon. And, as part of his campaign to destroy the judge, Long was supposed to have accused him of having Negro blood, a remark that would affect both Dr. Weiss's wife and his son. No one can know what finally drove Weiss to the decision, with what somber purpose he went to the Capitol, with what feelings he waited in the rotunda, with what thoughts he passed the endless moments, till, at last, the door of the chamber opened across the way, and the pudgy red-faced man emerged in the clatter of heels on the marble floor, and the muscles tightened in the stomach, and the steel of the gun clutched in the pocket felt cold and hot together, and, instantly, after the hours of waiting, the man was there, and one took the quiet swift step from the shadows and heard the deafening burst, and at last, as Mason Spencer foresaw, there was blood on the polished floor of the Capitol.

For thirty hours Long struggled for life. He had an operation and five blood transfusions, but his strength slipped away as he swam in and out of consciousness. Once he said, "Oh Lord, don't let me die, for I have a few more things to accomplish." Early in the morning of September 10, he died, still a young man, a dozen days past his forty-second birthday.

IX

For two days the body lay in state, with Huey incongruously dressed in the evening clothes he used to ridicule. One hundred thousand persons, white and black, swarmed upon Baton Rouge as officials prepared to bury him in the front lawn of the State Capitol. It was a hot day on September 12; over two hundred in the waiting crowd fainted. A huge mass of flowers covered the sea of green where the copper-lined vault was to be sunk. In the distance sounded the strains of "Every Man A King," now transposed to a minor key and played as a dirge. The Reverend Gerald L. K. Smith, never more sonorous, spoke over the bier. "This place marks not the resting place of Huey P. Long," Smith said, "it marks only the burial ground for his body. His spirit shall never rest as long as hungry bodies cry for food, as long as lean human frames stand naked, as long as homeless wretches haunt this land of plenty." He concluded with a side glance at Long's critics: "He was the Stradivarius, whose notes rose in competition with jealous drums, envious tomtoms. His was the unfinished symphony." That night people wept along the bayous and in bare cabins, chinks filled with mud, and in crossroad stores, — and possibly in the sleazy New Orleans apartments where Long's associates kept their loot and their girls.

There was not much grief among those who knew Long personally, except for a natural regret that the Lord had blown the whistle on a profitable racket. The Kingfish was hardly in his grave before the little fishes, the Reverend Mr. Smith foremost among them, were fighting over the spoils. In one outburst, Smith blamed the murder on the New Orleans newspaper publishers and Senator Theodore G. Bilbo of Mississippi, who, according to Smith, had made a sinister trip to New Orleans the week before with $35,000 in his pocket. Bilbo replied adeptly by calling Smith "a contemptible, dirty, vicious, pusillanimous, with-malice-afore-thought, damnable, self-made liar."

This vulgar scramble was in the spirit of Huey Long. But a certain dignity remained to him nevertheless. It was expressed in the Cajun ballad:

> O they say he was a crook
> But he gave us free school book
> Tell me why is it that they kill Huey Long?
> Now he's dead and in his grave
> But we riding on his pave'
> Tell me why is it that they kill Huey Long?

In Long's bones and his blood, Maury Maverick said, there was hatred born of the oppression, undernourishment, sorrow, misery, ignorance, and desperation of his people. Raging in his soul, he "slashed and cut and cursed the gods of oil and sulphur — his first hates — and then all the other gods across the national scene. He was like a violent Gargantua shouting his Rabelaisian song as he went. God rest his troubled soul in peace. There was much in him that was vicious but what he stirred up cannot be downed."

The news of Long's death reached Roosevelt over the luncheon table at Hyde Park. His companion was Father Coughlin, whom Joe Kennedy had brought to see the President in the usual effort at reconciliation. Coughlin was later quoted as calling Long's assassination "the most regrettable thing in modern history." The President, of course, condemned the murder and conveyed his sympathy to Long's widow. His more private reactions are not known; it is to be assumed that they were relief. A few weeks later, Jim Farley told Ickes that, if Long had lived, he would have polled six million votes in 1936. "I always laughed Huey off," Farley said, "but I did not feel that way about him." It is difficult to quarrel with Farley on political matters (especially on anything related to the election of 1936); but it may be put down as an axiom of politics that third parties are more formidable in May than in November. One doubts whether even Huey Long could have reversed that rule.

Still, skepticism about Long's power to affect matters in 1936 hardly alters the impact of his death in 1935. With a new appearance of tranquilization on the left, Franklin Roosevelt in September 1935 seemed to be sailing, for a moment, in quiet waters.[7]

19. The Battle of Relief

THE CONGRESSIONAL SESSION of 1935 ended for Roosevelt in a triumphant conquest of legislative objectives. There remained the problem of converting statutes into social results. Of the various questions of administration before him, none occupied Roosevelt more persistently through the year than the establishment of the new organization for federal relief. He had signed the joint resolution making appropriations of $4.8 billion for relief purposes on April 8, 1935. But this resolution could hardly have been more vague in its administrative injunctions. The next step was setting up a new relief agency. This step confronted the President with vexing issues both of personnel and of policy which he had for some months successfully evaded.

II

There were, of course, two active candidates for the top relief job — Harry L. Hopkins, the head of the Federal Emergency Relief Administration, and Harold L. Ickes, the head of the Public Works Administration. While the bill was before Congress, Roosevelt had carefully kept his own counsel about who would run the show. Some members of Congress, especially in the Senate, were sufficiently hostile to Hopkins to vote against any relief program which he might direct; others, especially in the House, were equally hostile to Ickes; so political discretion alone would have enjoined the President not to show his hand. One result was to plunge both Ickes and Hopkins into agonies of uncertainty.

Ickes was a more indignant man, and his anxiety was both

more peremptory and better documented. For a time he tormented himself in his diary with the thought that his one-time law partner and now detested administration colleague Donald Richberg might get the job; then he feared it might go to Admiral Christian J. Peoples, the Director of Treasury Procurement. In the meantime, resuming his mood of clumsy machiavellianism, he tried to enlist Hopkins in a campaign against Richberg and Peoples and then offered Hopkins his own support for the establishment of a cabinet department of social welfare with Hopkins as secretary. If this idea failed to go through, Ickes said generously that he would be glad to have Hopkins come in under him as Deputy Administrator of Public Works. For his part, Hopkins was distressed by what he took to be slighting references to the Civil Works Administration of 1933–34 in the President's message and for a long time had no idea where he would fit into the new program.

As late as March 1935 Ickes had persuaded himself that he was to have the job. But Roosevelt was already consulting privately with Hopkins on the design of the new agency. Thus on March 16 Hopkins, who hated organization charts, wrote in his diary, "We went over the organization of the work program — more charts in pencil — he loves charts — no two of them are ever the same, which is a bit baffling at times." When Hopkins accompanied the President on the train south to Warm Springs toward the end of the month, it seemed apparent that the FERA administrator was to emerge the dominant figure.

In fact, the presidential choice was less between personalities than between programs. Roosevelt wanted speed, flexibility, quick re-employment, and a sharp stimulus to consumer purchasing power. Wanting this, he inevitably favored light public works in the Hopkins style. "Ickes is a good administrator," Roosevelt explained to Richberg, "but often too slow. Harry gets things done. I am going to give this job to Harry." Yet Roosevelt shared Ickes's passion for beautifying the national estate through durable public works, and he trusted Ickes's capacity to keep graft out of the works program. The problem was to invent an organization which would retain Ickes's vigilance and drive while yet giving Hopkins primary control over the spending of money. Why not, Roosevelt mused, make Ickes chairman of an Advisory Committee on Allotments, which would pass on projects, and then make Hopkins responsible for the actual progress of the work?

This scheme disturbed Henry Morgenthau, Jr., who feared that from his vantage point on the Allotments Committee, Ickes would dominate the program. The notion of Hopkins in "some non-descript job," the Secretary of the Treasury noted in his dairy, "just made me sick." Morgenthau's proposal was to bring in Joseph P. Kennedy, the chairman of the Securities and Exchange Commission, as top man. Roosevelt liked the idea of some third person to keep the peace between Hopkins and Ickes; and, when Kennedy declined the job on the ground that he could not work with Ickes, Roosevelt appointed as third member the New Deal's prize harmonizer of sensitive bureaucrats, Frank Walker.

On the evening of April 26, 1935, Roosevelt called the key figures in the new works organization over to the White House. Impressing them all with his gravity, he said that he was committed personally to this new effort and planned to sit himself on the Allotments Committee. This undertaking meant a great deal to the American people, he added; its success or failure might determine the outcome of the 1936 election. He expected everything to go like clockwork, and he would take no excuses. Ickes reflecting on the evening, noted with rare detachment that it was probably just as well to have Walker in the picture. "Hopkins will fly off on tangents unless he is watched, and I am quite likely to be bulldoggish and want to have my own way."

As yet, Ickes felt set back but by no means defeated. Hopkins lost no time, however, in consolidating his position. What had been announced as the Works Progress Division, on a presumed level of equality with Walker's Division of Application and Information and Ickes's Works Allotment Division, grew in another fortnight into the Works Progress Administration — a designation selected by Hopkins with malice, Ickes always believed, in order to confuse the public between PWA and WPA. As first established in the executive order of May 6, WPA did not seem to be primarily an operating agency. But the small print in the executive order permitted Hopkins to initiate work projects of his own; and he proceeded to move fast into operations.[1]

III

"All day planning the work program," Hopkins noted in his diary on May 12, 1935, "which would be a great deal easier if

Ickes would play ball — but he is stubborn and righteous which is a hard combination. He is also the 'great resigner' — anything doesn't go his way, threatens to quit. He bores me." With swift agility, Hopkins pressed his WPA projects. "It is becoming ever clearer," Ickes wrote on June 18, "that Hopkins is dominating this program and this domination will mean thousands of inconsequential make-believe projects in all parts of the country." In the meantime Hopkins, in his sardonic way, tried to deprecate reports of a feud with Ickes. "The real low-down," he wrote in the draft of a speech to PWA personnel, "is that the fellow who is making all the trouble around here is Walker. He is the one that really stirs up all the trouble; if you want to blame anyone, blame Walker. That is one of the things he is here for, to be blamed for everything."

Such nonchalance did not cure the split. Nor could Walker himself do much to resolve the issues between Hopkins and Ickes. Beyond the alphabetical confusion, the line between PWA and WPA was far from clear. The effort to make cost the criterion — all construction projects over $25,000 to be automatically assigned to PWA — was frustrated by Hopkins's skill in subdividing his larger projects. And there were too many marginal cases to make possible a firm distinction between heavy and light public works. One difference was plain, that administratively Hopkins was in a much better position to get his projects under way. Ickes's projects, for example, had to go one by one before the Advisory Committee on Allotments — a process, Ickes termed it, of being cleared by a debating society. Then they went to Hopkins, who had an indirect veto of his own through his authority to decide whether the applicant community had enough unemployed labor to justify the project. Ickes was convinced that Hopkins was using this power to delay PWA and promote WPA. "It was something more than mere coincidence," he darkly observed, "that there were always workers available for one of Harry's projects, even if there were not for mine." (A reason in some cases was that PWA projects often required special labor skills, while WPA could usually get along with unskilled labor.)

Hopkins, on the other hand, did not have to go before the Committee on Allotments except to ask for lump-sum appropriations. "We vote him money by the carload," said Ickes resentfully, "and he spends it at his own sweet pleasure." Furthermore, where PWA required a monetary contribution from the local authority, WPA had the tremendous competitive advantage of being able to offer grants without demanding any local contribution in return. And WPA's advantages were compounded by what Ickes regarded as Hopkins's irresponsible delight in spending money. "He was not priming the pump," said the PWA administrator; "he was just turning on the fire-plug." Ickes knew by embittered experience Hopkins's uncanny capacity to lay his hands on any loose change floating around the government. More than once he discovered that unexpended PWA money was being impounded in order to finance Hopkins. "PWA was not being borrowed from," Ickes wrote later, "it was being politely held up at the point of a presidential executive order." He watched with particular envy Hopkins's success in carrying out what Morgenthau described as "squeeze plays" against the Treasury — that is, waiting until the last moment before letting the Treasury know that he was overspending, then appealing to Morgenthau's humanity by reminding him of the misery of the unemployed. "Hopkins," Morgenthau wrote ruefully, "could always get money." Ickes became convinced that Hopkins and Morgenthau were ranged in unholy alliance against him. "The President certainly has a blind side so far as Morgenthau is concerned," Ickes wrote, "and Hopkins seems to sing a siren song for him."

What perhaps exasperated Ickes most was the fact that, despite all the provocation, he could never properly hate Hopkins. A liking for him survived everything — "the liking," said Ickes, "of a man who had grown up under Scotch-Presbyterian restraint for the happy-go-lucky type who can bet his last cent, even if it be a borrowed one, on a horse race." Entering a conference with Hopkins, Ickes would resolve not to relent; but, as the evening wore on, he would sometimes find, as he later wrote indignantly, "that I, too, was succumbing to the blandishments of Harry's personality." [2]

IV

Throughout the summer of 1935 Ickes saw Hopkins gradually expand his power. By August the Secretary of the Interior was contemplating resignation from the Allotments Committee; "I can see all kinds of possible scandals ahead and I don't care to become involved." A fortnight later, when the remaining independent PWA funds were placed under the control of the Allot- ments Committee, Ickes angrily told the President that this order had put PWA out of business. The President told him not to be childish. Ickes responded hotly. "I never thought," he wrote later in his diary, "I would talk to a President of the United States the way I talked to President Roosevelt last night." Roosevelt said he would issue a statement reaffirming Ickes's position as Administrator of Public Works, and Ickes reluctantly decided to stay on despite the plots against him.

His wife's death in an automobile accident in New Mexico late in August increased the strain under which he was laboring. In the meantime Hopkins was making what Ickes regarded as slurring remarks against PWA in press conferences; and the whole controversy was becoming public property. "I am thoroughly convinced," Ickes said privately of his rival, "that he is a lawless individual bent on building a reputation for himself as a great builder." In one further plea to the President on September 7, Ickes asked how Democratic speakers next year could defend "the wholesale turning down of worthwhile and desirable public works projects proposed on a loan and grant basis while insisting on spending Federal money for less worthwhile works toward the building of which practically no local contribution has been made." He warned of the graft and corruption which seemed to him inevitable in WPA's helter-skelter administration; and added that if recovery to 1929 levels would not end unemployment because of the increase in productivity, there was all the more need for a carefully planned semipermanent public-works program to take up the slack. And if WPA failed, would Congress ever again appropriate enough to give PWA a real chance? Then the nation would once again find itself in social stalemate "until Communism in some form rears its ugly head to challenge an America that will not have elected to save its cherished civilization by a reasonable adaptation of its institutions to meet changing conditions."

A few days later Roosevelt asked Ickes to come up to Hyde Park. Ickes, seeing an opportunity for a showdown, accepted with alacrity. The harried Public Works Administrator spent a sleepless night, kept awake by the snoring of Frank Walker, with whom he was sharing a room. The next morning he met with Roosevelt, Hopkins, Walker, Bell, Tugwell, and a few others to make a final allocation of the $4.8 billion. For Roosevelt the determination to employ as many men as possible from relief rolls with as little as possible cost per man remained decisive. A month's employment on WPA cost $82; on a PWA project $330; and the secondary employment generated by PWA did not ordinarily reduce relief rolls. Of the total appropriation, Ickes found that he was coming out with less than $500 million. It was a rout.

There now remained for the President the job of binding the wounds. Later in the month he traveled across the country and then, boarding the cruiser *Houston*, sailing to Cocos Island and back through the Panama Canal. Both Hopkins and Ickes accompanied him. A story appeared one day in the ship's paper under the title "Buried at Sea"; it sounded as if the President had dashed it off himself.

> The feud between Hopkins and Ickes was given a decent burial today. With flags at half mast . . . the President officiated at the solemn ceremony which we trust will take these two babies off the front page for all time.
>
> Hopkins, as usual, was dressed in his immaculate blues, browns and whites, his fine figure making a pretty sight with the moon-drifted sea in the foreground.
>
> Ickes wore his conventional faded grays, Mona Lisa smile and carried his stamp collection. . . .
>
> Hopkins expressed regret at the unkind things Ickes had said about him and Ickes on his part promised to make it stronger — only more so — as soon as he could get a stenographer who would take it down hot. . . .
>
> The President gave them a hearty slap on the back — pushing them both into the sea. "Full speed ahead," the President ordered.

The tranquility of the ocean voyage, it seemed, might relax the acrimonies of Washington.[3]

v

Alas, it was not so simple. Once the holiday was over, Ickes and Hopkins resumed their struggle. In the spring of 1936 Hopkins made what Ickes regarded as a new attempt to gather in PWA under WPA. Ickes went wrathfully to the President to save what was left of his program. At a cabinet meeting on May 14, Roosevelt began to hold forth on work-relief policy. He cautioned Ickes against running down WPA in his scheduled appearance before the Senate Appropriations Committee and directed him to make no claims for the indirect employment stimulated by PWA. "It was as clear as day," Ickes noted angrily, "that the President was spanking me hard before the full Cabinet. . . . All the other members appeared to be embarrassed, but I could see Henry Morgenthau stealing a covert glance at me from time to time. Doubtless he enjoyed the spanking very much."

After cabinet, a few members waited to see the President privately. Miss Perkins got in ahead of the enraged Ickes; and though she knew that Roosevelt had to leave to greet a delegation of Navajo Indians, she avoided Ickes's eye and talked till the President's time was up. Ickes stalked out of the cabinet room in a fury. Back in his own office he received a call from Miss Perkins, who explained that she had deliberately ignored his signal because she thought he should not seek a showdown during the President's present mood. By now, Ickes was determined to get out. For the next few hours he wrote and rewrote a letter of resignation. Before the day was over, the letter was at the White House.

On the next day, Ickes had a luncheon engagement with the President, scheduled before the cabinet blow-up. In the morning he called Miss LeHand. Had the President seen the letter? Yes. Did he still want Ickes to come to luncheon? Miss LeHand said she would find out. A few moments later she called back; yes, the President was expecting the Secretary. When Ickes arrived in the presidential office, Roosevelt looked at him with an expression of mock reproach on his face and, saying not a word, gave him a handwritten memorandum.

The White House
Washington

Dear Harold:—
  1. P.W.A. IS NOT "repudiated."
  2. P.W.A. IS NOT "ended."

3. I did not "make it impossible for you to go before the
   committee."
4. I have not indicated lack of confidence.
5. I have *full* confidence in you.
6. You and I have the same big objectives.
7. You are needed, to carry on a big common task.
8. Resignation *not* accepted!

> Your affectionate friend,
> FRANKLIN D. ROOSEVELT

Ickes later remarked, "What could a man do with a President like
that?" [4]

VI

These had been years of testing for Hopkins and Ickes. The
freewheeling New York social worker and the embattled Chicago
lawyer, both unknown to the country on their arrival in Washington in 1933, had met large challenges and risen to large responsibilities. In the process, each developed a new personal author
ity, acerbity, and ambition. In short order, each became a national figure.

Hopkins, the younger and gayer of the two, concealed much
tension under his loose-jointed exterior. Already, as he journeyed
carelessly around the country or sat, perched on the small of his
back, through interminable conferences, he was experiencing severe
internal pain; it was the beginning of a duodenal ulcer. But
responsibility, though it produced worry, did not diminish his
insouciance. His hatred of formality seemed to grow. He took
perverse pride in his bare office in the Walker-Johnson Building,
with its shabby walls and its water pipes and its pervading smell
of disinfectant ("the very odor of Relief," remarked a *Fortune*
writer, ". . . at once prophylactic and unclean"), just as he exulted
in his contempt for red tape in government and pomposity in
business.

He was a first-class administrator. "I think," said Hugh Johnson,
"he has done the cleanest-cut job in the whole Recovery Show."
His staff was able and devoted. In charge of state relief organizations was a tall, tough, soft-spoken Alabaman named Aubrey

Williams. After serving in France during the First World War, studying philosophy with Bergson at the Sorbonne, and trying out as a Lutheran lay preacher, Williams had gone into social work. He knew what poverty was, hated it, and hated all those who, from privileged comfort, acquiesced in it. "If I sound bitter in describing life and liberty in the Union," he wrote in 1934, "I make no apology for it. It is time for us to be bitter." Radical by temperament, hard-working, relentlessly honest, relentlessly idealistic, he seconded Hopkins in charging FERA and WPA with an atmosphere of excitement and drive. Jacob Baker, an imaginative and resourceful engineer, had responsibility under Hopkins for the works projects, Corrington Gill, an economist, for statistics, and Colonel Lawrence Westbrook, an Army reserve officer, for rural rehabilitation and other special programs. Hopkins delegated authority to them freely, checked on them strictly, and kept his staff small. For their part, they all needled Hopkins and adored him.

Within the government, Hopkins fought for his agency with cool audacity. Once, in a conversation with Charles E. Merriam, he described his methods. "There are two kinds of administrators," he said, " — gentlemen and go-getters. When a gentleman learns that his appropriation is being cut by the Bureau of the Budget, he accepts it. But I'm no gentleman. If my appropriation is ever cut, I simply call up the White House and ask the President to issue a stop order, saying that I will go over in a few days and explain why. Then I never go over. That is how a go-getter always beats a gentleman." "What happens," inquired Merriam, "when two go-getters compete against each other?" "Then I pretend to be a gentlemen," said Hopkins; "and, when the other fellow finds out, it is too late."

His public image was of a quick, caustic, informal figure, without front or pretense. "Mr. Hopkins, I like you," wrote Ernie Pyle, "because you look like common people. I don't mean any slur by that either, because they don't come any commoner than I am, but you sit there so easy swinging back and forth in your swivel chair, in your blue suit and blue shirt, and your neck is sort of skinny, like poor people's necks, and you act honest, too." He had quickly acquired a reputation for laying things on the line without regard to consequence. "In an administration personnel which could have vied in objurgation with Marlborough's army in Flanders," wrote Arthur Krock, "he stands out in the use of vivid expressions." "He has," said Hugh Johnson admiringly, "a mind like a razor, a tongue like a skinning knife, a temper like a Tartar and a sufficient vocabulary of parlor profanity — words kosher enough to get by the censor but acid enough to make a mule-skinner jealous."

Robert E. Sherwood has noted that Hopkins's repertoire was less concrete and imaginative than that of Johnson or of Ickes; but few could surpass him in the swift, brutal retort. Thus, when challenged about relief spending, "Some people just can't stand seeing others make a decent living." Or, when Henry P. Fletcher, chairman of the Republican National Committee attacked him for overzealousness, "Hunger is not debatable." On Governor Eugene Talmadge of Georgia: "He doesn't contribute a dime but he's always yapping."

Sometimes his reckless tongue got him in trouble. Once, in defending white-collar projects in a press conference, he said angrily, "You know some people make fun of people who speak a foreign language, and dumb people criticize something they do not understand, and that is what is going on up there — God damn it!" The sentence was telescoped into "people are too damned dumb" and became a cant phrase for New Deal arrogance. But his candor could also have dramatic effect. On another occasion, speaking in his native Iowa, Hopkins descanted to the audience on the virtues of spending. Suddenly a voice came out of the crowd: "Who's going to pay for it?" Hopkins stopped, took off his coat, loosened his tie, rolled up his sleeves, while the crowd watched in silence. Then his voice cracked out like a whip across the auditorium: "You are!"[5]

VII

The purity of the social worker was beginning to melt under new allurements. The first tempter perhaps was politics. For a long time Hopkins struggled to hold the line. His appointments in FERA and CWA were on a strictly nonpartisan basis. Indeed, his whole early attitude toward politics threw Democratic leaders into helpless fury. "I am authoritatively informed," Key Pittman wrote Louis Howe in 1934, "that ninety per cent of the [CWA] appointees in the State of Nevada are Republicans. . . . I may say that the most desperate opposition that I will have in the next election will be from Democrats who attribute the failure of appointment to my neglect." The White House received a multitude of similar complaints from Democratic politicians across the country. In California Hopkins protected the state relief administrator, a Republican, from the McAdoo machine: he traded punches freely with local Democratic potentates like Martin Davey of Ohio, Talmadge of Georgia, and Long of Louisiana; and he kept the White House methodically informed about anticipated clashes with party leaders. Thus: "I am probably about to have a head-on collision with Senator McCarran. . . . The Senator wants to dominate the relief show politically, and I have no intention of allowing him to do it." Or: "There is going to be a case of dynamite unloosed pretty soon if the Census Bureau supervisers insist on going into the political records of people referred to them by the Reemployment Bureaus. . . . I simply want you to know that I have no intention of tolerating this kind of political interference with Civil Works." Hopkins found positive satisfaction in tangling with political organizations. "The evidence is complete on Ohio," he noted in March 1935; " — the political boys went too far this trip and I shall take great delight in giving them the 'works.'" And, when Davey assailed Hopkins for tearing down the Democratic party, the President gave Hopkins full support: "I wish you to pursue these investigations diligently and let the chips fall where they may. This Administration will not permit the relief population of Ohio to become the innocent victims of either corruption or political chicanery." "In fact," Hopkins noted, "I think the boss liked the idea of their being Democrats" — no doubt because it made possible a dramatic display of New Deal integrity.

"Politics," said Hopkins at the height of the Davey fight, "has no business in relief and wherever it gets in, we intend to get rid of it damned fast." Patronage was only one aspect of this problem. Another was the theory that relief was a means of purchasing elections. This accusation irritated a man who, when told that no one shot Santa Claus, responded that the old gentleman needed a bullet-proof vest. The last relief grants announced before the

1934 congressional election actually represented a reduction over
the month before. "If anybody thinks you can buy an election
through giving relief, or even work relief jobs," he said in 1935,
"I think it is the silliest thing in the world. I have been in
this game now for two years, and if there is one way not to do
it, it is by giving relief, because none of the clients like you. They
all think you're terrible, and you are not going to buy any elections that way." In this argument, Hopkins was probably right.
So experienced a Republican politician as Arthur Vandenberg
agreed with him. "For every vote the New Deal has 'bought,'"
Vandenberg remarked in 1936, "it has alienated two — one employable who has been able to hold out on his own resources
until too late to get back on work relief, and one unemployable
who has been thrown back on . . . local relief agencies." In addition, Hopkins in repeated public statements told WPA workers
that their politics was nobody's business but their own. "No em-
ployee of the Works Progress Administration shall at any time
solicit contributions for any political party. . . . No person shall
be employed or discharged by the Works Progress Administration
on the ground of his support or non-support of any candidate of
any political organization."

In time the political pressure began to tell. The turning point
came when Congress got its revenge and forced on him the amendment requiring senatorial confirmation for all WPA jobs over
$5,000 a year. From this moment, Hopkins knew he was licked;
from here on in, every top WPA appointment would have to be
cleared with Jim Farley and the local senators. For a while
he considered resignation; then, always the realist, he drew the
inevitable conclusion. "I thought at first I could be completely
non-political," he later said, "then they told me I had to be part
non-political and part political. I found that was impossible, at
least for me. I finally realized that there was nothing for it but
to be all-political."

He still was not political enough to satisfy the Democratic National Committee. When the chairman of the Democratic State
Committee in Massachusetts complained to Farley in late 1935
about Republican appointments to WPA, Farley responded with
appropriate indignation, "It is a situation which should not be
permitted to exist." As late as August 1936 Arthur Krock could

describe Hopkins as a man conceived by politicians "to be fanatically opposed to even the just claims of partisanship." But Hopkins, condemned to the political arena, had no intention of being eaten by the lions. By 1936 he was beginning to enter into friendly relations with Democratic bosses like Mayor Ed Kelly of Chicago and Mayor Frank Hague of Jersey City, as well as with conservative party figures like Bernard Baruch and Jesse Jones.[6]

VIII

His most powerful connection lay, however, with the White House. Mrs. Roosevelt was prepared by her own long interest in social work to support the activities of the top male social worker in the administration. Hopkins sought her advice and respected her judgment, and she introduced him into intimate presidential circles. His charm and informality quickly made him a White House favorite. No doubt he carefully cultivated his relations, not only with Eleanor Roosevelt, but with the President's mother, with Betsy Cushing Roosevelt, his daughter-in-law, with Anna Roosevelt Boettiger, his daughter, and with Missy LeHand. But this was not calculation on Hopkins's part so much as it was a delighted response to the world, social and political, which excited him more than any other. Above all, he soon won the President, who liked his quickness, his sympathy, and his unique mixture of cynicism and idealism.

Hopkins's qualities were secondary rather than primary. He had intelligence rather than wisdom, rapidity rather than originality, loyalty rather than faith. Nevertheless, his mind was unblinkered and unafraid, and every new experience came to him as a new opportunity. In Washington in the mid-thirties, he was reaching out wherever power lay. The White House was one area. Another was the Army. Seeking personnel capable of administering a public-works program, he turned to the Army Corps of Engineers; such figures as Colonel Brehon B. Somervell and Colonel Donald H. Connolly soon began to appear at WPA staff meetings. Still another was the society of the rich and fashionable. He was beginning to get immense relaxation from evenings in Broadway night clubs, weekends on Long Island, holidays in Palm Beach.

His circulation in the world of power was something the harnessmaker's son could not regard without continued wonder. Acceptance, whether by presidents or generals, by the poker-playing Democratic grandees of the Jefferson Island Club or by the glittering Manhattan circles of the Averell Harrimans and the John Hay Whitneys, gave him deep satisfaction. He carefully kept the formal invitations that came to him, the calling cards left at his house. This cosmopolitan liberalism of Hopkins was quite different from the austerity of a George Norris, so mistrustful of those who stuck their legs under the tables of the rich. Puritan reformers feared in Hopkins the possibility of another Ramsay MacDonald, exclaiming with delight, after he left the Labour party, "Tomorrow every Duchess in London will be wanting to kiss me!" But high society did not soften Hopkins's views. He took relish in lecturing the rich on their iniquities and warning them of taxes to come. Whether at the race track or at Jesse Jones's bridge table or weekending at Sands Point, he remained a gleeful and unregenerate New Dealer. As Joseph E. Davies summed it up ,"He had the purity of St. Francis of Assisi combined with the sharp shrewdness of a race track tout."

The experience of FERA and CWA was giving his social thought new concreteness. A radical in his willingness to experiment freely with social and economic reform, he had long since departed from his youthful flirtation with socialism. He was committed to the capitalistic system; but if that system were to survive, it had to change; in particular, it had to abolish the "outrage that we should permit hundreds and hundreds of thousands of people to be ill clad, to live in miserable homes, not to have enough to eat; not to be able to send their children to school for the only reason that they are poor." Why accept the evil of poverty? "I have never believed that with our capitalistic system people have to be poor. . . . I believe they are poor because we haven't wit and brains enough to divide up our national income each year so they won't be poor." The way out was through government intervention. "The government is ours whether it be local, county, State, or Federal. It doesn't belong to anybody but the people of America."

Yet the future contained tough problems. In particular, the steady improvement in productivity, accompanied by the steady growth in the size of the labor force, seemed to imply, Hopkins wrote to Roosevelt in 1936, "the prospect of a permanent problem

of unemployment and poverty of great magnitude." Even if the
1929 levels of industrial production could be regained, the nation
would have to expect 6.5 to 7.5 million unemployed. "It is probable," Hopkins thought, "that a minimum of 4 to 5 million
unemployed persons is to be expected even for future 'prosperity'
periods." To wipe out unemployment, production would have to
be increased 20 per cent over 1929 — or 45 per cent over 1936.
(Roosevelt, it should be noted, disagreed. "Some people tell you,"
he said in 1936, "that even with a completely restored prosperity
there will be a vast permanent army of unemployed. I do not
accept that.")

How were the unemployed to be taken care of? The first line
of defense, Hopkins contended in his book of 1936, *Spending to
Save*, was unemployment insurance. But this would not be enough.
He argued the necessity in addition for a permanent structure
of public works, responsive to the ebb and flow of the private
labor market — the big net under private employment designed to
catch the workers dropped from industrial payrolls. But even
more was required. "We are in a new fight," he said, " . . . the
war to insure economic and social security to every citizen of the
country." This meant social security, it meant compulsory health
insurance, it meant housing, it meant education, it meant jobs;
it meant a society where children would go to schools rather than
to the mills and the beet fields. A paragraph in a speech of
1934 summed up his position. "The end of Government is that
people, individuals shall be allowed to live a more abundant life,
and Government has no other purpose than to take care of the
people that live within our borders. There is a new day, and this
is it, and Roosevelt is its leader." [7]

IX

The growth of Ickes, an older man, was not so dramatic, but
was equally decisive. When he came to Washington, his pugnacity
concealed a flutter of inner doubts. Then his Washington career
turned out to be a succession of gratifying discoveries that he was
more wise, upright, and hard-working than anyone else. "I worked
every Sunday and every holiday, Christmas included. I signed
all of the Public Works contracts myself. I must have signed, at

first, at least 5,000, each one in triplicate. My desk used to be
piled so high with stuff for signature that it was appalling. I
was working beyond human endurance." Naturally such a record
induced a steady growth in self-confidence and self-esteem. "I've
known for a long time I'm not loved with all the fervor I think
I'm entitled to," he observed with characteristic satisfaction in
1935. "If a man worked hard at it, he couldn't get up a bigger
list of enemies than I." Given this opinion, Ickes saw few limits
to his capacity. Even the Presidency seemed a possible destiny.
"If I had resigned from the Cabinet a year ago," he confided
to his diary in 1936, ". . . there might have been a very real
possibility of my being nominated on the Republican ticket this
year. And in that event I would have had a good chance to be
elected" — presumably over the Democratic nominee, Franklin D.
Roosevelt.

The conviction that he was the only honest man in Washington
justified him in acts of egotism and vindictiveness from which less
perfect men would have shrunk. As an administrator, he was
sometimes petty and suspicious. His subordinates were subjected
to harassment for the most trivial of infractions. Louis Glavis,
his chief investigator, even (with Ickes's consent, though Ickes
finally stopped the practice) tapped the phones of Interior Department employees while his chief went around the country applaud-
ing the Bill of Rights. Some who worked for Ickes came to hate
him, while most who worked for Hopkins came to adore him.
Ickes's language reflected his irascibility: Hugh Johnson, he once
said, was "suffering from mental saddle sores"; and he addressed
an unfortunate Connecticut editor as "a cowardly, skulking cur
. . . eating your own vomit with relish but enjoying even more
the savor of the excrement in the pig-sty in which you root for
choice morsels."

But this was mostly concealed from the public. In the general
view, Ickes was emerging as the old curmudgeon — the terrible-
tempered but honest figure so beloved in American folklore. If
in some ways a flawed figure, Ickes still commanded respect for
his invincible integrity as a public administrator and for his out-
spoken public assertion of New Deal principles. In *The New
Democracy,* a book published in 1934, Ickes summed up his
political philosophy. American history as he saw it, was essen-

tially a record of exploitation — exploitation of natural resources, exploitation of human beings — conducted by greedy men in the name of individualism. "Rugged individualists," Ickes wrote, "may be compared to packs of wolves let loose to rend and tear fellow creatures. . . . The only law that they respect is the law of the jungle." Like Hopkins, Ickes envisaged an America where economic opportunity, housing, education, and medical care would be open to all; an America which could be achieved, he thought, only by "wise and comprehensive planning on a national scale."

Its objectives could be attained, Ickes emphasized, "under the Constitution and under the capitalistic system." The obstacle to attaining them lay, he believed, in the revival of rugged individualism. A year ago, he said in 1934, the business community had been "a frightened and penitent and docile group for once in its history." Now it seemed only to fear that government might hamper "its rugged-individualist right to pursue happiness in the good old eighty-miles-an-hour way." He saw growing danger that "the old and unteachable order, with its new breath and its new lease on boldness, will interfere with President Roosevelt's program of relief and reconstruction." [8]

x

Ickes and Hopkins had plenty to quarrel about when their own ambitions or agencies clashed. Fundamentally they agreed, however, on major political questions. And they agreed, too, on questions of tone. Neither had patience for business leaders who obstructed what they regarded as the general welfare. Both were prepared to use the prestige and power of government to blast the bulwarks of selfishness out of the paths of the New Deal. In this respect, they differed from the brain trust of 1932 and from Roosevelt's central advisers of 1933. Of the earlier group, only Tugwell and, to some extent, Johnson were prepared to go along with antibusiness rhetoric; and neither Johnson nor, on the whole, Tugwell sympathized with the divisive implications of the Ickes-Hopkins barrage. On policy Hopkins and Ickes were, like Roosevelt himself, pragmatists, capable of working both with the national planners of the Berle-Tugwell-Moley school and with trust-busters in the Brandeis tradition. But their constant emotional drive was away from business-government co-operation. Provoked by mounting business resistance to the New Deal, they increasingly demanded militance, the regulation of business, and the enlargement of government.

20. Power for the People

ANOTHER ISSUE which occupied Roosevelt considerably during 1935 and 1936 was the formation of national policy on electric power. Under the New Deal the federal government was moving into the production and distribution of electricity as never before. The Tennessee Valley Authority had gone into operation in 1933. By 1935 the government was building great dams in other parts of the country. Soon the power generated by the great new sluiceways and dynamos would be ready for distribution. At the same time, pressure was growing for the government to do something about rural electrification. On their side, naturally, private power companies were objecting vigorously to the emerging public competition. They were also mobilizing to resist the application of the deconcentration provisions of the Public Utilities Holding Company Act of 1935.

In these circumstances, it was increasingly urgent for government to work out a general policy both for public and for private power. In 1934 a National Power Policy Committee had been set up in PWA, with Benjamin V. Cohen as general counsel, to consider the basic principles of such a national policy. The National Resources Board was also studying the problem. And electric power was, of course, a long-time personal interest of the President's.

II

TVA was the first of the New Deal undertakings to have impact on the national power picture. Within TVA, the Board of Directors had early agreed on a division of responsibilities: Chairman Arthur

E. Morgan, the idealistic engineer, was to build dams and develop planning and educational programs; Harcourt A. Morgan, the experienced land-grant educator, was to supervise agricultural activities and especially to produce and distribute fertilizers; David E. Lilienthal, the astute and dedicated lawyer, was to develop power policy.

As Lilienthal saw it, the objective of the TVA power program was plain enough: it was to produce and distribute electric power in the Valley as rapidly and as cheaply as possible. And, since the Authority did not plan to undertake direct retail distribution of power, the next problem was to open up local outlets. Wendell Willkie's Commonwealth and Southern system, the main private distributive agency in the Valley, would have been glad to take over TVA power at the bus bar and pump it into its own operating companies at its own rates. The Act, however, directed the Authority to give preference to nonprofit agencies, such as munic-ipally owned power systems and farmers' co-operatives.

Lilienthal accepted this policy with enthusiasm. His preference in all matters was for the encouragement of local initiative and responsibility — "grass-roots democracy" — through the use of insti-tutions already existing in the Valley; and, when it came to electric power, the relevant local institution was in his view the local community itself — certainly not the power company, which was likely to be owned and controlled in Wall Street. Accordingly, he took every occasion to press the policy of decentralizing the distribution of electric power, urging municipalities to qualify for TVA power by buying up local private utilities or by building distribution systems of their own. In so doing, he was headed straight for a collision with Commonwealth and Southern — a pros-pect which dismayed A. E. Morgan. "If the TVA area must ex-perience the warfare of the duplication of facilities . . . with hard feeling and bitterness and other unfavorable developments," Morgan warned the Board in August 1933, " . . . then the TVA for a considerable period will be less effective, and will be less representative of what economic planning can accomplish." Morgan accordingly favored a treaty by which TVA and Common-wealth and Southern would divide the territory on geographical lines. "The Chairman's proposal," Felix Frankfurter wrote Lilienthal, "is fraught with every kind of danger, is wholly un-

scientific in proposing commitments at this stage of the development, and disregards past experience and the social purpose
back of the legislation." Lilienthal agreed, feeling that to found
TVA power policy on the idea of honest co-operation from the
power companies would be to run counter "to every reasonable
expectation under the circumstances, and to expose the work of
the Authority to the gravest hazards." But Roosevelt seemed inclined to go along with A. E. Morgan; and early in 1934 Lilienthal
and Willkie negotiated an interim agreement under which TVA
purchased certain local systems from Commonwealth and Southern
and carved out an integrated power area. In exchange TVA agreed
not to sell to present Commonwealth and Southern customers outside the area. The treaty was to stay in effect until three months
after the completion of the powerhouse at Norris Dam (or, in
Willkie's view, to the 1936 election, when all this nonsense would be
swept away at the polls).

For the moment, the standstill agreement seemed reasonable.
Then in the course of 1934 the power companies began a systematic
legal campaign against TVA. In September preferred stockholders
of the Alabama Power Company, led by George Ashwander, sued
to prevent the company from carrying out its part of the agreement it had helped negotiate in January. In November the Edison
Electric Institute, the fraternal association of the public utility
holding companies, got into the act, publishing a legal opinion
that surprised no one by finding TVA "palpably unconstitutional"; the opinion was signed by, among others, Wendell Willkie's old hero, Newton D. Baker.

The Ashwander case reached the federal district court of northern Alabama in the spring of 1935. In a sweeping decision the
judge enjoined municipalities in the area from buying TVA power
and ordered the annulment of the contract of January 1934.
According to this decision, it was all right for the Alabama Power
Company to buy power from the government at Muscle Shoals and
sell it to the people of Alabama, but unconstitutional for the
people of Alabama to buy Muscle Shoals power directly themselves.
The TVA promptly got John Lord O'Brian, a distinguished
Republican lawyer, to argue the case on appeal. While the case
made its gradual ascent through the federal courts in the next
months, the TVA power program was everywhere slowed down

and in some areas stopped. In February 1936 the Supreme Court in the Ashwander decision upheld the constitutionality of power distribution from Wilson Dam, thereby reversing the decision of the district court on the narrow issue of the transmission lines. However, the Court warily sidestepped the broader problem of the constitutionality of the TVA law. Formidable possibilities of harassment through litigation still remained.

III

Willkie originally denied that he was behind the Ashwander suit. "I say to you," he wrote fiercely to Steve Early in November 1934, "that any such statement made to you by anybody is an absolute and unqualified falsehood." He was, however, a member of the board of directors of the Edison Electric Institute, which took over the suit; and in time Commonwealth and Southern clearly adopted the cause as its own. One result was the aggravation of tension between TVA and the utilities. Willkie himself began to intensify his attacks upon TVA power policy. "When some of us faint-hearted utility operators say it will take years to use up the present existing generating capacity without taking into account that which is being built which will double the present excess and the plans already laid for the building of additional dams which will double again the recently created excess," he said sarcastically and a little incoherently in 1935, "we are told that we are faint-hearted and of little vision." By 1936 TVA had become for Willkie "the most useless and unnecessary of all the alphabetical joy-rides."

For Lilienthal, the attitude of the power companies confirmed his worst expectations, and he fought back without compunction. But Arthur E. Morgan, the Chairman, watched the rising bitterness with revulsion. Morgan had a prophet's passion to achieve "an integrated social and economic order." He believed that this could come only through "the democratic process of voluntary general agreement." The developing fight between Lilienthal and the power companies violated his benign dream of rational social change. He felt that the really important prospects for the Valley were being sacrificed to Lilienthal's mania for cheap electric power; and he considered Lilienthal's methods sharp and ruthless.

He publicly condemned what he called "that frequent shortcoming of revolutionists — a feeling that the destruction of what exists must be the first and major part of their program."

Still, Lilienthal's term as TVA director was to expire in May 1936. Morgan now proposed to Roosevelt a broad reorganization by which operating authority should go to a general manager, nominated by the Chairman, and policies should be adopted only by a unanimous vote of the Board. At the same time he lobbied energetically in Washington with Roosevelt, Norris, Ickes and others against Lilienthal's reappointment. For a moment, he thought Roosevelt would go along with him. But Morgan's objections to Lilienthal remained vague, and Lilienthal himself, cool and tough, began to fight back. The issue, Lilienthal told his Washington friends, was the relationship of TVA to the private utilities. He soon enlisted Norris's powerful support; and, after pondering the case, Roosevelt decided on his reappointment.

With the renewal of Lilienthal's term, the civil war in TVA came into the open. The engineers, construction superintendents, and foresters tended to line up with the Chairman; those concerned with power, agriculture, and personnel supported the Board majority. The issues assumed a variety of forms. From the Lilienthal viewpoint, the question was whether the TVA should capitulate to the power companies. From the Harcourt Morgan viewpoint, the question was whether outside planners should shove aside local interests and local institutions. From the Arthur Morgan viewpoint, the point was, as Oswald Garrison Villard put it, "the increasing danger that the electrical and water dam side of the project will swamp what may loosely be called the humanitarian side. . . . Cheap electricity is fine and most desirable, but saving and reconditioning human lives is far more vital."

By the end of 1936 the matter was beyond compromise. Lilienthal had proposed the appointment of John B. Blandford, Jr., the secretary of the Board, as General Manager. Blandford, an able public administrator, was generally on the side of Lilienthal and H. A. Morgan; and, though Arthur Morgan succeeded for a moment in staving off his final appointment as the man in charge of the organization, it was evident that the Chairman was hopelessly on the defensive. For a time he had considered resignation; but a sense of loyalty to his own staff persuaded him he should stay a while longer. It was a losing fight. Whereas the directors had made some effort before to submerge their differences, now decisions were made by a series of 2 to 1 votes. Lilienthal and Morgan gibed at each other indirectly in public speeches, and the hostility between them was compounded by the larger hostility between the Authority and Commonwealth and Southern.[1]

IV

After the Ashwander decision, Willkie continued a double strategy. On the one hand, hoping perhaps that Arthur Morgan might emerge victorious, he kept open the possibility of negotiation. But on the other hand, in the expectation that Lilienthal would win, he flourished the weapon of litigation. "The present status," he wrote Roosevelt in May 1936, "is practically one of open warfare and, as long as that status continues, the utilities in that district naturally feel they are fighting for their lives and are obliged to defend themselves by every legitimate means. This is the explanation of the numerous lawsuits that have been started recently." In this spirit, a few days after Willkie's letter to the President, nineteen operating companies brought suit against TVA. And it was becoming a grass-roots fight: TVA and Commonwealth and Southern crews were already building lines in the same areas — often in localities where the power companies for years had refused service.

In spite of the nineteen-company suit, the administration made one more try for agreement. But on what terms? "We are . . . justified, it seems to me," Willkie wrote Roosevelt, "in asking the Government either to accept our suggestion (repeatedly made during the last three years) to buy as systems all of our electric utility business in the southeast; or alternatively permit us to operate it free from the potential invasion of governmental agencies which are rendering us unable to operate successfully." In justice to utility investors, he argued, there had to be some understanding about the boundaries of government operation. His proposal was that TVA confine its power distribution for the next twenty or twenty-five years to a restricted area, tentatively defined as the watershed of the Tennessee River. Beyond that area, it should sell its power to private systems.

Lilienthal rejected the Willkie proposal. It would, he thought, allow the power companies to make money out of the government's cheap electricity; and it hardly seemed compatible with the preference clause in the TVA Act. The competitive spur provided by TVA would be blunted if TVA could not seek customers wherever it could supply power. Instead, Lilienthal suggested a southeastern power pool, in which both TVA and Commonwealth and Southern might set up a single distribution system under uniform rates with municipalities retaining the right to choose between TVA and C & S power. But the government offer proved equally unacceptable to Willkie.

The pool idea had sprung originally from the fertile mind of Dr. Alexander Sachs, who had left NRA in 1933 to return to the Lehman Corporation. Its introduction into the discussion complicated the internal conflict in TVA. As Arthur Morgan construed it, the primary requirement for success in negotiating a pool was "mutual confidence"; "if each side in negotiating tries to retain all possible arbitrary advantages and to exploit every need or disadvantage of the other in a process of ruthless strategy to drive the sharpest possible bargain, the undertaking probably will not fully succeed." These phrases constituted an evident allusion to Lilienthal's bargaining methods (even if they also described Willkie's); and the Board majority rejected Morgan's advice as both unrealistic and offensive. In addition, they began to detect signs that Morgan was succumbing to Willkie's hearty and disarming blandishments. As a consequence, Lilienthal, though initially in favor of a pool, began to turn against it.

Roosevelt, now taking a personal hand, called a conference to discuss a southeastern power pool in September 1936. He and Willkie had first met at a White House conference in 1934. (It was after this that Willkie sent his wife a famous wire: CHARM EXAGGERATED.) Their relationship was already prickly. On one occasion, when Willkie wrote the White House questioning a remark rumored to be Roosevelt's, the President drily replied, "I hope you give as little credence to the many statements you hear about me as I do to the many statements I hear about what you say and do." (He would repeat that sentiment in the future.)

The conference resulted in an agreement on a three-month truce, during which both sides would stick by the *status quo*. In the meantime the advocates of public power were swinging into action. Robert M. La Follette, Jr., and John Rankin denounced the pool idea as a conspiracy to destroy TVA. George Norris concluded that Arthur Morgan had gone over to the enemy, and protested the notion of concessions to Commonwealth and Southern, "an outfit," he wrote Roosevelt, "who would destroy you in a minute if they had the power." "No good can come," Norris said publicly, "from pooling interests with enemies of the TVA program." And there were difficulties in the interpretation of the truce. Thus Willkie, Arthur Morgan, and Louis B. Wehle, whom Roosevelt had brought in as an arbitrator, felt that the truce prohibited the TVA from continuing to seek PWA assistance for local public-power systems, though they did not feel that it prohibited the C & S from continuing to seek to enjoin TVA activities through the courts. Lilienthal disagreed on both these points. Then, on December 22, 1936, the nineteen companies won a broad injunction from the federal district court forbidding TVA to make any new contracts for six months. "Securing of the injunction by the C & S," Lilienthal wrote Roosevelt, "is a breach of faith with the Government." He recommended stopping negotiations until the injunction was dissolved. Roosevelt agreed. If not a violation of the letter of the negotiations, the injunction certainly strained the spirit. The pool talks came to an end, never to be resumed.[2]

v

Morgan now decided to carry his fight to the public. In an article early in 1937 in the *New Republic* he denounced, naming no names, men "ruled by a Napoleonic complex" conducting "essentially a war of social revolution" designed, not to come to terms with the power companies, but to destroy them. It was wrong, Morgan argued, to treat all utilities as if they were run by the buccaneers of the past. Power could be managed as well as any other business, and each company should be given the benefit of the doubt. "A spirit of tolerance and reasonableness on both sides is a public obligation." Doctrinaire hostility had to give way to an honest desire for accommodation. "I am of the opinion that for the haggling tradition to be largely replaced in our affairs by the policy of disinterested appraisal and planning would represent a substantial advance in the art of government." He concluded: "The power issue is not primarily a question of liberalism or conservatism, but of discovering how to do the job best."

There was in this a fine sense of the texture of the democratic process. But Morgan did not always live up to the values he so eloquently expressed. His fervent belief in his own mission made him condone in himself conduct which he would have abominated in others. Before the year was over, John Lord O'Brian, as TVA's special counsel, had to complain that Morgan's "disrupting and demoralizing" activities were hampering the preparation of the government case. On other occasions, Morgan seemed to express the interesting hope that the courts might enjoin part of TVA's power activities without challenging the rest of the law. To his fellow Board members, he seemed not a moral philosopher but a renegade, suborned by his own vanity and by the bearlike charm of Mr. Willkie.

In the process, Morgan lost the President's support. Roosevelt had originally shared Morgan's conception of TVA. "It was not initiated or organized for the purpose of selling electricity," he told the National Emergency Council in December 1934. "That is a side function. . . . There is a much bigger situation behind the TVA. . . . We are conducting a social experiment." Or, to his press conference the same year: "Power is really a secondary matter. What we are doing there is taking a watershed with about three and a half million people in it, almost all of them rural, and we are trying to make a different type of citizen out of them." But Roosevelt combined an ardor for planning with a deep distrust, founded in his gubernatorial experience, of the power companies. Morgan's roseate belief in the good faith of the utilities was progressively discredited, so far as the White House was concerned, by the series of injunctions the companies obtained in the courts. "Every time you do anything for them," Roosevelt said of the utilities in 1937, "they want something else. I am ready to sit down and work it out, but you can never pin them down. I had Wendell Willkie of the Commonwealth and Southern in here for a talk, but I couldn't get anywhere with him: you can't get anywhere with any of them."

Willkie's policies thus undermined his ally on the TVA Board.

In any case, the Chairman would have been undone by his own prophetic self-righteousness. "Morgan confused policies with principles," wrote Francis Biddle; "and when he reiterated that he would never compromise with principles he meant that he would not yield to someone who disagreed with him on policy." He had, Biddle thought, "the strength and the smaller weaknesses of the American zealot." "Morgan was an authentic descendant from the witch burners," said another New Deal observer, Harry Hopkins, "and his piety was sure to catch up with him." Beyond this, the horizons of policy were contracting a good deal between 1935 and 1936. It was perhaps this gradual change in the character of the New Deal, more than anything else, which doomed Arthur Morgan's dream.[3]

VI

"From 1936 on," Tugwell later wrote, "the TVA should have been called the Tennessee Valley Power Production and Flood Control Corporation." While this judgment was overharsh, there could be little doubt that, with Arthur Morgan's defeat, TVA's objectives were narrowed. In 1938 E. C. M. Richards, Chief Forester of TVA, presented the alternatives as the Arthur Morgan men saw them. One faction on the Board, Richards said, regarded TVA as simply a federally owned electric-power corporation. Allied to this group was one which regarded TVA as primarily a means of funneling money to local agencies, such as the land-grant colleges and the Extension Service. But the Morgan group continued to regard the TVA as an effort on the part of the American people, through the federal government, to solve the problems of a great watershed; in doing this job the TVA, it believed, should co-operate with other agencies but should not turn over to them the work of the TVA itself.

Even as Richards wrote, the coalition between the first and second groups had beaten the third. The Forestry Division remained a nearly solitary example of independent TVA action. Soon Richards left, and the TVA foresters began a painful rear-guard fight against absorption by the agricultural program and domination by the Extension Service. This development was typical. Instead of reconstructing life in the Valley, TVA seemed to be

accommodating itself to the strongest local interests and christen-
ing this accommodation "grass-roots democracy." Instead of moving
out toward a new utopia, it was concentrating on production of
power and fertilizer. "You had to win the power fight or you would
have been sunk," Morris Llewellyn Cooke, the champion of rural
electrification, wrote to Lilienthal in 1939. ". . . Electricity was
your 'spark plug.' But now that you have achieved some margin
here . . . you will be well advised to put the emphasis on other
parts of your task. The T.V. was chosen as the area for our first
National experiment in *over-all* conservation. . . . My major
criticism is that except in the one matter of dams — acquired, built,
building or to be built — you have given us laymen no picture
of the size and length of your job."

Under the new dispensation, TVA did more than retreat from
comprehensive social planning. It also began to question any
activity (aside from power) which might antagonize established
interests in the Valley — the interests with which H. A. Morgan
was so eager to enter into intimate association, and which the
champions of grass-roots democracy identified with the people.
The TVA agricultural program, for example, was directed to the
needs of the larger and more prosperous farmers rather than to
tenants and sharecroppers. Though Arthur Morgan had tried to
work with the Resettlement Administration, Harcourt Morgan regarded its activities with skepticism and did his best to ignore the
existence of its successor, the Farm Security Administration. After
Arthur Morgan, interest in co-operative efforts quickly declined.

The evolution of the TVA land acquisition and conservation
programs reflected a similar deference to local sensibilities — or
at least to the sensibilities of the Farm Bureau and the Extension
Service. Thus the Authority not only cut down Arthur Morgan's
Forestry Division, but recoiled from the Soil Conservation Service.
Equally symptomatic was the tacit acceptance of the racial mores
of the Valley, which led the TVA fertilizer program, for example,
to leave out the Negro agricultural colleges. If Lilienthal saw
in TVA the image of "democracy on the march," Tugwell considered it far more an example of democracy in retreat.

Yet Tugwell undoubtedly oversimplified the problems of planning. After all, TVA had been imposed on the people of the
Tennessee basin by benevolent congressional edict. This meant

that it was confronted from the start by the need for winning acceptance. It could hardly afford to alienate the established local institutions which, if hostile, could make the difference between its success and failure. For Lilienthal, with his militant ideas on public power, the impulse to avoid fights on other issues must have seemed particularly urgent. In a sense, a conservative agricultural policy was the price which TVA paid for a liberal power policy. And TVA's condition of legal jeopardy in these years inevitably influenced the organization toward a cautious construction of its own authority.

If the objectives of TVA became more narrow, it is likely that they also became more realistic, in the sober sense of the word — more, that is, within the limits of administrative and political possibilty. Nor should it be forgotten that the collaboration with the local community was by no means a one-way street. It may well be that TVA dragged existing institutions of the Valley further along than these institutions, through "grass-roots democracy," held TVA back.[4]

VII

And, even if TVA failed to create a new way of life in the Valley, no one could deny how magnificently it had improved the old. In a decade, TVA built twenty-one dams; their combined mass was more than a dozen times that of the great pyramids of Egypt. Copper and aluminum wires, glistening from lofty steel transmission towers, carried new life from the foaming waters of the river to the farthest corners of the Valley. In December 1932 there had been in all the rural homes served by the Alabama Power Company a total of 85 electric sewing machines, 185 vacuum cleaners, 645 refrigerators, 700 radios. One out of every 100 farms in Mississippi had electricity, 1 out of 36 in Georgia, 1 out of 25 in Tennessee and Alabama. TVA introduced a new age. Where people for decades labored by hand and lived by kerosene lamp, there was now the magic of electricity — light in the farmhouse, refrigerators in the kitchen, feed grinders in the woodshed, electric pumps in the farmyard. By the early forties one out of every five farms in the region was electrified.

TVA did more than spread electricity through the Valley. It

revolutionized the whole American philosophy of the marketing of electric power. Some TVA champions, indeed, went further than this, seeing in TVA a rate-yardstick, which could automatically measure the fairness of the rates structures of private utilities. In time experience demonstrated that TVA rates did not constitute an acceptable yardstick in the strict accounting sense. The vexing problem of the allocation of costs made precise comparisons between TVA and power company rates impossible.

What TVA did provide was, not a test of the equitableness of rates, but a new attitude toward the setting of rates. The philosophy of private power in America had been high rates and low consumption. Under Lilienthal's leadership, TVA embarked in September 1933 on the opposite policy — low rates, in the expectation that consumption would increase sufficiently to make up for the loss in unit revenue. This TVA decision was hardly the wild gamble which it seemed to the power companies. The province of Ontario, for example, had tried the low-rate policy with notable success. But the idea of widening of the market had never much attracted American utility magnates; their creative fervor had gone rather into manipulating financial structures.

From 1934 to 1938, consumption of electricity in the TVA area doubled. Nationally in this period it increased only 27 per cent. And, if TVA failed to furnish an exact yardstick for the cost of producing private power, at least its philosophy was infectious. The Tennessee and Georgia and Alabama Power companies hastily brought down their own rates after 1933 — and this, too, led not to disaster but to a great increase in demand. Nor, despite Willkie's pessimism, did the existence of TVA hurt the capital position of the neighboring power companies. In the twenty years after the establishment of TVA, the power capacity owned by private utilities in the eight states around the Valley increased 200 per cent, while private power capacity in the rest of the nation increased only 91 per cent. TVA power tactics had the effect of shocking adjacent private systems into profitability.

Power was but part of the multi-purpose design. In 1933 only one-fifth of the river had been navigable by boats drawing more than nine feet; one-third had been impassable for boats drawing more than three feet. But TVA engineers built locks and cleared a new channel from Paducah to Knoxville. In 1933, 32 million ton miles of freight moved along the river; in 1942, more than 161 million; by 1956, 2 billion. And at the same time the system of locks and dams helped tame the river and exorcise the curse of floods.

The agricultural program meanwhile conducted important researches into the preparation and production of fertilizers. Test demonstrations on farms throughout the Valley encouraged farmers to turn corn to legumes, especially clover and alfalfa, which would rebuild fertility in the soil. A million acres went into cover crops; almost another million into pasture; another million were terraced. Reforestation assisted the fight against erosion. And TVA laboratories worked out improved agricultural tools — a new side-hill terracing disk, for example, or a new cottonseed-oil cooker — which were made available at low cost to farmers and processors.

TVA brought an infinitude of stimuli to the Valley — to education, to industry, to labor relations, to road building, to state and local governmental agencies, to recreation, to nearly every form of public and private activity. "TVA," observed John Rankin, with his penchant for historical analogy, "is the most profitable investment the American people have made since the Louisiana Purchase."

And beyond the specified programs was the remarkable spirit of public service — a spirit which produced in the thirties such men as Gordon R. Clapp, John B. Blandford, James Lawrence Fly, Julius A. Krug, C. Girard Davidson. Protected by statute from political interference, TVA guarded its chastity jealously. Maury Maverick, visiting the Valley in 1936, reported the air as somewhat rarefied and noted the attitude "that all 'politicians' have red tails and work in sordid surroundings just as TVA'ers have wings and work in Green Pastures." The righteousness was doubtless excessive. But TVA did maintain an extraordinary enthusiasm and dedication. As Franklin Roosevelt said in 1945, TVA showed that "big government need not be absentee government . . . that great national powers can be exercised as government at hand, at home, working with the people and their local governments where the people are."

In the end, it was what TVA did for people that counted most. The result may have fallen below Arthur Morgan's dream. The Authority may have failed to reconstruct the total pattern of people's living. But TVA, with its shining dams and bright waters, gave them — millions of them — a wider opportunity to shape and fulfill their own lives.[5]

VIII

TVA was the nation's only valley authority. But it was by no means the only experiment in public power. While work went forward in the Tennessee Valley, other multipurpose dams were rising at key sites in rivers across the country, creating broad lakes behind high walls for purposes of navigation and flood control, of irrigation and electric power, of antipollution, afforestation, and recreation. The Army Corps of Engineers built some — especially Bonneville Dam on the Columbia and Fort Peck Dam on the Missouri. The department of the Interior's Bureau of Reclamation built others in the seventeen western states in which it was authorized to operate — especially Grand Coulee on the Columbia and Boulder on the Colorado. (Traditionally the Army Engineers, dedicated to navigation and flood control, worked downstream while the Bureau of Reclamation, dedicated to irrigation, worked upstream; but the multipurpose concept was beginning to confuse the old jurisdictional lines.) The Public Works Administration supplied most of the money.

Though power was not the first reason for many of the dams, it seemed to the government absurd not to use the impounded water for power purposes. The friends of utilities, however, regarded the federal manufacture of electric power as a step toward the socialization of the power industry. "Could anything be more unfair?" cried Thomas N. McCarter, president of the Edison Electric Institute. "Could anything be more outrageous? In all these respective localities there is a far greater abundance of power now existing in the resources already established other than is needed." Despite such vehement attacks, work went ahead. By 1936 nearly twenty major dams were under construction.

One project actually antedated the New Deal. This was Boulder Dam across upper Black Canyon on the turbulent Colorado. (The original legislation in the Coolidge administration established the name as Boulder; Hoover's Secretary of the Interior, Ray Lyman Wilbur, tried without congressional authorization to change it to the Hoover Dam; Ickes restored the original name in 1933; in 1947 Congress changed it to Hoover Dam.) The Boulder Dam legislation gave no preference to nonprofit-making distributive agencies and made no provision for federal transmission lines. However, since public agencies, including the Metropolitan Water District of Southern California, the City of Los Angeles, and others signed up for over 90 per cent of the dam's firm energy, there was no great pressure in the thirties to revise the terms of the law.

Of the New Deal projects, the most ambitious was Grand Coulee Dam in eastern Washington. The Columbia River, hurtling down from the Canadian Rockies across Washington and Oregon into the Pacific, was the greatest untapped source of energy in the country. For years citizens of the Northwest had dreamed of inter-cepting the river and using its waters for irrigation and power. Grand Coulee, the prehistoric riverbed of the Columbia, now a dry and endless gulch cut deep in the lava of central Washing-ton, provided the obvious site for a dam. By 1932 the Bureau of Reclamation, responding to local pressure, submitted plans for construction at Grand Coulee. Hoover, however, refused to ask for enabling legislation.

For some reason the Grand Coulee project roused particularly bitter opposition. Republican Representative Francis G. Culkin of New York called Grand Coulee "a vast area of gloomy tablelands interspersed with deep gullies"; there was no one in the region "to sell power to except rattlesnakes, coyotes, and rabbits. Every-one knows that. There is no market for power in the Northwest . . . absolutely no market for the power in this section and will not be for many years to come."

Roosevelt, although doubtful about the size of the dam as conceived by its euphoric northwestern advocates, was nonetheless willing to authorize a $60 million project. Later, when Ickes and the Special Board for Public Works momentarily turned the idea down, the President intervened to rescue the project. It soon grew to something far larger than Roosevelt himself had contem-plated. In the end, the dam became the largest man-made structure in the world, with a waterfall twice as high as Niagara, backing the Columbia into a wide blue lake — Roosevelt Lake — 150 miles long. As the key unit in the Columbia Basin Reclamation Project, the Grand Coulee Dam held out the promise, not only of cheap and abundant power, but of the reclamation of over a million acres of land and the regulation of the flow of the tumultuous river.

Everywhere interest in public power was rising. In western Oregon, the Army Engineers were building Bonneville, damming up the Cascade Rapids, a five-mile gorge of plunging water which had blocked navigation on the Columbia for years. Across the continent in Maine, Roosevelt, renewing an old personal enthusiasm, authorized inquiry into possibilities of harnessing the tidal power in Passamaquoddy Bay (though, after watching the preliminary results, Roosevelt cooled on 'Quoddy and resolved to get out of it as quickly as possible).[6]

IX

As the time approached when the new dams would begin to produce power, the administration faced the problem of disposing of the government-produced electricity. PWA's National Power Policy Committee, in co-operation with the National Resources Committee (the successor, in 1934, of the National Resources Board), was already formulating broad criteria for systems of government power distribution. By its plan, the Government would set up a central grid system — a power network co-ordinating both existing and new generating and transmission facilities into a single unit, making available large blocs of power at low rates uniform throughout the area. The northwestern grid would connect Bonneville and Grand Coulee and would make sure that nonprofit-making agencies would receive preference in the distribution of public power.

The Army Corps of Engineers, on the other hand, shared the view of the power companies that the northwestern dams would never have customers; nor did the Corps understand the mode in which low-cost power could begin to generate its own new markets. In 1936, bills began to appear in Congress authorizing the Engineers to operate the Bonneville Dam and to dispose of its surplus power as it chose — which meant sale to private utilities at the bus bar.

Early in 1937 Roosevelt established a new Committee on Power

Policy — in effect, an elevation of the old PWA committee onto an interdepartmental level. The new committee quickly proposed that the Army Engineers administer the navigation facilities at Bonneville but that the Secretary of the Interior appoint an independent power administrator to build the northwestern grid. A Bonneville Power Act, drawn up on these lines, passed Congress in 1937. With this victory, the administration set a pattern designed to make sure that the national investment in public power would result in lower rates for the consumers rather than in higher profits for the private utilities.[7]

X

Thus New Deal power policy began to take shape. One objective was to enlarge the publicly owned sector of the power industry as a means both of bringing down excessive private rates and of diminishing private control over the necessities of life. Another was to increase the effectiveness of federal regulation by strengthening the Federal Power Commission; another, to reduce the role of the holding companies by new federal legislation. But the essential purpose, which underlay New Deal programs in both the public and private areas, was to stimulate the use of electricity by lowering the price — to tap markets which the power companies, bound to a narrow faith in quick and certain profits, had thus far been unwilling or unable to open up. Nowhere was the New Deal contribution more striking than in the field of rural electrification.

Before the 1930's, farmers had been largely left out of the electric age. Power had lightened burdens, lowered costs, and multiplied energies of city dwellers a thousandfold. But on the countryside, nine out of ten American farms in 1933 relied on gas engines, horses, mule, and hand labor for power, and on kerosene lanterns for light. Of the thirty million Americans looking to agriculture for a living, nine-tenths had neither bathtub nor shower, three-quarters lived with privies and carried water from wells or brooks, half heated their homes from stoves and did their laundry and even bathed their children out of doors.

Electricity promised the farmers not just the transformation of the technology of farming, but the transformation of life on the farm. Yet years óf agitation had brought very little in the way of extending power lines into the countryside. Though the power companies were forced to show intermittent interest in rural electrification in the twenties, they always found it more profitable in the end to build their new lines in thickly populated areas. A special deterrent was a superstition, cherished by the utilities, that rural rates had to represent a mark-up on city rates. So long as profit determined power policy, it appeared increasingly evident that the farmers would remain at the end of the queue. Yet, so long as the power industry was in private hands, would policy ever be determined by anything else? "Unless rural service is worth more than it costs," as one utility magnate put it, "it should not be supplied" — and "worth" was to be measured solely in terms of financial return.

By such talk, the utilities eventually persuaded the countryside that it could hope for almost nothing from them. It seemed more and more obvious that rural electrification, if it was to come in anyone's lifetime, would have to be brought about by government. This supposition was dramatized when Gifford Pinchot, as governor of Pennsylvania in the early twenties, authorized what came to be known as the Pennsylvania Giant Power Survey under the direction of Morris Llewellyn Cooke. The survey laid great emphasis on the need for public support of rural electrification. Its proposals, though largely ignored in Pennsylvania, aroused national attention.[8]

XI

Cooke, a Philadelphian of good family and well-to-do background, with old-fashioned mustache, pince-nez, and courtesy of manners, had fallen early in life under the spell of Frederick W. Taylor, the prophet of scientific management. Like Tugwell, Cooke read Taylor in a social rather than a narrowly technical context. He was by profession a management engineer; but his larger dedication was to what might be termed technological liberalism — to freeing the mechanical possibilities of the power society for the good of all rather than permitting their sequestration for the profit of a few. In this spirit, Cooke had gone deeply into the utilities problem in Pennsylvania, and had advised Franklin Roosevelt in New York as a member of the New York Power Authority. In 1930 Cooke proposed a rural electrification program to Hoover, but received a brush-off from a White House secretary. He renewed the proposal in 1932, this time to Roosevelt, suggesting the possibility of utilizing "the present emergency as a means of accomplishing general rural electrification." In 1933 Roosevelt asked Cooke to make a survey of the Mississippi Valley for the Public Works Administration. The Mississippi Valley Committee repeated the plea for action under federal leadership in "the great task of rural electrification." The National Resources Board supported this recommendation. Ickes and Hopkins were encouraging. And, on the Hill, George Norris lent the movement his powerful backing. His boyhood memory of chores done in the flickering light of the coal oil lantern through autumn mud and winter snow had left him with a passion to bring electricity to the farms. "I could close my eyes," he said, "and recall the innumerable scenes of the harvest and the unending, punishing tasks performed by hundreds of thousands of women . . . growing old prematurely; dying before their time."

Roosevelt, too, shared the vision. He often recalled the astonishment with which he first inspected at Warm Springs an electricity bill with rates four times as high as those at Hyde Park. This had led him to look into the subject of electricity on the farm. "It can be said with a good deal of truth," he once remarked to a Georgia audience, "that a little cottage at Warm Springs, Georgia, was the birthplace of the Rural Electrification Administration."

Roosevelt's message to Congress in January 1935 urged rural electrification as part of the new works program. After the passage of the Emergency Relief Appropriation Act of 1935, he established on May 11 the Rural Electrification Administration and appointed Morris Cooke as administrator; it was Cooke's sixty-third birthday and the climax of a decade-long fight. Cooke recruited a staff, moved into the former residence of James G. Blaine on Massachusetts Avenue, and fell to work.[9]

XII

He soon encountered difficulties. REA, as part of the works relief program, was supposed to observe the standards under which the program as a whole operated — that is, 25 per cent of the funds were to be spent for labor and 90 per cent of the labor drawn from relief rolls. Cooke soon found that he could not operate under these conditions and, after a short time, became convinced that REA could perform its function best as a lending agency. By August he persuaded Roosevelt, Hopkins, and Ickes to let him go ahead on this new basis. The pattern of REA activity would now be to make low-interest loans for power and light lines in areas without electric service. Its funds would come from the ubiquitous RFC.

If REA meant to stimulate rural electrification through loans, the next problem was to decide to whom the money should go. Obviously private power companies were in the best theoretical position to carry out electrification programs. Past experience gave Cooke little hope of persuading the utilities to move out into the countryside; nevertheless, he was determined to give them every opportunity to do the job. Accordingly, he spent long hours of negotiation in an effort to induce the utilities to accept the low-cost government money and build lines in rural areas. His effort was in vain. The power companies were unchastened. They could see nothing wrong with their past record. As their representatives calmly concluded in a formal report, "There are very few farms requiring electricity for major farm operations that are not now served." If there were potential farm customers, these experts amazingly added, they must be people wanting electricity for household purposes. The essential problem, said the utilities, was not the lowering of rates; it was the financing of wiring and appliances. They would, they made clear, welcome government help in selling their appliances to the farmer.

This thought failed to excite Cooke. It was apparent that the power companies, already locked in struggle with the administration over TVA and over the attempt to regulate holding companies, had no intention of collaborating on the rural electrification front. This rebuff left Cooke no recourse but to follow up other means of carrying electric power to the farms. Municipal power systems afforded a possibility, of course; but few of them were situated — or even legally authorized — to move very far into the surrounding countryside. More and more, there seemed only one means of cracking the problem — the establishment of non-profit co-operatives by the farmers themselves.

The co-operative solution had difficulties of its own. The record of co-operatives in the United States was mixed. Moreover, some co-operative leaders — among them, James Warbasse of the Co-operative League — feared that the link with government would threaten the integrity of the movement. They begged Cooke not to try to organize rural electrification co-operatives. But the total lack of interest on the part of the power companies and the impotence of the municipal systems left co-operatives as the next best bet. "The rural electrification program," Cooke finally said, "is primarily an aid to self-help. It calls for the exercise of initiative on the part of the farmer."

As REA policy began to be clarified, George Norris was beginning to feel that electrification should be taken out of the relief program and given its own statutory identity. In 1936 he introduced a bill to make REA an independent agency. Sam Rayburn of Texas offered a similar bill in the House. The power companies, now openly hostile, fought the bill bitterly. Republicans raised standard cries of socialism and dictatorship. By now REA was gaining its own equally vociferous adherents. Led by fiery John Rankin of Mississippi, a group of public-power radicals, whom Cooke fondly called the "roughnecks," tried to ban the use of REA funds for loans to private corporations. "Let's electrify the country," was Rankin's motto. The Norris-Rayburn bill solidly established the principle of preference for nonprofit agencies in REA loans. It passed the Congress in the spring and became a law on May 20, 1936.[10]

XIII

The fight with the utilities was only beginning. Establishment of REA on a permanent basis galvanized the power companies into action. During the time when Cooke was still trying to win their co-operation, the utilities had sought to forestall REA by moving into the profitable rural areas themselves. They also moved to thwart REA's system of area coverage by building lines which would attract just enough potential REA customers to make it impossible to organize an REA co-operative. Thus "snake lines" — so called because they darted out in all directions — and "spite lines" — driven carefully through the center of a projected REA district — were important weapons in the utility "cream-skimming" policy.

For its part, REA early discovered that engineering, fiscal, and legal problems were slowing up the establishment of co-operatives by untutored farmers. By 1937 REA came to the decision that it must assume a larger responsibility itself in sponsoring and organizing local groups. In May of that year Cooke resigned and was succeeded as administrator by John M. Carmody, who had been his deputy. Carmody, an industrial engineer and, like Cooke, a Taylorite, believed wholeheartedly in the co-operative solution. "I gave recalcitrant private utilities no quarter," he later wrote. "Honest indignation sometimes is a useful administrative instrument." He began, for example, to build generating plants to end REA's dependence on the power companies for energy. Under his forceful leadership, the program moved rapidly forward between 1937 and 1939. Carmody resigned in 1939, when REA was placed in the Department of Agriculture. Harry Slattery, veteran of a generation of conservationist battles, from Ballinger-Pinchot through Teapot Dome to Muscle Shoals, took his place.

As REA assumed the offensive, its loan programs quickly expanded. By June 1939, REA loans amounted to $227 million; by December 1941, to $434 million. And, as a result of the competition for the rural consumer, electric cable lines began to crisscross the farm belt. By 1937, despite the depression, 1.25 million farms had electric power — 500,000 more than in 1934; by 1941, the figure rose to well over 2.25 mllion, or nearly 40 per cent of American farms. Moreover, REA brought general rates down, sometimes by threatening loans to co-operatives to enable them to build generating plants. And the REA concept of area coverage helped the low-income farmer, whose participation was necessary to build up the required level of consumer density. One way or another, REA broke down the barrier that had kept power off the farm. In 1934, one out of ten American farms was electrified; by 1950, nine out of every ten.

Where farm life had been so recently drab, dark, and backbreaking, it now received in a miraculous decade a new access of energy, cleanliness, and light. No single event, save perhaps for the invention of the automobile, so effectively diminished the aching resentment of the farmers and so swiftly closed the gap between country and city. No single public agency ever so enriched and brightened the quality of rural living.[11]

21. The Ideology of the Second New Deal

THE YEAR 1935 marked a watershed. In this year the strategy and tactics of the New Deal experienced a subtle but pervasive change. The broad human objectives remained the same. But the manner in which these objectives were pursued — the techniques employed, the economic presuppositions, the political style, the vision of the American future itself — underwent a significant transformation.

The early New Deal had accepted the concentration of economic power as the central and irreversible trend of the American economy and had proposed the concentration of political power as the answer. The effort of 1933 had been to reshape American institutions according to the philosophy of an organic economy and a co-ordinated society. The new effort was to restore a competitive society within a framework of strict social ground rules and on the foundation of basic economic standards — accompanied, as time went on, by a readiness to use the fiscal pulmotor to keep the economy lively and expansive.

II

Those opposed to all forms of government intervention could see little difference whether the intervention was for the purpose of controlling concentration or resuscitating competition; such people continued to detest the New Deal as heartily as ever. But within the New Deal the alteration in course had sharp impact. The disappearance of the National Recovery Administration and, with it, the conception of overhead industrial planning, was only the most spectacular expression of the new departure. There were many other evidences of the change: the growing domination of the Agricultural Adjustment Administration and other agricultural agencies by the more prosperous farmers — *i.e.* by the clients rather than by the planners; the shift in the Tennessee Valley Authority from an experiment in regional planning into a corporation for the production of power and fertilizer; the defeat of the attempt to make the Reconstruction Finance Corporation an instrument of government capital allocation rather than simply of government commercial banking; the establishment of unemployment compensation as a federal-state rather than a national program; the measures of the 1935 session of Congress looking toward the breaking up of business bigness; the increasing, though as yet largely unconscious, reliance on spending as a substitute for structural reform.

This did not, of course, happen all at once. But the rapid fading out of what remained of NRA after its exorcism by the Supreme Court showed how hostile the new atmosphere was to the old assumptions. Various efforts were first made to continue NRA agreements on a voluntary basis. Then, in September 1935, Roosevelt appointed George L. Berry of Tennessee Co-ordinator for Industrial Co-operation, with the mission of organizing industrial conferences to carry on the partnership ideas of NRA. Berry was the president of the Pressmen's Union. He also personally owned a 30,000-acre farm in Tennessee, a quarry, and the largest color-label printing plant in the country (which he had started with union funds). These varied interests no doubt qualified him for the job of reconciling business, labor, and the consumer. It was his professed belief that 70 per cent of the old NRA could be saved through spontaneous co-operation. But the efforts of Berry's Council for Industrial Progress to redeem NRA by voluntary methods produced a paper organization, a draft legislative program, and nothing more. "So far as NRA and the Blue Eagle are concerned," said Hugh Johnson, "the poor, pale ghosts that spook around their ancient place have not even the dignity of the honored dead. They are just funny phantoms." [1]

III

Some of the changes of 1935 were at first hard to detect. But what was unmistakable was the change in personnel. The key figures of the First New Deal were Moley, Tugwell, Berle, Richberg, Johnson. From 1935, their influence steadily declined. The characteristic figures of the Second New Deal were Frankfurter, Corcoran, Cohen, Landis, Eccles, in time William O. Douglas, Leon Henderson, and Lauchlin Currie. The shift in TVA from Arthur E. Morgan, the biographer of Edward Bellamy, to David Lilienthal, the protégé of Felix Frankfurter, was symptomatic.

The second New Deal was eventually a coalition between lawyers in the school of Brandeis and economists in the school of Keynes. But in 1935 the economists were still in the background; the neo-Brandeisian lawyers were at first the dominant figures in the new dispensation. As for the old Justice himself, he watched the events of the year with growing delight. Black Monday, the day the Supreme Court struck down NRA, seemed to him "the most important day in the history of the Court and the most beneficent." The three decisions, he said, far from rushing the country back to "horse and buggy" days, only "compelled a return to human limitations." The time had come to correct the "lie" that the country could make an advance as a whole; it could advance, he said, only locally — in particular communities and particular industries. Everything was beginning to look better — the reversion of social security to the states, the holding-company battle, the tax message, the rise to influence of his disciples. "F.D. is making a gallant fight," he wrote Norman Hapgood early in August, "and seems to appreciate fully the evils of bigness. He should have more support than his party is giving him; and the social worker–progressive crowd seems as blind as in 1912."

Brandeis's cry of triumph did not mean the literal triumph of Brandeis's ideas. His faith in smallness was too stark and rigorous. To Milo Perkins of the Department of Agriculture he held forth, as Perkins reported to Tugwell, on "the sanctity of littleness in *all* fields of human activity." To place men in jobs calling for superhuman abilities, Brandeis suggested, was to corrupt or to destroy human nature. The transition back to small units would be worth any cost in dislocation or suffering. As Perkins rose to leave, the old man told him earnestly to go back to Texas — back to the hinterland, where the real movement to reshape America would originate.

When Brandeis talked in this mood, when he told Tom Corcoran to send his boys back to the state capitals, when he decried the automotive industry on the ground that Americans ought to walk more, he was speaking for an America that was dead. His words were morally bracing but socially futile. There was, indeed, a conflict in the heart of Brandeis's social philosophy. Much as he admired competition, he admired smallness even more; and, when the two principles clashed, it was competition which had to go under. Thus he wanted government action not only to destroy bigness but affirmatively to protect smallness — even, if necessary, at the expense of competition. He had long ascribed vast importance, for example, to resale price maintenance and other fair-trade laws — laws which denied consumers the benefits of price competition in the interests of keeping the corner grocer and shopkeeper in business. Here the neo-Brandeisians left him. They could never get excited over such measures and were content to leave their advocacy to the independent grocers' and druggists' lobbies. Where Brandeis, in short, exalted smallness and localism per se, men like Cohen and Corcoran were trying to make competition work in an economy which would be technologically advanced as well as socially humane.

Cohen and Corcoran were not economists, any more than Brandeis was. Their specialty was statutes, not programs. Elsewhere in government, however, program-minded economists were working on alternatives to the First New Deal. Leon Henderson, the vigorous and resourceful chief economist of NRA, viewing the economic future late in 1935 from the rubble of his agency, outlined one program to test the possibilities of competition. Though Henderson could not yet be counted a member of the Corcoran-Cohen group, his suggestions ably stated the direction in which the Second New Deal might go.

The key problem, as Henderson saw it, was to restore price competition. He appreciated the strength of the tendencies toward economic concentration and price inflexibility. "Indeed, at the NRA," Henderson said, "so insistent and so convincing were the arguments for price protection measures against cutthroat competition that I was often compelled to ask: Has the nature of competition changed?" This was a fruitful question; and Henderson might have been wise to consider it more seriously. But his disposition was rather to wonder whether one more effort was not in order to revitalize the market. The antitrust laws were not enough;

they touched only a small part of the difficulties. More serious were the problems of productivity: obsolescent technology, as in textiles; unwieldy capital structures, as in steel; inflexible wage and transportation rate structures, as in construction; enforced scarcity as a result, for example, of tariff protection. "I favor a positive program for securing laissez faire," said Henderson — a multiple attack on concentration and price rigidity, including the active use of the taxing power; the revision of the patent laws; vigorous antitrust action; encouragement of co-operatives; yardstick competition; tariff reduction, and so on. "Perhaps the good old-fashioned kind of atomistic competition cannot exist everywhere in mass production," Henderson concluded. "If this be so, we need to know it realistically so that we may alter our concepts and our institutions to meet new demands. Certainly . . . a positive program to make it possible would liberate large areas for the agenda of market competition and reveal clearly those areas of production left for the agenda of the state." [2]

IV

Obviously the First New Dealers preferred the tempered and pragmatic spirit of a Henderson or Cohen to the extremism of a Brandeis. But in the end both were equally destructive to their vision. The essence of the First New Deal was affirmative national planning. The men of 1933 believed that, in a modern industrial society, the problems of price-wage-profit behavior and of the allocation of resources could not be left to solve themselves. These problems could be handled, in their view, only by a considerable integration of private and public planning; and their effort was to devise institutional means of associating business, labor, and government in this process. "For good or ill," as General Johnson said, "we are entering a managed economy. . . . It is not a question of whether we shall have a managed economy, but of who shall manage it. . . . The rout of laissez-faire is rampant through the world."

The First New Deal proposed to rebuild America through the reconstruction of economic institutions in accordance with technological imperatives. In the spring of 1934, Tugwell wrote with confidence, "We have turned our backs on competition and chosen control." But by autumn the bright hopes of 1933, when so much had seemed possible, were beginning to fade away. In October 1934 Tugwell mused in his diary about "the utter impossibility of achieving what it would be necessary to achieve in order to come close to solution of the socio-economic problem in our generation"; "we cannot," he said, "possibly move fast enough to stave off disaster."

Compared to the bold dream of making America over, the Brandeisian approach seemed mean and flat, a program of mending and tinkering. The New Dealers of 1935, Tugwell said, were denying the "operational wholeness," the intrinsic unity of the system. The running off into side issues, the constant tendency to escape from the structural problem into monetary manipulation or the redistribution of wealth through taxation or deficit spending — all this came, Tugwell thought, from a reluctance to take "the hard way," to accept the "harsh, relentless discipline" involved in a concerted national scheme "in which conflict disappears and the creative impulses of a people are fused in a satisfying effort." "Patching was all the [later] New Dealers knew how to do," he wrote subsequently, " — or, at any rate, all their enemies, as they regained their strength, would let them do." The result, he felt, was the trickling off of the energy of reform into painless — but, for that reason, trivial — measures which left the basic structure of American capitalism untouched. So, too, Charles A. Beard, in Moley's *Today,* condemned Roosevelt as he had once condemned Wilson: "The cult of littleness and Federal impotence prevails. It is the cult of 'the new freedom' which hurries us on into greater bigness. Only the depth of the crisis in 1933 made it possible for the President to abandon the admitted farce of trust-busting for a moment, and to seek the effective functioning of national economy." "The Anti-trust Acts," said Hugh Johnson, "are a throw-back to the Neolithic Age of statesmanship, and their blind sponsorship is a sort of jittering caveman ignorance."

Tugwell was always loyal and never vented his exasperation in public. Others among the First New Dealers were less restrained. "Think Fast, Captain!" said General Johnson in the *Saturday Evening Post* in the fall of 1935, blaming the trouble on what he called "the Harvard crowd" of "Happy Hot Dogs." Frankfurter, Johnson said in a burst of italics, was *"the most influential single individual in the United States."* Tugwell, reaching back further, blamed it all on Brandeis, the "doctrinaire parading as an instrumentalist." As a justice of the Supreme Court, Brandeis had to operate discreetly; but he had found, Tugwell said, two powerful means of influence on the President. "The first of these means was his disciples; the second was the threat of unconstitutionality." His evangelism was implacable. "It is my firm belief," Tugwell concluded, "that it was responsible for the failure of the New Deal." By 1935 Moley, Johnson, Richberg, and Berle had left Washington. Tugwell remained, but he was shunted off to a siding: in 1937 he left, too. The First New Dealers had had their chance. Now others were taking over.[3]

v

From the viewpoint of the men of 1935, the partnership of 1933 — government, business, labor and agriculture, planning together for the common good — had been an experiment noble in purpose but doomed in result. The neo-Brandeisians rejected national planning because they thought it put impossible intellectual and administrative burdens on the planners. Even if it had proved technically feasible, however, they would still have rejected it because they believed that, in a controlled capitalism, capitalism was bound to capture the machinery of control.

Tugwell later noted that the concept of national economic coordination underlying the effort of 1933 was "congenial, fundamentally, only to big business." For Tugwell, this was an ironic paradox; for the Corcoran crowd, it was inevitable and, by virtue of its inevitability, an overriding disqualification. Tugwell could further write, "We lost our battles because, before long, they ceased to be our battles. Our allies became more powerful than ourselves." To the neo-Brandeisians, watching the manufacturers rise to power in NRA and the processors in AAA, this admission only further proved the Brandeisian point. Obviously business would take over any agency of central planning in a capitalist society: the alternatives were therefore socialism, which the neo-Brandeisians rejected as incompatible with freedom, or a restoration of control through the market. The political expectations of the First New Deal seemed to the Second New Dealers hopelssly naïve.

Yet if the politics of the First New Deal were naïve, so, too, were the economics of the Second New Deal. Where the First New Deal sensed fundamental changes in the structure of the market and tried to adapt public policy to them, the Second New Deal too often supposed that the classical model of the market was somehow recoverable. It felt that government should confine itself to "general" policies, whether of ground rules or of fiscal stimulus, and that the pattern of resource use and the price-wage-profit relationship should be, within wide limits, "competitive" and unplanned. It was, as Corcoran correctly said, "ideologically far more 'capitalistic' than the First New Deal."

The basic conservatism of its economics was disguised by the aggressive radicalism of its politics. In part, this radicalism sprang from disenchantment with the experience of collaboration with business. In part, too, no doubt, it was an opportunistic improvisation, designed to neutralize the clamor on the left. And in part it emerged from a new conception of the problem. While the Second New Dealers wanted not a planned but a free economy, they felt that the way to restore the conditions of freedom was to use the powers of government to promote competitive enterprise in a society becoming increasingly interdependent; and this often seemed to involve the economic regulation and political chastisement of business.

In a memorandum to Hugh Johnson in 1933 Alexander Sachs had criticized the NRA approach as "monistic planning akin to state capitalism or state socialism" and proposed instead a system of "pluralistic planning . . . suited to a political and economic democracy." This distinction underlay the political philosophy of the Second New Deal. Where the First New Deal contemplated government, business, and labor marching hand in hand toward a brave new society, the Second New Deal proposed to revitalize the tired old society by establishing a framework within which enterprise could be set free. It was designed, Tugwell said, "to regulate industry, but not to require of it planning or performance."

A shift was taking place from a managed to a mixed economy: the one tried to convert business through new institutions, the other tried to discipline it through new laws. The First New Deal characteristically told business what it must do. The Second New Deal characteristically told business what it must *not* do.[4]

VI

The men of 1935 were somewhat different types from those of 1933. If, as Berle once remarked, Columbia was the "early intellectual home of the New Deal," the Harvard Law School was plainly its later home. The First New Dealers were characteristically social evangelists, with a broad historic sweep and a touch of the visionary, seeing America at a great turning of its history. The New Dealers of 1935 were characteristically lawyers, precise and trenchant, confining themselves to specific problems, seeing America as off on a tangent but capable of being recalled to the old main road of progress.

These distinctions should not be pushed too far. Part of the change was the erosion of politics. One group had been on the firing line too long; some of its members were simply worn out, or had been subjected to a political hammering which had destroyed their public usefulness. It seemed time for a change. And to a degree, some of those involved might as well have ended up on one side as the other; only the accident of circumstance placed one man in the class of 1933 and another in the class of 1935. Nonideological figures like Hopkins and Ickes (not to mention Roosevelt) coexisted happily with both. In any case, the issues involved were those of economic program, not of religious principle, and reasonable men might swing back from one to another according to the pressures of the time. The leader of the neo-Brandeisians, Frankfurter, had himself been a follower of Theodore Roosevelt and the New Nationalism in 1912. Walter Lippmann, whose *Drift and Mastery* of 1914 was the most lucid statement of the case for the New Nationalism, was now beginning work on *The Good Society,* to be published in 1937, the most lucid statement of the tradition of the New Freedom. William O. Douglas who in 1933 rejected Brandeisianism as obsolescent, became in a few years almost its most effective champion, while David Lilienthal, a Brandeisian in 1933, ended as the prophet of bigness.

Yet, for all the happenstance involved, a difference remains between the intellectual style and texture of the two New Deals. Each, of course, saw the distinction in different terms. Tugwell saw it as between men who had social vision and men who lacked it; Corcoran saw it as between men who disdained legal exactitude and men who valued it — and no doubt both were right. As New Deal social thought lost` richness and subtlety, its administrative thought was gaining clarity and precision. The two areas of economic analysis and legal draftsmanship best make the contrast.

In economics, the difference has been noted between the original and probing economic ideas of Berle, Means, and Tugwell and the free-market clichés of Brandeis and Frankfurter. The neo-Brandeisians often had not even thought through the economic implications of their own measures. Such enactments as the securities and exchange legislation, and especially the Public Utilities Holding Company Act, which were designed as exercises in "self-liquidating power" (in a phrase of Paul Freund's), often ended in government direction of precisely the sort to which the Second New Deal was theoretically opposed. "You start to set the patterns of right conduct," reflected Charles E. Wyzanski, Jr., years later, "and you may even get into the business that you have in the public utilities field of actually directing appropriate conduct through a public order enforcible through a judicial decree." He himself concluded that there was "no such thing as the mere elimination of improper practices, no such thing as the mere elimination of force and fraud. Whenever one goes into any area and purports to deal only with nefarious practices, one indirectly if not directly sets up standards of affirmative good conduct." Wyzanski wondered whether those who, like himself, were trained at the Harvard Law School were so clear about this as they should have been. (Cohen was an exception here, as to most generalizations; he well understood the subtle interplay of elements which made the differences between the First and Second New Deal, like those between the New Nationalism and New Freedom, less significant in practice than in principle. As Cohen later wrote, for example, "There was a measure of structural planning in the Holding Company Act which might have had more appeal to the First New Dealers if they had had clearer ideas of how they wished to give substance to their planning.")

In the field of law, however, the Second New Dealers were more accomplished and sophisticated. This difference, too, Wyzanski ascribed to the Harvard Law School and especially to the influence of Professor Thomas Reed Powell, whose exuberant insistence on the exact use of words made a generation of students, as Wyzanski put it, "think twenty times before you write that sentence quite that way." The difference emerged in the contrast between the sweeping and rhetorical legal strokes of, say, Donald Richberg, and the exquisite craftsmanship of Ben Cohen. Richberg, moved by a passionate feeling that the imperatives of history required drastic social reorganization, wanted to draft laws and fight cases in terms of prophetic affirmations; he resented the whole notion of pussy-footing around to avoid offending the stupid prejudices of reactionary judges. But Cohen, who felt it more important to make a particular statute stick than to promote a crusade, thought through every point with technical punctiliousness and always showed a meticulous regard for legal continuities. The laws drawn by the First New Deal tended to perish before the courts because of loose draftsmanship and emotional advocacy. The laws drawn by the Second New Deal were masterpieces of the lawyer's art; and they survived. Thus the National Recovery Act was, on the whole, a less complicated piece of legislation than the Holding Company Act; but, in the end, it turned out that one was, in the judgment of the Supreme Court, exhortation and the other, law.

VII

The First New Dealers, coming in at the bottom of the crisis, believing society to be almost on the verge of dissolution, attached a high value to social cohesion and viewed the governmental process as an exercise in conversion and co-operation. The Second New Dealers, coming in as things were on their way up, were less worried about the fragility of the system and saw the governmental process as an exercise in litigation and combat. They were quite prepared to risk straining the fabric of society in order to make their points and achieve their objectives. Moley ascribes a grim expression to Corcoran: "Fighting with a businessman is like fighting with a Polack. You can give no quarter." Corcoran does not remember saying this; it is perhaps the sort of thing he might have said without meaning it, with regard either to businessmen or Polacks; yet saying anything like this at all expressed the alteration in mood from 1933. Berle, deploring the change, tried to invoke the authority of Brandeis against "the would-be Brandeis follower of today," emphasizing Brandeis's ability "not only to attack an evil, letting the chips fall where they might; but to stand by and work out an appropriate arrangement by which all parties at the end could reach a stable relationship." Too often, Berle added, the neo-Brandeisian "has satisfied his lust for battle in mere punitive expeditions without having a clear picture of the result he intends to get; too often he has failed to recognize that the object is not winning a battle, but creating a socially workable result."

Arthur E. Morgan made a similar point in his bitter fight with Lilienthal. He attacked those who "use any method at hand, including intrigue, arbitrary force, and appeal to class hatred. In my opinion," he continued, "such methods, while they may be effective toward achieving a reputation for political realism, do not contribute to the public welfare." The militants, he suggested, were forgetting the moral dimension of public policy. "The manner in which we achieve our ends," he said in a noble sentence, "may have a more enduring influence on the country than the ends we may achieve. The art of planting the seeds of mutual confidence and of giving the young plants a chance to grow is a great art. Most of Europe has not learned it. Let us hope that we in America may do so." The men of 1935 vigorously objected to Morgan's application of these principles. Yet Morgan had a profound point: a battle won at the cost of tearing the nation apart might not be worth the winning. Still, to this the Second New Dealers might have replied that the big interests were not the nation, and that they had no choice but to fight hard to save their adversaries from their suicidal policies. The correctness of this decision, they could later claim, lay in the extent to which even their one-time opponents eventually accepted the statutes of the Second New Deal.

Fundamentally, perhaps, the First New Deal was destroyed by success. The economic disintegration of 1932 could only be stopped by a concerted national effort and a unified national discipline. The method and approach of the Brandeis school would have been ineffective and irrelevant in 1933. But once the First New Deal had reversed the decline and restored the nation's confidence in itself, then the very sense of crisis which made its discipline acceptable began to recede. The demand for change slackened, the instinct toward inertia grew, the dismal realities of life and mediocrities of aspiration reasserted themselves. New methods were required, relying less on deathbed repentance and crisis-induced co-operation than on older and stabler incentives, such as the desire to make money and avoid the policeman. Most important of all, the First New Dealers had expended themselves; they had run out of policy; they had nothing further convincing or attractive to recommend; and, for an administration which thrived on action, this was the ultimate disqualification.

In the end, the basic change in 1935 was in atmosphere — a certain lowering of ideals, waning of hopes, narrowing of possibilities, a sense that things were, not opening out, but closing in. The Hundred Days had been a golden spring, like Versailles in 1919, when for a moment a passionate national response to leadership which asked great things made anything — everything — seem possible. The First New Dealers had a utopian and optimistic and moral cast of mind; the Second New Dealers prided themselves on their realism. The First New Dealers thought well of human rationality and responsibility. It was their faith that man was capable of managing the great instrumentalities he had invented. The Second New Dealers accepted Brandeis's maxim, "Man is weak and his judgment is fallible"; they said with Frankfurter, "We know how slender a reed is reason — how recent its emergence in man, how deep the countervailing instincts and passions, how treacherous the whole rational process." If man could not be relied on to assume responsibility for his own creations, he could be saved from his weakness only as these creations were cut down to his own size.

The shift from the First to the Second New Deal was not a whimsical change of direction so much as it was an almost inevitable response to the new necessities of the American situation. The problem had changed between 1933 and 1935, so policies changed, too, and men with them. The next wave of New Dealers, more skeptical, more hard-boiled, more tough-minded, ostensibly more radical but essentially more conservative, were prepared to work within the existing moral attitudes and the existing institutional framework and to generate by sheer vigor and combativeness the energy to fuel their more limited purposes. As children of light, the First New Dealers had believed in the capacity for justice which, in Niebuhr's phrase, makes democracy possible. As children of darkness, the Second New Dealers believed in the inclination to injustice which makes democracy necessary.[5]

VIII

The fight of 1935 was essentially between the planners and the neo-Brandeisians, the devotees of bigness and the devotees of competition. But it would be a mistake to regard this contest as defining the ultimate content of the Second New Deal. For the neo-Brandeisians were but the shock troops of the 1935 coalition. They did the bureaucratic infighting and seized control of the strategic strong points. But they constituted only the cutting edge of the Second New Deal, not its inner essence. It was Marriner Eccles and the spenders, the silent partners of 1935, who eventually determined the fundamental policies.

The Second New Deal was not fully defined until the battle over spending in 1937–38. Still, the issue of fiscal policy did not go unperceived. It has been noted that Brandeis himself had favored government spending in 1933 and that Cohen from an early point was a thoughtful student of Keynes. The Supreme Court's condemnation of the structural approach of the First New Deal now heightened interest in a resort to fiscal policy. In 1934, when Frances Perkins had confided to Justice Stone her worries about the constitutionality of a social-security system, Stone whispered back, "The taxing power of the Federal Government, my dear; the taxing power is sufficient for everything you want and need." The same year Professor E. S. Corwin, in his *Twilight of the Supreme Court,* identified the independence of the spending power from constitutional control as the fatal weakness which threatened to envelop the entire institution of judicial review "in an atmosphere of unreality, even of futility." Thomas Reed Powell, reflecting on the NRA decision, now pointed out how the Supreme Court, without knowing it, had shoved the administration in new directions. "The waters dammed by judicial restrictions on the commerce power," Powell warned, "may break out in unwelcome fields of taxing and spending. What seems a great victory against national regulation may prove to be a Pyrrhic one. What is called the Ship of State has other controls than those with wires to where the Supreme Court is quartermaster."

And what was constitutionally possible might be socially desirable as well. In a brilliant column a few days after the NRA decision, Walter Lippmann forecast the development of the Second New Deal. Indeed, Lippmann's own evolution showed something of the urgencies which caused the Second New Deal to displace the First. In the spring of 1933, he had written that, "for the idea of an automatic return to normalcy we have to substitute the idea of a deliberate attempt to plan, to organize, and to manage our own economic system." This meant, he explained, managing money and banking, managing foreign trade, managing new capital investment, bringing basic industries under greater social control; "there is no escape." The "ideal of a consciously controlled society," he said later in the year, challenged men at last with a transcendent purpose. "I say to you, my fellow students [he was speaking at the University of California], that the purpose to make an ordered life on this planet can, if you embrace it and let it embrace you, carry through the years triumphantly."

All this expressed the first exhilaration of the planning idea. In another year Lippmann drew back somewhat from the enthusiasm of 1933. He began his remarkable Godkin Lectures of 1934, published under the title *The Method of Freedom,* with his familiar demonstration of the failure of laissez faire. The self-regulating and self-adjusting character of the old order had been destroyed: under modern conditions the state had no choice except to intervene. But it could intervene, he now emphasized, in two radically different ways. Here Lippmann distinguished between what he called the Directed Economy and the Compensated Economy. The Directed Economy, in its extreme version, was the centrally planned and physically regimented economy of the totalitarian state. The Compensated Economy, on the other hand, retained private intiative and decision so far as possible but committed the state to act when necessary to "redress the balance of private actions by compensating public actions" — by fiscal and monetary policy, by social insurance, by regulation of business, by the establishment of minimum economic levels below which no member of the community should be allowed to fall.

In substance, the state undertakes to counteract the mass errors of the individualist crowd by doing the opposite of what the crowd is doing: it saves when the crowd is spending too much; it borrows when the crowd is extravagant, and it spends when the crowd is afraid to spend . . . it becomes an employer when there is private unemployment, and it shuts down when there is work for all.

The shift from a Directed to a Compensated Economy forecast the directions in which the New Deal itself was beginning to move.

By 1935 Lippmann was sharply attacking the notion of detailed central planning. To him it seemed equivalent to trying to stop water from running through a sieve by plugging each hole. The principle of minute control, he had come to believe, was wrong; the economy needed only some from of "general social control"; and the most effective method would be, not to plug the individual holes in the sieve, but to control the flow of the water. What was necessary, he contended in his post-NRA column, were measures of "reflation" — government stimulus to promote expenditure — rather than measures of "regimentation." "If anything has been demonstrated in this depression which can be relied upon as a guide to policy, it is that reflation — not planning, not regimentation, and not laissez-faire — is the remedy." Not only would fiscal policy produce results, but it was compatible with freedom. It "affects only the general purchasing power of the whole nation, and can be administered without detailed intervention in each man's affairs." It could be used without destroying the federal character of the American government or the private character of the American economy. And the authority to use it lay beyond challenge within the federal power. "The power to fix the wages paid for killing chickens is negligible and would be totally unnecessary, and would not even be desired, if the great power to stabilize the total purchasing power of the nation were properly used." [6]

IX

The same issue had been considered at greater length a few months before when two Englishmen, Harold Laski and John Maynard Keynes, debated for the doubtless astonished readers of *Red-book* the question, "Can America Spend Its Way Into Recovery?" For the Socialist, the answer was No. As Laski saw it, the only hope was structural change — in his view, the nationalization of the means of production. "It is to avoid this end that the United States has embarked upon its present experiment." Keynes could not have disagreed more. Was salvation possible through spending? "Why, obviously!" he wrote. ". . . No one of common sense could doubt it, unless his mind had first been muddled by a 'sound' financier or an 'orthodox' economist." An economy produces in response to spending; how absurd to suppose that one can stimulate economic activity by declining to spend! When individuals fail to spend enough to maintain employment, then government must do it for them. "It might be better if they did it for themselves, but that is no argument for not having done it at all." While productive would be better than unproductive expenditure, "even pure relief expenditure is much better than nothing. The object must be to raise the total expenditure to a figure which is high enough to push the vast machine of American industry into renewed motion."

For Keynes, this was part of a larger argument. He was opposed to any system which would subject most of the economic life of the community to physical controls. "If the State," he believed, "is able to determine the aggregate amount of resources devoted to augmenting the instruments [of production] and the basic rate of reward to those who own them, it will have accomplished all that is necessary." The central controls necessary to influence these aggregates of economic activity would unquestionably mean an extension of state power; but a wide field remained for private initiative and responsibility. In this field, Keynes said, the traditional advantages of individualism — the decentralization of decision; the exercise of individual choice; variety and freedom — would still hold good. In stating this faith in indirect over direct planning, Keynes was putting in a more inclusive way what would become the ideals of the Second New Deal.

Of all the minds contending against dogmatism, both of right and left, and asserting the possibility of reasoned change, that of Keynes was the most luminous and penetrating. The Cambridge economist, indeed, represented almost the culmination of the British analytical tradition. He had grown up in the high noon of British rationalism — Cambridge before the First World War, G. E. Moore and Alfred North Whitehead and Bertrand Russell. But he tempered rationalism with rich cultivation; and he strengthened it with extraordinary practical instincts about public issues.

Keynes made clear his skepticism about laissez-faire capitalism in the twenties. That condition of perfect equilibrium imagined by the classical economists, in which the interest of each ministered to the interest of all, seemed to him a phantasm. The state obviously had to intervene all the time to keep the economy going; more than that, big enterprise was growing away from the old individualistic economic motives; it was socializing itself. What lay ahead was a new economic society, moving far ahead of the doctrines of both right and left. Classical socialism, indeed, seemed to him quite as stupid as classical capitalism. The socialist program was "little better than a dusty survival of a plan to meet the problems of fifty years ago, based on a misunderstanding of what someone said a hundred years ago." He marveled at how a doctrine "so illogical and so dull" as Marxism could ever have influenced anyone.

"For my part," Keynes said, "I think that Capitalism, wisely managed, can probably be made more efficient for attaining economic ends than any alternative system yet in sight." He proposed to manage capitalism "by the agency of collective action" — in particular, by a larger measure of public control over currency, credit, and investment, so that basic economic decisions would no longer be left entirely to the chances of private judgment and private profits. Such extensions of public authority need not, he felt, impair private initiative. But all this represented only theoretical possibilities. In the mid-twenties Keynes was pessimistic about actually reforming the system. "There is no party in the world at present," he ruefully concluded, "which appears to me to be pursuing right aims by right methods. . . . Europe lacks the means, America the will, to make a move."

By 1929 Keynes had succeeded in converting the Liberal party and Lloyd George to his doctrines. *We Can Conquer Unemployment*, a Liberal tract for the General Election that year, set forth an ambitious program of "national development," calling for public action to build roads and houses, to promote electrification, and to reclaim land. (A heckler asked how Keynes could support the man whom he had charged a decade earlier with wrecking the peace. "The difference between me and some other people," Keynes blandly replied, "is that I oppose Mr. Lloyd George when he is wrong and support him when he is right.") In a defense of the Liberal platform, entitled *Can Lloyd George Do It?* Keynes sharply distinguished the expansionist program from socialism. For their part, the Socialists attacked the Keynes program as a "quack remedy" and as "madcap finance" which would only increase the public debt.

Keynes was quick to recognize the depression as no passing squall, but rather a protracted storm which would test all democratic resourcefulness. He rejected the counsels of impotence so fashionable among his academic colleagues. "Our destiny is in our own hands," he said. In his *Treatise on Money* in 1930, he worked out the theory of a policy, arguing in effect that, when investment exceeded savings, the result was prosperity, and when savings exceeded investment, the result was depression. If this were so, then recovery required restoring the volume of investment to a point where it would once again offset savings; and this, as he saw it, called for a drastic reduction in the interest rate, a general rise in prices, and extensive government programs of public works.

But these policies presupposed more than ever political parties that were free, as he put it, of both the influence of Die-Hardism and of Catastrophe. Where were such parties to be found? Evidently not in Great Britain. The economic ideas of J. H. Thomas, the Labourite, seemed to Keynes as senseless as those of Neville Chamberlain, the Conservative. Ramsay MacDonald's Economy Report struck him as "the most foolish document I have ever had the misfortune to read." Both left and right retaliated in kind. The National Liberal Sir John Simon said it was tragic to see how Keynes had taken leave of his wits; the right-wing Socialist Philip Snowden called him a fool; and the left-wing Socialists considered him preposterous.

Shortly after Roosevelt's inauguration Keynes spoke once again in a brilliant pamphlet called *The Means to Prosperity*. Here he argued with new force and detail for public spending as the way out of depression. Employing the concept of the "multiplier" introduced by his student Richard F. Kahn, Keynes contended that deficit spending for public works would employ two additional men indirectly for each man directly employed in public projects. He even called for tax reduction; "given sufficient time to gather the fruits, a reduction of taxation will run a better chance, than an increase, of balancing the budget." The budget could only be balanced, after all, by enlarging the national income, and this could only be done by expanding employment. Make bank credit cheap and abundant; lower the interest rate; above all, demand massive and organized government action "to break the vicious circle and to stem the progressive deterioration." But would any government do this? "Unfortunately," Keynes wrote in April 1933, "it seems impossible in the world of today to find anything between a government which does nothing at all and one which goes right off the deep end! the former leading, sooner or later, to the latter." [7]

X

Then Roosevelt's message to the London Economic Conference in July 1933 came to cheer him. Here, perhaps, was a leader prepared to emancipate his nation from enslavement by defunct economists. In September, though, he confessed a certain disappointment. "I fear that the hesitation in American progress today," he said, "is almost entirely due to delays in putting loan expenditure in effect. . . . It seems to have been an error in choice of urgencies to put all the national energies into the National Recovery Act." Still, the flexibility and courage which lay behind New Deal policies continued to hearten him. Later in the autumn Keynes had talks with Frankfurter, who was then at Oxford; and in December Frankfurter forwarded to Roosevelt an advance copy of an open letter to the President scheduled for publication in the *New York Times* at the end of the year.

In this eloquent document Keynes summed up the vivid hope with which he viewed the American experiment. The problem, as he saw it, was Roosevelt's conflict of purpose between recovery and reform. "For the first, speed and quick results are essential. The second may be urgent, too; but haste will be injurious, and wisdom of long-range purpose is more necessary than immediate achievement." Too much emphasis on reform, Keynes suggested, might upset business confidence. It might weaken the existing motives to action before Roosevelt had time to put other motives in their place. And it might, in addition, confuse the administration by giving it too much to think about and do all at once. This was why Keynes considered concentration on NRA, despite its admirable social objectives, the wrong choice in the order of priorities.

Keynes questioned, moreover, the administration's devotion to raising prices as an end in itself. The techniques seemed to him bad: whether limiting production (though he approved the social purposes of NRA and "the various schemes for agricultural restriction. The latter, in particular, I should strongly support in principle"); or increasing the quantity of money ("like trying to get fat by buying a larger belt"); or fooling around with exchange depreciation and the price of gold ("the recent gyrations of the dollar have looked to me more like a gold standard on the booze than the ideal managed currency of my dreams"). In any case, the right way to get prices up was to stimulate output by increasing aggregate purchasing power; and not the other way round. Deficit spending was the answer; "nothing else counts in comparison with this." In the past, Keynes told Roosevelt, orthodox finance had regarded war as the only legitimate excuse for creating employment by government expenditure. "You, Mr. President, having cast off such fetters, are free to engage in the interests of peace and prosperity the technique which has hitherto only been allowed to serve the purposes of war and destruction."

There is no record of Roosevelt's reaction to this document. A few months later Keynes came to the United States to receive an honorary degree at Columbia. Frankfurter armed him with a note to the President; and on May 28, 1934, Keynes came to tea at the White House. The meeting does not seem to have been a great success. Keynes was a formidable person, and his urbanely arrogant manner may have annoyed Roosevelt. He was capable, for example, of saying publicly (as he did later that year), "The economic problem is not too difficult. If you will leave that to me, I will look after it." Such an attitude might well irritate statesmen. In addition, he was hopelessly quick and patronizing. "Annihilating arguments darted out of him with the swiftness of an adder's tongue," Bertrand Russell once wrote. "When I argued with him, I felt that I took my life in my hands, and I seldom emerged without feeling something of a fool." Still, Tugwell recalled Keynes's attitude in conversations with Roosevelt as "more that of an admiring observer than that of an instructor."

What is more certain is that Roosevelt shared the resentment which old Wilsonians felt toward Keynes ever since *The Economic Consequences of the Peace.* In 1923, for example, Roosevelt congratulated the author of a piece in *Foreign Affairs*; "I particularly love the way you hand things to Mr. Keynes." And in 1941, when Bernard Baruch, who had helped negotiate the reparations clauses which Keynes condemned as folly, warned Roosevelt against him, Roosevelt replied, "I did not have those Paris Peace Conference experiences with the 'gent' but from much more recent contacts, I am inclined wholly to agree." To Frankfurter, Roosevelt politely wrote after the first meeting that he had had "a grand talk" with Keynes and liked him "immensely"; and Tugwell mentions subsequent meetings in which Roosevelt talked to Keynes with "unusual" frankness. But to Frances Perkins Roosevelt complained strangely, "He left a whole rigamarole of figures. He must be a mathematician rather than a political economist."

For his part, Keynes, as was his custom, looked first at Roosevelt's hands and found them disappointing — "firm and fairly strong, but not clever or with finesse, shortish round nails like those at the end of a business-man's fingers." Also, they seemed oddly familiar; for some minutes Keynes searched his memory for a forgotten name, hardly knowing what he was saying about silver and balanced budgets and public works. At last it came to him: Sir Edward Grey! — more solid, cleverer, much more fertile, sensitive and permeable, but still an Americanized Sir Edward Grey. When Roosevelt got down to economics, Keynes's disappointment persisted. He told Frances Perkins later that he had "supposed the President was more literate, economically speaking"; to Alvin Johnson, "I don't think your President Roosevelt knows anything about economics."

XI

Keynes found others in Washington more receptive. Steered around by Tugwell, he met a number of the younger men and told them to spend — a monthly deficit of only $200 million, he said, would send the nation back to the bottom of the depression, but $300 million would hold it even and $400 million would bring recovery. A few days later he sent Roosevelt the draft of another *New York Times* article entitled "Agenda for the President." Here he continued his running review of the New Deal, saying he doubted whether NRA either helped or hurt as much as one side or the other supposed and again defending the agricultural policies. As usual, the best hope remained an increase in public spending; $400 million, through the multiplier, would increase the national income at least three or four times this amount. In detail, Keynes advocated special efforts in the housing and rail- road fields. "Of all the experiments to evolve a new order," he concluded, "it is the experiment of young America which most attracts my own deepest sympathy. For they are occupied with the task of trying to make the economic order work tolerably well, whilst preserving freedom of individual initiative and liberty of thought and criticism." With this, Keynes, pausing only to make astute investments in the depressed stocks of public utilities, re- turned home.

Newspapermen were quick but wrong to ascribe the increase in spending in the summer of 1934 to Keynes. No doubt Keynes strengthened the President's inclination to do what he was going to do anyway, and no doubt he showed the younger men lower down in the administration how to convert an expedient into a policy. But it cannot be said either that spending would not have taken place without his intervention or that it did take place for his reasons. In 1934 and 1935 the New Deal was spending in spite of itself. The deficit represented a condition, not a theory. What was happening was a rush of spending for separate emergency purposes. "I think that 95 per cent of the thinking in the admin- istration is how to spend money," said Henry Morgenthau in a morose moment in the summer of 1935, "and that possibly 5 per cent of the thinking is going towards how we can work ourselves out of our present unemployment." Certainly, except for Marriner Eccles, no leading person in Roosevelt's first administration had much notion of the purposeful use of fiscal policy to bring about recovery; and Eccles's approach, with its rough-and-ready empiri- cism, lacked the theoretical sophistication and depth of Keynes- ianism. Roosevelt's own heart belonged — and would belong for years — to fiscal orthodoxy. "I doubt if any of his reform legislation," wrote Stanley High, a close adviser in 1936, "would give him as much satisfaction as the actual balancing of the budget."

In 1935 Keynes was a potential rather than an actual influence. But circumstances were making the atmosphere increasingly propitious for his ideas — ideas which received their classic statement in February 1936, in his *General Theory of Employment, Interest and Money*. If Keynes's direct impact on Roosevelt was never great, his ideas were becoming increasingly compelling. They pointed to the alternatives to the First New Deal, and they provided an interpretation of what worked and what didn't in American economic policy. As no one knew better than Keynes, "The ideas of economists and political philosophers, both when they are right and when they are wrong, are more powerful than is commonly understood. Indeed, the world is ruled by little else." [8]

22. The Politics of the Second New Deal

THE SECOND NEW DEAL in 1935 was still in a state of only partial intellectual clarification. It was also in a state of partial political transformation. Underneath his nonparty stance of 1933–34, Roosevelt seems to have had two things in mind when he thought of the Democratic party — on the one hand, the traditional Democratic organization, "the princes and potentates of the party," as he called them, "who think they will be around long after I have gone"; and, on the other hand, a new and largely informal coalition of independent Democrats, Progressive Republicans, trade unionists, intellectuals, and independents. The traditional organization, with its classical alliance of city bosses of the North and the barons of the South, believed in little beyond states' rights and federal patronage; politics was its business — a way of life rather than a way to get things done. But the new coalition was bound together, not by habit and by spoils, but by ideas, by a sharp sense of alienation from the business culture and by a belief in positive government as the instrument of national improvement. Its members were in politics not to make office but to make policy.

The older conception of the Democratic party implied the politics of organization. The new conception implied the politics of ideology.[1]

II

The classical partnership between northern bosses and southern and western agrarians had been subjected to its first major strain soon after the First World War. That strain was not yet deep enough to threaten the idea that the partnership equaled the party; the rise of a new urban Democratic vote was only producing at this stage a demand by big-city Democrats for a larger share within the partnership — for party recognition, not just in smoke-filled rooms, but on national tickets. Yet even this limited challenge deeply disturbed the party. The result was the bruising fight in 1924 between Smith and McAdoo for the nomination, a fight which left deep wounds, as the South showed by its revolt against Smith four years later.

Smith was the great inadvertent revolutionist in Democratic politics. He precipitated the release of new energies without being able himself to follow them to their conclusion. He not only tried to reformulate the terms of the classical Democratic alliance; he also dimly perceived the possibility of strengthening the northern wing by supplementing the city machines with other voting groups — ethnic minorities, women, Negroes, even intellectuals. His instinct was penetrating; his vision, limited. He saw the coalition essentially in big-city and melting-pot terms. He never properly exploited his own following among the intellectuals, and the farmer he dismissed as "inherently a Republican" and beyond redemption. Nor did he ever have a program capable of animating a national coalition; he distrusted ideological politics and even tried to enlist big business in the Democratic party. Nor did he have a calamity like depression to induce disparate groups to submerge their differences in a common cause.

Roosevelt's first step was to heal the split within the alliance. He was admirably qualified to reunite the classical party. If Roosevelt was a New Yorker, he came from Dutchess County, not from the East Side; and he was also (and he never let the South forget it) a Georgian by adoption. As a person, he was plainly as much at home in the countryside as in the city, perhaps more at ease with farmers than with precinct committeemen or trade unionists. During the twenties he had worked zealously for reconciliation between the urban and rural wings of the party, between the followers of Smith and the followers of Bryan and McAdoo. He so identified himself with the country that during the 1932 campaign he even once complained that he could not rouse urban audiences; "Al Smith is good at that. I am not." The only states he lost that year were in the East.

Having restored the classical party, however, Roosevelt did not stop there. The classical party seemed to him still a minority party.

It could stay in power only by attaching to itself traditionally non-Democratic groups. Where would such groups come from? The mainspring of Roosevelt's own politics was the determination to rescue public policy — and the whole moral tone of politics — from what he regarded as the debasing consequences of business domination. He thereby became the natural leader of all Americans who felt themselves excluded by the business tradition — farmers, workers, intellectuals, southerners, Negroes, ethnic minorities, women.

He was even the natural leader of businessmen who felt themselves handicapped by Wall Street domination of the money market — and this included some of the ablest entrepreneurs in the country. It included representatives of the 'new money' of the South and West, like Jesse Jones, Henry J. Kaiser, and A. P. Giannini, who, without necessarily liking much of the New Deal, were in revolt against the *rentier* mentality of New York and wanted government to force down interest rates and even supply capital for local development. It included representatives of new industries, like communications and electronics; thus General Electric, the Radio Corporation of America, the National Broadcasting Company, the Columbia Broadcasting System, and International Business Machines were friendlier to the New Deal than business was generally, as were important elements in Hollywood. It included representatives of business particularly dependent on consumer demand, like Sears, Roebuck. And it included speculators like Joseph P. Kennedy, who invested in both new regions and new industries and was willing to bet on the nation's capacity to resume economic growth.

Few of these groups, from dissident businessmen to intellectuals, were represented in the traditional Democratic organization. Yet the Democratic party could not succeed until it won their allegiance with some degree of permanence. The need, as Roosevelt saw it, was for a broad national coalition, and the New Deal program offered the means of charging that coalition with meaning and vitality.[2]

III

In the 1932 campaign the politics of organization and the politics of ideology had coexisted without notable conflict. Even the party regulars acknowledged that the Democrats could win only by attracting independent voters and Republicans as well as the party faithful. As a candidate, Roosevelt struck a suitable number of familiar Democratic party chords at the same time that he made special appeals to the uncommitted and to the Progressive Republicans. His campaign organization contained independents as well as regulars. He recognized both groups in his cabinet, offering posts to Progressives and independents like Harold Ickes, Henry Wallace, Frances Perkins, and Bronson Cutting as well as to traditional Democrats like Cordell Hull, Daniel Roper, Carter Glass, and Claude Swanson.

In the next two years the politics of ideology became more important, and the politics of organization receded to the background. This happened for a simple and invincible reason. The old Democratic professionals just could not supply the ideas, the imagination, and the administrative drive which Roosevelt needed in the fight against depression. Inevitably, Roosevelt was forced to turn away from the Hulls and the Ropers, from the Newton D. Bakers and John W. Davises. "While the President has a certain number of such men around him," wrote the wisest of the Wilsonians, Colonel House, in 1933, "I believe he knows that their day is over." (House, doubtless recalling Wilson's own revolt against the Democratic professionals of his own day, added, "Men of the stamp of Hutchins and the La Follettes will hold the reins of government in the not distant future.") Roosevelt, staffing his emergency organizations, thus drew not on the organization but on the coalition: he confided the administration of industry to Hugh Johnson (independent) and Donald Richberg (Progressive), of agriculture to Henry Wallace (Progressive), of public works to Harold Ickes (Progressive), of relief to Harry Hopkins (independent), of social security to John G. Winant (Progressive), of securities regulations to Joseph P. Kennedy (new money), and James M. Landis (independent). Of the new agencies, only RFC had a chief whose face would have been recognized in the corridors of the Democratic convention of 1932.

And Roosevelt was probably glad enough to do it this way. He had won his fight for nomination against the party traditionalists, and he had long wanted to revitalize the Democratic party by infusing it with Uncle Ted's brand of Progressive Republicanism. The executive branch, under his direct control, became more and more the instrument of the politics of coalition and ideology. As this happened, the legislative branch became increasingly the stronghold of the professional politician. So the normal tension between the Congress and the President was aggravated by the rising tension between the old and the new politics.[3]

IV

But the tension was somewhat relieved by a curious series of paradoxes. Ironically, no greater obstacle stood in the way of Roosevelt's effort to build a progressive Democratic party than the resistance of the progressives in the Senate. Yet this very fractiousness of the Senate progressives forced Roosevelt to rely on the southern conservatives, thus giving him a bridge back to the professionals which somewhat mitigated his conflict with Congress.

Certainly the Senate progressives showed little disposition to accept the sort of discipline a coherent party strategy would imply. They were all individualists, and most of them were prima donnas. Even George Norris conceded of his progressive associates that they "do not take kindly to a movement . . . unless it originates with them. So often they seem to be jealous if it develops outside their own domain." This tendency had been aggravated, moreover, by their protracted absence from power and thus from responsibility. This made many of them value inner purity more than external results — a feeling conspicuously not shared by the New Dealers in the executive branch. In consequence, when liberals in political office made compromises, liberals in Congress and in editorial offices sometimes seemed excessively rapid in their willingness to pronounce adverse moral judgments. "I wonder why it is," Harold Ickes wrote to Oswald Garrison Villard, the editor of the *Nation*, in 1935,

that so-called liberals spend so much time trying to expose fellow liberals to the sneering scorn of those who delight to have their attention called to clay feet. There have been many occasions during my life when I have wished that I could go over to the political and social Philistines. I get very tired of the smug self-satisfaction, the holier-than-thou attitude, the sneering meticulousness of men and women with whose outlook on economic and social questions I often regretfully find myself in accord. It seems to be a fact that a reformer would rather hold up to ridicule another reformer because of some newly discovered fly· speck than he would to clean out Tammany Hall. Sometimes even the fly speck is imaginary.

The 1935 session strained feelings between the administrators and the purists. Even Tugwell, who might have been expected to sympathize with the congressional liberals, gave way at the end of the session to a stinging indictment of their behavior. When we turn to them for support, he wrote, "we find that they, like Baal, have gone upon a journey or are asleep." They complain incessantly that the administration is moving into the conservative camp, but do nothing to keep it from going there. "The progressive mind is stratified with dogmatism of the most appalling kind. . . . The progressive theme-song is 'I'll tell you about *my* panacea but you must not tell me about *your* panacea.'" The progressives seemed to Tugwell perennial skirmishers — free, like feudal chieftains, to change sides whenever the ideas to which each held allegiance prompted them to do so. "They are like Chinese warriors who decide battles, not by fighting, but by desertion. . . . They rush to the aid of any liberal victor, and then proceed to stab him in the back when he fails to perform the mental impossibility of subscribing unconditionally to their dozen or more conflicting principles." They would neither take presidential direction nor unite on a program of their own. "I think it can fairly be said," Tugwell observed, "that they cannot lead, they will not follow, and they refuse to cooperate."

By 1935 their behavior was becoming exceedingly irritating to an administration which prided itself amply on its own progressivism. Roosevelt began to repeat a story told him by Woodrow Wilson when similarly plagued. Conservatives, Wilson said, had the striking power of a closed fist. But progressives were like a man trying to hit with an open hand, each finger pointing in a slightly different direction; such a blow would accomplish nothing and probably break the fingers. "If we insist on choosing different roads," Roosevelt told the Young Democrats at the end of the long session in 1935, "most of us will not reach our common destination." In October he cited Wilson in a speech in California as saying that the greatest problem the head of a progressive democracy had to face was, not to fend off the reactionaries, but rather "to reconcile and unite progressive liberals themselves."

Even a radical like Tugwell had to acknowledge the practical conclusion. Given the character of the progressives, the administration had no choice, Tugwell agreed, but to regard the southern Democrats as "the only dependable body of men who can be counted on to stick by their bargains and pass legislation." It was this situation, even more than the fact that seniority gave the southerners control of key committees, which made Roosevelt turn increasingly in legislative matters to men like Joseph T. Robinson, Pat Harrison, and James F. Byrnes. Such men — at least in this period — could be relied on to support measures they did not want, where the Senate progressives could not always be relied on even to support measures they presumably favored. Such men had to remain more or less loyal to the Democratic party; while Roosevelt could never be sure that the progressives — even those he trusted most, like La Follette — might not (as he wrote House in 1935) be "flirting with the idea of a third ticket." [4]

v

Still, the Senate presented a special case. Within the executive branch, where Roosevelt's writ ran directly, the ideological and coalition conceptions of the Democratic party grew more and more powerful — a development which hastened the conflict with the professionals deferred since 1932. From the start of the Hundred Days, the two groups glared at each other across the distance separating the roads which had brought them to Washington. From time to time they met uncomfortably at party banquets. On one such occasion Vice-President Garner grimly indicated to the new boys the vast doubts with which the politicos regarded the practice of staffing a government with men who had never worked a precinct. Tugwell took away from another festive evening an impression of "thinly disguised bitterness against the influence of the younger and more liberal group. Robinson was especially nasty." He added, "These are our real enemies and will get rid of us if they can."

The New Dealers were far from blameless. They were men of ability and rectitude who too easily suspected others — espe-

cially practical politicians — of stupidity or corruption. They
exuded an atmosphere of rigidity and self-righteousness. They were
not aware how inexperienced they were in the business of government; and they did not seem interested in learning, at least
at the hands of men whose only qualification was their capacity to
get elected by the people. For many of them, Congress was an
eternal gantlet which all virtuous legislation had to run at imminent peril; and too many congressmen assumed the aspect of
automatic foes of the good and the beautiful. The New Dealers
looked forward to the growth of what Leon Henderson called in
1934 "a class of public administrators that we have known in this
country but little," and they jealously guarded their status and
prerogatives. They were not good at taking criticism. Whereas
the professional would shrug hard words off as all in a day's work,
the New Dealer, confident that whatever he was doing was for the
best, was astonished and resentful and given to questioning the
motives of his critics. "New Deal officials as a class," reported
W. M. Kiplinger, "are subjective, intellectually inbred and holier
by far than thou." For some of them the closeness to power
was heady and intoxicating. "When I hear them talk," said Rebecca West, "I can't make out whether they are drunk or sober."
("They're drunk all right," replied Agnes Meyer, who did not like
the New Dealers. "Drunk with power.") "Personally," said
Learned Hand, "the Filii Aurorae make me actively sick at my
stomach; they are so conceited, so insensitive, so arrogant."

The new politics and the old were bound to clash; and the
natural field of combat was the domain which the professionals regarded with such awe and the independents with such exasperation — patronage. In the middle, trying manfully to keep the peace,
stood Jim Farley, who, as Chairman of the National Committee,
was chief claimant and, as Postmaster-General, chief dispenser
of federal patronage. Farley's natural affinities were, of course,
with the professionals. But personal loyalty bound him to the
White House; and he was determined to keep the New Deal and
the Democratic organization from flying apart.[5]

VI

It was not an easy job, particularly after a patronage famine
of twelve Republican years. Office-seekers with hungry faces

haunted Farley's antechamber in the Post Office Department, tumbling in when the first stenographer unlocked the door in the morning; a mixed and unhappy lot, some were hopeful and suppliant, some, woeful, some, indignant. When the Postmaster-General arrived, he would pass soothingly into the tremulous crowd. He would say to one, "I'm working on your case and you'll hear from me"; to another, "See me later"; to others, "I'm sorry, but I can't do anything for you." ("There's no use in kidding them," he would explain, "so I tell them the truth.") Then those who were asked to wait later filed, one by one, into his cathedral-like office. To some he talked while perched, half leaning, half sitting, on the edge of his desk; this posture kept the visitors from sitting down themselves. Luckier ones were offered a chair and invited to pass the time of day. After a while the moment would arrive to catch up on developments around the country; and for an hour or so Farley would chat genially and efficiently with party leaders by long-distance telephone. Through it all, whether talking to a messenger boy or to the Secretary of State, Farley never seemed perfunctory, never preoccupied, never out of sorts. His bald head shone and his face broke into smiles of genuine delight as he thrust out his big hand and infallibly produced, not just the right name, but the right nickname. This large pink man, with his obviously spontaneous affability and his disarming candor, created a majestic impression of calm, solicitude, good humor, and reliability — all badly needed if he were to succeed in his mission.

For, as if the importunate mob on the office-seeking side was not enough, he confronted on the office-giving side, not sympathetic professionals who understood his problems, but high-minded amateurs inclined to recoil self-righteously from any suggestion of the spoils system. The buzz and confusion of the Hundred Days gave patronage a very low priority. In addition, Roosevelt was deliberately holding patronage to a trickle in order to guarantee congressional sympathy for his emergency legislation.

It was all a mess. Influential Democrats went directly to departments and agencies on behalf of their protégés, and uninstructed government officials turned applications down or gave jobs to the wrong Democrats or even to Republicans. As the man in the middle, Farley was the target for increasingly angry congressional complaint. Toward the end of the Hundred Days he called together representatives of each department in an effort to straighten out the situation. He began by laying down three rules: that the candidate should be qualified for the job; that he should be a Democrat; and that "a written request from the state leaders be in the [National] Committee files for every person appointed to a Federal position." Though Farley was willing to define the Democracy broadly to include "any person who worked and voted for the Roosevelt-Garner ticket," his rule that no one should be appointed from any state except at the request of the state leader seemed to give control to the regulars. This was, he insisted, "the only known method of protecting the Administration against the recognition of improper persons." To underline his point, he passed around lists of state leaders. He added that he had no one in the Post Office Department who did not qualify as a Democrat and announced that he saw no excuse for every other department's not achieving the same state of beatitude. On adjournment, he hoped he had set up a system by which all federal jobs would go to Democrats under the central clearance of the National Committee.[6]

VII

Such a system remained the National Chairman's dream. But it worked only intermittently. In NRA, Johnson and Richberg simply ignored it. "I can remember," Richberg later wrote, "the somewhat pathetic appeals of Jim Farley for notification at least of our intention to appoint someone so that he might clear it with the appropriate politician who would like to get the credit even for an appointment to which he was personally opposed." Farley's attempt to discuss patronage with Arthur E. Morgan of TVA ended in a fight, and they never spoke again.

After a time, though, the Postmaster-General, through affability and persistence, began to achieve a *modus vivendi* with most of the New Dealers. To Henry Morgenthau he explained that all he cared about were clerical and administrative jobs, and even here, "Just give me three chances to fill each job. If none of my people work out, then you fill the job as you please." Morgenthau later wrote, "I cannot remember a single instance that Farley ever asked me to do anything that was not honorable" — a particularly impressive testimonial in view of the Treasury's control over tax cases. The suspicious Rex Tugwell noted in his diary of Farley, "He is frank and open as well as resourceful. It is impossible not to like him." A State Department official, J. Pierrepont Moffat, wrote in *his* diary that Farley had "reduced the political patronage pressure on the [Foreign] Service and the State Department to a minimum." Frances Perkins reported him "extremely helpful to me in all kinds of things, such as getting senatorial endorsements for appointments that I wanted to make when the person didn't have any special political background." Even Harold Ickes, with all his contempt for machine politicians, freely acknowledged Farley's qualities — "I have always found him very considerate. He has never shown any disposition to press for the appointment of anyone not fit"; and "Farley has never in the slightest degree sought to influence my action as Public Works Administrator with respect to any project or any contract. His record is absolutely clean."

Though Farley improved his relations with the New Dealers, he still could not produce jobs in enough volume to satisfy the politicians. Morgenthau expressed a typical New Deal viewpoint when he noted in his diary, "I made up my mind that I am not going to aid the politicians, and I am going to tell them politely, but firmly, that I cannot accept their candidates." From faithful party Democrats over the country, letters poured in complaining that the local CWA office, or NRA board, or Farm Credit office, or Census Bureau, was in Republican hands. In Nebraska, for example, Arthur Mullen claimed that 60 per cent of the federal officeholders credited to his state were not Democrats at all. And on Capitol Hill, where senators and congressmen were hounded beyond endurance by constituents eager for jobs, resentment was concentrated and intense. As reported by George Creel, an intimate of old-line Democrats in Congress, the New Dealers were making legislators feel that interest in patronage practically signified moral turpitude. Harry Hopkins, said Creel, would callously refer requests to his personnel officer. Frances Perkins would keep senators waiting in her anteroom. Hugh Johnson would roar with rage. Tugwell's cold, forbidding glare made many a senator feel that he was lucky to be out on bail. Morgenthau caused Democratic politicians even more agony. And at the mere sight of a congressman Ickes "screamed for Glavis and the rest of his sleuths and the poor devils were trailed for weeks to see if some connection could not be established between them and Al Capone."

Creel exaggerated, but only a little. He was certainly correct in drawing a picture of congressional Democrats seething with indignation over the contempt displayed by these amateurs in government toward what was, after all, the perfectly normal behavior of professional politicians. If only, Farley thought, the New Dealers would co-operate! "Frankly, Mr. President," Farley wrote Roosevelt in 1935, "some of our fellows make the damnedest moves and it takes hours of explaining to rectify the wrongs which have been done, whereas, if we knew what they have in mind or if they would tip us off as to what they want to do, it would be a whole lot easier." The Postmaster-General's shoulders were broad, and he tried to handle his congressional clients himself as long as he could. When the heat became too great, he had no recourse except to call in the President.

As for Roosevelt, he had regarded political organizations with mistrust since the days of Blue-eyed Billy Sheehan, and he was determined to keep scandal out of his New Deal. Early in 1934 he shocked the professionals by declaring that Democratic National Committeemen should not practice before government departments — an announcement which drove several respected Democratic veterans from the National Committee. "Within a month," Frank Kent, the conservative columnist, wrote grudgingly in February 1934, "the Administration has itself, publicly revealed and denounced, in six separate directions, instances of graft, collusion, waste, corruption or irregularities." Similarly, the President supported — and sometimes spurred on — subordinates like Hopkins, Ickes, and Morgenthau who were zealous to keep politics out of federal activities. For a time in 1934, under pressure from Ickes, Roosevelt even toyed with the idea of picking a fight with the Democratic Kelly-Nash machine in Chicago, till Farley dissuaded him. Morgenthau moved cheerfully against political bosses of whatever party; both the Republican boss of Atlantic City, Enoch L. "Nucky" Johnson, and the Democratic boss of Kansas City, Thomas J. Pendergast, were sent to prison as a result of Treasury action.

On the other hand, Roosevelt was quite enough of a professional himself to feel that there was a legitimate sense of grievance on the Hill. He knew, in addition, that the success of his legislative program depended on keeping congressmen happy. In January 1934 a delegation of House Democrats waited on the President to protest snubs and run-arounds in the executive branch. Roosevelt listened patiently, called them by their first names, and invited them to drop in whenever they felt like it. They went away unsatisfied but bemused. Farley, who was present, recorded the meeting as a "social success." Roosevelt later pleaded with his cabinet to show a little more consideration for congressional sensitivities. ("I have tried to establish this as a principle in this Department," said Ickes, "although I suppose that all of us become overstrained at times and are brusque and lacking in courtesy.")

A year later another congressional deputation told Roosevelt that the executive branch still pushed them around and gave jobs to their political enemies. This time the President exploded at the next meeting of the National Emergency Council. "I would be awfully hot," he said, "if I were a member of Congress and had to put up with some of the things these Congressmen have had to put up with. I would be inclined to get up on the floor of Congress and say some pretty nasty things about the heads of Departments and Agencies." He told of one congressman who went to an agency with a problem and heard a voice from an inner office say, "To hell with it! I am too busy to see any Congressman!" "I was so gosh darn mad," Roosevelt said, "that I almost fired him out of hand!" Most congressmen, the President continued, were fairly reasonable about executive appointments. "They are not asking that these people work *for* the Congressmen, but they are asking that they be prevented from working *against* them, either for other Democrats or for Republicans, and they are entitled to that. . . . Nobody wants to put all these agencies into administration politics, but we must prevent them from being antiadministration. If they are not in sympathy with what we are doing, we do not need to use them." [7]

VIII

But Roosevelt's efforts to propitiate the organization Democrats were, on the whole, spasmodic and tactical. Both his own inclinations and the logic of the New Deal argued for the strategy of a broad liberal coalition based on ideological considerations. Indeed, the support he had received from Progressive Republicans in 1932 had already brought such a coalition into rudimentary existence. Confronted in several states with the choice between repaying his campaign debts or building up the regular Democratic organization against pro-Roosevelt Republicans, Roosevelt instructed Farley in the main to stick with the Progressives. Thus Hiram Johnson and Bob La Follette were given their share of federal patronage; and Bronson Cutting's fall from administration grace in 1934 was a product of things other than his Progressivism.

To many old-line Democrats, this policy verged on treason. "I am fundamentally opposed to any kind of coalition with the so-called 'Progressives,'" said Arthur Mullen. "Every so-called Progressive is opposed to the fundamental principles of the Democratic Party." But Mullen, who had labored so valiantly for Roosevelt in the 1932 convention, was a figure of the past. The defection of conservative Democrats from the New Deal in the course of 1934 was giving additional strength to the idea of a liberal coalition. As Harold Ickes said when told of the formation of the American Liberty League, "That's fine! I've been hoping ever since 1912 that we'd have political parties divided on real issues. . . . I'd like to see all the progressives together and all the conservatives together. Then you'd always be facing your enemy and not wondering what was happening behind your back." Henry Wallace added, "We badly need a new alignment: conservatives versus liberals. . . . The faster the showdown comes and the more definite the division between the Old Dealers and the New Dealers of both present parties, the better."

The congressional elections in November 1934 appeared to vindicate the coalition concept. A flood of Democratic votes gushing from traditionally non-Democratic sources washed the traditional Democratic party into the discard. In the new Congress, the Democratic party now stood forward as predominantly a northern and, to a new degree, an urban party. Of 69 Democratic senators, the South had but 24; of 322 representatives, the South had 108. And the turn toward the political left in 1935 accelerated the process of northernization. Though certain financial measures like the Holding Company Act received ardent southern support, the WPA, the Social Security Act, the Wagner Act, and the new, free-swinging antibusiness tone were laying the base for a new Democratic party in the cities of the North.

By 1935, in the desire to consolidate the new sources of Democratic support, Roosevelt was preparing to move boldly beyond the traditional party base. The South would now be just one element in a broad national coalition; the city machines, just another. Most of the other elements — labor, the newer immigrants, Negroes, women, intellectuals — were particularly accessible in great cities of the North, increasingly unresponsive to old-school bosses and machines, and increasingly insistent on direct representation in the new politics.

Consequently, the urban masses became the central preoccupation of the Second New Deal; and this fact profoundly affected both its politics and its policies. The means of forging the coalition were, not just patronage and handouts in the traditional manner, but the personality of Roosevelt and the social and ideological programs of the New Deal. So Roosevelt began to reshape the Democratic party in terms of the New Deal coalition, seeking to rally, not just the classical Democratic groups through the classical party methods, but forgotten men and women everywhere through new ideas and policies.[8]

23. The Roosevelt Coalition

ONE KEYSTONE of the emerging Democratic coalition was labor. The drift of labor into the Democratic party had been going on for some time — at least since Wilson's presidency. But it had been a vague and gradual matter. In the twenties, except for the quickly regretted adventure with La Follette, union leaders generally avoided politics. Some, like John L. Lewis, were unashamed Republicans. The depression changed all that. Hoover's inaction in face of depression killed the Republican party among wage-earners for a generation. And what had been in 1932 an anti-Republican vote was becoming by 1934 a pro-Democratic — or, at least, pro-Roosevelt — vote. Many workers had felt outside looking in during the twenties; nearly all felt that way during the depression. Now Roosevelt conveyed to them a sense of acute personal concern and sympathy. No President had ever seemed to care about them before. As a millworker in North Carolina put it, "I do think that Roosevelt is the biggest-hearted man we ever had in the White House. . . . It's the first time in my ricollection that a president ever got up and said, 'I'm interested in and aim to do somethin' for the workin' man.' " Another stated it more succinctly: "Mr. Roosevelt is the only man we ever had in the White House who would understand that my boss is a son-of-a-bitch."

The legislation of 1935 completed the identification of the cause of labor with the New Deal. The Social Security Act and the WPA clinched the loyalty of the ordinary worker; the Wagner Act, the loyalty of the trade unionists. And the condemnation of NRA pushed organized labor beyond the point of no return in national politics. Leon Henderson, wandering into Sidney Hillman's office at the National Industrial Recovery Board after the Schechter decision, found Hillman hastily throwing papers into a suitcase. "We're all through here," Hillman said, "I'm packing my bags and taking the next train to New York. I'm going to raise a war chest of a million dollars through my union to see to it that we hold onto the gains labor has won." The drive toward political action was a motive in — and an important result of — the rise of the CIO. By the end of 1935, the New Deal had pretty well annexed an entire political constituency. And, as workers moved steadily to join unions, it was a constituency growing fast in numbers and power.[1]

II

Elements in the emerging coalition overlapped, of course; many of the forgotten men felt themselves forgotten not only as workers or as poor people but as members of racial minorities. The New Deal took special care to cultivate ethnic groups. Thus Roosevelt named the first Italo-American and the first Negroes ever appointed to the federal bench. Catholics and Jews were recognized as never before. Of the 214 federal judges appointed by Harding, Coolidge and Hoover, according to the computations of Samuel Lubell, only 8 were Catholics and 8 Jews. Of the 196 judicial appointments made by Roosevelt, 51 were Catholics and 8 Jews. Roosevelt cared deeply about speeding the assimilation of minorities into all parts of national life. "If I could do anything I wanted for twenty-four hours," he once said, "the thing I would want most to do would be to complete the melting of the melting-pot." "Remember, remember always," he told the Daughters of the American Revolution, "that all of us, and you and I especially, are descended from immigrants and revolutionists."

The appeal to the Negroes represented the most dramatic and risky innovation in the New Deal design. After all, the Democratic party had shown a capacity to absorb whites of foreign stock since the days of Jefferson. But the inclusion of Negroes struck vitally at the conception of a party which had also, since the days of Jefferson, respected the peculiar claims of the white South. Moreover, it challenged a tradition in America politics almost as sacred as the one which kept the South voting Democratic

— the tradition that the Negroes should vote Republican. Nothing in the politics of the New Deal was more daring then the project of combining in the same party the descendants of the slaveholders and the descendants of the slaves.[2]

III

By the turn of the century, when the last Negro congressman from the South retired from the House of Representatives, the Negro seemed extinct in national politics. In the South he was effectively excluded from political life. In the North, he was a negligible minority, tamely voted by the local Republican machine. Then the First World War provoked a massive change in the life of the Negro. He began to go north, partly because of increasing troubles in southern agriculture, but mostly because of expanding job opportunities in northern cities. The industrial boom of the twenties furthered the great migration. By 1930, almost two million Negroes had moved out of the realm of political impotence into that of political potentiality. Between 1910 and 1930 the Negro population of Detroit, for example, increased nearly twentyfold; that of Chicago, nearly sixfold; of New York, well over threefold; of Philadelphia, nearly threefold.

The result was a dazzling new opportunity for urban politicians. Some Republicans, like William Hale Thompson of Chicago, worked hard to keep the Negroes faithful to the Grand Old Party. But Republicans too often assumed Negro devotion as unalterable, just at the time that the Democrats, the urban politicians par excellence, began to awaken to the existence of this new voting group. The first Democratic boss to woo and win the Negro electorate was Tom Pendergast of Kansas City. Though Al Smith in his personal brushes with James Weldon Johnson and Walter White of the National Association for the Advancement of Colored People displayed reserve about Negroes and cynicism about their political motives, he was ready, as the specialist in urban coalitions, to consider a national Democratic appeal to colored people.

In 1928 he told White, "I know Negroes distrust the Democratic Party, and I can't blame them. But I want to show that the old Democratic Party, ruled entirely by the South, is on its way out, and that we Northern Democrats have a totally different approach to the Negro." At his request, White drafted a statement making it clear that Smith, if elected, would be president of all the people, white and colored. As the campaign developed, however, Joe Robinson, the vice-presidential candidate, and other southern Democrats, already sufficiently fearful about the South and Smith, succeeded in killing the statement. Indeed, during the campaign anti-Smith forces inundated the South with photographs of the Negro Civil Service Commissioner of New York City dictating to his white secretary — a tableau presented as ominous indication of what northern Democrats planned for the country.

Nonetheless, the political urgencies behind Smith's interest in the Negro vote remained ceaselessly at work. Thus the 1928 election gave Northern Negroes their first representative in the House in Oscar De Priest of Chicago, a Republican. Tammany Hall began to make inroads in Harlem. Hoover himself, however, failed to read these lessons. Not only had he backed lily-white against black-and-tan (*i.e.* mixed) delegations from southern states in the 1928 Republican convention; not only had he failed to rebuke racist attacks on Smith; but his success in splitting the solid South evidently persuaded him and other Republican strategists that if he continued to behave with circumspection, he might permanently attach a large number of southern whites to the Republican party. So he disregarded the portent of Oscar De Priest and proceeded to act in a way which soon led Walter White to dub him "the man in the lily-White House."

For all his Quaker background, Hoover showed little personal sympathy for Negroes. The White House shortly faced what the Hoovers apparently regarded as an insoluble social problem. Mrs. Hoover wanted to invite the wives of members of Congress to a series of teas; but what was to be done about Mrs. De Priest? The White House social secretary insisted that she must be invited; others were doubtful; and four parties, covering nearly all the congressional ladies, went by while Mrs. De Priest remained under prayerful consideration. "The official angle was referred to the Executive Offices," reported the White House usher, "one of the President's secretaries pondering over it for days and days." Finally Mrs. Hoover decided to ask Mrs. De Priest to a special tea at which guests could be individually warned in advance about the ordeal to which they were about to be subjected. When the day arrived, Mrs. De Priest seemed to the White House usher the most composed person there. "In a short while Mrs. Hoover retired from the room, and Mrs. De Priest in perfect form made her exit, no doubt to the relief of all and yet leaving behind a feeling of admiration at the way she conducted herself."

For the rest, Hoover ignored the Negroes. He made, said W. E. B. Du Bois, "fewer first-class appointments of Negroes to office than any President since Andrew Johnson." Negroes were not admitted to government cafeterias in the federal buildings. When the administration sent the Gold Star mothers to visit their sons' graves in France, Negro mothers went on separate ships with inferior accommodations. When a mixed delegation called on Vice-President Charles Curtis, the Vice-President refused to shake the hands of the Negro. The lynching of fifty-seven Negroes during his term provoked no expression of presidential disapproval. And Hoover's nomination to the Supreme Court in 1930 of Judge John J. Parker of North Carolina, who had been quoted ten years earlier as saying that the participation of the Negro in politics was "a source of evil and danger," drove Negro leaders into open opposition. The NAACP played an important role in preventing Parker's confirmation.[3]

IV

In March 1931 a new event occurred to heighten the determination of Negroes to fight for their rights. In the swirl of the depression, wandering boys, some white, some Negro, were caught together on a slow freight train out of Chattanooga into Alabama. As the train jolted along, the two groups began to pick at each other. "Nigger bastard, this is a white man's train. You better get off. All you black bastards get off!" Soon, with quiet, repressed bitterness, they began to fight. Some of the white boys, thrown off the train at Stevenson, Alabama, complained to the station master, who obligingly called ahead to the next stop. When the train chugged into Paint Rock, a posse cleared the freight cars and took the Negroes to the county seat at Scottsboro. They also found somewhere in one of the cars two girl hobos, who promptly claimed to have been raped by the Negroes. The colored boys denied ever having touched them. But Scottsboro justice knew better. In two weeks the Negro boys, whose average age was about sixteen, were tried, convicted, and sentenced to death.

Somehow the incident did not stop there. Negro organizations rallied behind the Scottsboro boys. Then the Communists moved in and, with cold disregard for the boys themselves, exploited the case as a means of raising money for the party and of dramatizing their portrait of capitalist society. ("Had it not been for their senseless interference," W. E. B. Du Bois, who was no enemy of Communists, wrote in 1940, "these poor victims of Southern injustice would today be free.") The Alabama Supreme Court affirmed the conviction; but late in 1932 the United States Supreme Court threw the case out because the boys had not had proper legal representation. At a new trial in 1933, one of the girls recanted her testimony. By now Samuel Leibowitz had come down from New York to take over the defense. The prosecutor said ominously that "no Alabama jury would listen to witnesses bought with Jew money in New York." After a notably fair charge from the judge, the jurors found the boys guilty again. "If you ever saw those creatures," Leibowitz later said, "those bigots, whose mouths are slits in their faces, whose eyes pop out at you like frogs, whose chins drip tobacco juice, bewhiskered and filthy, you would not ask how they could do it." The judge, outraged at the result, ordered a new trial and thereby insured his own political death at the next election. And the next trial produced the same result.

The Scottsboro case had profound emotional impact on the Negro community. It made white indifference to wrongs perpetrated against Negroes more intolerable than ever. It strengthened Negro determination to strike out on their own. It increased Negro militancy and Negro despair.[4]

v

By 1932 Negro leadership had fairly well soured on Republican indifference. In addition, since the Negroes were at the bottom of America's economic structure, Hoover's resistance to federal relief hurt them more than any other group. The result was a new impulse toward political action.

For many years, for example, James Weldon Johnson, secretary of the NAACP and the most eminent Negro literary figure, had been a devoted Republican. But as early as 1928 Johnson, increasingly disturbed over Republican passivity, declined a Republican nomination for Congress in New York City. Now he openly counseled political independence. "An uprising of Negro voters against Mr. Hoover and his party," said Bishop R. C. Ransom of the African Methodist Episcopal Church in the autumn of 1932, "would free our spirits equally as much as Mr. Lincoln's Proclamation freed our bodies." "For the Negro people of this country," said the *St. Louis Argus*, "Mr. Hoover is a dangerous man. In his palmiest days Tillman was a better friend to the colored brother than is President Hoover."

One day in Pittsburgh her Negro manicurist told Emma Guffey Miller, the Democratic National Committeewoman, that "Mr. Vann" would like to see her brother Joseph F. Guffey. This was Robert L. Vann, publisher of the influential *Pittsburgh Courier*, the largest Negro paper in the state. When Vann and Guffey met, Vann said that the Democrats had a chance of winning a large share of the 280,000 Negro votes in Pennsylvania. Guffey was quick to press the opportunity. "It was hard work," he later said, "but I finally persuaded Jim Farley and Louis McHenry Howe to establish the first really effective Negro division a Democratic campaign committee ever had." Vann was put in charge. "My friends, go home and turn Lincoln's picture to the wall," Vann told Negro voters. "That debt has been paid in full."

The swing away from Hoover was still essentially a defection from the top. Negro voters on the whole stuck with the Republicans in 1932. But the opinion-makers had abandoned the Republicans, and it might only be a matter of time before opinion followed their example.[5]

VI

The new President's history up to 1933 was of a man fairly conventional in his racial attitudes. Back in 1911 he could pencil on the margin of a speech text a crisp reminder: "story of nigger." As Assistant Secretary of the Navy, he served with no visible discomfort under Woodrow Wilson and Josephus Daniels — two liberal southerners who rapidly dropped their liberalism when it came to the race question. In the middle twenties he made

Georgia his "second home" with no thought to its peculiar folk-ways.[6] As late as 1929, he wired the chairman of the Democratic State Committee in Virginia indignantly denying a Republican charge that he had entertained a large number of Negroes at a public luncheon. As Governor of New York, he showed no special concern for Negroes either in appointments or in legislation. In seeking the nomination in 1932, he courted southern support; and he took as running mate a man whom Negroes regarded as hopeless (unjustly: Garner, who came from west Texas, was relatively fair-minded on the race issue).

Still, Roosevelt had no more a closed mind on this than on other subjects. Both his natural openness of heart and his early training in Christian responsibility inclined him, when he thought of it, to sympathy for Negro aspirations. As far back as his student days, he had written an essay urging southern colleges to follow the Harvard example and admit Negroes. During the Wilson administration he had harassed the Surgeon General to get a commission for a Negro doctor. As the Negro vote increased, his astute political sense doubtless made him think of these things more often. If a decent policy toward the Negro was not in his own first order of priorities, he was responsive enough to the idea when anyone else proposed it. Negro leaders felt in his general stance a greater accessibility to Negro issues. "A liberal in politics and in economics," as *Opportunity,* the organ of the Urban League, said shortly after the election, "might well be expected to be a liberal in race relations and to adopt the viewpoint of the more advanced thinkers on the problems of race adjustment. As he assumes his duties, he will carry the hopes of millions of Negroes who see in him an exponent of the finest ideals of this great Democracy."

For a time, however, the Negro had little more than these hopes to live on. Under AAA, Negro tenant farmers and share-croppers were the first to be thrown off farms as a consequence of the crop-reduction policy. Under NRA, Negroes either had to accept racial differentials in wages or run the risk of displacement by unemployed white men; in the case of jobs still reserved for Negroes, a complicated system of exemptions minimized the application of the codes; and local control of compliance machinery made it almost impossible for the Negro to seek effective redress. TVA, for all its high ideals, adopted surrounding southern folkways in order not to risk its central program by fighting marginal battles. It hired Negroes as unskilled labor but would not admit them to the training programs; in the model government town of Norris, Tennessee, as one Negro writer bitterly commented, the Negro could not "even live on the outskirts of town in his customary hovel." Subsistence homesteads were no better: more than two hundred Negroes applied for admission to Arthurdale, West Virginia, to be told by the manager that the project was open only to "native white stock." The Federal Housing Administration sponsored restrictive covenants in its building and rental programs. "The Attorney General," said Walter White with scorn of the Department of Justice, "continues his offensive against crime — except crimes involving the deprivation of life and liberty to Negroes." Even the administration's support of independent labor organization meant little to Negroes who, up to this time, had been largely rejected by organized labor and found their main haven in company unions (not out of managerial idealism, but because Negroes offered a convenient supply of strikebreakers).[7]

VII

There was nothing new about such a record of discrimination. What was new was that anyone cared about it. In the summer of 1933 Edwin R. Embree of the Julius Rosenwald Fund suggested to Roosevelt that someone in government be responsible for seeing that Negroes got fair treatment. Roosevelt approved the idea, adding that this person should be attached to a department; he suggested Harold Ickes as the cabinet member most likely to be sympathetic. When Embree approached Ickes, Ickes said he would be glad to have such a person on his staff but had no money for it. The Rosenwald Fund then offered to pay the salary. Dr. Clark Foreman, a forceful young Georgian who had been director of studies for the Fund, was now appointed to the Department of the Interior.

Ickes made clear to Foreman that, though located in Interior, he was expected to function in the government generally. Foreman brought in Dr. Robert C. Weaver, a Harvard Ph.D. in economics, as his assistant, as well as a Negro secretary. Shortly after, Dan

Roper, though a South Carolinian, appointed E. K. Jones of the Urban League as an adviser on Negro affairs in Commerce. Foreman and Jones began to work together to stimulate Negro appointments in other departments. In addition, they tried to protect the interest of the Negro in the operations of the emergency agencies.

By February 1934 Foreman succeeded in setting up an interdepartmental committee to consider the problems created for Negroes by NRA minimum wages and by AAA crop-reduction policies. The NRA representative frankly admitted to the committee that NRA's effect in "decreasing the spread between the wages of white and colored labor has been nullified to an undetermined extent by discriminations against Negroes." AAA added, "It may be said that the smaller the administrative unit and the greater the degree of local control, the worse the conditions to which Negroes are subjected." But neither NRA nor AAA could figure out any solution which would safeguard the Negro within the program without threatening the program's essential objectives. The interdepartmental committee reached the reluctant conclusion that it had no choice but to expect displacement of Negroes and to try and salvage them by relief programs.

This situation, as well as the exhaustion of savings, accounted for the steady increase of the number of Negroes on relief — from about 18 per cent of the Negro population in October 1933 to almost 30 per cent in January 1935. The various Hopkins organizations rose nobly to the challenge, though their efforts provoked angry southern resentment. As Lorena Hickok reported from Georgia early in 1934, "For these people to be getting $12 a week — at least twice as much as common labor has ever been paid down there before — is an awfully bitter pill for Savannah people to swallow. . . . The Federal Reemployment director observed yesterday: 'Any Nigger who gets over $8 a week is a spoiled Nigger, that's all.' "

Still, Hopkins and his people persisted in their efforts to end racial discrimination in relief. As *Crisis*, the NAACP journal, conceded in 1936, "Even with their failures, they have made great gains for the race in areas which heretofore have set their faces steadfastly against decent relief for Negroes." Other New Deal agencies followed this example. CCC took in 200,000 Negroes —

30,000 of these, mostly in New England and the West, in integrated camps. One Negro described his CCC life in *Crisis:* "As a job and an experience, for a man who has no work, I can heartily recommend it." PWA built houses, schools, and hospitals for Negroes. It granted $3 million to Howard University and another $7.5 million to Negro schools and colleges in the South. The National Youth Administration set up an Office of Minority Affairs with a leading Negro educator, Mary McLeod Bethune, as director, and helped thousands of Negro students. Southern Negroes, denied the right to vote for political office, could vote in NLRB elections and AAA referenda. Over a million Negroes took part in the government's emergency education program, where 300,000 learned to read and write.[8]

VIII

Quite as important as what the administration did was how it felt. The fact that it felt about the Negro at all was a startling novelty. And, Roosevelt, in particular, was a figure to stir the imagination. His physical handicap, John Hope Franklin has suggested, was a special inspiration for Negroes: "He had overcome his; perhaps some day, they could overcome theirs." Privately Roosevelt for a time still kept the problem at arm's length. "I am told," he wrote a southern correspondent in 1933, "that many of the colored brethren of South Carolina are very certain that NRA means Negro Relief Association. They are at least partly right!" The tone suggested a certain detachment. But later, when Mrs. Bethune, as a member of the NYA advisory committee, told Roosevelt how much the agency meant to Negro young people — "We are bringing life and spirit to these many thousands who for so long have been in darkness" — she thought she saw, at the end of her discourse, tears streaming down the President's cheeks. If tears seem unlikely, Roosevelt may well have been moved enough by her recital to justify this impression in recollection.

Roosevelt always remained on the cautious side. Mrs. Bethune reports that, when she proposed drastic steps to him, he usually demurred, saying that a New Reconstruction in the South would have to keep pace with democratic progress on a national scale. "Mrs. Bethune, if we do that now, we'll hurt our program over there. We must do this thing stride by stride, but leaving no stone unturned." Yet he communicated a genuine sense of commitment in the midst of his recognition of complexity. "People like you and me are fighting and must continue to fight for the day when a man will be regarded as a man regardless of his race or faith or country," he once said with great earnestness to Mrs. Bethune. "That day will come, but we must pass through perilous times before we realize it."

Eleanor Roosevelt, operating as the extension of the generous side of the President's personality, was openly and vigorously identified with the cause of the Negro. Although some of the White House staff, notably Steve Early, regarded this enthusiasm with dismay, Louis Howe, always alert to new sources of political backing, wrote letters in support of Clark Foreman's eventually successful campaign to use Negroes as advisers and specialists in CCC camps (getting a reply, for example, from Douglas MacArthur that, so far as the CCC educational program was concerned, "The position taken by the Army representatives on this committee on every occasion is that there should be no discrimination on account of race, religion, or color").

In the cabinet Harold Ickes, who had once served as president of the Chicago chapter of the NAACP, now functioned as an informal Secretary of Negro Relations. He quickly ended segregation in Interior, employed Negro architects and engineers in PWA, brought in a brilliant young Negro lawyer, William H. Hastie, as assistant solicitor of the Department, and backed him for appointment as federal judge in the Virgin Islands. When Foreman left his post as adviser on Negro problems, Ickes replaced him by his Negro aide, Robert C. Weaver. In the next years Weaver became the center of a group of Negroes scattered through the administration, known — reviving a term in disuse since the administration of Theodore Roosevelt — as the "Black Cabinet." In 1936 Ickes, addressing the annual convention of the NAACP, could begin by saying, "I feel at home here" — an unprecedented declaration from a member of a Democratic administration. Roosevelt, Ickes continued, had changed the old attitude of laissez faire in race relations. "Under our new conception of democracy, the Negro will be given the chance to which he is entitled. . . . The greatest advance since the Civil War toward assuring the Negro that degree of justice to which he is entitled and that equality of opportunity under the law which is implicit in his American citizenship, has been made since Franklin D. Roosevelt was sworn in as President." Perhaps the testimony delivered later that year by Mary McLeod Bethune was even more impressive, coming as it did from a Negro. "Never before in the history of America," Mrs. Bethune said, "has Negro youth been offered such opportunities." [9]

IX

Word got round among Negroes, and intelligent Democratic politicians were quick to exploit the new possibilities. After the 1932 election, Joe Guffey got the administration to appoint Robert L. Vann assistant to the Attorney-General. This was only the beginning of the federal recognition which descended on Pennsylvania Negroes in the next two years. Democratic professionals watched the Guffey experiment with some skepticism, but not without interest. Then, in 1934, in an upset, Republican Pennsylvania sent Guffey to the Senate and George Earle, another Democrat to Harrisburg. It was guessed that about 170,000 Negroes had voted for the Democratic ticket. There were other omens in 1934. In Louisville, the traditionally Republican Negro vote shifted and elected a Democratic mayor and congressman. In Chicago, Oscar De Priest fell before a Democratic Negro, Arthur W. Mitchell, who himself had been a Republican a few years back. Impressed, the Democratic National Committee quietly began to cultivate Negro leaders.

In national politics, one issue mattered more to Negroes than any other. This was federal legislation against lynching — an objective long sought by the NAACP. As far back as 1922 an antilynching bill had come to vote in the Senate only to be defeated by a southern filibuster. The issue then lay dormant through the years of Republican supremacy; lynching itself declined after the big year of 1926. With depression, the art revived — over 60 Negroes were hanged or shot or burned by mobs between 1930 and 1934. In 1933, after the Republican Governor of California defended a lynching (in this case, of two white men) as "the best lesson California has ever given the country," Roosevelt spoke sharply against "that vile form of collective murder. . . . We do not excuse those in high places or in low who condone lynch law." In his annual message in January 1934, he denounced lynching, kidnaping, and other crimes, adding that "these violations of law call on the strong arm of Government for their immediate suppression." Two Democrats, Wagner of New York and Costigan of Colorado, promptly introduced a federal antilynching bill. It had been drafted by the NAACP and bore the endorsement of nearly a dozen northern governors.

The bill got nowhere in 1934, a year in which Negroes were lynched at a rate of better than one a month. Louis Howe put it in his files with a typewritten note: "Not favored at this time — may create hostility to other crime bills." In 1935 Wagner and Costigan reintroduced their bill. (Among those who now testified for it was H. L. Mencken: "No government pretending to be civilized can go on condoning such atrocities. Either it must make every possible effort to put them down or it must suffer the scorn and contempt of Christendom.") Late in April 1935 the Wagner-Costigan bill, with a favorable report from the Judiciary Committee reached the floor. Southern senators quickly deployed for their traditional response.

Except for a few demagogic interpolations about southern womanhood by Cotton Ed Smith of South Carolina, the filibuster was on a relatively high level. Josiah Bailey of North Carolina condemned the Wagner-Costigan proposal as a force bill and praised states' rights ("that's a cause worth dying for"). Hugo Black of Alabama said it was an antilabor bill ("in the name of antilynching, to crucify the hopes and the aspirations of the millions of workers of the country is beyond my conception") and would drive a wedge between the races ("is it fair to us at this time, when we are working in peace and harmony the one with the other, to do something which will bring about again the spread of the flame of race antagonism, and instill prejudices which, thank God! have been stifled in the hearts of most of the people of Alabama and the other States of the South?"). James F. Byrnes denounced the bill as unconstitutional.

As the filibuster droned on into May, the administration grew increasingly concerned about the rest of its legislative program. On a lovely spring Sunday, Eleanor Roosevelt brought Walter White to the White House. "I did not choose the tools with which

I must work," Roosevelt told White. "But I've got to get legislation passed by Congress to save America. The Southerners by reason of the seniority rule in Congress are chairmen or occupy strategic places on most of the Senate and House committees. If I come out for the antilynching bill now, they will block every bill I ask Congress to pass to keep America from collapsing. I just can't take that risk."

Nonetheless Roosevelt, while not sure himself about the constitutionality of the measure, induced Joe Robinson to permit consideration of the motion to bring up the bill. "I am absolutely for the objective," the President told his press conference, "but am not clear in my own mind as to whether that is absolutely the right way to attain the objective. However, I told them to go ahead and try to get a vote on it." Other liberals shared Roosevelt's constitutional doubts. George Norris, for example, opposed the bill; and toward the end of the filibuster William E. Borah delivered a powerful attack on it. It was Borah's speech which tipped the balance; the Senate now voted to adjourn, after having refused to do so on earlier occasions, and Costigan's original motion to bring up the bill was thereby vacated. . . . In that year, Negroes were lynched in America at a rate of a little better than one every three weeks.

Crisis, while deploring "the Great Silence of the Man in the White House," called the 1935 fight "the best of the many crusades against lynching." No one could miss the fact that the fight was initiated and largely conducted by northern Democrats. And Roosevelt's painful dilemma was understood, if not excused, in Negro circles. The antilynching fight further dramatized the northern Democrats as the only men to appear in national politics for years prepared to work and struggle for Negro rights. It provided new incentives for the Negro to sign up with the New Deal coalition.[10]

X

If a somewhat reluctant Al Smith had pioneered the way for Negroes in politics, he had done the same — and with the same reluctance — for women. Like many Irish politicians, Smith had personal doubts. He felt that a woman had no business, for example, as governor of a state — a belief confirmed for him when Governor Nellie Tayloe Ross proved not to have every vital statistic of Wyoming at her fingertips (as Smith did of New York). Still, after 1920, a woman's vote was as good as anyone else's; and, as in the case of Negroes, private reservations could be overcome by prospective rewards. So the New York organization, with Belle Moskowitz at Smith's side and Caroline O'Day, Eleanor Roosevelt, and Elinor Morgenthau working in the Democratic State Committee, began in the course of the twenties to make the grudging acknowledgment that women existed.

This acknowledgment was not widely shared in the party. In 1924 Eleanor Roosevelt, charged with presenting to the resolutions committee a series of platform planks of special interest to her sex, discovered where women stood at national conventions: "they stood outside the door of all important meetings and waited." But with Smith's nomination in 1928, the Democratic ladies enlarged their bridgehead. Belle Moskowitz and Eleanor Roosevelt ran a busy women's division at national headquarters. Women's activities in the Middle West were in the charge of Mary W. Dewson, the shrewd and engaging social worker who had been for some years secretary of the Consumers' League. Molly Dewson displayed such particular talents that Roosevelt asked her to direct women's activities in his gubernatorial campaign of 1930, and again to organize support for him before the 1932 convention. "I want to send you a line of appreciation," he wrote Miss Dewson after the 1932 election. ". . . Let's hope we can build up a women's organization which will be lasting and highly effective."

Such was certainly Molly Dewson's ambition. This tall, vigorous social worker, now almost sixty, with her low-heeled shoes and her sensible clothes, fitted oddly well into the world of politicians. But while she played the political game, she also sought subtly and persistently to show the professionals that women and adult education could produce as many votes as political clubs and ward heelers. And to women she tried to demonstrate that the Democratic party had the interests of their sex at heart. She fought hard, for example, to get women equal pay for equal work under NRA. She insisted on the appointment of women to important jobs — thus Frances Perkins in the Labor Department, Nellie Ross as Director of the Mint, Ruth Bryan Owen in Copenhagen as the first woman to achieve the rank of minister, Florence Allen on the Circuit Court of Appeals. And she nagged just as much to get equal representation for women within the party — that is, as she liked to put it, "fifty-fifty" between the sexes on all party committees.

But her deepest belief was that women were intelligent and could not be expected to support what they did not understand. In January 1934 she worked out what she called her Reporter Plan, calling on Democratic women to interest themselves in the local activities of New Deal agencies and pass on to others what they had learned. Farley, who cared little about the intellectual approach to politics and thought in any case that the Women's Division should be only a campaign operation, began to question the Dewson program. "Oh come, Jim," Molly finally said, "we've always got on so well, it's a pity to quarrel now. Let's go and see the Boss and let him decide." Roosevelt backed Miss Dewson, though giving her only $3,000 a month instead of the $4,000 she had requested. The professionals around Farley remained skeptical (except for Joe O'Mahoney, whom Molly Dewson later described as "the only one of Farley's colleagues I consulted with profit"); but Molly promptly went ahead, appointing a "senior reporter" on each of twenty-two agencies in all co-operating communities and then drafting Harriet Elliott of The Woman's College of the University of North Carolina to tour the country. By 1935 the Reporter Plan had become a highly effective way of funneling information about the government to thousands of localities where the press was hostile to the New Deal. The further result was to fold women into the center of the New Deal coalition. As for Molly Dewson, the veteran social worker was more than satisfied with her excursion into politics. As she said in 1937, "I consider I have done my best work for the objectives of social workers in the six political years." [11]

XI

During the First New Deal, the coalition concept had been submerged under the official thesis of national unity. But in 1934 and 1935 the various Democratic links with labor, with the ethnic minorities, with the Negroes, and with the women grew more clearly defined. With the movement against big business in the summer of 1935, there remained only the need to articulate the new conception. This need gave the intellectuals their indispensable role in the coalition. The philosophy of the New Deal welded the various groups together: not just the New Dealers themselves, but their sympathizers in schools and colleges, on newspapers and magazines, now transmitted this philosophy in all its ramifications. Some overdid it, of course, especially in their effort to stimulate the new politics. In late October 1935 Rex Tugwell, almost unique in combining the economic radicalism of the First New Deal with the political radicalism of the Second New Deal, declared in a speech in Los Angeles, "Our best strategy is to surge forward with the workers and farmers of this nation." Aubrey Williams, speaking about the same time in West Virginia, seemed to suggest that the issue was war to the death between the "have-nots" and the "haves." Others, however, set forth in less alarming language a potent and unifying ideology of social justice.

The Roosevelt conception of the Democratic party left professional politicians of the old school in a precarious and baffled position. They were used to dealing, not with coalitions, but with organizations; their lines of force moved from national committee to country courthouse, city hall, ward, and precinct, without regard to such odd groups as trade unions, nationality clubs, or women. And they were used to dealing, not with issues, but with jobs; they felt increasingly stranded in a political world grown more and more ideological. Some were flexible enough to make the adaptation. Others were not; and among them was Farley, the last and one of the greatest of the classical school.

Molly Dewson, who worked with him for years, once said, "I never heard Farley mention any of Roosevelt's plans or policies." He defended the New Deal, it is true, in speeches written for him by Charlie Michelson, but he doubtless could have defended opposite policies with equal zeal. He was nonideological in his political style. Consequently he was indifferent to the existence of the new groups which lay outside the machine politician's traditional constellation. In Roosevelt's gubernatorial campaign of 1930, when Frances Perkins suggested a committee to work with the intellectuals, Farley said tolerantly, "If you want to bother with that one and a half per cent of the voters, go ahead." He could see little point in Molly Dewson's activities with women. When Dan Roper brought up the Aubrey Williams speech in cabinet, Farley seconded the Secretary of Commerce's protest. Confident in his power and skill, Jim remained majestically oblivious to the new political conceptions rising about him. But by ignoring the importance of issues, by refusing to take seriously the disparate elements in the Roosevelt coalition, Farley was beginning to lose his central position in the politics of the New Deal. By 1935, he was already on his way to becoming little more than the New Deal's ambassador to the political bosses, almost on a plane of equality with its other ambassadors; Molly Dewson to women, John Lewis and Sidney Hillman to labor, Eleanor Roosevelt and Harold Ickes to Negroes, and Tom Corcoran and Charlie West to Congress.

Even with the political bosses, Farley was losing ground. For a new type of boss was emerging — the one who could make the adaptation to the forces whose significance Farley declined to recognize. Probably Guffey of Pennsylvania was the first deliberately to harness the drive of New Deal liberalism to a political machine. By organizing the CIO, Negroes, and independent liberals behind New Deal social policies, Guffey, the first of the liberal bosses, invented a new political formula destined to put the nonideological bosses out of business. His accomplishment would soon seem obvious enough. But it was revolutionary in its day. As Joseph Alsop and Robert Kintner observed in 1938, "When Joe did it liberalism was considered too refined a fuel for a political engine. His achievement was as novel, as mysterious and as daring as atom-smashing."

Some of the old-line bosses, notably Ed Flynn of the Bronx, Ed Kelly of Chicago, even Frank Hague of Jersey City, glimpsed the new vision, made the New Deal itself the issue, and began to get into line. But Farley, with his imperturbable confidence, continued along the only way he knew. He was beginning to feel that things weren't going altogether right; but he did not know — would never know — why he was in trouble. At times he struck out against the coalition tendencies, as when he tried to rouse Roosevelt's suspicions against Floyd Olson in 1935. By the spring of 1936 he was complaining that, of all people, Harry Hopkins was outflanking him in his relations with certain bosses — he mentioned Kelly and Hague. And, though this was only a tendency in Roosevelt's first term, it was indeed Hopkins, with his social passion, his tough audacity of temperament, and his command of the WPA funds, who was becoming the natural link between the liberal bosses and the Second New Deal. Hopkins could never become a professional in the Farley sense. There were always invisible niceties of the politician's code which he casually ignored or violated. But he saw the new political realities, as Farley would never see them; and he survived where Farley — like Moley, Richberg, and Johnson — eventually became a casualty of the shift from the First to the Second New Deal.[12]

XII

By the end of 1935 the New Deal was something different from what it had been before. Its intellectual content and its political method had undergone striking changes. It had renounced the dream of national planning through national unity and had become a coalition of the nonbusiness groups, mobilized to prevent the domination of the country by the business community. One consequence was the sloughing off of New Deal personalities too firmly committed to the old economic ideas or to the old political techniques. Yet these changes, striking as they were, should not be overemphasized. A consistency remained not only in top leadership but in moral purpose. The objective was unchanged — the determination to use democratic means somehow or other to give the plain people a better break in a darkly confusing world.

III

The Crisis of the Constitution

24. The Seat of Judgment

ROOSEVELT'S PROMULGATION of a breathing spell in the autumn of 1935 reduced political pressure against the New Deal for a moment. What reduced it even more was the apparent approach of recovery — the marked and seemingly steady upswing in business activity in late 1935, with increases in jobs, output, stock prices, and corporate dividends. But this momentary lull did not solve Roosevelt's problems. At this point the most insistent challenge to the New Deal was coming from another direction. The Supreme Court's evident readiness to throw out enactments of the New Deal Congress was creating a stampede of litigation and judgment beyond the power of benign presidential letters to halt. There was to be no breathing spell in the federal courts.

II

Under the laws of 1935, a single district judge could issue an injunction suspending the application of a federal statute. This would seem a power for a prudent judiciary to employ with utmost discretion. But in 1935–36, federal judges issued some sixteen hundred injunctions preventing federal officials from carrying out federal laws. "At no time in the country's history," observed the annual appraisal of the Court's work in the *Harvard Law Review,* "was there a more voluminous outpouring of judicial rulings in restraint of acts of Congress than the body of decisions in which the lower courts, in varying degree, invalidated every measure deemed appropriate by Congress for grappling with the great depression." The administration, noting (as Homer Cummings had informed Roosevelt in 1933) that only 28 per cent of the 266 federal judges were Democrats, regarded this explosion of judicial nullification as almost a political counteroffensive.

Unhappily, there was just enough in the tone of the campaign to lend plausibility to such suspicions. In Kentucky, for example, Judge Charles I. Dawson, finding for a coal company against the National Industrial Recovery Act, blasted the Coal Code as "the boldest kind of usurpation — dared by the authorities and tolerated by the public only because of the bewilderment of the people in the present emergency." (Judge Dawson resigned shortly thereafter to represent other coal companies in their suits against the government and to re-enter Republican politics.) Enough other judges delivered stump speeches as they struck down New Deal laws to remind historians of the "political harangues by early Federalist judges" in the young republic.

Given this predisposition on the bench — and over a hundred federal judges, well over a third of the entire corps, issued injunctions in this singular period — lawyers naturally rushed to exploit it to the full. They not only demanded injunctions on every hand; they freely resorted to an ingenious method by which they could apply for injunctions and challenge the constitutionality of laws while preventing the government from entering the court and defending the threatened enactment. This was done by raising the question through friendly private lawsuits, in which stockholders would sue their own companies to enjoin them from obeying the law. These cases obviously did not present any authentic conflict of interests. As Robert H. Jackson remarked, "Both sides wanted the same thing. There was no real isssue between them." But they were cunningly designed to keep the federal government out of court when federal legislation was under challenge.

Nor was this all. Beyond the actual testing in the courts, the conservative leaders worked hard to discredit the new legislation in the mind of the public. In particular, they sponsored a technique of constitutional prejudgment, in which eminent counsel, on their own, would hand down private decisions against irksome statutes. Thus by the end of 1935 elaborate opinions were in circulation holding the TVA Act, the Holding Company Act and the Labor Relations Act unconstitutional — the first, circulated by the Edison Electric Institute; the second, by Wendell Willkie of

Commonwealth and Southern; the third, by the American Liberty League — and all were signed by the leaders of the American bar. "Whether the purpose of such emanations is to influence the federal courts when such legislation shall be presented for consideration," said the *United States Law Review* editorially, "or whether it is to arouse public sentiment so that confidence in the courts will be impaired should the legislation be held constitutional, is not clear. But neither purpose has anything to commend it." [1]

III

The New Deal, it has been noted, regarded the courts in 1933 with sufficient wariness to defer judicial testing of its enactments. Yet most New Dealers had at bottom a strong faith, if not in the courts, at least in the Constitution. Roosevelt himself declared that faith in his Inaugural Address: "Our Constitution is so simple and practical that it is possible always to meet extraordinary needs by changes in emphasis and arrangement without loss of essential form." "We have undertaken a new order of things," he said again in 1935; "yet we progress to it under the framework and in the spirit and intent of the American Constitution." The Constitution, said the Attorney-General, has "always lent itself to experiment and has served to meet the needs of the time as those needs have developed — and it will do so now." "What we have done," said Tugwell, "is to rediscover the Constitution, to revitalize the powers it was intended to create."

This confidence in the Constitution was founded, plausibly enough, in the whole experience of American history. After all, a document drawn up for a few rural seaboard states with four million inhabitants had survived, with minimal changes, as the basis of a continental and industrial nation of 125 million. It was, as Tugwell said, a charter of government written by wise and bold men. There was no reason to suppose such men meant to foreclose on wisdom and boldness on the part of their successors.

Still, the Constitution was not a self-executing document. It had survived, not alone because of the words in the text, but even more because of the discretion with which succeeding generations had reinterpreted these words. The process of interpretation was centered in the Supreme Court. In the course of time this process had acquired certain rules. One was stated by Justice Bushrod Washington in 1827: "It is but a decent respect due to the wisdom, the integrity, and the patriotism of the legislative body, by which any law is passed, to presume in favor of its validity, until its violation of the Constitution is proved beyond all reasonable doubt." Another was stated by Roger B. Taney in 1851: that a definition, "originally correct," ought not to be persisted in after it had ceased, "from a change in circumstances, to be the true description" of the extent of federal authority. Another was stated by Morrison R. Waite in 1879: "One branch of the government cannot encroach on the domain of another without danger." Another was stated by Oliver Wendell Holmes in 1920: "The case before us must be considered in the light of our whole experience and not merely in that of what was said a hundred years ago."

In 1928, seven years before the Court handed down its judgment in the Schechter case, Charles Evans Hughes, not yet recalled to the bench, summed up in magistral terms the reasons for the Supreme Court's success. That success, Hughes said, "depended not upon constitutional formulas but on the quality of the men selected and the restraint imposed by the principles which they adopted for the control of their exercise of the judicial power." He enumerated four basic principles of judicial restraint. The first was that the Court should confine itself to the judicial duty of deciding actual cases; the second, that it would not deal with purely political questions. The third of Hughes's principles went to the problem of assessing the constitutionality of statutes. "The Court," he said, "will not undertake to decide questions of the constitutional validity of legislation unless these questions are necessarily presented and must be determined." In every case the Court must "avoid if possible the decision of a doubtful constitutional question." And the fourth Hughes principle enjoined the Court from reviewing the wisdom of legislative policy. "It is doubtless true," Hughes said, "that men holding strong convictions as to the unwisdom of legislation may easily pass to the position that it is wholly unreasonable. But the distinction nevertheless exists and it is ever present to the conscientious judge. He recognizes that there is a wide domain of legislative discretion before constitutional boundaries are reached." The survival of the Court, Hughes concluded, "has been due largely to the deliberate determination of the Court to confine itself to its judicial task, and, while careful to maintain its authority as the interpreter of the Constitution, the Court has not sought to aggrandize itself at the expense of either executive or legislative."

This was the grand constitutional tradition — the tradition so nobly stated by John Marshall when he said, "We must never forget that it is a *constitution* we are expounding . . . intended to endure for ages to come, and consequently to be adapted to the various *crises* of human affairs." Yet the whole dependency of the Constitution on those who expounded it was precisely the problem. It justified Hughes's dictum: "We are under a Constitution, but the Constitution is what the judges say it is." It created the possibility that the judges, in expounding the Constitution, might betray it — a possibility which, in the hands of recent Courts, seemed to have become almost an expectation.

This, indeed, was the problem: the modern Court seemed to have fallen away from the Marshallian tradition toward a more fixed image of the Constitution. As Frankfurter had pointed out in 1930, the Court up to 1912, in deciding nearly a hundred cases involving social and economic legislation, had interposed its veto only six times. Between 1913 and 1920, it decided adversely in nearly one-quarter of such cases. And between 1920 and 1930 it did so nearly one-third of the time. So a New Deal lawyer, Thurman Arnold, writing in the fall of 1933, could firmly entitle his essay "The New Deal is Constitutional," while conceding at the same time that recent decisions of the Court had understandably persuaded liberals that "anything they want is unconstitutional."

Nevertheless the Marshallian tradition remained, and in 1933 the great American scholars of constitutional law believed that the Supreme Court had pretty much a free choice to uphold the New Deal or to overthrow it. A month after Roosevelt's inauguration, Thomas Reed Powell, professor of constitutional law at Harvard, wrote, "In my judgment, there are sufficient doctrines of constitutional law to enable the Supreme Court to sustain any exercises of legislative or executive power that its practical judgment would move it to do." In his book of 1934, *The Twilight of the Supreme Court*, Professor Edward S. Corwin of Princeton documented this thesis at length, arguing that the justices had by now enough be-

hind them in the way of conflicting precedent on, say, the scope of
federal power over interstate commerce to produce within broad
limits nearly any constitutional result they pleased. In an expansive mood, for example, they could adopt Holmes's "current of
commerce" doctrine from the Swift case; in a restrictionist mood,
Melville W. Fuller's "direct-indirect" doctrine from E. C. Knight.
The choice was theirs to make.

By 1935 the Court had evidently made its choice. The succession
of judicial vetoes in critical areas of federal action — oil, railroad
pensions, farm debt relief, the President's removal power, industrial planning — seemed to express a clear determination on the
part of the Court to nullify the New Deal. In so doing, the Court
was vindicating the liberals' skepticism about judges as against
their faith in constitutions. "Legislation in the United States," said
Sir Wilmot Lewis of the *London Times,* "is a digestive process by
Congress with frequent regurgitations by the Supreme Court." [2]

IV

Franklin Roosevelt, who had come of political age while his
kinsman Theodore was bewailing the Supreme Court and demanding the recall of state judicial decisions, was not one to
regard the judiciary as sacrosanct. His view was the common-sense
one that the Supreme Court had always, more or less, been in
politics. During the 1932 campaign he remarked casually that
in 1929 the Republican party was in "complete control of all
branches of the Federal Government" — the executive, the legislative, "and, I might add for good measure, the Supreme Court
as well." This last remark was not in the script, but Roosevelt
said to James F. Byrnes the next day, "What I said last night
about the judiciary is true, and whatever is in a man's heart is
apt to come to his tongue — I shall not make any explanations or
apology for it!"

Viewing the Court as a secular rather than a sacred institution,
the President accordingly had few inhibitions about counterattack
when the Court began to move against the New Deal in 1935.
If an adverse decision threatened in the gold cases, he was prepared to frustrate the conclusions of the nation's highest bench.
After Black Monday, in the famous horse-and-buggy press confer-

ence, he conceived it his presidential duty to raise searching questions about where the Court was heading in its apparent redefinition of interstate commerce. As Walter Lippmann surmised, he had probably concluded "that if the Court was going to warn him [in the Schechter decision] not to go to extremes, it was necessary to remind the Court not to go to extremes," too; if they could destroy his legislative program, he could appeal to the people against them.

The reserved public reaction to the press conference evidently induced Roosevelt to desist from further comment. But he continued to ponder the judicial performance through the summer of 1935. In August he told Charles E. Wyzanski, Jr., the Solicitor of the Department of Labor, that it was becoming clear how many judges were deciding cases on the basis of partisan political views. "Of course, if the Supreme Court should knock out the AAA," Roosevelt said, "then the constitutional amendment would be *the* real issue. It probably will be anyway, and there will be less difficulty in phrasing it than many people think. If the Court does send the AAA flying like the NRA there might even be a revolution."

Later that month he dictated to George Creel an article to appear under Creel's signature in *Collier's*. The piece, entitled "Looking Ahead with Roosevelt," emphasized the President's "deep conviction" that the Constitution was not meant to be a " 'dead hand,' chilling human aspiration and blocking humanity's advance," but rather "a living force for the expression of the national will with respect to national needs." The President had acted "under the compulsion of terrific necessities," Roosevelt had Creel say, "and never at any time was there a doubt in his mind that such swift action would have had the approval of those great men who put such stress on life, liberty and the pursuit of happiness." (Apparently the President was confusing the Constitution and the Declaration of Independence.) If the Supreme Court continued to hold the present generation "powerless to meet social and economic problems that were not within the knowledge of the founding fathers, and therefore not made the subject of their specific consideration," then, said Roosevelt, he would have no alternative but to go to the country with a constitutional amendment.

"Fire that as an opening gun," he said grimly to Creel. But it was apparently only a popgun. Either the country did not much care about the Court, or else it was hypnotized by the impression that it was an institution above profane concerns. Still, the President's problem remained. And it was not solving itself in the way which had traditionally enabled Presidents to keep the Court abreast of their own policies. William Howard Taft had made five appointments to the Supreme Court in four years; Harding, four in two and a half years; Hoover, three in four years. But Roosevelt had made none at all in three years, and none was in prospect. At times in 1933 and 1934 he talked hopefully of new appointments (he told Moley that he had eastern, western, and southern candidates in mind — Frankfurter, Hiram Johnson, and Joseph T. Robinson), but by late 1935 he had pretty well abandoned this hope. More and more the problem of the Court was shaping up in his mind as a major conflict, comparable to that of the Liberal party in Britain with the House of Lords. As he told Ickes that November, Lloyd George, when the Lords refused to accept the bill for Irish home rule, threatened to pack the chamber by creating several hundred new peers. As usual, Roosevelt garbled his historical analogy; the threat was made by Asquith, and in connection with the bill to reform the House of Lords. But, whatever the precedent was, Roosevelt seemed moved by it. More and more it looked to him that, if the Supreme Court was the major obstacle to a national attack on the evils of depression, then somehow the Supreme Court would have to be dealt with.[3]

v

The Court had encountered presidential hostility before. "We are very quiet there," Oliver Wendell Holmes once said, "but it is the quiet of a storm centre." But the Court had been around far longer than any President; and it had been more than a match for most Presidents. Its dominant members were not unduly disturbed now.

The Court of 1935 had been created basically by Warren G. Harding. Though only two of his justices were still alive in 1935 — George Sutherland and Pierce Butler — his nominee as Chief Justice, William Howard Taft, had done most to give this Court its distinctive character. As Taft took early occasion to inform his brethren, he had been "appointed to reverse a few decisions" ("I looked right at old man Holmes when I said it"). Certainly under Taft the Court majority displayed a new solicitude for the rights of property. Moreover, it showed boldness in a field where such Chief Justices as Marshall and Taney had been reluctant to tread — that is, in condemning acts of Congress as unconstitutional. In the seventy-six years between 1789 and 1865, the Court vetoed only two provisions of acts of Congress. In the dozen years between 1920 and 1932, it vetoed twenty-two. For whatever reasons, the Court majority *knew*, as few of its predecessors had been given to know, what was constitutional and what was not.

Toward the end of his life Taft had moments of gloom. "I am older and slower and less acute and more confused," he wrote in 1929. "However, as long as things continue as they are, and I am able to answer in my place, I must stay on the Court in order to prevent the Bolsheviki from getting control." At times he despaired a little of the Court itself. "Brandeis is of course hopeless, as Holmes is, and as Stone is." The most that could be hoped for, he told Butler in 1929, "is continued life of enough of the present membership . . . to prevent disastrous reversals of our present attitude. With Van and Mac and Sutherland and you and Sanford, there will be five to steady the boat. . . . We must not give up at once."

In 1930 both Taft and Sanford died. The new Chief Justice was Charles Evans Hughes; the new Associate Justice, after the abortive nomination of John J. Parker, was Owen J. Roberts. These appointments somewhat diluted the Taft influence on the Court. Nonetheless Van and Mac — Willis Van Devanter and James C. McReynolds — were still there, along with Butler and Sutherland, a compact group of four, always able to outvote the three liberals — old man Holmes (replaced in 1932 by Benjamin N. Cardozo), Brandeis, and Stone. In the center, holding the balance of power, stood Hughes and Roberts.[4]

VI

In point of service, the senior justice was Willis Van Devanter of Wyoming. Van Devanter had grown up on the frontier, was chief justice of the supreme court of Wyoming Territory by the age of thirty, and thereafter was a prosperous railroad lawyer. He was an outdoor man, who used to go hunting with Buffalo Bill. But he was also a calm and thoughtful student of the law. No member of the Court had more influence on his colleagues and less on the outside world. Taft, who originally appointed him, called him his "lord chancellor," and relied on him utterly. In conference, Van Devanter's lucidity, knowledge, and sweetness of manner commanded the respectful attention even of brethren who detested his conclusions. But at his desk an awful paralysis overtook him; and he could only rarely get his views down on paper. By 1931 and 1932 his production had slowed down to one opinion a year. Sometimes Hughes would take cases back from him. "You are overworked," he would say with ambiguous and sardonic courtesy. "Let me relieve you of some of your burden."

The next senior member of the conservative bloc was James C. McReynolds, a Kentuckian who had once been Wilson's Attorney-General. In 1913 McReynolds had recommended a bill to authorize the President to appoint additional judges when judges in inferior federal courts remained in service beyond the age of seventy — an idea he would hear again. He was a lonely and crusty southern bachelor whose fierce internal resentments took the form of surliness toward his colleagues and a deliberate offensiveness toward those among them who happened to be Jews. Even Taft, who shared his constitutional views, described him as "one who seems to delight in making others uncomfortable" and resented his "continued grouch." His opinions sometimes exhibited industry of a scissors-and-paste variety, but never distinction.

George Sutherland of Utah was the chief spokesman for the conservative bloc. Sutherland was English by birth, but his parents took him to Utah while he was still a baby. He learned law at Michigan from the Thomas Cooley of *Constitutional Limitations,* as he learned social philosophy from the writings of Herbert Spencer. Evidently nothing happened after the eighteen eighties to cause him to doubt these teachings of his youth. A long career in the Senate made him an intimate of Harding's, and the result was his appointment to the Court in 1922. He was personally good-humored and kindly, liked by his colleagues for his stories. As a judge, he was forceful and fluent; and it was he who wrote the major conservative opinions. In the Adkins case he declared that Congress had no right to pass a law prescribing minimum wages for working women in the District of Columbia. In the Tyson case he declared that the New York legislature had no right to regulate the ticket brokerage business. In the Ribnik case he declared that the New York legislature had no right to control the charges of employment agencies. In the Oklahoma Ice case he declared that even depression did not justify the efforts of the Oklahoma legislature to restrain competition in the ice industry. In a series of vigorous decisions, Sutherland thus denied to both federal and state government power to intervene in the private economy.

His Harding classmate on the Court, Pierce Butler of Minnesota, pressed the same views with greater bellicosity. Butler was born in a log cabin, had risen in the world through his own efforts and, before his appointment to the Court, was counsel for the great northwestern railroads. He had the characteristics of a certain type of self-made man — an unshakable confidence in his own views, a contempt for those who had not risen from poverty as he had, a granite conviction that his own life summed up the great truths of human experience. Holmes used to call him a "monolith." As a trustee of the University of Minnesota, Butler had haled objectionable members of the faculty before him to tell them to reform or get out. Such habits of mind and personality were only faintly subdued on the Court. He was a bruiser, burly and contentious, untiring at his desk, bullying in conference, vigorous and dogmatic in his opinions.

Reed Powell once summed them up with characteristic pungency:

> The four stalwarts differ among themselves in temperament. I think that Mr. Justice Butler knows just what he is up to and that he is playing God or Lucifer to keep the world from going the way he does not want it to. Sutherland seems to me a naïve, doctrinaire person who really does not know the world as it is. His incompetence in economic reasoning is amazing when one contrasts it with the excellence of his historical and legal. . . . Mr. Justice McReynolds is a tempestuous cad, and Mr. Justice Van Devanter an old dodo.[5]

The first thing which united Van Devanter, McReynolds, Sutherland, and Butler was constitutional fundamentalism. The office of
the judge, Sutherland said, quoting Thomas Cooley, was to *"declare
the law as written."* For them the Constitution was a fixed and un-
ambiguous document, carrying its meaning, as Sutherland put it,
"in such plain English words that it would seem that the ingenuity
of man could not evade them." "As nearly as possible," he added,
"we should place ourselves in the condition of those who framed
and adopted it. . . . The whole aim of construction, as applied to
a provision of the Constitution, is to discover the meaning, to ascer-
tain and give effect to the intent of its framers." And that meaning,
Sutherland emphasized, was "changeless"; "the meaning of the Constitution does not change with the ebb and flow of economic events."
The judicial function "does not include the power of amendment
under the guise of interpretation." The Constitution, in short, was
rigid and complete, prescribing in every case one — and only one
— rational construction. The office of the judge was essentially
mechanical. He had, said Owen Roberts in one of his conservative
moods, "only one duty — to lay the article of the Constitution
which is invoked beside the statute which is challenged and to decide whether the latter squares with the former." "The Constitution
speaks for itself," Sutherland said, "in terms so plain that to mis-
understand their import is not rationally possible."

This slot-machine theory of constitutional interpretation had obvious epistemological and historical defects. And for all the earnestness with which the four conservative justices (joined on occasion by
Roberts; Hughes might on occasion endorse their judicial results,
but never their methodological solecisms) insisted on the literal
reading of the constitutional text, the literalness with which they
themselves read the Constitution was considerably greater in theory
than in practice. Indeed, it seemed that constitutional fundamentalism excluded "amendment by interpretation" only when
such interpretation bolstered the power of the community as
against the power of property. This was the second — and more
important — thing which united the conservative bloc. The guiding faith of the four justices was that civilization and progress depended on the massive and unending protection of property from

government. "It has been proved by centuries of experience, under all conceivable circumstances," Sutherland said, " . . . that government should confine its activities, as a general rule, to preserving a free market and preventing fraud." He deeply believed in "certain fundamental social and economic laws which are beyond the power, and certain underlying governmental principles, which are beyond the right of official control . . . are entirely outside the scope of human power."

Yet this belief in the sacredness of free contract, which the conservatives claimed to see as the essence of the Constitution, could be proved even less by the text than the liberal belief that the Constitution licensed a wide range of alternatives. Indeed, the judicial assault on the New Deal turned on a series of distinctions for which the text of the Constitution provided no warrant at all. Thus the Constitution contained no express bar against the delegation of legislative power, nor had even previous Supreme Courts rated this issue very high; yet it was on this "constitutional" ground that the Court vetoed the Petroleum Code and then the NRA. Similarly, the Constitution drew no distinction between "direct" and "indirect" effects on interstate commerce; yet it was on this "constitutional" distinction that NRA foundered. And it is beyond dispute that the framers of the Constitution meant something quite different by "due process" from the substantive meaning first endowed it by the Court seventy years after the Constitutional Convention and repeated by the Court of 1935 when it pronounced against railroad pensions.

Far from being engaged, as they supposed, in a process of immaculate interpretation, the conservative four, like the liberal three, were reading their own notions of social wisdom into a designedly ambiguous charter of government. But they differed in their conceptions of social wisdom; for the conservatives, wisdom lay in adherence to a rigid philosophy of laissez faire; for the liberals, it lay in adherence to a faith in orderly experiment, even if that faith produced measures which they personally deemed unwise. Both identified their conceptions with the Founding Fathers — the conservatives in the delusion that the men of 1787 were a collection of laissez-faire fundamentalists; the liberals in the Marshallian conviction that their responsibility was to construe a constitution.

In fact, the views of the conservative four were demonstrably not those of the framers, who included an admixture of mercantilists and Hamiltonians; the conservative commitment was actually to the Manchester economics imported from England almost a century after the Philadelphia convention. Sutherland was an avowed Spencerian; the others followed contentedly in the path. The fact that three were raised on the frontier (and McReynolds not far from it) doubtless gave them strong predispositions toward rugged individualism and social Darwinism. For them all, life was an evolutionary contest in which the survival of the fittest guaranteed the progress of the race, and in which the intervention of government, by permitting the unfit to survive, could only mean catastrophe. This view had seized the Supreme Court so deeply that its devotees might well have supposed that Herbert Spencer had been in Philadelphia in 1787. It was against this view that Holmes had vainly protested thirty years before when he wrote, in a celebrated dissent: "The Fourteenth Amendment does not enact Mr. Herbert Spencer's *Social Statics.*"

The difference between the conservatives and the liberals went to the whole conception of constitutionalism and law. As Harlan Stone wrote privately to a friend in 1930, the issue was *"not a contest between conservatism and radicalism, nearly so much as it is a difference arising from an inadequate understanding of the relation of law to the social and economic forces which control society."* The conservatives, in supposing that judges were the infallible expositors of an unchanging document, thought that "law, especially in our Court, is a system of mathematics." For them, the essence of the judicial process was conformity with abstractions; for the liberals, the essence was confrontation of concrete fact. In regarding interpretation and adjustment as the essence of constitutionalism, the liberals were trying never to forget that the Constitution was intended to endure for ages to come and consequently to be adapted to the various crises of human affairs.[6]

VIII

Against the four constitutional fundamentalists were ranged the three constitutional liberals. Of the liberal three, Brandeis had been longest on the Court. The approach of his eightieth birth-day hardly diminished the sharpness of his mind. But he had been a dissenter too long to be pugnacious about it. He had long since accepted the limitations of the Court. "Sonny, when I first came to this Court," he had told James M. Landis in the twenties, "I thought I would be associated with men who really cared whether they were right or wrong. But sometimes, Sonny, it just ain't so." Age only deepened the serenity of his nature. He had to hoard his strength, not expend it in arguments with his col-leagues.

Justice Benjamin N. Cardozo, in service the junior member of the Court, was by temperament even less disposed than Brandeis to rough-and-tumble controversy. His voice rarely rose, in his own phrase, "above the modulated level of equitable persuasion." A man of unusual sensitivity of nature and grace of spirit, now in his mid-sixties, Cardozo had the finest sensibility on the Court and the most exquisite understanding of the judicial process. He had no illusions about the objectivity of the art of adjudication. "I take judge-made law as one of the existing realities of life," he had written a decade earlier. By bringing to the level of con-sciousness the elements in the act of judgment — the judge's ex-perience of life, his understanding of the prevailing canons of justice and morality, his study of the social sciences, his intuitions and guesses, even his ignorance or prejudice — Cardozo hoped to strengthen the judge's own sense of austerity and discipline. True judicial consistency, he believed, lay not in mechanical repeti-tion of the past but "in fitting our statement of the relation to the new position of the objects and the new interval between them."

But his art was suasion, not combat; and these were not happy years for him. When he was Chief Judge of the New York Court of Appeals, the comradeship of the corporate life of the Court at Albany had overcome what he called his "vivid" loneliness. But in Washington each justice worked alone; Cardozo rarely saw his brethren except on the business of the Court. "I am in exile here," he used to say; and the rudeness of his conservative colleagues as well as what he deemed the folly of their constitutional dogmatism heightened his sense of frustration and futility. The 1935 term he called "a cruel year." Watching his cocksure associates ("Certi-tude is not the test of certainty," Holmes had once said. "We have been cock-sure of many things that were not so"), entrenched behind convictions beyond the reach of reason, Cardozo began to despair of suasion. "I don't worry any more about whether I can influence the vote of the other Justices," he once said. "I'm satisfied now if I can get myself to vote right."

His logic unavailing, his frail and gentle personality unsuited to contention, Cardozo nevertheless, with unassailable integrity of mind, continued with delicate precision to lay open the great issues. Beginning with the "hot oil" case, he assumed the intellectual leadership of the liberal group in expounding wider views of constitutional authority. "The Constitution of the United States," he protested then, "is not a code of civil practice." Whether wisdom or unwisdom resides in particular laws, he declared, "is not for us to say. The answer to such inquiries must come from Congress, not the courts. Our concern here, as often, is with power, not with wisdom." "There is a wise and ancient doctrine," he reminded his colleagues, "that a court will not inquire into the motives of a legislative body or assume them to be wrongful. There is another wise and ancient doctrine that a court will not adjudge the invalidity of a statute, except for manifest necessity. Every reasonable doubt must have been explored and extinguished before moving to that grave conclusion." [7]

IX

Given the age of Brandeis and the temperament of Cardozo, the brunt of battle fell on the youngest and most unexpected of the liberals, Harlan Fiske Stone. Stone, who was sixty-three in 1935, had served as Dean of the Columbia Law School and then as partner in Sullivan and Cromwell before his Amherst friend, Calvin Coolidge, brought him to Washington as Attorney-General in 1924 to clean up the Department of Justice. Coolidge named him to the Court the next year. In the meantime, Stone had become an intimate of Herbert Hoover's; during Hoover's presidency, he was a member of the medicine-ball cabinet. He came on the Court as a sensible, practical conservative, drawn to Butler and Van Devanter, mistrustful of Holmes, for all his charm, and positively repelled by Brandeis. "In no wise a reformer — at any time in his life — " as one of his law clerks later wrote, "he looked at the world as he found it, and reserved judgment on most of what he saw."

Yet, from the start, several things distinguished him from the Taft group. As a law-school professor, Stone had been exposed to the new breezes blowing through the legal-academic world. While he did not accept all the new sociological jurisprudence, he accepted enough to conclude, with Holmes, that the life of law was not logic but experience, and that the law grew as judges reinterpreted it against changing social settings. Within well-defined limits, he wrote in 1936, a judge had liberty concerning the rule of law he applies. "His choice," Stone added, "will rightly depend upon the relative weights of the social and economic advantages which will finally turn the scale of judgment in favor of one rule rather than another. Within this area he performs essentially the function of the legislator, and in a real sense makes law." If judges would only recognize their role, he thought, this would constitute the strongest assurance that the judicial function would become "a creative art by which legal doctrine, with due regard to its continuity, can be constantly molded to the social and economic needs of the times."

Stone's intellectual understanding of the relativity of adjudication was reinforced by the sturdily pluralistic view he took of society. Holmes had impressed on him that it was not the judge's role to try to play God; and Stone had a good New England respect for the conscientious opinions of others. And this meant the opinions of legislators who passed laws as well as of judges who passed on them. When the Oklahoma Ice case came up, Stone, noting privately that as an Oklahoman he would probably have voted against such regulation, joined with Brandeis in affirming the right of the Oklahoma legislature to do it anyway. "I think those are questions to be determined by the legislature and not by the Supreme Court," he explained. "I have never been able to persuade myself that the Fourteenth Amendment was ever intended to preclude the legislature from regulating business where regulation could not be said to be palpably arbitrary and unreasonable." On questions of constitutionality, he agreed with Marshall "that every law duly passed is presumed to be constitutional, and that the burden is on him who assails it to establish its unconstitutionality beyond the reasonable doubts of objective-minded men."

When Holmes resigned, Stone was apprehensive lest Hoover appoint a conservative; "I feared that great public harm might result and that some sort of explosion would occur." The choice of Cardozo delighted him, though the liberals remained a minority. For all his affection for Hoover, Stone evidently looked on his presidency with disappointment. He welcomed the change of spirit which came with the New Deal. As he wrote Roosevelt in December, 1933, "I have long wished to hear from a President such words as you uttered last night."

As the depression continued, Stone's discomfort over the conservatism of bar and bench increased. "In our own time," he said in 1934, "the Bar has not maintained its traditional position of public influence and leadership." He regretted the minor role played by the practicing lawyer "in the struggle, unique in our history, to determine whether the giant economic forces which our industrial and financial world have created shall be brought under some larger measure of control." As for the judiciary, he publicly proclaimed at the Harvard Tercentenary his doubt whether "a rigid adherence to the doctrine of *stare decisis*" was the way to save the nation. Boldly he declared for "the idea that the law itself is something better than its bad precedents"; he demanded recognition "that the bad precedent must on occasion yield to the better reason." "The law itself is on trial," Stone warned, "quite as much as the cause to be decided. . . . If our appraisals are mechanical and superficial, the law which they generate will likewise be mechanical and superficial, to become at last but a dry and sterile formalism." Tough, articulate, passionate, Stone had both the energy and the will to assume the burden of the fight for progressive constitutionalism against what he deemed an arid fundamentalism.[8]

x

Two justices remained in the middle — the Chief Justice and Associate Justice Owen J. Roberts, the youngest member of the Court. Youth was relative in these circles: Roberts was sixty in 1935. He had been a successful Philadelphia corporation lawyer, whose sense of public service had made him available for government assignments — espionage prosecutions in the First World

War and, later, the Teapot Dome cases — which he carried out with vigor and ability. Some of his more rhetorical utterances of the twenties — "Are we to go into a state of socialism, or are you men, and men like you, prepared to get out, take off your coats and root for old-fashioned Anglo-Saxon individualism?" — sound as if they were from the novels of Sinclair Lewis; but they belied a moderate, affable, and somewhat confused personality. Underneath his rugged exterior and his prosecutor's confidence in specific arguments, Roberts concealed a deep, wavering uncertainty about the Constitution and about the nature of the judicial responsibility.

Hughes had no such uncertainties. For him, the return to the Court was a notable challenge. In the age of Theodore Roosevelt, he had been a strongly progressive Governor of New York. In his first period of service, as Associate Justice from 1910 to 1916, he was the most consistent liberal on the Court. Thereafter he engaged in Republican politics and corporate law practice to such an extent that, when his name went to the Senate in 1930, Norris, Borah, and Wheeler led a bitter fight against his confirmation. Now he was chief of the Court, with all the power and responsibility that implied. It was his job to define issues at the weekly conference of judges, to lead off the discussion of cases, to assign the writing of opinions, to control the atmosphere of deliberation — in short, in Taft's phrase, to mass the Court.

Hughes was superbly equipped for this job; nor did his seventieth birthday (in 1932) signal any diminution of energy. He looked like the essence of Chief Justices, with his white hair and bristling beard, his searching eyes, strong nose, and noble brow. "To see him preside," said Felix Frankfurter, "was like witnessing Toscanini lead an orchestra." His formidable personality radiated authority and distinction; and his mind, so extraordinarily quick and clear and cold and penetrating, so highly moral and at the same time so flecked with a profound cynicism, made him the master of intricate issues of law, business, and government. When Holmes said, "Judges are apt to be naïf, simple-minded men, and they need something of Mephistopheles," he was providing the recipe for Hughes. Always aware, always disciplined, always resourceful, always urbane, he bent all his private charm, all his driving energy, all his ruthless genius toward the vindication of the Court as an institution and himself as a Chief Justice.

At the beginning, perhaps under the stimulus of the battle over his confirmation, Hughes took a markedly liberal course. Roberts followed his lead. For a moment in 1931 it looked as if Van Devanter and his friends would constitute a new minority. And Hughes's liberalism, which was particularly spontaneous in civil liberties cases, seemed to survive the early years of the depression. His own view of the social crisis did not diverge too much from the premises of the New Deal. "One increasingly finds himself controlled by a social urge," he said in June 1933. "Economic independence is now difficult. We cannot save ourselves unless we save society. No one can go it alone." This liberal mood continued through 1934, when the Court, speaking in one case through the Chief Justice, in another through Roberts, upheld the right of the state of Minnesota to declare a mortgage moratorium and the right of the state of New York to fix the price of milk.

But Hughes had a double problem: on the one hand, to reconcile the Court to the twentieth century; on the other, to do so without hopelessly dividing and embittering the Court itself. Both the Minnesota and New York cases of 1934 were 5–4 decisions. In the first New Deal case, hot oil, Hughes succeeded in gaining virtual unanimity, losing only Cardozo. But gold then went 5–4 for the New Deal; railroad pensions, 5–4 against. And the decision in the railroad-pension case was written significantly by a very different Roberts from *Nebbia v. New York*. Even Hughes was shocked when Roberts denied that Congress could ever pass any compulsory pension act for railway employees. Black Monday brought a passing rebirth of unanimity. But the end of the 1934–35 term left nerves frayed and tempers short.

What was the Chief Justice now to do? The split in the Court appeared to have passed the point where it could be closed by rational argument, even when enforced by so commanding a personality as his own. The only way, it must have seemed to Hughes, by which he could maintain at least a prospect of future influence was to throw his weight, now to one side, now to the other, and hope that by alternatively appeasing conservatives and liberals, he might maintain a superficial continuity of decision, keep the Court in balance, and even coax it to a higher degree of harmony.

This course created no particular technical problem. A judge of Hughes's skill could make the close constitutional cases come out one way or the other with equal ease. His attitude toward the law was precisely what he himself once described as his attitude toward the religion of his youth: "what interested me most was the dialectic rather than the premises." Never, in his most bemused moments, did he suppose that the process of adjudication meant laying a law beside a provision of the Constitution and seeing whether they squared. The Constitution, he well knew, was what the judges said it was; his problem was therefore the judges. His uncertainties were not over the constitutional substance, but over the Chief Justice's strategy.

And the balancing strategy created problems of its own, especially for the Chief Justice's reputation if he became too much identified with causes which might be passed over by history. Accordingly, Hughes took care, when he came down on the liberal side in controversial cases, to write a large share of the opinions himself. When he came down on the conservative side, however, he assigned the opinions to one or another of his conservative brethren. As Irving Brant pointed out in 1937, in the 43 cases in which Hughes helped form a liberal majority, he wrote 13 opinions himself; of his 15 times in the liberal minority, he wrote 7 dissents. But of his 51 times in the conservative majority, he wrote but *one* opinion. That opinion, in *Crowell v. Benson* in 1932, provoked such a devastating dissent from Brandeis and such a popular wisecrack from Stone ("Whenever I read one of his opinions I feel as if I'd been through a cyclone with everything but the kitchen stove flying in my face") that Hughes never ventured to speak for a conservative majority again. "When Charles Evans Hughes is a liberal," Brant concluded, "he proclaims it to the world. When he is reactionary, he votes silently and allows somebody else to be torn to pieces by the liberal dissenters." [9]

25. The Supreme Court Takes the Offensive

IN THE AUTUMN OF 1935 the justices returned from summer tranquility for the opening of a new term. They were already forming into distinct personal as well as constitutional blocs. The four conservatives used to ride to and from the Court together every day of argument and conference. To offset these riding caucuses, Stone and Cardozo began to go to Brandeis's apartment in the late afternoon on Fridays before conferences. Each group went over cases together and tried to agree on their position.[1]

II

For some weeks matters proceeded without difficulty. Then in the middle of October the Court heard argument over a Vermont law taxing the income of citizens from out-of-state loans at a higher rate than income from loans made within the state. For Brandeis, Cardozo, and Stone, the Vermont law seemed a valid, if peculiar, exercise of the state taxing power. But Hughes believed it to be a denial of equal protection under the Fourteenth Amendment; he did, however, dismiss as unworthy of consideration an argument proposed in the brief that it was also a violation of the privileges and immunities clause in the same amendment. Hughes then assigned the majority opinion in *Colgate v. Harvey* to the willing and voluble Sutherland.

When the opinion was circulated, Stone, speaking for the dissenters, assailed Sutherland's use of the equal protection clause with such power that Sutherland, after conferring with the Chief, decided to withdraw his draft for more work. Soon a new Sutherland piece appeared, this time resting the case against the law on the privileges and immunities point that had been passed over in conference. By now Stone was in a high state of irritation. He had resented Hughes's original presentation of the case in conference ("in his usual fashion of greatly over-elaborating the unimportant details . . . and disposing, by *ipse dixit,* in a sentence or two, of the vital question"). He now resented Sutherland's sudden resort to the privileges and immunities clause ("the matter had not been presented or considered in conference"). And he particularly resented Hughes's characteristic adroitness in controlling the opinion without assuming responsibility for it ("if the inventor would only sponsor his invention in public, I think I could write a really effective dissent"). Revising his dissent to meet the new Hughes-Sutherland argument, Stone had no difficulty in showing that the Court had refused on forty-four previous occasions to use the privileges and immunities clause to strike down state legislation. In short, the constitutional fundamentalists in what appeared to Stone an unseemly passion to deny power to public authority, were presenting an application of the clause hitherto unknown to constitutional history. The Court, Stone said in a grim dissent, was sitting as "a super-legislature, or as triers of the facts on which a legislature is to say what shall and what shall not be taxes."

Colgate v. Harvey caused general astonishment. "We are intellectually outraged here," wrote Reed Powell of the Harvard Law School. ". . . If the Court is going to pick new, strange clubs out of the air to swat anything that it doesn't like, the subject of constitutional law will be as stable as a kaleidoscope operated by an electric battery." He concluded somberly: "The Supreme Court is riding high, wide and handsome, and I see no likelihood of any serious movement to curb its powers." As for Stone, his biographer believes that the case marked the emotional turning point for him. Both the result and the surrounding maneuvers deeply angered him. He feared that the Court, by its novel application of the privileges and immunities clause, had created a fresh set of weapons with which to defend property against legislation. This fear may well have exaggerated the significance of the decision, which could also be interpreted as a blow against economic localism in favor of a federal economy. Yet Stone's very vehemence expressed the deeper tensions in the Court. The conservative justices, it seemed to him, were more determined than ever to rewrite the Constitution to block both state and national governments from doing anything; and Hughes, who in Stone's view should have known far better, was now spurring them on in some obscure game of his own.[2]

III

As Stone worried over the developing situation, the Court confronted a new testing of federal power. Early in December 1935 the justices heard argument on the constitutionality of AAA. The case of *U.S. v. Butler* involved the attempt of the government to collect processing taxes from the receivers of the Hoosac Mills; the Butler involved was William M. Butler, the former senator from Massachusetts and a crony of Calvin Coolidge's. Over seventeen hundred separate suits pending in lower courts — as well as the whole New Deal agricultural policy — hung on the outcome of the case. George Wharton Pepper, the lawyer for the cotton mill, lost eight pounds in the week before he appeared in the Court. "I am standing here today," he concluded an exceptionally eloquent argument, his voice throbbing with emotion, "to plead the cause of the America I have loved; and I pray Almighty God that not in my time may 'the land of the regimented' be accepted as a worthy substitute for 'the land of the free.'" Stanley Reed, replying for the government, was tense and ashen; immediately following the AAA case, he had to make another argument before the Court, and he fainted in the midst of the presentation.

In conference on the following Saturday, Hughes recommended that the AAA be struck down. It involved, he said, an unconstitutional regulation of agriculture within the states; it was both an invasion of the reserved powers of the states and a case of improper delegation. The five conservative justices agreed with his result but objected to resting the case on the delegation issue. Brandeis passed. Stone said federal gifts of money upon conditions which were consistent with a national purpose seemed to him clearly within the spending power. Cardozo said he agreed with Stone. Hughes, now stating that he was willing to rest the case on the issue of unconstitutional regulation, called for a vote. As Stone noted a few weeks later in a memorandum, "Thus the main question in the case was decided practically without discussion and with no analysis or consideration of the relation of conditional gifts for a national purpose to the spending power conferred upon Congress."

The next day Brandeis told Hughes that he was going with Stone and Cardozo. Hughes meanwhile had assigned the majority opinion to Roberts. Stone received the Roberts draft on December 30. "I had only two days to write the AAA dissent," Stone later said, "New Year's day and the day before, and on both days the Library was closed." Nevertheless, he managed to turn out a draft for circulation by January 3. Roberts promptly complained to Hughes of the tone of Stone's opinion; the Chief Justice, declining to interfere, suggested that Roberts speak to Brandeis. But Brandeis had already read Stone with approval, scribbling, "I join in a fine job." Stone nonetheless moderated his language, while Roberts revised the opinion of the Court in an effort to meet Stone's arguments. On the following Monday, January 6, 1936, the Court announced its results. "The whole history of the case," Stone later observed, "was characterized by inadequate discussions and great haste in the production and circulation of the opinions." One senses that the invincible Hughes, his Court now wholly out of his control, hoped somehow to abbreviate periods of tension by rushing things through, almost by main force.[3]

IV

This was the Supreme Court's first term in its new white temple, glittering in the winter sun across the way from the Capitol. An overflow crowd filled every seat in the ornate classical auditorium as Justice Roberts, in the hush of expectancy, began to deliver the opinion of six members of the Court in the case of *U.S. v. Butler*. The most accomplished member of the Court in the histrionics of adjudication, Roberts spoke his opinions as from memory, hardly glancing at the printed pages on the mahogany desk before him, dominating the room with the confident resonance of his voice, his rugged head and powerful frame rendered particularly impressive by the flow of his black judicial robes. Thomas L. Stokes, watching the scene, wrote later, "Never did a judge kill a legislative creature with more elegance and soft grace."

The Justice had laid the law against the corresponding section of the Constitution, and they had failed to square. The government, in presenting its case, had invoked, not the commerce clause, which the Schechter decision had largely emptied of power, but the clause giving the Congress power "to lay and collect Taxes, Duties, Imposts and Excises, to pay the Debts and provide for the common Defence and general Welfare of the United States." The general-welfare clause, the government argued, should be construed broadly to include anything conducive to the national welfare; it therefore added to the delegated powers of Congress. In urging this view, the government had adopted the Hamiltonian as against the Madisonian view of the spending power. Now the Court, speaking through Roberts, formally pronounced, for the first time in its history, the Hamiltonian view as correct. But what Roberts appeared to give, he quickly took away. The "new" power, it developed, was limited by the Tenth Amendment just the way the commerce power was. The processing tax under AAA, it seemed, was not a proper exercise of the taxing and spending power because it imposed contractual obligations on those accepting federal grants. It became therefore a means of coercion designed to force farmers into a plan to regulate agricultural production. And that plan, Roberts added, was an invasion of the reserved rights of the states. Thus the processing tax was an unconstitutional means to an unconstitutional end.

Roberts dismissed the idea that agriculture was a national problem. "It does not help," he said, "to declare that local conditions throughout the nation have created a situation of national concern; for this is but to say that whenever there is a widespread similarity of local conditions, Congress may ignore any constitutional limitations upon its own powers and usurp those reserved to the states." If Congress were permitted to get away with the Agricultural Adjustment Act, the welfare clause "would become the instrument for total subversion of the governmental powers reserved to the individual states." He pictured in dire terms an American future with "the independence of the individual states obliterated, and the United States converted into a central government exercising uncontrolled police power in every state of the Union."

Stone spoke for himself, Cardozo, and Brandeis. Both Stone and Brandeis disliked the Agricultural Adjustment Act; probably neither would have voted for it as legislators. But this was not, in their view, the problem they faced as judges. That problem was whether it was constitutional for other people to have enacted such legislation. Talking quietly in his dry Yankee voice, Stone began by dealing with Roberts's technical points. The doctrine that conditioning a federal grant canceled the federal spending power, he suggested, would wreck the operations of government. It was a "contradiction in terms to say that there is power to spend for the national welfare, while rejecting any power to impose conditions reasonably adapted to the attainment of the end which alone would justify the expenditure." The consequences of the majority doctrine would be that "the government may give seeds to farmers, but may not condition the gift upon their being planted in places where they are most needed or even planted at all. The government may give money to the unemployed, but may not ask that those who get it shall give labor in return." As for Roberts's view of the local character of agriculture: "As the present depressed state of agriculture is nationwide in its extent and effects, there is no basis for saying that the expenditure of public money in aid of farmers is not within the specifically granted power of Congress to levy taxes to 'provide for the . . . general welfare.' "

But Stone was concerned with much more than whether AAA stood or fell. He was concerned most of all with the attitude of mind displayed by the majority in its determination to strike AAA down. "A tortured construction of the Constitution," he said, "is not to be justified by recourse to extreme examples." Such suppositions could only be addressed to minds accustomed to believe "that it is the business of courts to sit in judgment on the wisdom of legislative action." Stone addressed a grave reminder to his brethren. "Courts are not the only agency of government that must be assumed to have capacity to govern. . . . Interpretation of our great charter of government which proceeds on any assumption that the responsibility for the preservation of our institutions is the exclusive concern of any one of the three branches of government, or that it alone can save them from destruction, is far more likely in the long run 'to obliterate the constituent members' of 'an indestructible union of indestructible states' than the frank recognition that language, even of a constitution, may mean what it says: that the power to tax and spend includes the power to relieve a nationwide economic maladjustment by conditional gifts of money."

The Supreme Court, Stone said, had its responsibilities too. The Court's authority to declare a statute unconstitutional was subject to two principles which ought never to be absent from judicial consciousness.

One principle was that courts were concerned with the *power* to enact statutes, not with their *wisdom*. For the removal of unwise laws from the statute book, appeal lay not to the courts but to the processes of democratic government.

And the other principle, said Stone with all the solemnity at his command, was "that while unconstitutional exercise of power by the executive and legislative branches of the government is subject to judicial restraint, the only check upon our own exercise of power is our own sense of self-restraint." [4]

v

"Your dissenting opinion," Homer Cummings wrote to Stone, ". . . may not be the law *now* — but it will be the law later, unless governmental functions are to be permanently frozen in an unescapable mold. You spoke at a great moment and in a great way." Stone replied that one had to be a little skeptical of one's judgment when outvoted two to one, "but I have sincere faith that history and long time perspective will see the function of our court in a different light from that in which it is viewed at the moment."

At the moment, however, as Stone commented to a former Columbia Law School colleague, the Court's approach to constitutional construction was only multiplying the "dead areas" in the Constitution, "the lacunae in which no power exists, either state or national to deal with the problems of government." How long could government continue under this dispensation? And the crisis seemed to be heightening with each new decision. To Frankfurter, Stone wrote of himself in February 1936, "A very moderate person is now a very wrought up one."

Stone's slowly accumulating wrath may have had its effect for a moment on the Court, or at least on the Chief Justice. The next New Deal case after AAA involved the Tennessee Valley Authority.

This was the Ashwander case, where a contract between TVA and the Alabama Power Company (and, with it, TVA's right to sell electric power directly to consumers) was under challenge, not by the company itself, but by a few holders of preferred stock. The immediate technical issue was whether minority stockholders had the right to bring such a suit. For Brandeis, Cardozo, Stone, and, in this instance, Roberts, this was the disposable issue. Courts did not usually mix into corporation policy at the behest of minority stockholders; so, acting in accordance with established judicial tradition, they saw no proper cause of action and wanted to dismiss the case at once.

The four conservative justices, however, wished to validate the suit. There were precedents for such suits; moreover, to give preferred stockholders the right to challenge a federal statute would strengthen the whole attack against the New Deal (especially in cases pending against the Guffey Act and the Holding Company Act). And Hughes, was prepared to join the conservative four in this conclusion. At the same time, and perhaps by going so far, he was able to persuade three of the conservative justices — all but McReynolds — to go along with him on the substantive question and sustain the constitutionality of the power operations at Wilson Dam — a result which the liberal justices thought correct but, by their canons of judicial economy, gratuitous. Evidently the three conservatives thought it more important to weaken the procedural defenses of the New Deal than to knock out an existing dam; moreover, Hughes, by resting part of the result on the federal war powers, was able to limit any precedents created for the future.

To outsiders it looked as if Hughes, in a monumental effort to wrest the majority from its anti-New Deal fixation, had outdone himself in constitutional dexterity. Not since the gold-clause cases had his talent for division and conquest been so successfully employed. The results were newspaper headlines proclaiming an 8–1 victory for the New Deal and a temporary lifting of pressure from the Court.

The TVA decision was handed down on February 17, 1936, while bands played and factories blew their whistles through the Valley. But six weeks later, in the next New Deal case, the Court returned to form. By the familiar 6–3 vote, it delivered a ve-

hement attack (marked, said Cardozo in his dissent, by "denuncia-
tory fervor") on the administrative methods of the Securities and
Exchange Commission. Sutherland, for the majority, compared
the SEC investigation, with some extravagance, to the "intolerable
abuses of the Star Chamber." Cardozo, noting that the SEC had no
coercive powers, could neither arrest nor imprison nor even punish for contempt, observed drily, "Historians may find hyperbole
in the sanguinary simile." Stone added privately that the majority
opinion was obviously written "for morons." Still, the majority,
while impeaching the methods of the SEC, did refrain from challenging its constitutionality.[5]

VI

But the conservative justices were less restrained when confronted by the Guffey Act. The case produced a titanic legal struggle. F. H. Wood of Cravath adopted against the government the
same device which W. D. Guthrie of the same firm had used forty
years before to defeat the federal income tax — a staged demand
by a stockholder for an injunction against his own company. James
W. Carter was asking the Court to enjoin the Carter Coal Company
from collaborating with the system of bituminous coal regulation
established the year before to replace the NRA Coal Code. "Coal
mining," as one of Carter's lawyers, the former Kentucky judge
Charles I. Dawson summarized his case, "is just as much a local
activity as is farming or manufacture"; hence the Guffey Act was
beyond the national power and infringed on the rights of the
states — this despite the fact that 97 per cent of Carter coal was
shipped outside West Virginia.

The actual issue presented concerned only the first part of the
law, which dealt with price stabilization and fair-trade practices.
Wages, hours, and collective bargaining were covered in a separate
part, not yet in effect and therefore not subject to direct suit.
Moreover, Congress, in enacting the law, had made the customary
stipulation that, if any provision of the statute should be held
invalid, the other provisions should not be affected thereby. Nonetheless, Carter asked the Court to declare the entire law unconstitutional.

John Dickinson of the Department of Justice made a brilliant presentation of the government's case; Reed Powell was among those who worked on the government brief. Seven coal-producing states filed briefs supporting the government's contention that the act did not endanger states' rights and that federal regulation was the only solution for the coal industry. But these efforts did not avail. Five justices — Roberts returning to the die-hard four — united in striking down the act on May 18, 1936.

Sutherland, speaking for the majority, declared the labor provisions of the act unconstitutional, in spite of the fact that they had not been put in effect and that therefore the Court was presented with no concrete question involving them. From this, he concluded that the other provisions of the act, as inseparably joined with the labor provisions, were unconstitutional, too, in spite of the fact that Congress had tried to pronounce the two parts separable. This second transgression of judicial practice was too much for Hughes. He agreed that the labor provisions must fall as beyond the federal power; but he forthrightly attacked the Court's disregard of the congressional declaration of separability and said that the price provisions were valid and should stand. Cardozo, joined by Stone and Brandeis, took higher ground in dissent. The liberal justices wanted to sustain the price provisions. As for the labor provisions, they declined, in the normal judicial tradition, to rule on these until they were confronted with a specific case. As Cardozo said, "The complainants have been crying before they are really hurt."

What the Carter case did was to develop the latent differences between Hughes's opinion and Cardozo's concurrence in the Schechter case. The unresolved question in the NRA decision was whether the distinction between "direct" and "indirect" effects on interstate commerce was, as Hughes said, a matter of kind, or, as Cardozo suggested, a matter of degree. The majority was now unequivocal on this point: "The distinction between a direct and an indirect effect turns, not upon the magnitude of either the cause or the effect, but entirely upon the manner in which the effect has been brought about." Evidently, as Irving Brant commented in his book of 1936, *Storm Over the Constitution*, the national commerce power could reach acts affecting interstate commerce directly and trivially but could not reach acts affecting it indirectly and tremendously — a result all the more ludicrous when the basic distinction involved could not be found in the Constitution at all. If Congress could not regulate an industry so patently interstate as coal, did the national government have any resources at all with which to meet the crisis? Cardozo protested in his dissent that Congress should not be thus condemned to inaction. "Commerce had been choked and burdened; its normal flow has been diverted from one state to another; there had been bankruptcy and waste and ruin alike for capital and for labor. The liberty protected by the Fifth Amendment does not include the right to persist in this anarchic riot." But he protested in vain: the Court, by a line-up of 6–3 (Hughes standing with the majority on the commerce issue), struck a staggering blow against the whole idea of national power. Anarchic riot was evidently immune to federal regulation.

The majority hammered this point home on May 25, 1936, when by a 5–4 vote (Hughes joining the liberals) it vetoed the municipal bankruptcy act. This law, passed in 1934, permitted a municipality, when authorized by the law of its state, to appeal to federal bankruptcy courts for a readjustment of their debts. It conferred no power on the federal government, and could not operate except when validated by state legislation. It simply extended to public corporations facilities long available to private corporations. Though the law was permissive and required positive state action to take effect, the majority declared that the law violated the rights of the states. As in the Carter case, the conservative justices were valiantly rescuing the states from themselves.[6]

VII

And did even the states now have power to check "anarchic riot"? This issue was presented in the last important case of the term. This case, *Morehead v. Tipaldo*, involved a New York law setting a minimum wage for women. Such laws had had a long and mixed judicial history. Brandeis had drafted some of the original state minimum-wage laws; Frankfurter had defended them before the Supreme Court; Molly Dewson and the Consumers' League had helped prepare the briefs. In 1917 the Court split 4–4 on the constitutionality of an Oregon minimum-wage law. But in 1923, after Harding had reconstructed the Court, a majority, speaking through Sutherland (but with Chief Justice Taft writing the dissent) declared in the Adkins case that the federal government had no power to enact minimum-wage legislation for the District of Columbia.

With the onset of depression, the Consumers' League made a new effort to outlaw women's sweatshops. Sutherland's Adkins opinion seemed to contain clues as to how a constitutional minimum-wage law might still be written. Utilizing these clues, Frankfurter and Ben Cohen drafted a model bill which was soon adopted in a number of states, among them New York. Promptly challenged, the New York law went before the New York Court of Appeals, which in March 1935, found it indistinguishable from Adkins and by a 4–3 vote declared it unconstitutional. Six weeks later the case came before the Supreme Court. Henry Epstein, the New York Solicitor General, and Dean Acheson, for the Consumers' League and for six states with similar laws, sought to show that the New York law could be distinguished from the statute which fell in the Adkins decision. Hughes accepted the argument that the New York law could be thus distinguished. He therefore wanted to uphold it without repudiating Adkins. The three liberal justices, however, considering Adkins bad law, wanted to seize the opportunity to overrule it.

The four conservatives, of course, were loyal to Adkins. This left Roberts in the unenviable but now familiar position of casting the deciding vote. His view, first expressed when the petition for *certiorari* came up, was that the New York law could not be distinguished and that the Court should not hear the case unless it was prepared to do something which New York was not requesting — overrule Adkins. The Court chose to grant *certiorari* nevertheless. When the time came to consider the merits, Roberts reaffirmed his position. The Court, he felt, should not reach out for issues. If the New York brief did not seek to reverse Adkins, it was not up to the Court to do so. The argument for distinction, however persuasive to Hughes, seemed "disingenuous and born of timidity" to Roberts. Prepared to reverse Adkins but not to distinguish it, Roberts felt that existing alternatives left him no choice but to vote with those who would strike down the New York law.

Butler, who was assigned the majority opinion, apparently agreed at first to rest his argument on the narrow ground proposed by Roberts. But the circulation of a biting dissent from Stone infuriated Butler; and he proceeded to expand his opinion, moving from the technical point of distinction to an impassioned defense of the principle of the Adkins decision. "The right to make contracts about one's affairs," he said, "is a part of the liberty protected by the due process clause. . . . In making contracts of employment, generally speaking, the parties have equal rights to obtain from each other the best terms they can by private bargaining." The conclusion of the majority opinion was so sweeping as to suggest that the due-process clause put minimum-wage legislation forever out of the reach both of state or federal power.

Roberts still had the opportunity to write a separate opinion explaining why he dissented from Butler's reasoning but concurred in his result. The rising public concern over the Court would seem to have made some such clarification all the more urgent. But Roberts inexplicably failed to write a concurrence — an omission which gave rise to the natural but evidently erroneous impression that he agreed with Butler's reasoning. His position, indeed, defied rational accounting. One can with effort understand why, if he really wanted to reverse Adkins, technical scruples might still keep him from joining Stone in open reversal or Hughes in reversal by distinction. But one cannot understand why these same scruples permitted him to join Butler in a vehement reaffirmation of the decision he believed to be so wrong at a juncture so critical to the position of the Court. The hopeless confusion of this entirely honest man suggests the tension of loyalties among the nine justices. It may well be that, at the crucial moment in 1936, Roberts, having identified himself emotionally with the bloc of conservatives, could not bear to desert them. The result of his failure to declare what he really believed was greatly to increase the Court's jeopardy.

Against Butler, Hughes simply stated that, in view of the differences between the two statutes, he could not regard Adkins as controlling. "I can find nothing in the Federal Constitution," he added, "which denies to the state the power to protect women from being exploited by overreaching employers through the refusal of a fair wage as defined in the New York statute." This was the artful judge's way out; but Hughes could persuade no one that it was the proper solution. While Cardozo and Brandeis joined in his dissent, they also joined with Stone who went on to attack Adkins, root and branch. "There is grim irony," Stone said, "in speaking of freedom of contract of those who because of their economic necessities, give their services for less than is needful to keep body and soul together." Why should the majority of the Court suppose that the contract of employment was too sacred a subject for regulation? "It is difficult to imagine any grounds," said Stone gloomily, "other than our own personal predilections. . . . [But] the Fourteenth Amendment has no more embedded in the Constitution our preference for some particular set of economic beliefs than it has adopted, in the name of liberty, the system of theology which we may happen to approve." Privately he commented that the Court had said in the Carter case the national government could not regulate minimum wages because it was a local matter; now it said that local governments could not do so even if it was a local matter: "we seem to have tied Uncle Sam up in a hard knot." (He was a little unfair: Carter did not state the majority's only objection to such legislation; the other objection — due process — became operative with state legislation.)

There was a further irony. The Court had now voted three times on minimum-wage cases — in 1917, 1923, and 1936. Irving Dilliard of the St. Louis Post-Dispatch, counting noses, discovered that a majority of the justices who had taken part in these cases believed the laws constitutional. Ten had voted for, nine against. But the conservative justices had lived longer and thus voted more often. Still, when a majority of voting justices sustained an act, who could conceivably say that its violation of the Constitution was proved beyond all reasonable doubt? [7]

VIII

The bitter term was at last coming to an end. In May, Charles Evans Hughes opened a meeting of the American Law Institute with the jovial remark, "I am happy to report that the Supreme Court is still functioning." His sedate audience cheered for two minutes. Then the Chief Justice, almost with a hint of apology, went on to make more sober points. No one should expect unanimity on the Court, he said; all history, after all, was a record of disagreement. "When we deal with questions relating to principles of law and their application, we do not suddenly rise to an atmosphere of icy certainty."

But was he not conceding the dissenters' case? If the judicial process lacked icy certainty, how could a bare majority ever be so sure in its wisdom that it could flatly deny government the power to act in national crisis? And was not Hughes, by accepting the paradox of the certitude of five men midst a process he deemed so uncertain, really abdicating his responsibility as Chief Justice? What was needed was, not this urbane throwing up of hands, but a massive effort to reorient the Court by exposition in the grand manner — exposition restating in fundamental terms the relationship between the Constitution and a changing society. But Hughes was no Marshall or Taney. His genius lay in the realm of tactics rather than that of principle. He bent his immense intellectual power, not to basic interpretation of the Constitution, but to the manipulation of technicalities in the vain hope of reconciling irreconcilable judicial blocs. He seemed to reach his decisions with an eye to preserving the balance *within* the Court rather than the balance *between* the Court and the nation.

Worse than this, his personal contribution actually held back the evolution of the Court. Defending judicial review in 1928, Hughes had spoken of the importance of maintaining "the consitutional restrictions of the powers of Congress" in order to protect the nation against "undue centralization." Seven years later, this aim still dominated him, insofar as he followed any consistent line at all. Instead of trying to see what the Constitution implied as a charter of government, he endorsed — sometimes devised — ingenious restraints on federal power (as in the Schechter, Butler, and Carter cases) and even on state power (as in *Colgate v. Harvey* and in *Morehead v. Tipaldo*, where his dissent still sustained the *Adkins* ruling). And when, as in the gold and TVA cases, he did speak for the power to govern, he often did so in terms so niggling and obscurantist that they savored far more of astute political trading than of Marshallian statesmanship. On balance, perhaps, it could be argued that he looked forward rather than back: in the railroad-retirement and minimum-wage cases his dissents took a broad view of federal and state power;

in Carter he held out for the validity of price regulation; even in Butler he rescued the Hamiltonian view of the spending power. Still, little emerged in the way of identifiable philosophy; and his vacillations between conservatism and liberalism only compounded the sense of a leaderless, floundering Court.

There had never been, Stone said in the course of the term, "a time in the history of the Court when there has been so little intelligent, recognizable pattern in its judicial performance as in the last few years." If Supreme Court decisions were to be "no better than an excursion ticket, good for this day and trip only" (an epigram later borrowed by Roberts for an opinion), they had "much better be left unsaid." "It just seems as though, in some of these cases, the writer and those who united with him didn't care what was said, as long as the opinion seemed plausible on its face, if not compared with any other." When Frankfurter commented that he could understand the role of everyone save Hughes, Stone replied, "The worst of it is that the one that you find most difficult to understand is the one chiefly responsible."

For once the very brilliance of his mind betrayed him. Concerned, as always, with dialectics rather than with premises, the Chief Justice thought that the troubles of the Court could be cured by maneuver, when what they really needed was wisdom. It was apparent by 1936 that he had failed, either through the persuasions of personality or the persuasions of philosophy, to mass the Court. Far from foreseeing and averting a major constitutional crisis, he was in some respects even inciting the Court in its onward rush.

As the Court recessed, Harlan Stone gave a verdict. "I suppose no intelligent person likes very well the way the New Deal does things," Stone said, "but that ought not to make us forget that ours is a nation which should have the powers ordinarily possessed by governments, and that the framers of the Constitution intended that it should have. . . . We finished the term of Court yesterday, I think in many ways one of the most disastrous in its history." [8]

26.   Storm over the Constitution

THE BEHAVIOR of the Supreme Court in 1935 and 1936 exposed a familiar sensitivity in the American system. The traditional respect for the priesthood of the Constitution had always mingled in the popular mind with an instinctive skepticism about any men, especially lawyers, who claimed infallibility. Nearly every forceful President in American history had come at one time or another into a collision with the Court. When he did, his objections discovered a surprising resonance among the people.

II

The suspicions of the Court were as old as the republic. "You seem to consider the judges as the ultimate arbiters of all constitutional questions," wrote Thomas Jefferson to an early supporter of the Court; "a very dangerous doctrine indeed, and one which would place us under the despotism of an oligarchy." "The opinion of the judges," said Andrew Jackson, "has no more authority over Congress than the opinion of Congress has over the judges, and on that point the President is independent of both." "If the policy of the government, upon vital questions affecting the whole people," said Abraham Lincoln, "is to be irrevocably fixed by decisions of the Supreme Court, the instant they are made, in ordinary litigation between parties in personal actions, the people will have ceased to be their own rulers, having to that extent practically resigned their government into the hands of that eminent tribunal." "One way or the other," said Theodore Roosevelt, "it will be absolutely necessary for the people themselves to take the control of the interpretation of the Constitution. . . . We cannot permanently go on dancing in fetters. For the last thirty years there has been a riot of judicial action looking to the prevention of measures for social and industrial betterment which every other civilized nation takes as a matter of course, and in some way or other this riot must be stopped." "The most obvious and immediate danger to which we are exposed," said Woodrow Wilson, "is that the courts will more and more outrage the common people's sense of justice and cause a revulsion against judicial authority which may seriously disturb the equilibrium of our institutions, and I can see nothing which can save us from this danger, if the Supreme Court is to repudiate liberal courses of thought and action."

This hostility stayed alive through the twenties. Robert M. La Follette made the Court an issue in the presidential campaign of 1924. "When the constitutionality of the law is tested," said Fiorello La Guardia in 1927, "Congress ought to have the right to overrule the decision of the Supreme Court." "It would be difficult to conceive of a real advance toward 'social justice' in the United States," said Donald Richberg in 1929, "that has not left, or would not leave, a vast wreckage of judge-made law in its pathway."

The revolt in the Senate in 1930 against the nominations to the Court of Hughes and of John J. Parker, as A. T. Mason has pointed out, was aimed far less at the nominees than at the Court itself. (That revolt had its ironies: Parker, who was defeated for confirmation in the name of liberalism, became an outstanding liberal judge, while Roberts, who made the Court fight inevitable, was confirmed in his place.) William E. Borah denounced the Court during these debates as an "economic dictator." "The real issue before the people of the country today," said Tom Connally of Texas, "is whether government should regulate and control vast aggregations of wealth, or whether they through the Supreme Court shall dominate and run government." "If the system of judicial law that is being written in defiance of state legislation and of congressional legislation is continued," said Senator C. C. Dill of Washington, "there is no human power in America that can keep the Supreme Court from becoming a political issue, nationwide, in the not far distant future." This senatorial uprising of 1930 should have alerted wise justices to the potential feeling against the Court. In retrospect, it was a dress rehearsal for graver challenges to come.[1]

III

Popular suspicions, moreover, were finding powerful support in new theories of jurisprudence. From the days of Holmes's *Common Law*, legal philosophers had been reconsidering the nature of the judicial process. Holmes's skepticism, the pragmatism of James and Dewey, the sociology of Brandeis, the psychology of Cardozo — all these had resulted in a new school of jurisprudence, which focused a sharp light on the nonrational elements in judicial decision and on the role of judges as unacknowledged legislators. Cardozo's *Nature of the Judicial Process* was the central text of the new jurisprudence. As Dean Roscoe Pound of the Harvard Law School summed up the impact of the new school in 1931, no one could believe any more in the "mechanical certainty of [judicial] result which the last century believed in. The dogma of a complete body of rules to be applied mechanically was quite out of line with reality."

The new jurisprudence found a host of persuasive teachers — notably, perhaps, Felix Frankfurter and Thomas Reed Powell of Harvard and Edward S. Corwin of Princeton. Under their influence, a new generation of lawyers and political scientists abandoned the notion that judicial pronouncements were delivered by the stork. They tried instead to reconstruct the various carnal factors — economic, political, psychological, as well as legal — which so evidently entered into every decision. In due course this effort produced an even more radical school. Two influential books of 1930 — Jerome Frank's *Law and the Modern Mind* and Karl Llewellyn's *The Bramble Bush* — along with the articles and teaching of such men as Herman Oliphant of Columbia, signaled the rise of legal realism.

The legal realists carried the desecration of the mysteries several steps further. Judicial opinions, said Llewellyn, ought to be regarded no more than "lawyers' arguments made by the judges . . . intended to make the decision seem plausible." Corwin's *Twilight of the Supreme Court* offered historical documentation for this thesis. And in 1935 Thurman Arnold of the Yale Law School provided a popular statement of the case in *The Symbols of Government*, a witty and irreverent commentary on the legal process. "The 'Law' as a body of principles and ideals which is above men," Arnold wrote, "lives in a vast metaphysical literature, and in a succession of ceremonial trials." None of this had anything to do with reality, he said, except insofar as man had to live by symbols and thus in some way fulfill himself by devising an "elaborate dream world where logic creates justice."

After the new jurisprudence, it became impossible — or at least exceedingly difficult — to share with the constitutional fundamentalists the belief that judicial decisions were the results of immaculate conception. "The absolute theory of one and only one rational construction of the Constitution," said Homer Cummings, "renders impossible any proper understanding of the nature of our American constitutional method." The flowing black robes still gave judges a kind of protective coloration; as Paul Porter once said, trying to discern the man behind the robes was like trying to guess the weight of a nun. But legal realism had had its effect. A judge — even a Justice of the Supreme Court — was no longer a high priest. He now seemed much less certainly the voice of the law than he did the voice of his own prepossessions speaking through the law.[2]

IV

While the higher criticism of the new jurisprudence divested the Court of its cloak of objectivity, the concrete decisions were awakening ancient and deep-seated popular resentments. As early as March 1935, Edward F. McGrady, the Assistant Secretary of Labor, told a labor audience: "With stupid judges on the bench . . . it is up to the workers to organize to such an extent that their economic strength will make it unhealthy for a judge to defy you." The Schechter decision touched off a major fusillade. James F. Byrnes of South Carolina was the first to speak. The successor of Calhoun and Hayne, returning to the birthplace of nullification to make a formal address, Byrnes argued eloquently for national power. He demanded a constitutional amendment to "give the Congress the power to legislate as to all matters that affect

interstate commerce and which experience has shown cannot, under present-day conditions, be effectively remedied by State action."
Much, Byrnes added with scorn, was being said about Thomas Jefferson and states' rights. "But it does not follow that when one
champions the states' rights doctrine of Jefferson, that by it is
meant the Federal Government must stand aloof in meeting broad
social and economic problems." Jefferson himself, after all, was
"a progressive, a liberal, and, above all, a champion of the masses."
"I venture the opinion," Byrnes said, "that if the sage of Monticello
were alive today, he would frown upon any effort to use his views
of states' rights to block social and economic reforms so badly
needed to improve conditions for those who labor in the factories
and toil in the fields."

Defenders of the Court were quick to reply. The terms of defense were exalted: thus William E. Borah asserted on January
2, 1936, that the Supreme Court was "the most nearly perfect human institution yet devised by the wit of man for dispensation
of justice." Four days after Borah had repented his skepticism
of 1930, the most nearly perfect human institution responded
by declaring agriculture to be a local problem, beyond the reach
of the national government. The outcry was immediate. "This
means," said Hugo Black, "that 120,000,000 are ruled by five men."
"There has been a great deal of talk about the sanctity of the Constitution," said Burton K. Wheeler. "But I suggest that constitutions are made for men, not men for constitutions. On what
does the Supreme Court base this claim to power?" "The Supreme Court now, in effect, for all practical purposes," said
George W. Norris, "is a continuous constitutional convention.
. . . The people can change the Congress, but only God can change
the Supreme Court." "So long as we intend to remain a free,
self-governing people," said Donald Richberg, "we cannot sanc-
tion any effort to establish the worship of a man-made document
and reverence for its human interpreters as a state religion." Near
Ames, Iowa, six figures in black robes, representing the justices
who voted against AAA, were hanged in effigy.

And the import of the decision went far beyond AAA — it was,
wrote Arthur Krock, "a decision so broad that few New Deal
acts before the court now seem to have any chance of being upheld." In a thoughtful article, Dean Lloyd K. Garrison of the Wis-

consin Law School pointed up the larger implications. Obviously forty-eight separate state legislatures could not deal with the national agricultural problem: now the federal government could not do so either. This situation, Garrison continued, existed not only in agriculture but in labor relations, in pension plans, and doubtless in other areas where the states could not practically and the federal government could not constitutionally assert power. "What we face now, at numerous and critical points, is the question, not how governmental functions shall be shared, but whether in substance we shall govern at all."

Each new adverse decision in the winter and spring of 1936 brought new bursts of hostility. As the Court alienated the farmers in the Butler case, so it alienated the workers in the Carter case. "If we understand correctly the decision of the United States Supreme Court in the Guffey law case," said the *United Mine Workers Journal,* "labor has no rights under the Constitution." "It is a sad commentary on our form of government," said John L. Lewis, "when every decision of the Supreme Court seems designed to fatten capital and starve and destroy labor." "Every worker of every class," said Dan Tobin, "is pledged tonight to President Roosevelt . . . as a result of the decision today." And finally, in June, with the minimum-wage case, it alienated nearly everybody. Even those who had enthusiastically supported earlier decisions recoiled from this one. Out of 344 editorials, only ten — mostly from textile towns — approved the Tipaldo decision. Nearly sixty papers — among them such conservative papers as the *New York Sun* and the *Baltimore Sun* — called for the submission of a constitutional amendment. "I am not criticizing the Supreme Court," said Hamilton Fish of New York, "but I was fairly shocked at the decision." It was even too much for Herbert Hoover. "Something should be done," the ex-President said, "to give back to the states the powers they thought they already had."

"I think we should be more than human," Cardozo wrote to Stone, a week after the decision, "if we failed to sit back in our chairs with a broad grin upon our faces as we watch the response. . . . Is it possible that both political parties hold the view that legislation condemned by the majority of our brethren as an arbitrary and capricious assault upon liberty is so necessary and beneficent that we cannot get along without it?" "It seems to be dawn-

ing on a good many minds," Stone agreed, "that after all there may
be something in the protest of the so-called minority." "Yes,"
said Brandeis, "the consternation of the enemy is encouraging." [3]

V

The consternation may have been encouraging, but the enemy
remained. In the autumn, it would be the same old Court, with
the same die-hard four and the same vacillating two. By principles
already handed down, the Wagner Act would surely fall, perhaps
social security, too, and much else beside; indeed, the whole New
Deal threatened to expire in an agony of 6–3 and 5–4 decisions. As
conservatives observed with relish, the New Deal was plainly
against the Constitution. "This is not a matter of opinion, but of
fact," said Raoul E. Desvernine, chairman of the Lawyers' Committee of the American Liberty League. "The Supreme Court, the
final and conclusive authority on such matters, has so determined."

If this were the case, could a showdown between the Supreme
Court and the New Deal be averted? Even if Hughes remained
unalarmed, Roosevelt saw the shadow of portending crisis as early
as the late summer and fall of 1935. Ickes noted in his diary,
"Clearly it is running in the President's mind that substantially
all of the New Deal bills will be declared unconstitutional." With
the present composition of the Court, Homer Cummings said, New
Deal cases would not stand much chance if "the Angel Gabriel
himself made the argument." In December 1935 Roosevelt outlined three possibilities to his cabinet: giving new substantive
powers to Congress; limiting the powers of the Court; or ("a distasteful idea") packing the Court by appointing new judges. If
the New Deal legislation were all nullified, the President said
somberly, there would be marching farmers and marching miners
and marching workingmen throughout the land.

In a few days the AAA decision brought the constitutional crisis
measurably nearer. If Stone and two of his brethren could speak
in language of unprecedented force of a "tortured construction
of the Constitution" and beg the Court majority to exercise self-
restraint, who was to blame the administration for feeling slightly
desperate? Roosevelt refrained from public comment. But in a
memorandum for the files he said that the President and the Con-

gress had been virtually denied "the right, under modern conditions, to intervene reasonably in the regulation of nation-wide commerce and nation-wide agriculture." This result, he added, was based on "the private, social philosophy" of the six justices. In cabinet, Cummings, backed by the old Bull Moosers Ickes and Wallace (whose book *Whose Constitution?* came out in the spring), warned urgently against the dangers of what Ickes called a "judicial tyranny." In government and out, proposals began to appear seeking in one way or another to surmount the roadblock laid down by the Court.

The plans mostly fell into the first two categories mentioned by Roosevelt. Some proposed to clarify the position of Congress by making an explicit constitutional grant of powers now in dispute. Tugwell and Moley favored something along these lines. Costigan of Colorado drew up an amendment giving Congress express authority to regulate business practices and conditions of labor. Floyd Olson wanted to confer on Congress the power to establish laws for the "ownership, operation, and management by the United States" of business and industry.

The other class of proposals — and these were somewhat more numerous — looked to curtailing the power of the Supreme Court to veto congressional legislation. One type, regarded with special interest by Roosevelt and Cummings and ardently backed by Richberg, gave a new Congress, an election having intervened, the right to re-enact a law declared unconstitutional. Senator Norris proposed taking from inferior courts authority to pass on constitutionality and requiring unanimity from the Supreme Court; "it takes twelve men to find a man guilty of murder. I don't see why it should not take a unanimous court to find a law unconstitutional." Senator Joseph C. O'Mahoney also favored the requirement of unanimity. Congressman Knute Hill wanted to withdraw altogether from the Court the power to strike down acts of Congress; after all, Holmes had said, "I do not think the United States would come to an end if we lost our power to declare an Act of Congress void." Senator La Follette wanted the Supreme Court to provide on presidential request an opinion concerning the constitutionality of federal statutes. Olson thought that federal judges should hold office only for ten-year terms.

After the New York minimum-wage decision, the Consumers'

League asked a group of lawyers and political scientists what to do next. Half of those consulted, including Felix Frankfurter, Charles A. Beard, and Ben Cohen, were against an amendment. "The *due process clause*," said Frankfurter, "if construed according to traditional law, puts no barriers against needed social legislation." "In view of Roberts' treatment of the general welfare clause in the AAA case," added Beard, "I fear that no gain would be made by adding another general clause." And among those favoring amendment there was such a bewildering diversity of opinion concerning its form that the Consumers' League committee concluded it "not advisable at this time" to start an amendment campaign.

Supporters of the amendment solution continued their efforts. Burt Wheeler asked Norris to head the movement: "You are the only one who can unite all forces upon a single plan." With some reluctance, Norris agreed. But no specific draft capable of winning the backing of even a majority of the pro-amendment forces appeared. In the confusion, the thought of solving the Court problem by amending the Constitution seemed increasingly academic and irrelevant.[4]

VI

The problem, it was becoming apparent, was one, not of changing the Constitution, but of changing its interpretation by the Supreme Court. The existing Court, it seemed likely, could outwit any amendment. "There is no substitute for wise and enlightened interpretation," said John Dickinson; "without it, the possibility of amendment is but a barren hope." Whatever the amendment, said E. S. Corwin, *"we must still trust the Court . . . to correct its own errors."* "Amendments designed to achieve specific purposes," said Dean Acheson, "will be seen to effect changes far greater than anyone desires and will merely substitute new problems and uncertainties for existing ones. . . . The change must be by the Court itself in the attitude with which it approaches judgment." (But these remained close issues, on which reasonable men might change their own minds. Both Corwin and Acheson, responding to the Consumers' League inquiry, had said they favored amendments.)

As for Roosevelt, in the winter and spring of 1936 he began

to back away from the amendment idea. It was partly the hard fact, as he put it, that "no two people agree both on the general method of amendment or on the language of an amendment." But, even if agreement were possible, he questioned the political feasibility of the approach. "To get a two-thirds vote, this year or next year, on any type of amendment is next to impossible." And, even if Congress passed an amendment, the problem of ratification by the states seemed overwhelming. "You could make five million dollars as easy as rolling off a log," he said to one correspondent, "by undertaking a campaign to prevent ratification by one house of the Legislature, or even the summoning of a constitutional convention, in thirteen states for the next four years. Easy money." "If I were John W. Davis and had five hundred thousand dollars," he would say, "I could stop a constitutional amendment cold" — and then he would explain in detail how much it would take to fix each of thirteen states. And, even if an amendment was finally ratified, it would provide only a "delusion of certainty"; a hostile Court could still interpret it out of existence.

If amending the Constitution were out, if the problem was getting a new judicial interpretation, how was this to be done? The justices appeared in excellent health; the Metropolitan Life Insurance Company calculated that even the oldest had five and a half more years of life expectancy. There remained, of course, a good possibility that elections might, as they had in the past, liberalize the Court's reading of the Constitution. As Arthur N. Holcombe of Harvard, looking forward to November, told the Consumers' League, "If these elections turn out satisfactorily, I cherish a strong hope that there will be a better prospect for liberal interpretation of the Constitution from the Supreme Court."

But was no more specific attack possible? In January 1935 Homer Cummings had proposed appointing enough justices to the Court to create a New Deal majority. Morris Cohen, the philosopher, also suggested in 1935 that Congress should enlarge the Court. "There is a general impression that this would be dishonest. Why so?" A year later, brooding over the matter some more, the Attorney-General wrote a long letter to the President. "The real difficulty," he began, "is not with the Constitution but with the Judges who interpret it." In present circumstances, the administration either had to try and meet the Court's terms or else go out for an amendment. "For the present, at least, I think our proper course is along the former line rather than the latter. The hand has not yet been played out. No one has yet suggested an amendment that does not do either too much or too little, or which does not raise practical and political questions which it would be better to avoid."

But, "if we had liberal Judges," Cummings continued, "with a lively sense of the importance of the social problems *which have now spilled over State lines,* there would be no serious difficulty." If amendment there must be, should it not aim at the compulsory retirement of all Supreme Court justices at the age of seventy? Such an approach would not change "in the least degree the structure of our Government, nor would it impair the power of the Court. It would merely insure the exercise of the powers of the Court by Judges less likely to be horrified by new ideas."

Roosevelt was sufficiently attracted by the idea to ask Cummings to study it further. Frances Perkins reports that in the latter part of 1936, during the "general go-around" in cabinet, Roosevelt repeatedly asked Cummings, "How is your plan coming along, Homer?" without ever making clear to the others what he was talking about. But he had reached no conclusion himself and, as usual, he kept his own counsel. After the failure of his "horse-and-buggy" press conference, he preserved equanimity in face of the series of adverse decisions. He did not even mention the Court publicly again until a year later when, after the minimum-wage decision, he mildly complained of the existence of a " 'no-man's-land' where no Government — State or Federal — can function," but declined to be drawn into any further comment on the matter. Yet within him there was crystallizing the firm conviction that, as he later put it, the whole line of decisions had cast a deep shadow "upon the ability of the Congress ever at any time to protect the Nation against catastrophe by squarely meeting modern social and economic maladjustments." He was biding his time, uncertain yet how to act. Still, unless the block disappeared, action at some future point was inevitable.[5]

VII

By the late spring of 1936, two viewpoints about the Court's assault on the New Deal were defining themselves with piercing

clarity. On the one hand: "When an act of Congress is thus rejected, it is the Constitution which is speaking. . . . The Supreme
Court, in such instance, is only the Constitution's voice" (Arthur H.
Vandenberg). On the other: "If we are to accept without right of
protest the unrestrained control of public policy which has been
exercised by the Supreme Court for the first time in history in the
last two years — let us clearly understand what we are doing. . . .
This is indeed the end of self-government in America" (Donald
Richberg).

For the New Dealers, the attitude of the Court imperiled the
whole hope of a decent society. "The basic grievance of the New
Deal," wrote Robert H. Jackson, "was that the Court has seemed
unduly to favor private economic power and always to find ways
of circumventing the efforts of popular government to control or
regulate it." If regulated capitalism was impossible, then what
could ensue but the anarchy of reaction, leading in the end to
the violence of revolution? The impasse threatened the future of
democracy in America.

It therefore clouded the future of free institutions everywhere.
"This is an age," an eminent English observer wrote in the summer
of 1936, "in which the citizen requires more, and not less, legal
protection in the exercise of his rights and liberties." This, he
surmised, was why the American administration had thus far been
so restrained in its response to the offensive launched by the Supreme Court against the New Deal. "The challenge may come at a
later date," he continued, adding astutely, "though it would perhaps be wiser to dissociate it from any question of the age of the
judges, lest it be the liberal element in the court which is weakened."

The Constitution, he said, was "the shield of the common man."
But it "ought not to be interpreted by pedants." In England
"we continually give new interpretation to the archaic language of
our fundamental institutions, and this is no new thing in the
United States. The judiciary have obligations which go beyond
expounding the mere letter of the law. The Constitution must be
made to work." A true interpretation of the Constitution would
not be "a chop-logic or pedantic interpretation. So august a body
as the Supreme Court in dealing with law must also deal with the
life of the United States, and words, however solemn, are only

true when they preserve their vital relationship to facts."

"It would certainly be a great disaster, not only to the American Republic but to the whole world," Winston Churchill concluded, "if a violent collision should take place between the large majority of the American people and the great instrument of government which has so long presided over their expanding fortunes." [6]

IV

The Campaign of 1936

27. Shadows Ahead

FOR AN ILLUSORY MOMENT in the mellow autumn of 1935, national politics almost achieved an appearance of tranquility. The President's breathing-spell letter to Roy Howard seemed to mollify the right. The assassination of Huey Long removed his most dangerous enemy on the left. The Supreme Court had not yet resumed its offensive against the New Deal. The resumption through the summer of progress toward economic recovery made everybody happy. Only the mounting Italian pressure against Ethiopia darkened the sky. Most Americans, worn out by the labors of their Congress, turned to more agreeable events, like the race between the Chicago Cubs and the St. Louis Cardinals for the National League title.

The President himself left in late September for a long holiday. Crossing the Great Plains and the Rockies in his slow-moving special train, he paused to dedicate Boulder Dam and then moved on through the golden countryside to the West Coast. In a series of speeches he redefined the purposes of his administration to express the particular emphasis of the Second New Deal. He talked much less about "planning" than in 1933, much more about the role of the "individual." "Serious as have been the errors of unrestrained individualism," he said in a characteristic passage, "I do not believe in abandoning the system of individual enterprise. The freedom and opportunity that have characterized American development in the past can be maintained if 'freedom' and 'opportunity' do not mean a license to climb upwards by pushing other people down." The purpose of government, he declared, was "service to the individual." Leaving a trail of conciliatory sentiments behind him, he boarded the U.S.S. *Houston* in early October and sailed south in the company of Hopkins and Ickes for a long-anticipated rest. After fishing on the high seas, visiting Cocos Island and passing pleasantly through the Panama Canal, he disembarked, tanned and revived, three weeks later in Charleston, South Carolina.[1]

II

On returning, Roosevelt found the September truce already beginning to wear thin. While his letter to Roy Howard had evoked a favorable reaction among people in the center, it did not deeply move those affiliated with either the organized left or the organized right. The breathing spell, Tom Amlie thus said for the radicals, signified "the end of New Deal liberalism." The *New Republic* muttered gloomily about "the final death rattle," and the *Nation* entitled its comment, "The New Deal Ends."

If the radicals disliked the breathing-spell letter because they supposed Roosevelt meant it, the conservatives disliked it for the opposite reason: because they were sure he didn't. "Business and financial judgment may be wrong," said the *Wall Street Journal* "but unmistakably the impression in such quarters was that Mr. Roosevelt favored a breathing spell for industry, not because industry needed it, but because it had become indispensable to Mr. Roosevelt and his party." If this were so, then it seemed time for the conservatives to move in for the kill.

Everything conspired to revive the political wars. The approach of the presidential election of 1936 led politicians to redouble their efforts to incite businessmen against the New Deal. The return to battle of the Supreme Court soon seemed to place on opposition the seal of high judicial approval. The lugubrious warnings of favorite columnists strengthened the renewal of conservative fears. Mark Sullivan, once a follower of Theodore Roosevelt, and David Lawrence, once a follower of Woodrow Wilson, indulged in Cassandra-like lamentations of precisely the sort they had ridiculed when applied by earlier conservatives to their own heroes. In November 1935 Sullivan even suggested that 1936 might offer "the last presidential election America will have. . . . It is tragic that America fails to see that the New Deal is to America what the early phase of Nazism was to Germany." Under such

counsel, business opinion steadily hardened against the administration through the fall and winter. Patriots began to emerge,
like the Minneapolis thermostat manufacturer who announced
late in 1935 that he would take a year off to work for Roosevelt's
defeat: "So many businessmen have been so deeply engrossed in
their private business that they have permitted half-wits to seize
the Government. . . . I believe businessmen everywhere should
follow my example!"

The annual meeting of the American Banking Association in New
Orleans in November 1935 displayed the resurgent bitterness. The
members of the ABA, as loyal Americans, had presumably accepted
the Banking Act of 1935. But when the nominating committee
proposed as second vice-president (and thus future president) of
the organization a former partner of the author of that act,
Marriner Eccles, the convention rose in angry protest, rejected the
nomination, and named in his stead another Utah banker who
had just won its affection by a statesmanlike speech urging the
bankers to boycott Treasury securities until the administration
abandoned its policies: "The bankers of America should resume
cooperation with the Federal Government only under a rigid economy, a balanced budget, and a sane tax program." On reading
this threat, Roosevelt remarked bitterly to the Comptroller of the
Currency that such a statement would have been treason in wartime.

This idea of a business boycott of the New Deal government
was suddenly much in the air. December 1 was the deadline for
registration under the Public Utilities Holding Company Act. But
a district court decision in November, declaring the law unconstitutional, inspired utility executives to defy the deadline. Now, in
nearly fifty suits, power companies sought injunctions to prevent
the government from enforcing the law. And this was only part of a
larger business offensive. "Industry, much against its will," as the
President of the National Association of Manufacturers explained
at the annual meeting on December 4, "has been forced in sheer
self-defense, to enter the political arena or be destroyed as a
private enterprise." And the fire was concentrating more than
ever on Roosevelt himself. On December 10, at an Edison Electric
Institute dinner, its president, Thomas N. McCarter, the utilities
czar of New Jersey, startled the assemblage by offering a toast to

the President of the United States. At first, only a few diners stood, grinning as they rose; then others began to catch the joke, and soon all were on their feet, lifting their glasses in derisive laughter. Later Floyd L. Carlisle of Consolidated Gas addressed the audience. With a bow to McCarter he said, "Never have I admired the 'Overlord of New Jersey' as much as I did tonight. That toast! ——" and he did not have to finish the sentence for the laughter and applause.

On December 16, 1935, the Republican National Committee, preparing for the presidential year, summed up the situation from the conservative viewpoint. "The United States," it declared, "is facing as grave a crisis as has arisen in its history. The coming election will determine whether we hold to the American system of government or whether we shall sit idly by and allow it to be replaced by a socialistic state honeycombed with waste and extravagance and ruled by a dictatorship that mocks at the rights of the States and the liberty of the citizen." [2]

III

It was in this atmosphere that Roosevelt began to prepare for the return of Congress in 1936. Much had happened between September and January. Observers declared that his popularity had never been so low. The Gallup poll gave him barely over half the electorate. His foes had never been more confident, his friends never more exasperated and apathetic. And the 1935 session had pretty well exhausted his agenda for immediate legislative action. Despite business cynicism about the breathing spell, he was personally inclined to soft-pedal further reform. ("If he will only stick to these principles for another year," Morgenthau reflected in October 1935, "I predict that we will be sufficiently along the path of recovery so that we can afford additional reform.")

Yet he faced a complex political problem: how to reawaken enthusiasm on his left without aggravating discontent on his right? His disposition, as he thought about the impending message to Congress, was not to abandon the policy of moderation but rather to conceal it in a garb of militancy. His formula was to combine a radical State-of-the-Union message with a conservative budget in the apparent hope that brave words would restore the faith of the left while lack of deeds might in time restore the hope of the right.

Roosevelt thus planned the annual message as a "fighting speech," almost as a keynote address for election year. To gain the widest audience, he demanded to deliver it to an evening session of Congress — a departure from precedent which naturally enraged the Republicans. Actually the speech began soberly enough with an inventory of the foreign situation. But Roosevelt's lucid warning that dictatorship confronted the world with the threat of war passed quickly into a general indictment of autocracy; and this thought afforded an easy transition to the problem of safeguarding democratic nations internally against the rise of those "autocratic institutions that beget slavery at home and aggression abroad." In the United States, for example, the struggle to return the government to the people had "earned the hatred of entrenched greed." Now the nation's former masters were conspiring to recapture their power. "Autocrats in small things, they seek autocracy in bigger things. . . . They steal the livery of great national constitutional ideals to serve discredited special interests. . . . Give them their way and they will take the course of every autocracy of the past — power for themselves, enslavement for the public."

This slam-bang attack on the "resplendent economic autocracy," phrased with felicity and delivered with evident relish, transformed the State-of-the-Union message into a campaign harangue. A few days later, speaking at the Jackson Day dinner, Roosevelt enthusiastically cast himself as the modern Andrew Jackson:

> An overwhelming proportion of the material power of the Nation was arrayed against him. The great media for the dissemination of information and the molding of public opinion fought him. Haughty and sterile intellectualism opposed him. Musty reaction disapproved him. Hollow and outworn traditionalism shook a trembling finger at him. It seemed sometimes that all were against him — all but the people of the United States. . . . History so often repeats itself.

Yet, for all the fierce talk, careful readers noted that, apart from pledging "unceasing warfare against those who seek a continua-

tion of that spirit of fear," Roosevelt's speeches were notably wanting in specifics: the budget was declared to be approaching
balance; reductions in relief appropriations were to be anticipated;
no additional taxes were demanded; nothing was said of new
reforms.

Congress thus confronted little in the way of a new presidential
program. And it had little on its own mind save a desire to
adjourn in plenty of time for the campaign. The bonus, of course,
was still around, and this provided the first action of the session.
Recognizing inexorable political pressures, Roosevelt was finally
ready to accept the inevitable. When both houses shouted through
a bill calling for the payment to veterans of nearly $2 billion in
1936 instead of in 1945, the President vetoed the bill for the record;
but his message was perfunctory, and he made no fight, as he had
the year before, to uphold the veto. As a result, Congress promptly
provided the necessary two-thirds to make the bill a law.

The Supreme Court's decision against the Agricultural Adjustment Administration provided the next action of the session. The
Department of Agriculture was not caught wholly unprepared. Henry
Wallace had long had his own doubts about aspects of AAA, such
as the processing tax; and serious thinking had gone on for some
time within AAA about how best to put the emergency program
on a permanent basis. As early as October 1935 Roosevelt himself
had outlined requirements for a long-term plan, laying particular
emphasis on the broadening of agricultural adjustment operations
"to give farmers increasing incentives for conservation and efficient use of the Nation's soil resources."

Now, with the old AAA dead, the Department of Agriculture came
up rather quickly with a plan based on the Soil Conservation Act
of 1935. The ostensible object of the new program was to pay
farmers for taking land out of soil-depleting crops and putting
it into soil-conserving crops. But since the leading soil-depleting
crops — wheat, corn, cotton, and tobacco — were also leading surplus crops, such an approach could achieve indirectly somewhat
the same effects in controlling production and increasing farm
income that AAA had achieved directly. And since farmers would
receive their benefit payments not for curtailing production but for
restoring soil fertility, Justice Roberts and his colleagues would
presumably not be offended. The Farm Bureau enthusiastically

seconded the measure. There were nominal opposition objections.
"It is an attempt to enslave the farmer," said Representative John
Taber mildly. ". . . It is communistic." "They are to be dominated
and regimented for all time," added Joe Martin. "No longer are
they to be free men. . . . Give the farmer a chance to live happily
but do not sell him into slavery." But most of Congress took a less
drastic view, and the bill became law in early March.[3]

IV

These events — the passage of the bonus and the outlawing of
AAA — destroyed the fiscal complacency induced by the budget message. Not only did the government now owe $2 billion to the
veterans; not only was the processing tax now eliminated as a
source of revenue; but the Supreme Court further ordered the
return to the processors of $200 million of taxes already collected
("probably the greatest legalized steal in American history," said
Henry Wallace, an opinion which produced demands for his impeachment from Republicans in the House). All this changed the
President's mind about not asking for new taxes. He did not like
deficits in any case; and it seemed, in addition, bad politics to
enter an election year without trying to do something about the
growing national debt.

At the same time, the impending election limited the choice of
taxes. Raising income or even estate taxes would be politically
unpopular. Reduced exemptions or a rehabilitated processing tax
would cut into consumer buying power. Something special was
required. On March 3, 1936, in a supplemental budget message
calling for new revenues to meet the new needs, the President
invited the attention of Congress to a tax on undistributed corporation profits.

Such a tax was by no means a new idea. During the Civil War,
for example, the personal income tax applied to corporate earnings, whether or not distributed to the individual. After the First
World War, there was interest in a modernized tax on undistributed
profits; David Houston, Secretary of the Treasury under Woodrow
Wilson, recommended such a tax in 1920. And since 1933 the
idea had been under quiet consideration in Roosevelt's Treasury
Department. It appealed to Morgenthau, as to Roosevelt, pri-

marily as a means of frustrating individual surtax avoidance in high-income brackets. As Roosevelt explained to a press conference, a tax on undistributed profits would prevent rich men "from continuing the practice of leaving their profits . . . in the company without paying income taxes on them, thereby increasing their wealth year by year without the Government getting any tax on that increase until they died." Probably as much as $4.5 billion of corporate income was thus withheld from taxation in 1936, depriving the government of over $1.3 billion in revenue. Roosevelt further claimed that the tax would equalize the burden between incorporated and unincorporated enterprises. He recommended it as the sole tax on corporate income; the corporate income tax, the capital stocks tax, and the excess-profits tax, he said, should be repealed.

The Roosevelt-Morgenthau case rested essentially on the desire to seal up tax leakages and increase revenue. But there were, in addition, deeper economic arguments for the tax — arguments of which Roosevelt and Morgenthau seemed largely unaware. "When every corporation turns its earnings into surpluses," R. G. Tugwell had once written, "a good deal of the purchasing power of the community is made sterile"; and on this theory both he and Marriner Eccles had called in 1933 for an undistributed-profits tax to force corporate profits into purchasing power as wages or dividends. Keynes gave powerful support to this argument in his *General Theory* in 1936, arguing that corporate oversaving "alone was probably sufficient to cause a slump" in the twenties and remained "a serious obstacle to early recovery" in the thirties.

The tax had a further purpose. A change was already beginning to take place in the function of the securities market: large corporations, instead of going to the market for capital, were tending more and more to generate capital within themselves through the retention of earnings. The effect of this change was to remove control over investment from the traditional checks of the money market, to concentrate it further in a few private hands, and to extend what Gardiner Means had called the "administered" system from price policy to investment. The undistributed-profits tax seemed a means to make corporations seeking new funds subject themselves to the control of the money market or of national investment policy. It therefore had appeal as a

device either to decentralize or to rationalize the whole process
of capital formation.

Herman Oliphant, Morgenthau's inexhaustible idea man at
the Treasury, was primarily responsible for reviving the idea in
1936, partly at Means's instigation. The tax appealed equally to
the First and the Second New Dealers. If Tugwell advocated it as
an indispensable part of a federal investment policy, David Cushman Coyle advocated it in order to restore competitive freedom
to the money market. And to some economists of conservative
bent, like Dr. Jacob Viner of the Treasury, it seemed a good thing
if only because it insured the investor the right to determine
what was done with his money.

While all these considerations produced interest in the tax,
it was doubtless its apparent political innocuousness which disposed Roosevelt to select it as the best way of raising extra revenue
in an election year. On paper, the tax not only promised to
improve and simplify the tax structure but to alienate the least
number of uncommitted voters. As Oliphant put it in a Treasury
meeting, "If we have to fight we might as well fight the people
who are our enemies anyway." [4]

v

Morgenthau, needing a vacation, now disappeared to Sea Island,
Georgia, leaving behind an erroneous impression that he disapproved of the taxation of undistributed profits. In his absence,
the burden of carrying the fight before the House Ways and
Means Committee fell to Guy Helvering, the Commissioner of Internal Revenue, and to Oliphant. The first business reaction to
the proposal was markedly unfavorable; but Oliphant's impressive testimony, delivered with stern eye and somber intensity of
voice, overbore all opposition. Most important, Oliphant's presentation converted the ablest member of the Committee, Fred M.
Vinson of Kentucky ("the most intelligent of the lot," Oliphant
reported to Morgenthau, "— and the most ruthless"). While the
Committee restored some of the existing corporation taxes, the
new tax remained the bill's most prominent feature. With Vinson's
backing, the bill passed the House handily on April 29, 1936.

This interval of two months, however, gave the opposition a

chance to organize its forces. By the time the bill reached the Senate Finance Committee — in any case a more conservative group than its House equivalent — the critics of the undistributed-profits tax were speaking with new confidence. Of the first hundred witnesses to appear before the Senate Committee, almost all, except for the Treasury spokesmen, denounced the tax. The arguments against it were of varying persuasiveness. A favorite was that it would prevent corporations from setting aside reserves for a rainy day. To this the tax's advocates replied that corporate reserves had never been larger than in 1929, and that they did more then to bring on the downpour than to provide shelter against the storm. As Robert H. Jackson put it, "If this wealth and purchasing power were better distributed, we might not have so many rainy days." A more impressive argument, used with particular effect by Harry Byrd of Virginia, was that the tax denied the small concern the accumulation of reserves it needed for expansion, and thus threatened to freeze the American corporate structure in its existing mix. Another argument, urged by Robert E. Wood of Sears Roebuck, was that, by forcing business into the money market for new funds, it placed enterprising businessmen "at the mercy of the bankers." The Treasury presented data designed to refute these arguments, but the evidence was inconclusive. Morgenthau himself was impressed by the contention that the bill was unfair to small business.

In the meantime, Eccles was working on an alternative version of the tax. Whereas the Treasury saw the proposal as the basic and exclusive corporation tax, Eccles saw it as primarily a surtax; and he proposed restricting its application to the large corporations where most of the undistributed profits lay. Early in May Eccles sold — or thought he sold — this new theory of the bill to the President. By now the parliamentary situation was hopelessly confused. Most of the Senate Finance Committee wanted to throw the tax out altogether. The House leaders were angry because it looked as if, after they had passed the Treasury version, the administration might now desert them. Morgenthau was both furious at the fact of Eccles's intervention and shaken by his reasoning. And the pressure for adjournment was growing as the Republican convention, scheduled for early June, came nearer.

Eventually the Senate Finance Committee rejected the House bill and proposed instead an increase in the corporate income tax. Then, after Pat Harrison and Bob La Follette threatened to withdraw unless the principle at least were recognized, the Committee added a nominal tax on undistributed profits. The plan passed the Senate in this form. The two divergent bills next went into conference. "With Vinson to lead the fight," Oliphant told Morgenthau, "the result will be altogether different than otherwise." His confidence was justified. Led by Vinson, the House conferees wrote a somewhat strengthened undistributed-profits tax into the final version.

The bill thus established the principle of a tax on undistributed profits. But, despite Vinson, the pulling and hauling of draftsmanship had so attenuated the application that the tax had the capacity neither for good, anticipated by its supporters, nor for evil, dreaded by its opponents. Still, the result gave Roosevelt a sufficient appearance of political success for him to retain the initiative at a time when attention was shifting from Washington to the sites of the two national conventions.[5]

VI

The battle over the undistributed-profits tax vaguely enlivened an exceptionally languid session of Congress; the degree of enlivenment, however, was severely limited by the intricacy of the issue. For the rest, members of Congress waited with restless impatience for the signal which would release them for the political excitements of the summer.

In the closing weeks two bills embodying parts of the legacy of NRA reached the statute books. Just after the Schechter decision Frances Perkins had proposed applying to industries doing business with the federal government the standards of wages, hours, and working conditions which NRA tried to impose on all industry. Now, as the Walsh-Healey bill, this proposal was coming to vote. "This is a measure to regiment the industries of the United States," sternly said Representative James W. Wadsworth of New York, leading the conservative opposition. ". . . It makes the Secretary of Labor the absolute dictator of all wages." But Congress as a whole took the idea with greater calm. The enactment of this rather modest measure kept alive the conception of national industrial standards and provided a basis for more comprehensive wage-and-hour regulation in the future.

The other post-NRA enactment was an instance of congressional rather than administration initiative. The Robinson-Patman bill aimed to extend to wholesalers and independent retailers certain protections which they had enjoyed (or to which they had aspired) under the NRA codes. Its particular objective was to deny the chain store the competitive advantages gained by quantity buying at low prices direct from the manufacturer. Though its backers spoke with deep emotion about the corner grocer and druggist, the bill was actually drafted by the counsel for the United States Wholesale Grocers' Association and was ardently backed by food and drug wholesalers; obviously, chain buying from the manufacturer threatened the wholesaler quite as much as the retailer. The chain stores, fighting back, succeeded in forcing important modifications in the bill during the spring. In the end, the legislative process purged the measure of its more sweeping rigidities, authorized price differentiation in response to differing production costs or competitive situations, and confined its prohibitions to definite abuses by the mass distributors of their market power. Though the bill was Brandeisian in its passion for smallness, the battle did not enlist New Deal emotions. It was essentially a family fight between two sections of the business community. New Deal liberalism had other clients; it had not yet embarked on its unrequited love affair with small business. Most New Dealers therefore regarded the Robinson-Patman bill as an irrelevance. Its enactment completed the major domestic record of an undistinguished congressional session.[6]

VII

Roosevelt had promised business a breathing spell in September 1935. So far as new programs were concerned, he substantially kept the promise. The one novelty of 1936 — the undistributed-profits tax — was forced on him by events which he could not easily have anticipated. In the administration of existing New Deal programs, he showed a comparable moderation. In particular, under the insistent pressure both of Henry Morgenthau and of election year, he displayed new sensitivity to the problems of public spending.

In August 1935 Morgenthau had begun to wonder whether he could stay as Secretary of the Treasury if the President "did not begin to show some signs of economic sense and interest in curtailing government expenditures." Pointing to the business up-swing, Morgenthau proposed liquidating PWA and RFC and can-celing all government projects (including programs such as rural electrification, conservation, and public works) which could not be completed by July 1, 1936. Early in 1936, the Secretary of the Treasury, returning to his favorite theme, warned Roosevelt that the cost of government was his greatest political vulnerability, that White House statements always stressed spending and never economy, and that, if he delayed retrenchment much longer, he would be accused of doing it for political effect. "To my great surprise," as Morgenthau recorded it later, "he sat there very quietly, nodded his head, smiled at me and said, 'You are right.'"

Through February and March 1936 Roosevelt made an earnest effort to cut back public spending. He convened meetings of the heads of emergency agencies and, over their aggrieved protests, reduced their authorizations. He ordered Hopkins and Ickes to make the $4.8 billion for public works last as long as possible. Hopkins was to cut down WPA rolls as winter came to an end. To Congressman Marvin Jones, Roosevelt spoke gravely about the need to reduce the deficit; if it continued to rise, the Treasury would be unable to market government securities. ("I wanted to go over in the corner and hide my face and grin," Morgenthau wrote in his diary, "but instead of that I sat back as though it was an entirely new idea to me . . . and . . . said, you are perfectly right, Mr. President.")

Morgenthau's crusade had some effect. Yet, as no one knew better than the compassionate Secretary of the Treasury, economy was not so easy when there were still over seven million out of work. "I think the next move is industry's," Roosevelt told his press confer-ence a few days after his February talk with Morgenthau. ". . . I am sitting here waiting for them to come and give some kind of solution. But, instead of doing that, they go around the country saying, 'We have to have a balanced budget. We have to have a balanced budget.' A balanced budget isn't putting people to work. I will balance the budget as soon as I take care of the unemployed. . . . Hell, I can stop relief tomorrow. What happens? Tell me that!" He paused and added soberly, "You know, as human beings, what happens if I stop relief tomorrow. It isn't any joke." It wasn't any joke, and it was this which most obstructed the economy drive.[7]

VIII

Morgenthau's campaign against government spending was paralleled by a bankers' campaign against the government's easy-money policy. The flow of gold from abroad into the United States had increased the reserves of the banking system. By the end of 1935, reserves amounted to about $5.5 billion — more than twice as much as the $2.6 billion required by law. These reserves could, in theory, produce a credit expansion of about $30 billion. Winthrop Aldrich of the Chase National Bank spoke for the banking community in calling attention to the supposed danger in the piling up of excess reserves. "There it is," he said darkly, "spread out, explosive material awaiting the match. It invites a far wilder speculation than that which culminated in 1929. . . . I believe that measures should immediately be taken to reduce these excess reserves." The American economy, said Aldrich, oddly overlooking the millions of unemployed, was "running with the throttle chained wide open and the air-brake system removed." A group of academic economists, led by E. W. Kemmerer of Princeton, echoed Aldrich's warning that inflation was the great danger. The Federal Reserve Advisory Council called for the reduction of excess reserves "to obviate the probability [sic] of an undue and dangerous credit inflation."

The panic was a delusion. Far from the excess reserves producing an inflationary expansion of credit, most banks were not able to dispose of the credit they had. There was no evidence of excessive extension of business loans. But the banking community, seeing an opportunity to force interest rates up and thus to increase banking profits, pressed its attack on the easy-money policy. Only the House of Morgan resisted the stampede. "Any premature effort to make money dear, in . . . anticipation of an inflation which does not exist," said Russell Leffingwell, "will defeat its own purpose by retarding recovery."

For some time the Federal Reserve Board held out. But — despite the fact that there was no marked increase in business loans during the early months of 1936 — the concentrated banking pressure finally began to stampede Eccles. In April the reconstituted Open-Market Committee proposed an increase of reserve requirements. Roosevelt told Morgenthau that he was eager to show that the New Deal was as alive to the inflation threat as the bankers, and that he had therefore asked Eccles to raise reserve requirements in May. Decision was delayed until the Treasury could complete its June financing. As the flow of gold from Europe continued to enlarge the reserves, Eccles finally went to the White House in July to recommend a 50 per cent increase in reserve requirements.

The action was not terribly significant. It was not nearly drastic enough for the Aldriches, who wanted a reversal of the easy-money policy and higher interest rates. At the same time, it was interpreted as meaning that the Federal Reserve Board accepted the view that the depression was over and inflation the main threat. "It in no way reversed the Board's easy-money and credit policies," Eccles said later, a little unconvincingly, "though, as expected, it was widely judged as doing just that." Whatever else it meant, it seemed again to indicate new moderation on the administration's part.

So far as policy was concerned, Roosevelt thus kept on his good behavior in 1936. This moderation at times made him restive. "Wait until next year, Henry," he told Morgenthau in May, "I am going to be really radical." "What do you mean?" asked Morgenthau. "I am going to recommend a lot of radical legislation," said Roosevelt with a quizzical look. Morgenthau said, "You are going to be very careful about money spending?" When Roosevelt replied "Yes, I am," Morgenthau said, "Well then, I do not care how radical you are in other matters."

He did remain fairly radical on other matters. If he offered business a breathing spell so far as legislation and administration were concerned, he did not let up in politics. "Nation-wide thinking, nation-wide planning and nation-wide action," he said in New York in April, "are the three great essentials to prevent nation-wide crisis for future generations to struggle through." "We do not change our form of free government," he said in Illinois in June, "when we arm ourselves with new weapons against new devices of crime and cupidity." It might have seemed that this oratorical extremism would nullify the effect of the legislative and administrative moderation. But no doubt Roosevelt hoped that, while the one gave new heart to his friends, the other might diminish the grievances of his enemies. In any case, as winter gave way to spring and spring to summer, everything else was increasingly drowned out in the premonitory roar of election-year politics.[8]

28. Dissidence among the Democrats

WITH THE APPROACH of the presidential election, the New Deal fell under ever more hostile scrutiny. But for a considerable time in 1935 and 1936, the more vociferous criticism came less from Republicans than from dissident Democrats. Of these dissident Democrats, there were two main groups: those who had left the New Deal and those who had never joined it.

II

The most active in the first group were Lewis Douglas and James P. Warburg. These attractive young men, who two years before had been the President's close advisers, were now hurrying back and forth across the country doing their best to bring him down. Both represented the honorable faith of classical economic liberalism, Douglas, with dogmatic certitude; Warburg, with qualification and sophistication. Consequently, both found traditional Republicanism almost as objectionable as Rooseveltian Democracy. "The New Era and the New Deal," as Douglas put it in a statement signed also by Newton D. Baker and Leo Wolman, "are two streams from the same source." That source was monopoly; and if, on balance, the New Dealers seemed worse, it was only because state monopoly was worse than private monopoly.

Douglas had not the shade of a doubt in his mind about where the New Deal was heading. "The present pseudo-planned economy," he said flatly, "leads relentlessly into the complete autocracy and tyranny of the Collective State." Or again: "If the spending policy continues . . . there will be wiped out all of the liberties for which the Anglo-Saxon race has struggled for more than a thousand years." "This is not mere fiction," he would say when producing a gloomy prediction. "It is confirmed by experience." The year 1936 added a new threat: recovery was now coming too fast; unless the "current boom" (as he termed the increase in business activity) was immediately checked, he guaranteed an even more catastrophic collapse in the future.

How were the imperiled Anglo-Saxon liberties to be saved? For Douglas, the "degenerate capitalism" of the Republican twenties was no answer. He saw everything in terms of the classical laissez-faire model; and the acid test of virtue, in his view, was the annual balancing of the budget. Government spending had to be ruthlessly cut. CCC, RFC, AAA, WPA, PWA — all must go. All forms of government favor, including tariffs, must be withdrawn. Power must be transferred from Washington to the states. In such terms Douglas sought to impose a Jeffersonian conception of the state on a society different from anything Jefferson had ever imagined.

Warburg was, as in 1933, far less doctrinaire. But his indictment of the New Deal was equally sharp. Two effective pamphlets — Hell Bent for Election in the fall of 1935 and Still Hell Bent in the spring of 1936 — summed up his case. He was still fond, he said, of the President: "It is much as if I had a brother who was a locomotive engineer and developed color-blindness. I should continue to love my brother, but I should certainly not feel justified in urging his employers to continue trusting him with the lives of others." With suave logic, Warburg tried to show how Roosevelt had meticulously fulfilled the Socialist rather than the Democratic platform of 1932. In so doing, he had led the nation into "an orgy of wild spending," had "flouted the Constitution which he swore on oath to support," and had "made a laughing stock of the sanctity of our national promises." His whole effort was "to lead this nation upon the heels of Russia, Germany, Austria and Italy, away from the democratic principle and toward dictatorship." This made the 1936 election peculiarly fateful. Warburg's view was clear: "barring an extreme radical or an extreme reactionary, almost anyone would be better than Mr. Roosevelt." To defeat him, Warburg suggested, might well turn the tide against dictatorship everywhere and seal the fate of Stalin, Hitler, and Mussolini. Warburg ended reaffirming Douglas's old prophecy: "I say that the decision we shall reach this year may well affect the history of Western civilization." [1]

III

Douglas and Warburg represented a rather new political type — the clean-cut young conservative, more businessman than politician, with tidy views about policy and a commendable desire for public service. For a moment, Franklin Roosevelt had given such men a cherished opportunity to bring sense and order in Washington, until finally the New Deal alienated them by its helter-skelter unorthodoxy. They were quite a different type from the professional politicians of the older Democratic school who, snubbed by Roosevelt and outraged by his policies, hated the New Deal from the start.

This latter group included the Democratic candidates for President in 1924 and 1928, John W. Davis and Al Smith. It included former executives of the Democratic National Committee, John J. Raskob and Jouett Shouse. Conservative Democratic governors, like Albert Ritchie of Maryland and Joseph B. Ely of Massachusetts, and Democratic elder statesmen, like Newton D. Baker, were in the general orbit. These men represented the old-line leadership of the Democratic party which Roosevelt had quietly but firmly deposed. "In some mysterious way," as John W. Davis mournfully put it, "the whole course and direction of our party seems to have changed."

The new course terrified them. In May 1936 Baker sent his old friend, John W. Clarke, the only living retired Justice of the Supreme Court, an impassioned arraignment of the Roosevelt administration — for breaking its campaign promises, for its "frightful extravagance," for "the wickedness of a political administration of these government favors." "Our present government," Baker said, "is a government by propaganda and terrorism, the like of which I have never seen and against the continuance of which I protest with all the vehemence I am capable of." No doubt, Baker added, Clarke had missed much of this in his "Arcadian retreat." (Clarke drily replied, "In my Arcadian retreat, I have not, as you say, seen anything of the 'propaganda and terrorism' of which you wrote and I should like to know what you refer to.")

Turning from the new Democratic party, a number of these displaced persons had joined together in 1934 to create a spiritual home away from home in the American Liberty League. In 1935 the League erupted into furious activity. It spent twice as much money that year as the Republican party. Its pamphlets, lavishly printed and widely circulated, depicted the United States on the verge of socialism, bankruptcy, and tyranny. Hardly any New Deal policy escaped the League's disapproval. AAA was a "trend toward Fascist control of agriculture"; the Holding Company Act, a "blow at invested capital"; the Guffey Act, "a step toward further aggrandizement of an ever spreading governmental bureaucracy"; relief and social security were "the end of democracy"; NRA had plunged the nation into a "quicksand of visionary experimentation." The New Deal was at once infinitely clever and infinitely incompetent. John W. Davis solemnly warned that the influence of the American Congress would soon be "little more than that of the present Congress of the Soviets, the Reichstag of Germany or the Italian Parliament."

But the American people seemed inadequately moved. Outside of the innumerable du Ponts, such talk won meager mass response. Early in 1936 the League decided to make one great effort to break through. For this purpose Raskob and Shouse prevailed upon the popular hero of the twenties, Al Smith, to deliver their message.

Smith had traveled a long distance from his days as progressive governor of New York. He had largely turned his back, for example, on his old humanitarianism. Thus in 1934 he joined a committee to fight a proposed amendment abolishing child labor. Even more improbably, by the early autumn of 1935 common hatred of the New Deal had dissolved his historic feud with William Randolph Hearst. In a bull from San Simeon excommunicating the "imported, autocratic, Asiatic Socialist party of Karl Marx and Franklin Delano Roosevelt," Hearst actually proposed his once hated foe as Jeffersonian Democratic candidate for President. Roosevelt's one-time friend and patron now seemed eaten up with bitterness. Telling Emil Ludwig how Roosevelt had betrayed the party, Smith, in his office high in the Empire State Building, snatched a book, rose to his feet, and thundered forth the ancient dogmas of states' rights. "There he stood, a threatening figure, black against the dazzling sun of the world city." After hearing him pour out his aggrieved feelings, his heavy cigar twisting between his lips as he talked, Ludwig concluded, "Smith lacks, in age and defeat, that inner equilibrium which alone can save a disappointed man." [2]

IV

Two thousand guests gathered in the banquet hall of the Mayflower Hotel in Washington on January 25, 1936. Among them were an even dozen du Ponts, old Democratic leaders like Davis and Ritchie, dissident younger Democrats like Warburg and Dean Acheson, businessmen like Winthrop Aldrich and Ernest T. Weir, and a miscellany of other figures, like Elizabeth Dilling and her husband. The audience, according to the *New York Times* "represented, either through principals or attorneys, a large portion of the capitalistic wealth of the country." For an hour Smith, resplendent in white tie and tails, assailed Roosevelt and all his works. "It is all right with me," Smith said of the New Dealers, "if they want to disguise themselves as Karl Marx or Lenin or any of the rest of that bunch, but I won't stand for their allowing them to march under the banner of Jackson or Cleveland." (While he no longer mispronounced the word "radio," he still frequently employed "ain't," enchanting listeners who had been repelled by precisely such solecisms eight years earlier.) His peroration summed up his message. "Let me give this solemn warning: There can be only one capital, Washington or Moscow. There can be only one atmosphere of government, the clean, pure, fresh air of free America, or the foul breath of communistic Russia."

Pierre S. du Pont said afterward, "It was perfect." It may have been perfect for the du Ponts, but it was disaster for the Liberty League. Joe Robinson, who had been Smith's running mate in 1928, was selected to make the administration's response. Armed with a speech by Charles Michelson and additional notes from Cordell Hull (whose fading liberalism was momentarily renewed by Smith's performance), Robinson delivered a slashing answer to the "unhappy warrior." "It was the swellest party ever given by the du Ponts," Robinson said. Smith had "turned away from the East Side with those little shops and fish markets, and now his gaze rests fondly upon the gilded towers and palaces of Park Avenue." Appealing directly to Smith, Robinson concluded: "It was as difficult to conceive you at that Liberty League banquet as it would be to imagine George Washington waving a cheery good-bye to the ragged and bleeding band at Valley Forge while he rode forth to dine in sumptuous luxury with smug and sanctimonious Tories in near-by Philadelphia." John L. Lewis expressed contempt more crisply. Smith's speech, Lewis said, was the act of "a gibbering political jackanapes."

On hearing that Smith was coming to Washington, Roosevelt had promptly asked him to spend the night at the White House, an invitation which Smith as promptly declined. "I just can't understand it," Roosevelt said to Frances Perkins. "Practically all the things we've done in the federal government are like things Al Smith did as governor of New York. They're things he would have done if he had been President. . . . What in the world is the matter?" Roosevelt doubtless knew well enough what the matter was. And he had reason to be grateful to his old friend. Arthur Krock of the *New York Times* subsequently dated the revival of Roosevelt's popularity in 1936 from the Liberty League dinner.[3]

v

The Mayflower banquet proved conclusively that the Liberty League was not a potent political instrumentality. Indeed, some of its backers had already begun to search for an alternative with greater popular appeal. Raskob and the du Ponts in particular were prepared to support almost anyone who promised to stir the masses — even, it developed, Governor Eugene Talmadge of Georgia.

Nothing better demonstrated the naïveté — or the desperation — of the American right than this decision. Since his election as governor in 1933, Talmadge had become a strident figure on the national scene. He seemed a character out of Erskine Caldwell, with black rumpled hair, suspicious eyes glaring behind thick horn-rimmed glasses, a black cigar jutting out of his wide fleshy mouth, and a collection of poor-white prejudices ejaculated with restless and rabid intensity. Talmadge, who held a law degree from the University of Georgia, was actually much less the uncouth backwoodsman from Sugar Creek than he pretended. But his clientele were the wool-hat boys; and he went around the state, his thumbs in his famous red galluses, giving them what they wanted. "I expect I know nearly every pig path in the State and every creek, and river and branch," he said in his inaugural address on his re-election in 1935. And he went on to offer his creed: "The only way to have an honest government is to keep it poor. You can't help the people by giving them something. You weaken their soul and their heart, and dry up their muscles."

From the governor's mansion in Ansley Park, Talmadge spat at the New Deal with contempt. Little riled him more than NRA standards of wages and hours, unless possibly it was the WPA standards of relief. When Ben Stolberg asked him what he would do for the unemployed, Talmadge roared back, "Let 'em starve." The Governor then added, "What you need in New York is not La Guardia but Mussolini. A little castor oil would go a long ways toward starting the wheels of industry goin' again." (Stolberg concluded he was talking to Buzz Windrip.) By 1935 Talmadge had engaged in bitter fights with Hugh Johnson, with Harry Hopkins, and with Harold Ickes (who called him "his chain-gang Excellency" and described him as looking "more like a rat than any other human being that I know . . . [with] all of the mean, poisonous, and treacherous characteristics of that rodent"). By now Talmadge courteously referred to Roosevelt as "that cripple in the White House." His deepest emotion, however, was his belief in white supremacy. "No niggah's 's good as a white man," he told William Bradford Huie, "because the niggah's only a few shawt year-ahs from cannibalism."

At some point Talmadge began to glimpse larger horizons. In 1935 he engaged in friendly political discussions with Huey Long. Talmadge had no use for Share Our Wealth ("I believe in small government and small taxes and getting the government out of business"); but, like Long, he was ready to make any deal which might stop Roosevelt and, hopefully, benefit himself. With Huey gone, Gene's ambitions soared higher than ever. A Texas lumberman named John Henry Kirby presently waited on him as chairman of the Southern Committee to Uphold the Constitution. Kirby and Talmadge soon conceived the idea of a convention of grassroots Democrats to denounce the New Deal and (though this was less advertised) to launch the Talmadge presidential boom.

Talmadge's retrenchment policies — especially the across-the-

board reduction of the property tax, which gave immense benefits to the Georgia Power Company while saving the average
Georgia farmer 53 cents a year — had won him a good name
among businessmen. When a political promoter named Vance Muse
now applied to the du Pont group on his behalf, he found a more
than amiable response. Raskob, a couple of du Ponts, and Alfred
Sloan soon offered the money to stage the meeting.

Late in January 1936 the forces gathered at Macon, Georgia, to
save the republic — Thomas L. Dixon, the author of *The Clans-
man*, Gerald L. K. Smith, an assortment of other southern spellbinders, and Talmadge himself, in a green double-breasted suit
with a sapphire pin on his black necktie. Above the platform hung
the Stars and Bars of the Confederacy. On every seat lay a copy
of the *Georgia Woman's World* with a two-column photograph
splashed across the page; it was, as described by Vance Muse,
"a picture of Mrs. Roosevelt going to some nigger meeting, with two
escorts, niggers, on each arm." The *Woman's World* went on to
complain that the President was permitting "negroes to come to
the White House banquets and sleep in the White House beds."
And it thoughtfully inquired whether the voters of Georgia really
wanted the New Deal to "get the anti-lynching bill passed — for
the purpose of permissive ravishment."

Even in Georgia the grass-roots convention played only to a
half-filled auditorium (and for those present, Gerald Smith
stole the show from its supposed star). What gave the episode
significance was the readiness of northern businessmen — who presumably knew by 1936 all that it was necessary to know about
Gene Talmadge — to give him money to advance his ideas and ambitions. Some of them — Sloan and Henry du Pont, for example
— actually sent along their contributions *after* the revelations of
Macon. Arthur Krock ascribed it not to malice but to gullibility,
and he was doubtless right. The frightened rich were evidently at
the mercy of every fast-talking political adventurer who came down
the street.

Other attempts on the part of the Liberty Leaguers, du Pont
section, to break through to the masses were even more ludicrous.
One shrewd promoter sold them the idea of establishing something
called the Farmers' Independence Council. The only known address
of the organization was the Liberty League office in Washing-

ton. "The biggest contributor," remarked the *Philadelphia Record*, "was that old hayseed, Lammot du Pont, who kicked in $5000. (Crops pretty good this year, ain't they Lammot!)" Other interested agriculturists were Sloan, Ogden Mills, Winthrop Aldrich, and Pew of Sun Oil. Relentless congressional investigation failed to disclose a single working farmer in the membership.

In the spring of 1936 Hugo Black's Special Committee to Investigate Lobbying Activities got around to looking at the du Pont political subsidiaries — the Southern Committee to Uphold the Constitution, the Farmers' Independence Council, the Crusaders, the Sentinels of the Republic. The result of the unfeeling exposure of rich men as political suckers was merriment in the press and a permanent conviction that the American Liberty League was a political bust. By midsummer, in the cruelest blow of all, the Republican party begged the Liberty League to stay away from its presidential ticket.[4]

29. Revival among the Republicans

WHILE THE DISSIDENT DEMOCRATS were expending themselves in comic political exercises, the official opposition was engaged in business both more serious and more complex. The Republican party had been in inner turmoil since its staggering losses in the mid-term election of 1934. This disaster had reopened the perennial family dispute whether the party should stand by its ancient principles or whether it should liberalize itself to keep up with changing times.

William E. Borah put one side of the issue with characteristic disheveled force. Unless the Republican party was delivered from its "reactionary" leadership, he said, it would die like the Whig party "of sheer political cowardice." "I don't think there is any room in this country for an old conservative party"; "the driving power in politics in this country for years to come will come from labor, from the producer, from small business, and from millions who have, through no fault of their own, been stripped of their life's savings and life's opportunities." What was the Grand Old Party offering such people? "They are offered the Constitution. But the people can't eat the Constitution. . . . I should like to see the Republican party reorganized." [1]

II

Hiram Johnson dourly responded, "First you will have to have something to reorganize." But other progressives backed Borah. "The trouble with our beloved party," said William Allen White, "is that it is shot through with the plutocratic conquest. . . . It cannot live with fatty degeneration of the heart." The party's future, said Gerald Nye, "must be that of [the] liberalism which some Republicans have been voicing for years, only to have their voices drowned by the jeers of Republican leaders, who cried: 'Red,' 'Insurgents,' 'Traitors' "; the party must turn its back "upon that which has been its undoing, namely the private money bags." "The Republican party," said Gifford Pinchot, "must go Progressive or go bust." "It should now be plain," said Charles McNary, the Republican Senate leader, "that a party cannot gain the attention of a people distraught by business and employment worries by extolling the nobility of the forefathers and the sanctity of the Constitution, and by spreading alarms over regimentation and bureaucracy. . . . We ought to accept and acknowledge the good that is to be found in the Administration program."

Such latitudinarian views enraged the traditional party bosses. The Republican chairman Henry P. Fletcher pronounced "constitutional government" the issue: "the Constitution is not so 'resilient' as Mr. Roosevelt imagines; on the contrary, it is as rigid as every foundation must be." Charles Hilles of New York, the most influential of the Old Guard leaders, thought that "the only useful purpose" which the Republican party could serve was to offer "a resolute resistance to economic heresies." "The Republican party, Hilles added, "cannot stagger to the left." ("No," cried William E. Borah, ". . . we are not going to stagger, but we are going to the left as sure as I am alive.") Ogden Mills and Herbert Hoover joined in opposing the liberalization movement.

In the meantime, Republican prospects appeared to be looking up. In August 1935 they won a congressional by-election in Rhode Island. In November they held the city of Philadelphia and recaptured the New York Assembly. Through the fall they were unduly impressed by the big-name conservative Democrats who seemed ready to defect to their ranks. As Roosevelt's popularity sagged to unprecedented lows in the early winter, some Republicans succumbed to euphoria about 1936. In an only slightly heightened version of a general optimism, H. L. Mencken, still smarting perhaps from the Gridiron dinner, analyzed the process of national disenchantment. In 1933, he said, America had been told that utopia was on the way. "Wizards of the highest amperage, it appeared, were at hand to do the job, and they were armed with new and infallible arcana." They would produce the more abundant life, with everyone rich and happy and the very birds in the trees singing hallelujah. But what did these wizards turn out to be, once they had got into the ring? — "the sorriest mob of mountebanks ever gathered together at one time, even in Washington . . . vapid young pedagogues, out-of-work YMCA secretaries, third-rate journalists, briefless lawyers, and soaring chicken farmers." On only one point did they agree — that any man who worked hard, saved his money, and tried to provide security for his children was a low and unmitigated scoundrel. "To hand over to such incandescent vacuums the immensely difficult and complicated problems which now confront the country is as insane as it would be to hand over a laparotomy to a traffic cop." As for the President, he had survived for a long time through the very flexibility of his principles. "If he became convinced tomorrow that coming out for cannibalism would get him the votes he so sorely needs, he would begin fattening a missionary in the White House backyard come Wednesday." But the people were at last catching on. They were grasping the fact that, if they can beat Roosevelt at all, "they can beat him with a Chinaman or even with a Republican." [2]

III

No eligible Chinaman seemed available; but a number of Republicans were prepared to make the great sacrifice. First in any speculation stood, of course, Herbert Hoover. In power of mind and personality, he was still the dominant figure in the party. He plainly felt that his Presidency had been a success, that he had been betrayed by events beyond his control and traduced by unscrupulous propagandists; and he gave every indication of a passionate desire for vindication.

In 1935 he burst into new activity, traveling around the country more than in any year since his defeat. His publicity built him up as "the new Hoover" — mellow, pungent, and human. His speeches did now have surprising flashes of a certain grim humor. The New Deal, he would say, is about to run out of letters for its alphabetical agencies; "but, of course, the new Russian alphabet has thirty-four letters." In content, however, his addresses showed little change. In the main, they repeated the indictment he had

made the year before in *A Challenge to Liberty.* He denounced
spending, he denounced regimentation, he denounced centralization. For a positive program he offered only his old formula:
retrenchment, the balanced budget, the gold standard, the tariff,
the return of relief to the states. "Hoover feels that our property
rights are set in the cement of the bill of rights," wrote William
Allen White after a visit with the ex-President. ". . . I believe we
can give up a good deal of vested interest and still survive as a
democracy. We wrangled a little about that." Still, a crusading
fervor shone through his fierce determination to awaken the
country to its danger; and at times he achieved eloquence in
invoking the older America of individual enterprise and individual
responsibility. "The real sympathy from the national heart," he
said early in 1936, "flows far more truly through personal leadership in the community than through Federal agents. There is a
spiritual loss in all this which cannot be estimated. . . . One
need of the nation today is a recall of the spirit of individual
service. That spirit springs from the human heart, not from politics.
Upon that spirit alone can this democracy survive." He added, "No
greater call to service could be made than to remobilize local
administration of relief."

But Hoover frightened most Republican politicians. His embrace, they believed, meant political death; the party could pros-
per only as it got as far away as possible from its last President
— a feeling which told not only against Hoover but also against
Ogden Mills. By the end of 1935 the politicians were talking
much more of four other names, all suitably removed from the
Hoover contamination. They were Borah, Colonel Frank Knox, the
publisher of the *Chicago Daily News,* Governor Alfred M. Landon
of Kansas, and, as a permanent Republican dark horse, Senator
Arthur H. Vandenberg of Michigan. All more or less — Borah most,
Knox least — represented the liberal wing of the party, and regarded the New Deal, not in Hoover's terms of unalloyed evil,
but as a mixture of good and bad.[3]

IV

Borah, indeed, had voted for many more New Deal measures
than he had opposed. The old man was seventy in 1935; he had
served in the Senate for over a quarter of a century; but his

vigor was undiminished, and he was showing a personal interest
in the presidential nomination as never before in his long
career. So surprising was this on the part of one who had always
seemed the lone wolf of American politics that many insisted he
could not really mean it — he was launching a presidential boom,
they said, to build himself up for a tough re-election campaign
in Idaho against a popular Democratic governor, or he was doing
it in order to have enough power at the convention to force the
Republican party to take a liberal platform and candidate. Doubtless both motives played their part, as well, perhaps, as the inex-
tinguishable confidence of an aging giant who, in a time of pyg-
mies, thought he might as well condescend to the Presidency.

The essence of Borah's liberalism was an attack on monopoly.
He had little new to propose in the way of solution — federal
incorporation and regulation for all business in interstate commerce — but he flourished the issue with threatening political
effect against other Republican leaders. For labor and the farmers,
Borah offered deep concern, if little new in the way of a program.
He displayed such warm sympathy for Dr. Townsend (who had many
followers in Idaho) that, though Borah reluctantly came out against
the Townsend Plan early in 1936, Townsend still was ready to
change his registration to Republican in order to support him for
President. And he preserved his standing as a constitutional expert not by ritual genuflections alone, but by opposing at some
political disadvantage measures he considered constitutionally objectionable, like the antilynching bill.

Borah's liberalism always had its perverse aspects, however, and
nothing more sharply distinguished him from his fellow Progressive Republicans than his inexorable regularity in presidential years
— even supporting Hoover in 1932, even William Howard Taft in
1912. In this respect he also differed from his active rivals in
1936, Knox and Landon, both of whom had followed Teddy Roosevelt into the Bull Moose heresy. Knox, indeed, had been a Rough
Rider in Cuba as well as chairman of the credentials committee
at the Progressive convention (though a misunderstanding with
T. R., later repaired, kept him out of the campaign); and T. R.
remained the hero of his life. He served overseas in the First World
War, enlisting as a private at the age of forty-three and ending
with a commission as colonel in the Field Artillery Reserve. For

the rest, he had been a newspaper publisher in Michigan, New Hampshire, and Massachusetts; for three years in the late twenties he was general manager of the Hearst newspapers. He now owned the *Chicago Daily News*, which he ran along intelligent conservative lines; it had admirable coverage of the nation and the world; and its impartiality in news play applied even to its publisher's presidential aspirations. As a politician, Knox modeled himself on T. R. — toothy grin, jerky movements, vigorous epithets, bristling reactions. He once gave a radio talk entitled "Roosevelt vs. Roosevelt." "I draw the parallelism," he told his wife, "between the Europeanized Regimentation of Franklin Roosevelt with the stalwart Americanism of Theodore." What the nation needed, he said in 1935, was "fewer and better Roosevelts." He was sixty-one years old; and with his still reddish hair, his ruddy complexion, his heavy face, he had the gruff look of an aging country squire.

Knox somehow convinced himself that there was a deep anti-New Deal groundswell throughout the nation. His editorials and speeches therefore took a rather mechanical anti-New Deal line, with much forthright talk about Marxism, "Tovarich Tugwell," state socialism, and coercion supplanting individual liberty. "Upon what food does this our Caesar feed?" Knox cried in Los Angeles in 1935. "What madness has seized upon him? Does he not see how dangerously close this comes to conspiracy to break down our institutions of government?" (After a certain amount of this, a newspaperman asked Roosevelt whether Knox and Hoover were on the Democratic payroll. "Strictly off the record," the President replied, "it is a question of how much longer we can afford to pay them. They have been so successful that they are raising their prices.")

His public expressions did Knox something of an injustice. Like Ickes, Pinchot, Richberg, and other T. R. devotees, the Colonel had adopted the Bull Moose rhetorical convention of picturesque exaggeration by which nothing seemed worth saying if not said at the top of one's voice. Behind the ring of Liberty League clichés he remained rather flexible and pragmatic. His advisers were not the Old Guard, but rather younger and more imaginative people, like James P. Warburg. After several talks with Knox, Raymond Swing wrote that he remained in many respects the old Bull Mooser, "as anyone will learn in private conversation with him."

"He and I are still good personal friends," said Ickes, "and he doesn't overstep all the bounds of decency as does the *Tribune*." [4]

v

The other veteran of the Bull Moose crusade, Alfred M. Landon, had been the only Republican elected governor west of the Mississippi in 1932, and the only Republican governor re-elected anywhere two years later. His success in the midst of the rout of 1934 first attracted eastern Republican politicians; and the reports of his annual success in balancing the Kansas budget further whetted professional interest. Newspapers started to call him "the Kansas Coolidge." This was an appealing thought for conservatives disturbed by the supposed orgy of New Deal spending. In Kansas a small group, headed by Roy Roberts and Lacy Haynes of the *Kansas City Star* and consisting largely of Landon's former collegemates, began in 1935 to promote him for President.

Landon was forty-eight years old. He was born in Pennsylvania; but his father, an oil company superintendent, had taken the family west to Kansas when young Alfred was in his teens. The boy went on to the state university, where his proficiency in campus politics won him the nickname, detested ever after, of "Fox." He was evidently a gay dog, and introduced one of the first dinner jackets into university society. Though he took a law degree, he never practiced, trying his hand at banking instead. When this seemed unpromising, he turned to the oil business. Here his shrewdness and drive brought relatively quick success. By the nineteen twenties, he was well known as an independent oil producer and had become a comparatively wealthy man. He became known as Alf in the oil fields, and thereafter rarely used his full name.

He was also growing increasingly interested in Republican state politics. Within the party, he worked with the liberal faction. When William Allen White ran as an independent candidate for Governor in protest against the influence of the Ku Klux Klan in both major parties, Landon unhesitatingly backed him. He was afterward associated with the political fortunes of the erratic progressive Clyde Reed. In 1932 he entered the gubernatorial race against the Democratic incumbent, Harry Woodring, and a political adventurer named Dr. John ("Goat Glands") Brinkley. Landon campaigned on the need for economy: "Our great danger lies in lack of courage to retrench. . . . We must attack the cost of government from every angle. Nothing is too small to overlook." Brinkley took enough votes away from Woodring to give Landon the election.

What the nation heard most about Landon was his dedication to fiscal austerity. But his achievements in government economy were not so notable as they looked on the surface, and in any case they misrepresented his real qualities. It is true enough that he balanced the budget. But so had his Democratic predecessor; and it would have been extremely difficult for any governor in Kansas — precisely because of laws enacted under the Woodring administration — to spend more than he received. Moreover, Landon could hardly have balanced the budget and survived if it had not been for the nearly $400 million of federal money the New Deal put into the state. His passion for retrenchment was sincere enough: between 1932 and 1935 the per-capita cost of state government fell from $15.68 to $13.41. Landon accomplished this in part, though, by passing responsibility from the state to local governmental units. Characteristically, he once wrote, "Kansas should change its way of handling the state institutions. . . . We should charge each county for the patients which they send to the state institutions." At the same time, it should be said, he did his best to enforce the pay-as-you-go principle on counties, towns, and school districts.

Some of the general reduction in government costs inevitably took place at the expense of public services. Landon's critics claimed that his policies left schools, jails, and hospitals for the insane in distressing shape. Part of this criticism blamed Landon for things beyond his direct control. The state government had never, for example, given aid to the common schools; so the Governor was hardly responsible for the fact that the average annual salary of grade teachers in 1933–34 was only $615. He was, it is true, responsible for closing down some 700 of these schools, but this represented, not just the economy drive, but also a consolidation of four- or five-pupil rural schools long urged by the state's educators.

Landon also regarded relief as a local rather than a state responsibility. "The Governor of Kansas," said Harry Hopkins in a moment of irritation, "has never put up a thin dime for the unemployed in Kansas. [He exaggerated: the state gave nothing for relief, but did contribute some $200,000 to help pay the administrative expenses of the program.] . . . Of course some cities and counties in Kansas have done well, but the State has not done anything. The last thing I knew about the Governor he was trying to get money out of me to keep his schools open." Someone interrupted to say that, after all, the Landon administration had balanced the budget. Hopkins said caustically, "They have taken it out of the hides of the people."

VI

While it was true enough that Landon cared deeply about retrenchment, this concern did not, as it did with Coolidge, constitute his entire social philosophy. The picture of "the Kansas Coolidge" did him an injustice. "He is neither tight nor taciturn," said William Allen White. "I never liked to be called 'the Kansas Coolidge,'" Landon wrote White after reading *A Puritan in Babylon* in 1939. ". . . The Coolidge family were always, apparently, all regulars — my family were always insurgents." Landon was no unfeeling penny pincher, persuaded that economy was the only public virtue. He was rather a modest and decent embodiment of small-town liberalism, who had an excellent record on civil liberties (when Norman Thomas came to town in 1934, Landon chaired the meeting) and who retained something of the old Bull Moose progressivism in his attitude toward government. It is no accident that White, who expressed better than anyone else the humane civic spirit of the middle border, was Landon's friend. "His father was a leader in the Rooseveltian revolt from 1909 to 1916," as White put it, "and the boy was brought up in the way he should go. . . . He naturally believes in using the Government as an agency of human welfare."

Landon had not only been on the liberal side in state politics, but he had maintained an interest in larger liberal affairs. He had been an admirer of Woodrow Wilson and a supporter of the League of Nations. He had subscribed to the *New Republic* in the days of Herbert Croly. "I looked with much interest on the Russian experiment," he wrote in 1937. "Contrary to a great many folks, I felt the leaders who initiated that move were sincere." He never denied that he voted for La Follette and Wheeler in 1924. "The scandals of the Harding Administration," he later wrote, "warranted the defeat of the Republican Party." In his inaugural address he could say, in hardly the conventional accents of Republicanism, "Our problems have been intensified by the great industrial plutocracy we have built since the last depression of 1893." He had no faith in a return to laissez faire. "I do not believe," he said, "the Jeffersonian theory that the best government is the one that governs the least can be applied today. I think that as civilization becomes more complex, government power must increase."

As governor, he contemplated for a while the establishment of a state-owned gas system for Kansas — wells, pipelines, and local distribution. He even solicited the aid of Harold Ickes in advance planning, but finally (to his later regret) decided not to go ahead on the ground of expense. He had no liking for the power companies, and secured the passage of a law requiring them to pay the costs of investigation by the state public-utilities commission. "The utilities," he wrote to a friend, "by refusing to recognize their semi-public position, are driving the country to public ownership as the choice of the lesser of two evils."

Holding these views, Landon showed himself (at least till the Presidency loomed up ahead) generally sympathetic to the purposes of the New Deal. "From the very first," he said in 1934, "I advocated the granting of unusual powers to the President because of the national emergency." And again: "I have cooperated with the New Deal to the best of my ability." In the spring of 1935 he even issued public praise of Rexford G. Tugwell — an extreme act. Nor did he flinch from New Deal economics. "I do not think there is anything new or revolutionary about the redistribution of wealth theory," he wrote privately. "Every wise statesman in every period of history has been concerned with the equitable distribution of property in his country." Nor did the New Deal seem to him to portend the end of everything he held sacred. "America bids fair to join the procession of nations of the world in their march toward a new social and economic philosophy," he said in his 1935 inaugural. "Some say this will lead to socialism, some communism, others fascism. For myself I am convinced that the ultimate goal will be a modified form of individual rights and ownership of property out of which will come a wider spread of prosperity and opportunity."

In December 1935 Charles P. Taft, the younger son of William Howard Taft, came to Topeka to speak to the young Republicans. Taft, who had served the Roosevelt administration as a conciliator in labor disputes, was known as a liberal Republican. Once asked to give a speech damning F.D.R. and all his works, Taft replied, "I can't and won't, and some of the Republican orators and candidates who do, give me an acute pain in the neck." At Topeka, Taft pointed out that the Republicans could win in 1936 only by reclaiming about 15 per cent of the voters from the New Deal. "Surely it is not a switch of the standpatters that will defeat Roosevelt. This leads to one inevitable conclusion. We must not yield to the standpatters' idea of policy. We don't want to insult them or drive them unnecessarily off the reservation, but it seems to me that we should act 'like they wasn't there.' " Taft added, "We cannot sit back and let people starve, and no more can we let individual human beings live in hopeless squalor, drudgery and fear." The Democrats have taken us on a spending spree of confused government expansion, "but the answer to that policy is not masterly inactivity."

This address very much impressed Landon, who asked Taft to send him a number of copies. Government, in Landon's view, had to act; but, as he put it, "it is something to be approached slowly, with caution, not with inertia but with competency. We have had too much of the slap-dash, jazzy method." It was here that he dissented from the New Deal — not from its objectives but from its execution. He felt that Roosevelt "had asked a good many proper questions. To me, he seems increasingly to find the wrong answers." He summed up his position in a frank letter to a close friend in August 1935:

If we should succeed in reelecting a president, there is enough legislation already on the statute books that has received haphazard administrative methods to keep him busy for the next four years. Many of the things which Roosevelt has tried have failed because of the lack of clear-cut, definite and vigorous administrative leadership. Any good administrator will have his hands full for the next few years trying to bring order out of chaos, because we are not going to unscramble all of these eggs. Some of these experiments might work satisfactorily if they had a chance. . . .

So I want to see a man who will go in with a fair and open frame of mind and attempt to adjust and manage them, plus a genuine budget-balancing, tax-reducing program; then in a few years we can tell which of the New Deal experiments are basically wrong. I suspect a good many of them are, but I feel that some of them might be made to work. . . .

The next president who succeeds Mr. Roosevelt, when, as and if, is in a good bit the same position as the captain of a tugboat which is hitched to a liner that is on the rocks. If he tightens up the cable too quickly, it will part, and the liner with its load of passengers will then be completely wrecked. His job is to ease the liner off the rocks, and he can't do that by any sudden strain on his cable. In other words, if we reverse too quickly I believe it will put too much of a strain on our social and political institutions.

The moral of this for Republican policy seemed evident.

My fear is . . . that those who will have considerable to say in the next Republican convention will want to hang, quarter, and shoot at sunrise, — that the bitter-enders will control. If we should succeed in winning with that kind of program, the crisis will simply be deferred until 1940 or later. Action, of course, always brings reaction, and the pendulum, swinging so far back to the right, if we succeed in winning, will undoubtedly follow a counter-swing possibly even further to the left than even now.

Landon, in short, was a rather rigid conservative in fiscal policy; he disliked the national debt, feared inflation, and wanted a balanced budget and the gold standard. He was somewhat conservative in a broad preference for states' rights as against federal action. He was hardly conservative at all in such areas as civil liberties or the regulation of business or conservation or the objectives of social welfare. He occupied a middle ground between the old-fashioned Republicans and the New Deal. "I think four more years of the same policies that we have had will wreck our parliamentary government," he wrote in November 1935, "and four years of the old policies will do the job also."

He enforced these views with a mild but determined personality. He was a man of medium height with a bland Midwestern face, gray eyes behind rimless glasses, flat and drawling speech, and the general appearance of a small-town businessman. Kansas knew him best in riding trousers, with high-laced boots, a leather jacket, and an old brown hat, driving in from the oil fields in his old coupé. In the evening he relaxed in the big white house in Independence filled with old-fashioned mahogany furniture; here he chatted lazily on the front-porch swing in summer twilight or played poker in the parlor and raided the icebox in the late evening. The foxiness which had marked him in college still had its moments; "nothing in Alfred Landon's life," wrote William Allen White, "has ever been casual." But his essentially self-contained quality was offset by the peculiarly engaging smile, the forthright candor, the lack of front or pretense. His bad qualities, said White, were "a mulish stubbornness and a Napoleonic selfishness." They were not often displayed in public. For all the quiet deliberation of his manner, he was warm and friendly in personal relations. His charm captivated such diverse people as Raymond Swing and William Randolph Hearst.[5]

VII

Did he have, in addition, presidential qualities? "I have never been able to visualize him as President," White wrote in July 1935. Still, he would not exclude the possibility. "Responsibility does a lot to a man. If he has any iron, it becomes steel, any quartz, it becomes gold." For the moment, however, White thought that Landon had better ripen in the Senate. But Roy Roberts and Lacy Haynes had other ideas; so did Landon himself. The presidential gleam had entered his eyes some time before the mid-term election. "It doesn't mean anything to me," he wrote deprecatingly to Ben Hibbs of *The Country Gentleman* as early as June 1934, "because I have no idea that the Republican party will be so hard up as to name a man from Kansas." A year later, in June 1935, he confided to a friend that eastern Republicans like Bertrand H. Snell of New York and George Moses of New Hampshire were reported to feel "that I was the most available candidate." "The value of the nomination," Landon added, "has steadily increased."

Soon the amateurs around Landon were reinforced by the addition of John D. M. Hamilton, the Kansas National Committeeman. Hamilton had been associated with the Old Guard faction in the state, but he was a smooth and effective politician with valuable eastern contacts, and he threw his considerable talents into promoting the boom. He wrote encouragingly to Landon after a ten-day swing through New England in July 1935, "Even I was astounded to find that you were so well known." At the same time, he persistently warned Landon against yielding to his own liberal inclinations. Thus Hamilton reported Jim Watson of Indiana as saying "one thing that I hear expressed more and more as time goes on and that is that the party can't stand for a candidate who has a record of supporting the New Deal and he asked me in detail as to what attitude you had taken. . . . I believe it would be good tactics for you to open up gradually on Roosevelt taking subjects on which he has patently been wrong at first and then slowly increase your fire as we go into next Spring."

Landon responded somewhat to this pressure. "As I see it," he told Ben Hibbs in August 1935, "our basic issue should be the waste and extravagant expenditure of this administration. He is the most magnificent spender since King Solomon." "Frankly, as a matter of cold blooded politics," he told Mark Sullivan, "I am willing to make this fight along whatever line it seems to have the best hope and chance of winning." Spending seemed the best issue, though "it may be that six months from now we shall want to be stressing something else."

In the fall of 1935 interest in Landon whirled up almost overnight. After all, he came from the Middle West, had progressive leanings, was not identified with the Hoover wing, and might bring the farmers back into the party. Yet he was a businessman, a budget-balancer, showed none of the stigmata of the wild jackass, and could well be acceptable to eastern financial interests. Did he not meet the specifications for the ideal Republican candidate?

Certainly William Randolph Hearst was coming to think so. In the same editorial in which he had called for Al Smith as the Jeffersonian Democratic candidate, Hearst, after a survey of Republican possibilities, concluded, "Landon and Knox would make a very appealing ticket." As the Jeffersonian Democratic dream faded away through the autumn, Hearst now turned the full force of his organization into generating Landon publicity. Why Hearst should have cared so much is not clear, unless one assumes a disinterested desire to find the strongest candidate against Roosevelt. Many of the things his agents uncovered about Landon, except for the invaluable budget, were distasteful. Landon himself asked one Hearst emissary, "Did you find any ring-bones on the pony that would show up in dry weather?" The Hearst man replied, "We wish your position had been clearer on the League of Nations and the World Court," both of which Landon had favored. Still, the old man, for all his successive disillusionments in politics — most recently and notably after 1932 — retained a basic innocence which enabled him to the end to miscalculate the object of his political enthusiasms. Once again, he was staking all on a candidate whose Hearstianism was essentially a figment of his own imagination.

Hearst columnists puffed Landon; Hearst papers ran features about him; Damon Runyon, the author of *Guys and Dolls,* was improbably summoned from Lindy's to Topeka to write a piece for Hearst's *Cosmopolitan* entitled "Horse and Buggy Governor"; Adela Rogers St. John arrived under instructions to make the Landon family "the best-loved family in America." In December 1935 two private railroad cars and a chartered Pullman pulled into the yards at Topeka. From them debouched Hearst, Marion Davies, Arthur Brisbane, the top Hearst columnist, Cissy Patterson, the publisher of the *Washington Herald,* and Paul Block, the publisher of the *Pittsburgh Post-Gazette.* After an audience with Landon, the pilgrims came out glowing with satisfaction. "I think he is marvelous!" said Hearst. "An even bigger man than I had previously thought," said Block. "I thought of Lincoln," said Mrs. Patterson.

The visitation of the publishers was the start of Landon's ordeal. If he wanted the Republican nomination, how far was he prepared to go in compromising his progressive principles? John Hamilton was ready to have him go quite far; William Allen White, who considered Hearst "on the whole the most sinister human being on the American continent," thought that Landon had gone quite far enough. "Professionally, Hearst is a form of poison," White wrote. "Politically, he has degenerated into a form of suicide. Whoever ties up with him begins to smell of lilies and attract the undertaker. . . . Hearst is a hitch-hiker on the Landon bandwagon. Sooner or later Landon will have to throw him off." Landon and his managers may well have agreed. Still, for the moment, they needed his help. And, in making his decision, Landon had the august precedent of Franklin Roosevelt four years before. Indeed, Roosevelt's experience may well have persuaded the Landon group that Hearst was better at providing support than in cashing in on it, and that association with him need be no worse than a bad cold.

As for Hearst, his suggestions to Landon were few and vague. His general advice was "not to talk now." The issues "have been made by Roosevelt. It is these issues which are creating the demand for Landon. People think he is the antithesis of Roosevelt. He represents Americanism. That is all people want to know. If other issues are declared and defined, a lot of people may disagree and oppose Landon." He added, "I would diffidently suggest . . . that he denounce Communism." Hearst's capacity for political self-delusion remained monumental. "I personally believe," he wrote in the spring of 1936, "that Landon is what is called 'a man of destiny.' "

Landon's more serious alliances were both more respectable and more private than the tie-up with Hearst. These were with the eastern financial leaders. The conservative old-line bosses — Charles O. Hilles in New York, J. Henry Roraback in Connecticut, David A. Reed in Pennsylvania — stayed mistrustfully away from the Landon boom. But the more sophisticated business politicians — Ogden Mills, Eugene Meyer, Winthrop Aldrich — recognized that the nomination of Hoover or another conservative would be a disaster and were probably persuaded by Hamilton that the mildly progressive Landon might be adapted to their own purposes. Hoover even believed — incorrectly — that Mills was making clandestine visits to Topeka, getting off furtively at remote railroad stations and traveling by car under cover of darkness to confer with Landon.

VIII

By now the preconvention campaign was beginning in earnest. The December Gallup poll showed Landon leading the field, with Borah, Hoover, Knox, and Vandenberg following in that order. Late in January, Landon opened his bid in a nation-wide broadcast. He pronounced himself a "constitutional liberal." "The policy of condemning everything the opposition party does has never produced better government," he forthrightly observed. ". . . But I do condemn half-baked legislation, maladministration and the dangerous short-cuts to permanent change attempted in the name of emergency." "The greatest reform we could have," he added forcibly, "is recovery."

Borah announced his candidacy a week later. Where Landon hoped through ringing generalities to overcome differences within the party, Borah obviously planned to sharpen the differences in order to expose what he regarded as the party's hopelessly reactionary leadership. The Republican party, Borah said, "is shot to pieces, demoralized and without influence in national affairs. I am good enough a Republican to fight as long as I have power against the men who brought the party to its present condition." As the campaign wore on, Borah grew increasingly specific. "The high place in the counsels of the party which corporate and monopolistic interests have long occupied," he said (mentioning oil in particular — a presumed slap at Landon), "is known to all the world. . . . The supreme party problem is this: Can, and will, the party drive these forces from its councils, disregard their satellites and break their grip upon its policies?" If not, Borah hinted, he meant himself to take a walk. (Roosevelt actually bet Farley a dollar even money that Borah would come out for him before November.)

Borah's campaign was badly organized and financed. But he won the support of antimachine Republicans in the East like Gifford Pinchot of Pennsylvania and Hamilton Fish, Jr., of New York, and his capacity for making trouble seemed considerable, especially after he swept the Wisconsin primaries and beat Knox in Illinois outside of Cook County.

In 1935 Landon had played around with the idea of entering primaries in a systematic way; but when the time came, it now seemed better to stay out in order to avoid both factional bitterness and entangling commitment. "My fixed purpose," he wrote, "is to keep the party in the best possible shape to win the election. Furthermore, we haven't been under any embarrassing obligations for contributions to finance these primary campaigns." Accordingly, he campaigned in no state primaries, though in several states local politicians entered slates in his name. Thus, without campaigning, he took the Massachusetts primary, a demonstration that he could win votes in the East. The next important test came in California. Here Hoover had entered an uninstructed slate headed by a young man named Earl Warren, district attorney of Alameda County. Hearst promptly countered by filing a slate pledged to Landon and headed by Governor Frank Merriam. Landon wisely refused either to approve or to repudiate the Hearst strategy. The Warren slate, campaigning against Hearst rather than Landon, won rather handily, but Landon was not much hurt by the defeat and, indeed, somewhat relieved of the onus of Hearst. And any bad effect of California was soon canceled out when a slate pledged to Robert A. Taft, the older son of William Howard Taft, beat Borah in Ohio, and even more when Landon himself trounced Borah four to one in New Jersey. ("I have always felt personally," Farley told Roosevelt, "that Borah was a quartermile runner. He generally broke well at the barrier with those who always ran, but by the time they reached the head of the stretch, he was well back in the field, and never heard from after that.")

As the Republicans began to descend on Cleveland early in June for the convention, Borah and Knox seemed to be out of the running, and Hoover and Vandenberg were not even in sight. Yet New York and Pennsylvania were holding out; Borah was always an unpredictable quantity; there was even a fear that the Hoover men might try to stampede the convention after the former President made his address. As for Knox, he considered himself vigorously in the contest. He rejected the whole Landon approach ("if he is right, I am entirely wrong because I feel the public psychology requires a slashing, frontal attack"), and he treasured an assurance from Hoover that, if it came down to a choice between himself and Landon, he would receive the former President's backing. Still, the professionals generally expected Landon's nomination on the first ballot.[6]

IX

The preconvention campaign had been a brilliant success. Without stirring from Topeka, Landon had made himself the man to beat at Cleveland. He had done so without deals or commitments: "there have been no promises to anyone," he wrote shortly before the convention. And he had done so without violating his own style or character. Raymond Swing, in a surprisingly sympathetic account of Landon for the *Nation,* had raised the question how he would meet the test of the White House. "Frankly," Landon wrote to Swing, "I quite agree with you that I do not know how I would stand up on the job. Who does? You never can tell how a hoss will work until you hitch him up. But I still believe in the old-fashioned motto that one who is faithful in little things will be faithful in the big things."

A few hours before William Allen White left for Cleveland, he sat chatting with Landon on the front porch of the Governor's house. White returned to a favorite theme — the impact of responsibility on men who came to the White House. Would Landon himself crumble or crystallize under the tremendous heat and pressure? Landon, with his quiet candor, said, "Mr. White, I don't know." "I think he is frightened," White noted, "which is a good attitude. The fear of the Lord is the beginning of wisdom."

The first problem in Cleveland was the platform. Landon had asked Charles P. Taft to take charge of drafting the Landon positions. As Taft saw it, the platform should be socially progressive while remaining constitutionally and fiscally conservative — in other words, it should endorse most New Deal goals but insist on carrying them out through the states. And Landon's representative on the Resolutions Committee was (despite Hamilton) William Allen White, who could be relied on to second the fight for a liberal document.

The platform confronted the Landon managers with a special problem of some delicacy: how to keep Borah happy enough about the platform so that he would not feel called upon to stage an all-out fight against Landon's nomination. White, who had known Borah since they went to the University of Kansas together nearly half a century before, went to Borah's hotel one day around noon. Borah was lying on his bed in his dressing gown in a darkened room. White explained that his principal was eager that Borah have every consideration in the expression of his views. Borah seemed to White a bit surprised and greatly pleased. The old man had two planks to submit to the committee. The first, substantially a condensation of the antimonopoly plank in the Democratic platform of 1912, was acceptable to Landon. The other, on foreign affairs, disappointed him by its repudiation of the World Court; but Borah would not yield on his demand for a thoroughgoing isolationist position. Though Borah submitted no plank on monetary policy, he insisted that there be no mention of a re-establishment of the gold standard.

While negotiations were going on with Borah, conservative pressure on the committee forced the dilution of other planks. Landon wanted White to bring out a minority report, but the aging editor was too exhausted for a floor fight. Still, if the final text was less liberal than Landon had hoped, it accepted much more of the New Deal than the conservatives could have anticipated. If it denounced reciprocal trade agreements and public spending, it endorsed federal regulation of the marketing of securities and of interstate public utilities. And if it wanted to do most things through state governments, it also tacitly acknowledged the validity of one after another of the major New Deal objectives. The fury of its rhetoric ("America is in peril. The welfare of American men and women and the future of our youth are at stake") could hardly conceal the moderation of its substance.[7]

x

There remained a vast gap between the mood of the platform and the mood of the convention. The delegates were solemn and dedicated. The band roused them less with gay tunes like "Oh! Susanna," the Landon song, than with "Onward, Christian Soldiers" and "The Battle Hymn of the Republic." The atmosphere in the hall, reporters noted, was like a religious revival. "Landon," wrote Mark Sullivan, expressing the mood, "is as old as the Bible and the Constitution, as modern as the radio and the automobile" — qualities which Elmer Davis supposed could be ascribed only to Him who is from everlasting to everlasting. A Kansas delegate, more restrained, said, "God has His hand on Alf Landon's shoulder."

The platform did not articulate the deeper emotions which brought these earnest men and women to Cleveland. But on Wednesday night, when Herbert Hoover made his way to the rostrum, the underlying desperation found its voice. For fifteen minutes everything stopped as the delegates yelled and cheered. The former President waited patiently, a happy smile of vindication on his face. Then, as the uproar died down, he began his speech — a long, bitter, deeply felt attack on the New Deal as the first phase of American fascism: "If there are any items in the march of European collectivism that the New Deal has not imitated it must have been an oversight." With earnest passion, the former President set forth a drastic indictment, his left hand working in and out of his pocket, his right, pounding the speaker's desk. If Roosevelt were re-elected, if he put his own men on the Supreme Court, America could expect "the succeeding stages of violence and outrage by which European despotisms have crushed all liberalism and all freedom." Gigantic expenditures and waste had piled up a national debt which two generations could not repay. "If this is to continue the end result is the tears and anguish of universal bankruptcy." On every hand there had been the most flagrant violation of economic law, of political law, of moral law. "For the first time in the history of America we have heard the gospel of class hatred preached from the White House. That is human poison far more deadly than fear." The only hope was to return to the old safe ground of American individualism. "There are some principles that cannot be compromised. Either we shall have a society based upon ordered liberty and the initiative of the individual, or we shall have a planned society that means dictation no matter what you call it or who does it. There is no half-way ground."

By now there was a crescendo of excitement: at last a leader was expressing what the delegates deeply felt the election was all about. Sentence after sentence brought them to their feet, cheering wildly and without restraint. Hoover's words, as the *New York Times* described it, whipped the audience into "a wild and uncontrollable burst of frenzy." "Fundamental American liberties are at stake. Is the Republican Party ready for the issue?" "Yes," answered the crowd, "Will you, for expediency's sake, also offer will-o'-the-wisps which beguile the people?" "No," the crowd roared back. "Or have you determined to enter in a holy crusade for liberty which shall determine the future and the perpetuity of a nation of free men?" "Yes," shouted the crowd. "Thus can America be preserved," said Herbert Hoover. ". . . Thus you will win the gratitude of posterity, and the blessing of Almighty God." And as he concluded, the crowd stood on its seats, cheering, waving, weeping, shaken by shout after shout of "We want Hoover."

A thin line of worry etched the face of John Hamilton as he assured newspapermen: "Everything's all right. This is just a personal tribute." But the chant continued, delegations lifting their standards high started to parade around the auditorium, while the former President, a half smile on his face, stood irresolutely on the platform, starting several times to leave, but always returning as his movements provoked new outbursts of applause. Even after he finally went, the demonstration continued. In vain the chairman, Bertrand Snell of New York, announced that Hoover had left the building to catch a train for New York. And, in fact, Hoover had not left the building. He was waiting in a room nearby, wistfully hopeful that the ovation would lead to his renomination.

Eventually order was restored. The convention, after this enormous discharge of its affection and its guilt, returned to the practical world of presidential nominations — a world from which they knew Herbert Hoover was excluded. Yet the emotional explosion on June 10, 1936, showed once again that Hoover was the most powerful personality in the Republican party.[8]

XI

Everything else was anticlimax. The attempts to form a combination against Landon were not working. Borah worried only about the platform. Hoover had gambled everything on his speech. Knox was beginning to think of the Vice-Presidency. Arthur Vandenburg made an effort early in the week to put together a stop-Landon coalition; but, even as he attempted it, he had to resist the importunities of the Landon managers that he accept the nomination for Vice-President. Hamilton and Roberts, for men inexperienced in national politics, were operating with cool effectiveness. Having bought off Borah with a couple of planks and

Hoover with an ovation, they were now bringing their work to completion.

Hamilton himself delivered the nominating speech. He began by reading a telegram from Landon clarifying his understanding of the platform. In this supplementary expression, Landon pledged himself to seek a constitutional amendment if under existing law states could not enact wages-and-hours legislation; and he put the gold standard back into the currency plank. Then Hamilton launched into the standard inventory of his candidate's providential characteristics. Making one of his few mistakes of the convention, he mentioned Landon's name in the first few minutes of the speech and thereby set off the demonstration. But nothing mattered now. Vandenberg ("I belong to but one bloc and it has but one slogan — stop Roosevelt!"), Frank Knox, and Robert A. Taft rose to second the nomination. It became evident that Landon would be named without opposition. The banners rose again, the band played "Oh! Susanna," and the hall burst into a dazzle of sunflowers.

There remained only the Vice-Presidency. Some hopefuls had been eliminated earlier in the week — Governor Styles Bridges of New Hampshire, for example, when someone dreamily remarked, "Landon-Bridges falling down." Vandenberg finally agreed to accept the nomination if it came by acclamation. The Landon managers worked hard to bring this about; but at a crucial moment in the negotiations Hamilton could not reach Vandenberg by telephone (though Arthur Krock could), and evidently did not think of going down the street to his hotel to knock on his door. In the meantime, Knox's people astutely got a commitment from the Pennsylvania delegation to put the doughty Colonel in nomination. When Vandenberg heard this, he gratefully withdrew, noting later in his diary, "I think I should die of inaction in the VICE presidency." Robert A. Taft, who had thought of trying for it, also changed his mind. The result was the unanimous nomination of Frank Knox, who heard the news in a hotel dining room as he was driving back to Chicago. In his exhilaration, the new candidate lost control over his syntax and wired Landon: WE ARE AT ARMAGEDDON . . . CONDITIONS CALL FOR A DISPLAY OF THE SAME GREAT QUALITIES WHICH ENDEARED US BOTH TO THEODORE ROOSEVELT.

When Herbert Hoover arrived in New York, a reporter asked him about the platform. "If you will look through the speeches I have been making for the past nine months," Hoover said, "you will find that practically every recommendation I made in them is in the platform." And the candidate? "For a year and a half," said Hoover, "I have been conducting a crusade vital to the American people to regenerate real, individual freedom in the United States. The election of Governor Landon is the next step to the attainment of that purpose."

The "holy crusade for liberty," 1936 model, was under way.[9]

30. Mumblings in the Night

THE YEAR 1935 had seen the political ferment of interior America rise to a new height. The economic improvement in the succeeding fall and winter exerted something of a tranquilizing effect, but discontent retained considerable momentum well into 1936 — to a degree among the radicals and to a much greater degree among the demagogues. So long as a sense of frustration and grievance continued, a call for a revolt against the major parties might yet detonate a genuine political explosion. So, at least, believed observers who watched Father Coughlin's still enormous radio audience and Dr. Townsend's still multiplying clubs and remembered the appeal of Huey Long. In early 1936 Republican and Democratic politicians alike followed third-party possibilities with acute concern.

II

Actually the group which had thought most about launching a third party was the small but articulate collection of native radicals organized around *Common Sense* and the American Commonwealth Federation. The first meeting of the Federation in July 1935, however, had avoided commitment on the subject of a third party in 1936, though Tom Amlie himself wrote optimistically in *Common Sense*, "In my opinion it should be possible for a third party in 1936 to secure a total vote of between five and ten million." The reason for the ACF's reluctance to commit itself to such a venture became more troubling as the presidential election itself came nearer — should the radicals, in the interests of a purer radicalism, start a third party, which, if it won any support at all, would only deliver the country to the reactionaries?

Whatever practical political importance the group had derived from its tenuous association with Governor Olson of Minnesota. But Olson, while as generous as ever with third party rhetoric ("We must have a new national third party," he obligingly said for *Common Sense* in January 1936, "and I am particularly interested in the growth of the American Commonwealth Federation"), remained as wary as ever about specific action. In February 1936 Alfred Bingham wrote him, "The danger of not taking advantage of latent possibilities this year is that the national third party movement, having no dramatic center or head, will remain impotent for several years more, during which time the forces of fascism and reaction will be organizing." But Olson admired Roosevelt, got along satisfactorily with the administration, and was, in every respect, a practical man. Moreover, he was an increasingly sick man. His persistent illness had been diagnosed as pancreatic cancer, and he could only fitfully stir himself to his old energy. When the Minnesota Farmer-Labor Federation called a national conference in May to consider setting up a third party, Olson said he would go along with the movement only so long as it confined itself to running candidates for Congress. A third presidential ticket, he warned, might defeat "our liberal President" and elect a "Fascist Republican."

There were other objections to the proposed conference. Olson's control over the Minnesota party had loosened with his illness; and fellow travelers and Communists were starting to move into key positions. The Minnesota call included, among other groups, the Communists. Tom Amlie denounced the meeting as "apparently to be under the domination of the Communists," and refused to attend. Bingham, Paul Douglas, and the American Commonwealth Federation group followed his example; so, too, did the Wisconsin Progressives and the Socialists. The meeting came to nothing.

In the meantime, the ACF was pushing hard on its own for a non-Communist third party. "1936 Is The Time!" cried a *Common Sense* editorial in April; the nation could not risk further delay. If economic disintegration continued, *"there may well be no election of 1940."* Since Olsen would not head a third-party

ticket, the editorial continued, how about Gerald Nye? A new
party, uniting all the elements of discontent, might carry two
to five states and poll "a probable minimum of five million votes."
But this pleasant vision represented a last burst of optimism.
Olson's logic was too convincing. In June the *Common Sense*
editorial was sadly entitled "Roosevelt: Radicals' Nemesis." A
third party, it concluded, was "generally conceded by even the
most hopeful radicals to be impossible"; Roosevelt's genius for
appearing all things to all men had won him the support of the
groups that would make the strength of a third party. "This leaves
the genuine Left in an embarrassing position. And it leaves those
who realize the futility of the New Deal but who have no great
hope in Socialist or Communist parties without a political home."
The one solution, added John T. Flynn ("Both Parties Are Wrong!"),
was to organize a third party after the election, dedicated to bringing about "a wider and juster distribution of the nation's produce"
and, in the meantime, to make the radical criticism of Roosevelt,
"vocal, incessant, emphatic, unmistakable." On this querulous note,
the radical third-party dream faded away.[1]

III

But the demagogues had the third-party dream, too. It had
already possessed Huey Long; if he had lived, he would almost
certainly have organized a new party in 1936. And in the latter
part of 1935 it began to afflict even the unassuming Dr. Townsend.
The Townsendites had plainly given up on Roosevelt. The
Doctor himself had been early offended by Roosevelt's refusal to
grant him an interview. "That is an insult that the masses of
the people should resent," the *Townsend Weekly* declared in
February 1935. "We have aristocracy in the White House — not
democracy." When an orator said of the President at the 1935
Townsend convention, "If only he would spend as much time
looking after the welfare of the people as he does playing on his
yacht, he might be of more help," the delegates cheered wildly
for several minutes. Townsend himself called the social-security
program "wholly unfair, inadequate and unjust." "The New
Deal," added the *Townsend Weekly*, "seems to promise little except more debt."

But the Republicans did not look much better, except on the slim chance that they might nominate Borah or Vandenberg. Dr. Townsend's deeper hope was to break loose from the old politics altogether. "The people are heartily sick and disgusted with both old parties," he wrote Co-Founder Robert E. Clements after a tour of the Northwest in August 1935. ". . . The cry everywhere I go is, 'Why don't we have our own party?' Now, that is just the thing I believe we should begin to do, talk about the Townsend Party, not wait in the foolish hope that one of the old groups will adopt us. If they ever do they will treat us like poor adopted trash. To hell with them. If we begin to announce ourselves soon and work like the dickens for the next year we shall be able to lick the stuffing out of both of them."

Late in 1935 a Townsend candidate won the Republican nomination and then a congressional by-election in Michigan. "I am predicting now," Townsend exulted, "that, by next fall, there won't be half a dozen congressmen who have a chance to return unless they cease being Democrats and Republicans and get behind our movement." A third party, he said, would win the support of the Progressives, the Farmer-Labor party, the Nonpartisan League, and the American Commonwealth Federation. When someone asked whether he really had the strength to put up an independent candidate, he replied "very quietly," "We have strength enough to ELECT a candidate. We have at least 30,000,000 votes."

After the Michigan episode, the Townsend movement, with its claim to a membership of two million and its prairie-fire rush from California across the Great Plains to the Middle West, seemed to present a clear and present danger to both major parties. Democrats and Republicans in Congress might be able to co-operate on little else, but they could at least take steps to eliminate the common nuisance. In the spring of 1936 they decided to close ranks in order to smash Townsend once and for all. The chosen mechanism was a congressional investigation. In order to divide political risks evenly, the investigating committee, contrary to usual practice, had an equal number of Democrats and Republicans. Its chairman was a Kansas City Democrat named C. Jasper Bell.

The investigation brought to a head the developing conflict between Townsend and his Co-Founder. They had wrangled over the internal organization, which Townsend wanted to democratize; over the regressive transaction tax, which Townsend was willing to abandon; and over the third-party project, which Clements rejected. A few hours before the investigation started, Clements dramatically resigned from the Townsend organization. He then appeared as the first witness before the Bell Committee. While the necessity of protecting himself limited his ability to smear Townsend, his testimony gave a convincing picture of financial muddle and chicanery in the movement. He admitted, for example, that on his departure he had received $50,000 from Townsend for his share of the *Townsend Weekly*. "Both Dr. Townsend and Robert E. Clements have taken from the treasury much larger amounts than we thought," said one Townsend leader sadly. As for the movement's books, their hopeless confusion even defeated the best auditing efforts of Price Waterhouse.

Townsend tried fairly convincingly to defend his own financial honor. He had assigned 90 per cent of his profits to the Old-Age Revolving Pensions, Ltd., he said, and at the moment only had $300 in the bank. But the committee was not interested in a balanced investigation. Instead, it brutally bored in for the kill. Finally, Townsend, confronted by unscrupulous and invincible hostility, declined to testify further. (He was cited for contempt, found guilty, and sentenced to thirty days in the District of Columbia jail, from which he was eventually preserved by a presidential pardon.)

As he carried out a quavering defiance of the congressional committee, a big man strode out of the crowd to his side, took him protectively by the arm, shouldered bystanders out of the way, and conducted him to a waiting taxi. When the two men alighted an hour later in Baltimore, the stranger identified himself: "I am the Reverend Gerald L. K. Smith, national head of the Share-Our-Wealth Society. I am the successor of Huey Long." Turning to Townsend, he said, "The program of persecution is the thing that has drawn me to Dr. Townsend." Smith continued: "We symbolize the following of one leader who was shot and another who is being persecuted. How's that, Doctor?" "That's all right," said Townsend.

Smith, that indefatigable political freebooter, was now a leader in search of a movement. The politicians who took over the Long machine in Louisiana had lost no time in shoving him out into the cold. Gene Talmadge, his next hope, could not forgive him for his oratorical success at Macon; in May, Smith repaid Talmadge's hospitality by describing him with contempt as "buried." For a few weeks Smith had no place to go. Then, as Clements walked out of the Townsend movement, Smith fixed his eye on the vacant slot and pursued Dr. Townsend without rest (as he confided to a newspaperman, "like a bridegroom still trying to catch up with my bride"). The courting made rapid progress. Soon Smith announced, "We here and now join hands in what shall result in a nationwide protest against this Communistic dictatorship in Washington." For a moment Townsend shyly hung back: "That was simply a friendly gesture. There will be no amalgamation of the Townsend movement with any other." Smith persisted. Finally, in early June, he won the necessary consent. "Dr. Townsend and I," Smith solemnly announced, "stood under the historic arch at Valley Forge and vowed to take over the government." [2]

IV

Townsend and Smith thus laid part of the foundation for a new party. But the party itself was still remote. Of all the demagogues, the one who most often and firmly stated his opposition to third-party movements was Father Coughlin. It should have surprised no one, therefore, that it was he who, in the end, brought the third party into existence.

When Walter Davenport asked him about a third party in the spring of 1935, Coughlin replied gloomily, "I foresee none. I see no need. . . . What would it be? A gathering of political malcontents with personal political grudges to air?" He continued through the year to gallop off in a variety of directions. Thus he warmly applauded Hearst's proposal for a Jeffersonian Democratic party ("Norman Thomas is a piker compared to Roosevelt. After all, Thomas stands for a fairly good brand of American Socialism, but Roosevelt stands for a poor brand of Russian Communism"). Then a few months later, in January 1936, he was in Washington paying his respects at the White House and praising the New Deal monetary policy to Henry Morgenthau. At the same time he was instructing his radio flock that the party conflict was a "sham battle" and that the American people were "on Calvary's heights," crucified between the two thieves symbolic of the two political parties.

There were indications through the winter that he was preparing for at least limited political action in the fall elections. In March he founded a weekly paper called *Social Justice*. In April he called for the reorganization of the National Union for Social Justice by congressional districts. Soon the National Union was emulating the Townsend movement and endorsing candidates in primaries. But Coughlin kept insisting that he planned to go no further. "The National Union for Social Justice — it cannot be too often reiterated — is not in the presidential campaign," he said in May. "The endorsation of candidates for Congress ... is the sole activity of the National Union." As late as May 28 Coughlin told the *New York Times* that if Landon and Roosevelt were the nominees, he proposed to concentrate on the congressional elections. He told the *New York Sun*, "I have not contemplated the launching of a so-called third party."

In the meantime, he had acquired a new method of uniting his old inflationist program with the still lively agricultural protest. Senator Lynn Frazier and Congressman William Lemke, both of North Dakota, were sponsoring a new Frazier-Lemke bill to refinance farm mortgages through the issuance of $8 billion worth of greenbacks by the federal government. Early in 1936 Coughlin began a hectic campaign to mobilize support for the measure. When Congressman John O'Connor of New York tried to bottle it up in the House Rules Committee, Coughlin assailed him without mercy (O'Connor responded by offering to kick Coughlin from the Capitol to the White House, "with clerical garb and all the silver in your pockets which you got by speculating in Wall Street"). Eventually the bill was discharged from committee by petition. Then on May 13 it was voted down in the House. Coughlin called the defeat of the Frazier-Lemke bill "the last straw." It was probably then that he decided to go ahead with a new party.

v

"Within two or three weeks," he wrote in *Social Justice* on May 29, "I shall be able to disclose the first chapter of a plan which, if followed out, will discomfort the erstwhile sham battlers, both Republican and Democratic." The inner history of the next week is still unknown. Evidently Coughlin or his representatives conferred with Congressman Lemke, the co-sponsor of the martyred bill, and the two men agreed to unite behind Lemke's presidential candidacy. On June 12 Coughlin told his followers, "I shall lay down a plan for action which will thrill you and inspire you beyond anything that I have ever said or accomplished in the past." He added that, no matter what newspaper headlines might say, "I pledge and promise you that I still remain your leader!" — evidently a warning that someone else might be the candidate. As his deadline approached, he poured scorn on Roosevelt and Landon ("Neither is worth a nickel and a plugged one at that. One is a promise breaker. The other is dumb. The Democrats have put the country on the dole standard. The Republicans want to put it on the booby standard").

In the meantime, Coughlin's people were also negotiating with Gerald Smith and Townsend. As early as May 22 Smith predicted that the followers of Coughlin, Townsend, and himself were about to "congeal under a leadership with guts." Then, on June 16, Smith, who could not bear to see anyone else's name in the headlines, jumped the gun and announced the formation of a Coughlin-Townsend-Smith-Lemke united front with "more than 20 million" votes unified by common opposition to "the communistic philosophy of Frankfurter, Ickes, Hopkins and Wallace." Coughlin doubtless gritted his teeth, but kept to his own timetable. Three days later Lemke announced that he was running for President on a new ticket — the Union party. That night Coughlin in a radio address declared Lemke "eligible for endorsation"; his platform, "delivered to me last week, is in harmony with our principles." For Vice-President, Coughlin announced Thomas C. O'Brien of Boston, an attorney for the railroad brotherhoods. The Union party, Coughlin said, offered the only escape from the two major parties, both of which were in thrall to Wall Street. His old slogan, "Roosevelt or Ruin," he belatedly explained, should have read, "Roosevelt and Ruin." As for the Republicans, their stupidity had "bred more radicals than did Karl Marx or Lenin." He summed up the merits of his candidates in a glowing peroration: "Lemke and Yale and Agriculture and Republican.

O'Brien and Harvard, Labor and Democrat. East and West, Protestant and Catholic sharing one program of driving the money changers from the temple."

The fifteen points of the Union party platform were essentially a condensation of the sixteen principles of the National Union for Social Justice. The predominating concern was with the currency question. (The Union's demand for the "nationalization of all public necessities" was omitted; this was no doubt an awkward item in a campaign against the communism of the New Deal.) Coughlin added to his own list full and explicit endorsement of Lemke's agricultural proposals. He did not show equal interest in the ideas of his other allies. Instead of endorsing the Townsend plan, the platform simply called for "reasonable and decent security for the aged." Instead of endorsing Share Our Wealth, it called vaguely for "a limitation upon the net income of any individual in any one year." So far as its platform provided a test, the Union party was evidently Father Coughlin's personal creation.[3]

VI

This indifference was not accidental: Coughlin could hardly conceal his contempt for his partners. He had once characterized the Townsend Plan as "economic insanity"; and, as late as May 8, 1936, *Social Justice* carefully stated, "The National Union is in no way affiliated with the Townsend Clubs. While the Townsend Club principles are very beneficial and their motives well intentioned, they are absolutely not practical." In August Coughlin coolly told a press conference that Townsend had no right even to dream of his plan until the Federal Reserve System had been nationalized. As for Share Our Wealth, Coughlin had never had much use for Huey Long. They stood for different social tendencies, as shown by their attitudes toward NRA, which Long had opposed in the name of the small businessman and Coughlin had welcomed in the name of the corporate state. The first issue of *Social Justice* even contained an article praising the Supreme Court for overturning one of Long's newspaper statutes. Of Gerald Smith's alleged following, Coughlin remarked in August that, so far as he knew, Smith did not even have any files. "You can't have much of an organization without at least a mailing list of members."

Townsend and Smith, undoubtedly aware of Coughlin's disdain, did not rush to endorse his candidate. "Any bid for our support," said Smith guardedly, ". . . will have to convince us that the bidders have the intention and power to carry out the Huey Long and Townsend programs." Late in June Smith and Townsend conferred with Lemke and a Coughlin representative, but still withheld endorsement. In mid-July, on the eve of the Townsend convention in Cleveland, they indicated that, while they personally favored Lemke, they did not want to involve the Townsend movement in a losing contest.

For several days, under sweltering Ohio heat, the Townsend delegates, earnest and elderly, inundated Cleveland, the men in shirt sleeves, their wash pants held up by wide suspenders, the women without make-up, in flat shoes and plain print dresses. As they waited in the auditorium where a few weeks before the Republicans had nominated Landon, they sang the good old hymns which recalled the pleasant dreams of youth. Some of the delegates were placid and hopeful, others were embittered by disappointment and age, but all represented an older America baffled by a harsh new time.

They listened intently as their beloved leader, unwontedly embittered by his experience before the investigating committee, denounced the Roosevelt administration. Then Gerald Smith sauntered quietly on to the platform. He began by telling his audience that he had been informed of a plot to break up his speech. How many, he asked, would promise to hang anyone who interrupted? Every hand in the hall (according to the *New York Times*) shot up. The enemies of Townsend had sneered at us as the "lunatic fringe," Smith continued, but now the lunatic fringe was about to "take over the government." Gerald himself promised to deliver the six million followers of Huey Long. By now he was in the full passion of oratory, his coat flung to one side, his blue shirt wringing with sweat, his great voice booming to the far corners of the auditorium, a Bible brandished in his left hand as with his right he pounded the rostrum. Occasionally he issued orders to the audience — "Give that a hand!" — and paused to drink deep from a pitcher of iced water, while the delegates chanted "Amen."

The audience was in ecstasies of pleasure; so, too, was H. L. Mencken, who, renewing his enthusiasm for the orator, described the speech as "a magnificent amalgam of each and every American species of rabble-rousing, with embellishments borrowed from the Algonquin Indians and the Cossacks of the Don. It ran the keyboard from the softest sobs and gurgles to the most ear-splitting whoops and howls, and when it was over the 9000 delegates simply lay back in their pews and yelled. . . . Never in my life, in truth, have I ever heard a more effective speech." Nor was it, Mencken added, only the true believers who panted under his eloquence; even the reporters began to shout. Everyone in the hall was transported, though, when Gerald at last sat down, "no one could remember what he had said."

Some did remember: certain Townsend leaders, notably Sheridan Downey of California and Gomer Smith of Oklahoma, were Democrats. They resented both Townsend's anti-Roosevelt position and Gerald Smith's rising influence in the movement. Gomer Smith now undertook a defense of the administration. It was a display of old-fashioned oratory almost matching Gerald's own. He would not, Gomer said sarcastically, take off his shirt or his shoes or whip up a Bible out of his pocket. He ridiculed the notion of Gerald's six million followers: the place to look for them was in the swamps of Louisiana, and, if one looked carefully, "they would turn out to be bullfrogs." The audience cheered Gomer's praise of Roosevelt quite as wildly as it had cheered Gerald's attack; it was evidently the decibel value of the oratory, not the content, which mattered.

Troubled by the sudden surge of Roosevelt sentiment, Townsend (at least according to Coughlin) sent out a hurry call to the Detroit priest to come to his rescue. "I want," Coughlin later said, "to try to keep Dr. Townsend's following behind him." He arrived in Cleveland on July 16, geared to make a supreme oratorical effort. The priest was not at his best before a live audience. As Mencken noted, he was almost totally lacking in dramatic gesture. His radio experience taught him to stick firmly to the microphone; and since no orator with passion in him could remain wholly immovable, Coughlin, as Mencken recorded it, had "developed a habit of enforcing his point by revolving his backside. This saves him from going off the air, but it is somewhat

disconcerting, not to say indecent, in the presence of an audience."
But the shouting crowd of old folks spurred him to new heights.
He took off his black coat and then, as his clerical collar began
to wilt from sweat, the collar itself, passing them back to Gerald
Smith, who stood behind him: Intoxicated by the screams, he
denounced "the great betrayer and liar, Franklin D. Roosevelt." A moment later, when he referred to "Franklin Double-
crossing Roosevelt," the crowd went wild. The convention, as
such, could not technically endorse candidates; but the movement's
leaders now had clear authorization to go for Lemke.

Before adjournment, Gerald Smith proposed the organization
of 100,000 Townsendite youth to serve as storm troopers and guard
the polls on election day. For the photographers, Father Coughlin
put one arm around Dr. Townsend, poked the Reverend Mr.
Smith gaily in the ribs, and declared they stood four-square together in their crusade.[4]

VII

The beneficiary of this harmony, William Lemke of North Dakota,
was a man of fifty-eight, well weathered in the agrarian storms
of the middle border. Raised on a farm on the wintry Dakota
plains, he had escaped to work his way through the University of
North Dakota and the Yale Law School. He then spent a few
years in Mexico; in 1915 he wrote a book entitled *Crimes Against
Mexico*, bitterly criticizing Wilson for refusing to recognize the
Huerta regime. Returning to North Dakota, he became a leader
in the Nonpartisan League and, for a turbulent year, Attorney-
General of the state when Lynn Frazier was Governor. Both
Frazier and Lemke were recalled from office following a banking scandal; but both had fully established themselves in the confidence of the farmers, and they soon restored their partnership
when one went to the Senate and the other, to the House.

As a congressman Lemke, though nominally a Republican, had
supported most of the New Deal, from AAA and NRA to work
relief and the Holding Company Act. But his driving commitment was to the debt-ridden farmers of the Great Plains; and,
along with Frazier, he fought their case with dogged fervor. He
could hardly do otherwise. His own district was a study in eco-

nomic desperation: two-thirds of the farms had been foreclosed since 1929. The succession of Frazier-Lemke bills tried to postpone foreclosures, to scale down inflated appraisals, and to facilitate mortgage refinancing through real-estate loans and greenbacks. Populism had two rhetorical styles: high-flown extravagance, like Ignatius Donnelly's; or detailed, factual, impersonal, quasi-economic analysis. Lemke's was the second; and he could rattle off statistics in his flat high-pitched voice at a great rate of speed for an interminable time. His economic knowledge was considerable and, while it often verged on crankiness, the crankiness was sometimes no more wrong-headed than the certitudes of economic orthodoxy.

He looked like a farmer, with his long face, his ill-fitting clothes, and his gray cloth cap. Smallpox contracted in Mexico had left his face pitted and seamed; he disliked shaving and often appeared with a gray stubble on his chin. He had a glass eye. He neither drank nor smoked, probably as a result of his Lutheran background. He was a novice in national politics; he permitted Coughlin, for example, to dub him "Liberty Bill" Lemke in spite of the notorious fact that the Liberty Bell was cracked. Even many farmers assumed from constant repetition that Lemke's first name must be Frazier. But no one could question the somber ferocity with which Bill Lemke had fought for the farmers' welfare.

The administration's opposition to the most recent Frazier-Lemke bill soured Lemke on the New Deal. "I look upon Roosevelt," he said, "as the bewildered Kerensky of a provisional government. He doesn't know where he came from or where he's going. . . . As for Landon he represents the dying shadow of a past civilization." He added, "The public is looking for a real statesman yet to come." As head of the ticket, Lemke confirmed the Populist flavor of the Union party. It was his participation which caused a man like Tom Amlie, while rejecting the new party, to suggest that it raised perplexing questions for progressives. "Many of the elements that have been united in this movement have deep roots in the American tradition." Moreover, Lemke had a constituency of his own in Nonpartisan League country, and especially among farmers of German descent. When political observers added the potential Lemke vote to what Coughlin could pull among Irish Catholics in urban areas, Townsend among his old folks, especially in the Far West and Michigan, and (though this was more speculative) Smith among the remnants of Share Our Wealth, it looked as if the Union party could hardly fail to be a significant factor in the election.[5]

VIII

The native radicals, who desired a third party, failed to get one. The demagogues, including some who rejected a third party, now set one up. But the radicals in the Marxist orbit already had existing parties of their own. Both the Socialists and the Communists dreamed in 1935 of broadening their appeal and of becoming *the* effective third party in 1936.

Within the Socialist party, the Militant faction had gained a precarious victory over the Old Guard in 1934. But the closeness of the margin in the party referendum only sharpened the bitterness. The Militant hard core was increasingly catastrophic in its views; at times, only a thin line seemed to separate its doctrine from Communism. On the other hand, the Militants were also the young, the adventurous, and the idealistic in the movement; they seemed in closer contact with vital currents on the left; and men like Norman Thomas, while disliking their dogmatic extremism, felt nevertheless that Socialist growth would more probably come from Militant ferment than from Old Guard rigidity. The struggle centered in New York, where, by early 1936, the Old Guard was engaged in public warfare with Thomas and the Militants. For the next months, each side laid plans for a showdown in the party convention.

Late in May the Socialists gathered in Cleveland under great pictures of Marx, Debs, Victor Berger, and Morris Hillquit. The convention faced the choice between Militant and Old Guard delegations from New York. After bitter debate and vain attempts at compromise, it voted to accept the Militant group. With the atmosphere still tense from the fight, most of the delegates rose to sing the "Internationale." Suddenly David Lasser, head of the Workers' Alliance, pointed to the right-wing leaders, Louis Waldman and Algernon Lee, still seated on the platform. There was a rumble of boos from the floor. Waldman said grimly, "I would not rise to sing a song of solidarity with the group of delegates who have just voted to break the Socialist Party."

That evening the old-line Socialists walked out to form the Social Democratic Federation. They took with them about a third of the membership, a good deal of the financial backing, and much of the labor support, as well as such party institutions as the *New Leader,* the *Jewish Daily Forward,* and the Rand School. The defection was hardly unexpected; it seemed almost inevitable after the fight in Detroit two years before. "To some extent it may help us," Thomas wrote. "Our great loss will come anyway on account of the Roosevelt sentiment and many of the votes that our right-wing friends think they can control would have gone to Roosevelt anyway."

The problem remained how to deal with Roosevelt. Thomas, again the Socialist candidate, regarded the President as a decent, well-intentioned man, incapable of breaking through either the political organization or the economic system of which he was the willing prisoner — "a good man in a bad party, a good man, moreover, who at best is doing nothing except to try to reform capitalism a little." Nothing irritated Thomas more than the suggestion, popularized by James P. Warburg and Al Smith, that Roosevelt had carried out the Socialist platform of 1932. "Roosevelt did not carry out the Socialist platform," said Thomas with scorn, "unless he carried it out on a stretcher." He had given the nation, not the co-operative commonwealth, but the same state capitalism the Fascist demagogues of Europe used when they came to power. "I do not mean that Mr. Roosevelt is himself a Fascist. . . . I credit him with as liberal intentions as capitalism and his Democratic colleagues of the South permit." But the New Deal was headed remorselessly toward war or economic collapse. "After the New Deal — What?" asked Thomas in August. "The probable answer is: After the New Deal — Fascism."

Roosevelt was "unquestionably . . . more progressive, more alert to the human problems of his time than Mr. Landon." But this was not enough; Landon, while a conservative, was not in Thomas's view a fascist; and the gap between Roosevelt and Landon was not great enough to make any difference to a Socialist. Only the workers could build their own protection against the fascist future. The Socialist mission, Thomas said, was "to insist that nothing short of socialism will save us. We must show that *within capitalism* every scheme will fail as the New Deal has failed."

He soon perceived that this was a thankless task. "This campaign," he wrote in late July, "is going to be hard for me because so many of my liberal and labor friends are caught up in this idea that Roosevelt can somehow save us from reaction or fascism." The galaxy of liberals who had backed Thomas in 1932 had now dwindled to a valiant few; there remained John Dewey, Reinhold Niebuhr, Morris Cohen, Sidney Hook, Van Wyck Brooks, Max Eastman, Oswald Garrison Villard, Freda Kirchwey, James Burnham. A vote for Thomas, wrote John T. Flynn, was "the only way to vote and not to waste one's vote." But few listened. Even old-time Socialists in the Amalgamated Clothing Workers and the International Ladies' Garment Workers were following Sidney Hillman and David Dubinsky into the New Deal camp. In vain Thomas warned, "This is to repeat the mistake of the German Social Democrats who voted for Hindenburg because they did not want Hitler."

Thomas spoke as gallantly as ever, exposing in caustic terms the liberal pretensions of the administration ("Roosevelt or reaction? What does that phrase mean to the exploited peons of the cotton fields or to the slaves of Florida's flogging belt?"), dealing glancing blows at the Republicans and, as the campaign wore on, devoting increasing attention to what seemed to him the genuinely fascist potential in the Union party. But he was uneasily conscious from the start that it was too late — that Roosevelt had long since captured his audience.[6]

IX

If the Socialists plugged away at the same old line, the Communists had suffered a transformation from the austere and dedicated revolutionists of 1932. Nothing was more startling than their new appearance in 1936 — reasonable, benevolent, self-effacing men, professing views closer in many respects to those of the Old Guard Socialists than to those of any other radical sects. This metamorphosis was the consequence of a new world strategy adopted by the Soviet Union in response to its own necessities and generalized for all Communist parties at the Seventh World Congress of the Communist International at Moscow in July and August 1935.

On August 2 Georgi Dimitrov, a brave Bulgarian Communist who had defied and survived the Nazis, entered the Hall of Columns in Moscow to speak on "The Tasks of the Communist International in the Fight for the Unity of the Working Class Against Fascism." He began by defining fascism in conventional Marxist terms as "the power of finance capital." But he added that, in appealing to the masses, fascism often disguised itself as radicalism (as, he said, with Share Our Wealth in the United States). When fascism came to power, it was primarily because this appeal was successful. Consequently, fascism's greatest ally, Dimitrov emphasized, was working-class disunity. While such disunity was mainly, of course, the fault of the Social Democrats, it was also, he added. in part the fault of the Communists themselves, who had underrated the danger of fascism and had ignored the concrete needs of the masses. In the United States, for example, Dimitrov said sarcastically, Communists had described the New Deal itself as fascist. "One must indeed be a confirmed addict of the use of the hackneyed schemes," Dimitrov commented, "not to see that the most reactionary circles of American finance capital, which are attacking Roosevelt, represent first and foremost the very force which is stimulating and organizing the fascist movement in the United States." If fascism were to be halted, it could only be done through the organization of a united front of *all* antifascist forces. In helping to build the united front, Dimitrov said, Communists must be prepared to subordinate their long-range objectives in the interests of antifascist unity.

Dimitrov then began a country-by-country analysis, with an extended discussion of the United States. American fascism, he noted, appeared principally "in the guise of an opposition to fascism, which it accuses of being an 'un-American' tendency imported from abroad." As yet, it was not a directly menacing force. But, if it came to power, it "would change the whole international situation quite materially." In these circumstances the American proletariat could not content itself with the organization of just its revolutionary vanguard. It must strive to prevent fascism from winning over the broad discontented masses.

How was this to be done? Through the organization of a Workers' and Farmers' party; *"such a party,"* Dimitrov said, *"would be a specific form of the mass people's front in America* that should be set up in opposition to the parties of the trusts and the banks, and likewise to growing fascism." The party would be neither Socialist nor Communist. It would seek "a *common language* with the broadest masses." It would oppose big business, it would fight for social legislation, it would reduce the burden of debt on the farmer, it would demand equal status for the Negro, it would defend the sharecropper, the war veteran, the small businessman, the artisan. "We should develop the most widespread movement for the creation of such a party, and take the lead in it." His peroration contained a warning which too many non-Communist enthusiasts for the popular front later ignored.

We want all this because only in this way will the working class at the head of all the toilers, welded into a million-strong revolutionary army, led by the Communist International and possessed of so great and wise a pilot as our leader Comrade Stalin (a storm of applause) *be able to fulfill its historical mission with certainty — to sweep fascism off the face of the earth and together with it, capitalism!*

Dimitrov's speech was followed by prolonged cheering, shouts of "Hurrah!" "Rot Front!" and "Banzai!" and the singing of the "Internationale" in twelve languages. Among those joining in the ovation was the general secretary of the American party, Earl Browder.[7]

x

The reason for the reversal in Communist policy was plain enough. The rise of Hitler confronted the Soviet Union with the threat of war. The policy of revolutionary extremism, designed to destroy bourgeois governments, now appeared only to benefit the fascists. To avert the war — or win it if it came — Russia needed every possible ally against fascism. Nor was the switch in Communist policy exclusively the result of the changing requirements of Soviet foreign policy. The Comintern had always to take some, if limited, account of the situation faced locally by national Communist leaders; its action could not be wholly unilateral, unless it was prepared to dispense with whatever basis in mass support a national party enjoyed. The new line also responded to needs felt by local Communist leaders for common action with "progressive" forces — needs that had already produced the premature Dimitrovism which caused the expulsion of Jacques Doriot from the French Communist party.

This need had been felt particularly in the United States. The American Communist leaders were uneasily aware that their policy of ferocious opposition to the New Deal was only isolating their party at a time when the whole nation appeared to be swinging left. As Browder said as early as September 1934, "the mass demand for united action is clearly growing into a mighty movement." The tactics of the united-front-from-below and the endeavor to establish mass organizations for peace, youth, and culture were all responses to this demand. The First American Writers' Congress early in 1935 showed the extent to which the desire for unity, at least among the intellectuals of the left, was undermining the slogans of revolutionary militance from within. Thus John Chamberlain found the conference "a very agreeable surprise. . . . I felt more at home in conversation with Left writers than at any time since 1932." (There was, however, one bad moment when Kenneth Burke dared propose that Communists talk, not about "workers," a term which had limited appeal in America, but about "the people." The Communists angrily denounced this as a fascist formulation; "we must not encourage such myths," said Joseph Freeman.)

Only a few weeks before the Comintern meeting, Browder had been blackguarding Roosevelt, John L. Lewis, Floyd Olson, Norman Thomas, and all other American liberals. Nine days after the new revelation, Browder walked to the podium of the congress and admitted a "too narrow understanding" of the united front policy, as evidenced, for example, in the mistaken rejection of the name 'farmer-labor party.' Communists, he said, should not "at the present moment" stipulate that the united front required an absolute recognition "of the principle of the proletarian dictatorship and the Soviet power." To newspapermen in Moscow, he said that the American party would hereafter appeal "to all opponents of fascism and not demand of all that they subscribe to the principles of Soviet government."

On September 17, 1935, he returned to New York. Two days later he issued a call for the formation of a farmer-labor party.

The Communists, he said disarmingly, could play only a small part in such a party. "We are far too weak to achieve our major objectives, and too weak to even present, alone, effective resistance to the advance of political reaction." All the Communists wanted was to unite with other forces opposed to fascism and war. They proposed a farmer-labor party "as a bulwark against reaction, not as an instrument for introducing socialism."

The new line gave many American Communists and fellow-travelers a sense of vast release. "It was what we wanted," said Granville Hicks, "and it seemed to us a great step ahead for the revolutionary movement." "I felt better about being a communist," said James Wechsler. "I deeply believed that the Popular Front was not a momentary tactic but a great turning point in political history." It was now not only possible but mandatory to believe in America and talk about "the people."

Browder's efforts to build the people's front were more energetic than effective. Though he prevailed upon Norman Thomas to speak with him at a meeting in Madison Square Garden, and though the two men jointly led the audience in the "Internationale," Thomas remained wary. In the next months the Socialist leader backed steadily away from the Communist embrace. In the end, the Socialist party overwhelmingly rejected a formal Communist proposal for a Thomas-Browder presidential ticket. And while Communist agents prodded the Minnesota Farmer-Labor organization into calling the Chicago convention in May, this effort failed too. Unable to entice either the Socialist or the Independent progressives into a new party, Browder had to settle for his old party in a new and more genial mood.

The new line had meanwhile won for the party an entree into places where doors had heretofore been firmly closed. By June 1936 membership was reported at 40,000 — an increase of about 15,000 over the year before and of 66 per cent since 1934. At the American League Against War and Fascism convention in Cleveland, Mayor Harold Burton gave a welcoming address and sat on the platform with Browder. In Minnesota the Communists operated with increasing skill and ruthlessness within the Farmer-Labor organization. When the Republican senator died, Floyd Olson resisted pressure from the pro-Communists and others to name Elmer Benson to the Senate in his place; but a group in the Farmer-Labor party gave the party organ, the *Minnesota Leader,* a false story that Benson had been appointed, and the publication of the story forced the dying Governor's hand.

As for the united-front idea, it was now in circulation in the oddest places. George Sokolsky could say in April 1936, "We must band together, Republican and Democrat, capitalist and communist — every citizen of whatever party — in a union of strength for the protection of those liberties guaranteed us by the Constitution." And, as quoted in the *Daily Worker* in June, Westbrook Pegler said, "This idea of forming a Farmer-Labor Party to put through real social legislation and progressive policies in government is okay. Call it any name you want to — People's Party, American Party, Progressive Party or Farmer-Labor — but go ahead and form one!" Pegler added, "Undoubtedly the Communist Party convention will be a more important event than ever before." [8]

XI

Whether the convention was as important as Pegler supposed, it certainly dramatized the new face of Communism. Giant banners carried the bold slogan: "Communism Is Twentieth Century Americanism." Speakers, avoiding the usual reverent allusions to Marx, Lenin, and Stalin, invoked instead such unfamiliar deities as Jefferson and Lincoln. Robert Minor, nominating Browder, presented him as *"the new John Brown from Osawatomie."* (Westbrook Pegler himself called Browder "more Kansan than Alf Landon if it comes to a showdown.") Browder exhorted the delegates to talk American. "We [American Communists] cannot think of any other spot on the globe where we would rather be than exactly this one. We love our country." From beginning to end, Communism was unveiled as the climax of the American revolutionary tradition.

This was all very well; but a problem of tactics remained. At Moscow Dimitrov had directed the American party to stop the march of fascism and had identified American fascism, in effect, with the Liberty League, Hearst, and the Republican party. How were the Communists now to discharge their mission? What would their policy be toward the only realistic alternative to Republican rule, Franklin Roosevelt and the New Deal?

Their attitude toward Roosevelt up to this point had been one, of course, of political rage flavored by nasty personal animosity. In their anger against the President, the American Communists had even ignored a signal from Stalin, who in his interview with H. G. Wells in 1934 had lavishly praised Roosevelt's "initiative, courage, and determination," his "energy and abilities," and pronounced him "one of the strongest figures among all the captains of the contemporary capitalist world." Where Stalin credited Roosevelt with the honest if vain intention of trying to plan within the capitalist system, the American Communists dismissed him as a capitalist stooge and exploiter.

The Dimitrov directive, however, was definitive on this point. Browder soon after his return began to revise the Communist theory of the Roosevelt administration. But the revision was grudging. Roosevelt, Browder told the party in November 1935, "seeks to achieve fundamentally the same class objectives as his Right opponents," though he was pursuing a different path and basing himself on different groups within the bourgeoisie. If the difference was important, it would still be a "mistake to think that Roosevelt had no basis among the finance capitalists." "While no longer as in 1933–34 representing . . . the main fascist camp," Roosevelt offered no obstacle to the growth of fascist forces. As for the proposal that the left should "rally around Roosevelt, unsatisfactory as he is, as the only bulwark against reaction and fascism," Browder rejected this with contempt. "We cannot fight against reaction by supporting Roosevelt, whose whole strategy of fighting against reaction consists in making one concession after another to it." With some of the old-time bitterness, Browder admonished the advocates of this view, "When Roosevelt spit in your face, you looked up at the sky and complained that the weather was getting bad. This is what you recommend to us as a means of fighting against reaction."

In March 1936 he repeated his indictment. "The House of Morgan is the real ruler today," he said. ". . . It has strengthened its rule under Franklin D. Roosevelt." Under the two-party system, Wall Street always won, the people always lost. "Tweedledum and Tweedledee are still twins, even when one wears the cold mask of Hoover and the other the professional smile of Roosevelt." The New Deal was "bankrupted and in ruins." At the Communist convention in June, he declared it a "fatal mistake to depend upon Roosevelt to check the attacks of Wall Street, or to advance the fundamental interests and demands of the masses." But now a new theme had begun to enter his speeches. However hopeless Roosevelt was, it was necessary to differentiate sharply between Roosevelt and Landon. "The Republican Party, with its Hearst–Liberty League allies," said Browder, "is the main enemy that must be defeated at all costs." The Communist strategy was therefore to direct "our main fire" against Landon and do everything possible to shift votes away from him "even though we cannot win their votes for the Communist Party, even though the result is that they vote for Roosevelt." Yet Communists could not support Roosevelt. If the left were to unite behind Roosevelt "and he felt secure in their support," Browder said, "he would move over in the direction of Landon and the Fascists."

In a way the Communist slogan — "Defeat Landon At All Costs, Vote For Browder!" — was ludicrous. But it was perhaps not so entirely ludicrous as it sounded. Given the Communist analysis of the situation, it was important both to defeat Landon and to maintain an independent left-wing party; and this the Browder strategy was designed to do. The Communists were not telling Communists or fellow-travelers to vote for Roosevelt; those within the Communist orbit were expected to vote for Browder; but they hoped at the same time that their campaign might induce people who would never in the world vote for Browder at least to vote against Landon. The dubiety of the statement that the Communists "really" backed Roosevelt in 1936 can be proved by comparing the Communist vote for governor and for President in the state of New York. The party obviously did its best to deliver the vote of the faithful to its own presidential candidates; Communist voters did not cut Browder for Roosevelt. But the thrust of the Communist campaign was entirely against Landon.[9]

31. The Democrats on the Brink

As for Franklin Roosevelt, the election had been on his mind for many months. There was much, of course, to induce optimism. The nation had seen great changes since that gloomy March day in 1933. The national income had risen by more than 50 per cent — from $39.6 billion in 1933 to $64.7 billion in 1936. Unemployment had fallen by nearly half — from between 12 and 13 million to between 6 and 8 million; 6 million more people were at work than in 1933. In May 1936 the *New York Times* index of business activity reached 100 for the first time since 1930.

Nowhere were improvements more striking than in corporate profits, which had risen from minus $2 billion in 1933 to nearly $5 billion in 1936. The Dow-Jones industrial average of stock prices was 80 per cent higher than in 1933. Automobile manufacturers were looking to their biggest year since 1929. The earnings of du Pont in the first half of 1936 were 72 per cent higher than in the same period the year before; of General Motors, 70 per cent. Company earnings as a whole were reported over 50 per cent higher than in 1935. In August United States Steel declared gross earnings in the second quarter of 1936 70 per cent higher than in the first quarter. So dramatic, indeed, was the revival, that Winthrop Aldrich and the banking crowd were shouting that the great danger was inflation. For the first time since 1929 people could worry about a boom. It was a propitious climate for a presidential election.[1]

II

On January 30, 1936, after a few calculations on a scratch pad, Roosevelt estimated a probable Democratic vote in the electoral college of 325 and a Republican vote of 206. He had no expectations of a walkover. "We are facing a very formidable opposition on the part of a very powerful group among the extremely wealthy and the centralized industries," he wrote a friend early in 1936. "Ours must be a truth-telling and falsehood exposing campaign that will get into every home." If this were so, then the party should lose no time in setting to work. "We ought to conduct a very aggressive campaign, Jim," he told Farley as early as December 1935. "Every effort should be made to get public sentiment in our favor before the Republican convention meets."

If this was the indicated campaign, there was some presidential dissatisfaction over Jim Farley's preparations for it. Indeed, there had been for a little time elusive suggestions of strain between the White House and the Democratic National Committee. As early as January 1934 the *New York Times* ran a story saying that Farley was going to resign as National Chairman and run for Governor of New York. In June of that year Farley told Josephus Daniels, "My wife is not enamored of Washington life and prefers our old home life, and I am interested more in our party's victories in the future than in holding any job." Persistent rumors said that Bess Farley disliked not only Washington but the Roosevelts. Yet Jim's loyalty to Roosevelt seemed undiminished. Thanking the President for a Christmas gift in January 1935, Farley said in a longhand note, "No words are adequate to express to you my real appreciation of not only this act, but of the many fine things you have done for me. . . . I pray God that you will be spared to see accomplished everything you said and everything you have in your heart for humanity."

The active center of White House dissatisfaction with Farley was Steve Early, who felt that Farley was spending too much time going about making speeches and not enough time working on the impending campaign or on party organization. Harold Ickes shared Early's concern over Farley's casting himself as the spokesman for the Democratic party; not only was the Postmaster-General invidiously identified with machine politics, but "he carries no conviction because people know he hasn't any settled views on any subject and no background against which to set up any views if he did have them." As the *New York Times* soon commented, "Even of a good thing like Chairman Farley it is possible to have too much. There are multiplying signs that his constant speaking is making other managers of his party a bit nervous, not to say weary. . . . His tendency to berate all who disagree with him, his incessant boasting and predictions, pall a little after a time." It seemed imperative to take steps both to move Farley toward the background and to refurbish the neglected party organization. Beginning in January 1936, Early and Roosevelt consequently began to infiltrate their own people into the National Committee.

The first White House agent was Edward L. Roddan, an experienced newspaperman who had been covering the President for the International News Service. In a series of meetings Roosevelt personally briefed Roddan on how he wanted things run, following this up with a series of notes and chits on campaign strategy, sent directly to Roddan, not through the Chairman. The keynote of the Roosevelt plan was: "Take the initiative." The Committee should ignore the Republicans and center its fire on the Liberty League. Early added definite instructions to Roddan that he was not to write speeches for Farley.

The next White House recruit for the Committee was a man well known in Protestant circles, Stanley High. Though never an ordained minister, High had a divinity degree, was editor for a time of the *Christian Herald,* and had recently been a speaker on current events for the National Broadcasting Company. He was a fluent writer and an affable person, easy to get along with and free (wrote Sam Rosenman) "from the ordinary occupational diseases of speech writing — argumentativeness and stubbornness." More than this, Rosenman added, "he had a happy facility of expression and phrase-making, perhaps a better one than anyone else with whom I worked on Roosevelt's speeches" — a judgment evidently meant to include not only Raymond Moley but Robert E. Sherwood. High had been a Republican before 1936, and would be again; but in 1936 he displayed both an impassioned liberalism and a facility for memorable utterance which hardly marked his later speech-writing assignments for Thomas E. Dewey and Dwight D. Eisenhower. Perhaps, as Rosenman surmised, "the inspiration of a Roosevelt, the direction which Roosevelt gave our thinking and our writing, were absent — and when High no longer had these, he did not do as well." High's chief drawback was his bubbling exuberance over the fact that he was writing speeches at all; he once startled Michelson by "prancing through Democratic headquarters at the Biltmore proclaiming that he was off to write a speech for the President — a rather shocking violation of the rules of the game, as a ghost is never supposed to admit that he is the author of a great man's utterance." High may have gone even further than this in self-promotion; at least Ickes was moved to fury in June on hearing that High claimed authorship of a speech that Ickes had written himself.[2]

III

Farley worked hard and skillfully at his particular job of maintaining contact with other professional politicians through the country. But 1936 was to be a coalition campaign, and Farley never understood the coalition idea. Through High, Roddan, and Early (and later through Leon Henderson, who became economist for the National Committee), the New Dealers were able to have some influence on campaign planning. And, to a surprising degree Roosevelt himself took over personal command.

In December 1935 he laid down broad campaign strategy to the National Emergency Council. It was necessary, he suggested, to offset the mass media and to correct the "very large amount of misinformation, part of which is innocent, and a large part of which is not innocent," in circulation concerning the New Deal. "It probably should be the policy of the Government not to call people names," he continued, "but, in a very gentle and happy way, to explain that things which are not proved, though we do not necessarily call them lies, are not exactly the truth and that the truth is as follows, and so on." He added: "Bring in as much as possible the simple illustrations that appeal to the average person back home. . . . Get down to the human element. Don't tell them in Georgia what is being done in Alabama; take the nearest project to where you are speaking in Georgia and tell them about that." Above all, "emphasize the rounded picture" — the interdependence of various groups in the country. "People in the cities, when they find pork chops are going up, are perfectly reasonable most of them, and if we explain their relationship to the farmers' problems we are going to get away from the division between different regions of the country — North against South, and East against West."

He watched the tactical problems with equal concern. In January and February we find him giving J. F. T. O'Connor specific instructions about making up a California delegation designed to heal the split in the party; the President carefully named those he wanted on the delegation and those he did not want. In March he sent Farley a memorandum reorganizing the Committee's activities — speech material to clear through Michelson, pamphlets through High, and so on. He also brought constant pressure on the Chairman to set up committees for businessmen, independent voters, Republicans, and other groups. Farley, of course, accepted the presidential direction; but his own conception of the campaign remained stubbornly traditional and nonideological. In April, for example, Henry Wallace came up with the manuscript of his book *Whose Constitution?* Farley, playing by the rules, sharply opposed its publication: new ideas might have unexpected repercussions. Roosevelt told Wallace, "I have not had a chance to read it very carefully but what I have read I like enormously. May you sell 100,000 copies!"

During 1935 Roosevelt had hoped that Hoover would be his opponent in 1936. This was only partly because he supposed Hoover would make a weak candidate. It was more that he considered Hoover the one Republican leader to possess (in Moley's words) "the massive convictions and intelligence to provide an alternative to the New Deal." With Hoover heading the Republican ticket, the electorate would confront a genuine choice.

But this was evidently not to be. Of the remaining Republican possibilities, Roosevelt seems to have hoped for Landon's nomination on the ground that the Kansas Governor would be easiest to beat. But he intended to take no chances. In late May Farley, speaking at the Michigan Democratic convention, brushed off Landon as governor of "a typical prairie state." This remark from a New York Irish Catholic caused a factitious uproar throughout the Middle West. Soon throwaways appeared with a picture of Abraham Lincoln and the caption: "He, Too, Came From 'A Typical Prairie State.' " Roosevelt sent Farley a plaintive memorandum: "I thought we had decided that any reference to Landon or any other Republican candidate was inadvisable." The President added that as a general rule no section of the country should ever be spoken of as "typical"; there should always be a laudatory adjective. "If the sentence had read 'one of those splendid prairie states,' no one would have picked us up on it, but the word 'typical' coming from any New Yorker is meat for the opposition."

Farley, unconvinced, soon put.out a statement attacking Landon as a "synthetic" candidate. Roosevelt then called Farley and Michelson in and told them to issue no more statements about Landon without White House clearance. He also told Farley to stop giving public speeches and interviews. And he asked Harold Ickes, the former Republican, to deliver a speech on the Republican record on the eve of the Republican convention. (This Ickes did with delight and effect; it was the speech which High claimed to have written.)

To complete his personal staff, Roosevelt now invited his old friend Judge Samuel Rosenman to spend the Memorial Day weekend cruising down the Potomac on the presidential yacht. Another guest was High. Roosevelt was obviously eying them as the autumn's speech-writing team.[3]

IV

The summons to Rosenman expressed the President's gradual recognition that he and Moley could no longer work together. The first serious argument between the two men had taken place in the fall of 1935, over the reciprocal trade agreement with Canada and over what Moley regarded as the administration's excessive sympathy with Ethiopia in the Italo-Ethiopian war. In November Moley sent Roosevelt a long, vehement justification of his isolationist position in foreign affairs. "Nothing so hurts as to disagree with you," he concluded; luckily these particular issues constitute "a small — however important — minority of the public policies you profess."

Alas, the field of disagreement was larger, and its more sensitive part was in domestic policy. Moley, though nominally in favor of a sort of national planning, had always believed that business should be at least an equal partner in the planning effort. For a time, during the period of the Moley business dinners, he saw himself as the man who might bring business and the New Deal together. When this hope was frustrated — as he thought, because of the rise of malice and radicalism in the President's councils — his distaste for the New Deal increased. His new associates in New

York were mostly businessmen, and he spoke with increasing frequency to business groups. Radicalism, he was coming to feel, was "an ebbing tide" in political life; people were getting tired of the "habit of belaboring business with a big stick." He was delighted when the Gallup poll reported that over half the people, confronted with a choice between two parties called liberal and conservative, preferred the conservative party. "In the mysterious ebbing and flowing of the tide of public opinion," Moley said, "the moment has come, or nearly come, when the case of business is going to get a mighty respectful and sympathetic hearing."

Feeling this, he resented the new rhetorical directions of the Second New Deal. Though he himself helped write the State-of-the-Union message in January 1936, he decided afterward never again to lend himself to what he considered presidential demagoguery. The effect of the new course, he believed, would be to transform the Democratic party into a labor party and to establish American politics on a class basis. He later said that he watched with relief the entry of High and of Tom Corcoran into the speech group; "my one concern was to inch out of my responsibilities without a fuss." In the meantime, he was stepping up his public criticism. Speaking before the National Association of Manufacturers, Moley condemned "petty bickerings" and "inordinate ambitions" inside the New Deal. The administration, he said, was "too likely to accept the new merely because it is new."

On the weekend following Rosenman's and High's visit, Moley was a guest on the presidential yacht. Sitting placidly on the deck on a Sunday afternoon, Moley and his host got into a tedious wrangle about the administration's attitude toward business. The conversation was resumed at the White House later in the month. Moley contended as an editor for his right to criticize New Deal policies. Roosevelt asked coldly whether Moley realized that the press played him up only because he had been a member of the administration. Moley replied that this couldn't be helped; his obligation now was to the profession of journalism, where the essential virtue was independence. Roosevelt waved this away impatiently. A presidential campaign was on; and in a campaign the issues narrowed. "It's not what you say or think about an individual in the administration or about a specific issue," Moley remembers Roosevelt saying. "There's one issue in this campaign.

It's myself, and people must be either for me or against me."

For Roosevelt this was no doubt a realistic statement of what the issue in the campaign would be. It turned out to be a correct statement; as Farley later put it, "The only issue in the campaign was Franklin D. Roosevelt." But Moley regarded it as a sudden and blinding revelation of Roosevelt's essential character. "That, really, was all I needed to know." The hopes of the First New Deal, he felt had been swallowed up in presidential megalomania. The breaking point had been reached.

Nevertheless, Moley consented for some reason to work with Corcoran on a draft of the President's acceptance address. (Moley later claimed that he was inveigled into doing this against his will; Rosenman said that Roosevelt had not wanted to bring Moley in, but did so because of his old-time inability to hurt people's feelings.) During convention week Moley and Corcoran dined at the White House with Rosenman and High (who had also written a draft), Missy LeHand and the President. Roosevelt started ribbing Moley in a heavy-handed and offensive way over his "new, rich friends" and their influence on his views. Missy, sensing unpleasantness ahead, tried to change the subject. But Roosevelt could not be stopped. He said that no one would pay any attention to Moley except for his one-time intimacy with the President. Moley replied that Roosevelt could not take criticism. The exchange became heated and bitter. "It was an ordeal for all of us," said Rosenman. ". . . For the first and only time in my life, I saw the President forget himself as a gentleman." Corcoran was equally shocked.

It was one of those evenings which apparently distressed the spectators more than it did the combatants. Moley later wrote that he and the President had always extended to each other the privilege of plain, even rough, talk; "this particular exchange of asperities was no different from the rest." The next morning, when Roosevelt, going through Moley's draft, came on the line, "Governments can err, Presidents do make mistakes," he read the sentence aloud, laughed genially, and, in his manner, conveyed an apology. For a moment, things seemed back to normal.

But it was the end for both men. In late September Frank Walker, the indefatigable conciliator, arranged a last meeting. It was Moley's fiftieth birthday, and he came to luncheon at Hyde

Park. The President went through the motions of inviting him to help in the campaign; Moley declined with imperturbable politeness. It was too late. The heart of their relationship — the evenings shared around the fireplace in Albany, the excitement and fulfillment of the 1932 campaign, the springtime hopes of the Hundred Days — all, all were gone. They met only once again after 1936. In a short while Moley became a strong and unrelenting administration critic. . . . He once said, years later, that whenever he dreamed of Roosevelt, it was a dream of their reconciliation.[4]

v

Alfred M. Landon was nominated on June 11. William Lemke announced his candidacy on June 19. The Democratic convention opened in Philadelphia three days later. A great electric sign improbably violated the decorous façade of the Union League Club: LANDON AND KNOX, 1936. LOVE OF COUNTRY LEADS. But Philadelphia displayed few other evidences of Republican sentiment. Jim Farley, meticulously describing Kansas to reporters as a "splendid state," exuded a modest but invincible optimism. Everywhere there was the fraternal glee of Democrats gathering for a quadrennial celebration in a victory year.

Nothing could ruffle the delegates. The appearance of the Union party roused only the most tepid interest. Nor were they any more excited when the newspapers published an exhortation by Al Smith, Bainbridge Colby, who had been Wilson's Secretary of State and law partner, former Senator James A. Reed of Missouri, former Governor Joseph B. Ely of Massachusetts, and a New York politician named Daniel F. Cohalan. As the Lewis Douglas–Newton Baker letter earlier in the month had spoken for anti-New Deal Democrats of the old-fashioned, low-tariff, antimonopoly sort, this new manifesto spoke for the high-tariff, big-business Democrats to whom Smith himself had catered in 1928. In the name of Jefferson, Jackson, and Cleveland (the omission of Wilson, apparently on the insistence of Reed, caused comment), the Smith letter called on the convention to declare for a balanced budget, a protective tariff, a foreign policy "free from entangling alliances with Old World powers," and an end to efforts "to turn our Republic into a dictatorship on the European model or an Asiatic absolutism." These goals could be achieved, the message added, only by "the putting aside of Franklin D. Roosevelt and the substitution of some genuine Democrat."

The delegates could not have cared less about Al Smith and his friends. What roused them was Alben Barkley's keynote address with its sonorous defense of the New Deal. The great Kentucky orator had rarely been in happier form. Connoisseurs admired, for example, his passage on the little pigs so beloved to Republican spellbinders.

They shed tears over these little pigs as if they had been tender human infants nestling at the breasts of their mothers. They have cried over these little pigs as if they had been born, educated and destined for the ministry — or for Republican politics. My friends, their bitter tears are not shed for the little pigs. Their real grief comes from the fact of the slaughter of the fat hogs of Republican plunder which they had fed on the substance of the American people.

In more sober vein Barkley discussed the Supreme Court. "Over against the hosannas of Hoover for the tortured interpretation of the Constitution of this nation," he said to uproarious applause, "I place the tortured souls and bodies" of its working men, women, and children. The trouble lay, not with the Constitution, but with the men who interpreted it. The Democratic party wanted the Court to treat the Constitution "as a life-giving charter, rather than an object of curiosity on the shelf of a museum." "Is the Court beyond criticism?" he asked. "May it be regarded as too sacred to be disagreed with?" The convention roared back: "No! No!"

Only one issue threatened the prevailing equanimity. Since its first national convention one hundred years before in 1836, the Democratic party had required a two-thirds vote for nomination. In recent years that rule had become increasingly irksome — first in 1912, when Champ Clark held a majority for eight consecutive ballots, only to fail of nomination; again in 1924, when for an interminable period the rule prevented any nomination at all. Nonetheless, the South cherished the rule because it assured a minority veto over the party ticket. Four years before, the Roosevelt forces had been compelled to abandon a movement for repeal. "Now

that the party is in power and there is no question about my renomination," Roosevelt told Farley, "we should clear up the situation
for all time." And in Senator Bennett Champ Clark of Missouri
the President had available a conservative Democrat who could
not be happier than in leading the fight against the rule ("my
father would have been elected in 1912 . . . this country would
not have gone into the World War"). Clark pursued his goal, as
James F. Byrnes later said, "with all the energy of an avenging
fury"; and newspapermen tried to whip up the picture of a great
impending struggle. But the opposition (though loud enough
when "ayes" and "noes" were called) was perfunctory, even from
the South, and the party was painlessly relieved of a century-old
burden. "That was a job completely engineered by Mr. Roosevelt,"
Farley said later. "I did it under his direction." The result was to
accelerate the transformation of the Democracy into a more thoroughly northern party.

The platform promised little trouble. Assistant Attorney-General
John Dickinson had been assigned the job of preparing a basic
draft. A week before the convention he read the result to Senator
Wagner, the chairman of the Resolutions Committee, William C.
Bullitt, Rosenman, High, Miss LeHand, and the President. Roosevelt, wanting a simpler and more compelling document, told
Rosenman to make a redraft. "I would like to have as short a
platform as possible this year," he said as he wheeled off to bed,
"and . . . I would like to have it based on the sentence of the
Declaration of Independence, 'We hold these truths to be self-
evident.' "

Rosenman and High labored most of the night. They cast the
new draft in the form of a succession of self-evident truths; but
they could not think what to say about foreign affairs or about the
Supreme Court; and they had no peroration. The next morning
they met with the President and Donald Richberg. Roosevelt approved the general form. Then Richberg pulled out of his pocket
a plank pledging the party to seek a "clarifying amendment" in case
pressing national problems could not be solved within the Constitution. There had been controversy over the question of making
the Supreme Court and the Constitution campaign issues. Homer
Cummings, the militant in these matters, had urged Roosevelt for
months to take the issue to the people. Farley, on the other hand,
demurred. Frances Perkins could remember his saying, "Mr. Presi-

dent, the funny part of it is that although the lawyers go on about the Supreme Court having exceeded its powers, and all that, the people of the United States don't understand it. You couldn't possibly get a sufficient excitement among the people about it." The Frankfurter group, too, feeling that the issue was not the Constitution but the judges, disliked the idea of coming out for an amendment. Richberg's proposal thus caused a momentary rumpus. But in the confusion it went through. In the meantime, Bullitt produced a foreign-policy plank; it was never shown to Cordell Hull, and the Secretary of State later pronounced it "a jumble of ideas or theories in which different persons had stuck their respective notions"; but the convention cheerfully accepted it. Harry Hopkins then came up with a peroration, which lasted until Bob La Follette, who had supplied it, warned that it had been copied from the Progressive platform of 1924; then Rosenman and High prepared a new one. The convention adopted the platform in a series of automatic ovations.

And so the proceedings moved on, one day's business stretched into five, for what Oswald Garrison Villard called "the dreariest, dullest, stupidest, loudest, most inane" convention he had ever seen. In the White House the President worked away on his acceptance address. The draft from Corcoran and Moley was serene and conciliatory in tone; the one from Rosenman and High was tough and hard-hitting. Roosevelt characteristically told Rosenman to weave the two incompatible speeches together. This Rosenman did, with assists from High and Richberg. Jostling uneasily next to each other, the two moods were smoothed out in Roosevelt's redictation into a single sustained document.[5]

VI

It was still raining gently on the evening of June 27 when people began to fill the great outdoor stadium at Franklin Field. A large white half-moon, rising to the south, cast a dim light through the misty air. Then, around nine-thirty, the showers stopped, the skies cleared, and the moon, still veiled with clouds, rose steadily overhead. By now over 100,000 men and women were crowded into the stands. The quiet splendor of the scene was a change from the blaring vulgarities of the week. Instead of a brass band, the Philadelphia Symphony played Tschaikowsky; and when Lily Pons sang "Song of the Lark," even the reporters were on their feet cheering. "Something had happened to that audience," wrote Raymond Clapper. "It had been lifted, not to a cheap political emotional pitch, but to something finer. It was ready for Roosevelt."

In the meantime, John Garner formally accepted renomination as Vice-President. The light was poor, and he could barely make out the script on the rostrum before him. Jim Farley, standing near, whispered out words like a prompter, while the Vice-President stumbled through to his conclusion. Then there was a stir in the background; the President's car had arrived. The limousine was on the same level as the floor of the platform; and Roosevelt was supposed to walk, leaning on his son James's arm, from the automobile to the stage. The orchestra went into "Hail to the Chief"; spotlights, scurrying through the black sky, stabbed at the President; and the side curtains suddenly drew back, showing Roosevelt in a pool of brilliant light, a smile on his face, his hand raised high. The crowd went wild. Then, shaking hands as he went, the President began to walk in his stiff-legged, halting way toward the stage.

As he walked, he saw, in the blur of faces, the unmistakable white beard and lofty brow of the poet Edwin Markham, whose "Man With the Hoe" had been a battle-cry for the forgotten man nearly forty years before. Roosevelt waved to Markham; and Markham, now eighty-four years old, came forward to greet him. The crowd, surging behind Markham, pressed him on. As the poet moved to shake the President's hand, someone pushed him, he stumbled heavily against James Roosevelt, and James, off balance, stumbled against his father. Under the pressure, the steel brace holding Roosevelt's right leg snapped out of position. To the horror of those near him, the President suddenly toppled over. Mike Reilly of the Secret Service dived and caught him, his shoulder under Roosevelt's right arm, just before he hit the ground. Meanwhile, the pages of the speech floated from the President's hand into the crowd. While Farley, Homer Cummings, and other tall men clustered around to hide the scene, Gus Gennerich, Roosevelt's bodyguard, knelt down and snapped the brace back to position. Reilly, fearing that some Secret Service man might shoot down the white-bearded stranger in the confusion, shouted frantically to Markham, "Don't move!"

Roosevelt was pale and shaken as they raised him to his feet. "Clean me up," he ordered; then, thinking of his speech, told those around him to keep their feet off "those damned sheets." ("I was the damnedest, maddest white man at that moment you ever saw," he said later; and, again, "it was the most frightful five minutes of my life.") While someone brushed the dirt off his clothes, others rushed to retrieve the scattered manuscript. "Okay, let's go," Roosevelt said after a minute. Now noticing Markham close to tears, a look of agony on his face, Roosevelt stopped again, smiled, and took the poet's hand in his. In a moment the President was on the platform, his expression tranquil and unperturbed, while he quietly reassembled the smudged and crumpled pages in the proper order. And in another moment Senator Robinson presented him to the madly cheering crowd.[6]

VII

The ocean of faces stretched out illimitably into the darkness, and the applause came back, wave after wave, while Roosevelt, his poise regained, smiled and waited. He began his speech with sober thanks for the sympathy, help, and confidence with which the nation had sustained him in his task. "In those days we feared fear. That was why we fought fear. And today, my friends, we have won against the most dangerous of our foes. We have conquered fear." But problems remained — the problem, above all, of preserving freedom against the pressures created by the rush of modern civilization. "Philadelphia is a good city in which to write American history." As Americans in 1776 had sought freedom from the tyranny of a political autocracy, so Americans in 1936 sought freedom from an economic autocracy — from the "economic royalists" (the phrase was Stanley High's). "For too many of us the political equality we once had won was meaningless in the face of economic inequality"; against organized economic tyranny, "the American citizen could appeal only to the organized power of Government." Government must fulfill its obligations to its citizens. "These economic royalists complain that we seek to overthrow the institutions of America. What they really complain of is that we seek to take away their power."

We were poor indeed, Roosevelt said, if this nation could not lift from every recess of American life the dread fear of the unemployed that the world needed them no longer. "We cannot afford to accumulate a deficit in the books of human fortitude." The issue here was whether democracy as a form of government could survive in industrial society. In eloquent words, Roosevelt defined the challenge:

> Governments can err, Presidents do make mistakes, but the immortal Dante tells us that divine justice weighs the sins of the cold-blooded and the sins of the warm-hearted in different scales.
>
> Better the occasional faults of a Government that lives in a spirit of charity than the consistent omissions of a Government frozen in the ice of its own indifference.
>
> There is a mysterious cycle in human events. To some generations much is given. Of other generations much is expected. This generation of Americans has a rendezvous with destiny.

A "rendezvous with destiny!" (Tom Corcoran's phrase; perhaps suggested by a phrase "appointment with destiny," used in 1935 by Walter Lippmann.) Roosevelt went on to make clear what he meant: on the success or failure of the American attempt to make industrial society livable might rest the future of free society everywhere. "We are fighting to save a great and precious form of government for ourselves and for the world."

He reached his conclusion. "I accept the commission you have tendered. . . ." But the applause, thundering up from the audience against the dark sky, overwhelmed his last words. "The greatest political speech I have ever heard," said Harold Ickes; and most of those present agreed. For ten minutes the shouts and cheers went on. Then, as the President stood with his mother and family around him, the orchestra played "Auld Lang Syne." Roosevelt called for the song again, began singing himself, and soon the whole stadium joined him. Presently the President returned to his car. The car circled the stadium's track, Roosevelt erect and waving, to an intense and sustained ovation. Even after he had left the grounds, most of the crowd remained, as if in a sort of trance. Then silently they dispersed into the soft summer night.[7]

32. The Coalition in Action

THE ACCEPTANCE SPEECH launched the Democratic campaign in a mood of high fervor. It also laid out the ideological lines of the campaign and, in so doing, marked the final liquidation of the First New Deal. Where in 1933 Roosevelt had summoned the people to a great experiment in national planning, he now abandoned the phrase, obscured the idea, and held forth at Franklin Field the new goal of "equal opportunity in the market place." And where in 1933 he had called for a united national effort, with business, labor, and farmers, and the government working together in partnership, now he read a powerful section of business out of the community, as the "enemy within our gates." The vision of the managed and co-ordinated society had receded. As Tugwell said, with this address "the original New Deal was now definitely abandoned." [1]

II

A fortnight after the speech, Roosevelt cheerfully set off on a cruise in the waters off New England. He left behind the campaign in a state of considerable confusion. The early polls showed surprising Landon strength, and Emil Hurja in mid-July regarded the situation as "very serious." The National Committee statisticians saw little chance of carrying New York or Illinois, an outside chance perhaps in Ohio, Indiana, and Minnesota; plainly it would be "the toughest kind of a fight." In Farley's view, the main reasons for the Democratic troubles were spending and relief. WPA summed up what people disliked in the New Deal; and Hopkins, with his "injudicious wisecracks," only made matters worse. The first requirement of a successful campaign, Farley thought, was to keep the extreme New Dealers, especially Hopkins and Tugwell, out of the public eye. Since Farley had already consented to silence himself, this greatly reduced the number of administrative spokesmen. He considered Morgenthau and Dern of little use; Cummings would campaign only if the President ordered him to; Miss Perkins was no good outside New York. "I'd use Wallace in the farm areas," Farley told Roosevelt, "and keep him away from the industrial sections." As for the Vice-President, both Roosevelt and Farley wanted him in the campaign. But Garner, now in summer retirement at Uvalde ("The gnats, mosquitoes, and red-bugs are sometimes a little annoying. . . . I am hardened up, have blistered and peeled off twice and am getting very brown"), was as reluctant as ever to go on the hustings. "I know my weakness," he wrote Roosevelt. ". . . and I know if I get to 'swashbuckling' around speech-making I am liable to do something like the 'Mad Priest' did at Cleveland, which would destroy whatever I accomplished, as it has him." Of all the cabinet members, the most usable seemed, surprisingly, to be Ickes. Farley well understood the value of attack in politics; and in Ickes the administration had an orator whose record of solid if testy achievement had earned him a national license for bellicosity. He had proved himself in his speech on the eve of the Republican convention. From that moment, Roosevelt and Farley turned to him whenever they wanted a hard-hitting, free-swinging, well-documented assault on the Republican enemy. Ickes assumed the role of hatchet man with grim relish.

But the chief campaigner, of course, had to be Roosevelt himself. As Garner told Farley, "Jim, after all, the people in this country are going to vote for or against Roosevelt and it doesn't make a great deal of difference just what is done by the campaign other than get out votes to the polls. The personality of the Chief is the principal issue."

III

The technical organization of the campaign was still sketchy. Eleanor Roosevelt made a tour of inspection to Democratic headquarters in the middle of July. Her memorandum to Farley is worth quoting at length for the light it throws not only on the campaign but on the way Mrs. Roosevelt operated for her husband. "I hear from outside sources," she began, "that the Landon headquarters are set up and ready to work full time. They have continuity people writing for the radio, they have employed advertising people to do their copy, and the whole spirit is the spirit of a crusade. My feeling is that we have to get going and [get] going quickly." How did the Democrats look? "My impression," said Mrs. Roosevelt, who was, of course, a veteran on the working side of political campaigns, "is that the women are further along in their organization and more ready to go than any other unit as yet." She then raised a series of pointed questions:

1. . . . Because of the importance of this [publicity] committee, I hope a meeting will be held immediately for organizing and defining the duties of the members and that you will have the minutes kept at every meeting in order that a copy may go to the President. . . .

2. Who is responsible for studying news reports and suggesting answers to charges, etc.?

3. Who is responsible . . . for the planning of a radio campaign, getting the speakers through the speakers' bureau, making the arrangements in the states for people to listen?

4. Who is in charge of research? Have we a department with complete information concerning all activities of the New Deal, and also concerning Landon and his supporters?

5. What definite plans have we made for tying in the other publicity organizations, both of men and women with the national publicity organization? . . .

6. Have you mapped out continuous publicity steps which will be taken between now and November? Is there any way at least of charting a tentative plan of strategy for the whole campaign? . . .

7. In the doubtful and Republican states what special attention do you plan to give? . . .

8. Who is handling news reels? . . .

9. Has your committee assigned as yet to each member definite fields for supervision?

10. How many people are now working on campaign speeches? . . .

11. Who is your man making contacts with newspapers all over the country?

12. Who is responsible for sending regular news to friendly newspapers? By this I mean feature stories, pictures, mats, boiler plate, etc.

I feel Mr. Rayburn should come at once to plan the policy and mechanics of the speakers' bureau. . . .

I think it would be well to start some Negro speakers, like Mrs. Bethune to speak at church meetings and that type of Negro organization.

Eleanor Roosevelt concluded: "I hope the answers will be mailed to reach us at Eastport, Maine, on the 27th or 28th of July, when the President expects to be there."

With the President largely out of reach, with Farley unwilling or perhaps unauthorized to make crucial decisions in his absence, the campaign seemed to be drifting dangerously. Early told Ickes on July 20 that there were "no campaign plans and no budget." "If this campaign is run much longer as it is being run," noted Ickes in his diary, "there will be little chance of defeating Landon. . . . We are losing ground every day." In his irritation he even mused about what might have happened had he responded to suggestions that he seek the Republican nomination. "As I see the thing now, if I had been nominated, in all probability I could have won in November with the situation standing as it does today." And Roosevelt? "Meanwhile," Ickes wrote indignantly, "the President smiles and sails and fishes and the rest of us worry and fume." [2]

IV

The President was off on blue water in the small schooner *Sewanna* with three of his boys and a crew of two. "I haven't the faintest idea where I'm going, except to work to the eastward," he told the press. "I'm just going to loaf and have a good time." Relaxed in his old clothes and a floppy white hat, a straggle of beard on his chin, his skin tanning under the wind and sun,

Roosevelt weighed anchor at Pulpit Harbor, Maine, and sailed happily down east past Mount Desert into the Bay of Fundy and along the gray shores of Nova Scotia. But as he smiled and sailed and fished, he also thought about the campaign ahead.

His main problem, as he saw it, was the business domination of the media of opinion. "If the Republicans should win or make enormous gains," he wrote, "it would prove that an 85 percent control of the Press and a very definite campaign of misinformation can be effective here just as it was in the early days of the Hitler rise to power. Democracy is verily on trial." But he had one great weapon to counter the opposition of the newspapers. That was his own capacity as President to make news, and this he proposed to use to the utmost. In a letter of July 19 to Garner, Roosevelt outlined his plans. In August and early September he contemplated a series of "nonpolitical" trips to parts of the country stricken by flood or drought ("absolutely no political speeches, but a number of short talks on the flood problem, the drought problem, the soil erosion problem, etc., etc."). "I am inclined to think," he wrote Josephus Daniels, "that the Republican high command is shooting off all their ammunition too soon and that people will be rather sick of their same old story by the end of September." Then in October he would turn politician and deliver four or five major addresses.

In the meantime, the New Deal also could make news: its deeds constituted his most powerful political asset. Roosevelt was acutely aware of the electoral implications of federal policy. In February, for example, he told Wallace, "Henry, through July, August, September, October and up to the fifth of November, I want cotton to sell at 12 cents. I do not care how you do it. That is your problem. It can't go below 12 cents. Is that clear?" Again, when a WPA decision to cut back relief funds threatened the dismissal of many workers on October 1, Roosevelt told Morgenthau, "You tell Corrington Gill that I don't give a goddam where he gets the money from but not one person is to be laid off on the first of October."

Though WPA reductions were thus postponed, there is no persuasive evidence to support the charge that WPA rolls were enlarged for election purposes. According to a WPA study, relief figures, excluding drought cases, went steadily down from June to November 1936. In any case, those on the WPA rolls were deluged by instructions from Hopkins that they were under no obligation to any political party and that they should vote as they pleased. More than this, Democratic politicians continued to complain that in many localities WPA was under Republican domination and was being used against the administration. Thus Fred M. Vinson of Kentucky to Farley:

I do not want relief in politics and I know that the President does not, but when it gets to the point that the Republicans are in charge of it and Democrats are discriminated against . . . it is no wonder that our folks are wondering how such a thing could happen.

C. M. Brown of California:

The WPA is our worst set-up. It is under Republican administration and everybody who does not get a job damns the Democratic Administration.

M. C. Wallgren of Washington:

Federal employees are afraid to be at all politically active. It is understood that they are receiving constant notices from Washington to the effect that there must be no political activity whatever. The men on WPA and PWA are fearful of even carrying stickers on their cars.

Margaret O'Riordan of Massachusetts:

The only thing that hurts is the old story of WPA domination by the Republicans.

Still, even if WPA caused local resentments, it stood as a symbol of a determination to help the forgotten man. The press might be Republican, but the New Deal would continue to do things for people, and Roosevelt himself could move nonpolitically around the land as the visible embodiment of federal humanitarianism.[3]

v

As for the actual organization of the campaign, Roosevelt envisaged this as a much larger matter than simply the Democratic party. Seeing himself increasingly as the leader, not just of a party, but of a coalition, he saw the traditional party organization as perhaps the central constituent, but by no means the whole works. Indeed, the President himself hardly ever mentioned the party by name, and did his campaigning, as Stanley High noted, "not as a Democrat, but as a New Deal liberal fighting not for party success but for a cause."

As the campaign developed, the Democratic party seemed more and more submerged in the New Deal coalition. The most active campaigners in addition to Roosevelt — Ickes, Wallace, Hugh Johnson — were men identified with the New Deal, not with the professional Democratic organization. Loyalty to the cause superseded loyalty to the party as the criterion for administration support. In Minnesota, the Democratic ticket thus withdrew in favor of the Farmer-Labor ticket; in Nebraska, Roosevelt ignored the Democratic candidate and endorsed George Norris; in Wisconsin, the New Deal worked with the Progressives; in Massachusetts, the administration declined to back James M. Curley, the Democratic candidate for senator. It was evident that the basis of the campaign would be the mobilization *beyond* the Democratic party of all the elements in the New Deal coalition — liberals, labor, farmers, women, minorities. To do this required the elaborate structure of subsidiary organizations and committees which Roosevelt began urging on Farley as early as January 1936. To the building of this structure the architects of the Democratic campaign now gave their chief attention.[4]

VI

The most powerful new element in the coalition represented a major departure from classical Democratic politics — and one with which Jim Farley was little qualified to deal. This was organized labor, endowed by NRA and the Wagner Act with a new stake in the federal government and now determined to keep a friendly administration in Washington. In 1932 Roosevelt had not even bothered to make a major labor speech, despite pleas from Dan Tobin, the head of the Democratic National Committee's Labor Division; nor had the labor vote made a distinctive contribution to the outcome. But by 1934 the federal guarantee of collective bargaining had transformed the prospects of the labor movement. "Labor knew this," Francis Biddle wrote Roosevelt in 1935, "and looked to you as their leader. This faith in you was very largely responsible for the swing in Pennsylvania last Autumn, particularly in the steel mills and coal mines, where employer domination had been synonymous with Republican control." Organized labor promised to be an active factor in 1936 as it had never been in American history.

In the past the Labor Division was but one of a miscellany of the National Committee's ritualistic gestures toward special groups — more for show than for use. When it became evident that Farley, who displayed little appreciation of the possibilities of the labor vote, meant to hand the Labor Division over to Tobin again in 1936, the labor militants decided they would have to organize for Roosevelt on their own. This was not just to prevent the old-line unionists from freezing the CIO leaders out of the campaign. It was also to make sure that the labor vote was mobilized in quantity — something the Labor Division, operating on traditional lines, had never been able to do.

Accordingly, in early April 1936 John L. Lewis, Sidney Hillman, and George L. Berry announced the formation of Labor's Nonpartisan League. The immediate aim of the new organization was the re-election of Roosevelt — "the greatest statesman of modern times," as Lewis called him. "President Roosevelt has undertaken and accomplished more for the workers than any other president in the history of the nation," Lewis said, "and labor owes him a debt of gratitude that can be liquidated only by casting its solid vote for him at the coming election." Hillman added, "We know that the defeat of the Roosevelt Administration means no labor legislation for decades to come." Beyond 1936, they contemplated continuing the League as the political arm of labor and as the basis for what Berry described as "the permanent establishment of a liberal party, if necessary, in the United States in 1940."

The League swung into action over the summer. David Dubinsky of the International Ladies' Garment Workers and Emil Rieve of the Hosiery Workers resigned from the Socialist party to join its campaign. Though Bill Green disapproved, a number of A.F. of L. craft unions took part. In New York, the League invented a new party — the American Labor party — to get support for Roosevelt and for Herbert Lehman from people reluctant to vote for them on the Democratic ticket. While the League did not generally attempt ward-and-precinct organization, it worked through local trade-union people in nearly every state to stimulate a sense of urgency. It went on the radio, passed out leaflets by the thousand, staged rallies (109 in Chicago alone), and spent nearly a million dollars. Lewis himself set the tone for the fight against the Republican candidate — "this little man out in Topeka, Kansas, who has no more conception nor idea of what ails America or what to do about it than a goat herder in the hills of Bulgaria." Landon, Lewis said, was "as empty, as inane, as innocuous as a watermelon that has been boiled in a washtub"; in another mood, Lewis saw him as a "bootlicker of plutocracy . . . as with quibble and quirk he seeks to cozen the American people."

Labor's greatest contribution to the campaign, however, was money. Lewis, Hillman, and Berry chipped in to keep the League going; and the United Mine Workers, in particular, became in the end the chief support not only of the Democratic party but of other campaign subsidiaries, such as the Progressive National Committee. The history of the financial transactions of the 1936 campaign remains obscure. According to one detailed account (George Creel's), Lewis originally proposed to hand Roosevelt a check from the UMW for $250,000. Roosevelt replied, "No, John, I don't want your check, much as I appreciate the thought. Just keep it, and I'll call on you if and when any small need arises." Lewis grumbled to his associates that they had been outsmarted; now there would be no limit to the amount for which they would be asked. Certainly, as the campaign proceeded, the Democrats subjected the UMW to a series of requisitions until the bill ran up to just under half a million dollars (of which $40,000 was a loan, eventually repaid). With gifts from other unions, the total labor contribution to the Democratic campaign was almost three-quarters of a million dollars. At a time when contributions from big business were falling sharply (bankers and brokers, who had given about one-quarter of the funds received by the Democrats in 1932 in amounts over $1,000, gave less than one twenty-fifth in this same category in 1936), labor enabled Roosevelt and Farley to campaign in the style to which they had become accustomed. Later in the autumn Matthew McCloskey of Philadelphia invented the $100-a-plate dinner, thereby providing the coalition its indispensable fund-raising device.[5]

A second element in the coalition were those middle-class liberals, independents, and intellectuals more attracted by the New Deal than by the Democratic party. Progressivism had by no means been a Democratic monopoly before 1933; indeed, the term itself implied primarily a dissident Republican. Roosevelt, seeing himself (in 1936 over the protests of T.R.'s widow) as the residuary legatee of his great kinsman's Bull Moose heritage, started early in the year to prod Farley and Ickes into setting up a new edition of the committee of progressives which had backed him in 1932.

The two key figures in the wooing of progressive support were Floyd Olson and Bob La Follette. Both were wholly friendly "I liked your acceptance speech," Olson wrote the President at the end of June. ". . . The thing that pleased me most was that you did not pull your punches.'" But Olson's health continued to decline. He now spent most of his time in the Mayo Clinic at Rochester, Minnesota. Pain was constant and racking (said Dr. Will Mayo, "The Governor absolutely is the most courageous person I ever saw"); he could be fed only through a tube; and he steadily wasted away, his weight falling to 130 pounds. In mid-August, as the final crisis approached, Olson sent off a last message. The choice, he said, was between Roosevelt and Landon. He had the "utmost respect" for Lemke and Coughlin; but "for the liberals to split their votes is merely to play into the hands of the Wall Street gang. . . . The defeat of Landon is of the utmost importance to the great masses." A few days later Olson died. Roosevelt said, "The nation has lost a personality of singular force and courage . . . year by year . . . a more massive figure in our national life." This most powerful of the radical politicians was only forty-four years old.

In the meantime, La Follette had agreed to head the progressive drive for Roosevelt. Early in September La Follette, joined by Norris, La Guardia, Frank P. Walsh, Homer Bone, Adolf Berle, Elmer Benson of Minnesota, and other progressives, called a national conference. On September 11, Lewis, Hillman, Hugo

Black, Lewis Schwellenbach, Tom Amlie, and others met with them in Chicago to organize the Progressive National Committee and advocate Roosevelt's re-election (Amlie prevented an endorsement of the Democratic party as well by arguing that the time might come when progressives wanted to stand alone.)

Norris, though not present in Chicago, gave the movement effective support. The old man was stancher in his faith than the younger liberals, who applauded Roosevelt one moment and denounced him the next. "All of us are apt to get discouraged when we compare things today with a year ago and see no difference," Norris said in July. "But when we look back twenty-five years, say, we can see that there has been a great change." Franklin Roosevelt, he said, had gone further "in the protection of those who toil, both on the farm and in the factory, than any other man who has held this high office. . . . Out of the New Deal, under his leadership, will come a new civilization for America."

Roosevelt's decision to back Norris against the regular Democratic candidate, Terry Carpenter (then dallying with the nostrums of Townsend and Coughlin; he later had a moment of fame when he spoke for the mythical Joe Smith in the Republican convention of 1956), confirmed his claim to progressive support. Liberal Republicans like James M. Couzens and Peter Norbeck and the Farmer-Laborite Henrik Shipstead endorsed Roosevelt. Other liberal Republicans like Hiram Johnson, Gerald Nye, even Charles McNary and William E. Borah, took no part in the campaign rather than oppose Roosevelt. Louis Waldman and the right-wing Socialists came out for Roosevelt in August. Even Alfred Bingham, Tom Amlie, and the radicals around *Common Sense*, after watching the third party dream fade away, concluded that they had to support Roosevelt ("a support limited only to the next few weeks, and [to be] withdrawn the day after Election Day"). A poll of *Common Sense* readers showed 50 per cent for Roosevelt, 44 per cent for Thomas, 4 per cent for Lemke, and less than one per cent each for Browder and Landon. "I'm going to vote for Roosevelt," said Frank Hanighen, "because I believe that his election will provide the best chance of preventing the formation of a fascist set-up in this country." "I'm going to vote for Roosevelt, but without enthusiasm," said John Chamberlain. "He probably won't do anything *for* those who see him as the nearest available symbol of a People's Front, but he is likely to do *less* against them."

The Progressive National Committee aimed at politically conscious liberals. But there were, in addition, liberal-minded people — churchmen, educators, social workers, intellectuals — who did not think primarily in political terms. Before his death, Louis Howe suggested the formation of a Good Neighbor League as a means of bringing such people into the campaign. This became Stanley High's particular project. The League was organized in April, with the social worker Lilian Wald and the philanthropist George Foster Peabody as co-chairmen; among its directors were Frank Graham of North Carolina, George Harrison of the Railway Clerks, Carrie Chapman Catt, Fannie Hurst, Charles Edison, and A. P. Giannini. By August High claimed that the League was organized in twenty states and that 40 per cent of its membership was Republican. Together the Progressive National Committee and the Good Neighbor League made a powerful appeal to the independent-minded middle-class voter. And, on their own initiative, groups of intellectuals — especially members of college faculties — declared their support for Roosevelt and his administration.[6]

VIII

The mobilization of women was once again in the more than competent hands of Molly Dewson. The months of hard work spent in 1934 and 1935 in developing the Reporter Plan now paid off; and the Women's Division, as Eleanor Roosevelt had noted, was far ahead of the rest of the National Committee in its preparations. When the Democratic delegates assembled at Philadelphia, the Women's Division had on every seat a packet of Rainbow Fliers, each printed on different colored paper and carrying the basic facts on a different government activity. These fliers became the basis of the information effort of the campaign. Roosevelt was delighted by them: "Make it simple enough for the women to understand," he said, "and then the men will understand it." Over eighty million were distributed; indeed, 80 per cent of the printed material distributed by the National Committee in 1936 came from the Women's Division.

Molly Dewson also saw to it that the convention dramatized the recognition the Democratic party was according women: eight women seconded Roosevelt's nomination; and, more important, each state was authorized to add a female alternate to the Resolutions Committee. The Democrats had 219 women delegates and alternates at Philadelphia as compared to 60 Republican women at Cleveland. All this constituted a strong bid for the women's vote.

In the same way, the campaign was marked by a new concentration on the foreign nationality groups. Roosevelt even came up with the dubious idea of calling back ministers and ambassadors: "they could speak effectively in cities where there are a goodly number of inhabitants from the countries they represent abroad." The labor movement, and especially the industrial unions, represented the more potent means by which recent immigrants were made to feel their stake in national politics.

IX

What was perhaps most striking was the successful Democratic effort to consolidate its gains among the Negroes. In this effort, Roosevelt was greatly assisted by the performance of Cotton Ed Smith and other anti-Negro extremists at the Philadelphia convention, where there were thirty-two Negro delegates and alternates. When a Negro Baptist minister opened one session with a prayer, Smith, accompanied by Mayor Burnet Maybank of Charleston and one or two other South Carolina delegates, walked ostentatiously off the floor, saying that he would not support "any political organization that looks upon the Negro and caters to him as a political and social equal." He was, Smith said, "sick of the whole damn thing." (The minister commented, "Brother Smith needs more prayer.") Smith repeated the performance the next day when Congressman Mitchell of Illinois was speaking; and the South Carolina delegation subsequently adopted a resolution protesting the presence of Negroes on the program. All this called Negro attention to the recognition accorded their race in the Democratic convention — a marked contrast to the Republican convention, which had seated lily-white delegations from southern states.

Two southern Democratic primaries further raised the race issue to Roosevelt's advantage. James F. Byrnes had conspicuously not imitated his South Carolina colleagues in protesting the Negroes in Philadelphia; he had further committed the offense of once trying to get a grand jury to indict a white man for shooting a

Negro. His opponent in the South Carolina primary now used the "nigger issue" against him: "Little Jimmy Byrnes is not the man we sent to Washington as a Senator, else he would have walked out too." In Georgia, Gene Talmadge, fighting for his political life, did his best to defeat Richard B. Russell on the ground of Russell's support of the nigger-loving New Deal. The fact that both Byrnes and Russell won their fights in the course of the summer seemed to show that even the Southern Democracy was moderate rather than rabid on the race question.

Negro leaders had sharply condemned the Republican platform, among other things for pledging "protection" of the Negro's economic status. "That is precisely what the Negroes do not want," said *Crisis*. "His present economic status is the chief cause of his discontent." While they liked the Democratic platform no better, they consoled themselves somewhat by recalling that Roosevelt had "indicated on numerous occasions his personal differences with the traditional attitudes of his party." So great a friend of the Negro as J. E. Spingarn, president of the National Association for the Advancement of Colored People, who had not endorsed a presidential candidate since T.R., came out for F.D.R.; "he has done more for the Negro than any Republican President since Lincoln." In the end, *Crisis* recommended in effect that Negroes vote their economic interests. For both *Crisis* and the majority of Negroes, this meant supporting the New Deal.

The National Committee, committed to its orthodox view of party tactics, was slow to exploit the new possibilities. Early in September Congressman Thomas C. Hennings, Jr., of Missouri pointed out to Farley that the 100,000 Negroes in his own St. Louis district had been instrumental in holding the city for the Republicans since the Civil War. "I am wondering just what the National Committee is planning to do in this regard," Hennings wrote. ". . . I feel that there is a great deal of constructive work to be done in this connection." J. F. Quinlivan of Toledo had a word of advice for Farley: "We do not feel that this is the proper time to bring Southern speakers in Ohio because for the first time in history the outlook is very favorable for the Democratic Party to have a majority of the Negro vote."

Given the inflexibility of the regulars, the job of rallying the Negroes fell particularly to Stanley High and the Good Neighbor

League. On September 21 the League sponsored a great Roosevelt rally in New York. The professionals predicted that Negroes would never come all the way from Harlem to attend a Democratic rally in Madison Square Garden. But they filled the vast auditorium long before the meeting began. On the same night, similar rallies were held in twenty-five other northern cities. The proceedings at Madison Square Garden were even broadcast nationally (southern stations were carefully omitted from the hookup). Negroes turned out with wild enthusiasm to see Roosevelt, but looked on Landon parades with evident coolness. It seemed clear by October that the Negro vote was going Democratic by a considerable margin.

The year 1936 was, so to speak, the springtime of the New Deal coalition. Labor, liberals, intellectuals, women, minorities — all were charged with extra energy by the sense of a new role and dignity in national affairs; as Sidney Hillman put it for labor in a moment of exultation, "We have participated in making the labor policy of this Administration." As for the old-line Democratic politicians, they were rushed along by the current, hardly aware of what was going on around them, continuing in a stately manner to execute their classical strokes.[8]

33. Saving the American Way of Life

IT WAS TOPEKA's largest crowd and almost its hottest day: and now, at evening, after the long parade in the sweltering sun, the people stood under the floodlights before the State House, waiting cheerfully in shirt sleeves and summer dresses, eating sandwiches and ice cream, cooling themselves with fans shaped in the form of huge sunflowers. Flares lit the State House dome, and searchlights dashed rapidly over the scene below. At last the moment arrived, and Governor Alfred M. Landon, his face serious, his voice a trifle nervous, appeared to accept the Republican nomination.

II

Landon, presenting himself in his third sentence as "the everyday American," spoke as a man who had given the New Deal the benefit of every doubt but now concluded that its administrative incompetence and intellectual confusion were defeating its own ends. "The nation has not made the durable progress, either in reform or recovery, that we had the right to expect." The time had come to stop fumbling with recovery, "to unshackle initiative and free the spirit of American enterprise." Once business was liberated from governmental hostility and extravagance, "the energies of the American economic system will remedy the ravages of depression." And, in the meantime, government would not forget its obligations to the farmer, the worker, and the unemployed. In quiet, general and earnest terms, Alf Landon issued, not a summons to the "holy crusade" against the New Deal Herbert

Hoover had declared in Cleveland, but a plea that he could manage the New Deal better and cheaper — provide all its benefits and balance the budget, too.

The address lacked force, both in substance and in delivery. Landon looked down at his script too often, spoke too fast, and, on occasion, killed his own applause. It disappointed nearly everybody, except the Democrats. "It sounded to me," Jim Farley told Roosevelt joyfully, "like a country candidate running for office in an upstate New York county." "If this is the best that Landon can do," said Ickes, "the Democratic Campaign Committee ought to spend all the money it can raise to send him out to make speeches." But it accurately reflected both Landon's own personality and the Kansan's theory of the campaign.

"It is an extremely difficult thing to be yourself in a position like mine," Landon had written a friend in January, "but I have not stepped out of character, and if I do have any strength it is because everything around me and about me is the direct antithesis of the present executive." He was determined to stay himself, and he was convinced that his very flatness as a political performer might constitute a campaign virtue. "The American people always have been fearful, in the end, of a *great* man," he said in the spring. The tide of national support leading to his nomination seemed to him to be a response to "simple virtues which the rank and file understand and like to think they themselves possess." He wanted to emphasize the contrast between the slick, eloquent, and insincere Democrat and the sound, humdrum, common-sense Republican, the "everyday American," whose very lack of polish attested to his sincerity. His advisers agreed. As Mark Sullivan put it, "The public is getting tired of Roosevelt's personality, of his evasiveness, his adroitness, his showmanship and especially of his everlasting smile. . . . The thing they will seek in the election will be the opposite."

Landon had declined to fly to the convention to accept the nomination lest he seem to be aping Roosevelt's 1932 flight to Chicago. Nor were all his supporters dismayed by the address at Topeka. "Let Il Duce make his ringing speeches with his dramatic inflections," wrote Richard E. Berlin of the Hearst papers. "You have now hit the formula, stick to it!" Amos Pinchot even told William Hard of the Republican National Committee, "Do urge Governor Landon not to try to improve his delivery."

III

As for the moderate substance of the speech, this, too, expressed
Landon's own considered views. He simply did not see the New
Deal, as Hoover did, as a conspiracy to subvert American institutions. He was, after all, a man who had offered to enlist with
Roosevelt in 1933, who supported the administration's agricultural
and conservation programs, endorsed the principle of social security, had never criticized the securities or banking or holding company or labor legislation, and seemed to hold against the New
Deal chiefly its administrative inefficiency and its fiscal deficits.
His Kansas intimates, moreover, supported by Charles P. Taft,
the head of his brain trust, conceived moderation to be not only
right but the best politics. They calculated that fanatical anti–
New Dealers would vote for Landon in any case, having no place
else to go; enough raw meat could be inserted from time to time
(as in the preamble to the platform) to keep the troops happy.
The campaign's main target should therefore be the troubled
citizens on Main Street who liked the New Deal's goals but distrusted its methods. "None of my campaign speeches will be
merely an attack upon the opposition," Landon wrote Borah early
in August. ". . . I cannot criticize everything that has been done
in the past three years and do it sincerely. Neither do I believe
that such an attack is good politics."

In fact, this was the strategy Roosevelt most feared. Once in
October he told friends how he would run the Landon campaign: "First, I would repudiate Hearst. Then I would repudiate
the du Ponts and everything they stand for. Then I would say:
'I am for social security, work relief, etc. etc. But the Democrats
cannot be entrusted with the administration of these fine ideals.'
I would cite chapter and verse on WPA inefficiency — and there's
plenty of it."

Not all Republicans, however, accepted this conception of the
campaign. The party was torn in its chronic conflict between
those, like Landon and Charles Taft, who favored what would later
be called a "me-too" policy toward liberalism, and those, like
Hoover, who favored a root-and-branch assault on every liberal
idea as a menace to the republic. Powerful forces in the party were

demanding all-out attack. This is what the Hearst press, which represented the second largest single contributor, wanted. It was what the *Chicago Tribune* wanted, with its daily reminders that only a stated number of days remained to save the American way of life; what the du Ponts and Pews wanted, who between them gave the campaign more than a million dollars; what many of Landon's eastern supporters wanted; what many Republican professionals believed necessary in order to stir the zeal of the rank-and-file. "You can't win the coming campaign by being nice," John Hamilton, now the National Chairman, had said the year before. "Those Republicans who say we should talk on constructive issues don't know their politics. You beat men in office, you don't elect men. . . . People vote their dislikes. It may not be sportsmanlike to work on that basis, but this is not the time to sit back and be nice."

From the start, the conflict divided the headquarters. "As soon as the Magi get up a speech," William Allen White observed in August, "the Shepherds come and tear it down." But the candidate was confident he could deal with the situation. He planned to surround himself with Republicans of the Bull Moose stripe — men like Gifford Pinchot of Pennsylvania, Robert Bass of New Hampshire, Harold Johnson of New York. He asked Pinchot to arrange meetings with labor leaders, and wrote him in early August, "I note there are many strong partisans who would like to 'smell blood,' but again I quite agree with your views." To Frank Knox he explained that the Constitution could not be a winning issue for the Republicans. When Hamilton tried to send out a businessman as an advance man, Landon objected to it as one more "illustration of getting too many businessmen, employers of labor, in our campaign organization." He added, "I am hearing again and again that the Old Guard is functioning too prominently in the picture, that the great effect of the new leadership in the party as demonstrated at the Cleveland convention is being lost." To Frank Altschul he reiterated his guiding determination: "I don't want to get too much out of character."[1]

IV

For the moment, the candidate's ideas remained in the ascendancy. He took care in his first campaign trips that no Republican associated with the Harding, Coolidge, or Hoover administrations, with big business or the Old Guard — with what he called "the stuffed-shirt leadership of the party" — should be in his entourage. But Hoover himself remained an overhanging presence; and when the former President predictably offered his services to the campaign, Landon headquarters was filled with consternation.

Hoover had explained to Hamilton that he did not wish to speak until Roosevelt started to campaign, at which point he proposed three speeches to be billed as specific answers to Roosevelt and to be delivered in New York, Chicago, and Philadelphia. He added, as Hamilton informed Landon, "that he was quite certain that there had never been a time when the Republican nominee did not invite the Republican ex-President to participate." Landon had no wish to see the campaign turn into a debate between Roosevelt and Hoover. But Hamilton kept pressing him to send Hoover a letter asking him to take part. With Landon still reluctant, Hamilton asked Hoover whether he would settle for a telephone call. Hoover said that he would; and in due course Landon called.

An Associated Press reporter now queried Hoover as to whether he had heard from Landon. Hoover referred the reporter to the Chicago headquarters for the details of their conversation. The next morning a member of the Landon staff denied that the two men had talked. Hoover, who had taken the precaution of having his secretary record the conversation, responded indignantly, "This is the first time anyone has ever dared challenge the integrity of a statement I made. . . . If this denial is persisted in by members of Landon's staff I will . . . have published the complete stenographic notes of my conversation yesterday morning with Governor Landon." At this, Republican headquarters took back the story. Hoover promptly wrote a letter to Landon, acknowledging what he called Landon's urgent plea for his help and adding ominously that somewhere along the line he planned to take occasion to indicate publicly that Landon had made such a request. Then the former President went on to Chicago. He was chilled by his reception at Landon's headquarters. No one seemed interested in arranging speeches for him; and, in the end, he played little part in the campaign. When he did speak, he hardly mentioned the Republican candidate.

If Landon could control his own speeches and entourage he could

not always control the rest of the campaign. Indeed, in the weeks
after the acceptance speech, he went away on a prolonged vacation
in Colorado. ("Considerable mystery," wrote Westbrook Pegler,
"surrounds the disappearance of Alfred M. Landon of Topeka,
Kansas, who has been missing from his regular haunts for some time.
. . . Anyone having information of his whereabouts is asked to com-
municate direct with the Republican National Committee.") During the long silence, Frank Knox and John Hamilton set the tone of
the campaign. Where Landon dealt in moderation and generality,
their speeches resounded with fearful predictions of calamity
and doom.

This was not necessarily a mistake. A campaign is a matter of
orchestration. If the presidential candidate meant to strike only
the high notes, there was an advantage in having party spokesmen who could bang the drums and slap the bass, so long as
they were not mistaken for the conductor. Knox and Hamilton
took for the Republicans the role which Ickes filled for the Democrats. But they blanketed Landon as Ickes never blanketed Roosevelt. "The New Deal candidate," said Knox, "has been leading
us toward Moscow." The Democratic party "has been seized by
alien and un-American elements." "I preach to you," he cried in
the accents of T.R., "the doctrine, not of the soft and spineless kept
citizens of a regimented state, but of the self-respecting and self-
reliant men who made America. . . . Next November you will
choose the American way." And the National Chairman, who had
denied any intention of sitting back and being nice, made trips
around the country speaking darkly of the "makings of a dictatorship." He charged the New Dealers with planning to supplant
the Constitution by "some other mechanism" or simply by "the
vague principles and aspirations of Franklin Roosevelt." He spoke
so much and so furiously (he, too, hoped to draw a useful contrast
between his own clean-cut, Yankee personality and the image
of Irish machine politics embodied in Farley) that it left headquarters without direction, irritated Republican leaders and provoked Harold Ickes to the inquiry: "Who is the Republican
candidate anyway — Landon or Hamilton?"

Landon, who had urged Hamilton to make the trips, considered
the criticism unfair: "You have done a whale of a job in rebuilding
the state organizations. . . . You have carried the banner well,

and were the only one who could carry the banner during these past few weeks." Toward the end of the month, the candidate emerged from his Colorado holiday to take charge himself. He opened his own first trip with a speech at his birthplace in Pennsylvania — an exceedingly innocuous declaration in favor of local initiative and the American way, almost entirely lacking in any attack on the New Deal. (This speech contained the immortal line, "Wherever I have gone in this country, I have found Americans.") A few days later at Chautauqua, New York, he offered a courageous defense of civil liberties. "The right of free inquiry," he said, ". . . is the very bedrock of democracy." He supported the freedom of teachers to concern themselves with political and economic problems; more than that, he sharply condemned the project of a teachers' oath — not only a favorite idea of Hearst's but the measure which New York Republicans, under the leadership of Assemblyman Irving Ives, had only recently fastened on New York schools. ("You might call the attention of some of your liberal friends," Landon wrote to William Allen White, "that the President made a mouthful sounding address on freedom of speech at Harvard, but he didn't get down to brass tacks like I did at Chautauqua.") In Buffalo Landon attacked the administration's "reckless spending" and finally came out against a specific New Deal measure — the undistributed-profits tax ("the most cock-eyed piece of legislation ever imposed in a modern country"). He completed his New York and Pennsylvania tour, his aides carefully pointed out to the press, without any private conferences with the Old Guard bosses, Charles Hilles and Joe Grundy. And he returned to Kansas in time to appear before a state convention of the American Legion and bravely denounce racial and religious intolerence. ("The evidence of the need of this speech," Landon explained to W. W. Waymack of the *Des Moines Register,* "is the fact that I have received a large number of letters from legionnaires all over the country protesting against it.")

"The Republican gospel of salvation being preached by Alf Landon on one hand and that being preached by John Hamilton and Frank Knox on the other," commented *Time,* "seemed about as dissonant and confusing to voters as the competing Christianities of a Boston Unitarian and a hard-shell Southern Baptist would be to Hottentot bushmen." [2]

V

"Straight from the shoulder," Representative William P. Connery, Jr., of Massachusetts wrote James A. Farley in August: "From where I sit at present time it looks like 60-40 in favor of Landon." The continued presidential inactivity seemed inexplicable to many Democrats. "What in the hell is the use of having a General in this battle of words if he is not going to lead us?" a Kansas politician wrote. "Roosevelt is the only man who can do the job. . . . The Democratic enthusiasm is lessening every day, simply because of the President's silence."

But the President, when he returned from his cruise at the end of July, was unperturbed. Three weeks before the Republican convention, he had made a slight downward revision of his estimates of January, giving the Republicans 216 votes in the electoral college and the Democrats 315. Landon's nomination increased his optimism; on August 2, he wrote on a piece of paper, "FDR, 340, AML, 191." And he proceeded thoughtfully to conduct the first — the "nonpolitical" — phase of his campaign. He began with a trip through parts of Pennsylvania and Ohio recently damaged by floods. On August 14 he paused for a major speech at Chautauqua in New York; here he identified the administration and himself with the cause of peace ("I hate war"). Then he resumed the inspection of flooded areas. Along the way, he delivered off-the-cuff speeches displaying the federal government in a posture of humane concern. He never mentioned the election or the Republicans.

If too much water was a problem in one part of the country, too little was the problem in another. The year 1936 brought drought once again. The fierce sun beat relentlessly through the summer across Minnesota, the Dakotas, Montana, Wyoming, as far south as Oklahoma and the Texas Panhandle. Crops withered under the hot wind, livestock sickened and died, the black soil crumbled into dust and began again to blow away. Father Coughlin described it as divine punishment inflicted upon the American people by the hand of God for the sin of electing Franklin Roosevelt President in 1932.

Late in July the La Follettes, who took a more secular view, proposed a conference of the governors of the affected states.

There was doubt in Washington about the idea; Tugwell and Aubrey Williams, who were in charge of bringing relief to the farmers, said they had the situation in hand. But Roosevelt himself saw other possibilities. Early in August he told his press conference of his plan to go to the Dakotas for a few days and confer on the drought problem with the governors of those states, Wyoming, and Montana; then to Wisconsin to confer with the governors of Wisconsin and Minnesota; then to Iowa to confer with the governors of — now he leaned back in his chair and closed his eyes — Iowa, Nebraska, Missouri, Oklahoma and — Kansas. When he said Kansas, he opened one eye and genially winked.

For Roosevelt, the drought tour was no junket. The conferences with the governors had long and technical agendas — overgrazing, water storage, emergency credit. The presidential train moved along tracks which had not carried a passenger train for years, and stopped at every community of size along the way; the President spoke extemporaneously to crowds which always materialized amazingly out of nowhere; then, very often, he took automobile trips through the scorched countryside, inspecting farms and water-conservation projects, and talking with farmers and local officials. He was, of course, in his element. This was a field in which he was an expert himself; and his personal appearance communicated both his knowledge and his concern. "When he says, 'my friends,'" Governor Tom Berry of South Dakota used to say in introducing the President, "he means 'my friends.'" Roosevelt, speaking warmly and simply, would tell them that they had done fine, that the government would help in every way it could and that, with planning and foresight, this kind of crisis might be avoided again ("I hear the word 'planning' is not popular with some people, but one reason why the water table has sunk as low as it has is that we did not think about the future twenty years ago"). The trip roused deep enthusiasm not only for Roosevelt but for all his works: at Pierre, South Dakota, the crowd even shouted, "We want Tugwell!" Most extraordinary of all was the fact that the President, by his very presence, seemed to bring rain; his trip was followed by dark clouds, overcast skies, and a long, welcome drizzle. Father Coughlin was evidently wrong.

Early in September the President arrived in Des Moines for the conference with the governors of the central Midwest. This was a test for both men — of Roosevelt's self-restraint and of Landon's self-possession. Both met the test admirably. Roosevelt took care to avoid any appearance of political exploitation; no Democratic posters or banner hung in Des Moines during his visit. Landon motored quietly over from Topeka and won respect for his courtesy and dignity. (Tugwell said afterward, "Landon is a swell guy.") The conference followed the usual agenda; but one exchange was interesting and characteristic.

> GOVERNOR LANDON: Mr. President. You will not remember, but
> the first talk with me when you invited
> me to Washington in 1933 ——
> PRESIDENT ROOSEVELT: About the water ——
> GOVERNOR LANDON: You remember that?
> PRESIDENT ROOSEVELT: Yes.
> GOVERNOR LANDON: I am amazed you remember.

Later a newspaperman asked Landon what he thought of Roosevelt. "He's a very fine, charming gentleman," the Republican candidate replied. As they parted, Roosevelt said, "Governor, however this comes out, we'll see more of each other. Either you come to see me or I'll come to see you." "I certainly shall," Landon replied. "And Governor," added Roosevelt, "don't work too hard!"

"Harmony dripped so steadily from every rafter," Senator Arthur Capper of Kansas observed, "that I fully expected one of the candidates to withdraw." [3]

VI

If the Des Moines rapprochement was a tribute to the personal amiability of the two candidates, it was also, in the view of leading Republicans, a poor way to run a presidential campaign against a highly popular incumbent. Nothing in the whole strange autumn reflected Landon's personality more faithfully than the Pennsylvania–New York trip in August and the Des Moines meeting; but it was increasingly evident that this was all too mild for the hard-core partisans. Something tougher and more forceful was required — something to give the lagging campaign lift and hope.

Ogden Mills now proposed that Landon make an unscheduled dash to Maine, where his intervention might possibly save a Republican senator in the impending September election. "This is going to be a fighting campaign," Landon said vigorously on departure; and his speech in Portland, with its scornful attacks on New Deal industrial and agricultural policies, certainly expressed a new and harsher tone. NRA and AAA, he said, were the products of the philosophy of the planned economy; and a "planned economy is incompatible with the democratic form of government." Either America must have "the system of free competitive enterprise" or "a system under which the minutest doings of every citizen are scrutinized and regulated; under which the privacy of our homes is invaded"; there is, he said, "no half-way house between these two systems."

It was not altogether a happy occasion. Toward the end of the speech a cold mist began to roll in from the sea. When a few Republican stragglers, the last of a political parade, entered the stadium, they looked to Landon like ghosts in the fog. Thoroughly chilled, he returned to Senator Hale's house. The Senator, filled with enthusiasm, repeated several times that this was one of the warmest meetings ever held in Maine. Finally Landon said, "Senator, it may have been warm for Maine, but it was damn cold for Kansas." Still, the new tone produced a response; this either-or talk was more like it. The Republicans won in Maine; and, on September 18, Arthur Krock of the New York Times predicted that "the Republican party will poll a far larger popular and electoral vote than in 1932. . . . Roosevelt's big majorities are over." Two days later he described this as a "conservative" forecast. In the meantime, Landon got ready for his most crucial speeches thus far — in Des Moines, on agriculture; in Minneapolis, on foreign trade; and in Milwaukee, on social security.

These speeches would substantially determine the tone for the rest of the campaign. Landon called a strategy meeting to discuss them at Lacy Haynes's farm near Kansas City. It was a furiously hot day, in one of the hottest summers Kansas had ever known (there were almost sixty days when the temperature went over 100); the heat, Roy Roberts said later, "made tempers short and efficient thinking almost impossible." Argument was vehement. On agriculture, Landon had before him a program which, in effect, considerably outpromised the AAA. Some of the eastern group, willing to do anything to get the farm vote, supported this idea. Roberts vigorously fought it, less because he was against the program than because he felt that this complete reversal, after the build-up of Landon as the budget-balancing candidate, would be disastrous. On social security, Landon had a draft from Charles P. Taft which, while sharply critical of parts of the Roosevelt program, nonetheless accepted the idea of social security in principle. John Hamilton and the eastern crowd opposed even going this far.

Speaking dates were inexorable; the campaign had to go ahead. Landon made up his mind, went to Des Moines, assured the farmers they would collect all their present checks (the phrase "cash benefits" occurred four times in the speech) and much more, too; at the same time, he added in a curious conclusion, he would reduce public spending, cut taxes, and start paying off the national debt. The *Des Moines Register* applauded the speech: "Landon has dumped 'laissez-faire' ideology clear out of the window. He has plumped for a broad fine policy of national planning." But the *New York Times* commented acidly that his farm program would "infallibly swell Federal appropriations and increase the deficits" and presumed that Landon's final plea for economy was "irony." In any case, such a program sounded strange on the lips of the man who had denounced reckless spending at Buffalo and economic planning at Portland.

The Minneapolis speech two days later caused even more complications. The recent trade agreement with Canada was supposed to be deeply unpopular in the Northwest. Landon (proudly introduced as the candidate who was no "radio crooner") assailed the whole reciprocal trade agreements program. While he declared himself against isolation and in favor of the principle of reciprocity (by which he seemed to mean George Peek's Yankee trading), he denounced the most-favored-nations clause and accused the program of having "sold the American farmer down the river." This speech further shook his advisers: Charles Taft and William Allen White both opposed it. Frank Kellogg, a former Secretary of State, sat sourly on the platform at Minneapolis while Landon spoke and declined to applaud at the end. Cordell Hull, who had not planned to take an active part in the campaign, was galvanized into action by the attack; soon he was in Minneapolis himself, denouncing Landon's "wild misrepresentations." Indeed, the Minneapolis speech was a far cry from the Landon of May who would have reportedly liked the Republican platform to endorse reciprocal trade agreements, or from the Landon of 1930 who had wired congratulations to the only Kansas Republican congressman to vote against the Smoot-Hawley tariff. "In every campaign," he wrote a year later about the Minneapolis speech, "the candidate must trim his sails — not to suit his own personal ideas, but to what seems to fit the political situation. So, for better or for worse, the decision was mine — no one persuaded me . . . although it was not a position that really expressed my own personal views."

VII

Going on to Milwaukee, Landon turned to social security and with doomed ingenuity contrived to alienate at once both its friends and its enemies. He had not been up to this point a particular critic of the social-security system. As Governor, he had put through the legislature a resolution amending the Kansas constitution to validate social-security legislation modeled on the federal statute. When he gave his acceptance address, he displayed no special concern over the program. For that matter, his party had voted in favor of the act in both houses of Congress.

The underlying thrust of the Milwaukee address remained an acceptance of the idea in principle. But he had been genuinely disturbed for some time about financial aspects of the system. Early in 1936 he exchanged letters with Raymond Swing about social-security problems; and, later in the year, Charles Taft gained access to a preliminary report, prepared by Swing and J. Frederic Dewhurst, for a Twentieth Century Fund study of the social-security system. This report, though favorable, raised questions about the existing program, especially about the reserve fund. In August, Swing, with Dewhurst's concurrence, sent Landon a carefully worked-out speech on social security. This draft, as revamped by Taft, formed the basis for the Milwaukee speech; but the process of translating an economic analysis into a political oration expelled the reservations and subtleties in the original. As a result, on September 26 in Milwaukee Landon suddenly portrayed the law as "unjust, unworkable, stupidly drafted and wastefully financed." The contributory feature was "a cruel hoax." Moreover, the program threatened dangerous regimentation; "the Republican party will have nothing to do with any plan that involves prying into the personal records of 26 million people." As for unemployment compensation, this, Landon said, should be a matter for the states. On old-age pensions, trying to sound conservative without alienating possible Townsend support, he promised "a workable, commonsense plan," to be financed by a special tax, which would at once be direct, visible, and widely distributed.

Landon himself evidently had compunctions about the Milwaukee speech. "I wondered several times why I didn't hear from you," he wrote Swing after the campaign. "I thought maybe you were offended at the way I handled the Twentieth Century Social Security report." And its effects justified his doubts. The attack on social security, on top of the condemnation of reciprocal trade agreements and the increasing vehemence of his either-or assault on the New Deal, destroyed any question liberals might have had about the importance of opposing Landon. It was symptomatic that John G. Winant, the Progressive Republican chairman of the Social Security Board, promptly resigned in order to enter the campaign and answer Landon.

Ironically, Landon's acceptance of the basic philosophy of social security, on top of the extravagance of his farm speech, distressed conservatives nearly as much. These two speeches, as John Hamilton saw them, went so far in the direction of the New Deal that they emptied the Landon campaign of intellectual consistency and denied the voters the clear-cut choice to which Hamilton thought them entitled. When Landon replied to Hamilton's protests that his only chance of winning was to gain votes from the liberals and from the lunatic fringe (presumably those who were tempted to vote for Lemke), the National Chairman, discouraged, took a less active part during the rest of the campaign.

The Iowa-Minnesota-Wisconsin trip marked the turning point. The Landon campaign now seemed rudderless. The Republican candidate had destroyed any consistent image of himself: he was free to say almost anything in the weeks remaining, but his words had lost whatever impact they might have had. He was moving at once both to the right and to the left — to the right in the sense of seeing American survival in either-or terms and identifying the

New Deal with total catastrophe; to the left in the sense of trying to outbid the New Deal in promises to special groups, like farmers and old people. William Allen White, looking back four years later, described the campaign as "nightmare. It had neither logical sequence in its conception and execution nor any touch of reality." [4]

VIII

Political campaigns tend to be exercises in progressive degeneration. The steady increase, week after week, in excitement and strain and weariness produces an oversimplification of issues, an overdramatization of alternatives, a growing susceptibility to extreme and catastrophic statements. Candidates find themselves shouting things in the fall that they would never dream of whispering in the summer. "I have always thought," William Allen White warned Landon, "that emotion in October . . . is mighty dangerous. It develops so easily into malice, and malice is poison." And candidates will be particularly vulnerable to pressure if they feel that their campaign is faltering and if they are surrounded by hard, determined men who claim to know how to win.

Landon had counted on having liberals at his side to fight for liberal policies. But one by one they eliminated themselves or were eliminated. White, who feared from the start that Landon's decency would be a casualty of the campaign, was quick to step out of the inner circle. He blamed the deterioration of the campaign on Hamilton: "John has a seven-devil lust to live and shine under the blessing of the rich, and he has turned over what ought to have been a good middle-of-the-road campaign to the hard-boiled political reactionaries . . . and their financial supporters." White later reflected, "Probably I could have horned away some of the conservative and reactionary influences, and I might have given the campaign a slightly more liberal cast. But, if I had stayed under the kleig lights that beat about a throne, if I had won a point now and then, I should have had to make compromises which I could not make and be happy." Borah, upset by Landon's gold standard telegram and by the big business contributions to his war chest, declined to give the ticket his endorsement. The Pennsylvania organization tried to keep Gifford Pinchot out of the campaign until Landon personally intervened;

as Landon wrote later, "then, for some reason or other, Hamilton failed to use him as I expected he would." Roy Roberts substantially dropped out after early October. Swing, after watching the distortion of his social-security speech and the rejection of a labor speech, gave up. Taft lasted longer than any of the others, but in due course he was shunted aside. "One of the things that was wrong with the campaign," Landon wrote subsequently, "was that I didn't have enough help on the Progressive and Liberal side to pick up the ball and emphasize our really liberal stand on many questions." He explained to another friend: "Frankly, I couldn't get John to appreciate the necessity of getting away from the appearance that the Old Guard was still doing business at the same old stand. . . . We have too many stuffed shirts in the Republican organization."

He had a small, reliable team of writers — Calvert Smith, Sherwin Badger, and Ralph Robie. But, deprived of liberal support on larger issues, he found it harder and harder in the tumult of campaigning to maintain his sense of direction. After his Portland speech, Raymond Clapper told him that the reactionaries in the party were a millstone around his neck. Landon replied sadly, "Who else can I get?" He wanted desperately to win, and he was beginning to lose grip on his true beliefs; at last he was getting out of character. From that moment on, he had declining confidence in his own instincts and was increasingly at the mercy of the militants.[5]

IX

In retrospect, it is perhaps astonishing that Landon preserved his moderation as long as he did. It was Hoover at Cleveland who had expressed the mood of the Republican party; and, as the campaign wore on, the Hoover mood — the hysterical certitude that the republic was on the verge of collapse — surged up more and more from Republican crowds. This mood was compounded as the advertising men, for zealous public manipulation, made their first large-scale entrance into presidential politics. "To my mind," Robert Choate of the *Boston Herald* had written Landon in the spring, "the handling of Republican publicity should be on the same basis as handling any other article that wants to be merchandised to the public." If Coca-Cola or Shredded Wheat wished to sell a product between June and November, "they would go to the best advertising agencies in the country and get the best brains, the best artists and the best copywriters that their appropriations would allow." They would use billboards, radio, newspapers, Choate added; "but the last thing they would do would be to send one hundred thousand or a million copies of the speech of the president of the corporation to prospective purchasers." (It was no doubt similar faith in the advertising mind that led one newspaper publisher to ask the Associated Press to identify Landon in its wire stories as "budget-balancer" — to which the AP replied that it might then be expected to comply with someone else's request and identify the other candidate as "humanity's savior" Roosevelt.)

This notion that images were more important than issues had an early expression when the Republican National Committee prepared a series of radio spots, presenting the case against the New Deal in the homely terms of soap opera.

> MARRIAGE LICENSE CLERK: Now what do you intend to do about the national debt?
> PROSPECTIVE BRIDEGROOM JOHN: National debt? Me?
> CLERK: You are going to establish a family and as the head of an American family you will shoulder a debt of more than $1017.26 — and it's growing every day. . . . Do you still want to get married?
> JOHN: You — er — I — I —What do you say, Mary!
> MARY: Maybe — maybe — we better talk it over first, John. . . . All those debts! When we thought we didn't owe anybody in the world.
> JOHN: Somebody is giving us a dirty deal. . . . It's a lowdown mean trick.
> VOICE OF DOOM: And the debts, like the sins of the fathers, shall be visited upon the children, aye, even unto the third and fourth generations! (Music)

In the innocent days of 1936, however, both the Columbia Broadcasting System and the National Broadcasting Company turned down these programs; as the NBC president said, it "would place the discussion of vital political and national issues on the basis of dramatic license rather than upon a basis of responsibility for stated fact or opinion."

Despite this rebuff to Madison Avenue, the manipulators, exploiting an atmosphere of genuine anxiety, began to charge the later stages of the Republican campaign with a pseudo-apocalyptic quality. A leaflet issued by the Republican National Committee summed up the case. Election Day, it said, "seals the fate of America. . . . That day will set the future pattern of government in the United States for years to come. . . . If the present Administration is not beaten in 1936, the American plan of government may be lost forever."

Frank Knox, hoarse-voiced and commanding, repeated this theme several times a day. Often he supplied interesting detail, as when he told the citizens of Allentown, Pennsylvania, "Today no life insurance policy is secure; no savings account is safe." (The force of this statement was reduced when, by sheer coincidence, six insurance executives met the next day with Roosevelt to report that the combined assets of life insurance companies had increased more than $3 billion since January 1933.) And on October 1 a new and more powerful voice reinforced the Republican thesis. It belonged to Al Smith, who delivered at Carnegie Hall a speech which oddly mixed the old gleeful humor with long, sad wails of personal bitterness. He had not gone high hat, Smith protested; and he wasn't mad because he had not been offered a place in the cabinet ("as a matter of fact, I couldn't afford to take a position in the cabinet"). But he could not abide Roosevelt's ingratitude ("I insisted upon his nomination at Rochester in 1928 over the protest of practically every leader of the party"), nor could he stand for so "narrow, personal and partisan" an administration. His conclusion was defiant: "I firmly believe that the remedy for all the ills that we are suffering from today is the election of Alfred M. Landon." (The next day, at a Democratic club on Second Avenue, they took Smith's portrait from the wall: "We don't want the picture of any Benedict Arnold around here." Later Landon said to Smith, "Governor, I know what this step has meant to you — how difficult it is for you to fraternize with the party that has fought you as they have in past campaigns. . . . Only the firm belief that your country was in danger could impel you to such a step." Smith, his eyes filling with tears, said, "I thought you would understand it.")

The anti-New Deal thesis was pushed still further. On September 19, in a front-page editorial, the Hearst papers said that, on orders from Moscow, the Communists were working to re-elect Roosevelt. For some reason, this charge wobbled the White House. Steve Early immediately issued a statement disclaiming Communist support and denouncing Hearst: "The American people will not permit their attention to be diverted from real issues to fake issues which no patriotic, honorable, decent citizen would purposely inject into American affairs." Hearst, who was abroad, fired back that, whether wittingly or not, Roosevelt was plainly receiving the support of such "enemies of the American system of government" as the Karl Marx Socialists, the Frankfurter radicals, Communists and anarchists, the Tugwell Bolsheviks, and the Richberg revolutionists.

John Hamilton moved quickly to drive the issue home. Among the Roosevelt electors in the state of New York, adopted jointly by the Democratic and American Labor parties, was David Dubinsky of the International Ladies' Garment Workers. Dubinsky had always been an inveterate foe of the Communists. Resigning from the Socialist party a few months before, he had condemned it for the mortal sin of holding a joint May Day parade with the Communists; "I can no longer be identified with a party that is making alliances with the Communists." But all this was less important than the facts that Dubinsky's name had a sinister foreign ring and that his union had contributed money to Labor's Red Cross for Spain. "How long, Mr. Roosevelt," cried Hamilton in tones of anguish, "do you intend to affront the voters of America by retaining as one of your presidential electors on the Democratic ballot a man who has rendered financial aid to the Communists in Spain so that they might continue to horrify the civilized world with their murders of clergymen?"

In the last weeks of September, Communism suddenly flared up as a major issue. Ogden Mills pointed to the "collectivist" tendencies in the New Deal. "Even a Communist with wire whiskers and a torch in his hand is welcome," said Al Smith, "so long as he signs on the dotted line." Bill Lemke joined in the chorus: "I do not charge that the President of this nation is a Communist but I do charge that Browder, Dubinsky and other Communist leaders have laid their cuckoo eggs in his Democratic nest and that he is hatching them." For a moment, it seemed possible that the administration might be on the defensive.[6]

X

Not for long: the nonpolitical phase was coming to an end. On September 29 Franklin Roosevelt, after two months of strictly presidential speech-making, was a candidate again. He opened the campaign at the New York State Democratic convention at Syracuse in scenes of wild enthusiasm. The opposition, he said, was up to its old game of dragging out red herrings "to divert attention from the trail of their own weaknesses." In times past they had said that George Washington wanted to make himself king; they had called Jefferson a revolutionist, Lincoln a Roman Emperor. Now Communism was the stock accusation.

> Here and now, once and for all, let us bury that red herring and destroy that false issue. . . . I have not sought, I do not seek, I repudiate the support of any advocate of Communism or of any other alien "ism" which would by fair means or foul change our American democracy. That is my position. It has always been my position. It always will be my position.

There was no difference between the major parties in what they thought about Communism, Roosevelt added. But there was a great difference in what they were doing about Communism. The Republicans, by rejecting the obligations of social justice, encouraged the economic and social unrest which bred Communism. The Democrats, by tackling the causes of unrest, struck Communism at the roots. "The most serious threat to our institutions," Roosevelt said, "comes from those who refuse to face the need for change. Liberalism becomes the protection for the far-sighted conservative. . . . 'Reform if you would preserve.' I am that kind of conservative because I am that kind of liberal."

It was a highly successful speech, setting forth in effective language the tone and thesis of the campaign. And it had characteristic touches of humor:

In the summer of 1933, a nice old gentleman wearing a silk hat fell off the end of a pier. He was unable to swim. A friend ran down the pier, dived overboard and pulled him out; but the silk hat floated off with the tide. After the old gentleman had been revived he was effusive in his thanks. He praised his friend for saving his life. Today, three years later, the old gentleman is berating his friend because the silk hat was lost.

This story was Roosevelt's own; the bulk of the work on the Syracuse speech had been done by Rosenman, High, and Corcoran. (They were working on it at Hyde Park when Moley arrived on his final visit. Not wishing to hurt the feelings of his old collaborator, Roosevelt ordered the others out of sight until he departed.)

The next major address was scheduled for Pittsburgh on October 1. This involved embarrassments because it was at Pittsburgh, four years before, that Roosevelt had made his celebrated promise to cut government expenditures. The earlier speech weighed on Roosevelt's conscience; moreover, Farley had lost no opportunity during the campaign to tell Roosevelt that (in the words of an assistant postmaster-general, whose letter Farley actually sent twice to the President), "The one criticism which is being constantly hammered home and which seems to be having the most effect is the charge that the President and his Administration are carrying on an orgy of spending and incurring a tremendous public debt." Roosevelt accordingly instructed Rosenman to prepare a Pittsburgh draft for 1936 which would give "a good and convincing explanation" of what he had meant in 1932. Rosenman, after prayerful re-examination of the earlier document, told the President that he could think of only one possible explanation. "Fine," said Roosevelt eagerly, "what sort?" "Mr. President," said Rosenman, "the only thing you can say about the 1932 speech is to deny categorically that you ever made it."

Roosevelt and Rosenman underestimated their own ingenuity. The new Pittsburgh speech, under the guise of a report on the administration's battle against depression, made it amply clear why they felt recovery had to take priority over retrenchment. "The only way to keep the Government out of the red," Roosevelt argued, "is to keep the people out of the red. And so we had to balance the budget of the American people." Government had accepted its responsibility "to spend money when no one else had money left to spend"; and the money spent constituted an investment in the future of America. As the national income increased, government receipts increased too. The result "within a year or two" would be sufficient to cover all ordinary and relief expenses of the government. (Herbert Hoover, who had finally extracted an invitation from Landon to visit him at Topeka, listened to the speech with Landon and some newspapermen in a chicken restaurant outside of town. As Roosevelt spoke, Hoover said: BOO. A little later: BOO. Again: BOO. The newspapermen were getting visibly restless and irritated. Landon finally broke in and took Hoover away, saying, "We had better rush if we're going to catch the train.")

In the Syracuse and Pittsburgh speeches, Roosevelt tried to meet Republican charges of Communism and extravagance. Others joined in the effort to put these issues out of the campaign. "If it is 'Communism' to urge a squarer deal for labor and the farmers," said the *New York Daily News*, "then there are a lot of 'Communists' in this country." "There has been scarcely a liberal piece of legislation during the last sixty years," said Joseph P. Kennedy, "that has not been opposed as Communistic." "You can be nailed as a Communist," said John T. Flynn disgustedly, "if you complain about the service in a railroad diner." "The charge of Communism directed at President Roosevelt," said Monsignor John A. Ryan, "is the silliest, falsest, most cruel and most unjust accusation ever made against a President in all the years of American history . . . ugly, cowardly and flagrant calumnies." Bishop James H. Ryan of Nebraska added, "Such a charge goes beyond the limits of the permissible in political debate. . . . There is not one shred of evidence, direct or indirect, to connect the name of President Roosevelt with Communism." "You might as well suspect atheism in a cathedral," said John Garner, "as Communism in the environment of Hyde Park."

And the friends of the New Deal deployed to defend other parts of the edifice. Robert H. Jackson dealt sardonically with Landon as a budget-balancer. The Kansas budget, he pointed out, was about the same as that of Schenectady; but "we would hardly think of running the Mayor of Schenectady for President solely on the ground that he balanced the Schenectady budget."

Moreover, over three-fourths of the public money spent in Kansas in 1935 came from the federal government. "It may be true, as our friends have charged, that President Roosevelt has not yet balanced his budget. But he certainly has balanced Governor Landon's." When George Peek came out for Landon, his one-time partner Hugh Johnson poured out derision: "Farmers will not go from the man who rescued them back to the men who ruined them — no, not even to gratify the wounded pride of a man who once served them valiantly." Even the Landon sunflower was not exempt. As Roosevelt told his press conference (off the record), a neighbor had pointed out to him that the sunflower was yellow, that it had a black heart and that it was only good for parrot food; to which someone added that it was dead in November.[7]

XI

By October Landon had broken loose from his moorings. He had always had in his mind — as he had explained to Knox soon after the convention — that "we must drive Mr. Roosevelt into a corner where he will say what he is going to do." Now this legitimate intention was disintegrating into a barrage of extreme and terrifying accusations. Franklin Roosevelt, Landon said at Detroit, had started the nation on the road to dictatorship. Economic planning "violates the basic ideals of the American system. . . . No nation can continue half regimented and half free." In Los Angeles he denounced the New Deal as "obsessed with the idea that it had a mandate to direct and control American business, American agriculture and American life. . . . If we are to preserve our American form of government, this administration must be defeated." "There can be no question as to the road down which we are being led," he said at Phoenix. ". . . . They have allowed nothing to deter them in their plan to make over our political, social and economic life." New Deal policies, he actually said at Baltimore, would lead to the guillotine. "Our homes, our communities, our jobs and our business are to be directed from Washington. The profit motive is to be eliminated. Business as we know it is to disappear."

An incident in mid-October illuminated the gap between the old Landon and the new. Assailing him as the "changeling candidate,"

Ickes produced evidence from his convenient Department of the Interior files showing that Landon had favored liberal ideas, including the state-owned gas system. Landon replied forthrightly, "I have always been in favor of public ownership as a gun behind the door in the adjustment of proper and fair utility rates" and boasted of his success in using this threat to scale rates down in Kansas. This reversion to New Dealism was a long way from the Hoover cries he was now uttering at Phoenix and Baltimore. (Ickes commented, "I wonder how many other concealed weapons he carries about. The utility interests had better frisk him before they go any further.") But it was a last glimpse of the real Landon. The man of modesty and moderation and charm had turned into a tired, groping, stumbling figure, moving somnambulistically from railroad train to limousine to hotel to auditorium, reading strident speeches in a flat earnest voice before crowds which came to cheer him and, after ten minutes, sank into fretful apathy. The less responsive the crowds, the sharper the attempt to rouse them: Landon's notes for his whistle-stop speeches sum up the last phases of his campaign.

> We have a choice to make between the American system of government and one that is alien to everything this country ever before has known.
> I do not mean to seem an alarmist, but the result of this election will determine what sort of a nation we are to hand down to our children.
> In the utmost seriousness I say this is the battle of our century.

He affected to believe what he said; or perhaps no longer knew what he believed. Ray Clapper told him one day, "That's terrible to spread that stuff. . . . It isn't true. Roosevelt isn't a Communist, and you know it." Landon said grimly, "His policies are leading to dictatorship. When a President gets hold of the purse strings, you have dictatorship."

The Republican campaign grew increasingly shrill. Frank Knox compared Roosevelt to George III and gave it as his "sober and solemn judgment that four more years of such a government may destroy our system." (Ickes called his old friend from Bull

Moose days "the Paul Revere of doom . . . the rough-riding, rough-spoken political trooper [who] rides facing his horse's tail.") The Republican National Committee pronounced Roosevelt "the Kerensky of the American revolutionary movement."

> The poor lamb does not realize that his fantastic planned economy . . . leads directly to the destruction of the capitalistic system.
> But Browder . . . knows it and is supporting him.
> Rexford G. Tugwell knows it . . .
> Felix Frankfurter knows it, and is keeping mighty quiet for the moment.
> Mordecai Ezekiel knows it, and you haven't heard his name for months.
> Stalin over in Russia knows it and has ordered his following in the United States to back Roosevelt.

"Let Tugwell get one of these racoon coats that the college boys wear at a football game," said Al Smith, "and let him go to Russia, sit on a cake of ice and plan all he wants. Let him buy six or seven more one-way tickets and take the rest of the brain trust with him" — and the audience whooped and shrieked with enthusiasm. Bainbridge Colby, the old Wilsonian, declared that Roosevelt had "gone over hook, line, and sinker to the Communists and Socialists, by whom he is surrounded." Fritz Kuhn and his German-American Alliance endorsed Landon — an act neither repudiated by the Republicans nor mentioned by the Democrats.

The tough tactics seemed to work. "Landon is like Coolidge," said Henry Ford, "I am for Landon. I haven't voted for twenty years, but I am going to vote this time." Many others appeared to be flocking to the Republican candidate. Throughout October, the *Literary Digest* poll, which had correctly forecast the outcome in 1932, predicted a Landon victory.[8]

34. The People Speak

ONE CANDIDATE, at least, should have been without illusions. The campaign, it was clear by late October, had no greater flop than the Union party. In mid-July at Cleveland, Father Coughlin, Gerald Smith, and Dr. Townsend were photographed with arms entwined and smiles of unctuous affection on their faces. The harmony, alas, was transient. Fortune could hardly have picked out three crusaders less likely to hang together until they reached the Holy City. Bill Lemke became the hapless victim of their incompatibilities.

II

Old Doctor Townsend, anxious and bewildered, played almost no role at all. For a time his contribution to the campaign was largely a parroting of the table talk of Gerald Smith. Thus he said to Selden Rodman that, if worst came to worst, he would favor Landon over Roosevelt since "at least he is not a Communist." But he really cared about little except the Townsend Plan; "I would vote for a native-born Chinaman," he once said, "if he was for the plan." Such influence as he commanded seemed to be used less for Lemke than against Roosevelt. Hugo Black reported to Farley from Alabama, "The followers of Townsend in this state are practically one hundred per cent against the Administration." In response to Landon's friendly gestures, Townsend eventually told his followers to vote Republican in states where Lemke was not on the ballot. This statement was designed particularly to help Landon in California; but California Democrats had long since taken the precaution of infiltrating the Townsend clubs in order, as Culbert Olson explained to Farley, "to hold them in line for their party and the President." Townsend's declaration probably had little effect.

As for Gerald Smith, he seemed at this point a curious combination of rogue and fanatic. Newspapermen rather liked him, under the impression that he recognized himself as a mountebank. He grinned, reported Tom Stokes, when they kidded him about his trade and its tricks. If he complained of Communist plots against his life, or said he wanted to identify himself so indelibly with the discontent that, when chaos came, his name would be on every lip, the reporters laughed and admired him for the general cynicism of his performance. They did him an injustice. The fact was that he believed these things, or was beginning to believe them. Whatever may be said for Gerald Smith's subsequent career, it certainly represented a triumph of principle over success. Far from being a jolly racketeer, he genuinely supposed himself a man of destiny. Drunk with the shrieks from the crowd, he perceived no limits to his power. "Religion and patriotism, keep going on that. It's the only way you can get them really 'het up.' " Once "het up," they would follow a strong man anywhere. "Certain nerve centers in the population will begin to twitch — and the people will start fomenting, fermenting, and then a fellow like myself, someone with courage enough to capture the people, will get on the radio and have the people with him, hook, line, and sinker. I'll teach 'em how to hate. The people are beginning to trust true leadership."

Coughlin, increasingly appalled by his partners, soon began to behave as if he had been thrust into the company of a dolt and an idiot. In Smith's case, he had, in addition, a reluctance to compete with the man whom Mencken called "the greatest rabble-rouser since Peter the Hermit." There was more perhaps than this: in 1955 Coughlin told an interviewer, "I was frightened by Smith." Originally the three men planned to stump the country together, but the priest soon vetoed this idea. A newspaperman asked him what would happen if all three chanced to be in the same town. Coughlin responded sourly, "Why should they tag me around?" When the time came for the convention of the National Union for Social Justice in August, Coughlin wanted nothing which might dilute his own charismatic attractions. These were still considerable: the moment he appeared, according to the *New York Times,* "men and women in a semihypnotic state jumped and gyrated around the hall, shrieking and screaming." Still, he took no chances, and kept Smith and Townsend off the platform until late one afternoon when the audience was presumably sated with oratory. Even then, Coughlin, sitting apprehensively on the platform behind Smith, tried to sabotage the performance by looking bored, winking at friends, and pretending to doze away. Smith, not much perturbed, roused the audience to the usual fury, proclaiming, "The blood memory of Huey Long is still hot in my eyes."

III

For all his conviction of superiority, Coughlin was driven to excesses by crowd hysteria quite as much as Smith. In addition, he was now lashed on by a determination to outdo the Louisiana preacher. The next day he climaxed a fiery speech with an astonishing apostrophe to the Jews on the subject of Christian brotherhood: "I challenge every Jew in this nation to tell me that he does or doesn't believe in it." A few moments later, moved beyond endurance, he broke down and had to be helped from the platform.

This extreme language aggravated the Union party's troubles. "If certain groups of politically-swayed Jews," *Social Justice* said menacingly at the end of the month, ". . . care to organize against Father Coughlin or the National Union they will be entirely responsible for stirring up any repercussions which they will invite." Soon Coughlin was forced into involved explanations that he was not really anti-Semitic. (His off-the-record comment to Dale Kramer was: "Jew-baiting won't work here. Fascism is different in every country.") And, in the meantime, his July description of Roosevelt as a liar had got him into trouble with his fellow Catholics. At least one archbishop and two bishops publicly rebuked him. "Coughlin is killing himself politically at a very rapid rate," Monsignor Ryan reported in August. "Everybody in California is for Roosevelt, especially the nuns." "Everybody resents his attack upon the President," the Democratic

National Committeeman from Connecticut told Farley. "All feel, and particularly the Irish Catholics, that he has stepped from the high place of priest and holy man."

Even the faithful Bishop Gallagher of Detroit deplored his language, and Coughlin made a prompt if somewhat double-edged apology to the President. This did not end the episode: it had repercussions in the Vatican and brought Coughlin a poor notice in *Osservatore Romano*. When Gallagher now came to Coughlin's defense, *Osservatore Romano* replied coldly that Gallagher's reported claim that the Holy See approved Coughlin's activities did not "correspond with the truth" and that Gallagher knew "quite well what he was told on the subject."

If the Vatican ever intimated displeasure, Coughlin must have decided to ignore the message. His own contributions to the campaign became wilder every day. At the National Union convention he rashly boasted, "If I don't deliver 9,000,000 votes for William Lemke, I'm through with radio forever." At Providence, he said that, if Hoover had been re-elected, "there would be more bullet holes in the White House than you could count with an adding machine." ("Hoover with his rugged individualism," he continued, "was more dangerous than Stalin with his communism . . . the worst menace America has ever known.") At New Bedford, he called Roosevelt "the dumbest man ever to occupy the White House." In Boston, he declared, "Every international banker has communistic tendencies." In New York, he pronounced the choice between Roosevelt and Landon a choice "between carbolic acid and rat poison." In Cincinnati, he called Roosevelt "anti-God." In Des Moines, he spoke to Dale Kramer of "Hull, the internationalist and No. 1 Communist. Then comes Ma Perkins, Ickes, Morgenthau, Tugwell, Mordecai Ezekiel — all Communists." (Kramer asked whether Wallace was a Communist; "Coughlin said he was a nothing and demonstrated how he runs into the bathroom and hides when he hears anyone coming.") The outbreak of civil war in Spain increased his sense of urgency. What if there were a popular-front government in the United States? "I'd be out with a gun!" said Coughlin. ". . . Democracy is doomed, this is our last election . . . It is fascism or communism. We are at the crossroads." "What road do you take, Father Coughlin?" "I take the road of fascism."

The Lemke campaign meanwhile staggered along. About this

time, the Union party reached its height when 5 per cent of re-
spondents to the Gallup poll said they intended to vote for Lemke.
Somewhere money appeared: thus Philip Johnson and Alan
Blackburn, the two young Harvard men who had been trailing
after Huey Long, gave $5,000 in September. It is not known
whether there was Republican support in addition. (One Republican, on the stationery of the Republican Radio Council, wrote in
Social Justice in August, "Permit this hard-boiled old-line Republican to pay tribute to the brilliance, candor and high moral courage
of your leader, Father Coughlin.") But the three prophets devoted
less and less time to their common cause and more and more to
themselves. "When it comes to Show-down," Roosevelt had astutely
predicted to Colonel House eighteen months earlier, "these fellows
cannot all lie in the same bed and will fight among themselves
with almost absolute certainty." By mid-October the preposterous
alliance was plainly falling to pieces. On October 18 Gerald Smith
announced that he planned to lead a new nationalist movement
designed to "seize the government of the United States." Townsend immediately disowned his lieutenant ("I am against fascism;
it is un-American and smacks of the dictator-like policies of the
New Deal"); and Lemke followed suit. As for Coughlin, he ignored
Smith and nearly everyone else, including his own candidate. In
his last New York rally, he did not even mention Lemke's name.[1]

IV

For Roosevelt, October assumed the aspect more and more of one
long victory parade. He had never seen such crowds — they
cheered and swarmed and roared, surging from the sidewalks onto
the streets and leaving only a narrow lane for the presidential
car. They cried "Thank you, Mr. President!" and "God bless
you!" and "You saved my home!" They shouted and wept and
pushed to touch the automobile and screamed with excitement
when he entered the auditorium.

On October 14 he came to Chicago. He rode slowly to the stadium
through streets packed with cheering men and women. Bands of
every conceivable sort — from fife and drum to bagpipes — played
along the route. People sang and danced, threw confetti from
upstairs windows, shouted from rooftops, waved his portrait at the

end of long poles. Great calcium flares lit the front of the stadium as the President arrived; fireworks went off in the sky above; the crowd rushed forward; and the police could hardly keep the path clear for the car to enter the stadium. When he appeared on the platform there was such an explosion of sound from the nearly one hundred thousand people that even Roosevelt seemed for a moment to lose his composure.

In his speech, Roosevelt boldly addressed himself to the group supposedly most hostile to him — the businessmen of America. He asked a series of questions. Did his hearers have bank deposits? They were safer today than ever before; October marked the first full year in fifty-five years without a single national bank failure. Were they investors? Stocks and bonds were up to five-year high levels. Were they merchants? Now they had customers again. Were they in industry? Profits were the highest in half a dozen years; bankruptcies were at a new low. And these things had not just happened. "Behind the growing recovery of today is a story of deliberate Government acceptance of responsibility to save business, to save the American system of private enterprise and economic democracy."

Why had the previous administration done so little? Because, said Roosevelt, it was high-finance minded — controlled by a handful of men who by one financial trick or another took their toll from the rest of business. The men of high finance had made free with other people's money, built huge monopolies, stifled independent enterprise. "There was no power under Heaven that could protect the people against that sort of thing except a people's Government at Washington. All that this Administration has done, all that it proposed to do . . . is to use every power and authority of the Federal Government to protect the commerce of America from the selfish forces which ruined it."

"I believe," Roosevelt said, "I have always believed, and I will always believe in private enterprise as the backbone of economic well-being in the United States." But

this concentration of economic power in all-embracing corporations does not represent private enterprise as we Americans cherish it and propose to foster it. On the contrary, it represents private enterprise which has become a kind of private government, a power unto itself — a regimentation of other people's lives. . . . The struggle against private monopoly is a struggle for, and not against, American business. It is a struggle to preserve individual enterprise and economic freedom.

In one speech after another Roosevelt drew a vivid contrast between conditions before and after the New Deal. On and on the presidential train went almost in the spirit of a carnival, with the President's unashamed delight in campaigning infecting the staff, the newspapermen, the visiting politicians, and the cheering crowds gathered at every whistle stop. There were occasional sour moments. Roosevelt was twice subjected to sustained booing, once in the Wall Street district in New York, once in Cambridge, Massachusetts, where students clustered on Massachusetts Avenue to hiss the most distinguished living Harvard graduate as he passed by (though a long list of faculty members had already declared publicly for him). But nearly everything else was festive. Thus Syracuse, New York: Roosevelt pausing to sing "Pack Up Your Troubles In Your Old Kit Bag," with an American Legion chorus. ("Imagine Hoover doing it," wrote Raymond Clapper, "or Coolidge or Wilson. And I don't think Governor Landon sings either.") Thus Emporia, Kansas: "My friends, I am very glad to come to Emporia. But I do not see Bill White." Laughter and applause from the crowd. "I wish he were here because I have known him for a great many years, and he is a very old friend of mine. He is a very good friend of mine for three and a half years out of every four years." In a doorway at the station stands Bill White, as far back as he could get in the crowd, fearing that too conspicuous an appearance would expose him to presidential kidding, but that no appearance at all would seem inadequate respect to the office. A shout from the crowd: "Mr. White is here and is coming up." "Where is he?" Roosevelt says, smiling broadly. White tries to hang back, but the President says, "Make a gangway there for Mr. White" and "Come on up, I want to see you a minute." William Allen White warily approaches the rear platform. "Hello, Bill, glad to see you. Come on over here." "Shoot not this old gray head," says White with a rueful smile. The President speaks a few more words to the crowd, then, "I hope I shall be able to come back to Emporia . . . and, when I get back, it may be in one of those three-and-a-half year periods when Bill White is with me." Finally a warm handshake with White. Great cheers and applause. The editor, vanquished, returns to his office to dictate an editorial about "the old American smiler."

v

Roosevelt's main fear about the election had been the press. His own estimate that 85 per cent of newspapers were against him was an exaggeration. Study of 150 leading papers showed that Landon had a combined circulation of about 14 million as against slightly under 7 million for Roosevelt. Of the small circulation papers, Roosevelt may even have had something close to a majority. But in the large cities he fell badly behind. Of the big dailies, about 75 per cent were for Landon, about 20 per cent for Roosevelt. In the *Chicago Tribune* days went by at the height of the campaign in which Roosevelt did not make the front page — one day in which he did not even make the paper at all. A typical *Tribune* lead: "Governor Alfred M. Landon tonight brought his great crusade for the preservation of the American form of government into Los Angeles." A *Tribune* headline: ROOSEVELT AREA IN WISCONSIN IS HOTBED OF VICE.

Though the President complained a good deal about this situation privately, he did little to dramatize it as an issue. Yet the people themselves seemed to understand and resent the attitude of the newspapers. During the great demonstration in Chicago, for example, the crowd shouted epithets at the *Tribune* and Hearst's *Herald-Examiner* as the press cars drove by ("Where's the *Tribune?*" "Down with the *Tribune!*" "To hell with the *Tribune!*"). "These people no longer had any respect for the press, or confidence in it," commented Tom Stokes, watching the scene. "The press had finally overreached itself." This episode was symptomatic, indeed, of a deeper resentment against the old order — a resentment bursting into bitter expression as the masses stirred with a new sense of power under their fighting leader. Stokes saw it in Pittsburgh as a local politician warmed up the crowd before Roosevelt's arrival.

"The President," the orator said as the crowd roared, "has decreed that your children shall enjoy equal opportunity with

the sons of the rich." Then Governor Earle appeared to call the
roll of the people's enemies:

> There are the Mellons, who have grown fabulously wealthy
> from the toil of the men of iron and steel, the men whose
> brain and brawn have made this great city; Grundy, whose
> sweatshop operators have been the shame and disgrace of
> Pennsylvania for a generation; Pew, who strives to build a
> political and economic empire with himself as dictator; the
> du Ponts, whose dollars were earned with the blood of Ameri-
> can soldiers; Morgan, financier of war.

After each name he had to pause while the crowd howled its contempt. "He stood, smiling and confident, enjoying the tempest
he produced," wrote Stokes. ". . . You could almost hear the
swish of the guillotine."

The old order had made Roosevelt the issue, and the people
now accepted the issue as they defined it. The hatred of the rich
had transformed him into a national hero. The trip to New
England in the third week of October startled even Roosevelt; it
brought out, he wrote Joe Robinson, "the most amazing tidal
wave of humanity I have ever seen." (The President was still
wary; he added cautiously, "I think we have a real possibility in
Massachusetts and some chance in Connecticut and Rhode
Island.") On he went, directing speeches to particular elements
in the coalition: at Howard University, to the Negroes ("among
American citizens there should be no forgotten men and no forgotten races"); at the Statue of Liberty, to the foreign nationalities ("by their effort and devotion they made the New World's
freedom safer, richer, more far-reaching, more capable of growth");
everywhere, to the men and women whom government before the
New Deal had forgotten.

When his own arguments did not work, Landon's errors did:
even doubters were coming back to his camp. If Roosevelt had
lost the *St. Louis Post-Dispatch* and the *Baltimore Sun,* the *New
York Times* was out for him. If Walter Lippmann and Lewis
Douglas stayed with Landon even after Minneapolis, James P.
Warburg and Dean Acheson, Will Clayton and Russell Leffingwell,
even Newton D. Baker, returned to his side. If H. L. Mencken
continued to denounce him, Westbrook Pegler, imagining the

Baltimore sage with a sunflower in his lapel and Mabel Walker Willebrandt on his arm, predicted that the next step would be for the former editor of the *American Mercury* to join the Tennessee fundamentalists and undergo total immersion in Goose Crick wearing a white night shirt and blubbering "Hallelujah." Even Huey P. Long, Sr., was for him. "Things seem to be going extraordinarily well in every State except Vermont and Maine," Roosevelt wrote on October 26, "though I am frankly a little worried about George Norris' chances in Nebraska." [2]

VI

But the Republicans still had one card to play. Landon's September speech on the Social Security Act had been only a beginning. On January 1, 1937, the payroll tax would go into effect, which meant that workers would start making compulsory contributions to their own retirement pensions. Would not this impending deduction from wages provide an opportunity to split Roosevelt's labor support and win votes for Landon? In early October a group of Detroit industrialists worked out a social-security campaign; and the Republican National Committee adopted it with enthusiasm.

The thesis was simple: the government was taking away the workers' money, and heaven alone knew whether the worker would ever get it back. (Nothing was said, of course, about employers' contributions.) In the last two weeks before election, placards began to go up in plants: YOU'RE SENTENCED TO A WEEKLY PAY REDUCTION FOR ALL YOUR WORKING LIFE. YOU'LL HAVE TO SERVE THE SENTENCE UNLESS YOU HELP REVERSE IT NOVEMBER 3. Workers opening their pay envelopes found a solicitous message:

Effective January, 1937, we are compelled by a Roosevelt "New Deal" law to make a 1 per cent deduction from your wages and turn it over to the government. Finally, this may go as high as 4 per cent. You might get this money back . . . but only if Congress decides to make the appropriation for this purpose. There is NO guarantee. Decide before November 3 — election day — whether or not you wish to take these chances.

At last the Republicans felt they had found an issue. Excited reports rolled in to Landon: thus from Ohio — "The labor vote has stayed unimpressed and adamant until now that the Social Security issue is brought home to them. This state is all agog over payroll reduction." As voting day came nearer, Republican orators harped with ever-increasing intensity on the horror which lay ahead. The Social Security Act, said Frank Knox, "puts half the working people of America under federal control." Republican spot broadcasts told workers that they would not have a name under the program, only a New Deal number.

The climax came the weekend before the election, when administration denials would presumably not have time to catch up with the allegations. In St. Louis on the last Saturday, Landon asked how any administration could keep track of 26 million Americans. "Imagine the field opened for federal snooping. Are these 26 million going to be fingerprinted? Are their photographs going to be kept on file in a Washington office? Or are they going to have identification tags put around their necks?" In Boston John Hamilton took up this last suggestion, declaring that each one of the enslaved 26 million workers would have to wear metal dog-tags ("such as the one I hold in my hand"). The only indication that the administration still thought of these unfortunates as human beings, Hamilton added, was that the tags were to be made of stainless steel so that they would not discolor the skin of the wearers. And on Monday the Hearst newspapers featured on page 1 an arresting spread: "Do You Want A Tag And A Number In The Name Of False Security?" On page 2 was a picture of a bare-chested man somberly wearing a tag on a long chain: below was the stark caption: YOU.

At first the administration could not take the social-security scare seriously. The *New York Times* sensibly pointed out that Landon, in attacking the contributory feature, was attacking one of the most conservative provisions of the act; did the Republicans, asked the *Times,* really want to charge the whole social-security system to the income tax? James M. Cox, the only former presidential candidate to stick by the Democratic party, wrote comfortably, "Why didn't the boss put any political propaganda in your pay envelopes four years ago? Because there wasn't any pay envelopes." But the apparent success of the pay-envelope gimmick ended Democratic complacency. Democratic headquarters began to hear unnerving stories of Roosevelt buttons thrown away in front of plants, of Roosevelt stickers ripped from automobiles, of Roosevelt posters in industrial towns spattered or torn down. On October 27, for example, Roosevelt received urgent messages from Frank Murphy in Michigan, from David Lawrence in Pennsylvania, and from Labor's Nonpartisan League that he must act quickly to counter the smear. The whole affair, said Stanley High, precipitated a "near-panic" in the Democratic command.

It did not panic the President, but it deeply angered him. Its patent cynicism summed up for him the contempt with which he believed all economic royalists viewed the democratic process. He had already in the course of 1935 passed out of the George Washington mood of the First New Deal. Now he saw himself increasingly as Andrew Jackson. "It is absolutely true," he had written of Jackson, "that his opponents represented the same social outlook and the same element in the population that ours do." "The more I learn about Andy Jackson," he told Garner, "the more I love him." (He evidently had not learned enough to know that contemporaries never called Jackson "Andy.") Sometime during 1935 Ickes passed him a note which Roosevelt kept in his papers: "It is the fight of Jackson against the U.S. Bank all over again with concentrated capital in the place of the Bank."

The attack on the social-security program completed the conversion of Roosevelt to a thoroughly Jacksonian wrath. For some time he had brooded over the venom with which the American rich regarded him. George Biddle reported in July 1936 as one of the "recurrent themes" in his mind — "Why do the Tories hate me?" The unpleasant incidents of the campaign renewed his feeling that the business classes were out to destroy anyone who threatened their wealth or prerogatives. In October he could have read Ernest T. Weir's businessman's indictment of himself in *Fortune:*

He never went through the grim competitive battle that every man must endure who fights his way from scratch. His experience with business has been narrowly limited. Most of his life has been spent in politics. He has never experienced the anxiety of the man who must find work for a large group

of employees and must meet a payroll week after week. He
has never occupied an executive post where he was responsible for the manufacture of products or the performance of
services under competitive conditions.

Weir concluded: "Today he is opposed, not by a 'small minority'
as he says, but almost unanimously by the business and professional
men of the country."

The evident determination of such men now to deprive the ordinary people of social security drove Roosevelt to fury. He told
Rosenman, Corcoran, Cohen, and High to take their gloves off when
it came to the campaign wind-up at Madison Square Garden.[3]

VII

Rarely in Roosevelt's political career was there such a night
as October 31, 1936. The Garden, packed to the rafters, erupted
into thirteen minutes of cheering and shrieking when Roosevelt
appeared, with the band blaring "Happy Days Are Here Again,"
and cowbells, horns, and clackers adding to the uproar. To the
President, unwontedly nervous before a major speech, it seemed
as if the applause would never stop. But there stuck in his mind
a picture of Landon trying ineffectually to halt applause by calling "Mr. Chairman," "Mr. Chairman," so he did nothing but raise
his hands. At last the great hall was quiet. "In 1932," Roosevelt
began, "the issue was the restoration of American democracy;
and the American people were in a mood to win. They did win.
In 1936 the issue is the preservation of their victory." He enumerated the gains of the years since 1933 — peace of mind for the
individual, peace for the community, peace for the nation, peace
with the world. But "we have not come this far without a struggle
and I assure you we cannot go further without a struggle." The
"old enemies" — "business and financial monopoly, speculation,
reckless banking, class antagonism" — were seeking to regain their
power. But "we know now that Government by organized money
is just as dangerous as Government by organized mob."

The audience was constantly on its feet. The applause, reported
the New York Times, came in "roars which rose and fell like the
sound of waves pounding in the surf." Roosevelt continued, his

voice growing hard, almost vengeful: "Never before in all our history have these forces been so united against one candidate as they stand today. They are unanimous in their hate for me — and I welcome their hatred." Again a scream from the crowd. The President spoke for a moment with deceptive mildness. "I should like to have it said of my first Administration that in it the forces of selfishness and of lust for power met their match." Over the cheers, he went on: "I should like to have it said ——"; but the mounting roar of anticipation threatened to drown out his words; he paused and cried, "Wait a moment!"; then "I should like to have it said of my second Administration that in it these forces met their master." The crowd's roar was like thunder.

He passed swiftly on to the social-security campaign; "only desperate men with their backs to the wall would descend so far below the level of decent citizenship." When they suggested that some future Congress would divert the reserve funds to some other purpose, they were "already aliens to the spirit of American democracy. Let them emigrate and try their lot under some foreign flag in which they have more confidence." Then, having expressed his "indignation," he moved to the affirmations — to the "vision for the future." Of course, we would continue to improve conditions for the workers and farmers of America, to fight against monopoly, to regulate financial practices, to wipe out slums, to enlarge opportunities for our young men and women, to strive for peace in the world. "For all these we have only just begun to fight." And economic objectives were only the beginning. "The recovery we are winning is more than economic. In it are included justice and love and humility, not for ourselves as individuals alone, but for our nation. That is the road to peace." [4]

VIII

Alfred M. Landon would be an easy victor, predicted the *Literary Digest*: 32 states with 370 electoral votes against 16 states with 161 electoral votes for Roosevelt. At Harvard, the professor of statistics, applying his own coefficient of error to the *Digest* poll, gravely reported to Landon that, even after correction, Landon would be sure to have 241 votes to Roosevelt's 99, with

91 votes uncertain. Landon himself was not so sure. For a moment, the night after his own Madison Square Garden address, when he saw an advance release on the last *Digest* poll, he thought he might win. As he went to bed that night, he mused over appointments he would like to make: Charles P. Taft as Solicitor General, J. Reuben Clark as Undersecretary of State, Raymond Clapper in some capacity. But when he woke the next morning, he knew he had been deluding himself.

The public-opinion polls of George Gallup and Elmo Roper, based on statistical sampling rather than direct-mail ballots, reported a marked swing to Roosevelt in the last weeks and forecast a Roosevelt victory of considerable proportions. The President, figuring the score with pencil and paper, now gave himself 360 electoral votes as against 171 for Landon. ("What frightened you?" a newspaperman asked him later. "Oh, just my well known conservative tendencies," Roosevelt replied.) The North American Newspaper Alliance wired William Allen White for a story to be released in case of a Landon victory. "You have a quaint sense of humor," White replied. "If Landon is elected I'll write you a book about him, bind it in platinum, illustrate it with apples of gold and pictures of silver, and won't charge you a cent. Why waste good telegraph tolls on a possibility so remote as the election of Landon?" Jim Farley was prepared to go further than anybody. "After looking them all over carefully and discounting everything that has been given in these reports," he wrote Roosevelt on November 2, "I am still definitely of the opinion that you will carry every state but two — Maine and Vermont."

Problems remained. No one knew how much damage the last-minute Republican drive on social security had done. The Social Security Board itself denied Hamilton's weird inspiration about the dog tags; but who read denials? And Roosevelt's Madison Square Garden flourish about making himself the "master" of the forces of selfishness fell with a dubious sound even on the ears of some of his friends. It "frankly horrified me," said Richberg; Moley was "stunned"; even a sympathetic newspaperman like Tom Stokes was shocked. The Republicans made the most of it in the last forty-eight hours. Some Democrats, succumbing to election nerves, begged the President to do something to qualify it. Roosevelt went calmly back to Hyde Park, ignoring the clamor.

The day passed, but the sentence remained an uneasy memory. Others wound up the campaign in their own ways. On October 26, William Randolph Hearst, moved perhaps by some presentiment, cabled his papers from Great Britain to give news about Roosevelt equal play with news about Landon. "I wish to close this campaign," said Father Coughlin, "by apologizing . . . for words which ordinarily do not issue from the lips of a gentleman." And on election eve, Gerald L. K. Smith, back in New Orleans, was jailed for using obscene language and disturbing the peace.

Election day dawned clear and unseasonably warm in the east. Around the Great Lakes there was light snow; in the Mississippi Valley, showers of rain. In the Far West the weather was clear and cold. Franklin Roosevelt wore for luck an engraved watch chain which had once belonged to Andrew Jackson; it showed a hound chasing a fox. Teletype machines were set up in the smoking room in his mother's house at Hyde Park. There was a spread in the library, with sandwiches and doughnuts and pitchers of freshly pressed sweet cider. As the returns began to come in, the President retired to a room by himself with a pencil, a pad, and a large voting chart.

Early in the evening the bulletin flashed through that New Haven had gone for Roosevelt by 15,000 votes. The returns "must be wrong," Roosevelt said; "they couldn't be that large"; and he demanded that the figures be checked. A few moments later he was assured of their accuracy. There could no longer be any doubt. Roosevelt leaned back, blew a smoke ring into the air, and said, "Wow!"

In New York City, nearly a million people milled about in good-humored frenzy in Times Square. In Chicago, crowds threw eggs at the *Tribune* building and burned a truckload of its bulldog edition. In Topeka, Alf Landon, a pipe in his mouth, moved thoughtfully among friends at the Executive Mansion. From Chicago, John Hamilton told him to ignore the first reports, to concede nothing; wait for the returns from the rural counties. At first Landon indicated that he would let the night pass before making a statement. But soon, with sober realism, he acknowledged the outcome. Around one in the morning, Topeka time, he sent a telegram of concession to Roosevelt: THE NATION HAS SPOKEN. EVERY AMERICAN WILL ACCEPT THE VERDICT AND WILL WORK

FOR THE COMMON CAUSE OF THE GOOD OF THE COUNTRY. In New York, the Republicans sat on in gloom. A *Herald Tribune* editorial writer, thinking it might cheer him, called out to Ogden Mills, "Well, Ogden, I see we still have those great Republican strongholds, Vermont and Utah!" Mills turned angrily. "This is no joking matter." he said, "It is a great national disaster." Soon Utah fell. "This is a ground swell," commented William Allen White. "The water of liberalism has been dammed up for forty years by the two major parties. The dam is out. Landon went down the creek in the torrent."

At Hyde Park, Tom Corcoran now had his accordion on his arm and was playing gay tunes. Jim Farley called up exultantly from New York: "Who are the fourteen persons who voted against you in Warm Springs? You ought to raise hell with them." Sara Delano Roosevelt moved in a glow of excitement and wonder. Around ten-thirty there was a glitter of lights and a blare of music in the grounds outside. The Democrats of Hyde Park, with red-fire torches, calcium flares, and a brass band, had come to salute the President. Roosevelt went out and greeted them. From their bedroom window on an upper floor Roosevelt grandchildren looked down at the spectacle with shining eyes, their faces pressed to the pane. As the President finished a quiet talk, some in the crowd shouted, "How about 1940?" . . . The last thing Roosevelt did before going to bed at three was to call Nebraska to inquire about George Norris. "Of all the results on November third," he wrote Norris later, "your re-election gave me the greatest happiness."

Never had there been such a victory. Farley had been right: as Maine went, so went Vermont. Roosevelt had gained the largest presidential vote in history, the largest presidential plurality, the largest proportion of electoral votes since 1820, the largest House majority since 1855, the largest Senate majority since 1869. He polled 27,476,673 votes to 16,679,583 for Landon, which meant that the Democratic vote had increased by nearly 5 million votes from 1932, while the Republican increased by less than a million. Roosevelt's percentage of the popular vote rose in every section of the country (except for imperceptible declines in the South and West Central regions). The most conspicuous increases — all 5 per cent or over — were in the Middle Atlantic and East

Central states and on the West Coast. The stock market promptly shot up. Seventeen great corporations proclaimed wage increases. Father Coughlin, whose candidate had polled 8,120,000 votes less than stipulated, announced that he was quitting the air. On the bridge over the Salmon Falls River, where automobiles crossed from New Hampshire into Maine, someone hung a sign: YOU ARE NOW LEAVING THE UNITED STATES.

As for Alf Landon, he took his defeat philosophically. He wrote to Raymond Clapper, "I don't think it would have made any difference what kind of campaign I made as far as stopping this avalanche is concerned. That is one consolation you get out of a good licking." One thing disappointed him: William Hard summed it up in a remark to Landon which the defeated candidate repeated with relish for years after. "One reason I was sorry you never became President," Hard said, "was that I missed seeing the astonishment on the faces of all those stuffed shirts who really thought you would be a Kansas Coolidge."

Landon finally did get to Washington when he came in December for the annual banquet of the Gridiron Club. "If there is one state that prepares a man for anything," he told the assembled newspapermen in the annual off-the-record evening,

> it is Kansas. The Kansas tornado is an old story. But let me tell you of one. It swept away first the barn, then the out buildings. Then it picked up the dwelling and scattered it all over the landscape.
>
> As the funnel-shaped cloud went twisting its way out of sight, leaving nothing but splinters behind, the wife came to, to find her husband laughing.
>
> She angrily asked him: "What are you laughing at, you darned old fool?"
>
> And the husband replied: "The completeness of it."

The completeness of it was unanswerable. From William Randolph Hearst to the striking employees of his paper in Seattle went an improbable telegram commending Roosevelt's "absolutely stunning" victory. "If Andrew Jackson's policies were essentially democratic," Hearst said, "why is it not reasonable to concede that Mr. Roosevelt's policies may be equally so — dictatorial in manner and method but democratic in essence? When I was a great admirer and supporter of Mr. Roosevelt . . . I gave him a picture of Andrew Jackson and a letter of that great Democrat. I thought then that Mr. Roosevelt resembled Jackson. Perhaps I was more nearly right then than later. Perhaps Roosevelt, like Jackson, has given essential democracy a new lease of life and will establish it in power for a generation."

"The election has shown one final thing conclusively," said William Randolph Hearst, "and that is that no alien theory is necessary to realize the popular ideal in this country." [5]

35. "Trustee for Those in Every Country"

"This problem of unemployment," wrote Winston Churchill, "is the most torturing that can be presented to a civilized society." In 1930 Churchill raised a question which troubled many in these dark years — the question whether this was a problem with which representative democracy could ever deal. Democratic governments, he suggested, drifted along the line of least resistance, took short views, smoothed their path with platitudes, and paid their way with sops and doles. Parliaments, he pessimistically concluded, could deal with political problems, but not with economic. "One may even be pardoned for doubting whether institutions based on adult suffrage could possibly arrive at the right decisions upon the intricate propositions of modern business and finance." What to do? "You cannot cure cancer by a majority. What is wanted is a remedy." And the remedy? With Parliament impotent before the economic crisis, the question arose, said Churchill, whether we must not, "while time remains, create a new instrument specially adapted for the purpose, and delegate to that instrument all the necessary powers and facilities."[1]

II

The distance which Churchill was prepared to travel remained obscure; but the ebb and flow of discussion in the United States as well as in Britain in the early thirties revealed an increasingly dour sense of existing alternatives; on the one hand, political democracy and economic chaos; on the other, economic direction and political tyranny. Even more dour was the sense that history

had already made the choice — that the democratic impulse had
been drained of vitality, that the free state was spent as a means
of organizing human action. Consider a selection of statements
from American writers between 1934 and 1936, all of whom, in
arguing for democracy and liberalism, wrote with the gallant
desperation of champions of a lost cause:

> The rejection of democracy is nowadays regarded as evidence
> of superior wisdom.
>
> — Ralph Barton Perry, Autumn 1934

> The moral and intellectual bankruptcy of liberalism in our
> time needs no demonstration. It is as obvious as rain and as
> taken for granted.
>
> — Nathaniel Peffer, August 1934

> To attempt a defense of democracy these days is a little like
> defending paganism in 313 or the divine right of kings in
> 1793. It is taken for granted that democracy is bad and that
> it is dying.
>
> — George Boas, September 1934

> Political democracy is moribund . . . Civil liberties like democ-
> racy are useful only as tools for social change. Political democ-
> racy as such a tool is obviously bankrupt throughout the
> world.
>
> — Roger Baldwin, April 1933

> Why is it that democracy has fallen so rapidly from the high
> prestige which it had at the Armistice? . . . Why is it that
> in America itself — in the very temple and citadel of democ-
> racy — self-government has been held up to every ridicule, and
> many observers count it already dead?
>
> — Will Durant, September 1934

> Modern Western civilization is a failure. That theory is now
> generally accepted.
>
> — Louise Maunsell Field, May 1936

> "Liberalism is dead." So many people who seem to agree
> upon nothing else have agreed to accept these three sweeping
> words.
>
> — Joseph Wood Krutch, May 1936

Could this be true? Was no middle way possible between free-dom and tyranny — no mixed system which might give the state more power than Herbert Hoover would approve, enough power, indeed, to assure economic and social security; but still not enough to create a Hitler or a Stalin? This was the critical question.

To this question the Hoovers, no less than the Hitlers and Stalins, had long since returned categorical answers. They all — the prophets of individualism and the prophets of totalitarianism — agreed on this if on nothing else: no modified capitalism was possible, no mixed economy, no system of partial and limited gov-ernment intervention. One could have one thing or the other, but one could never, never, never mix freedom and control. There was, in short, no middle way.

If this conclusion were true, it would have the most fateful consequences for the future of the world.[2]

III

The assumption that there were two absolutely distinct eco-nomic orders, capitalism and socialism, expressed, of course, an unconscious Platonism — a conviction that reality inhered in theo-retical essences of which any working economy, with its compro-mises and confusions, could only be an imperfect copy. If in the realm of essences capitalism and socialism were wholly separate phenomena based on wholly separate principles, then they must be rigorously kept apart on earth. Thus abstractions became more "real" than empirical reality: both doctrinaire capitalists and doc-trinaire socialists fell victim to what Whitehead called the "fallacy of misplaced concreteness." Both ideological conservatism and ideological radicalism dwelt in the realm of either-or. Both pre-ferred essence to existence.

The distinction of the New Deal lay precisely in its refusal to approach social problems in terms of ideology. Its strength lay in its preference of existence to essence. The great central source of its energy was the instinctive contempt of practical, energetic, and compassionate people for dogmatic absolutes. Refusing to be intimidated by abstractions or to be overawed by ideology, the New Dealers responded by doing things. Walt Whitman once

wrote, "To work for Democracy is good, the exercise is good —
strength it makes and lessons it teaches." The whole point of
the New Deal lay in its faith in "the exercise of Democracy," its
belief in gradualness, its rejection of catastrophism, its denial of
either-or, its indifference to ideology, its conviction that a managed and modified capitalist order achieved by piecemeal experiment could best combine personal freedom and economic growth.
"In a world in which revolutions just now are coming easily,"
said Adolf Berle, "the New Deal chose the more difficult course
of moderation and rebuilding." "It looks forward toward a more
stable social order," said Morgenthau, "but it is not doctrinaire, not
a complete cut-and-dried program. It involves the courage to experiment." "The course that the new administration did take,"
wrote Ickes, "was the hardest course. It conformed to no theory,
but it did fit into the American system — to meet concrete needs,
a system of courageous recognition of change." Tugwell, rejecting
laissez faire and Communism, spoke of the "third course." *Hold
Fast the Middle Way* was the title of a book by John Dickinson.

Roosevelt hoped to steer between the extreme of chaos and
tyranny by moving always, in his phrase, "slightly to the left of
center." "Unrestrained individualism" had proved a failure; yet
"any paternalistic system which tries to provide for security for
everyone from above only calls for an impossible task and a regimentation utterly uncongenial to the spirit of our people." He
deeply agreed with Macaulay's injunction to reform if you would
preserve. Once, defending public housing to a press conference,
he said, "If you had knowledge of what happened in Germany
and England and Vienna, you would know that 'socialism' has
probably done more to prevent Communism and rioting and
revolution than anything else in the last four or five years."

Roosevelt had no illusions about revolution. Mussolini and
Stalin seemed to him "not mere distant relatives" but "blood
brothers." When Emil Ludwig asked him his "political motive,"
he replied, "My desire to obviate revolution. . . . I work in a contrary sense to Rome and Moscow." He said during the 1932
campaign:

Say that civilization is a tree which, as it grows, continually
produces rot and dead wood. The radical says: "Cut it down."

The conservative says: "Don't touch it." The liberal compromises: "Let's prune, so that we lose neither the old trunk nor the new branches." This campaign is waged to teach the country to march upon its appointed course, the way of change, in an orderly march, avoiding alike the revolution of radicalism and the revolution of conservatism.

His "speech material" file contained a miscellany of material indexed according to the random categories of the President's mind. One folder bore the revealing label: "Liberalism vs. Communism and Conservatism."

As Roosevelt saw it, he was safeguarding the constitutional system by carrying through reforms long overdue. "The principal object of every Government all over the world," he once said, "seems to have been to impose the ideas of the last generation upon the present one. That's all wrong." As early as 1930 he had considered it time for America "to become fairly radical for at least one generation. History shows that where this occurs occasionally, nations are saved from revolution." In 1938 he remarked, "In five years I think we have caught up twenty years. If liberal government continues over another ten years we ought to be contemporary somewhere in the late nineteen forties." [3]

IV

For Roosevelt, the technique of liberal government was pragmatism. Tugwell talked about creating "a philosophy to fit the Rooseveltian method"; but this was the aspiration of an intellectual. Nothing attracted Roosevelt less than rigid intellectual systems. "The fluidity of change in society has always been the despair of theorists," Tugwell once wrote. This fluidity was Roosevelt's delight, and he floated upon it with the confidence of an expert sailor, who could detect currents and breezes invisible to others, hear the slap of waves on distant rocks, smell squalls beyond the horizon and make infallible landfalls in the blackest of fogs. He respected clear ideas, accepted them, employed them, but was never really at ease with them and always ultimately skeptical about their relationship to reality.

His attitude toward economists was typical. Though he acknowledged their necessity, he stood in little awe of them. "I brought down several books by English economists and leading American economists," he once told a press conference. ". . . I suppose I must have read different articles by fifteen different experts. Two things stand out: The first is that no two of them agree, and the other thing is that they are so foggy in what they say that it is almost impossible to figure out what they mean. It is jargon; absolute jargon." Once Roosevelt remarked to Keynes of Leon Henderson, "Just look at Leon. When I got him, he was only an economist." (Keynes could hardly wait to repeat this to Henderson.) Roosevelt dealt proficiently with practical questions of government finance, as he showed in his press conferences on the budget; but abstract theory left him cold.

Considering the state of economic theory in the nineteen thirties, this was not necessarily a disabling prejudice. Roosevelt had, as J. K. Galbraith has suggested, what was more important than theory, and surely far more useful than bad theory, a set of intelligent economic attitudes. He believed in government as an instrument for effecting economic change (though not as an instrument for doing everything: in 1934, he complained to the National Emergency Council, "There is the general feeling that it is up to the Government to take care of everybody . . . they should be told all the different things the Government can not do"). He did not regard successful businessmen as infallible repositories of economic wisdom. He regarded the nation as an estate to be improved for those who would eventually inherit it. He was willing to try nearly anything. And he had a sense of the complex continuities of history — that special intimacy with the American past which, as Frances Perkins perceptively observed, signified a man who had talked with old people who had talked with older people who remembered many things back to the War of the Revolution.

From this perspective, Roosevelt could not get excited about the debate between the First and Second New Deals. No one knew what he really thought about the question of the organic economy versus the restoration of competition. Tugwell, perhaps the most vigilant student of Roosevelt's economic ideas, could in one mood pronounce Roosevelt "a progressive of the nineteenth century in economic matters" (1946) who "clung to the Brandeis-Frankfurter view" (1950) and "could be persuaded away from the old progressive line only in the direst circumstances" (1950); in another, he could speak of Roosevelt's "preference for a planned and disciplined business system" (1957) and for "overhead management of the whole economy" (1940), and question whether he ever believed in Brandeis (1957). Corcoran and Cohen, who helped persuade Roosevelt to the Second New Deal, thought he never really abandoned the NRA dream of directing the economy through some kind of central economic mechanism. Roosevelt himself, confronted with a direct question, always wriggled away ("Brandeis is one thousand per cent right in principle but in certain fields there must be a guiding or restraining hand of Government because of the very nature of the specific field"). He never could see why the United States has to be all one way or all the other. "This country is big enough to experiment with several diverse systems and follow several different lines," he once remarked to Adolf Berle. "Why must we put our economic policy in a single systemic strait jacket?"

Rejecting the battle between the New Nationalism and the New Freedom which had so long divided American liberalism, Roosevelt equably defined the New Deal as the "satisfactory combination" of both. Rejecting the platonic distinction between "capitalism" and "socialism," he led the way toward a new society which took elements from each and rendered both obsolescent. It was this freedom from dogma which outraged the angry, logical men who saw everything with dazzling certitude. Roosevelt's illusion, said Herbert Hoover, was "that any economic system would work in a mixture of others. No greater illusions ever mesmerized the American people." "Your President," said Leon Trotsky with contempt, "abhors 'systems' and 'generalities.' . . . Your philosophic method is even more antiquated than your economic system." But the American President always resisted ideological commitment. His determination was to keep options open within the general frame of a humanized democracy; and his belief was that the very diversity of systems strengthened the basis for freedom.[4]

v

Without some critical vision, pragmatism could be a meaningless technique; the flight from ideology, a form of laziness; the middle way, an empty conception. For some politicians, such an approach meant nothing more than splitting the difference between extremes; the middle of the road was thus determined by the clamor from each side. At times it appeared to mean little more than this to Roosevelt. But at bottom he had a guiding vision with substantive content of its own. The content was not, however, intellectual; and this was where he disappointed more precise and exacting minds around him. It was rather a human content, a sense of the fortune and happiness of people. In 1936 a Canadian editor asked him to state his objectives. Roosevelt's off-the-cuff reply defined his goal in all its naïveté and power:

> . . . to do what any honest Government of any country would do; try to increase the security and the happiness of a larger number of people in all occupations of life and in all parts of the country; to give them more of the good things of life, to give them a greater distribution not only of wealth in the narrow terms, but of wealth in the wider terms; to give them places to go in the summer time — recreation; to give them assurance that they are not going to starve in their old age; to give honest business a chance to go ahead and make a reasonable profit, and to give everyone a chance to earn a living.

The listing was neither considered nor comprehensive, but the spirit was accurate. "The intellectual and spiritual climate," said Frances Perkins, "was Roosevelt's general attitude that *the people mattered*." Nothing else would count until ordinary people were provided an environment and an opportunity "as good as human ingenuity can devise and fit for children of God."

Developed against the backdrop of depression, his philosophy of compassion had a particular bias toward the idea of security — "a greater physical and mental and spiritual security for the people of this country." "Security," he once said,

> means a kind of feeling within our individual selves that we have lacked all through the course of history. We have had to take our chance about our old age in days past. We have had to take our chance with depressions and boom times. We have had to take chances on buying our homes. I have believed for a great many years that the time has come in our civilization

when a great many of these chances should be eliminated from our lives.

The urgencies of depression carried the concern for security to a degree which later generations, who thought they could assume abundance and move on to problems of opportunity and self-fulfillment, would find hard to understand. The old American dream, Roosevelt told a collection of young people in 1935, was the dream of the golden ladder — each individual for himself. But the newer generation would have a different dream: "Your advancement, you hope, is along a broad highway on which thousands of your fellow men and women are advancing with you." In many ways this was a dispiriting hope. In the longer run, security, while indispensable as a social minimum, might be cloying and perhaps even stultifying as a social ideal.

But this was a nuance imposed by depression. His essential ideals had an old-fashioned flavor. He was unconsciously seeing America in the Jeffersonian image of Dutchess County and Hyde Park. He hoped, as he said, to extend "to our national life the old principal of the local community, the principle that no individual, man, woman or child, has a right to do things that hurt his neighbors." "Our task of reconstruction does not require the creation of new and strange values. It is rather the finding of the way once more to known, but to some degree forgotten ideals." He wanted to make other people happy as he had been happy himself. Lifting his right hand high, his left hand only a little, he would say, "This difference is too big, it must become smaller — like this. . . . Wasn't I able to study, travel, take care of my sickness? The man who doesn't have to worry about his daily bread is securer and freer." He spoke of his philosophy as "social-mindedness." He meant by this essentially the humanization of industrial society.

A viewpoint so general provided no infallible guide to daily decision. Roosevelt therefore had to live by trial and error. His first term had its share of error: the overextension of NRA; the fumbling with monetary policy; the reluctant approach to spending; the waste of energy in trying to achieve the communitarian dream; the bungling of the London Economic Conference; the administrative confusion and conflict; the excessive reliance on ballyhoo and oratory. At times Roosevelt seemed almost to extemporize for the joy of it; his pragmatism appeared an addition to playing by ear in the nervous conviction that any kind of noise was better than silence. "Instead of being alarmed by the spirit of improvisation," wrote George Creel, "he seemed delighted by it, whooping on the improvisers with the excitement of one riding to hounds."

The chronic changing of front exposed the New Deal to repeated charges that it had no core of doctrine, that it was improvised and opportunistic, that it was guided only by circumstance. These charges were all true. But they also represented the New Deal's strength. For the advantage enjoyed by the pragmatists over the ideologists was their exceptional sensitivity to social and human reality. They measured results in terms not of conformity to *a priori* models but of concrete impact on people's lives. The New Deal thus had built-in mechanisms of feed-back, readjustment, and self-correction. Its incoherences were considerably more faithful to a highly complicated and shifting reality than any preconceived dogmatic system could have been. In the welter of confusion and ignorance, experiment corrected by compassion was the best answer.

Roosevelt's genius lay in the fact that he recognized — rather, rejoiced in — the challenge to the pragmatic nerve. His basic principle was not to sacrifice human beings to logic. Frances Perkins describes him as "in full revolt against the 'economic man.' " He had no philosophy save experiment, which was a technique; constitutionalism, which was a procedure; and humanity, which was a faith.[5]

VI

The depression, the Social Science Research Council Committee on Studies in Social Aspects of the Depression declared in unwontedly nonacademic language, "was like the explosion of a bomb dropped in the midst of society." It shook and strained the American community in a multitude of ways and profoundly challenged the nation's will to survive. The American people, in recording in 1936 so astonishing a vote of confidence in the New Deal, were by no means endorsing everything that had taken place in the tumultuous years since March 4, 1933. But they were voting unmistakably for the capacity of a representative democracy under strong leadership to produce energetic, resourceful, and free government in the face of an economic holocaust. And their vote came at a time when, throughout the west, faith in government by the people — faith in free society itself — was flickering and fading. While the men of Washington wrote their laws and established their agencies and set out to make America over, other men in Berlin and in Moscow looked confidently forward to the collapse of free institutions — and too few in free countries dared say them nay. In a real sense, the New Deal was testing the resources of democracy, not just for Americans, but for all mankind. Roosevelt's victory, said *The Times* of London, "is a matter of supreme importance at the moment when English-speaking nations are becoming more isolated as the champions of democracy in a world 'blown about by all the winds of doctrine.'"

Could the pragmatic experiment possibly work? Would not its failure hurtle the nation — and perhaps the western world — into darker and more desperate experiments? "I can hardly describe," said Winston Churchill, "with what eagerness, not only our working people, but all those who think about social problems in this island are watching the results of President Roosevelt's valiant effort to solve the riddle of the sphinx." "My whole impression," wrote Sir Stafford Cripps after visiting Roosevelt in 1935, "is of an honest anxious man faced by an impossible task — humanising capitalism and making it work." "It takes an opportunist and a moderate liberal to wreck capitalism in an hour of crisis and to prepare the way for the radical dictator," said Lawrence Dennis hopefully, adding, "Mr. Roosevelt is the Kerensky of American capitalism." Roosevelt sometimes used to make the Kerensky joke himself. No one can guess to what extent such jokes ventilated the interior doubts and fears which might well surge up in rare moments of solitude, when the shouting died away and he could not longer evade the ultimates. But Roosevelt had had private agonies before, and had conquered doubts and fears. There were historical consolations, too: Tugwell has compared the ordeal of Roosevelt's struggle against depression with the ordeal of Lincoln's struggle against disunion — the generals tried and dismissed, the strategic plans adopted and discarded, the troubles with Congress and the Supreme Court, the resistance of the faint of heart and the stubborn of mind, the waste and the tears, until at last national energies came into focus and produced victory.

Whatever might haunt Roosevelt in the dark of night, he showed nothing in the daylight but confidence and decision. He well knew that more was at stake than America — that the challenge of achieving economic security within a framework of freedom offered civilized society a decisive test. No one stated the challenge more exactly than John Maynard Keynes in his letter to Roosevelt at the end of 1933.

"You have made yourself," Keynes said, "the trustee for those in every country who seek to mend the evils of our condition by reasoned experiment within the framework of the existing social system.

"If you fail, rational choice will be gravely prejudiced throughout the world, leaving orthodoxy and revolution to fight it out.

"But, if you succeed, new and bolder methods will be tried everywhere, and we may date the first chapter of a new economic era from your accession to office." [6]

VII

He was apparently succeeding; and people could start to believe again in the free state and its capacity to solve problems of economic stability and social justice. Free society, in consequence, might not yet be finished; it had a future; it might have the strength and steadfastness to surmount the totalitarian challenge. Franklin Roosevelt and Adolf Hitler had come to power together in 1933. Four years later their two images were more sharply juxtaposed than ever, symbolizing a conflict between profoundly different views of society and humanity.

When Roosevelt was re-elected in 1936, the French Chamber of Deputies passed, without dissent, a resolution of congratulations. "Henceforth democracy has its chief!" said *Paris-Soir*. "After his brilliant triumph President Roosevelt has become the statesman on whom every hope is to be pinned if the great liberal and democratic civilization of the west is one day threatened, either by Bolshevism or by autocracy." "No dictator, whether Fascist or Communist," said *The Times* of London, "can challenge the solid basis of his backing. None can afford so securely to take the course which he believes to be right without regard for any need of a spell-bound popularity."

In England, Winston Churchill, roused from his pessimism of 1930, took a new look at the prospects of freedom. "His impulse," Churchill wrote of Roosevelt, "is one which makes toward the fuller life of the masses of the people in every land, and which, as it glows the brighter, may well eclipse both the lurid flames of German Nordic self-assertion and the baleful unnatural lights which are diffused from Soviet Russia."

For all his absorption in the struggle for American recovery during these years, Roosevelt had watched the spread of fascism and aggression with increasing apprehension. The only answer, he felt, was the strengthened vitality of democracy. When he accepted renomination at Franklin Field on June 27, 1936, he seemed also to accept a larger challenge. There were, he said, people in other lands who had once fought for freedom, but who now appeared too weary to carry on the fight, who had "sold their heritage of freedom for the illusion of a living."

"I believe in my heart," Roosevelt said, "that only our success can stir their ancient hope. They begin to know that here in America we are waging a great and successful war. It is not alone a war against want and destitution and economic demoralization. It is more than that: it is a war for the survival of democracy. We are fighting to save a great and precious form of government for ourselves and for the world.

"I accept the commission you have tendered me. I join with you. I am enlisted for the duration of the war." [7]

Notes

IN ORDER to avoid a hopelessly large number of notes, I have followed the practice of collecting the references necessary to a particular passage in a single note. The full citation of each title is to be found on the first mention in each chapter, with the exception of the following works, which receive abbreviated citation throughout:

Franklin D. Roosevelt, *Public Papers and Addresses,* S. I. Rosenman, comp. (New York, 1938–50), cited as F.D.R., *Public Papers,* with the year covered by the volume in parenthesis.

Franklin D. Roosevelt, *His Personal Letters: 1928–1945,* Elliott Roosevelt, ed. (2 vols., New York, 1950), cited as F.D.R., *Personal Letters,* III, IV.

Annals of the American Academy of Political and Social Science, cited as *Annals.*

Bureau of the Census, *Historical Statistics of the United States, 1789–1945* (Washington, 1949), cited as *Historical Statistics.*

Harold L. Ickes, *The First Thousand Days, 1933–1936* (New York, 1935), cited as Ickes, *First Thousand Days.*

Raymond Moley, *After Seven Years* (New York, 1939), cited as Moley, *After Seven Years.*

Henry Morgenthau, Jr., Diary, Morgenthau Papers, cited as Morgenthau, Diary.

Arthur M. Schlesinger, Jr., *The Age of Roosevelt: The Crisis of the Old Order* (Boston, 1957), and *The Age of Roosevelt: The Coming of the*

New Deal (Boston, 1958), cited as Schlesinger, *Crisis,* and Schlesinger, *Coming.*

Rexford G. Tugwell, "A New Deal Memoir: Early Days, 1932–1933," Tugwell Papers, cited as Tugwell, "New Deal Memoir"; and Diary, Tugwell Papers, cited as Tugwell, Diary.

Additional abbreviations are:

AAA, for the Agricultural Adjustment Administration
NRA, for the National Recovery Administration
PWA, for the Public Works Administration
WPA, for the Works Progress Administration.

Of the manuscript collections cited, the following are at the Roosevelt Library at Hyde Park, New York: Franklin D. Roosevelt Papers; Franklin D. Roosevelt, Press Conferences; Roosevelt Foundation Papers; Democratic National Committee Papers; Morris L. Cooke Papers; Mary W. Dewson Papers; Harry L. Hopkins Papers; Louis Howe Papers; Henry Morgenthau, Jr., Papers; Herbert Claiborne Pell Papers. The following are at the National Archives, Washington, D.C.: Department of Agriculture Papers; Bureau of the Budget Papers; National Recovery Administration Papers; National Resources Planning Board Papers; Proceedings of the Executive Council and the National Emergency Council. The Henry L. Stimson Diary is at the Sterling Library, Yale University; the Jay Pierrepont Moffat Diary is in the Moffat Papers at the Houghton Library, Harvard University. The Oswald Garrison Villard Papers are also at the Houghton Library. The Diary of J. F. T. O'Connor is at the Bancroft Library, University of California. The Maury Maverick Papers are in the possession of the Maverick family; I am indebted to Professor Richard B. Henderson for examining these papers on my behalf. The papers of Francis Biddle, Raymond Moley, Rexford G. Tugwell, and Charles E. Wyzanski, Jr., are in the private possession of the persons named. The Oral History Research Office, that indispensable aid to the contemporary historian, is at Columbia University.

CHAPTER 1 *(Pages 1–11)*

1. *New York Times,* Nov. 7, 11, 1934; *Time,* Nov. 19, 1934.
2. *Historical Statistics,* A 117, D 65; National Emergency Council, Report, March 5, 1935; Morgenthau, Diary, July 3, 1935; F.D.R. to Sir Arthur Steel Maitland, Feb. 4, 1935, Roosevelt Papers.
3. F.D.R., *Public Papers* (1935), 25; Moley, *After Seven Years,* 300.
4. *New York Times,* Jan. 17–30, Feb. 24, 27, 1935; Henry L. Stimson to F.D.R., Feb. 2, 1935, Roosevelt Papers; Tom Connally, *My Name Is*

Tom Connally (New York, 1954), 210–11; Ickes, *First Thousand Days,* 284–85, 293, 306; *Time,* Feb. 11, 1935.

5. *New York Times,* March 3, 1935; Ickes, *First Thousand Days,* 293, 305; Pittman to F.D.R., Feb. 19, Farley to F.D.R., March 12, 1935, Roosevelt Papers; *Congressional Record,* 74 Cong., 1 Sess., 3659 (March 14, 1935); *Time,* March 18, 1935; *Literary Digest,* March 9, 1935.

6. F. D. R. to Daniels, March 1, 1935, *Roosevelt and Daniels: A Friendship in Politics,* Carroll Kilpatrick, ed. (Chapel Hill, 1952), 156; National Emergency Council, Proceedings, March 12, 1935; F.D.R. to House, Feb. 16, March 20, to Baker, March 20, Schlesinger to F.D.R., May 8, F.D.R. to Schlesinger, May 14, 1935, Roosevelt Papers; Eleanor Roosevelt to Molly Dewson, March 9, 1935, Dewson Papers; Grace Tully, *F.D.R., My Boss* (New York, 1949), 159; Morgenthau, Diary, May 22, 1935; *Time,* March 18, 1935.

CHAPTER 2 *(Pages 15–28)*

1. H. G. Wells, *The New America: The New World* (New York, 1935), 31.
2. L. B. Ward, *Father Charles E. Coughlin* (Detroit, 1933); Ruth Mugglebee, *Father Coughlin* (Garden City, 1935); "Father Coughlin," *Fortune,* Feb. 1934; Forrest Davis, "Father Coughlin," *Atlantic,* Dec. 1935; George N. Shuster, "Radio Sky Pilot," *Review of Reviews,* April 1935; R. G. Swing, *Forerunners of American Fascism* (New York, 1935), Ch. 2; House Committee to Investigate Communist Activities, *Investigation of Communist Propaganda: Hearings,* 71 Cong., 2 Sess. (1930), 19–25.
3. Charles E. Coughlin, *United States, Incorporated* (discourse of Feb. 25, 1934); Coughlin, "How Long Can Democracy and Capitalism Last?" *Today,* Dec. 29, 1934; Ward, *Coughlin,* 165–66; Coughlin, *Come, Follow Me* (Oct. 18, 1931); House Coinage Weights and Measures Committee, *Gold Reserve Act of 1934: Hearings,* 73 Cong., 2 Sess. (1934), 56; J. E. Reeve, *Monetary Reform Movements* (Washington, 1943), Ch. 9; "Coughlin," *Fortune;* Coughlin, *By Their Fruits They Shall Be Known* (Nov. 26, 1933).
4. "Coughlin," *Fortune;* Swing, *Forerunners,* Ch. 2; Marquis Childs, "Father Coughlin," *New Republic,* May 2, 1934; *Boston Pilot,* April 18, 1932; Ward, *Coughlin,* x, 264–70; Rupert Hart-Davis, *Hugh Walpole* (New York, 1952), 386–87; Selden Rodman, "God's Angry Men," *Common Sense,* Sept. 1936; Frank R. Kent, *Without Gloves* (New York, 1934), 154–55; Mugglebee, *Coughlin,* 127, 218.
5. [Guernsey Cross?] to Coughlin, July 24, 1931, Coughlin to F.D.R., June 14, Sept. 24, 1933, Coughlin to McIntyre, March 21, 1934, Roosevelt Papers; Coughlin, *Share the Profits with Labor* (Dec. 2, 1934); House Coinage Wt. and Meas. Com., *Gold Reserve Act,* 54, 60; *Time,* Jan. 29, 1934; *New York Times,* April 5, 1934.
6. See the following seven works by Charles E. Coughlin: "How Long Can Democracy and Capitalism Last?"; *The New Deal in Money*

(Royal Oak, 1933), 119; *A Series of Lectures on Social Justice* (Royal Oak, 1935), 17–18, 147; *President Roosevelt and Social Justice* (Jan. 6, 1935); *Sovietizing or Saving America?* (Feb. 10, 1935); *Two Years of the New Deal* (March 3, 1935); *The New Deal and the Way Out* (June 2, 1935). Also *New York Times*, Nov. 5, 1934, Jan. 7, 1935; A. B. Magil, "Coughlin Crusades Against Labor," *New Masses*, April 23, 1935; Ickes, *First Thousand Days*, 472; James A. Farley, *Jim Farley's Story* (New York, 1948), 52; *Social Justice*, May 15, 1936.

7. See the following five works by Coughlin: *Money! Questions and Answers* (Royal Oak, 1936), 184; *The Bonus and Neutrality* (Jan. 5, 1936); *The Federal Reserve Bank Case* (Jan. 12, 1936); *Sovietizing or Saving America?; Two Years of the New Deal*. Also House Judiciary Committee, *Birth Control: Hearings*, 73 Cong., 2 Sess. (1934), 129; James Rorty, *Where Life Is Better* (New York, 1936), 174–75; John L. Spivak, *America Faces the Barricades* (New York, 1935), 214–16; Ward, *Coughlin*, 170; Swing, *Forerunners*, 48.

CHAPTER 3 *(Pages 29–41)*

1. F. E. Townsend, *New Horizons: An Autobiography* (Chicago, 1943), especially 78, 95, 128, 131; Richard Milne, *That Man Townsend* (Indianapolis, 1935), 2, 4; Russell Owen, "Townsend Talks of His Plan and Hopes," *New York Times Magazine*, Dec. 29, 1935; interview with Dr. Townsend, April 16, 1959.

2. Townsend, *New Horizons*, especially Ch. 21; Richard L. Neuberger and Kelley Loe, *An Army of the Aged* (Caldwell, Idaho, 1936), especially Chs. 3–4, also 123, 162, 225; Townsend interview; House Committee Investigating Old-Age Pension Organization, *Old-Age Pension Plans and Organizations: Hearings*, 74 Cong., 2 Sess. (1936), 3, 26, 124–25, 605, 751, 757–64; Abraham Holtzman, "The Townsend Movement" (Ph.D. thesis, Harvard University, 1952), 77–81; High to Early, Aug. 29, 1935, Roosevelt Papers; *Townsend Weekly*, Aug. 20, 1935; S. L. Solon, "Life Begins at Sixty," *Modern Monthly*, June 1936; Don Wharton, "Uncle Mose," *Today*, Jan. 11, 1936; Duncan Aikman, "Townsendism: Old-Time Religion," *New York Times Magazine*, March 8, 1936; *Time*, Nov. 4, 1935; S. N. Lake, "If Money," *Saturday Evening Post*, May 11, 1935; Frank Kent, *Without Grease* (New York, 1936), 270–71.

3. Old Age Revolving Pensions, Ltd., *The Townsend Plan* (Chicago, 1936); Twentieth Century Fund, *The Townsend Crusade* (New York, 1936); Neuberger and Loe, *Army of the Aged*, 58, 79–109, 163; *Townsend Weekly*, Jan. 28, Feb. 4, June 17, 1935; *Congressional Record*, 74 Cong., 1 Sess., 4474 (April 1, 1935), 5541 (April 12, 1935); House Ways and Means Committee, *Economic Security Act: Hearings*, 74 Cong., 1 Sess. (1935), 680, 682.

4. Neuberger and Loe, *Army of the Aged*, 95, 128, 141–58; Owen, "Town-

send Talks"; Townsend, *New Horizons,* 170, 187; House Investigating Com., *Old-Age Pension Plans,* 119, 329, 346, 457–58, 463, 484, 491–92, 595, 596–97, 732–33, 785, 795, 901; M. L. Walker, *The Townsend Plan Analyzed* (New York, 1936), 4; Milne, *Townsend,* 35; High to Early, Aug. 29, E. E. Witte to M. G. Murray, Dec. 11, 1935, Roosevelt Papers; Frances Perkins, *The Roosevelt I Knew* (New York, 1946), 278, 294; W. E. Borah, "The Farmer's Enemy," *Collier's,* Feb. 1, 1936; Raymond Moley, "The Townsend Threat," *Today,* Dec. 28, 1935; Holtzman. "The Townsend Movement," 186–87.

CHAPTER 4 *(Pages 42–68)*

1. Huey P. Long, *Every Man A King* (New Orleans, 1933), Chs. 1–2; V. O. Key, Jr., *Southern Politics in State and Nation* (New York, 1949), 151–61; Grady McWhiney, "Louisiana Socialists in the Early Twentieth Century," *Journal of Southern History,* Aug. 1954; James Rorty, "Callie Long's Boy Huey," *Forum,* Aug. 1935; Forrest Davis, *Huey Long, A Candid Biography* (New York, 1935), Chs. 3–4; Carleton Beals, *The Story of Huey Long* (Philadelphia, 1935), Ch. 2; H. T. Kane, *Louisiana Hayride* (New York, 1941), Ch. 2; H. B. Deutsch, "Prelude to a Heterocrat," *Saturday Evening Post,* Sept. 7, 1935.

2. Long, *Every Man A King,* Chs. 3–12, 15–16; Davis, *Long,* Chs. 4, 6; Beals, *Long,* Chs. 3–16; Walter Davenport, "Yes, Your Excellency," *Collier's,* Dec. 13, 1930; A. M. Shaw, "The First Time I Saw Huey," *Southwest Review,* Winter 1950; Senate Committee on Investigation of Campaign Expenditures, *Senatorial Campaign Expenditures, 1932 (Louisiana): Hearings,* 72 Cong., 2 Sess. (1933), 817, 822, 841, 953, 957, 964–67; *Congressional Record,* 73 Cong., 1 Sess. (March 13, 1933), 275.

3. Davenport, "Yes, Your Excellency"; Walter Davenport, "How Huey Long Gets Away With It," *Collier's,* June 17, 1933; Davenport, "The Robes of the Kingfish," *Collier's,* Nov. 22, 1935; Sen. Com. on Investigation of Campaign Expenditures, *Senatorial Campaign Expenditures,* 954–56, 963; John Dos Passos, "Washington: The Big Tent," *New Republic,* March 14, 1934; "Talk of the Town," *New Yorker,* Sept. 2, 1933; Jerome Beatty, "You Can't Laugh Him Off," *American,* Jan. 1933; Mildred Adams, "Huey the Great," *Forum,* Feb. 1933; Russell Owen, "Huey Long Keeps Washington Guessing," *New York Times Magazine,* Jan. 29, 1933; Owen, "Huey Long Gives His Views of Dictators," *New York Times Magazine,* Feb. 10, 1935; M. O. Frost, "Huey Long 'Purifies' Louisiana," *Today,* Aug. 4, 1934; Hamilton Basso, "Huey Long and His Background," *Harper's,* May 1935; Raymond Moley, *27 Masters of Politics* (New York, 1949), 221; Alben Barkley, *That Reminds Me* (New York, 1954), 159; *New York Times,* Oct. 18, 1932; Long, *Every Man A King,* especially Chs. 14, 27; Davis, *Long,* especially Chs. 5–6; H. T. Kane, "Louisiana Story," *New York Times*

Magazine, Sept. 27, 1959; Sherwood Anderson, *Letters,* H. M. Jones, ed. (Boston, 1953), 310–11.

4. Farley is mistaken when he says that Long and Roosevelt never met again after the hat incident. Long made another White House call in January 1934. For other references in this section, see James E. Watson, *As I Knew Them* (Indianapolis, 1936), 304; Long, *Every Man A King,* Ch. 29; Davis, *Long,* Ch. 9; Barkley, *That Reminds Me,* 159; Clinton Gilbert, "Swan Song," *Collier's,* June 10, 1933; James A. Farley, *Behind the Ballots* (New York, 1938), 170–71, 239–43; *New York Times,* Jan. 26, Oct. 11, 1932; *New York Herald Tribune,* Oct. 10, 1932; Tugwell, Diary, Jan. 17, 1933; R. G. Tugwell, *The Democratic Roosevelt* (New York, 1957), 350; Moley, 27 *Masters,* 227; *Time,* Jan. 30, Aug. 7, 1933; Walter Davenport, "Catching Up With Huey," *Collier's,* July 1, 1933; Kane, *Louisiana Hayride,* 101; Frazier Hunt, *One American* (New York, 1938), 389–90.

5. Elmer Irey, *The Tax Dodgers* (New York, 1948), Ch. 4; Davis, *Long,* Chs. 9–10; Beals, *Long,* Chs. 21–33; Sen. Com. on Investigation of Campaign Expenditures, *Senatorial Campaign Expenditures,* 964; *Time,* Sept. 11, 1933; *New York Times,* Oct. 17, 1933; Raymond Swing, *Forerunners of American Fascism* (New York, 1935), 65; A. P. Sindler, *Huey Long's Louisiana* (Baltimore, 1956), 87–95; Deutsch, "Prelude to a Heterocrat"; H. B. Deutsch, "Huey Long — The Last Phase," *Saturday Evening Post,* Oct. 12, 1935; Moley, 27 *Masters,* 222; Hodding Carter, "Huey Long, American Dictator," in Isabel Leighton, ed., *The Aspirin Age* (New York, 1949), especially 341; Hodding Carter, *Where Main Street Meets the River* (New York, 1953), Ch. 5; Kane, *Louisiana Hayride,* Ch. 4; T. H. Williams, "The Gentleman from Louisiana," *Journal of Southern History,* Feb. 1960.

6. Rorty, "Callie Long's Boy Huey"; Long, *Every Man A King,* Chs. 30–31; Davis, *Long,* 42–43, Appendix; Beals, *Long,* 309–15; "People of America" (Share-Our-Wealth Society throwaway); *Congressional Record,* 73 Cong., 1 Sess., 3321, 3329 (May 12, 1933); Alva Taylor in *Christian Century,* Aug. 9, 1933; Hodding Carter, "How Come Huey Long?" *New Republic,* Feb. 13, 1935, and Gerald L. K. Smith in same issue; Gerold Frank, "Huey Long the Second," *Nation,* July 25, 1936; G. L. K. Smith to W. D. Pelley, Aug. 15, 1933; John Roy Carlson, *Under Cover* (New York, 1943), 317; Gerald L. K. Smith, "An Open Letter To His Christian Mother," *The Cross and The Flag,* Dec. 1952; H. L. Mencken, *Heathen Days* (New York, 1943), 295; H. B. Deutsch, "Hattie and Huey," *Saturday Evening Post,* Oct. 15, 1932; Deutsch, "Huey Long — The Last Phase"; Tobin to Howe, Jan. 17, Howe to F.D.R., Feb. 21, 1935, Roosevelt Papers; Swing, *Forerunners,* 73; *American Progress,* Jan. 4, 1935.

7. He is supposed to have said this to Robert Cantwell; but Mr. Cantwell informs me (June 6, 1951), "It is not what Long said in his talk with me; but it is not basically opposed to what he said." Actually the epigram ascribed to Long would be much more characteristic of some-

one like Lawrence Dennis. Indeed, Dennis said very much the same thing: "Nothing could be more logical or in the best political tradition than for a type of fascism to be ushered into this country by leaders who are now vigorously denouncing fascism" (*Coming American Fascism*, New York, 1936, ix), or "It may be good minor tactics to call the socialism [fascism] they are inaugurating antisocialism" (*Dynamics of War and Revolution*, n.p., 1940, xxxi). Cf. Dimitrov at the Comintern in 1935: "It is a peculiarity of the development of American fascism that at the present time it appears principally in the guise of an opposition to fascism" (W. Z. Foster, *History of the Communist Party of the United States*, New York, 1952, 321).

8. H. G. Wells, *The New America: The New World* (New York, 1935), 29; Rebecca West, "The Kaleidoscope That Is Washington," *New Republic*, May 12, 1935; Rebecca West to author, Jan. 20, 1959; *Congressional Record*, 84 Cong., 1 Sess., 3637 (April 13, 1955); Owen, "Long Keeps Washington Guessing"; Russell Owen, "Huey Long Gives His Views of Dictators," *New York Times Magazine*, Feb. 10, 1935; *New York Times*, March 26, 1933; Rose Lee, "Senator Long At Home," *New Republic*, May 30, 1934; George Sokolsky, "Huey Long," *Atlantic*, Nov. 1935; Huey P. Long, *My First Days in the White House* (Harrisburg, 1935); F. Raymond Daniell, "Land of the Free," in Hanson Baldwin and Shepard Stone, eds., *We Saw It Happen* (New York, 1938), 90–91; Davis, *Long*, 22, 41, 204, 287; *Time*, April 1, 1935; Carter, "Huey Long," 343; B. L. Hoteling, "Long as a Journalist," *Journalism Quarterly*, March 1943; Williams, "Gentleman from Louisiana."

CHAPTER 5 *(Pages 69–95)*

1. For divergent, but suggestive, views of American fascism, see V. C. Ferkiss, "Populist Influences on American Fascism," *Western Political Quarterly*, June 1957; Seymour M. Lipset, *Political Man* (New York, 1960), especially 139–40, 170; Morris Schonbach, "Native Fascism During the 1930's and 1940's: A Study of Its Roots, Its Growth and Its Decline" (Ph.D. thesis, U.C.L.A., 1958); V. C. Ferkiss, "The Political and Economic Philosophy of American Fascism" (Ph.D. thesis, University of Chicago, 1954).

2. Seward Collins, "Editorial Notes," *American Review*, April 1933; Collins, "The Revival of Monarchy," *American Review*, May 1933; Collins, "The American Review's First Year," April 1934; George Sokolsky, *Labor's Fight for Power* (New York, 1934), 201, 205; Allen Tate, Seward Collins, Grace Lumpkin, letters in the *New Republic*, May 27, June 10, 1936; John Roy Carlson, *Under Cover* (New York, 1943), 198–203.

3. *New York Herald Tribune*, Dec. 18, 1934; *New York Times*, Dec. 18, 1934; Henry Hoke, *It's a Secret* (New York, 1946), 122; [J. F. Carter]

American Messiahs (New York, 1935), 24–25; and the following seven works by Ezra Pound: *Jefferson and/or Mussolini* (London, 1935), 12, 104; "Mug's Game?" *Esquire,* Feb. 1935; *ABC of Economics* (London, 1933); *Culture* (Norfolk, Conn., 1938), especially 105, 109, 254, 256; *An Introduction to the Economic Nature of the United States* (London, 1950), 12; *What Is Money For?* (London, 1951), 12; "A Thing of Beauty," *Esquire,* Nov. 1935. Also W. V. O'Connor and Edward Stone, eds., *A Casebook on Ezra Pound* (New York, 1959), 146, 156–57; V. C. Ferkiss, "Ezra Pound and American Fascism," *Journal of American Politics,* May 1955; "Ezra Pound, Silvershirt," *New Masses,* March 17, 1936.

4. See the following six works by Lawrence Dennis: *Is Capitalism Doomed?* (New York, 1932), viii, 85, 135, 178, 193, 310; "Fascism for America," *Annals,* July 1935; "Portrait of American Fascism," *American Mercury,* Dec. 1935; *The Coming American Fascism* (New York, 1936), 15, 49–50, 52, 105–06, 115, 121, 170–71, 198–99, 201, 229, 304, 308; *Dynamics of War and Revolution* (n.p., 1940), xiv; "H. G. Wells's Internationalism," *Saturday Review of Literature,* Sept. 9, 1933. Also Senate Finance Committee, *Investigation of Economic Problems: Hearings,* 72 Cong., 2 Sess. (1933), 741–44; *New York World Telegram,* April 16, 1935; *In Fact,* Jan. 17, 1944; Schonbach, "Native Fascism," 247; B. S. Lane, "The Theory and Practice of American Fascism" (honors essay, Harvard University, 1952), 10–12.

5. *New York Times,* July 15, Sept. 18, Oct. 13; 17; Dec. 13, 14, 1933; Nathaniel Weyl, "The Khaki Shirts," *New Republic,* Sept. 21, 1932; "Murder and the Khaki Shirts," *Nation,* Nov. 20, 1933; *Time,* May 7, 1934; Norman Thomas, *The Choice Before Us* (New York, 1934), 192.

6. For Pelley, see: S. D. McCoy, "Hitlerism Invades America," *Today,* April 7, 1934; Arthur Graham, "Crazy Like a Fox," *New Republic,* April 18, 1934; *Liberation,* Feb. 18, 1933, Jan. 20, 1934; Jean Burton, "The Shirts," *Modern Monthly,* Feb. 1934; *Time,* May 7, 1934; House Committee on Un-American Activities, *Investigation of Nazi and Other Propaganda,* House Report No. 153, 74 Cong., 1 Sess. (1935), 11; House Committee on Un-American Activities, *Investigation of Un-American Propaganda Activities: Hearings,* 76 Cong., 3 Sess. (1940), 7233, 7234, 7539; Eric Sevareid, *Not So Wild a Dream* (New York, 1946), 69–70; Sokolsky, *Labor's Fight for Power,* 202–04; Carlson, *Under Cover,* 399–400; Travis Hoke, *Shirts!* (New York, 1934), 9–11; John L. Spivak, *America Faces the Barricades* (New York, 1935), 221–30. For Winrod, see: Gerald B. Winrod, *Communism and the Roosevelt Brain Trust* (Wichita, 1933); Carlson, *Under Cover,* Ch. 10; R. L. Roy, *Apostles of Discord* (Boston, 1953), Ch. 3; Will Chasan and Victor Riesel, "Keep Them Out!" *Nation,* July 4, 1942; "A Report on Winrod," *Democracy's Battle,* June 1, 1949. For a perceptive analysis, Oscar Handlin, *The American People in the Twentieth Century* (Cambridge, 1954), 179–85.

7. Senate Special Committee to Investigate Lobbying Activities, *Investi-*

gation of Lobbying Activities: Hearings, 74 Cong., 2 Sess. (1936), 2070, 2073; *New York Times*, April 18, 1936; House Committee on Un-American Activities, *Investigation of Nazi Propaganda Activities and Investigation of Certain Other Propaganda Activities: Hearings*, 73 Cong., 2 Sess. (1934), especially 17–23, 113; House Com. on Un-American Activities, *Investigation of Nazi and Other Propaganda*, House Report No. 153, 74 Cong., 1 Sess. (1935), 10; *New York Times*, Nov. 23, Dec. 30, 1934; Walter Wilson, "Where Smedley Butler Stands," *New Masses*, Nov. 12, 1935.

8. Raymond Swing, *Forerunners of American Fascism* (New York, 1935), 19, 144–52; E. D. Coblentz, *William Randolph Hearst* (New York, 1952), 106, 114; John Tebbel, *Life and Good Times of William Randolph Hearst* (New York, 1952), 249, 255–59; Eugene Lyons, *The Red Decade* (Indianapolis, 1941), 118; W. R. Hearst, "Government by the Proletariat," *Vital Speeches*, Jan. 14, 1935; Ferdinand Lundberg, *Imperial Hearst* (New York, 1936), 347–52; Oliver Carlson and E. S. Bates, *Hearst: Lord of San Simeon* (New York, 1936), 252–63; Hamilton Basso, "Mr. Hearst Sees Red," *New Republic*, Jan. 16, 1935; James Wechsler, *Revolt on the Campus* (New York, 1935), 222–68; Eric F. Goldman, "Sinister Forces on Campus," *National Republic*, Aug. 1933; Nancy Bedford-Jones, "My Father Is A Liar!" *New Masses*, Sept. 3, 1935; Elizabeth Dilling, *The Red Network* (Chicago, 1934); Chard Powers Smith, "Static on the Red Network," *Scribner's*, May 1936; American Civil Liberties Union, *"Land of the Free": The Story of the Fight for Civil Liberty, 1935–36* (New York, 1936); W. S. Steele, "School Reds and Immorality," *National Republic*, May 1935; "The Enemy Within the Gates," *National Republic*, Dec. 1935; Ann Weedon, *Hearst: Counterfeit American* (New York, 1936), 21; Roger Baldwin, "Red Scare: 1935," *Common Sense*, March 1935.

9. John T. Flynn, "Other People's Money," *New Republic*, Nov. 27, 1935; Swing, *Forerunners*, 13, 167–68; W. A. White, *Selected Letters*, Walter Johnson, ed. (New York, 1947), 354; Sinclair Lewis, *It Can't Happen Here* (New York, 1935), especially 21–22, 74, 88, 103, 344–45; Elmer Davis, "Ode to Liberty," *Saturday Review of Literature*, Oct. 19, 1935; R. P. Blackmur, "Utopia or Uncle Tom's Cabin," *Nation*, Oct. 30, 1935; Winston Churchill, "What Good's a Constitution," *Collier's*, Aug. 22, 1936.

10. Ickes, *First Thousand Days*, 349–50, 354, 402; F.D.R., Press Conference #223, July 24, #226, Aug. 2, 1935; Lucille Milner, *Education of an American Liberal* (New York, 1954), 196; Harold Ickes, "Academic Freedom," *School and Society*, June 8, 1935; *New York Times*, April 23, Aug. 17, Dec. 5, 1935; Pell to Easley, July 19, 1935, Pell Papers; House Military Affairs Committee, *To Make Better Provision for the Government of the Military and Naval Forces of the United States by the Suppression of Attempts to Incite the Members Thereof to Disobedience: Hearings*, 74 Cong., 1 Sess. (1935), especially 2, 11, 17, 21, 36, 40–44, 50, 67; House Military Affairs Committee, *To Punish for*

Exerting Mutinous Influence Upon Army and Navy, House Report No.
1603, 74 Cong., 1 Sess. (1935), especially 13; House Judiciary Committee, *Crime to Promote the Overthrow of the Government: Hearing,*
74 Cong., 1 Sess. (1935), 114–15; American Civil Liberties Union,
Beat the "Incitement to Disaffection" Bill! (New York, 1935), 7; White,
Selected Letters, 353, 354; *Time,* July 20, 1936.

CHAPTER 6 *(Pages 96–108)*

1. Irving Brant, "Harry S. Truman," *New Republic,* May 7, 1945.
2. J. S. McGrath and James J. Delmont, in their memorial volume *Floyd
   Bjornsterne Olson: Minnesota's Greatest Liberal Governor* (St. Paul,
   1937), give a different version of Olson's middle name. I follow the
   form in *Who's Who,* presumably submitted by Olson himself, and used
   by G. H. Mayer in *The Political Career of Floyd Olson* (Minneapolis,
   1951).
3. Floyd Olson, "A National Third Party," *Common Sense,* Nov. 1933;
   Olson, "My Political Creed," *Common Sense,* April 1935; *Congressional
   Record,* 73 Cong., 1 Sess., 4571–72 (May 29, 1933), 9248–53 (May 22,
   1934); Selden Rodman, "A Letter from Minnesota," *New Republic,*
   Aug. 15, 1934; Fred C. Kelly, " 'You Bet Your Life I'm a Radical,' "
   Today, Dec. 22, 29, 1934; Herbert Lefkovitz, "Olson: Radical and
   Proud Of It," *Review of Reviews,* May 1935; R. L. Duffus, "Two States
   Test Third Party Hopes," *New York Times Magazine,* May 19, 1935;
   New York Times, Nov. 16, 1935; John Janney, "Minnesota's Enigma,"
   American Magazine, Sept. 1935; "Revolt in the Northwest," *Fortune,*
   April 1936; Selden Rodman, "Floyd Olson: A Tribute," *Common
   Sense,* Oct. 1936; C. R. Walker, "The Farmer-Labor Party of Minnesota," *Nation,* May 20, 1937; Lorena Hickok to Hopkins, Dec. 12, 1933,
   Hopkins Papers; F.D.R. to Farley, n.d., Hopkins to F.D.R., Aug.
   25, 1935, Roosevelt Papers; Walter W. Liggett, "Third Parties for
   Sale," *Modern Monthly,* Feb. 1935; Selden Rodman, "Walter W.
   Liggett for Sale," *Modern Monthly,* April 1935; V. F. Calverton, "Who
   Killed Walter Liggett?" *Modern Monthly,* Jan. 1936; Mayer, *Olson,*
   especially 4–6, 132, 142–49, 158, 255, 289–90; McGrath and Delmont,
   Olson, especially 121, 266–67, 312–14, 333; C. R. Walker, *American
   City* (New York, 1937), 66–71, 199–204; Sherwood Anderson, *Puzzled
   America* (New York, 1935), 268; James Gray, *Pine, Stream and Prairie*
   (New York, 1945), 128–29; James Rorty, *Where Life Is Better* (New
   York, 1936), 182–87.
4. C. E. Cason, "The La Follettes Begin a New Crusade," *New York
   Times Magazine,* Oct. 21, 1934; F.D.R., Press Conference #133, June
   27, 1934; R. L. Duffus, "Two States Test Third Party Hopes," *New
   York Times Magazine,* May 19, 1935; Louis Adamic, "A Talk with
   Phil La Follette," *Nation,* Feb. 27, 1935; Adamic, *My America* (New
   York, 1938), 551–64; *Congressional Record,* 74 Cong., 1 Sess., 13529

(Aug. 16, 1935); *New York Times,* May 20, Aug. 10, 17, Oct. 23, Nov. 9, 1934, July 28, 1935; *Time,* Nov. 19, 1934; Philip La Follette, "Capital on Strike," *Common Sense,* July 1934; Lincoln Steffens, *Letters,* Ella Winter and Granville Hicks, eds. (New York, 1938), 957; Marquis Childs, *I Write from Washington* (New York, 1942), 20; Thomas L. Stokes, *Chip Off My Shoulder* (Princeton, 1940), 364; D. R. McCoy, "The Formation of the Wisconsin Progressive Party in 1934," *Historian,* Autumn 1951.

CHAPTER 7 *(Pages 109–124)*

1. Upton Sinclair, *I, Candidate for Governor and How I Got Licked* (Pasadena, 1935), Chs. 1–2; Sinclair, *The Way Out* (Pasadena, 1933), 33; Walter Davenport, "Sinclair Gets the Glory Vote," *Collier's,* Oct. 27, 1934; Oliver Carlson, *A Mirror for Californians* (Indianapolis, 1941), Ch. 12; George Creel, *Rebel At Large* (New York, 1947), Ch. 35; Luther Whiteman and S. L. Lewis, *Glory Roads* (New York, 1936), Chs. 2–6, 19; [J. F. Carter] *American Messiahs, by the Unofficial Observer* (New York, 1935), Ch. 3; William Manchester, *Disturber of the Peace* (New York, 1951), 260; Ezra Pound, "A Matter of Modesty," *Esquire,* May 1935.
2. See the following eight works by Upton Sinclair: *We, People of America and How We Ended Poverty* (Pasadena [1935]), 14; *I, Governor of California* (Los Angeles, 1933), 7, 61; *I, Candidate,* 110–11; "An Open Letter to the American People," *Liberty,* June 10, 1933; "The EPIC Plan," *Common Sense,* May 1934; "Making Democracy Work," *Common Sense,* Sept. 1934; "National EPIC," *Common Sense,* Aug. 1935; "End Poverty in Civilization," *Nation,* Sept. 26, 1934. Also Whiteman and Lewis, *Glory Roads,* Ch. 19; Creel, *Rebel At Large,* 285–86; Carey McWilliams, "Upton Sinclair and His EPIC," *New Republic,* Aug. 22, 1934; Webb Waldron, "Can Sinclair Win?" *Today,* Oct. 6, 1934; *Time,* Sept. 3, 1934.
3. Upton Sinclair, *The Lie Factory Starts* (Los Angeles, 1934), 24, 57; Sinclair, *I, Candidate,* 54–56, 74–79, 190; Sinclair, "Open Letter"; Howe to Hopkins, March 5, Sinclair to L. A. Rochford, July 30, 1934, Roosevelt Papers; F.D.R., *Public Papers* (1934), 158; Sinclair, *I, Governor,* 2; Mary Craig Sinclair, *Southern Belle* (New York, 1957), 349; Sinclair to *The Call,* July 16, 1947; F.D.R., Press Conference #141, Sept. 5, #142, Sept. 7, 1934; Theodore Dreiser, "The Epic Sinclair," *Esquire,* Dec. 1934; Report of a Conference with the President, Nov. 9, 1939, National Resources Planning Board Papers; J. F. T. O'Connor, Diary, Oct. 3, 1934; Frances Perkins, *The Roosevelt I Knew* (New York, 1946), 124; R. G. Tugwell, *The Democratic Roosevelt* (New York, 1957), 298; R. G. Cleland, *California in Our Time* (New York, 1947), 226; *Time,* Sept. 10, 17, 1934; *New Masses,* Aug. 14, Sept. 11, 1934.

4. Sinclair, *I, Candidate*, 45–46, 141, 151–56, 172–88, 203; Sinclair, *We, People*, 1; Sinclair, *Lie Factory;* Irwin Ross, *The Image Merchants* (New York, 1959), 70; Leo Rosten, *Hollywood* (New York, 1941), 135–39; Johnson to Ickes, Sept. 17, Sinclair to F.D.R., Oct. 5, 18, F.D.R. to Pittman, Oct. 9, 1934, Early to Eleanor Roosevelt, n.d., Roosevelt Papers; Sinclair, "End Poverty in Civilization"; Upton Sinclair, "The Future of EPIC," *Nation,* Nov. 28, 1934; *New York Times,* Oct. 27, 1934; Whiteman and Lewis, *Glory Roads,* Ch. 20; Theodore Roosevelt, *Letters,* E. E. Morison, ed. (Cambridge, 1952), V, 209; F.D.R., Press Conference #153, Oct. 26, 1934; Moley, *After Seven Years,* 298–99; O'Connor, Diary, Oct. 26, 28, 29, 31, Nov. 1, 2, 7, 13, 15, 1934; Sinclair, *Southern Belle,* 354, 358.

5. Sinclair, *I, Candidate,* 46–48, 101, 200, 211–13; Sinclair, *We, People,* 21, 31; *New Masses,* Aug. 14, 1934; Jerry Voorhis, *Confessions of a Congressman* (Garden City, 1947), 17–18; Rosten, *Hollywood,* 135–39.

6. "The Shape of Things," *Nation,* June 24, 1936; Alfred Bingham, *Insurgent America* (New York, 1935), 190, 224; John Gunther, *Inside U.S.A.* (New York, 1947), 99; *Newsweek,* Feb. 16, 1948.

CHAPTER 8 *(Pages 125–133)*

1. F. H. La Guardia, *The Making of an Insurgent* (New York, 1948); Arthur Mann, *La Guardia: A Fighter Against His Times, 1882–1933* (Philadelphia, 1959), especially 114, 242–44; L. M. Limpus and Burr Leyson, *This Man La Guardia* (New York, 1938), especially 18, 153, 164–65; Jay Franklin, *La Guardia: A Biography* (New York, 1937), especially 148; Ernest Cuneo, *Life With Fiorello* (New York, 1955), especially ix–xi, 33, 39, 48, 62; Newbold Morris, *Let the Chips Fall* (New York, 1955), Ch. 5; La Guardia to Maverick, May 26, 1939, Maverick Papers; *New York Times,* Jan. 3, May 29, 1934; Russell Owen, "The Mayor," *New York Times Magazine,* July 1, 1934; Karl Schriftgiesser, "Portrait of a Mayor," *Atlantic,* Jan. 1938; Milton MacKaye, "Fiorello H. La Guardia," *Ladies' Home Journal,* Jan. 1938. I am particularly indebted to "The Era of La Guardia" (Ph.D. thesis, Harvard Univ., 1957), a doctoral dissertation by my student Charles Garrett, both for discriminating insights and for the what's-the-matter-with-a-little-guy story.

2. E. J. Flynn, *You're the Boss* (New York, 1947), Ch. 11; J. A. Farley, *Jim Farley's Story* (New York, 1948), 42–43; Limpus and Leyson, *La Guardia,* Ch. 20; Garrett, "The Era of La Guardia."

3. Robert Moses, "La Guardia — A Salute and a Memoir," *New York Times Magazine,* Sept. 8, 1957; Owen, "The Mayor"; La Guardia, "New York Must Clean House," *Liberty,* Jan. 20, 1934; Franklin, *La Guardia,* 166; James Marshall, "Memories of La Guardia," *New York Herald Tribune,* Dec. 11, 1954; Morris, *Let the Chips Fall,* 118; *Time,* Sept. 29, 1947; Daniel Bell, "Crime as an American Way of Life,"

Antioch Review, Summer 1953; *New York Times,* Oct. 23, 1934, May 28, June 20, 1935; Benjamin Stolberg, *The Story of the CIO* (New York, 1938), 57.

CHAPTER 9 *(Pages 134–146)*

1. Harry S. Truman, *Memoirs: Year of Decisions* (New York, 1955), 144; George Creel, "The Retiring Senator," *Collier's,* Jan. 25, 1936.
2. In view of manifest defects in editing, the Dodd Diary cannot be taken as an exclusive source. However, Tugwell was sufficiently impressed by the evening to get independent statements the next day from both Appleby and Carter; and these, along with Tugwell's own diary notations, support Dodd's general account.
3. On Wheeler: [J. F. Carter] *American Messiahs* (New York, 1935), Ch. 7; C. W. Gilbert, *You Takes Your Choice* (New York, 1924), 160–67; Ray Tucker and F. R. Barkley, *Sons of the Wild Jackass* (Boston, 1932), Ch. 12; John Gunther, *Inside U.S.A.* (New York, 1947), 174–78; Marquis Childs, *I Write from Washington* (New York, 1942), 186–90; E. G. Lowry, "The Senate's No. 1 Investigator," *Today,* Sept. 14, 1935; Hamilton Basso, "Burton the Bronc," *New Republic,* April 22, 1940; Robert Bendiner, "Burton K. Wheeler," *Nation,* April 27, 1940; Richard Neuberger, "Wheeler of Montana," *Harper's,* May 1940; Joseph Kinsey Howard, "The Decline and Fall of Burton K. Wheeler," *Harper's,* March 1947; Blair Coan, *The Red Web* (Chicago, 1925); Alva Johnston, "President Tamer," *Saturday Evening Post,* Nov. 13, 1937; "Where Are the Pre-War Radicals," *Survey,* Feb. 1, 1926; Tugwell, Diary, Feb. 2, 1935, with statements by Paul Appleby and J. F. Carter; W. E. Dodd, *Ambassador Dodd's Diary,* W. E. Dodd, Jr., and Martha Dodd, eds. (New York, 1941), 212–13; F.D.R., Press Conference #714, Jan. 31, 1941; Max Lowenthal, *The Federal Bureau of Investigation* (New York, 1950), 365. On Cutting: Tucker and Barkley, *Sons of the Wild Jackass,* Ch. 9; Norris to F.D.R., Jan. 19, F.D.R. to Norris, Jan. 24, 1934, Roosevelt Papers; *New York Times,* May 7, 21, 1935; Oswald Garrison Villard, "Senator Cutting," *Nation,* May 22, 1935; Moley, *After Seven Years,* 125, 191, 193; Richard Neuberger and S. B. Kahn, *Integrity:The Life of George W. Norris* (New York, 1937); Ickes, *First Thousand Days,* 217, 358–59; Henry S. Commager to the author, Feb. 5, 1957.
4. Maury Maverick, *A Maverick American* (New York, 1937), especially 16–17, 28, 58, 63; Maverick, *In Blood and Ink* (New York, 1939); Maverick to Jennings Perry, Jan. 6, 1936, Maverick Papers; Jonathan Mitchell, "Front-Fighters in Congress," *New Republic,* June 19, 1935; *New York Times,* March 10, 15, 17, 22, 1935.
5. Thomas R. Amlie, "The Collapse of Capitalism," *Common Sense,* Oct. 1933; Amlie, "Dialectics Adrift," *Common Sense,* July 1934; Alfred Bingham, "The Farm Labor Political Federation," *Common Sense,*

Oct. 1933; Robert Whitcomb and Selden Rodman, "Amlie: New Party Builder," *Common Sense*, May 1936; House Judiciary Committee, *Crime to Promote the Overthrow of the Government: Hearing*, 74 Cong., 1 Sess. (1935), 123; Marguerite Young, "Congressman Amlie Sees Red," *New Masses*, Aug. 13, 1935; "An Exclusive Labor Party," *New Masses*, July 16, 1935.

CHAPTER 10 *(Pages 147–161)*

1. Alfred Bingham, *Insurgent America* (New York, 1935), 5, 47, 62, 178, 189–90, 196–98, 210–11, 226–27, 237–46; Bingham, *Man's Estate* (New York, 1939), 34–36; Bingham to author, July 2, 1956; Selden Rodman to author, June 25, 1956; Alfred Bingham and Selden Rodman, eds., *Challenge to the New Deal* (New York, 1934), 133–34; *New York Times*, Jan. 1, 5, Dec. 9, 10, 1934, March 6, May 5, 30, July 1, 5–7, Aug. 21, 23, 1935; R. M. Lovett, "A Party in Embryo," *New Republic*, July 24, 1935; Thomas Amlie, "The American Commonwealth Federation," *Common Sense*, Aug. 1935; Marguerite Young, "Congressman Amlie Sees Red," *New Masses*, Aug. 13, 1935; Donald McCoy, *Angry Voices* (Lawrence, Kansas, 1958), 36–42, 75–82.

2. C. A. Beard and Mary Beard, *The Rise of American Civilization* (New York, 1933), II, 253; Beard and Beard, *The American Spirit* (New York, 1942), 472; John Dewey, "A Great American Prophet," *Common Sense*, April 1934; Heywood Broun, *It Seems to Me* (New York, 1935), 207–10; *New York Times*, March 15, 1935; Bingham, *Insurgent America*, 5, and reviews of Beard's *Open Door* and Dewey's *Liberalism and Social Action*, *Common Sense*, Feb., Sept. 1935; Schlesinger, *Crisis*, Ch. 17.

3. Beard and Beard, *American Spirit*, 163–67; C. A. Beard "That Promise of American Life," *New Republic*, Feb. 6, 1935, and *A Charter for the Social Sciences in the Schools* (New York, 1932), 33, 79–80, and "Written History As an Act of Faith," *American Historical Review*, Jan. 1934, and "The World As I Want It," *Forum*, June 1934, and "America Must Stay Big," *Today*, Sept. 14, 1935, and "The Anti-Trust Racket," *New Republic*, Sept. 21, 1938; American Historical Association, *Report of the Commission on Social Studies: Conclusions and Recommendations* (New York, 1934), 16–17; C. A. Beard and G. H. E. Smith, *The Future Comes: A Study of the New Deal* (New York, 1933), viii; Beard, *The Open Door at Home* (New York, 1934), 213–14, 313–19; Beard and Mary R. Beard, *America in Mid-Passage* (New York, 1939), 452; Beard, "National Politics and War," *Scribner's*, Feb. 1935; Harry D. Gideonse, "Nationalist Collectivism and Charles A. Beard," *Journal of Political Economy*, Dec. 1935; Cushing Strout, "The Twentieth Century Enlightenment," *American Political Science Review*, June 1955.

4. John Dewey, "Prospects for a Third Party," *New Republic*, July 27, 1932, and "The Future of Radical Political Action," *Nation*, Jan. 4,

1933; League for Independent Political Action, *Audacity! More Audacity! Always Audacity!* (New York, 1933); John Dewey, Introduction to in Bingham and Rodman, eds., *Challenge to the New Deal,* vi; Dewey, "The Future of Liberalism," *School and Society,* Jan. 19, 1935; Dewey, *Liberalism and Social Action* (New York, 1935), 48, 54–55, 62, 70–73, 88–91 (my italics).

5. *World Tomorrow,* May 10, 24, 1934; S. Wells Utley, "Render Unto Caesar," *Nation's Business,* Nov. 1935; Jerome Davis, "Capitalism and the Churches," *Harper's,* Jan. 1937.

6. See the following six works by Reinhold Niebuhr, *Reflections on the End of an Era* (New York, 1934), 24, 30, 53, 59, 230; "After Capitalism — What?" *World Tomorrow,* March 1, 1933; "Our Romantic Radicals," *Christian Century,* April 10, 1935; "The National Elections," *Radical Religion,* Winter 1936; "Roosevelt's Merry-Go-Round," *Radical Religion,* Spring 1938; "Politics and the Christian Ethic," *Christianity and Society,* Spring 1940. Cf. also Arthur M. Schlesinger, Jr., "Reinhold Niebuhr's Role in American Political Thought and Life," in C. W. Kegley and R. W. Bretall, eds., *Reinhold Niebuhr: His Religious, Social and Political Thought* (New York, 1956), Ch. 5.

7. Alfred Bingham, Introduction to *Challenge to the New Deal,* 4; Bingham, *Insurgent America,* 184–85; "Franklin Delano Roosevelt," *Common Sense,* Sept. 1934; W. H. Hale, "The Opium Wears Off," *Common Sense,* Sept. 1934; R. S. Lynd, *Knowledge for What?* (Princeton, 1939); L. S. Mitchell, *Two Lives* (New York, 1953), 552; R. S. Lynd, "The Implications of Economic Planning for Sociology," *American Sociological Review,* Feb. 1944; "Questionnaire on Social Objectives," *New Republic,* April 17, 1935; John T. Flynn, "The New Capitalism," *Collier's,* March 18, 1933; Flynn, "NRA: 1934," *Common Sense,* May 1934; Flynn, "The Collapse of the New Deal," *Common Sense,* Nov. 1934; Flynn, "Roosevelt Faces 1936," *Scribner's,* July 1934; Flynn, "Who Started This Regimentation?" *Scribner's,* Sept. 1934.

8. William Saroyan, "Aspirin Is a Member of the NRA," *American Mercury,* May 1934.

CHAPTER 11 *(Pages 162–180)*

1. C. A. and Mary R. Beard, *The American Spirit* (New York, 1942), 527, 531; Max Eastman, *Heroes I Have Known* (New York, 1942), 312; See the eleven following essays by Reinhold Niebuhr: "Marx, Barth and Israel's Prophets," *Christian Century,* Jan. 30, 1935; "Communism and the Clergy," *Christian Century,* Aug. 19, 1953; "Our Romantic Radicals," *Christian Century,* April 10, 1935; "Socialist Decision and Christian Conscience," *Radical Religion,* Spring 1938; "Russia and Karl Marx," *Nation,* May 7, 1938; "The Religion of Communism," *Atlantic,* April 1931; "Optimism and Utopianism," *World Tomorrow,*

Feb. 22, 1933; "Religion and Marxism," *Modern Monthly*, Feb. 1935; "Modern Utopians," *Scribner's*, Sept. 1936; "The Revolutionary Moment," *American Socialist Quarterly*, June 1935; "Liberals and the Marxist Heresy," *New Republic*, Oct. 12, 1953. Cf. also Arthur M. Schlesinger, Jr., "Reinhold Niebuhr's Role in American Political Thought and Life," in C. W. Kegley and R. W. Bretall, eds., *Reinhold Niebuhr: His Religious, Social and Political Thought* (New York, 1956), 125–50.

2. *New York Times*, Feb. 17, 1934; "To John Dos Passos," *New Masses*, March 6, 1934; letter from Algernon Lee, *New Republic*, March 7, 1934.

3. For an earlier discussion of the Marxist appeal, see Schlesinger, *Crisis*, 209–23.

4. Henry Hart, ed., *American Writers' Congress* (New York, 1935), 10–11, 45, 58, 83; Scott Fitzgerald, *The Crack-Up*, Edmund Wilson, ed. (Norfolk, Conn., 1945), 311; Lionel Trilling, "Politics and the Liberal," *Nation*, July 4, 1934; W. B. Rideout, *The Radical Novel in the United States, 1900–1954* (Cambridge, 1956), 171; Philip Rahv, "Proletarian Literature: A Political Autopsy," *Southern Review*, Winter 1939; Murray Kempton, *Part of Our Time* (New York, 1955), Ch. 4; Eugene Lyons, *The Red Decade* (New York, 1941), Ch. 12; Granville Hicks, *Where We Came Out* (New York, 1954), Ch. 4; "Communism and the American Writer," *Newberry Library Bulletin*, Aug. 1959.

5. Lewis Corey, *The Decline of American Capitalism* (New York, 1934), 11, 113, 506; Corey, *The Crisis of the Middle Class* (New York, 1935), 331; Alfred Bingham in *Common Sense*, Oct. 1934; Theodore Draper, *The Roots of American Communism* (New York, 1957), 229–32, 293–300.

6. See the following eight works by H. J. Laski, *Authority in the Modern State* (New Haven, 1919), 374; "The Prospects of Constitutional Government," *Political Quarterly*, July–Sept. 1930; *Democracy in Crisis* (Chapel Hill, 1933), 9, 30, 40, 46–47, 84, 189, 213; *The State in Theory and Practice* (New York, 1935), 163; "Why I Am a Marxist," *Nation*, Jan. 14, 1939; "The Roosevelt Experiment," *Atlantic*, Feb. 1934; "What Is Vital in Democracy?" *Survey Graphic*, April 1935; "Communism Faces the Wrath to Come," *New Republic*, Oct. 30, 1935. Cf. also Laski and J. M. Keynes, "Can America Spend Its Way Into Recovery?" *Redbook*, Dec. 1934; Henry Hazlitt, "The Twilight of Capitalist Democracy," *Nation*, April 12, 1933; Mark DeW. Howe, ed., *Holmes-Laski Letters* (Cambridge, 1953), 1470; Kingsley Martin, *Harold Laski* (London, 1953), especially 82–85, 91; H. A. Deane, *The Political Ideas of Harold J. Laski* (New York, 1955), especially 19, 43, 177, 191, 197.

7. James Wechsler, *The Age of Suspicion* (New York, 1953), 44; Benjamin Stolberg and W. J. Vinton, *Economic Consequences of the New Deal* (New York, 1935), 5, 11, 63–64, 85; John Strachey, *The Coming Struggle for Power* (New York, 1935), 405; Strachey, "To Explain — Or To

Change?" *New Masses*, Jan. 22, 1935; Abelard [I. F.] Stone, "Roosevelt Moves Toward Fascism," *Modern Monthly*, June 1933; Max Lerner, "What Is Usable in Veblen?" *New Republic*, May 15, 1935; Louis M. Hacker, *The Farmer Is Doomed* (New York, 1933), 24; Elliot Cohen, "Stalin Buries Revolution — Prematurely," *Nation*, May 9, 1934; "An Open Letter to American Intellectuals," *Modern Monthly*, March 1934; "Social Control vs. the Constitution," *New Republic*, June 12, 1935 (my italics).

When one considers the panic-stricken intellectuals of 1934, one cannot but reflect how many of these men have remained in a state of panic ever since. For them, the capitalist system has always been a fragile thing on the verge of imminent collapse before a revolutionary conspiracy; but, whereas they looked on this situation with complacency in the thirties, they looked on it with horror in the fifties. Still, the suppressed hysteria, the sense of crisis, the conviction of impending catastrophe have remained constant. This doubtless explains why, for example, Mr. Burnham backed revolution in 1934 and Senator McCarthy twenty years later. He had changed a good deal less than it might seem on the surface.

8. Daniel Bell, "The Background and Development of Marxian Socialism in the United States," in D. D. Egbert and Stow Persons, eds., *Socialism and American Life* (Princeton, 1952), I, 369–83; D. A. Shannon, *The Socialist Party of America* (New York, 1955), Ch. 10; "Full Stenographic Report of the Declaration of Principles Adopted at the National Convention," *American Socialist Quarterly*, supp., July 1934; John Herling, "The Socialist Convention," *New Republic*, June 20, 1934; Norman Thomas, *A Socialist Looks at the New Deal* (New York, 1933), 4, 7; Thomas, *The Choice Before Us* (New York, 1934), 92, 126, 151, 198–99, 235; D. P. Berenberg, " 'Pie in the Sky,' " *American Socialist Quarterly*, March 1935; Norman Thomas, "On Our Way," *Saturday Review of Literature*, April 14, 1934; Thomas, "The Campaign of 1934," *American Socialist Quarterly*, Autumn 1934; William Hard, "Left, Right," *Redbook*, April 1935; Eunice Clark, "The Failure of the Socialist Party," *Common Sense*, Oct. 1934; Louis Waldman, *Labor Lawyer* (New York, 1944), 184; *New York Times*, Oct. 21, 1932, Oct. 18, 21, 1934, Feb. 9, 1935.

CHAPTER 12 *(Pages 181–207)*

1. Lincoln Steffens, *Letters*, Ella Winter and Granville Hicks, eds. (New York, 1938), 878, 949, 988, 1001, 1051; Lorena Hickok to Harry Hopkins [late 1934], Hopkins Papers; "No Rights for Lynchers," *New Masses*, Jan. 12, 1934; Gil Green, *Youth Confronts the Blue Eagle* (New York, 1933), 27–28.

2. R. M. Lovett, Introduction to James Wechsler, *Revolt on the Campus* (New York, 1935), ix; Steffens, *Letters*, 1002, 1028; Granville

Hicks, *I Like America* (New York, 1938), 144–45; Benjamin Davis, Jr.,
"Paul Robeson," *Soviet Russia Today*, Aug. 1936; Cecil B. De Mille in
A. Arossev, ed., *Soviet Cinema* (Moscow, 1935), 263; Eugene Lyons,
The Red Decade (New York, 1941), Chs. 9–11; Marcel Proust, *Remembrance of Things Past* (New York, 1934), I, 190.

3. *Time*, April 16, 1934; Steffens, *Letters*, 983, 988; Lincoln Steffens, "A
Muckraker's Memoirs," *Nation*, Dec. 20, 1933; Dwight Macdonald,
"The Defense of Everybody," *New Yorker*, July 18, 1953; Janet Flanner, "A Woman in the House," *New Yorker*, May 8, 1949; Clifford
Odets, *Waiting for Lefty and Till the Day I Die* (New York, 1935),
3–4, 50–54.

4. Chambers in *New York Herald Tribune*, Feb. 1, 1950; Lawrence
Gately, "Almost a Red," *American*, Nov. 1935; House Committee on
Un-American Activities, *Hearings Regarding Communism in the
United States Government*, 81 Cong., 2 Sess. (1950), 2845; Nathaniel
Weyl, " 'I Was in a Communist Unit with Hiss,' " *U.S. News and
World Report*, Jan. 9, 1953; John Gates, *The Story of an American
Communist* (New York, 1958), 18–19; Murray Kempton, *Part of Our
Time* (New York, 1955), 303; Hicks, *I Like America*, 215–16; Whittaker
Chambers, *Witness* (New York, 1952), 358.

5. House Committee on Un-American Activities, *Investigation of Nazi
and Other Propaganda*, House Report No. 153, 74 Cong., 1 Sess.
(1935), 14; W. Z. Foster, *Toward Soviet America* (New York, 1932);
W. Z. Foster, *Pages from a Worker's Life* (New York, 1939), 284; Earl
Browder, *Report of the Central Committee to the Eighth Convention
of the Communist Party of America* (New York, 1934), 20–21; Browder,
Communism in the United States (New York, 1935), 14, 115; *Daily
Worker* (New York), July 10, 1933, Jan. 2, 1934, Feb. 9, 1935; "Not a
Sweep for the New Deal," *New Masses*, Nov. 27, 1934; Green, *Youth
Confronts the Blue Eagle*, 3; Editorial Notes, *New Masses*, April 2,
16, 1935; Harold M. Ware and Webster Powell, "Planning for Permanent Poverty," *Harper's*, April 1935; Richard H. Rovere, "Vito
Marcantonio," *Harper's*, March 1944; House Ways and Means Committee, *Economic Security Act: Hearings*, 74 Cong., 1 Sess. (1935),
845.

6. Ickes, *First Thousand Days*, 62; Hopkins interview, *New York Times*,
Aug. 24, 1934; L. H. Robbins, "Ickes Defines the Task Ahead," *New
York Times Magazine*, April 1, 1934; Jerome Frank obituary, *New
York Times*, Jan. 14, 1957; Paul Appleby to F. W. Loring, March 3,
1934, Department of Agriculture Papers; "On the Dole: 17,000,000,"
Fortune, Oct. 1934; Raymond Moley, "Our Present Discontent," *Today*, Sept. 8, 1934; Browder, *Communism in the United States*, 325–26;
Archibald MacLeish, "Preface to an American Manifesto," *Forum*,
April 1934; Adolf A. Berle, Jr., in *Nation*, Sept. 12, 1934.

7. MacLeish, "Preface to an American Manifesto"; Felix Frankfurter,
"The Young Men Go to Washington," *Fortune*, Jan. 1936; Upton
Sinclair in *New Masses*, Aug. 14, 1934; Gertrude Springer, "Rising to

a New Challenge," *Survey*, June 1934; D. C. Coyle, "Illusions Regarding Revolution," *Survey*, July 1934; H. A. Wallace, *New Frontiers* (New York, 1934), 51; H. L. Ickes, "Academic Freedom," *School and Society*, June 8, 1935; Frances Perkins, "Eight Years as Madame Secretary," *Fortune*, Sept. 1941.

8. Raymond Moley, "Common Sense about Communism," *Today*, May 26, 1934; MacLeish, "Preface to an American Manifesto"; Henry Wallace, "Violence, For and Against," *Common Sense*, Jan. 1938; John T. Flynn, "To Get Rich Scare the Rich," *New Republic*, Sept. 9, 1936; American Federation of Labor, *Proceedings of the Fifty-Fifth Annual Convention* (Washington [1936]), 746-47; J. M. Keynes, *Essays in Persuasion* (London, 1931), 311.

9. Browder, *Report . . . to the Eighth Convention . . .*, 56, 76, 81, 123; House Labor Committee, *Unemployment, Old-Age and Social Insurance: Hearings*, 74 Cong., 1 Sess. (1935), 457; Browder, *Communism in the United States*, 244; Moley, "Common Sense about Communism,"; Herbert Solow, "Stalin's Great American Hoax," *American Mercury*, Dec. 1939; Lyons, *Red Decade*, Chs. 12-13; *Program of American Youth Congress* (New York, 1934); Wechsler, *Revolt On the Campus*, 171-77; Orrick Johns, "The John Reed Clubs Meet," *New Masses*, Oct. 30, 1934; *New Masses*, Feb. 26, 1935.

10. Chambers, *Witness*, 275-443; House Un-American Activities Committee, *The Shameful Years: Thirty Years of Soviet Espionage in the United States*, House Report No. 1229, 82 Cong., 2 Sess. (1952), 5-21; David Dallin, *Soviet Espionage* (New Haven, 1955), 1-24, 289-413; Weyl, " 'I Was in a Communist Unit' "; H. J. Wadleigh, "Why I Spied for the Communists," *New York Post*, July 11-24, 1949; Alexander Foote, "Watching a Spy," *London Observer*, Oct. 2, 1955; Foote, *Handbook for Spies* (New York, 1949), 3, 31, 46-47; Hede Massing, *This Deception* (New York, 1951), 163-90; House Un-American Activities Committee, *Communist Espionage in the United States Government: Hearings*, 80 Cong., 2 Sess. (1948), 1180-91, 1279, 1349-52; *New York Times*, Nov. 3, 1949.

11. *Time*, February 14, 1955; Weyl, " 'I Was in a Communist Unit' "; Wallace to Cummings, Feb. 8, 1934, Department of Agriculture Papers; F.D.R. to Perkins, Aug. 29, Sept. 18, 1935, Roosevelt Papers; Don Whitehead, *The FBI Story* (New York, 1956), Ch. 18.

CHAPTER 13 *(Pages 211-241)*

1. Charles A. Beard, "The President Loses Prestige," *Current History*, April 1935.

2. *New York Times*, April 22, 1934; Raymond Moley, "And Now Give Us Good Men," *Today*, May 19, 1934; F.D.R., *Public Papers* (1934), 125, 298; Ickes, *First Thousand Days*, 244, 303, 342; *Time*, Feb. 18, 1935; Tugwell, Diary, Feb. 24, 1935; J. David Stern to Joseph Guffey,

Feb. 6, 1935, Roosevelt Papers; Bruce Bliven, "Washington Revisited," *New Republic*, March 13, 1935; Beard, "The President Loses Prestige"; Francis Brown, "Washington Tempo," *Current History*, May 1935.

3. R. G. Tugwell, "The Experimental Roosevelt," *Political Quarterly*, July-September 1950. Moley wrote as late as 1945: "I happen to be one of those who believe that much the NRA accomplished will have to be done over again in other ways and much it failed to accomplish will have to be undertaken sooner or later in any industrial society as intricate as ours." Cf. Raymond Moley, *The Hays Office* (Indianapolis, 1945), 203.

4. Mordecai Ezekiel, *$2500 A Year* (New York, 1936), 30, 38, 83; Ezekiel, *Jobs for All* (New York, 1939), 12, 20, 186; Executive Council, Report, Oct. 2, 1934; Ezekiel, "AAA in Reverse," *Common Sense*, June 1937; Harold Loeb, "Economic Planning Through 'Industrial Adjustment,'" *Common Sense*, June 1937; T. R. Amlie, "The Answer to Fascism," *Common Sense*, Aug. 1937; Herbert Harris, "'This Bill Bears Watching,'" *Survey Graphic*, April 1938; Wagner to Ezekiel, Feb. 28, Ezekiel to Wagner, March 14, 1936, Ezekiel to D. L. Thompson, Feb. 2, 1937, Ezekiel to R. W. Sibly, Oct. 31, 1939, Department of Agriculture Papers; L. M. Graves, "The Folly of Industrial Planning," *Harper's*, Feb. 1938; Clair Wilcox, "Can We Legislate Abundance?" *Plan Age*, Jan. 1939; N. I. Stone, "Mordecai Ezekiel's Jobs for All," *Plan Age*, June 1939.

5. G. C. Means, *Industrial Prices and Their Relative Inflexibility* (Sen. Document No. 13, 74 Cong., 1 Sess., Jan. 17, 1935), 12-13, 36; Caroline F. Ware and G. C. Means, *The Modern Economy in Action* (New York, 1936), 208; "Statement submitted by G. C. Means, Industrial Committee, National Resources Committee, October 12, 1935," National Resources Planning Board Papers.

6. 285 U.S. 311; A. T. Mason, *Brandeis: A Free Man's Life* (New York, 1946), 602, 616, 621; Brandeis to Laski, Sept. 21, 1921; A. M. Bickel, "Passion and Patience: Centennial-year Thoughts on 'The Brandeis Way,'" *New Republic*, Nov. 12, 1956; Henry L. Stimson, Diary, Jan. 15, 1932; Charles E. Wyzanski, Jr., "Brandeis," *Atlantic*, Nov. 1956; (and Dean Acheson to Wyzanski, Feb. 27, 1956); Mark DeW. Howe, ed., *Holmes-Laski Letters* (Cambridge, 1953), 1298-99; Felix Frankfurter, "Mr. Justice Brandeis and the Constitution," *Harvard Law Review*, Nov. 1931; Ickes, *First Thousand Days*, 6; Marquis W. Childs, *I Write from Washington* (New York, 1942), 43-44; Edith B. Helm, *The Captains and the Kings* (New York, 1954), 128; Catherine Drinker Bowen, "The Magnificence of Age," *Harper's*, April 1953; Harold J. Laski, "Mr. Justice Brandeis," *Harper's*, Jan. 1934; Elizabeth Glendower Evans, "Mr. Justice Brandeis," *Survey*, Nov. 1, 1931; *Harvard Law Review*, Dec. 1941; James M. Landis, "Mr. Justice Brandeis: A Law Clerk's View," *Publications of the American Jewish Historical Society*, June 1957; Paul A. Freund, "The Liberalism of Justice Brandeis," *American Jewish Archives*, April 1958; Freund, "Mr. Justice Brandeis,"

in Allison Dunham and P. B. Kurland, eds., *Mr. Justice* (Chicago, 1956), 98, 101.

7. Dean Acheson, "Mr. Justice Brandeis," *Harvard Law Review*, Dec. 1941; Paul Freund, "Mr. Justice Brandeis," *Harvard Law Review*, Dec. 1941; Richard L. Neuberger, "A Citizen of the Entire Country," *Progressive*, Oct. 25, 1941; Paul Freund, "Mr. Justice Brandeis: A Centennial Memoir," *Harvard Law Review*, March 1957; Jonathan Daniels, *The Man of Independence* (Philadelphia, 1950), 185–87; Felix Frankfurter, draft for Democratic platform, June 1936, Roosevelt Papers; Frankfurter, "Democracy and the Expert," *Atlantic*, Nov. 1930; Frankfurter, "The Young Men Go to Washington," *Fortune*, Jan. 1936; Frankfurter, *The Public and Its Government* (New Haven, 1930), 127–28, 137, 139; Frankfurter, *Law and Politics* (New York, 1939), 246–49; Felix Frankfurter in *New York Times*, March 17, 1944; Joseph Alsop and Robert Kintner, *Men Around the President* (New York, 1939), 47–52; H. B. Phillips, *Felix Frankfurter Reminisces* (New York, 1960), 256, 266.

8. Grace Tully, *F.D.R., My Boss* (New York, 1949), 141–42; Alsop and Kintner, *Men Around the President*, 54–61; Alva Johnston, "White House Tommy," *Saturday Evening Post*, July 31, 1937; Walter Davenport, "It Seems There Were Two Irishmen," *Collier's*, Sept. 10, 1938; Charles Michelson, *The Ghost Talks* (New York, 1944), 190–92; Benjamin V. Cohen, "The Goblins Will Get You," *Today*, Sept. 29, 1934; Amos Pinchot to F.D.R., May 17, 1938, *Congressional Record*, 75 Cong., 3 Sess. (May 23, 1938), 7258; "Mr. Kennedy the Chairman," *Fortune*, Sept. 1937; T. G. Corcoran to author, April 1, 1958; Charles E. Wyzanski, Jr., "Reminiscences" (Oral History Research Office), 153; Oscar Cox, "Wartime Interpretation of Legal Orders," quoted by H. D. Lasswell, *The Analysis of Political Behavior* (London, 1948), 84.

9. See following articles and books by D. C. Coyle: "Illusions Regarding Revolution," *Survey*, July 1934; "Free Initiative and Free Prices," *Scribner's*, June 1935; "Decentralize Industry," *Virginia Quarterly Review*, July 1935; "The Twilight of National Planning," *Harper's*, Oct. 1935; "Tax for Democracy!" *Survey Graphic*, Aug. 1937; *The Irrepressible Conflict: Business vs. Finance* (New York, 1932); *Brass Tacks* (Washington, 1936), especially 121–26; *The American Way* (New York, 1938), especially 28–31, 37–44; *Roads to a New America* (New York, 1938), especially Chs. 21–23, 31–39. Also Hapgood to Brandeis, Aug. 3, 1935, Roosevelt Papers; F.D.R., Press Conference #318, Sept. 8, 1936; Corcoran to author, April 1, 1958.

10. Adolf A. Berle, Jr., and G. C. Means, *The Modern Corporation and Private Property* (New York, 1932), viii; Felix Frankfurter, ed., *Mr. Justice Brandeis* (New Haven, 1932), 129–30; Moley, *After Seven Years*, 24, 289; Tugwell, Diary, April 15, 1933, April 23, 26, 1934; F.D.R., *Personal Letters*, III, 562; Raymond Moley, "The March of Circumstance," *Today*, July 13, 1935; Tugwell, "New Deal Memoir," Ch. 2; F.D.R., Press Conference #184, Feb. 15, 1935; Jay Franklin,

"Big Bad Wolves vs. Little Hot Dogs," *Today*, Nov. 2, 1935; W. M. Kiplinger, "What's Ahead in Washington," *Nation's Business*, Aug. 1935.

11. Moley, *After Seven Years*, 375; Raymond Moley, "What Are Security Payments?" *Today*, Feb. 2, 1935; Tugwell, "New Deal Memoir," Ch. 2; Frankfurter to Moley, Feb. 9, 1933 (enclosing Brandeis to Frankfurter, Jan. 31, 1933), Moley Papers; Frankfurter to F.D.R., Sept. 14, 1931, Roosevelt Papers; W. T. Foster, "Economic Consequences of the New Deal," *Atlantic*, Dec. 1933; Schlesinger, *Crisis*, 134–36; *Balancing the Budget: Federal Fiscal Policy During Depression. A Statement by a University of Chicago Round Table* (Chicago, 1933).

12. Senate Finance Committee, *Investigation of Economic Problems: Hearings*, 72 Cong., 2 Sess. (1933), 705–33; M. S. Eccles with Sidney Hyman, *Beckoning Frontiers* (New York, 1951), Parts I–III; M. S. Eccles, *Economic Balance and a Balanced Budget*, R. L. Weissman, ed. (New York, 1940), 1–12; National Emergency Council, Reports by the Governor of the Federal Reserve Board, March 27, April 24, 1935, National Archives; Dern to F.D.R., Dec. 20, 1934, Roosevelt Papers; Raymond Clapper, "Banker or Bureaucrat?" *Review of Reviews*, July, 1935; "Marriner Stoddard Eccles," *Fortune*, Feb. 1935; George Creel, "A Banker Who Can Talk," *Collier's*, June 29, 1935; Paul W. Ward, "Morgenthau and His Friends," *Nation*, Aug. 14, 1935.

CHAPTER 14 *(Pages 242–262)*

1. Forrest Davis, *Huey Long* (New York, 1935), 244–61; Marquis Childs, *I Write from Washington* (New York, 1942), 18; Howe to F.D.R., Jan. 24, Feb. 21, F.D.R. to Stimson, Feb. 6, to Breckinridge Long, March 9, 1935, Roosevelt Papers; National Emergency Council, Proceedings, Feb. 5, 1935; H. S. Johnson, "Pied Pipers," *Vital Speeches*, March 11, 1935.

2. *Congressional Record*, 74 Cong., 1 Sess., 2933, 2938 (March 5, 1935); *New York Times*, March 5, 6, 8, 10, 12, April 13, 1935; Huey Long and Charles E. Coughlin in *Vital Speeches*, March 25, 1935.

3. Walter Davenport, "The Shepherd of Discontent," *Collier's*, May 4, 1935; Long and Coughlin, *Vital Speeches*, March 25, 1935; Davis, *Huey Long*, 244–61, 267; *Congressional Record*, 74 Cong., 1 Sess., 2935 (March 5, 1935); *New York Times*, April 25, 28, May 23, 1935; *Time*, May 6, 20, 1935; R. M. Lovett, "Huey Long Invades the Middle West," *New Republic*, May 15, 1935; "Father Coughlin at the Garden," *Nation*, June 5, 1935; Charles E. Coughlin, *The New Deal and the Way Out* (June 2, 1935).

4. *New York Times*, April 17, 19, 21, 23, June 14, 1935; Ickes, *First Thousand Days*, 346; J. A. Farley, *Jim Farley's Story* (New York, 1948), 52; Morgenthau, Diary, May 23, 1935; Elmer Irey, *The Tax Dodgers* (New York, 1948), 97; Alexander Holtzoff, "Re: Constitutional Guar-

anty to the States of a Republican Form of Government," April 12, Cummings to F.D.R., April 18, F.D.R. to Lemann, July 23, Frankfurter to LeHand [Aug. 16], Farley to F.D.R., Sept. 26, 1935, Roosevelt Papers; F.D.R., Press Conference #137, Aug. 24, 1934; Raymond Moley, 27 *Masters of Politics* (New York, 1949), 229; James M. Burns, *The Lion and the Fox* (New York, 1956), 214; interview with Felix Frankfurter, March 8, 1958; H. S. Truman, *Memoirs: Year of Decisions* (New York, 1954), 145-46.

5. A. T. Mason, *Harlan Fiske Stone: Pillar of the Law* (New York, 1956), 384; *New State Ice Co. v. Liebmann*, 285 U.S. 307-08; *Home Building and Loan Association v. Blaisdell*, 290 U.S. 426, 437, 442, 447-48, 483; *Nebbia v. New York*, 291 U.S. 523, 524, 537-38, 555, 556; Morton Keller, *In Defense of Yesterday: James M. Beck and the Politics of Conservatism* (New York, 1958), 254.

6. R. H. Jackson, *The Struggle for Judicial Supremacy* (New York, 1941), 87-95; *Panama Refining Co. v. Ryan*, 293 U.S. 443; F.D.R., Press Conference #173, Jan. 9, 1935; Raymond Moley, " 'Hot' Oil and a Cool Temper," *Today*, Jan. 19, 1935.

7. F.D.R., *Public Papers* (1935), 8; Cummings to LeHand, Jan. 8, 1935, Roosevelt Papers; *Norman v. Baltimore and Ohio Railroad, United States v. Bankers Trust Company*, 294 U.S. 256, 257, 268; *New York Times*, Jan. 9-16, 1935; Ickes, *First Thousand Days*, 273-74; George Creel, "Looking Ahead with Roosevelt," *Collier's*, Sept. 7, 1935; Morgenthau, Diary, Jan. 14-15, 1935; J. M. Blum, *From the Morgenthau Diaries: Years of Crisis, 1928-1938* (Boston, 1959), 125-31.

8. Mason, *Stone*, 390-92; F.D.R., *Personal Letters*, III, 445-60; Grace Tully, *F.D.R., My Boss* (New York, 1949), 157-61; Morgenthau, Diary, Feb. 18, 1935; Allison Dunham, "Mr. Chief Justice Stone," in Allison Dunham and P. B. Kurland, eds., *Mr. Justice* (Chicago, 1956), 49; *Wall Street Journal*, Feb. 23, 1935 (McReynolds remarks); Delbert Clark, "Stanch States' Righter of Our High Court," *New York Times Magazine*, May 23, 1937; Tugwell, Diary, Feb. 19, 1935.

9. Roosevelt to Angus D. MacLean, Feb. 21, 1935, Roosevelt Papers; George Creel, "The Tall Man," *Collier's*, Jan. 4, 1936; H. R. Fraser, "Attorney General Cummings," *American Mercury*, Dec. 1934; *Time*, March 25, 1935; Ickes, *First Thousand Days*, 247; J. F. Carter, "No More Legal Pushovers," *Today*, March 14, 1936; Lewis Wood, "A Hard-Working Lawyer Joins the Supreme Court," *New York Times Magazine*, Jan. 30, 1938; *New York Times*, Feb. 3, 10, 19, 23, 28, March 3, 17, 1935.

CHAPTER 15 *(Pages 263-290)*

1. *Foreign Relations of the United States: 1933* (Washington, 1950), I, 655; F.D.R., *Public Papers* (1934), 174; F.D.R., Press Conference #172, Jan. 5, 1935.

2. Schlesinger, *Coming*, Chs. 16-17; Ickes, *First Thousand Days*, 228,

239; Ickes to McIntyre, March 8, 1934, Roosevelt Papers; R. E. Sherwood, *Roosevelt and Hopkins* (New York, 1948), 64–65; Morgenthau, Diary, Dec. 3, 1934; Tugwell, Diary, Dec. 5, 1934; Tugwell, "New Deal Memoir," Ch. 4; Moley to Hopkins, Feb. 29, 1936, Hopkins Papers; Raymond Moley, "Men At Work," *Today*, Aug. 10, 1935; Moley, "Commonsense — 1936 Model," *Vital Speeches*, May 18. 1936; A. W. Macmahon *et al.*, *Administration of Federal Work Relief* (Chicago, 1941), 30.

3. Morgenthau, Diary, Dec. 26, 27, 1934; F.D.R., *Public Papers* (1935), 10–22, 35; Aubrey Williams to author, Aug. 1957.

4. *New York Times*, Feb. 5, 1935; Philip La Follette to Robert M. La Follette, Jr., Feb. 8, 1935, Roosevelt Papers; *Congressional Record*, 74 Cong., 1 Sess., 4073, 4160 (March 20, 21, 1935); Edith Abbott, "Don't Do It, Mr. Hopkins!" *Nation*, Jan. 9, 1935; Macmahon *et al.*, *Administration of Federal Work Relief*, Ch. 2.

5. T. W. D. Duke to author, April 24, 1958; Tugwell, Diary, Jan. 29, 1935; H. I. Harriman, "American Business Turns a Page," *New York Times Magazine*, Dec. 2, 1933; *New York Times*, May 2–4, 1935; *Time*, May 13, 1935; Watson to F.D.R., May 3, 1935, Roosevelt Papers.

6. F.D.R. to Watson, May 6, 1935, Roosevelt Papers; F.D.R., *Public Papers* (1935), 156–63; Elmer Davis, "Roosevelt: The Rich Man's Alibi," *Harper's*, Oct. 1939; Richard Hofstadter, *The American Political Tradition* (New York, 1948), 330; Ickes, *First Thousand Days*, 195, 241–42, 316, 363; Tugwell, Diary, May 19, 1935.

7. 295 U.S. 374–75; A. T. Mason, *Harlan Fiske Stone* (New York, 1956), 393, 397; Tugwell, Diary, May 9, 1935; the President's Committee on Industrial Analysis, *The National Recovery Administration* (Washington, 1937), Ch. 19; O. P. Field, "The Constitutional Theory of the National Industrial Recovery Act," 18 *Minnesota Law Review*, 291–92; Donald Richberg, "Constitutional Aspects of the New Deal," *Annals*, March 1935; T. R. Powell, "Recovery and the Supreme Court," *Today*, Nov. 18, 1933; J. M. Beck in *Congressional Digest*, Dec. 1933; Hugh S. Johnson, "In Commerce We Are One Country," *Vital Speeches*, April 8, 1935; Johnson, *Where Do We Go From Here?* (New York, 1935), 7; Donald Richberg, *The Rainbow* (New York, 1936), Ch. 12; Richberg, *My Hero* (New York, 1954), Ch. 17; *New York Times*, March 26, April 5, 1935; interview with Paul A. Freund, April 29, 1957.

8. *Schechter v. U.S.*, *Brief for the United States*, (Washington, 1935), especially 14–20, 30–45; *Local 167 v. U.S.*, 291 U.S. 293; Victor Weybright, "Chickens Come Home to Roost," *Survey Graphic*, July 1935; Johnson, *Where Do We Go From Here?*, 7; Richberg to F.D.R., April 3, Corcoran to F.D.R., April 4, Early to F.D.R., April 4, F.D.R. to Cummings, April 4, Reed to F.D.R., April 11, Cummings to F.D.R., July 5, 1935, Roosevelt Papers; J. M. Landis, "Mr. Justice Brandeis: A Law Clerk's View," *Publications of the American Jewish Historical Society*, June 1957; Richberg, *My Hero*, Ch. 17; Richberg, *The Rain-*

bow, Ch. 12; Richberg, "Lessons of the NRA," *New York Times Magazine,* June 18, 1939; *New York Times,* May 3, 4, 28, 1935; Harry Hopkins, "A Statement to Me by Thomas Corcoran Giving His Recollection of the Genesis of the Supreme Court Fight," April 3, 1939, Hopkins Papers; Freund interview; interview with T. G. Corcoran, Oct. 21, 1957.

9. 295 U.S. 542, 548, 553, 554; Mason, *Stone,* 397; Stone to Powell, Aug. 23, 1935, Powell Papers; T. R. Powell, "Would the Supreme Court Block a Planned Economy?" *Fortune,* Aug. 1935; Powell, "Commerce, Pensions and Codes," *Harvard Law Review,* Nov.–Dec. 1935; Felix Frankfurter and Henry M. Hart, Jr., "The Business of the Supreme Court at October Term, 1934," *Harvard Law Review,* Nov. 1935; Joseph L. Rauh, Jr., to author, April 9, 1958.

10. Hadley Cantrill, ed., *Public Opinion, 1935–1946* (Princeton, 1951), 344; Hillman in *New York Times,* June 30, 1935; *American Federationist,* July 1935; *United Mine Workers' Journal,* Aug. 1, 1935; *New York Daily News,* June 9, 1935; "Social Control and the Constitution," *New Republic,* June 12, 1935; Long in *New York Times,* June 2, 1935; *Literary Digest,* June 8, 1935; Frank Kent, *Without Grease* (New York, 1936), 136, 139; Samuel I. Rosenman, *Working With Roosevelt* (New York, 1952), 111; interview with Felix Frankfurter, March 8, 1958; Krock in *New York Times,* June 2, 1935; F.D.R., *Public Papers* (1935), 200–22; Woodrow Wilson, *Constitutional Government in the United States* (New York, 1908), 169; Stimson to F.D.R., June 4, F.D.R. to Stimson, June 10, F.D.R. to Bullitt, June 3, 1935, Roosevelt Papers; R.F.A., "In Washington," *Today,* June 15, 1935.

11. Powell, "Commerce, Pensions and Codes: II"; Tugwell to F.D.R., May 28, F.D.R. to David Gray, June 17, 1935, Roosevelt Papers: Tugwell, Diary, May 30, 31, June 5, 1935; Frances Perkins, "Reminiscences" (Oral History Research Office), 3342, 3386; Charles E. Wyzanski, Jr., "Reminiscences" (Oral History Research Office), 232–33; Wyzanski, "What the Schechter Case Does and Does Not Decide with Respect to Congressional Power Over Commerce," n.d. [Aug. 1935], Wyzanski Papers; Frances Perkins, *The Roosevelt I Knew* (New York, 1946), 248–53; Johnson, *Where Do We Go From Here?,* 13; Richberg, *The Rainbow,* 250, 262–67; Richberg, *My Hero,* 197–99; Moley, *After Seven Years,* 307; Raymond Moley, "Beyond the NRA," *Today,* June 8, 1935; Ickes, *First Thousand Days,* 371–74; F.D.R., *Public Papers* (1935), 223–33; *Time,* May 27, 1935.

CHAPTER 16 *(Pages 291–301)*

1. F.D.R. to Norman Davis, June 10, 1935, Roosevelt Papers; *New York Times,* June 14, 1935.

2. F.D.R. to D. U. Fletcher, Feb. 4, 1935, *New York Times,* Feb. 6, 1935; Marriner Eccles, *Beckoning Frontiers* (New York, 1951), 166–76; House Banking Committee, *Banking Act of 1935: Hearings,* 74 Cong.,

1 Sess. (1935), 180–84, 195, 206–07, 229, 269; Senate Banking Committee, *Banking Act of 1935: Hearings*, 74 Cong., 1 Sess. (1935), 261, 290, 674–75; Eccles in `New York Times*, Feb. 9, 1935; Marriner Eccles, *Economic Balance and a Balanced Budget*, R. L. Weissman, ed. (New York, 1940), 13–38; John M. Blum, *From the Morgenthau Diaries: Years of Crisis, 1928–1938* (Boston, 1959), 343–54.

3. J. F. T. O'Connor, Diary, Jan. 16, March 21, 25, 1935; Daniels to F.D.R., Oct. 11, 1934, F.D.R. to Glass, July 6, 1935, Eccles, "Memorandum on Commerce Committee's Report on Permanent Monetary Policy," May 21, 1936, Roosevelt Papers; J. E. Palmer, Jr., *Carter Glass* (Roanoke, 1938), especially 255–58; S. J. Woolf, *Here Am I* (New York, 1941), 334; Eccles, *Beckoning Frontiers*, 194–230, 248; *New York Times*, Feb. 6, 9, 13, March 10, 21, 29, April 14, 16, 17, 29, May 9, 10, 16, 26, 29, June 20, July 2, 25–27, Aug. 17, 24, 1935; F.D.R., Press Conference #205, May 17, 1935; Sen. Banking Com., *Banking Act of 1935*, 72, 76, 389, 422; Walter Lippmann, *Interpretations, 1933–1935* (New York, 1936), 194; Elliott V. Bell, "Who Shall Rule the Money Market?" *Current History*, July 1935; John T. Flynn, "Our Daily Dollars," *Collier's*, June 8, 1935; A. P. Giannini, "I Favor the Banking Bill," *Today*, June 1, 1935.

CHAPTER 17 *(Pages 302–324)*

1. F.D.R. to Fred I. Kent, March 27, 1934, Roosevelt Papers.
2. National Executive Council, Proceedings, Dec. 11, 1934; Tugwell, Diary, Dec. 12, 1934; Ickes, *First Thousand Days*, 244–5; Raymond Moley, "The Failure of Private Socialism," *Today*, Jan. 26, 1935; "Report of National Power Policy Committee on Public-Utility Holding Companies," House Document No. 137, 74 Cong., 1 Sess. (March 12, 1935), 4–8; House Interstate and Foreign Commerce Committee, *Public Utility Holding Companies: Hearings*, 74 Cong., 1 Sess. (1935), 122, 2200; *New York Times*, Jan. 28, 1935; Felix Frankfurter, "Public Services and the Public," *Yale Review*, Sept. 1930.
3. *New York Times*, Jan. 5, 12, 1935; Moley, *After Seven Years*, 303; "SEC," *Fortune*, June 1940; House Interstate and For. Commerce Com., *Public Utility Holding Companies, passim*, especially testimony of Healy and Splawn; Senate Interstate Commerce Committee, *Public Utility Holding Company Act of 1935: Hearings*, 74 Cong., 1 Sess. (1935), *passim*, especially testimony of Corcoran, and 65, 177–79; Walter Lippmann, *Interpretations, 1933–1935* (New York, 1936), 383; B. V. Cohen to author, Oct. 4, 1957; T. G. Corcoran to author, April 1, 1958.
4. Senate Special Committee to Investigate Lobbying Activities, *Investigation of Lobbying Activities: Hearings*, 74 Cong., 1 Sess. (1935), 1077, 1093; House Interstate and For. Commerce Com., *Public Utility Holding Companies*, especially 589–90, 606, 654, 680, 837, 1069, 1197, 1435–37, 2057; Sen. Interstate Com. Com., *Public Utility Holding Company*

Act of 1935, especially 201, 206–7; "Light Up with Politics," *Electrical World,* Oct. 14, 1933; W. L. Willkie, "Government and the Public Utilities," *Vital Speeches,* Feb. 11, 1935; Willkie, "The Campaign Against the Companies," *Current History,* May 1935; Willkie, "The New Fear," *Vital Speeches,* May 20, 1935; Willkie, "Horse Power and Horse Sense," *Review of Reviews,* Aug. 1936; Owen D. Young to Herbert Pell, Jan. 5, 1938, Pell Papers; Joseph Barnes, *Willkie* (New York, 1952), Ch. 6; Harry S. Truman, *Memoirs: Year of Decisions* (New York, 1955), 151–52; *New York Times,* Jan. 22, March 7, April 2, May 9, June 5, Dec. 4, 1935, Aug. 26, 1936; *Time,* June 17, Oct. 7, 1935; Morris L. Cooke, "Power and Its Social Control," *Plan Age,* May 1936.

5. F.D.R., *Public Papers* (1935), 98–101; Will Rogers, *Autobiography,* Donald Day, ed. (Boston, 1949), 373; interview with Burton K. Wheeler, Nov. 19, 1959; Marquis W. Childs, *I Write from Washington* (New York, 1942), 118–19; Raymond Moley, *27 Masters of Politics* (New York, 1949), 69; *New York Times,* March 13, June 9, 12, 14, 1935; *Time,* July 8, 22, 1935; F.D.R., Press Conference #216, June 28, 1935; Sen. Lobbying Com., *Investigation,* 817, 828.

6. Sen. Lobbying Com., *Investigation,* 61–64; *New York Times,* June 20–30, July 2, 3, 7, 1935; T.R.B., "Washington Notes," *New Republic,* July 17, 1935.

7. House Rules Committee, *Investigation of Lobbying on Utility Holding Company Bills: Hearings,* 74 Cong., 1 Sess. (1935), especially 21, 32, 85–86 and *passim; Time,* July 28, 1935; F.D.R. to Corcoran, July 6, Corcoran to F.D.R., July 9, 1935, Roosevelt Papers.

8. Sen. Lobbying Com., *Investigation, passim;* Willkie, "The Campaign Against the Companies"; *Time,* July 29, 1935; Hugo Black, "Lobby Investigation," *Vital Speeches,* Aug. 26, 1935; Paul Ward, "Shenanigans of the Power Lobby," *Nation,* Aug. 28, 1935; *New York Times,* July 13, 28, Aug. 14–24, 1935.

9. *New York Times,* March 6, 12, 21, 24, 27, Nov. 10, 1936, Jan. 7, 1941, June 18, 1957; *Congressional Record,* 74 Cong., 2 Sess., 3328–30 (March 5, 1936), 4094–104 (March 20, 1936); Sen. Lobbying Com., *Investigation,* 990, 1001, 1003; Lippmann in *New York Herald Tribune,* March 5, 1936; A. A. Mavrinac, "Congressional Investigations," *Confluence,* Dec. 1954; Sylvia C. Mitchell, "The Black Committee" (seminar paper, Harvard University, 1952).

10. *New York Times,* Aug. 2–27, 1935; Moley, *After Seven Years,* 316; Moley, *27 Masters of Politics,* 158; W. L. Willkie, "Sober Second Judgment," *Vital Speeches,* Dec. 30, 1935.

CHAPTER 18 *(Pages 325–342)*

1. F.D.R., *Public Papers* (1935), 36.
2. E. D. Coblentz, *William Randolph Hearst* (New York, 1952), 178; Moley, *After Seven Years,* 305, 308–12; John M. Blum, *From the Morgenthau Diaries: Years of Crisis, 1928–1938* (Boston, 1959), 298–301;

Morgenthau, *Diary*, June 16, 1935; Ickes, *First Thousand Days,* 384, 472; *New York Times*, Feb. 11, March 21, April 27, June 2, 1935.

3. *New York Times*, March 15, April 29, June 20–28, July 8, 1935; F.D.R., *Public Papers* (1935), 270–76; Coblentz, *Hearst*, 170; Long to F.D.R., June 22, 1935, Roosevelt Papers; La Follette in *Congressional Record,* 74 Cong., 1 Sess., 4148 (March 21, 1935), 13202–04 (Aug. 15, 1935); Francis Brown, "Old Wars for 'Young Bob,'" *New York Times Magazine*, Aug. 18, 1935; Francis Brown, "La Follette: Ten Years a Senator," *Current History*, Aug. 1935; R. G. Tugwell, *The Democratic Roosevelt* (New York, 1935), 220; Adolf A. Berle, Jr., "Revenue and Social Progress," *Survey Graphic*, Oct. 1935; *Time*, July 1, 1935; Blum, *From the Morgenthau Diaries*, 301–04.

4. House Ways and Means Committee, *Proposed Taxation of Individual and Corporate Incomes, and Inheritances and Gifts: Hearings*, 74 Cong., 1 Sess. (1935), 5–6; Senate Finance Committee, *Revenue Act of 1935: Hearings*, 74 Cong., 1 Sess. (1935), 99, 173–78, 213, 228; Moley, *After Seven Years*, 312; Herbert Hoover, *Addresses Upon the American Road, 1941–1945* (New York, 1946), 229; F.D.R., Press Conference #225, July 31, 1935; Lehman to F.D.R., Aug. 6, F.D.R. to Lehman, Aug. 9, 1935, Roosevelt Papers; House Banking Committee, *Banking Act of 1935: Hearings*, 74 Cong., 1 Sess. (1935), 238; *New York Times,* March 20, July 26–Aug. 16, 1935; R. G. and G. C. Blakey, "Revenue Act of 1935," *American Economic Review*, Dec. 1935; Berle, "Revenue and Social Progress."

5. J. F. Guffey, with John Sullivan, *Seventy Years on the Red-Fire Wagon*, Roosevelt Foundation Papers; F.D.R. to S. B. Hill, July 6, 1935, F.D.R., *Public Papers* (1935), 297–98; *New York Times*, May 23, June 5, Aug. 12–23, 1935; Ray Tucker, "Ex-King Coal," *Today*, March 9, 1935; S. D. Spero, "Trouble in Coal," *New Republic*, July 3, 1935; Charles A. Beard, "The New Deal's Rough Road," *Current History,* Sept. 1935.

6. *Congressional Record*, 74 Cong., 1 Sess., 12788–89 (Aug. 9), 14722 (Aug. 26, 1935); Charles A. Beard, "The Labors of Congress," *Current History*, Oct. 1935; Howard to F.D.R., Aug. 26, F.D.R. to Howard, Sept. 2, 1935, F.D.R., *Public Papers* (1935), 352–57; Moley, *After Seven Years*, 317–18.

7. *New York Times*, Sept. 9–13, 1935; *Time*, Sept. 16, 23, 1935; F.D.R., Press Conference #237, Sept. 11, 1935; Harnett Kane, *Louisiana Hayride* (New York, 1941), 133–44; Carleton Beals, *The Story of Huey P. Long* (Philadelphia, 1935), Ch. 34; Hodding Carter, *Where Main Street Meets the River* (New York, 1953), 59; Maury Maverick, "The South Is Rising," *Nation*, June 17, 1936; Ickes, *First Thousand Days*, 462.

CHAPTER 19 *(Pages 343–361)*

1. Ickes, *First Thousand Days*, 264–65, 275–77, 288, 293, 311, 337–39,

341-43, 351-52; John M. Blum, *From the Morgenthau Diaries: Years of Crisis, 1928-1938* (Boston, 1959), 241-42; Corrington Gill, *Wasted Manpower* (New York, 1939). 270-71; Robert E. Sherwood, *Roosevelt and Hopkins* (New York, 1948), 68-71; Donald R. Richberg, *My Hero* (New York, 1954), 241; Harry L. Hopkins, Diary, March 16, 1935, Hopkins Papers; Tugwell, Diary, April 27, 1935; S. F. Charles, "Harry L. Hopkins: New Deal Administrator, 1933-1938" (Ph.D. thesis, University of Illinois, 1953), Ch. 6.

2. Hopkins, Diary, May 12, 1935; H. L. Ickes, "My Twelve Years with F.D.R.," *Saturday Evening Post*, June 12, 19, 1948; Henry Morgenthau, Jr., "The Fight to Balance the Budget," *Collier's*, Sept. 27, 1947; Ickes, *First Thousand Days*, 378, 410, 427-29; Charles, "Hopkins," Ch. 6.

3. Ickes, *First Thousand Days*, 410, 424-29, 434-38; Ickes to F.D.R., Sept. 7, 1935, Roosevelt Papers; Sherwood, *Roosevelt and Hopkins*, 78-79; Ickes, "My Twelve Years"; Daniel Bell, "President's Conferences," Sept. 14, 1935, Bureau of the Budget Papers; A. W. Macmahon *et al.*, *The Administration of Federal Work Relief* (Chicago, 1941), 123-26. An account of the activities of the WPA will be found in a subsequent volume.

4. Ickes, *First Thousand Days*, 581-83, 589-95; Ickes, "My Twelve Years."

5. Sherwood, *Roosevelt and Hopkins*, 59-61, 80; H. S. Johnson, *The Blue Eagle* (New York, 1935), 426; "Harry Hopkins," *Fortune*, July 1935; Raymond Clapper, "Who Is Hopkins?" *Forum*, Dec. 1937; M. W. Childs, "The President's Best Friend," *Saturday Evening Post*, April 19, 1941; Arthur Krock in *New York Times*, July 20, 1934; I am indebted to Rexford G. Tugwell for the Hopkins-Merriam story; Aubrey Williams, "Standards of Living and Government Responsibility," *Annals*, Nov. 1934; Charles, "Hopkins," Ch. 3.

6. Hopkins to McIntyre, Jan. 4, Dec. 31, to Garner, March 29, 1934, Farley to Joseph McGrath, Nov. 12, 1935, Hopkins Papers; Pittman to Louis Howe, Feb. 9, Hopkins to Early, Oct. 31, 1934, Roosevelt Papers; Sherwood, *Roosevelt and Hopkins*, 68, 77-78; Harry L. Hopkins address, *Proceedings: Conference of State Administrators, Works Progress Administration, June 17-19, 1935* (Washington, 1935), 27; H. B. Hinton, "And What about Senator Vandenberg?" *New York Times Magazine*, May 17, 1936; Hopkins, order of March 13, 1936, Hopkins Papers; Lillian Symes, "Politics vs. Relief," *Survey Graphic*, Jan. 1935; Ickes, *First Thousand Days*, 586; *New York Times*, Aug. 21, 1936.

7. Philip Snowden, *Autobiography* (London, 1936), II, 957; Sherwood, *Roosevelt and Hopkins*, 49; Harry L. Hopkins, Speech before Catholic Charities, New York, May 4, before the Citizens' League, Cleveland, May 24, 1935, before the Conference of WPA State Administrators, Feb. 12, 1937, Hopkins to John A. Kingsbury, April 16, 1934, Hopkins Papers; Hopkins to F.D.R., Nov. 17, 1936, Roosevelt Papers; Hopkins, "Beyond Relief," *New York Times Magazine*, Aug. 19, 1934; Hopkins, "Social Planning for the Future," *Social Service*

Review, Sept. 1934; Hopkins, "Employment in America," *Vital Speeches,* Dec. 1, 1936; Hopkins, "The Future of Relief," *New Republic,* Feb. 10, 1937; Hopkins, *Spending to Save* (New York, 1936), Ch. 10; R. L. Duffus, "Unemployment: Must It Be Permanent?" *New York Times Magazine,* Aug. 25, 1935; Sherwood, *Roosevelt and Hopkins,* 21, 83–85; "On the Dole," *Fortune,* Oct. 1934; F.D.R., *Public Papers* (1936), 162.

8. Senate Public Lands Committee, *Nomination of Elbert K. Burlew: Hearings,* 75 Cong., 3 Sess. (1938), 7, 19, 94; Ickes, *First Thousand Days,* 676; *New York Times,* Feb. 4, 1952; *Congressional Record,* 77 Cong., 2 Sess., Appendix, 813 (Feb. 26, 1942); *Time,* Feb. 4, 1935; H. L. Ickes, *The New Democracy* (New York, 1934), 32–33, 120; L. H. Robbins, "Ickes Defines the Task Ahead," *New York Times Magazine,* April 1, 1934.

CHAPTER 20 *(Pages 362–384)*

1. Wendell Willkie to Early, Nov. 19, 1934, A. E. Morgan to F.D.R., May 18, 1936, Roosevelt Papers; Willkie, "Government and the Public Utilities," *Vital Speeches,* Feb. 11, 1935; Schlesinger, *Coming,* 327–28; *Ashwander v. TVA,* 297 U.S. 288; C. H. Pritchett, *The Tennessee Valley Authority* (Chapel Hill, 1943), Ch. 3; M. E. Dillon, *Wendell Willkie* (Philadelphia, 1952), 74–77; Joseph Barnes, *Willkie* (New York, 1952), 69, 75–77, 101–05; Alfred Lief, *Democracy's Norris* (New York, 1935), 481–82; Ickes, *First Thousand Days,* 566–67; O. G. Villard to A. E. Morgan, Sept. 24, 1936, A. J. Ackerman to Villard, Jan. 5, 1937, Villard Papers; James D. Lorenz, Jr., "Arthur E. Morgan and the TVA" (honors essay, Harvard University, 1960).

2. Willkie to F.D.R., May 21, Lilienthal to F.D.R., May 18, F.D.R. to Willkie, Jan. 8, Arthur E. Morgan, "Memorandum on Proposed TVA and C & S Corporation Power Transmission Pool," Sept. 28, La Follette to F.D.R., Sept. 26, Rankin to F.D.R., Sept. 28, Willkie to F.D.R., Sept. 30, Wehle to F.D.R., Oct. 26, 1936, Lilienthal to F.D.R., Jan. 12, 1937, Roosevelt Papers; Norris to F.D.R., Nov. 13, 1936, in F.D.R., *Personal Letters,* III, 630; *Time,* Jan. 25, 1937; L. B. Wehle, *Hidden Threads of History* (New York, 1953), 161–74; Barnes, *Willkie,* 77, 106–09.

3. A. E. Morgan, "The Next Four Years in the TVA," *New Republic,* Jan. 6, 1937; *New York Times,* Jan. 17, 1937; A. E. Morgan, "Public Ownership of Power," *Atlantic,* Sept. 1937; Joint Committee on the Investigation of the Tennessee Valley Authority, *Investigation of the Tennessee Valley Authority: Hearings,* 75 Cong., 3 Sess. (1939), 222–29; National Emergency Council, *Proceedings,* Dec. 11, 1934; F.D.R., Press Conference #160, Nov. 23, 1934; E. B. Nixon, ed., *Franklin D. Roosevelt and Conservation, 1911–1945* (Hyde Park, 1957), I, 333–34; Francis Biddle, "The TVA Investigation," Biddle Papers;

Hopkins to M. C. Harrison, April 6, 1938, Hopkins Papers; J. A. Farley, *Jim Farley's Story* (New York, 1948), 105.

4. This analysis owes a great deal to Philip Selznick, *TVA and the Grass Roots* (Berkeley, 1949). See also M. L. Cooke to Lilienthal, Nov. 7, 1939, Cooke Papers; N. I. Wengert, *Valley of Tomorrow: The TVA and Agriculture* (Knoxville, 1952); R. G. Tugwell and E. C. Banfield, "Grass Roots Democracy — Myth or Reality?" *Public Administration Review*, Winter 1950; Grant McConnell, *The Decline of Agrarian Democracy* (Berkeley, 1953), 124.

5. David E. Lilienthal, *TVA: Democracy on the March* (New York, 1953); Gordon Clapp, "TVA After Two Decades," *New Republic*, Sept. 22, 1952; Richard Hellman, "The TVA and the Utilities," *Harper's*, Jan. 1939; Bernard Frank and Anthony Netboy, *Water, Land and People* (New York, 1950), 215–23; Gordon Clapp, *The T.V.A.: An Approach to the Development of a Region* (Chicago, 1955); F.D.R. to Estes Kefauver, March 2, 1945, Roosevelt Papers; Maury Maverick, "TVA Faces the Future," *New Republic*, Nov. 18, 1936; John Rankin in Joint Com. on the Investigation of the TVA, *Investigation of the TVA*, 5491; Lilienthal, "Senator Norris and the TVA," *Nation*, Sept. 23, 1944.

6. *Edison Electric Institute Bulletin*, II, 354; George Sundberg, *Hail Columbia: The Thirty-Year Struggle for Grand Coulee Dam* (New York, 1954), Chs. 22–23; *Congressional Record*, 74 Cong., 1 Sess., 13727–29 (Aug. 19, 1935); Richard L. Neuberger, "Power as an Issue," *Current History*, Sept. 1936; Ickes, *First Thousand Days*, 543; Margaret Chase Smith, "Brief History of Passamaquoddy Tidal Power Project," *Congressional Record*, 83 Cong., 1 Sess., Appendix, 4756 (July 21, 1953).

7. E. H. Foley, Jr., "Federal Power Legislation for the Pacific Northwest," *Conference on Distribution of Bonneville Power* (Eugene, Ore., 1937); National Resources Committee, *Regional Planning, Part 1: Pacific Northwest* (Washington, 1936), ix; Arthur Maass, *Muddy Waters* (Cambridge, 1951), 198–99.

8. F. R. Muller, *Public Rural Electrification* (Washington, 1944), Ch. 1; M. W. Childs, *The Farmer Takes a Hand* (New York, 1952), Ch. 2; M. L. Cooke, "The Early Days of the Rural Electrification Idea: 1914–1936," *American Political Science Review*, June 1948; K. E. Trombley, *Life and Times of a Happy Liberal: A Biography of Morris Llewellyn Cooke* (New York, 1954), 166; Cooke to author, Oct. 17, 1958.

9. Cooke to Frank P. Walsh, March 12, 1932, Roosevelt Papers; Cooke to Hoover, Oct. 20, Lawrence Richey to Cooke, Oct. 21, 1930, Cooke to F.D.R., June 5, 1933, Cooke Papers; George W. Norris, *Fighting Liberal* (New York, 1945), 319; F.D.R., *Public Papers* (1938), 463; Trombley, *Happy Liberal*, Ch. 10.

10. W. W. Freeman to Cooke, July 24, 1935, House Committee on Interstate and Foreign Commerce, *Rural Electrification: Hearings*, 74 Cong., 2 Sess. (1936), 34–38; H. S. Person, "The Rural Electrification Adminis-

tration in Perspective," *Agricultural History*, April 1950; Jesse Jones, with Edward Angly, *Fifty Billion Dollars* (New York, 1951), Ch. 14; M. L. Cooke, "Light Up the Farm," *Bureau Farmer*, Aug.–Sept. 1935; John M. Carmody, "Power Supply Seen Greatest Weakness Since Early Days of REA Program," *Public Power*, May 1956; REA, "Proceedings and Addresses, Sixth Annual Staff Conference, April 15–18, 1941," 20; Childs, *Farmer*, 66–70; Cooke, "Early Days"; Cooke to Judson King, March 23, 1939, Cooke Papers.

11. Muller, *Public Rural Electrification*, 17, 31, 121–22; Carmody, "Power Supply"; Claude R. Wickard, "Power Revolution on the Farm," *New York Times Magazine*, Sept. 9, 1951; Person, "REA in Perspective"; Childs, *Farmer*, Chs. 3–4.

CHAPTER 21 *(Pages 385–408)*

1. *Council for Industrial Progress* (Washington, 1937); Herbert Corey, "Up from a Dusty Road," *Nation's Business*, Oct. 1936; Hugh S. Johnson, *Where Do We Go From Here?* (New York, 1935), 10.
2. A. T. Mason, *Brandeis: A Free Man's Life* (New York, 1946), 620, 622; Perkins to Tugwell, June 5, 1935, Tugwell Papers; interview with T. G. Corcoran, Oct. 21, 1957; Leon Henderson, "The Consumer and Competition," *Annals*, Jan. 1936.
   The distinction between a First and Second New Deal was often noted by contemporaries, though rarely with agreement as to what the exact difference was. Basil Rauch brought the distinction into historical literature in his early and valuable *History of the New Deal* (New York, 1944); his conception, however, differs from the one presented here. Rexford G. Tugwell deals with the problem searchingly in *The Democratic Roosevelt* (New York, 1957). The distinction outlined in this chapter has won the assent of most veterans of both the First and Second New Deal kind enough to read these pages or to submit to interrogation. However, I would like to record a powerful *caveat* filed by Leon Keyserling (in a letter to me of April 9, 1958). With Mr. Keyserling's permission, I quote a few passages from his counterstatement:
   "When Roosevelt came to Washington in 1933 he did not have what could be called a systematic economic program and he certainly had not spelled one out in his campaign. There did come to Washington in 1933, drawn by the crisis of the times, a great array of vigorous thinkers and doers of all kinds. It is perfectly feasible to pluck from the writings and speeches of some of these a series of statements which would seem to add up to the fairly coherent economic philosophy which you seem to attribute to the First New Deal. I suspect that it might be equally possible to pick from the writings and speeches of the same group a series of statements adding up to something quite

different. In any event, the important thing seems to me to be that
what Roosevelt adopted and the Congress approved during the First
New Deal was highly experimental, improvised and inconsistent. . . .

"As the program of the First New Deal was largely incoherent, so
the individuals whom you cite as the most important influences in the
First New Deal were a medley of forceful people almost defying a
single classification. Some of them were sincere people struggling for
the ascendancy of their respective views; others were opportunists
struggling for an ascendancy of personal power; still others were representatives of group interests struggling for the advancement of these
interests. Those who stemmed from Mr. Baruch, such as General Johnson and George Peek, or who stemmed from Gerard Swope, can hardly
be said, despite some of their polemics, to have desired structural
changes or a transfer of fundamental power in the sense that Tugwell
did. They were really crusaders for the modification of the anti-trust
laws toward the strengthening of business cartels. The National Recovery Act as they wanted it would not have included either Section
7(a) or the wage or hour or labor standard provisions. These emerged
through a series of haphazard accidents reflecting the desire to get rid
of the Black bill and to put something in to satisfy labor. . . .

"The reform measures of the First New Deal stemmed from entirely
different sources and were its great achievement. They stemmed from
all of the schools of reformers who for years had been working for
social security systems, housing improvements, etc. Most of these,
incidentally, did not flow from any of the people whom you classify
as the primary influences of the First New Deal. . . .

"The period beginning with 1935 does not seem to me to represent
primarily the kind of dividing point which you suggest. It represents
rather a gradual weakening of the momentum and ideas of the Roosevelt Administration, and furthermore I think that this process was
continuous (despite the election of 1936) from 1934 until World War
II. This weakening was in part due to the natural political trends
characteristic throughout American history. It was in part due to the
fact that practically every type of experiment having been tried by
1935, there was not much more to offer in the absence of much coherence in any quarter. The President, personally, was inclined to
slow down and draw back whenever things began to look a little better.

"The transfers in influence from those whom you call the First New
Dealers to those whom you call the Second New Dealers does not seem
to me to represent primarily a basic philosophic shift on the part
of the President but rather to reflect what would have happened
naturally in the course of the developments that I have just described.
The First New Deal did so many things that so many powerful people
disliked that the people who had been identified with them became
whipping boys and were consequently eased out by the President. The
practical, agile and vigorous people who took their places in influence
were able to do so because fate had made them less vulnerable, and,

of course they were smart enough to translate their drive for power into appealing generalizations. . . .

"Aside from the gradual wearing away of program and momentum, the real change from the First New Deal to the Second New Deal was a change in political strategy and semantics, illustrating the degree of improvisation and the lack of deep commitment to a fundamental program except for the general idea on the part of most to do what was right and to help the country. Political and economic conditions in 1933 were such as to call for effort to unite everybody. When the New Dealers found to their surprise that no program could unite everybody and that those who in some ways had benefited most were turning to bite the hand that fed them, they shifted from the political strategy of unity to the political strategy of division."

3. Hugh Johnson, "American Recovery and the European Situation," *Vital Speeches,* Jan. 1, 1937; R. G. Tugwell, *The Stricken Land* (New York, 1946), 22, 681; Tugwell, *Battle for Democracy* (New York, 1935), 264-67; Tugwell, "The Progressive Task," *Vital Speeches,* Nov. 16, 1935; Tugwell, "The Preparation of a President," *Western Political Quarterly,* June 1948; Tugwell, "The New Deal in Retrospect," *Western Political Quarterly,* Dec. 1948; Charles A. Beard, "America Must Stay Big," *Today,* Sept. 14, 1935; Johnson, *Where Do We Go from Here?* 13; Tugwell, "America Takes Hold of Its Destiny," *Today,* April 28, 1934; Tugwell, "After the New Deal," *New Republic,* July 26, 1939; Tugwell, Diary, Oct. 18, 1934; Ickes, *First Thousand Days,* 303; H. S. Johnson, "Think Fast, Captain!" *Saturday Evening Post,* Oct. 26, 1935; Tugwell, "New Deal Memoir," Part 8; Tugwell, *The Art of Politics* (New York, 1958), 247.

4. Tugwell, *Democratic Roosevelt,* 415, 454, 465; Tugwell, "New Deal Memoir," Part 8; T. G. Corcoran to author, April 1, 1958; Sachs to Johnson, May 20, 1933, C. F. Roos, *NRA Economic Planning* (Bloomington, Ind., 1937), 34.

5. Berle in *New York Times,* Aug. 17, 1933, and "The Way of an American," *Survey Graphic,* Nov. 1936; Charles E. Wyzanski, Jr., "Reminiscences" (Oral History Research Office), 108, 110, 217; Paul A. Freund, "The Liberalism of Justice Brandeis," *American Jewish Archives,* April 1958; Brandeis, 285 U.S. 310; Felix Frankfurter, *The Public and Its Government* (New Haven, 1930), 128; Arthur E. Morgan, "Intelligent Reasonableness and the Utilities," *Vital Speeches,* Feb. 1, 1937; Moley, *After Seven Years,* 290; Raymond Moley, "There Are Three Brains Trusts," *Today,* April 14, 1934; Reinhold Niebuhr, *The Children of Light and the Children of Darkness* (New York, 1944), xi.

6. Frances Perkins, *The Roosevelt I Knew* (New York, 1946), 286; E. S. Corwin, *Twilight of the Supreme Court* (New Haven, 1934), 178; T. R. Powell, "Commerce, Pensions and Codes," *Harvard Law Review,* Nov. 1935; and the following works by Walter Lippmann: "The New Deal," *American,* May 1933; *Interpretations, 1933-1935* (New York, 1936), 288-90; *A New Social Order* (New York, 1933), 16-17, 21-22,

24–25; *The Method of Freedom* (New York, 1934), 18, 46, 59, 74.
7. J. M. Keynes and H. J. Laski, "Can America Spend Its Way Into
   Recovery?" *Redbook*, Dec. 1934; J. M. Keynes, *The General Theory
   of Employment, Interest and Money* (London, 1936), 378–80; and *The
   End of Laissez-Faire* (London, 1926), 34, 43, 45, 48, 52, 53; and *Essays
   in Persuasion* (New York, 1932), 306, 329; Liberal Party, *We Can
   Conquer Unemployment* (London, 1929); Keynes and Hubert Hender-
   son, *Can Lloyd George Do It?* (London, 1929); Labour Party, *Labour's
   Reply to Lloyd George* (London, 1929), 5, 9; R. F. Harrod, *Life of
   John Maynard Keynes* (New York, 1951), 390–413, 438–39; Keynes,
   The Means to Prosperity (London, 1933); *London Times*, April 27,
   1933; Hugh Dalton, *Back to Yesterday* (London, 1953), 261, 290;
   Keynes, "The Dilemma of Modern Socialism," *New Republic,* April
   13, 1932; Seymour E. Harris, *John Maynard Keynes: Economist and
   Policy Maker* (New York, 1955), Chs. 9–10.
8. *Time,* Sept. 25, 1933; *New York Times,* Dec. 31, 1933; F.D.R. to G. P.
   Auld, Oct. 13, 1923, Frankfurter to F.D.R., Dec. 16, 1933, May 7,
   Keynes to Marvin McIntyre, June 5, F.D.R. to Frankfurter, June 11,
   1934, Wallace to F.D.R., May 8, 1936 (with memorandum by A. P.
   Chew of talk with Keynes), Baruch to F.D.R., July 9, F.D.R. to Baruch,
   July 11, 1941, Roosevelt Papers; Bertrand Russell, "Portraits from
   Memory," *Harper's,* Jan. 1953; J. M. Keynes, "Shaw on Wells on
   Stalin," *New Statesman and Nation,* Nov. 10, 1934; Tugwell, *Demo-
   cratic Roosevelt,* 375; Perkins, *Roosevelt I Knew,* 225–26; Harrod,
   Keynes, 20, 447–50; Alvin Johnson, *Pioneer's Progress* (New York,
   1952), 244; Harris, *Keynes,* Ch. 24; J. H. Williams, "Federal Budget:
   Economic Consequences of Deficit Financing," *American Economic
   Review,* Feb. 1941; Morgenthau, Diary, July 3, 1935; Stanley High,
   Roosevelt — and Then? (New York, 1937), 9; Keynes, "A Self-Adjust-
   ing Economic System?" *New Republic,* Feb. 20, 1935; Keynes, *General
   Theory,* 383.

CHAPTER 22 *(Pages 409–423)*

1. I owe the Roosevelt quotation to Felix Frankfurter (interview, March
   8, 1958).
2. Alfred E. Smith, *Up to Now* (New York, 1929), 314; Raymond Moley,
   27 Masters of Politics (New York, 1949), 40.
3. Edward M. House, "This Crisis," *Liberty,* Nov. 25, 1933.
4. G. W. Norris, *Fighting Liberal* (New York, 1945), 353; F.D.R., *Public
   Papers* (1935), 343, 404; R. G. Tugwell, "The Progressive Tradition,"
   Western Political Quarterly, Sept. 1950; Tugwell, *The Democratic
   Roosevelt* (New York, 1957), 413–14; Ickes to Villard, June 8, 1935,
   Villard Papers; Tugwell, Diary, especially Dec. 28, 1934, Feb. 24, Sept.
   10, 1935; F.D.R., *Personal Letters,* III, 452.
5. Russell Lord, *The Wallaces of Iowa* (Boston, 1947), 352–54; Tugwell,

Diary, April 2, 1934; Leon Henderson to Robert E. Wood, April 5, 1934, NRA Papers; Agnes Meyer, *Out of These Roots* (Boston, 1953), 142; W. M. Kiplinger. "What's Ahead in Washington," *Nation's Business*, June 1934, Sept. 1935; A. T. Mason, *Harlan Fiske Stone* (New York, 1956), 384.

6. Ray Tucker, "Guardian at the Cupboard," *Collier's*, Sept. 23, 1933; James A. Farley, *Behind the Ballots* (New York, 1938), 225–38; T.R.B., "Washington Notes," *New Republic*, May 31, 1939; Harold Brayman, "Roosevelt and the Spoilsmen," *Current History*, Oct. 1934; James A. Farley, "66," *American*, Aug. 1933; Delbert Clark, "Portrait of a Political Strategist," *New York Times Magazine*, March 22, 1936; "Proceedings of the First Meeting of the Democratic Coordination Council, June 16, 1933," Howe Papers; *New York Times*, June 17, 1933.

7. Donald Richberg, *My Hero* (New York, 1954), 236; Farley, *Behind the Ballots*, 232–33; interview with Henry Morgenthau, Jr., Oct. 12, 1954; John M. Blum, *From the Morgenthau Diaries: Years of Crisis, 1928–1938* (Boston, 1959), xv, 49, 96–97; Tugwell, Diary, Feb. 26, 1933; J. P. Moffat, Diary, Jan. 3, 1934, Moffat Papers; Frances Perkins, "Reminiscences" (Oral History Research Office), 3529; Ickes, *First Thousand Days*, 39, 67, 143–44, 297–98; Arthur Mullen, *Western Democrat* (New York, 1940), 338; George Creel, "The Amateur Touch," *Collier's*, Aug. 3, 1935; Farley to F.D.R., Dec. 5, 1935, Roosevelt Papers; F.D.R., *Public Papers* (1934), 55; Frank Kent, *Without Gloves* (New York, 1934), 178; Raymond Clapper, *Watching the World* (New York, 1944), 83–84; *New York Times*, Jan. 30, 1935; National Emergency Council, Proceedings, Feb. 5, 19, 1935.

8. Mullen, *Western Democrat*, 316–17; *Newsweek*, Sept. 1, 1934; *Time*, Sept. 3, 1934.

CHAPTER 23 *(Pages 424–443)*

1. *These Are Our Lives* (Chapel Hill, 1939), 209–10; Eric Goldman, *Rendezvous with Destiny* (New York, 1952), 344–45; Matthew Josephson, *Sidney Hillman* (New York, 1952), 380.

2. Samuel Lubell, *The Future of American Politics* (New York, 1952), 78; interview with George Fischer, Dec. 13, 1956; F.D.R., *Public Papers* (1938), 259.

3. E. Franklin Frazier, *The Negro in the United States* (New York, 1957), 230; Walter White, *A Man Called White* (New York, 1948), Chs. 13–14; White, *How Far the Promised Land* (New York, 1955), 77; I. H. Hoover, *42 Years in the White House* (Boston, 1934), 301–03; Henry Lee Moon, *Balance of Power: The Negro Vote* (New York, 1948), Ch. 6; W. E. B. Du Bois, "Herbert Hoover," *Crisis*, Nov. 1932; James Weldon Johnson, *Along This Way* (New York, 1933), 239, 407; Ella Reeve Bloor, *We Are Many*·(New York, 1940), 239.

4. Haywood Patterson and Earl Conrad, *Scottsboro Boy* (New York, 1950), Part I; Walter White, "The Negro and the Communists," *Harper's,* Dec. 1931; W. E. B. Du Bois, *Dusk of Dawn* (New York, 1940), 298; Mary Heaton Vorse, "The Scottsboro Trial," *New Republic,* April 19, 1933; editorial note, *New Republic,* April 26, 1933; F. Raymond Daniell, "Land of the Free," in Hanson Baldwin and Shepard Stone, eds., *We Saw It Happen* (New York, 1938).

5. White, *Man Called White,* Ch. 16; Johnson, *Along This Way,* 393; Bishop R. C. Ransom in *Crisis,* Nov. 1932; *St. Louis Argus,* Sept. 16, 1932; Joseph R. Guffey, *Seventy Years on the Red-Fire Wagon* (privately printed, 1952), 170; Joseph Alsop and Robert Kintner, "The Guffey," *Saturday Evening Post,* March 26, 1938.

6. On the other hand, he did not, as has been charged, insert a racial restriction clause into deeds conveying farmlands in Georgia. On May 27, 1957, Senator Herman Talmadge put into the appendix of the *Congressional Record* a letter from R. Carter Pittman of Dalton, Georgia, making this charge and adding that the clause was known locally as "the Roosevelt restriction." (The rest of the Pittman letter was a denunciation of the Supreme Court, suggesting that Alger Hiss "led the Court away from the Constitution" in the restrictive-covenant case of *Shelley v. Kraemer* in 1948.)

I am indebted to William F. Snyder, general counsel of the Georgia Warm Springs Foundation, for the following comment: "The statement . . . that the restriction is referred to by some Georgia lawyers as the Roosevelt restriction 'because Mr. Roosevelt was one of the few persons ever to insert such a clause in a deed conveying farmlands in Georgia' is not true. (1) Thousands of deeds contained such restriction before Mr. Roosevelt ever went to Georgia. (2) The restriction was not inserted by Mr. Roosevelt in any deed of his own property. (3) The restriction was included in the printed form used by Meriweather Reserve, Inc. for the conveyance of subdivision lots [for private dwelling purposes] — not farm lands. (4) Neither of the deeds referred to by Mr. Pittman was a conveyance by Mr. Roosevelt personally and both deeds conveyed subdivision lots. As a matter of fact the deed recorded in Book 24, page 388, was a conveyance *to* Mr. Roosevelt. When he later conveyed this property to Meriweather Reserve, Inc. (Book 29, page 183) the deed merely stated that the property was conveyed subject to restrictions of record, which is the uniform practice in all states.

"It is true that Mr. Roosevelt, as President of Meriweather Reserve, Inc. signed some of the deeds containing the said restriction (the last such deed appears to have been on May 23, 1932), but it is doubtful that he knew the deed contained such restriction. In every case the deed was completed by a Georgia attorney and was sent to Mr. Roosevelt. . . . The form consisted of three full legal-size pages. The restriction was printed in small type on the second page and Mr. Roosevelt signed on the third page. It should also be remembered that lawyers of one state are not familiar with the real estate laws of another state and when a deed is prepared by a lawyer of another state they assume that the printed terms, conditions and restrictions therein are in accordance with the laws of that state.

"Mr. Roosevelt was also President of the Georgia Warm Springs Foundation. . . . The [Warm Springs] property was acquired by Georgia Warm Springs Foundation from Meriweather Reserve, Inc. in 1940. No deed containing a restriction such as appeared in the Meriweather Reserve, Inc. deeds was ever executed by Mr. Roosevelt as President of Georgia Warm Springs Foundation. . . . It is noteworthy that the deed from Meriweather Reserve, Inc. to Georgia Warm Springs Foundation did not contain the restriction as to racial usage because in this case a Georgia printed form was not used and also the property conveyed by this deed included farm land."

Cf. *Congressional Record*, 85 Cong., 2 Sess., A4048 (May 27, 1957); and W. F. Snyder to author, Nov. 20, 1957.

One other incident reflecting Roosevelt's attitude toward the Negro should perhaps be noted. In 1923, a Harvard graduate wrote Roosevelt, as a Harvard overseer, and asked him to do something for "the maintenance of the Harvard tradition of liberal and democratic treatment" by speaking up for a Negro boy excluded from the freshman dormitories. Roosevelt replied, "It seems to be a pity that the matter ever came up in this way. There were certainly many colored students in Cambridge when we were there and no question ever arose." Mrs. Merle Fainsod informs me that two Negro students in particular, both prominent in Harvard College, lived in dormitories in 1904, Roosevelt's last year at Harvard. Southerners who didn't like it could live elsewhere. The issue of 1923 apparently arose over a recent ruling that, up to capacity, all members of the freshman class should reside in freshman halls. There is no indication of further action by Roosevelt in this matter. Cf. R. S. Wallace to Roosevelt, February 1, F.D.R. to Wallace, February 7, 1923, Roosevelt Papers.

7. F.D.R., speech before Saturn Club of Buffalo, Dec. 23, 1911, F.D.R. to W. C. Gorgas, Aug. 7, 1917, F.D.R. to J. Murphy Hooker, Oct. 31, 1929, Roosevelt Papers; Ickes, *First Thousand Days*, 16; editorial, *Opportunity*, Dec. 1932; Report of the Agricultural Committee of the Inter-Departmental Group concerned with the Special Problems of Negroes, May 1934, National Archives; E. E. Lewis, "Black Cotton Farmers and the AAA," *Crisis*, March 1935; NRA Division of Research and Planning, Report on Effect of NRA Codes Upon Negroes, March 21, 1934, NRA Papers; John P. Davis, "Blue Eagles and Black Workers," *New Republic*, Nov. 14, 1934; Davis before Senate Finance Committee, *Investigation of the National Recovery Administration: Hearings*, 74 Cong., 1 Sess. (1935), 2140 ff.; Davis, "The Plight of the Negro in the Tennessee Valley," *Crisis*, Oct. 1935; Davis, "A Black Inventory of the New Deal," *Crisis*, May 1935; Cranston Clayton, "The TVA and the Race Problem," *Opportunity*, April 1934; Walter White, "United

States Department of (White) Justice," *Crisis*, Oct. 1935; Charles Abrams, *Forbidden Neighbors* (New York, 1955), 8, 162.

8. Report on Special Problems of Negroes; Agric. Com. NRA Div. of Res. and Planning, Effect of NRA Codes Upon Negroes; Minutes of the Third Meeting of the Inter-Departmental Group, March 20, 1934, NRA Papers; C. F. Roos, *NRA Economic Planning* (Bloomington, 1937), 173; Davis, "Black Inventory"; Lorena Hickok to Harry Hopkins, Jan. 16, 1934, Hopkins Papers; "The Campaign," *Crisis*, Nov. 1936; Luther C. Wandall, "A Negro in the CCC," *Crisis*, Aug. 1935; C. P. Harper, *The Administration of the Civilian Conservation Corps* (Baltimore, 1937), 89–90; Kenneth Holland and F. E. Hill, *Youth in the CCC* (Washington, 1942), 111–12; Stanley High, *Roosevelt — And Then?* (New York, 1937), 201–02; Robert C. Weaver, "The New Deal and the Negro," *Opportunity*, July 1935.

9. F.D.R. to Mrs. William C. Eustis, Dec. 12, 1933, Roosevelt Papers; Mary McLeod Bethune, "My Secret Talks with President Roosevelt," *Ebony*, April 1949; Allan Morrison, "The Secret Papers of F.D.R.," *Negro Digest*, Jan. 1951; J. H. Franklin, *From Slavery to Freedom* (New York, 1947), 516; Eleanor Roosevelt to Hopkins, July 16, 1935, Hopkins Papers; Douglas MacArthur to Louis Howe, March 30, 1934, Howe Papers; Harold Ickes, "My Twelve Years with F.D.R.," *Saturday Evening Post*, June 26, 1948; Ickes, *First Thousand Days*, 416; Ickes, "The Negro as a Citizen," *Crisis*, Aug. 1936; Mary McLeod Bethune, radio address, Oct. 26, 1936, Roosevelt Papers.

10. Guffey, *Seventy Years on the Red-Fire Wagon*, Ch. 21; Alsop and Kintner, "The Guffey"; Harold Gosnell, *Negro Politicians: The Rise of Negro Politics in Chicago* (Chicago, 1935), 90–92; Mary White Ovington, *The Walls Came Tumbling Down* (New York, 1947), 258; F.D.R., *Public Papers* (1933), 519, (1934), 12–13; antilynching file in Howe Papers; Senate Judiciary Committee, *Punishment for the Crime of Lynching: Hearings*, 73 Cong., 2 Sess. (1934), 17–20; Senate Judiciary Committee, *Punishment for the Crime of Lynching: Hearing*, 74 Cong., 1 Sess. (1935), 23; *New York Times*, Nov. 21, 1933, April 25–May 2, 1935; *Congressional Record*, 74 Cong., 1 Sess., 6529, 6533 (April 29, 1935); White, *Man Called White*, 169–70; O. G. Villard, "The President's Worst Failure," *Nation*, June 5, 1935; F.D.R., Press Conference #125, May 25, 1934; editorial, *Crisis*, June 1935.

11. Eleanor Roosevelt, *This Is My Story* (New York, 1937), 346–54; Eleanor Roosevelt, *This I Remember* (New York, 1949), 41–42; Mary W. Dewson, "An Aid to the End" (mss), I, F.D.R. to Dewson, Dec. 12, 1932, Dewson to F.D.R., Dec. 15, 1934 (and Miss Dewson's note on carbon), Dewson to Farley, Aug. 27, 1937, Dewson Papers; Eleanor Roosevelt and Lorena Hickok, *Ladies of Courage* (New York, 1954), 12–20; Mary W. Dewson to author, Aug. 5, 1949; Frances Perkins, *The Roosevelt I Knew* (New York, 1946), 121; Mary Anderson, *Woman at Work* (Minneapolis, 1951), Ch. 17.

12. R. G. Tugwell, "The Progressive Task," *Vital Speeches*, Nov. 16, 1935;

New York Times, Oct. 29, 1935; R. G. Kelly to J. A. Farley, Oct. 29, Farley to F.D.R., Nov. 14, 1935, Hopkins Papers; Frank Kent, *Without Grease* (New York, 1936), 260–63; Alsop and Kintner, "The Guffey"; Farley to F.D.R., Feb. 26, 1935, Roosevelt Papers; Dewson, "An Aid to the End"; Ickes, *First Thousand Days,* 579.

CHAPTER 24 *(Pages 447–467)*

1. Felix Frankfurter and Adrian S. Fisher, "The Business of the Supreme Court at the October Term, 1935 and 1936," *Harvard Law Review,* Feb. 1938; Robert H. Jackson, *The Struggle for Judicial Supremacy* (New York, 1941), 115–23; Cummings to F.D.R., Nov. 8, 1933, Roosevelt Papers; Thomas Reed Powell, "Fifty-Eight Lawyers Report," *New Republic,* Dec. 11, 1935.

2. F.D.R., *Public Papers* (1933), 14–15 (1935), 15; Homer Cummings, *Liberty Under Law and Administration* (New York, 1934), 72–73; Harold Ickes, *The New Democracy* (New York, 1934), 43; R. G. Tugwell, *The Battle for Democracy* (New York, 1935), 12–13; *Ogden v. Saunders,* 12 Wheaton 270; *Propeller Genesee Chief v. Fitzhugh,* 12 How. 455; Sinking Fund Cases, 99 U.S. 718; *Missouri v. Holland,* 252 U.S. 433; Charles Evans Hughes, *The Supreme Court of the United States* (New York, 1928), 29–41; *McCulloch v. Maryland,* 2 Wheaton 407, 415; Charles Evans Hughes, *Addresses and Papers . . . 1906–1908* (New York, 1908), 139; Thurman Arnold, "The New Deal Is Constitutional," *New Republic,* Nov. 15, 1933; T. R. Powell to R. W. Hale, April 4, 1933, Powell Papers; E. S. Corwin, *Twilight of the Supreme Court* (New Haven, 1934), xxvii, 182; Felix Frankfurter, "The Supreme Court and the Public," *Forum,* June 1930; Drew Pearson and Robert S. Allen, *The Nine Old Men* (New York, 1936), 44.

3. F.D.R., *Public Papers* (1932), 837; James F. Byrnes, *All in One Lifetime* (New York, 1959), 65; Walter Lippmann, *Interpretations: 1933–1935* (New York, 1936), 121; C. E. Wyzanski, Jr., to Mrs. C. E. Wyzanski, Aug. 2, 1935, Wyzanski Papers; George Creel, "Looking Ahead with Roosevelt," *Collier's,* Sept. 7, 1935; Creel, *Rebel At Large* (New York, 1947), 290–92; Charles Fairman, "The Retirement of Federal Judges," *Harvard Law Review,* Jan. 1938; Raymond Moley, *27 Masters of Politics* (New York, 1949), 237; Ickes, *First Thousand Days,* 468, 495.

4. Oliver Wendell Holmes, *Collected Legal Papers* (London, 1920), 292, 295; Edward S. Corwin, "President and Court: A Crucial Issue," *New York Times Magazine,* Feb. 14, 1937; Henry F. Pringle, *Life and Times of William Howard Taft* (New York, 1939), II, 967, 1044.

5. 310 U.S. especially vi; 316 U.S. especially xxxiii; 323 U.S. especially xxi; Merlo Pusey, *Charles Evans Hughes* (New York, 1951), I, 284, II, 667–70; Felix Frankfurter, "Chief Justices I Have Known," *Virginia Law Review,* Nov. 1953; Pringle, *Taft,* II, 971; Delbert Clark, "Stanch

States' Righter of Our High Court," *New York Times Magazine*, May 22, 1937; *Report of the Attorney General*, 1913, 5; Robert D. Hill, "James Clark McReynolds: Prosecutor and Judge" (James Gordon Bennet Prize Essay, Harvard University, 1942); J. F. Paschal, *Mr. Justice Sutherland* (Princeton, 1951); F. J. Brown, *The Social and Economic Philosophy of Pierce Butler* (Washington, 1945); Pearson and Allen, *Nine Old Men;* "The Honorable Supreme Court," *Fortune,* May 1936; Ernest Sutherland Bates, "The Diehard Justices," *New Republic,* June 17, July 1, 1936; R. M. Lovett, *All Our Years* (New York, 1948), 170; T. R. Powell to J. N. Ulman, Jan. 27, 1937, Powell Papers.

6. *Home Building and Loan Association v. Blaisdell*, 290 U.S. 449, 450, 451, 452, 453; *United States v. Butler*, 297 U.S. 62–63; *West Coast Hotel v. Parrish*, 300 U.S. 402, 404; *Carter v. Carter Coal Co.*, 298 U.S. 296; *Lochner v. New York*, 198 U.S. 74; A. T. Mason, *Harlan Fiske Stone* (New York, 1956), 302–03; Paschal, *Sutherland,* 109–10.

7. J. M. Landis, "Mr. Justice Brandeis: A Law Clerk's View," *Publication of the American Jewish Historical Society,* June 1957; G. S. Hellman, *Benjamin N. Cardozo: American Judge* (New York, 1940), vii, 179, 254, 287; Joseph L. Rauh, Jr., review of Hellman, *Cardozo,* in *Harvard Law Review,* June 1940; Benjamin N. Cardozo, *The Growth of the Law* (New York, 1924), 96; Cardozo, *Paradoxes of Legal Science* (New York, 1928), 12; Louis L. Jaffe in *University of Chicago Law Review,* April 1947; *Panama Refining Co. v. Ryan*, 293 U.S. 447; *Helvering v. Davis*, 301 U.S. 644–45; *U.S. v. Constantine*, 296 U.S. 200; Holmes, *Collected Legal Papers,* 311; Babette Deutsch, "The Cloister and the Bench," *New Yorker,* March 22, 1930.

8. Alfred McCormack, "A Law Clerk's Recollections," *Columbia Law Review,* Sept. 1946; Mason, *Stone,* 322, 332–33; T. R. Powell, *Vagaries and Varieties in Constitutional Interpretation* (New York, 1956), 47; Stone to F.D.R., Dec. 7, 1933, Roosevelt Papers; H. F. Stone, "The Public Influence of the Bar," *Harvard Law Review,* Nov. 1934; Stone, "The Common Law in the United States," *Harvard Law Review,* Nov. 1936.

9. Pearson and Allen, *Nine Old Men,* 149; Pusey, *Hughes,* I, 25, II, 733; Frankfurter, "Chief Justices"; Mason, *Stone,* 210–11, 387; Henry F. Pringle, "Chief Justice," *New Yorker,* June 29–July 13, 1935; Irving Brant, "How Liberal is Justice Hughes?" *New Republic,* July 21, 28, 1937.

CHAPTER 25 *(Pages 468–483)*

1. Joseph L. Rauh, Jr., to author, April 9, 1958.
2. A. T. Mason, *Harlan Fiske Stone* (New York, 1956), 399–402; *Colgate v. Harvey*, 296 U.S. 440–41, 445–56; T. R. Powell to L. P. Smith, Jan. 3, to F. R. Coudert, March 9, 1936, Powell Papers; "Notes," *Harvard Law Review,* April 1936.

3. Mason, *Stone*, 405–16; George Wharton Pepper, *Philadelphia Lawyer* (Philadelphia, 1944), 244, 384; *New York Times*, Dec. 10, 11, 1935; Stone to Powell, Jan. 22, 1936, Powell Papers.

4. *U.S. v. Butler*, 297 U.S. 1, *passim;* Thomas L. Stokes, *Chip Off My Shoulder* (Princeton, 1940), 480–81; Allison Dunham and P. B. Kurland, eds., *Mr. Justice* (Chicago, 1956), 49, 109.

5. Cummings to Stone, Jan. 8, Stone to Cummings, Jan. 9, 1936, Roosevelt Papers; Mason, *Stone*, Ch. 26; R. H. Jackson, *The Struggle for Judicial Supremacy* (New York, 1941), Ch. 5; Charles P. Curtis, Jr., *Lions Under the Throne* (Boston, 1947), 121–53; Felix Frankfurter and Adrian S. Fisher, "The Business of the Supreme Court at the October Term, 1935 and 1936," *Harvard Law Review*, Feb. 1938; *Jones v. Securities Commission*, 298 U.S. 28, 33.

6. *Carter v. Carter Coal Company*, 298 U.S. 269, 307–08, 331; R. T. Swaine, *The Cravath Firm* (New York, 1948), II, 564–65; Irving Brant, *Storm over the Constitution* (New York, 1936), 144; T. R. Powell, "The Next Four Years: The Constitution," *New Republic*, Jan. 13, 1937.

7. Josephine Goldmark, *Impatient Crusader* (Urbana, 1953), 170–78; interview with Owen J. Roberts, March 14, 1951; Felix Frankfurter, "Mr. Justice Roberts," *University of Pennsylvania Law Review*, Dec. 1955; *Morehead v. New York* ex rel. *Tipaldo*, 298 U.S. 610–11, 618–19, 632–35; for Dilliard, O. G. Villard, "Issues and Men," *Nation*, Oct. 7, 1936.

8. *New York Times*, May 8, 1936; C. E. Hughes, *The Supreme Court of the United States* (New York, 1928), 95–97; Mason, *Stone*, 419–40, 425–26; Mason, "Charles Evans Hughes: An Appeal to the Bar of History," *Vanderbilt Law Review*, Dec. 1952.

CHAPTER 26 *(Pages 484–496)*

1. Thomas Jefferson, *Writings* (Memorial ed.), XV, 276; Andrew Jackson, Message to Congress, July 10, 1832; Abraham Lincoln, First Inaugural Address; Theodore Roosevelt, *Letters* (Cambridge, 1951–54), vii, 512; Roy Stannard Baker, *Woodrow Wilson* (New York, 1937), vi, 117; L. M. Limpus and B. W. Leyson, *This Man La Guardia* (New York, 1938), 225; Donald Richberg, *Tents of the Mighty* (New York, 1930), 162–63; A. T. Mason, *The Supreme Court: Vehicle of Revealed Truth or Power Group, 1930–1937* (Boston, 1953), 10–13; [Drew Pearson and Robert S. Allen] *More Merry-Go-Round* (New York, 1932), 63; A. T. Mason, *The Supreme Court from Taft to Warren* (Baton Rouge, 1958), 73–74.

2. Roscoe Pound, "The Call for a Realist Jurisprudence," *Harvard Law Review*, March 1931; Karl Llewellyn, "Some Realism about Realism," *Harvard Law Review*, June 1931; E. S. Corwin, *Twilight of the Supreme Court* (New Haven, 1934); Thurman Arnold, *The Symbols of Government* (New Haven, 1935), 34, 45; Homer Cummings, *Selected Papers*, C. B. Swisher, ed. (New York, 1939), 140; Herman Oliphant,

"The New Legal Education," *Nation*, Nov. 5, 1930; F. V. Cahill, *Judicial Legislation* (New York, 1952), especially 93–95, 123–26.

3. *Time*, March 11, 1935; Byrnes in *Congressional Record*, 74 Cong., 1 Sess., 8747–48 (June 6, 1935); *New York Times*, Jan. 3, 7, 8, 17, Feb. 13, 17, May 19, June 3, 1936; Lloyd K. Garrison, "The Constitution and the Future," *New Republic*, Jan. 29, 1936; *United Mine Workers' Journal*, June 1, 1936; Charlotte Williams, *Hugo Black* (Baltimore, 1950), 49; Evelyn Miller Crowell, "Who Wants a Constitutional Amendment?" *New Republic*, July 15, 1936; G. S. Hellman, *Benjamin N. Cardozo* (New York, 1940), 230; A. T. Mason, *Harlan Fiske Stone* (New York, 1956), 425.

4. R. E. Desvernine, *Democratic Despotism* (New York, 1936), 194–95; Ickes, *First Thousand Days*, 467, 495, 524; Joseph Alsop and Turner Catledge, *The 168 Days* (New York, 1938), 18; F.D.R., *Personal Letters*, III, 548–49; *Congressional Digest*, Dec. 1935; J. S. McGrath and James J. Delmont, *Floyd Bjornsterne Olson* (Minneapolis, 1937), 308, 314–15; Cummings *Selected Papers*, 147–48; Donald Richberg, "The Constitution and the New Deal," *Annals*, May 1936; *New York Times*, Jan. 12, 1936; O'Mahoney to F.D.R., Jan. 10, 1936, Roosevelt Papers; O. W. Holmes, *Collected Legal Papers* (London, 1920), 296; letters from Felix Frankfurter, Sept. 16, Charles A. Beard, Aug. 8, and "Report of the Committee of Inquiry to the Board [of the National Consumers' League]," Nov. 5, 1936, Dewson Papers; Alfred Lief, *Democracy's Norris* (New York, 1939), 492–95.

5. Cummings, *Selected Papers*, 140; E. S. Corwin, *The Commerce Power vs. States Rights* (Princeton, 1936), 263–67; Dean Acheson, "Roger Brooke Taney: Notes Upon Judicial Self-Restraint," address before the Maryland Bar Association, July 4, 1936; letters from Holcombe, Aug. 7, Acheson, Sept. 21, and Corwin, Sept. 24, 1936, Dewson Papers; F.D.R. to Charles C. Burlingham, Feb. 23, 1937, Cummings to F.D.R., Jan. 29, 1936 (cf. also Cummings, *Selected Papers*, 148–49), Roosevelt Papers; interview with T. G. Corcoran, Oct. 21, 1957; R. G. Tugwell, *The Democratic Roosevelt* (New York, 1957), 415; Morris Cohen in *Congressional Digest*, Dec. 1935; Frances Perkins, "Reminiscences" (Oral History Research Office), 3395; F.D.R., Press Conference #344, Feb. 12, 1937; F.D.R., *Public Papers* (1935), 13 (1936), 192; *New York Times*, June 3, 1936; *Newsweek*, Jan. 18, 1936.

6. *New York Times*, March 3, 1936; Donald Richberg, "Memorandum for the President — in re Constitutional Issues," June 16, 1936, Roosevelt Papers; Robert H. Jackson, *The Struggle for Judicial Supremacy* (New York, 1941), xii–xiii; Winston S. Churchill, "What Good's a Constitution," *Collier's*, Aug. 22, 1936.

CHAPTER 27 *(Pages 499–514)*

1. F.D.R., *Public Papers* (1935), 341–42, 406.
2. *New York Times*, Sept. 8, Nov. 26, Dec. 5, 11, 17, 1935; "Washington

Notes," *New Republic,* Sept. 25, 1935; "The New Deal Ends," *Nation,* Nov. 27, 1935; *Time,* Sept. 23, Oct. 14, Nov. 25, 1935; Mark Sullivan in *Erie Star,* Nov. 17, 1935; Marriner Eccles, *Beckoning Frontiers* (New York, 1951), 233-34; J. F. T. O'Connor, Diary, Nov. 15, 1935; Charles A. Beard, "Industry's Attack on the New Deal," *Current History,* Feb. 1936.

3. *Time,* March 2, 1936; Morgenthau, Diary, Oct. 31, 1935; Moley, *After Seven Years,* 330-31; Raymond Moley, "Speak Softly, But ——" *Newsweek,* Feb. 4, 1957; F.D.R., *Public Papers* (1936), 8-18, 40; Morgenthau to F.D.R., Sept. 4, 1935, Roosevelt Papers; Russell Lord, *The Wallaces of Iowa* (Boston, 1947), 456-57; P. L. Murphy, "The New Deal Agricultural Program and the Constitution," *Agricultural History,* Oct. 1955; *Congressional Record,* 74 Cong., 2 Sess., 2362, 2551 (Feb. 19, 21, 1936).

4. F.D.R., *Public Papers* (1936), 102-07; A. G. Buehler, *The Undistributed Profits Tax* (New York, 1937), Ch. 1; F.D.R., Press Conference #545, May 12, 1939; George W. Ball to author, Jan. 14, 1959; J. M. Keynes, *General Theory of Employment, Interest and Money* (London, 1936), 100; Eccles, *Beckoning Frontiers,* 130, 256-60; R. G. Tugwell, *The Battle for Democracy* (New York, 1935), 188; Tugwell, *The Industrial Discipline* (New York, 1933), 204-07; D. C. Coyle, *Brass Tacks* (Washington, 1935), 90; Morgenthau, Diary, Feb. 26, 1936.

5. Morgenthau, Diary, April-June 1936, especially Eccles to F.D.R., May 11, 1936; *New York Times,* April-June 1936; J. M. Blum, *From the Morgenthau Diaries: Years of Crisis, 1928-1938* (Boston, 1959), 305-19; interview with Henry Morgenthau, Jr., Nov. 7, 1954; Robert H. Jackson, "The Proposed Revision of Corporation Taxes," *Vital Speeches,* March 18, 1936; Robert E. Wood to F.D.R., Oct. 13, 1937, Roosevelt Papers; Raymond Moley, "Toward Insecurity," *Today,* March 14, 1936; Max Lerner, "The Corporate Tax Battle," *Nation,* May 27, 1936; Eccles, *Beckoning Frontiers,* 261-65; Bernard Sternsher, "The Undistributed Profits Tax" (seminar paper, Harvard University, 1953).

6. *Congressional Record,* 74 Cong., 2 Sess., 10007 (June 18, 1936); Frances Perkins, "Eight Years as Madame Secretary," *Fortune,* Sept. 1941; Perkins, *The Roosevelt I Knew* (New York, 1946), 253-54; Wright Patman, "Curbing the Chain Store," *Nation,* Nov. 28, 1936; Patman, "New Battle Lines Are Forming," *Nation's Business,* Dec. 1936; F. P. Stockbridge, "What Does Mr. Patman Mean?" *Today,* Nov. 7, 1936; Stockbridge, "Let the Buyer Beware," *Today,* Nov. 14, 1936; J. C. Palamountain, Jr., *The Politics of Distribution* (Cambridge, 1955), 188-234; B. A. Zorn and G. J. Feldman, *Business Under the New Price Laws* (New York, 1937), 46-57.

7. Morgenthau, Diary, especially Morgenthau to F.D.R., Aug. 17, diary notes, Sept. 6, 1935, Feb. 2, April 20, June 18, Aug. 19, 1936; F.D.R., Press Conference #275-A, Feb. 14, 1936; Blum, *From the Morgenthau Diaries,* 259-68.

8. Blum, *From the Morgenthau Diaries,* 354-57; Eccles, *Beckoning Fron-*

tiers, 287–90; Herbert Elliston, "Blaming the Money Managers," *Atlantic,* July 1938; Winthrop Aldrich, "Business Revival and Government Policy," *Vital Speeches,* Dec. 30, 1935; Russell Leffingwell, "Economic Recovery and Monetary Stabilization," address before Academy of Political Science, April 2, 1936; F.D.R., *Public Papers* (1936), 181, 220.

CHAPTER 28 *(Pages 515–523)*

1. The following by Lewis W. Douglas: "Recovery by Balanced Budget," *Review of Reviews,* Jan. 1935; *Baltimore Sun,* March 15, 1935; "Over the Hill to the Poorhouse," *Review of Reviews,* June 1935; "There Is One Way Out," *Atlantic,* Sept. 1935; "Can Government Spending Cure Unemployment?" *Atlantic,* Oct. 1935; "Sound Recovery Through a Balanced Budget," *Atlantic,* Dec. 1935; *New York Times,* Nov. 26, 1935; letter from Douglas, Newton Baker, and Leo Wolman, *New York Times,* June 3, 1936; *The Liberal Tradition* (New York, 1935), 11, 101. Also Herbert Elliston, "The World's Business," *Christian Science Monitor,* Nov. 13, 1935; James P. Warburg, *Hell Bent for Election* (New York, 1935); Warburg, *Still Hell Bent* (New York, 1936); Warburg, "What of 1936?" *Vital Speeches,* Jan. 15, 1936.
2. John W. Davis, "Principles," *Vital Speeches,* Oct. 20, 1936; H. L. Warner, *The Life of Mr. Justice Clarke* (Cleveland, 1959), 192–93; Gretta Palmer, "The Spirit of '76," *Today,* April 11, 1936; George Creel, "The True Friend," *Collier's,* Dec. 14, 1935; *New York Times,* April 16, 1934, Aug. 29, 1935, March 22, 1936; *Time,* Sept. 9, 1935; Emil Ludwig, *Roosevelt* (New York, 1938), 168–70.
3. Alfred E. Smith and Joseph T. Robinson in *Vital Speeches,* Feb. 10, 1936; Hull to F.D.R., Jan. 27, 1936, Roosevelt Papers; Alva Johnston, "Hundred-Tongued Charlie," *Saturday Evening Post,* May 30, 1936; Frances Perkins, *The Roosevelt I Knew* (New York, 1946), 157; *New York Times,* Jan. 25, 26, 29, 1936.
4. Eugene Talmadge, *Inaugural Address* (Atlanta, 1935), 14; Benjamin Stolberg, "Buzz Windrip — Governor of Georgia," *Nation,* March 4, 1936; William Bradford Huie, "Talmadge: White Man's Governor," *American Mercury,* Feb. 1942; Edward Angly, "Talmadge: Czar of All Georgia," *Today,* Feb. 2–23, 1935; Rufus Jarman, "Wool-Hat Dictator," *Saturday Evening Post,* June 27, 1942; Hamilton Basso, " 'Our Gene,' " *New Republic,* Feb. 19, 1936; Walter Davenport, "The Shouting Dies," *Collier's,* May 2, 1936; John Gunther, *Inside U.S.A.* (New York, 1947), 777–78; *New York Times,* Jan. 30, Feb. 2, April 17, July 1, Aug. 7, 1936; *Time,* Feb. 10, 24, 1936; Johnson to F.D.R., Aug. 15, 1934, Roosevelt Papers; Ickes, *First Thousand Days,* 675; A. P. Sindler, *Huey Long's Louisiana* (Baltimore, 1956), 113; Senate Special Committee to Investigate Lobbying Activities, *Investigation of Lobbying Activities: Hearings,* 74 Cong., 2 Sess. (1936), 1762, 1850–54, 1963, 1972–73; O. M. Kile, *Farm Bureau Through Three Decades* (Baltimore, 1948), 218–19.

CHAPTER 29 *(Pages 524–547)*

1. *New York Times*, Nov. 9, 1934; *Time*, Nov. 19, 1934; Frank Rising, "What Can the GOP Do?" *Today*, Jan. 5, 1935.
2. *Time*, Dec. 24, 1934; Walter Johnson, *William Allen White's America* (New York, 1947), 446; Rising, "What Can the GOP Do?"; J. S. Mason, "Wanted: A New Normalcy," *Today*, July 16, 1935; *Nation*, Nov. 28, 1934; H. L. Mencken, "Three Years of Dr. Roosevelt," *American Mercury*, March 1936; R. E. Low, "The Republican Reaction to the New Deal" (seminar paper, Harvard University, 1952).
3. Herbert Hoover, *Addresses Upon the American Road, 1933–1938* (New York, 1938), 77, 128–36, 162, 191–92; Johnson, *White's America*, 446; George Creel, "The New Hoover," *Collier's*, Oct. 12, 1935; Don Wharton, "Whither Hoover?" *Today*, Nov. 16, 1935.
4. C. O. Johnson, *Borah of Idaho* (New York, 1936), 484, 488; Jonathan Mitchell, "Borah Knows Best," *New Republic*, Jan. 29, 1936; Richard Neuberger and Kelley Loe, *An Army of the Aged* (Caldwell, Idaho, 1936), 8–9, 246–50; *New York Times*, March 23, 1936; "Who Is Frank Knox?" *Fortune*, Nov. 1935; Raymond Swing, "Knox — Publisher into Candidate," *Nation*, Feb. 19–26, 1936; G. H. Lobdell, Jr., "Biography of Frank Knox" (Ph.D. thesis, University of Illinois, 1954), 259; S. J. Woolf, "A Rough Rider Has His Hat in the Ring," *New York Times Magazine*, Nov. 10, 1935; Don Wharton, "Go-Getter Candidate," *Today*, Sept. 21, 1935; H. T. Moore, "Candidate Knox," *New Republic*, March 18, 1936; Frank Knox, "What I Stand For," *Vital Speeches*, April 6, 1936; F.D.R., Press Conference #212, June 12, 1935; Ickes, *First Thousand Days*, 211.
5. William Allen White, *What It's All About* (New York, 1936), Ch. 4; Willis Thornton, *The Life of Alfred M. Landon* (New York, 1936), especially 36–37; Frederick Palmer, *This Man Landon* (New York, 1936), especially 67; William Allen White to David Lawrence (n.d., mimeographed sheet), Landon to Richard Lloyd Jones, March 21, Aug. 2, J. G. Stutz to Harry Hopkins, Oct. 31, Landon to Raymond Clapper, Nov. 2, Landon to Charles P. Taft, Dec. 11, 1935, Landon to W. A. Bailey, March 31, Willard Mayberry to H. J. Allen, Oct. 4, 1936, W. A. Stacey *et al.*, "A Statement of Fact Concerning Governor Landon and the Public Schools of Kansas" (n.d., mimeographed sheet), Landon to O. P. Swift, Jan. 28, Landon to W. W. Waymack, Sept. 11, 1937, Landon Papers; interviews with Landon, April 1–3, 1959; Charles P. Taft, "Remarks Before Young Republican Clubs Convention," Dec. 7, 1935; Taft, *You and I — and Roosevelt* (New York, 1936), 4; Democratic National Committee, *Governor Landon vs. Candidate Landon* (Washington, 1936), 28–29, 40; Olive E. Clapper, *Washington Tapestry* (New York, 1946), 118–19; William Allen White, *Selected Letters*, Walter Johnson, ed. (New York, 1947), 367; Johnson, *White's America*, 452; Don Wharton, "They Call Him Another Coolidge," *Today*, Aug. 10, 1935; *Time*, Nov. 11, 1935; Raymond

Swing, "Alf Landon Is Not Cal Coolidge," *Nation,* Jan. 8-15, 1936; Morton Taylor, "Budget-Balancer Landon," *New Republic,* Jan. 15, 1936; "The Landon Boom," *Fortune,* March 1936; Avis D. Carlson, "The Man from Kansas," *Harper's,* April 1936; *Newsweek,* June 13, 1936; E. K. Lindley, "This Man Landon," *Today,* Aug. 22, 1936.

6. Landon to Ben Hibbs, June 9, 1934, to Richard Lloyd Jones, June 19, Hamilton to Landon, July 1, 30, Landon to Hibbs, Aug. 26, to Mark Sullivan, Nov. 4, 1935, to W. M. Kiplinger, Jan. 8, R. E. Berlin to Landon, Jan. 13, Landon to J. A. Meckstroth, March 10, W. A. White to Emory Bucke, Aug. 17, 1936, Landon Papers; interviews with Landon, March 30-31, 1959; White, *Selected Letters,* 357; "The Landon Boom," *Fortune,* March 1936; John Tebbel, *Life and Good Times of William Randolph Hearst* (New York, 1952), 259-60; E. D. Coblentz, *William Randolph Hearst* (New York, 1952), 183; H. L. Stimson, Diary, Nov. 1, 1937; F.D.R. to Farley, Feb. 19, Farley to F.D.R., March 4, 1937, Roosevelt Papers; Lobdell, "Knox," 273-74, 276-77; *New York Times,* Jan.–May, 1936; *Time,* Sept. 9, Dec. 23, 1935, May 11–June 1, 1936; *Newsweek,* May 16, 1936; Roy Roberts to author, March 26, 1958.

7. Landon to Frederick Palmer, May 16, to Raymond Swing, Jan. 15, 1936, Landon Papers; Johnson, *White's America,* 456-57; White, *Selected Letters,* 366; White, *What It's All About,* Ch. 3; David Hinshaw, *A Man from Kansas* (New York, 1945), 39-40; Republican National Committee, *Text Book of the Republican Party, 1936* (Chicago, 1936), Ch. 11.

8. *New York Times,* June 11, Oct. 12, 1936; Elmer Davis, "Post-Convention Reflections," *Harper's,* Sept. 1936; Hoover, *Addresses Upon the American Road, 1933-1938,* 173-83; Thomas L. Stokes, *Chip Off My Shoulder* (Princeton, 1940), 428-29; *Time,* June 22, 1936; David Hinshaw, *Herbert Hoover: American Quaker* (New York, 1950), 313-14.

9. *New York Times,* June 4-14, 1936; *Time,* June 22, 1936; A. H. Vandenberg, *Private Papers of Senator Vandenberg,* A. H. Vandenberg, Jr., ed. (Boston, 1952), xvi; Grove Patterson, *I Like People* (New York, 1948), 148-49; Knox to Landon, June 12, 1936, Landon Papers; Jonathan Mitchell, "The Republicans Hate Roosevelt," *New Republic,* June 24, 1936.

CHAPTER 30 *(Pages 548-570)*

1. *New York Times,* July 7, Aug. 21, 23, 1935, March 28, May 31, June 1, 1936; Thomas R. Amlie, "The American Commonwealth Federation — What Chance in 1936?" *Common Sense,* Aug. 1935; Floyd Olson, "Why a New National Party?" *Common Sense,* Jan. 1936; "1936 Is the Time!" *Common Sense,* April 1936; "Roosevelt: Radicals' Nemesis," *Common Sense,* June 1936; John T. Flynn, "Both Parties Are Wrong!"

Common Sense, June 1936; Donald R. McCoy, *Angry Voices* (Lawrence, 1958), Ch. 4.

2. House Committee Investigating Old-Age Pension Organizations, *Old-Age Pension Plans and Organizations: Hearings,* 73 Cong., 2 Sess. (1936), 87, 213, 330, 336-37, 596-97, 614-15; Townsend in March of Time film, "The Townsend Plan"; *Townsend Weekly,* Feb. 4, March 4, 1935; E. Merriam, "Impressions of the First Convention of Townsend Clubs, Oct. 24-27, 1935," Roosevelt Papers; H. T. Moore, "Just Folks in Utopia," *New Republic,* Nov. 13, 1935; Russell Owen, "Townsend Talks of His Plan and Hopes," *New York Times Magazine,* Dec. 29, 1935; *New York Times,* Nov. 25, Dec. 13, 15, 1935, May 23, 1936; Richard Milne, *That Man Townsend* (Indianapolis, 1935), 35; Richard Neuberger and Kelley Loe, *An Army of the Aged* (Caldwell, Idaho, 1936), 259, 265-92; Abraham Holtzman, "The Townsend Movement: A Study in Old Age Pressure Politics" (Ph.D. thesis, Harvard University, 1952), 453-54; F. E. Townsend, *New Horizons: An Autobiography* (Chicago, 1953), Chs. 28-29; *Newsweek,* May 30, June 13, 1936.

3. Walter Davenport, "The Shepherd of Discontent," *Collier's,* May 4, 1935; Ferdinand Lundberg, *Imperial Hearst* (New York, 1936), 375; Morgenthau, Diary, Jan. 8, 1936; Coughlin, *Shall the Sham Battle Go On?* (Jan. 26, 1936); *Social Justice,* March 13, April 3, 17, May 8, 22, 29, June 5, 12, 22, 1936; *New York Times,* Feb. 12, May 23, 28, June 15, 17, 20, 1936; Robert Ripin, "The Union Party of 1936" (seminar paper, Harvard University, 1952).

4. *Social Justice,* March 13, May 8, July 27, 1936; *New York Times,* June 20, 24, July 14, 16, 17, 24, Aug. 14, 1936; Thomas L. Stokes, *Chip Off My Shoulder* (Princeton, 1940), 412-20; H. L. Mencken, *Heathen Days* (New York, 1943), 296-99; *Time,* July 27, 1936.

5. Paul W. Ward, "Lemke: Crackpot for President," *Nation,* July 11, 1936; Duncan Aikman, "Lemke's New Party," *New York Times Magazine,* July 26, 1936; Jonathan Mitchell, "Liberty Bill Lemke," *New Republic,* Aug. 12, 1936; Don Wharton, "Prairie Messiah," *Today,* Aug. 29, 1936; George Creel, "The Old Homesteader," *Collier's,* Oct. 3, 1936; Walter Davenport, "Mr. Lemke Stops to Think," *Collier's,* Oct. 17, 1936; Thomas Amlie, "How Radical Is the New Deal?" *Common Sense,* Aug. 1936.

6. The following four articles by Norman Thomas appeared in *American Socialist Monthly:* "Roosevelt Faces Re-election," Jan. 1936; "Symposium on Important Problems of the Socialist Party," June 1936; "Why Labor Should Support the Socialist Party," July 1936; "The Election of 1936," Dec. 1936. Cf. also *New York Times,* Feb. 3, May 23-26, July 7, 18, 1936; John Herling, "The Socialists Meet," *New Republic,* June 10, 1936; S. J. Woolf, "Thomas: 'If I Were Elected President,'" *New York Times Magazine,* June 7, 1936; Thomas to H. C. Pell, July 30, 1936, Pell Papers; Thomas, "After the New Deal — What?" *Modern Monthly,* Aug. 1936; John T. Flynn, "Other People's Money," *New Republic,* Nov. 4, 1936; Thomas, *Shall Labor*

Support Roosevelt? (New York, 1936); McAlister Coleman, *Symbols of 1936* (New York, 1936); Daniel Bell, "Marxian Socialism in the United States," in D. D. Egbert and Stow Persons, eds., *Socialism in American Life* (Princeton, 1952), I, 377-84; D. A. Shannon, *The Socialist Party of America* (New York, 1955), Ch. 10.

7. Georgi Dimitrov, *The United Front Against Fascism and War* (New York, 1935), 7, 10, 20, 27-29, 90, 97.

8. *New York Times*, Aug. 7, 12, Sept. 19, Oct. 4, Nov. 28, 1935, May 10, 20, 1936; *Foreign Relations of the United States . . . The Soviet Union, 1932-39* (Washington, 1952), 239-41; Earl Browder, *Communism in the United States* (New York, 1935), 167-68; Granville Hicks, "Communism and the American Intellectuals," in I. DeW. Talmadge, ed., *Whose Revolution?* (New York, 1941), 94; James Wechsler, *The Age of Suspicion* (New York, 1953), 86; W. P. Mangold, "Forming a People's Front," *New Republic,* Jan. 22, 1936; G. H. Mayer, *The Political Career of Floyd B. Olson* (Minneapolis, 1951), 283-87; George Sokolsky, "Is Our Freedom in Danger?" America's Town Meeting of the Air, April 30, 1936; *New York Daily Worker,* June 18, 1936.

9. W. P. Mangold, "The Communist Convention," *New Republic,* July 15, 1936; Irving Howe and Lewis Coser, *The American Communist Party* (Boston, 1958).

CHAPTER 31 *(Pages 571-585)*

1. *Historical Statistics*, A 117, 128; Paul Webbink, "Unemployment in the United States, 1939-40," *American Economic Review*, Feb. 1941; George Haas to Herbert Gaston, May 19, 1936, Morgenthau Papers; *Newsweek,* Aug. 1, 8, Sept. 5, 1936. A detailed analysis of the economic situation of the mid-thirties will be provided in a subsequent volume in connection with the debate over the resumption of public spending in 1937-38.

2. F.D.R., Press Conference #325, Nov. 6, 1936; F.D.R., *Personal Letters*, III, 560, 565-66, 574; James A. Farley, *Jim Farley's Story* (New York, 1948), 57-59; Josephus Daniels, *Shirt-Sleeve Diplomat* (Chapel Hill, 1947), 461; *New York Times*, Jan. 20, 1934, May 23, 1936; Farley to F.D.R., Jan. 4, 1935, High to Early, April 2, 1936, Roosevelt Papers; Edward L. Roddan, "Thou Shalt Not Bear False Witness," Roosevelt Foundation Papers; Ickes, *First Thousand Days*, 517-18, 619; Samuel Rosenman, *Working With Roosevelt* (New York, 1952), 99, 117-18; Charles Michelson, *The Ghost Talks* (New York, 1944), 193; Mary Scribner, "Introducing Stanley High," *Today*, Oct. 3, 1936; Silas Bent, "Apostle of the New Deal," *Nation's Business,* Nov. 1936.

3. National Emergency Council, Proceedings, Dec. 17, 1935; J. F. T. O'Connor, Diary, Jan. 10, Feb. 1, 7, 1936; F.D.R. to Wallace, April 20, Early to F.D.R., April 23, 1936, Roosevelt Papers; Raymond Moley, *27 Masters of Politics* (New York, 1949), 26; Grace Tully, *F.D.R.,*

My Boss (New York, 1949), 201; Ickes, *First Thousand Days*, 467, 606, 613, 617–18; F.D.R., *Personal Letters*, III, 574, 591–92.

4. Rosenman, *Working With Roosevelt*, 98–105; Moley, *After Seven Years*, Ch. 9; *New York Sun*, July 1, 1936; *Time*, May 11, 1936; James A. Farley, *Behind the Ballots* (New York, 1938), 311; Farley, *Jim Farley's Story*, 62; T. G. Corcoran to author, April 1, 1958; interview with Raymond Moley, Dec. 16, 1958.

5. *New York Times*, June 18–28, 1936; Farley, *Jim Farley's Story*, 57; Rosenman, *Working With Roosevelt*, 100–05; Donald Richberg, *My Hero* (New York, 1954), 204; Ickes, *First Thousand Days*, 602; Moley, *After Seven Years*, 343–48; James F. Byrnes, *All in One Lifetime* (New York, 1958), 95; James A. Farley, "The 'Pros' Analyze Their 'Art,' " *New York Times Magazine*, Aug. 10, 1958; Alben Barkley, *That Reminds Me* (New York, 1954), 152; Donald Richberg, "Memorandum for the President — in re Constitutional Issues," June 16, 1936, Cummings to F.D.R., June 20, 1936, Roosevelt Papers; Cordell Hull, *Memoirs* (New York, 1948), I, 485–86; Frances Perkins, "Reminiscences" (Oral History Research Office), 3390; O. G. Villard, "The Donkey Brays Again," *Nation*, July 4, 1936.

6. Raymond Clapper, *Watching the World* (New York, 1944), 86–87; *New York Times*, June 28, 1936; Tom Connally, *My Name Is Tom Connally* (New York, 1954), 182; Michael Reilly, *Reilly of the White House* (New York, 1947), 98–101; William D. Hassett, "The President Was My Boss," *Saturday Evening Post*, Oct. 10, 1953; Tully, *F.D.R.*, 202; Ross McIntire, *White House Physician* (New York, 1946), 74.

7. Ickes, *First Thousand Days*, 625–26; Laura Crowell, "The Franklin Field Address," *Franklin D. Roosevelt Collector*, May 1952; Rosenman, *Working With Roosevelt*, 106–07; D. C. Coyle, *Brass Tacks* (Washington, 1935), 148; F.D.R., *Public Papers* (1936), 230–35.

CHAPTER 32 *(Pages 586–600)*

1. F.D.R., *Public Papers* (1936), 234; R. G. Tugwell, *The Democratic Roosevelt* (New York, 1957), 420.

2. Ickes, *First Thousand Days*, 580, 603, 632, 638–46; James A. Farley, *Jim Farley's Story* (New York, 1948), 57, 63–64; F.D.R., *Personal Letters*, III, 598–600; Early to Eleanor Roosevelt, July 22, Farley to Eleanor Roosevelt, July 25, Garner to F.D.R., July 27, 1936, Roosevelt Papers; Morgenthau, Diary, Aug. 24, 1936; James A. Farley, *Behind the Ballots* (New York, 1938), 314–15, 323.

3. *Time*, July 27, 1936; F.D.R., *Personal Letters*, III, 601–06; John M. Blum, *From the Morgenthau Diaries: Years of Crisis, 1928–1938* (Boston, 1959), 272; Vinson to Farley, Aug. 10, Wallgren to Farley, Aug. 19, O'Riordan to Farley, Sept. 11, Brown to Farley, Sept. 14, 1936, Democratic National Committee Papers; E. W. Gilboy, *Applicants for Work Relief* (Cambridge, 1940), 204–05; R. E. Sherwood, *Roosevelt and Hopkins* (New York, 1948), 83.

4. Stanley High, *Roosevelt — And Then?* (New York, 1937), 255–58; Farley, *Jim Farley's Story*, 59.
5. Tobin to Farley, Oct. 16, 1932, Biddle to F.D.R., July 16, 1935, Berry to Moley, May 16, Berry to F.D.R., Sept. 9, 1936, Roosevelt Papers; *Louisville Courier Journal*, Oct. 29, 1935; John L. Lewis, "Why Labor Should Support Roosevelt," *American Socialist Monthly*, July 1936; Matthew Josephson, *Sidney Hillman* (New York, 1952), 394–401; Sidney Lens, *Left, Right and Center* (Hinsdale, 1949), 316; George Creel, *Rebel At Large* (New York, 1947), 300–02; Louise Overacker, "Labor's Political Contributions," *Political Science Quarterly*, March 1939; *New York Times*, April 2, 10, July 17, Oct. 21, 28, 1936; *Time*, Aug. 24, 1936; *United Mine Workers' Journal*, Nov. 1936; L. B. Wehle, *Hidden Threads of History* (New York, 1953), 106–08.
6. [Margaret Durand?] to Marvin McIntyre, Jan. 30, Olson to F.D.R., June 29, George Berry to F.D.R., Sept. 9, 1936, Roosevelt Papers; E. A. Walsh to Kathryn Godwin, July 18, 24, Aug. 12, 1936, Hopkins Papers; *New York Times*, April 25, Aug. 19, 20, 23, Sept. 2, 12, Oct. 26, 1936; *Time*, Aug. 31, 1936; Ickes, *First Thousand Days*, 655; D. R. McCoy, "The Progressive National Committee of 1936," *Western Political Quarterly*, June 1956; H. B. Hinton, "Norris, 75, Sees Much Still to Be Done," *New York Times Magazine*, July 12, 1936; Richard Neuberger and S. B. Kahn, *Integrity: The Life of George W. Norris* (New York, 1937), 317–18; Alfred Lief, *Democracy's Norris* (New York, 1939), 313–19, 483–84; "How Shall I Vote," *Common Sense*, Oct. 1936; "What It's All About," *Common Sense*, Nov. 1936; "How They Are Voting," *New Republic*, Sept. 30, Oct 7, 1936; Farley, *Behind the Ballots*, 301–02.
7. Mary W. Dewson, "Campaign of 1936: Work of the Women's Division," Dewson Papers; Mary W. Dewson to author, Aug. 5, 1949; Eleanor Roosevelt and Lorena Hickok, *Ladies of Courage* (New York, 1954), 15–19; Frances Perkins, *The Roosevelt I Knew* (New York, 1946), 121; Farley, *Jim Farley's Story*, 63.
8. *New York Times*, June 25–28, Sept. 22, Oct. 19, 1936; *Newsweek*, July 4, 1936; *Time*, Aug. 17, 24, Sept. 7, 1936; the following editorials in *Crisis:* "The G.O.P. Speaks," July, "The Democrats Speak," Aug., "The Campaign," Nov., "Roosevelt's Opportunity," Dec. 1936; Hennings to Farley, Aug. 17, Sept. 8, Quinlivan to Farley, Oct. 3, 1936, Democratic National Committee Papers; High, *Roosevelt — And Then?*, 198–200.

CHAPTER 33 *(Pages 601–625)*

1. Landon to W. M. Kiplinger, Jan. 8, May 14, to J. A. Meckstroth, May 26, to Henry J. Allen, June 20, to Borah, Aug. 3, to Gifford Pinchot, Aug. 7, to Cornelia Bryce Pinchot, n.d., to Hamilton, Aug. 7, to Altschul, Sept. 2, to Raymond Clapper, Nov. 16, R. E. Berlin to Landon, July 24, Amos Pinchot to William Hard, July 28, 1936,

Landon to J. L. Wright, Feb. 9, 1937, Landon Papers; *New York Times*, July 24, Aug. 30, 1936; Farley to F.D.R., July 25, 1936, Roosevelt Papers; Ickes, *First Thousand Days*, 648–49; *Time*, Sept. 21, 1936; Walter Johnson, *William Allen White's America* (New York, 1947), 457–58; Samuel I. Rosenman, *Working With Roosevelt* (New York, 1952), 131–32; Walter Davenport, "The Doubtless Democrats," *Collier's*, Sept. 26, 1936; Louise Overacker, "Campaign Funds in the Presidential Election of 1936," *American Political Science Review*, June 1937.

2. Landon to Hamilton, Aug. 7, 17, Hamilton to Landon, Aug. 21, Hoover to Landon, Sept. 2, Landon to Waymack, Sept. 2, Landon to White, Sept. 21, Landon to Clapper, Nov. 16, 1936, Landon Papers; David Hinshaw, *Herbert Hoover: American Quaker* (New York, 1950), 313–16; *Time*, June 29, Aug. 10, 31, Sept. 21, 1936; *Newsweek*, Aug. 15, 1936; *New York Times*, Aug. 18–Sept. 8, 1936.

3. Connery to Farley, Aug. 12, W. H. Carpenter to F.D.R., Sept. 19, 1936, Democratic National Committee Papers; F.D.R., Press Conference #325, Nov. 6, 1936; R. G. Tugwell, *The Art of Politics* (New York, 1958), 10–14; F.D.R., *Public Papers* (1936), 271–330; "The Hand of God," *Social Justice*, July 20, 1936; Early to F.D.R., July 27, 1936, "Presidential Drought Conference . . . held at the State House, Des Moines, Iowa, 3 Sept. 1936" (stenographic report), Roosevelt Papers; *Time*, Aug. 17, Sept. 7, 14, 1936; Thomas L. Stokes, *Chip Off My Shoulder* (Princeton, 1940), 386–89; *New York Times*, Sept. 5, 6. Oct. 10, 1936.

4. Interview with Landon, April 2, 1959; Landon to Swing, Feb. 26, May 15, Swing to Landon, May 19, Aug. 11, Dewhurst to Landon, Aug. 14, Landon to Swing, Nov. 28, 1936, Landon Papers; Swing to author, April 21, 1959; Dewhurst to author, May 5, 1959; *Time*, Sept. 21, 1936; *New York Times*, Sept. 13–27, 1936; Stokes, *Chip Off My Shoulder*, 436–44; G. C. Fite, *George N. Peek and the Fight for Farm Parity* (Norman, Okla., 1954), 291–92; G. N. Peek, "World Market — Closed," *Today*, Oct. 24, 1936; W. A. White, *Selected Letters*, Walter Johnson, ed. (New York, 1947), 13. For valuable insights, I am not only indebted to Governor Landon but to communications from several of his associates, notably Charles P. Taft (March 6, 1958), Roy Roberts (March 26, 1958), and John D. M. Hamilton (April 18, 1958). Of course none of these veterans of the campaign is to be held responsible for facts or interpretations offered here, but I wish to express my gratitude for their good sportsmanship (which I would be glad in due course to reciprocate, if future historians ever have any interest in the losing campaigns of 1952 and 1956).

5. White to Landon, Oct. 6, Frank Gannett to Landon, Oct. 20, Landon to Henry J. Haskell, Nov. 13, 1936, Landon to Calvert Smith, May 14, 1937, Landon Papers; Johnson, *White's America*, 460; White, *Selected Letters*, 369; Olive E. Clapper, *Washington Tapestry* (New York, 1946). 108–11; Swing to author, April 21, 1959.

6. Robert Choate to Landon, April 25, 1936, Landon to Charles J. Bullock, April 21, 1937, Landon Papers; Kent Cooper, *Kent Cooper and the Associated Press* (New York, 1959), 206; *Time*, Jan. 27, 1936; Republican National Committee, *For Country and For Self* (n.p., 1936); *New York Times*, Sept. 16–Oct. 3, 1936; *Time*, Sept. 21, Oct. 12, 1936; W. R. Hearst, *Selections from the Writings and Speeches* (San Francisco, 1948), 129–30; Max D. Danish, *The World of David Dubinsky* (New York, 1957), 95; *New York Herald Tribune*, Sixth Annual Forum (New York, 1936), 162.

7. F.D.R., *Public Papers* (1936), 383–408; Rosenman, *Working With Roosevelt*, 86–87, 109–13; Harllee Branch to Farley, Aug. 5, 1936, Democratic National Committee Papers; *New York Daily News*, April 12, 1936; *New York Times*, Sept. 29–Oct. 18, 1936; Bishop James H. Ryan in *The True Voice*, Oct. 2, 1936; John T. Flynn, "Other People's Money," *New Republic*, Oct. 21, 1936; Fite, *Peek*, 292; F.D.R., Press Conference #322, Sept. 25, 1936; Mrs. J. H. Kahn to F.D.R., Oct 2, Joseph P. Kennedy, Address before Democratic Businessmen's League of Massachusetts, Oct. 24, 1936, Roosevelt Papers.

8. Landon, whistle-stop cards [1936], Landon to J. L. Wright, Feb. 9, 1937, Landon Papers; *New York Times*, Oct. 12–Nov. 1, 1936; Clapper, *Washington Tapestry*, 111; Early to LeHand, Nov. 9, 1936, with transcript of Bainbridge Colby's address of Nov. 2, Roosevelt Papers; *Newsweek*, Oct. 24, Nov. 7, 1936; *Time*, Nov. 2, 1936.

CHAPTER 34 *(Pages 626–644)*

1. Olson to Farley, July 28, Aug. 10, David E. Fitzgerald to Farley, July 22, Olson to Farley, July 28, Ryan to P. H. Callahan, Aug. 3, Black to Farley, Aug. 10, 1936, Democratic National Committee Papers; Selden Rodman, "God's Angry Men," *Common Sense*, Sept. 1936; Thomas L. Stokes, *Chip Off My Shoulder* (Princeton, 1940), 416; Herbert Harris, "That Third Party," *Current History*, Oct. 1936; H. L. Mencken, *Heathen Days* (New York, 1943), 298; *New York Times*, July 19, 21, 24, 25, 26, Aug. 3, 11, 14, 15, 16, Sept. 3, 12, 26, Oct. 12, 20, 21, 30, 1936; *Boston Transcript*, Aug. 3, 1936; "The Bandwagon," *New Republic*, Nov. 11, 1936; Dale Kramer, *Coughlin, Lemke and the Union Party* (Minneapolis, 1936), 45–47; Jonathan Mitchell, "Father Coughlin's Children," *New Republic*, Aug. 26, 1936; *Newsweek*, Aug. 22, 1936; Gerold Frank, "Huey Long the Second," *Nation*, July 25, 1936; F. Raymond Daniell, "Land of the Free," in Hanson Baldwin and Shepard Stone, eds., *We Saw It Happen* (New York, 1938), 98–99; "Father Coughlin on the Jewish Question," *Social Justice*, Aug. 31, 1936; *Social Justice*, Sept. 7, 1936; *Time*, Sept. 14, 1936; Duncan Aikman, "Third Party Slipping as a Campaign Force," *New York Times Magazine*, Oct. 18, 1936; Hadley Cantril, ed., *Public Opinion, 1935–46* (Princeton, 1951), 591; F.D.R., *Personal Letters*, III, 453; "Calm for a Stormy Priest," *Life*, Nov. 14, 1955.

2. Ickes, *First Thousand Days*, 695; Anne O'Hare McCormick, "The Big Moment," *New York Times Magazine*, Nov. 1, 1936; Marquis Childs, *I Write from Washington* (New York, 1942), 112–18; Stokes, *Chip Off My Shoulder*, 447–61; F.D.R., *Public Papers* (1936), 480–88, 537–44; Walter Johnson, *William Allen White's America* (New York, 1947), 460–61; Michael Reilly, *Reilly of the White House* (New York, 1947), 101; Raymond Clapper, *Watching the World* (New York, 1944), 88–89; Betty Millard, "The Press Places Its Bets," *New Masses*, Oct. 27, 1936; *Time*, Oct. 26, Nov. 2, 1936; F.D.R., *Personal Letters*, III, 622–23; Westbrook Pegler, *Dissenting Opinions* (New York, 1938), 312–15; *New York Times*, Oct. 7–30, 1936.

3. Landon to Malcolm Bingay, Oct. 24, 1936, Landon Papers; *New York Times*, Oct. 24–Nov. 4, 1936; *New York American*, Nov. 2, 1936; *Time*, Nov. 2, 1936; Stanley High, *Roosevelt — And Then?* (New York, 1937), 187–88; memoranda to F.D.R. of messages from Frank Murphy, David Lawrence, Labor's Nonpartisan League, Oct. 27, 1936, from Harold Ickes, n.d. [1936], F.D.R. to E. A. O'Neal, Dec. 1, 1933, Roosevelt Papers; F.D.R., *Personal Letters*, III, 433; Biddle to Maury Maverick, July 18, 1936, Maverick Papers; E. T. Weir, "I Am What Mr. Roosevelt Calls an Economic Royalist," *Fortune*, Oct. 1936; Samuel I. Rosenman, *Working With Roosevelt* (New York, 1952), 133–35.

4. Olive E. Clapper, *Washington Tapestry* (New York, 1946), 114–15; J. M. Burns, *The Lion and the Fox* (New York, 1956), 282–83; F.D.R., *Public Papers* (1936), 522–73.

5. *New York Times*, Nov. 1–7, 1936; C. J. Bullock to Landon, Oct. 29, 1936, Landon Papers; interview with Landon, March 31, 1959; Cantrill, *Public Opinion*, 591; F.D.R., Press Conference #325, Nov. 6, 1936; Johnson, *White's America*, 460; James A. Farley, *Jim Farley's Story* (New York, 1948), 65–66; Donald Richberg, *My Hero* (New York, 1954), 206; Moley, *After Seven Years*, 352; Stokes, *Chip Off My Shoulder*, 462–63; Rosenman, *Working With Roosevelt*, 135–39; *Time*, Nov. 2, 9, 16, 23, 1936; *Newsweek*, Nov. 14, 1936; Nicholas Roosevelt, *A Front Row Seat* (Norman, Okla., 1953), 241–42; W. A. White, *Selected Letters*, Walter Johnson, ed. (New York, 1947), 370; F.D.R., *Personal Letters*, III, 628; Clapper, *Washington Tapestry*, 118; Landon to Clapper, Nov. 16, 1936, Landon, Gridiron Banquet Speech, Dec. 21, 1936, Landon Papers.

CHAPTER 35 *(Pages 645–657)*

1. Winston Churchill, *Amid These Storms* (New York, 1932), 232, 238, 240, 278; Churchill, "Who'll Pay the Jobless," *Collier's*, Feb. 25, 1933.

2. Ralph Barton Perry, "The Alleged Failure of Democracy," *Yale Review*, Autumn 1934; Baldwin in *New York Times*, April 11, 1933; Nathaniel Peffer, "Why Liberalism is Bankrupt," *Harper's*, Aug. 1934;

George Boas, "A Defense of Democracy," *Harper's*, Sept. 1934; Will Durant, "Is Democracy Doomed?" *Saturday Evening Post*, Sept. 15, 1934; Louise Maunsell Field, "Our Destructive Idealism," *Scribner's*, May 1936; Joseph Wood Krutch, "How Dead Is Liberalism?" *Nation*, Sept. 12, 1936. For the views of Hoover, Ogden Mills, and others on this point, see Schlesinger, *Coming*, 479.

3. Walt Whitman, "Notes for Lecturers on Democracy and 'Adhesiveness,'" in C. J. Furness, *Walt Whitman's Workshop* (Cambridge, 1928), 57–58; Adolf A. Berle, Jr., "The Social Economics of the New Deal," *New York Times Magazine*, Oct. 29, 1933; Morgenthau in *New York Times*, May 28, 1933; R. G. Tugwell, "The Third Economy," *Vital Speeches*, April 22, 1935; John Dickinson, *Hold Fast the Middle Way* (Boston, 1935); E. K. Lindley, *The Roosevelt Revolution* (New York, 1933), 61; F.D.R. to J. A. Kingsbury, May 12, to H. G. Leach, Dec. 11, 1930, Roosevelt Papers; Anne O'Hare McCormick, "Roosevelt's View of the Big Job," *New York Times Magazine*, Sept. 11, 1932; F.D.R., Press Conference #161, Nov. 28, 1934; Emil Ludwig, *Roosevelt* (New York, 1938), 229–30; Rosita Forbes, *These Men I Knew* (New York, 1940), 173; Anne O'Hare McCormick, "As He Sees Himself," *New York Times Magazine*, Oct. 16, 1938.

4. R. G. Tugwell, *The Battle for Democracy* (New York, 1935), 220; Tugwell, *The Industrial Discipline* (New York, 1933), 11; F.D.R., Press Conference #193–B, April 8, 1935; Leon Henderson, "I Came to Know FDR First" (1947), Roosevelt Foundation Papers; J. K. Galbraith, "On the Economics of F.D.R.," *Commentary*, Aug. 1956; National Emergency Council, Proceedings, Jan. 23, 1934; Frances Perkins, *The Roosevelt I Knew* (New York, 1946), 33; Tugwell, "Must We Draft Roosevelt?" *New Republic*, May 13, 1940; Tugwell, *The Stricken Land* (New York, 1946), 681; Tugwell and E. C. Banfield, "Grass Roots Democracy," *Public Administration Review*, Winter 1950; Tugwell, "The Experimental Roosevelt," *Political Quarterly*, July–Sept. 1950; Tugwell, *The Democratic Roosevelt* (New York, 1957), 355, 454; interview with Thomas G. Corcoran, Benjamin V. Cohen, and Leon Henderson, Oct. 2, 1954; F.D.R., *Personal Letters*, III, 561; Adolf A. Berle, Jr., *Power Without Property* (New York, 1959), 16; Franklin D. Roosevelt, *On Our Way* (New York, 1934), x; Herbert Hoover, *Memoirs . . . The Great Depression, 1929–1941* (New York, 1952), 355; Leon Trotsky, "If America Should Go Communist," *Liberty*, March 23, 1935.

5. F.D.R., *Public Papers* (1933), 340; (1934), 288; (1935), 236–37, 339, 341–42; (1936), 574–75; Perkins, *Roosevelt I Knew*, 173; Frances Perkins, *People At Work* (New York, 1934), 286–87; Anne O'Hare McCormick, "An Unchanging Roosevelt Drives On," *New York Times Magazine*, Aug. 15, 1937; Ludwig, *Roosevelt*, 229–30; George Creel, *Rebel At Large* (New York, 1947), 275; Frances Perkins, "Memoirs" (Oral History Research Office), 1725.

6. Social Science Research Council, Committee on Studies in Social

Aspects of the Depression, Foreword, *SSRC Bulletins* 27–39 (1937–38); (London) *Times*, Nov. 5, 1936; Winston S. Churchill, "The Bond Between Us," *Collier's*, Nov. 4, 1933; Eric Estorick, *Stafford Cripps* (New York, 1949), 122; Lawrence Dennis, "Down the Dollar Toboggan Slide," *Common Sense*, Oct. 1933; Tugwell, Diary, March 24, 1934; H. F. Pringle, "Mr. President," *New Yorker*, June 16, 23, 1934; Keynes in *New York Times*, Dec. 31, 1934.

7. *Time*, Nov. 16, 1936; (London) *Times*, Nov. 5, 1936; Winston S. Churchill, "While the World Watches," *Collier's*, Dec. 29, 1934; F.D.R., *Public Papers* (1936), 235–36.

Index

Index

Bituminous Coal Code, 334. *See also* Coal Code

Black, Hugo, in Ku Klux Klan, 45; on holding companies, 313; heads investigation of lobbyists, '318–20; methods criticized, 320–23; on the antilynching bill, 437; protests power of Supreme Court, 488; and the Progressive National Committee, 595–96; on the followers of Townsend in Alabama, 626

Black Monday, 387, 466

Blackburn, Alan, 72, 630

Blandford, John B., Jr., 366, 375

Blanshard, Paul, 180

Bliven, Bruce, 213

Block, Paul, 538

Boas, George, 646

Boettiger, Anna Roosevelt, 356

Boileau, Gerald J., 143

Bone, Homer, 123, 135, 595

Bonneville Dam, 376, 378–79

Bonneville Power Act, 379

Bonus bill, veterans', F.D.R. resolves to make fight over, 10–11; becomes law, 504

Bonus Expeditionary Force, 79

Bookman, 70

Borah, William E., opposed to U.S. participation in World Court, 4; on Townsendism, 40; called Communist by Mrs. Dilling, 87; and Cutting's death, 141; insists relief funds not be used for warships and munitions, 270; backs La Follette on tax program, 330; attacks antilynching bill, 438; opposed to confirmation of Hughes, 465; on the Supreme Court, 485; defends Supreme Court against Byrnes's attack, 488; on the Republican party, 524, 525; as possible candidate in 1936, 527–28, 540–41; Landon managers negotiate with, 542–43, 545; takes no part in 1936 campaign, 596; declines to endorse Republican ticket, 615; mentioned, 135

Boulder Dam, 376–77, 499

Bramble Bush, The, Llewellyn, 486

Brandeis, Louis D., Laski and, 170; and the New Deal, 220–21; as source of inspiration, 222–23, 224; Richberg

and Berle on, 233; and internal struggle in the New Deal, 234; urges comprehensive public-works program, 236; dissent to Oklahoma Ice case, 252; dissent to Railroad Retirement Act decision, 275; and the Myers case of 1926, 279; pronounces end to government centralization, 280; pronounces Frazier-Lemke Act unconstitutional, 280; delighted with Second New Deal, 387; conflict in social philosophy, 388; Tugwell blames for failure of New Deal, 391; Berle on, 395–96; favors government spending, 398; on limitations of the Court, 461; Stone repelled by, 462; dissents to decision in *Crowell v. Benson*, 467; and *Colgate v. Harvey*, 468; and *U.S. v. Butler*, 470, 471, 472–73; and the TVA case, 475; and the Guffey Act case, 477; and minimum-wage laws, 478; and the N.Y. minimum-wage case, 481; influence, 486; encouraged by "consternation of the enemy," 490; F.D.R. on, 651; mentioned, 227, 230, 455

Brandeis, Mrs. Louis D., 223

Brandt, Raymond P., 331

Brant, Irving, 467, 477–78

Brewster, (Ralph) Owen, 316–18

Bridges, Harry, 206

Bridges, Styles, 546

Brinkley, Dr. John ("Goat Glands"), 531

Brisbane, Arthur, 538

Brooks, Van Wyck, 563

Broun, Heywood, 139

Browder, Earl, Laski on, 173; on the CPUSA, 189; on Roosevelt, 190, 569–70; as Communist party leader, 190; on pragmatism, 192; on Communist party membership, 197, 198; denounces Norman Thomas *et al.*, 198; on the leadership of the party, 199; at Communists' Seventh World Congress, 565, 566; calls for formation of farmer-labor party, 566–67; at 1936 Communist party convention, 568, 570; and *Common Sense* readers poll, 596; mentioned, 170, 625

Brown, C. M., 591

McSwain, John J., 87
Madero, Francisco, 142
Madison Square Garden, Communists break up meeting in, 164; Thomas and Browder speak at, 567; Roosevelt's wind-up meeting at, 638–39
Magnuson, Warren, 123
Magruder, Calvert, 220
Marbury v. Madison, 259
Marcantonio, Vito, 128, 143–44, 150
Markham, Edwin, 583–84
Markin, Valentin, 203
Marshall, Justice John, 259, 451, 455, 463
Martin, Joseph W., 505
Martindell, Jackson, 82
Marxism, intellectual rejection of, 162–65; and the demi-intellectuals, 165–66
Mason, A. T., 485
Massing, Hede, 204
Matthews, Dr. J. B., 199
Maverick, Maury, 142–44; on Communists, 93–94; on Huey Long, 341; on TVA, 375; mentioned, 129
Maybank, Mayor Burnet, 598
Mayer, Louis B., 118
Mayo, Dr. Will, 595
Means, Gardiner, 218–19, 233, 263, 506
Means to Prosperity, The, Keynes, 403
Mein Kampf, Hitler, 67
Mencken, H. L., on Gerald L. K. Smith, 65, 627; on Mrs. Dilling's list, 87; on Upton Sinclair, 111; testifies for anti-lynching bill, 437; attack on Roosevelt and New Deal, 525–26; on Gerald L. K. Smith's speech, 558; on Father Coughlin, 558; denounces F.D.R., 634; Pegler on, 634–35
Merriam, Charles E., 352
Merriam, Frank, 38, 119, 120–21
Merz, Charles, 267
Method of Freedom, The, Lippmann, 399
Methodist General Conference, 157
Metropolitan Life Insurance Company, 493
Meyer, Agnes, 416
Meyer, Eugene, 54, 225, 539
Michelson, Charles, 519, 574, 576
Militants, Socialist, 177–78, 561
Miller, Emma Guffey, 430
Millis, H. A., 237

Mills, Ogden, and Treasury investigation of Huey Long, 57; opposed to banking bill, 297; and the Liberty League, 523; and Landon, 539; proposes Landon go to Maine, 611; on "collectivist" tendencies in New Deal, 619; on Landon's defeat, 642; mentioned, 176, 527
Milner, Lucille, 91
Minimum-wage laws, constitutionality argued, 478–81
Minnesota Farmer-Labor party, 26, 149; 1934 convention, 100–101; in power, 103; conference considers third party, 549; Communist agents prod, 567
Minnesota Leader, 568
Minnesota Mortgage case, 253, 254, 275
Minor, Robert, 568
Minton, Sherman, 251
Mississippi, U.S.S., 118
Mississippi Valley Committee, 381
Mitchell, Arthur W., 436, 598
Modern Corporation and Private Property, The, Berle, 233
Moffat, J. Pierrepont, 419
Moley, Raymond, on Townsendism, 40; and Huey Long, 54; favors disengaging the administration from Sinclair, 119, 120; endorses McKee's candidacy, 130; on Roosevelt's anger at Cutting, 140; sees no threat from socialism or communism, 192; 5-point program to combat Communism, 195; differs with Tugwell on the New Deal, 212; finds Corcoran indispensable, 226; rejects Wilson-Brandeis philosophy, 233; and New Deal differences of opinion, 234, 236; predicts NRA will be declared unconstitutional, 260; and Hopkins's work relief program, 266; gives New York dinners for businessmen, 270; proposes voluntary trade association codes, 287; on holding-company legislation, 303; objects to F.D.R.'s proposed tax program, 327; on Roosevelt, 327; opposed to tax bill, 333; helps F.D.R. draft reply to Roy Howard, 338; influence declines, 387, 443; and the Supreme Court crisis, 491; on Hoover, 575; increasing disagreement with F.D.R. and the New Deal, 576–79; final visit

to F.D.R., 578–79, 621; as speech-writer for F.D.R., 582; "stunned" at Roosevelt speech, 640; mentioned, 235, 263, 395, 573
Moody, Dan, 250
Moore, G. E., 402
Moral Man and Immoral Society, Niebuhr, 157
More, Paul Elmer, 70
Morehead v. Tipaldo, 478, 482, 489
Morgan, Arthur E., and TVA policy, 362–63, 366, 369–70, 372; objects to Lilienthal's methods, 365–66, 368; on the end vs. the means, 396; quarrels with Farley, 418; mentioned, 387
Morgan, Harcourt A., 363, 366, 372
Morgenthau, Henry, Jr., on unemployment, 2; urges Roosevelt to make a fight of the bonus bill, 11; Father Coughlin denounces, 24, 629; and investigation of Huey Long, 57; and Upton Sinclair, 116; proposes Eccles for Treasury and Federal Reserve Board, 240; Long angry at, 242; disagrees with F.D.R. over the gold case, 257; and relief policy, 264, 265, 266; determined to hold federal spending down, 267; views on open-market operations, 293–94; and Glass's fight against the banking bill, 298, 299; divergence from Eccles, 299, 300; ideas on taxes, 326; favors balancing budget, 327; declines to give views on income-tax bill, 332; proposes Kennedy to head relief organization, 345; on Hopkins, 347; on the rush to spend money, 407; on Farley, 418; Creel on, 419; on F.D.R.'s inclination to soft-pedal reform, 502; and the undistributed profits tax, 505, 506, 507, 508; presses curtailment of government expenditures on F.D.R., 510–11, 513; Father Coughlin praises New Deal monetary policy to, 553; Farley on, 587; on the New Deal, 648; mentioned, 590
Morgenthau, Elinor, 439
Morris, Newbold, 132
Morse, Wayne, 60
Moses, George, 537
Moses, Robert, 131–32
Moskowitz, Belle, 439

Muenzenberg, Willi, 198
Mugglebee, Ruth, 27
Mullen, Arthur, 419
Mumford, Lewis, 168
Murphy, Boss, 125
Murphy, Frank, 24, 250, 637
Muscle Shoals power, 364
Muse, Vance, 522
Museum of Modern Art, 72
Mussolini, 71, 78, 147, 648
My First Days in the White House, Long, 67
Myers case (1926), 279

Nation, 184, 500, 542
National Association for the Advancement of Colored People (NAACP), 426, 428, 435, 436
National Broadcasting Company, 411, 573, 617
National Catholic Welfare Conference, 157
National Civic Federation, 196
National Conference of Social Work, 193
National Education Association, 87
National Emergency Council, 8, 240, 243, 574
National Executive Council, 302
National Home Library Foundation, 232–33
National income: in 1934, 1, 2; in 1936, 571
National Industrial Recovery Act, suits challenging provisions of, 6, 254; Section 7a found unconstitutional, 260; constitutional foundations of, 275–76
National Labor Relations Act, 448. *See also* Wagner Act
National Power Policy Committee, 362; Cohen in, 226, 362; proposes rigid limitation of holding companies, 305; investigation of holding companies, 303, 304–5, 312; and problem of power distribution, 378
National Recovery Act (NRA), in state of turmoil, 3; in increasing trouble, 214; Brandeis's ideas on, 220; declared unconstitutional, 280; debate concerning how best to continue principles of, 287–89; various attempts to continue agreements on

ABOUT THE AUTHOR

Arthur M. Schlesinger, Jr., won the Pulitzer Prize for History in 1946 for *The Age of Jackson* and the Pulitzer Prize for Biography in 1966 for *A Thousand Days: JFK in the White House*. He is the Albert Schweitzer Professor in the Humanities at the City University of New York. A graduate of Harvard, Schlesinger also studied at Peterhouse, Cambridge, and has been a professor of history at Harvard. He lives in New York City.